The Blackwell City Reader

Blackwell Readers in Geography

Each volume in the *Blackwell Readers in Geography* series provides an authoritative and comprehensive collection of essential readings from geography's main fields of study, edited by the discipline's leading authorities. Designed to complement the *Blackwell Companions to Geography* series, each volume represents an unparalleled resource in its own right and will provide the ideal platform for course use.

Published

The Blackwell City Reader
Edited by Gary Bridge and Sophie Watson

In preparation

The Blackwell Cultural Economy Reader
Edited by Ash Amin and Nigel Thrift

The Blackwell City Reader

Edited by

Gary Bridge and Sophie Watson

Blackwell
Publishing

Editorial material and organization © 2002 by Gary Bridge and Sophie Watson

350 Main Street, Malden, MA 02148-5018, USA
108 Cowley Road, Oxford OX4 1JF, UK
550 Swanston Street, Carlton South, Melbourne, Victoria 3053, Australia
Kurfürstendamm 57, 10707 Berlin, Germany

First published 2002 by Blackwell Publishing Ltd

Library of Congress Cataloging-in-Publication Data

The Blackwell city reader / edited by Gary Bridge and Sophie Watson.
    p. cm. – (Blackwell readers in geography)
    Includes bibliographical references (p.).
    ISBN 0-631-22513-7 – ISBN 0-631-22514-5 (pb)
    1. Cities and towns. 2. Cities and towns–Cross-cultural studies. I. Bridge, Gary.
    II. Watson, Sophie. III. Series.

HT111 .B53 2002
307.76–dc21

                                                   2002022630

ISBN 0-631-22513-7 (hbk) 0-631-22514-5 (pbk)

A catalogue record for this title is available from the British Library.

Set in 9.5/11.5pt Sabon
by Kolam Information Services Pvt. Ltd, Pondicherry, India
Printed and bound in Great Britain by TJ International, Padstow, Cornwall

For further information on
Blackwell Publishing, visit our website:
www.blackwellpublishing.com

Contents

Acknowledgments   ix

Introduction   xiii

Part I: Reading City Imaginations   **1**
Introduction   3

1   The Metropolis and Mental Life   11
    Georg Simmel

2   from *The City of Tomorrow and its Planning*   20
    Le Corbusier

3   from *The Image of the City*   30
    Kevin Lynch

4   from *Dreaming the Rational City*   39
    M. Christine Boyer

5   Bodies in Space/Subjects in the City   46
    Antony Vidler

6   from *City of Bits: Space, Place, and the Infobahn*   52
    W. J. Mitchell

7   Literary Geography: Joyce, Woolf and the City   60
    Jeri Johnson

8   The Hem of Manhattan   71
    Djuna Barnes

9   from *Bleak House*   76
    Charles Dickens

10 from *Dubliners*   80
    James Joyce

11   from *Mrs Dalloway*   86
     Virginia Woolf

12   from *The Sea Wall*   90
     Marguerite Duras

13   from *Beirut Blues*   93
     Hanan al-Shaykh

Part II: Reading Urban Economies   **105**
Introduction   107

14   The Urban Process Under Capitalism: A Framework for Analysis   116
     David Harvey

15   An Introduction to the Information Age   125
     Manuel Castells

16   from *Metropolis: From the Division of Labor to Urban Form*   135
     Allen J. Scott

17   Flexibilization Through Metropolis: The Case of Postfordist Seoul, Korea   147
     Myung-Rae Cho

18   from *Globalization and its Discontents*   161
     Saskia Sassen

19   from *Nature's Metropolis: Chicago and the Great West*   171
     William Cronon

20   Six Discourses on the Postmetropolis   188
     Edward W. Soja

21   from *Landscapes of Power: From Detroit to Disney World*   197
     Sharon Zukin

22   Reinventing the Johannesburg Inner City   208
     Lindsay Bremner

23   from *The Dialectics of Seeing: Walter Benjamin and the Arcades Project*   219
     Susan Buck-Morss

24   from *The End of Capitalism (As We Knew It): A Feminist Critique
     of Political Economy*   225
     J. K. Gibson-Graham

25   from *Changing the Rules: The Politics of Liberalization and
     the Urban Informal Economy in Tanzania*   229
     Aili Mari Tripp

Part III: Reading Division and Difference   **235**
Introduction   237

26   The Growth of the City   244
     Ernest W. Burgess

27   from *City Trenches: Urban Politics and the Patterning of Class in the US*   251
     Ira Katznelson

28   from *The Truly Disadvantaged: The Inner City, the Underclass,*
     and Public Policy   261
     William Julius Wilson

29   Bastee Eviction and Housing Rights: A Case of Dhaka, Bangladesh   270
     Mohammed Mahbubur Rahman

30   After Tompkins Square Park: Degentrification and the Revanchist City   279
     Neil Smith

31   City A/genders   290
     Sophie Watson

32   Bodies-Cities   297
     Elizabeth Grosz

33   from *Geographies of Disability*   304
     Brendan Gleeson

34   from *Flesh and Stone: The Body and the City in Western Civilization*   315
     Richard Sennett

35   from *City of Quartz: Excavating the Future in Los Angeles*   323
     Mike Davis

Part IV: Reading City Publics   **333**
Introduction   335

36   from *The Fall of Public Man*   342
     Richard Sennett

37   from *The Death and Life of Great American Cities*   351
     Jane M. Jacobs

38   Spatializing Culture: The Social Construction of Public Space
     in Costa Rica   357
     Setha M. Low

39   The Right to the City   367
     Henri Lefebvre

40   from *Discipline and Punish: The Birth of the Prison*   375
     Michel Foucault

41   from *The Practice of Everyday Life*   383
     Michel de Certeau

42   from *The Arcades Project*   393
     Walter Benjamin

43   from *Evictions: Art and Spatial Politics*   401
     Rosalyn Deutsche

44 from *City of Dreadful Delight: Narratives of Sexual Danger in
    Late-Victorian London*   410
    Judith R. Walkowitz

45 from *The Sphinx in the City: Urban Life, the Control
    of Disorder, and Women*   419
    Elizabeth Wilson

46 The Ideal of Community and the Politics of Difference   430
    Iris Marion Young

47 The Overexposed City   440
    Paul Virilio

Part V: Reading Urban Interventions   **449**
Introduction   451

48 From Managerialism to Entrepreneurialism: The Transformation in
    Urban Governance in Late Capitalism   456
    David Harvey

49 from *Urban Fortunes: The Political Economy of Place*   464
    John R. Logan and Harvey L. Molotch

50 from *Cities of Tomorrow: An Intellectual History of Urban Planning
    and Design in the Twentieth Century*   477
    Peter Hall

51 from *Collaborative Planning: Shaping Places in Fragmented Societies* 490
    Patsy Healey

52 Between Modernity and Postmodernity: The Ambiguous Position
    of US Planning   502
    Robert Beauregard

53 from *The Modernist City: An Anthropological Critique of Brasília*   513
    James Holston

54 from *Urbanism, Colonialism, and the World-economy*   524
    Anthony D. King

55 The Dark Side of Modernism: Planning as Control of an Ethnic Minority 535
    Oren Yiftachel

56 from *Edge of Empire: Postcolonialism and the City*   542
    Jane M. Jacobs

57 Mega-cities and the Urban Future: A Model for Replicating Best Practices 549
    Akhtar A. Badshah and Janice E. Perlman

Index   559

Acknowledgments

Al-Shaykh, Hanan, extract from *Beirut Blues*, reproduced by permission of David Higham Associates.

Badshah, Akhtar and Janice Perlman, "Mega-Cities and the urban future: a model for replicating best practices", City, Vol 3 no 4. Reproduced by permission of Taylor and Francis journals (http://www.tandf.co.uk/journals) and the author.

Beauregard, Robert, "Between modernity and postmodernity: the ambiguous position of US planning", from *Environment and Planning D: Society and Space*, 1989, vol 7, reproduced by permission of Pion Ltd.

Benjamin, Walter, reprinted by permission of the publisher from "The Arcades of Paris; in *The Arcades Project*, by Walter Benjamin, translated by Howard Eiland and Kevin McLaughlin, pp 873–884, Cambridge Mass.: Harvard University Press, copyright © 1999, by the President and Fellows of Harvard College. Originally published in German by Surhkamp Verlag.

Boyer, Christine M., "The City of Collective Memory", from *Dreaming the Rational City*. The MIT Press, 1983. Reproduced by permission of The MIT Press.

Bremner, Lindsay, "Reinventing the Johannesburg Inner City", reproduced from *Cities*, vol 17, Issue 3, June 2000, with permission from Elsevier Science.

Buck-Morrs, Susan, extracts from *The Dialectics of Seeing*, 1989, MIT Press. Reproduced by permission of The MIT Press.

Castells, Manuel, "An Introduction to the Information Age", from City 7. Reproduced by permission of Taylor and Francis journals (http://www.tandf.co.uk/journals) and the author.

Cho, Myung-Rae, "Flexibilization through metropolis: the case of postfordist Seoul, Korea". Copyright 1997 Blackwell Publishers and Joint Editors, reproduced by permission of Blackwell Publishing.

Cronon, William, extracts from *Nature's Metropolis: Chicago and the Great West*. Copyright William Cronon 1991. Used by permission of W. W. Norton & Company Inc.

Davis, Mike, extracts from *City of Quarz*, reproduced by permission of Verso.

Certeau, Michel de, extracts from *The Practice of Everyday Life*, University of California Press, 1984. Reproduced by permission of the University of California Press.

Deutsche, Rosalyn, extracts from *Evictions: Art and the spatial politics*, 1996 The MIT Press. Reproduced by permission of The MIT Press.

Duras, Marguerite, excerpt from *The Sea Wall* (1986), translated by Herma Briffault. Copyright © 1952 by Marguerite Duras. Reprinted by permission of Farrar, Straus and Giroux, LLC. and Faber and Faber Limited.

Foucault, Michel, extracts from *Discipline and Punish*, Pantheon, 1977. Originally published in French as *Surveiller et Punir*. Copyright © 1975 by Editions Gallimard. Reprinted by permission of Georges Bourchardt Inc. for the Editions Gallimard.

Gleeson, Brendan, extracts from *Geographies of Disability*, Routledge, 1999. Reproduced by permission of Taylor and Francis.

Grosz, Elizabeth, extracts from "Bodies-Cities", from Beatriz Colomina, ed., *Sexuality and Space*, © 1992 Princeton Architectural Press, www.papress.com

Harvey, David, "From managerialism to entrepreneurialism: the transformation in urban governance in late capitalism". *Geografiska Annaler*, series B, human geography, vol 71 B, no 1, 1989, reproduced by permission of Blackwell Publishing. Copyright © The Swedish Society for Anthropology and Geography.

Harvey, David, "The Urban Process Under Capitalism: A framework for analysis", from *International Journal of Urban and Regional Research*, vol 2 1978. Reproduced by permission of Blackwell Publishing.

Healey, Patsy, extracts from *Collaborative Planning: shaping places in fragmented societies*, Macmillan, 1997. Reproduced by permission of Palgrave.

Holston, James, extracts from *The Modernist City: An anthropological critique of Brasilia*, University of Chicago Press, 1989. Reproduced by permission of Chicago University Press.

Jacobs, Jane, extract from *Death and Life of American Cities*, published by Jonathan Cape. Used by permission of The Random House Group Limited.

Jacobs, Jane, extracts from *Edge of Empire*, Routledge 1996. Reproduced by permission of Taylor and Francis.

Johnson, Jeri, "Literary Geography: Joyce, Woolf and the City", *City* Vol 4. No 2, 2000. Reproduced by permission of Taylor and Francis journals (http://www.tandf.co.uk/journals) and the author.

Joyce, James, "Two Gallants'from *Dubliners*, reproduced with permission of the Estate of James Joyce, © copyright, The Estate of James Joyce.

Katznelson, Ira, extract from *City Trenches*, copyright © 1981 by Ira Katznelson. Used by permission of Pantheon Books, a division of Random House, Inc.

King, Anthony, extracts from *Urbanism, colonialism, and the world economy*, 1990, Routledge. Reproduced by permission of Taylor and Francis.

Le Corbusier, text extracts and illustrations from *The City of Tomorrow and its Planning*, third edition, London: Architectural Press, 1971. © FLC/Adagp, Paris 2002. Reproduced by permission of FLC/Adagp/DACS.

Logan, John, and Harvey L. Molotch, excerpts from *Urban Fortunes: the political economy of place*, University of California Press, 1987. Reproduced by permission of the University of California Press.

Low, Setha, extracts from "Spatializing Culture: the Social Production and Social Construction of Public Space in Costa Rica", from *Theorizing the City*, edited Setha Low, copyright © 1999 by Setha Low. Reprinted by permission of Rutgers University Press.

Lynch, Kevin, extracts from *The Image of the City*. Cambridge: The MIT Press, 1960. Reproduced by permission of The MIT Press.

Mitchell, W. J., extracts from *City of Bits: Space, Place, and the Infobahn*, 1995. The MIT Press. Reproduced by permission of The MIT Press.

Rahman, Mohammed Mahbubur, "Bastee eviction and housing rights: a case of Dhaka, Bangladesh", reproduced from *Habitat International*, 25 (2001), with permission from Elsevier Science.

Scott, Allen, excerpts from *Metropolis: From the division of labour to urban form*, University of California Press, 1988. Reproduced by permission of the University of California Press.

Sassen, Sakia, excerpts from *Globalization and its Discontents*, copyright © 1998. Reprinted by permission of The New Press. (800) 233–4830.

Sennett, Richard, extract from *The Fall of Public Man*, copyright © 1974, 1976 by Richard Sennett. Used by permission of Alfred A. Knopf, a division of Random House, Inc.

Sennett, Richard, extract from *Flesh and Stone* (1994) reproduced by permission of Faber and Faber Limited and W. W. Norton & Company Inc.

Simmel, Georg, extracts from "The Metropolis and Mental Life", trans. Edward Shils, from *Social Sciences III, Selections and Selected Readings*, vol 2, 14th edn, Chicago University Press 1948. Reproduced by permission of Chicago University Press.

Smith, Neil, extracts from "After Tomkins Square Park" from *(Re)Presenting the City*, King A (ed), Macmillan, 1996. Reproduced by permission of Palgrave.

Soja, Ed, extracts from "Six Discourses on the postmetropolis", from *Imagining Cities* edited by S. Westwood, Routledge 1997. Reproduced by permission of Taylor and Francis.

Tripp, Aili Mari, extracts from *Changing the Rules: The politics of liberalization and the urban informal economy Tanzania*, University of California Press, 1992.

Vidler, Anthony, extracts from "The City", from *Differences: A Journal of Feminist Cultural Studies*, Fall 1993. Reproduced by permission of Indiana University Press.

Virilio, Paul, "The Overexposed City", from *Rethinking Architecture*, N. Leach (ed), Routledge 1997. Reproduced by permission of Taylor and Francis.

Extracts from Walkowitz, Judith R, *City of Dreadful Delight* (1992), reproduced by kind permission of The University of Chicago Press and Little Brown & Co.

Watson, Sophie, "City A/Genders" from *Engendering Social Policy* edited by Sophie Watson and Lesley Doyal (1999) reproduced by permission of the Open University Press.

Wilson, Elizabeth, excerpts from *The Sphinx in the City*, University of California Press 1992. Reproduced by permission of the author and the University of California Press.

Wilson, William Julius, extracts from *The Truly Disadvantaged*, University of Chicago Press, 1987. Reproduced by permission of Chicago University Press.

Woolf, Virginia, extract from *Mrs Dalloway*, reproduced by permission of The Society of Authors as the Literary Representative of the Estate of Virginia Woolf.

Young, Iris Marion, extracts from "The Ideal of Community and the Politics of Difference" from *Social Theory and Practice*, vol 12, no 1, spring 1986.

Zukin, Sharon, excerpts from *Landscapes of Power*, University of California Press, 1991. Reproduced by permission of the University of California Press.

Introduction

In the twenty-first century cities are once again at the center of intellectual and political debate. For the first time in history the majority of the world's population live in cities and even greater proportions are affected by urban processes. This makes for a complex range of urban experiences across the globe, within cities, and even in single neighborhoods. There is a great diversity of contemporary thinking on cities which this *Reader* intends to capture.

To introduce the reader to the wide range of contemporary and early twentieth-century writing on the city we have brought together extracts from a variety of disciplinary backgrounds – from economics to critical theory, from physical planning to psychoanalysis. We also reflect a diversity of theoretical positions – Marxism and positivism, feminism, poststructuralism, modernist and postmodernist thought. These are organized under the five themes of imagination; economies; division and difference; the public; and politics, planning, and urban interventions. The *Reader* seeks both to reflect well-established themes in urban studies and also to critique and develop these through its wider theoretical and disciplinary scope. The inclusion of literary pieces, for example, we hope highlights the role of the imagination and the psychological experience of cities. Several feminist pieces expose the masculinity of cities and the resistance of women through their urban subjectivities. We include extracts that are intended to disrupt categories. For example the Susan Buck-Morss piece on Walter Benjamin would traditionally be more at home in a city cultures section. We locate it in reading economies to suggest the deep connections between ideas of "culture" and "economy," between aesthetics and the "hard stuff" of instrumental economic exchange. Equally Lynch's piece on the visibility of cities, normally associated with urban planning, is included in the urban imagining section to represent the dominant visuality of the modernist urban imagination. The *Reader* also intends to disrupt the hegemony of western thought and action in urban studies by including examples of nonwestern cities and nonwestern thinking as well as including extracts that unsettle the influence of western imaginings.

The extracts themselves are selected to illustrate different analyses or empirical examples of cities within the themes. So for example David Harvey's piece in the economy section represents the classic statement of the role of cities in capital accumulation from a Marxist perspective. Soja's extract in the same section explores postmodern perspectives on the economies of the contemporary metropolis. There are also extracts that extend and unsettle our assumptions within the categories. The *Reader* is not a historical overview of thinking about cities. The extracts are thematically organized and mostly concern analysis and experience of the "modern" metropolis (mid-nineteenth century onwards), although certain pieces, such as Sennett's on the Jewish Ghetto in Venice, also apply modern sensibilities to more historical contexts.

The five organizing themes of the *Reader* reflect the structure of *A Companion to the City* (Bridge and Watson, 2000; Blackwell). This allows continuity of analysis between the commissioned pieces of contemporary scholarship in the *Companion* with the landmark, previously published extracts in this *Reader*. The *Reader* and *Companion* together are intended to provide a comprehensive, multidisciplinary overview of thinking on the city in the modern era.

Gary Bridge and Sophie Watson

Part I Reading City Imaginations

Introduction: Reading City Imaginations

Gary Bridge and Sophie Watson

No city stands in bricks and mortar which is not also a space of the imagination or of representation. The effect of the city on the imagination exists in a constant tension represented on the one hand as stimulating the imagination and enabling creativity and on the other as constraining it. These two opposing perspectives, or positive and negative imaginaries of the city, have long been embedded in pro- and anti-urbanist movements. Cities are places which enable the realization of the self, or conversely cities separate the self from creativity and imagination in spaces of alienation and estrangement (Bridge and Watson, 2000, p. 9). There is a long Western tradition of representing cities as both dystopia or hell – Sodom, the city of corruption – and utopia or heaven – Athens, the city of enlightenment, democracy and reason – and the force of these representations has shifted over time. Literature and more recently film play a crucial part in forming dominant representations of the city, as we shall see. James Donald quotes Burgin (1999, p. 48): "the city in our actual experience is *at the same time* an actually existing physical environment, and a city in a novel, a film, a photograph, a city seen on television, a city in a comic strip, a city in a pie chart, and so on." We could adapt here Spinoza's notion of the imagination as a form of bodily awareness and the mind as an idea of the body, or as the mind and body coming together in the most immediate way (Gatens and Lloyd, 1999, p. 12), and suggest the mind and the city are also intertwined.

City life is highly ambiguous, fluid, unreal, and difficult to pin down, and a wide range of traditions of analysis or understanding have dominated in different countries at different times. J. C. Oates (1981, p. 12) points to the emphasis in the United States on the city as an expression of the marketplace struggle that should yield individual success in financial and social terms. Late nineteenth and early twentieth century American writers, she suggests, have tended to represent the city as a place where human beings die as a result of the terrible conditions of slum life and mistreatment by employers or one another. For example, Upton Sinclair equated Chicago with the jungle, while for Stephen Crane the city is a dark region of gruesome doorways. After the second world war urban struggle became an internalized philosophical enquiry. For example, Saul Bellow in Mr. Sammler's Planet (1970) was obsessed with what it means to be an urban man in secular mass-market culture where there is no coherent sense of tradition (Oates, 1981, p. 26). On the question of poetry Stephen Spender (1981, p. 45) suggests that since the industrial revolution poets have seen the city as destructive of the conditions from which the best poetry came. Thus the modern metropolis is represented as ugly, overwhelming, and materialistic and antipoetic – particularly by the Romantic poets (for example, Blake's 'dark satanic mills'). Ambiguity towards the city is part of the modern tradition.

We can also see the city as a site of desire and fantasy, or as a space of anxiety, fear, or, as Vidler (1992) does, a site of the uncanny, drawing on Freud. Much writing on the city or on characters living in cities, as we shall see, sees subjectivity as constructed in the real and imagined, or formal and informal, spaces of the city. While for Modjeska (1989, p. 2) the imaginative lives of women are already in themselves cities, and cities which have an existence on the margins which survive the vicissitudes of time: "maybe ... the imaginative life of women, those 'inner cities' can prove durable. The shadows her city casts are not of battlements or ramparts. Women are practised on the peripheries. Our memories, our stories, like the ways we love, are formed in movement between inner and outer, past and future, center and margin, between the physical environment and the social world. We shape our cities, and re-shape them from the edge, we always have; just as our cities shape us. We live in houses that weren't built for dreams, in suburbs connected by transport systems we can't control. We fit our stories to the worlds we inherit." Dreaming in the city, as we see here, is yet another metaphor for city life, while memory is formed in the buildings and spaces of the city and thus spatialized.

Walter Benjamin (see Part 4), and Georg Simmel (1858–1918) in different ways (for Benjamin it is the *flâneur*) were early theorists of the relation between the city and mental or psychic life. For Simmel the city is overwhelming in its mass of impressions and activity, it literally bombards the senses so that people have to develop a blasé attitude in order to protect themselves. The city also operates in a field of social, cultural, and economic forces which for Simmel are inextricably firmly interconnected. Individual and collective activities are interdependent and central to urban experience which is noisy and unforgettable. In the 'Metropolis and Mental Life' (1903) Simmel explores the modern intellectual and rational individual whose disinterested circulation within the metropolis reflects the circulation of commodities and capital.

In this section of readings on city imaginations the focus, with one or two exceptions, is on the city in literature and on representations of the city which have spatial effects – namely through planning and architecture. There is another imaginary terrain – that of cinema, which is usefully explored elsewhere (see e.g. Donald, 1999, Caldwell, 2000). Modern cinema, Donald (1999, p. 132) argues, has had the effect of exposing people to complex representations of modern urban experience – the dangers, fears, and eroticism of streets, at the same time as placing people above it, thereby creating a panoramic vision of the city. The cinema he suggests embodies peoples' visual experience of the city, while providing a distanced perspective of rational vision: "The modern city and its cinematic projection can be seen in terms of a dramatic encounter between the irrational and instinctual forces, the fearful elements of the city, the unconscious and the uncanny, on the one hand, and the powers of reason, vision and control, that is to say conscious powers, on the other."

The new global city, for Donald, now exceeds our field of vision as it is more and more implicated in global communication networks and virtual space. This links with postmodern ideas of hyperreality and hyperspace (Baudrillard), where the idea of the 'real' pre-existing and separate from the image has fallen away, and any boundary between real and imagined space is increasingly blurry. Others such as Kevin Robbins (1995, p. 47) take a different tack in arguing that the new media have caused a weakening of urban imagination either of the city as a site of pleasure or of violence.

Planning, Urban Design, and Architecture

"Designing a dream city is easy; rebuilding a living one takes imagination." (Jane Jacobs, cited in Donald, 1999, p. 121)

Park, influenced by Simmel, is well known for his comment "the city is a state of mind." How cities are envisioned has effects and nowhere is this more apparent than in the planning, architecture, and design professions.

Many planning or architectural imaginations have characterized the city as irrational; subject to disruptive internal forces, chaos, disorder, and disease. And thus many city plans and designs have been motivated by a desire to impose order and rationality on the unplanned, fluid, complex, and fragmented city. Le Corbusier, with his desire to produce the transparent and readable city, was a key figure of this kind of modern utopianism.

There have been many visions of the good city (see Hall, 1988) in the late nineteenth and early twentieth century (following many who went before – the Renaissance urban designers, the Aztecs, Mayans, or early Greeks – to name but a few). The point here is that the imaginations of planners and architects have had profound effects in terms of the shape of the cities we inhabit today. Thus, the garden city movement initiated by Ebenezer Howard (1850–1928) in his Garden Cities of Tomorrow (1902) came up with the idea of building new communities on the edge of cities away from the overcrowding, squalor, and congestion of the Victorian slum. These were models of industrial decentralization where the skills of a diversity of people would be harnessed cooperatively to create a new socioeconomic order. His ideas were reinterpreted and realized in several places including Hampstead Garden Suburb, Letchworth, and Welwyn Garden City in Britain, and in Onkel Toms Hutte in Germany (Hall, 1988, pp. 86–136). Other important city visionaries include the Americans Frank Lloyd Wright with his plan for decentralized rural communities (Broadacre City, 1935) and Frederick Law Olmsted (1822–1903), with his advocacy of public parks as a solution to many of the perceived urban ills.

Whereas these earlier visions emphasized compact settlements with a rural flavor, Le Corbusier was a fully fledged urbanist. Le Corbusier is probably the most well known of these grand urban visionaries, and though only one city was ever built according to his plans – Chandigarh in India – his ideas had profound influence on the planning and development of cities in the postwar years across the world. Le Corbusier (1887–1969) is one of the key figures in the Modernist movement and one of the founders of the International Style in architecture. Le Corbusier is famous for his notion of the house as "a machine to live in" and his quest to build houses and cities according to a rational and ordered plan. He published a number of books, *La Vie Contemporaine* (1922), *La Vie Radieuse* (1933), and *Urbanisme* (1924) (retitled *The City of Tomorrow* in the 1929 English edition), extracted here, where he developed his ideas of centrally planned cities which were defined by a symmetrical and spatially differentiated grid structure in which where people lived depended on their employ-ment, and residence was separated from work in large uniform apartment blocks. His ideas were extremely influential on the building of public housing in many countries in the 1950s and 1960s, particularly before they came to be discredited, as after many years of poor maintenance and upkeep, many tower blocks became little more than sink estates for the poor. The growing unpopularity of Corbusian-style urban renewal hit an all-time high with the dynamiting of the failed Pruitt-Igoe high-rise housing project in St. Louis in 1972, and a similar destruction of Ronan Point in Britain.

Kevin Lynch (1918–89) is included in this *Reader* since his visions have had considerable influence on the planning and design professions with his focus on ordinary peoples' perception of cities and the need for practitioners to take these into account. A student of Frank Lloyd Wright and a man committed to finding a balance between human life and the built environment, Lynch suggested that people organize their city images into patterns – paths, edges, nodes, districts, and landmarks – which should be taken into account by design professionals in order to create a more imageable and livable city. Christine Boyer has written extensively on city planning and design, and the last chapter of her book, "Dreaming the Rational City," provides a useful overview of the crisis of modernism and its impact on planning. Central to her own critique is the hope for a new kind of physical planning which is humane and humanistic, and which confronts what she sees as the key characteristics of the modern city: "its alienating abstractions, rational efficiency, fragmented and malign configuration, ruptured tradition and memory."

Emanating from a more radical tradition of architectural thought, Antony Vidler, an architectural historian, has linked modernist planning practices with psychoana-lytic and other philosophical traditions, bringing Freud's notion of the uncanny to explain feelings of disquiet and unease in urban in urban space (Vidler, 1992). The metropolis, he suggests, represented a fear of contact and was an amalgam of urban experience and imaginary fear. In the article abstracted here, Vidler explores the connections between philosophical and psychoanalytic ideas and the modernist pro-duction of urban space. The nineteenth-century metropolis carried all sorts of stigmas – as the breeding ground for disease, as the site of dangerous crowds or social and political movements – and thus was linked to the development of agoraphobia, particularly in women, for whom the streets were represented as a site of repressed desire. Modernist urban space with its erasure of the old city and transparency was seen to cleanse the city of mental disturbance. In this article Vidler examines the ways in which an apparently serene and positivist, and also masculine, version of modernist urban space, masks all sorts of suppressed anxieties and phobias which its architects are attempting to cure.

Finally, from an entirely different tradition, Mitchell in his book *City of Bits*, extracted here, suggests that with new forms of technology and telecommunication the very idea of the city has to be reformulated and old urban design questions have to be rethought. Cyberspace, he proposes, offers new opportunities for mutual interests, new identities, and self-representation, despite the existence of an organizing frame-work, and the fact that peoples' rights to create private and public – or rather semi-public – spaces in cyberspace is fiercely contested. Virtual communities, the different sites where people meet, are, like grand urban designs, large-scale structures of places and connections which are organized to meet the needs of their inhabitants which are governed according to certain norms and customs.

Literature

'If the City is a text, how shall we read it?' (Joyce Carol Oates, 1981, p. 111)

The second part of this section of reading city imaginations moves from the visions of urban planning and design to the imaginations of the city in literature. Cities are so integral to literature shaping the day-to-day lives, feelings, and experiences of characters that many great works of literature almost depend on the city for their existence. At the same time our urban experience is integrally embedded and formed from our literary readings of the city – from the books and poetry we have read or the films and plays that we have seen. In other words, city life and literature are so intertwined that our experience of each is mutually constitutive. The possibilities that the city appears to offer and our daily urban imaginings are influenced as much by the literature we have encountered as by lived experiences that have gone before. We could even go so far as to argue that there is no understanding of the city that is not mediated by our literary imaginations. Jaye and Watts (1981, ix) put it this way: "the literature of the city yields experiences that become integral parts of our lives through time; we seek to revisit, discover, locate or avoid, or create those imaginative impressions and journeys anew." The boundaries between the real and imagined city are ill-defined, shifting, and slippery. Resonating strongly with contemporary geographical approaches to the city, Moretti (1983, p. 111) has argued that "what *distinguishes* the city... is that its spatial structure (basically its *concentration*) is functional to the intensification of *mobility* spatial mobility naturally enough, but mainly *social* mobility. The dazzling rapidity of success and ruin is the great theme of the nineteenth century novel from Balzac to Maupassant: with it the city enters modern literature and becomes, as it were, its obligatory context." In foregrounding the ideas of the city as a physical place which operates as a backdrop to the network of developing social relationships, Moretti claims its importance to the narrative temporality: "The novel reveals that the meaning of the city is not to be found in any particular place, but manifests itself only through temporal trajectory. Whereas the great aspiration of mythic narration exacts the metamorphosis of time into space, the urban novel turns the axiom on its head and seeks to resolve the spatial in terms of the sequential" (p. 112). Thus in Balzac's novels the urban landscape is present to reinforce the plot as plot – to emphasize its complexity and unpredictability – rather than vice versa. The same thing is going on in Hitchcock's films, for example, where the city is always simply background, framed and defined by the exigencies of a temporal order (p. 126).

There are many literary texts in which, however, the city plays a much more central role and which the extracts in this reader have been selected to illustrate. In contrast to other Victorian writers, who tended in their more metaphoric treatment of the city to eschew its literal reality (Knoepflmacher, 1973, p. 517), and arguably, more than any other writer, Dickens (1812–70) transposed the materiality, sensuality, and texture of London into text. It is impossible to think of his books without at once being immersed in the windy dirty streets of East London, or smelling the fog rising off the Thames, or listening to the sounds of street hawkers selling their wares. The themes of his novels resonate with salient urban issues of today – crime, law, streets, shops, transport, and popular pastimes or popular culture, and at the less tangible question of urban alienation (anomie). Dickens loved to walk the streets of London exploring every nook and cranny of the city, and though he tends more often to write about the central areas, he explored every suburb from Richmond to Finchley in his wanderings. Dickens was drawn to the underbelly of London life, its tawdriness and its dirt; as Forster (1928, p. 11) argues, "He had a profound attraction to repulsion...If he could only induce whomsoever took him out to take him to Seven Dials, he was supremely happy. 'Good heavens' he would exclaim 'what wild visions of wickeness, want and beggary, arose in my mind out of that place.'" As Dickens himself acknowledged, he was dependent on London for his writing, so much so that during a trip to Genoa in 1844, he craved the London streets and missed his nightly walks (Collins, 1973, p. 539). Like Baudelaire's *flaneur*, he loved the crowds and activities of the city which nourished his imagination, but for him the pleasure was not Benjamin's phantasmagoria of the bright lights and new commodities, rather it was the dereliction of the city and its juxtaposition to wealth and riches which suited his genius. This attention to the connections and disconnections and the extreme juxtapositions of the rich and the poor which he describes, prefigures so many of the academic writings on the city more than a century later (see e.g. Massey, Allen, and Pile, 1999). So Nicholas Nickleby, for example, contemplates "the very dirty and dusty suburb" containing "pale and pinched up faces...hungry eyes, half naked shivering figures" illuminated by "the brilliant flood of light that streamed from the windows of the shops...emporiums of splendid dresses...vessels of burnished gold and silver" (Dickens, quoted in Collins, 1973, p. 542).

This was the age of the fast-growing industrial capitalist city with all its associated ills as well as pleasures, its pollution, congestion, noise and poverty, its new civic and public life, and Dickens sets out to be its chronicler. As Bagehot (1965, p. 85) put it, "he describes London like a special correspondent for posterity", and for many a nonmetropolitan reader or reader from overseas, the London they knew was Dickens' London (Collins, p. 551), and his images of the city were immensely powerful. Thus in the journals of Francis Parkman, a visitor from the United States (Wade, 1947, p. 221), we find: "When I got to London, I thought I had been there before. There in flesh and blood, was the whole host of characters that figure in Pickwick...the hackney coachmen and cabmen," while similar observations figure in the autobiography of Henry James (Collins, pp. 551–2). Fog was a particularly salient feature of every Victorian Londoner's experience which Dickens used as an "outward and visible sign of spiritual and social disgrace" (Collins, p. 542), and we find it seeping through the lines in this extract from *Bleak House*.

Johnson's article "Literary Geography," through a discussion of *Ulysses* and *The Years* introduces the reader to the work of James Joyce (1882–1941) and Virginia Woolf (1892–1941). These two modernist writers, she argues, were concerned with both interrogating the effect of the metropolis on individuals and also significantly figured the cities of London and Dublin in material terms. Oates (p. 91) sees Joyce's work this way: his "boldly new art renders the city but refuses to present it (p. 19)...the city speaks through everyone and everything, in a multitude of voices," while Raymond Williams (1973, p. 243), writing about *Ulysses* (1922), suggests that "in a way there is no longer a city, there is only man walking through it." Though there is a recent tendency to attribute notions of the fragmentary, ephemeral, fleeting, complex, and so on to postmodern writing, these aspects of city life are fully present in Joyce's Dublin. Here too the city is internalized as consciousness; as Donald puts it (p. 5), "The Dead" "conveys something of the modern city-dweller's imagination, the ability to live both here and elsewhere." The internet has provided a different route into this state of being. In "Two Gallants," an essay from *Dubliners*, discussed by

Johnson in her article, the two men walk through the streets of Dublin redolent with Ireland's history of political betrayals.

Virginia Woolf, as Johnson argues, includes the "facts" of the material world not to present them as objective, but rather, as "perception filtered through the affective response of a narrated subject." In Woolf's novels the subjectivities of characters are constituted in the very spaces of the city. In *Mrs Dalloway*, extracted here, Woolf describes the streets and locations of London with the same detail as Dickens, but they are always mediated through the subjective thoughts of the protagonists, and the experience of London is rendered as a psychic space (Donald, 1999, p. 130).

Djuna Barnes (1892–1982), is a less well-known modernist figure, but is claimed by some critics to be one of the most original and ingenious novelists of the twentieth century. Born into a bohemian and poor family living in an artists' colony north of New York, Barnes' works include the *The Ladies Almanack, Ryder, Nightwood* – "a brilliant satirical tragedy that is as rife with profound insight into the human condition as it is with the grotesquely carnivalesque" (according to one Barnes website), and *The Antiphon*. Djuna Barnes was an enigmatic literary figure, who was dubbed the "Garbo of Letters" for her glamor and zealous insistence on privacy. In 1940 she became a recluse living in a small flat in Greenwich village which earned her premature and undeserved obscurity.

The essay here comes from a collection of 41 pieces of journalism (collected in the volume *New York*) written between 1913 and 1919 which capture a magical and mythical city. They reflect Barnes's style, which is filled with radical metaphors, aphoristic sayings, and original quotations, as well as exploring serious social issues of her time (Messerli, p. 11). "The Hem of Manhatten" was written for the *Morning Telegraph* about a 40-mile ferry-boat trip up the East River, through the narrow channel called Hell Gate, to Sputen Creek, south along the steep cliffs of the Palissades to Battery Park and under the Brooklyn Bridge, past the first of New York's great skyscrapers, the highest of which was the magnificent gothic Woolworth building, completed in 1913.

Shifting from the center to the margins, *The Sea Wall* conjures up the French colonial city of Saigon in the 1920s. Marguerite Duras (1914–) is probably best known for her film scripts *Hiroshima mon amour* (which won the 1959 International Critics' Prize at Cannes) and *Une aussie longue absence*. Duras was born in Indochina in a French colonial family where she stayed until moving to Paris to enroll for political science and law. This period of her life profoundly influenced her writing in particular, *The Sea Wall* and *The Lover* – a tale of a passionate encounter between a young French girl and a Chinese man. Duras is not an easy writer to classify or categorize, though some people have described it as part of the French "antinovel school" (Cismaru, 1971). She was influenced by Hemingway, and her books are filled with a psychological intensity and a concern with the problems of her day, while there is a haunting quality to her writing. As Duras said of herself in an interview (1990, p. 1): "I don't have general views about anything except social injustice . . . I don't drag the millstone of totalitarian, i.e. inflexible, thought around with me. That's one plague I've managed to avoid." But what does come through these interviews, and her books, is the sense of a woman who, like Virginia Woolf (whose writings she admired), believes profoundly in the independence of women, but who is somewhat pessimistic about the possibilities for real change.

The final extract in the section is by Hanan al-Shaykh, who was a well known journalist in Beirut, and is now writing in London as part of a diaspora of Arab intellectuals and artists. She is, according to Edward Said, the "premier woman writer in Arabic" (Jaggi, 2001, p. 4). *Beirut Blues* (1992) is a story about a everyday life in a city transformed by war into a city beset violence and division and by problems with the water, sewage, electricity, garbage collection. Here too, like in Woolf, the internal thoughts of the protagonist are voiced through the spaces of the city she walks through. But it is also a narrative which captures the smells as well as its destruction from colonial elegance to a pile of neglected ruins, selected here to provide another urban picture from the margins.

These and other literary writings on the city, western and nonwestern alike, can tell us as much about city life and its senses as a political-economic analysis of urban housing and labor markets. They are simply narratives of a different kind, drawing on the power of the imagination, rather than the power of concrete arguments and evidence.

REFERENCES

Bagehot, W. 1965: Charles Dickens. In N. St. John Stevas (ed.), *Literary Essays*, vol. 11.

Bridge, G. and Watson, S. (eds.) 2000: *A Companion to the City*. Oxford: Blackwell.

Caldwell, L. 2000: Imagining Naples: The Senses of the City. In Bridge, G. and Watson, S. (eds.), *A Companion to the City*. Oxford: Blackwell, 55–64.

Cismaru, A. 1971: *Marguerite Duras*. New York: Twayne Publishers.

Collins, P. 1973: Dickens and London. In Dyos, J. and Wolff, M. (eds.), *The Victorian City*, vol. 2. London: Routledge, 537–57.

Dickens, C. 1947–59: *Nicholas Nickelby*. Oxford: New Oxford Illustrated Edition.

Donald, J. 1999: *Imagining the Modern City*. London: The Athlone Press.

Duras, M. 1990: *Practicalities* (Interviews with Jerome Beaujour), tr. B. Bray. London: Collins.

Forster, J. 1928: *Life of Dickens*. J. W. T. Ley edition. London: Cecil Palmer.

Gatens, M. and Lloyd, G. 1999: *Collective Imaginings: Spinoza, Past and Present*. London: Routledge.

Hall, P. 1988: *Cities of Tomorrow*. Oxford: Blackwell.

Jaggi, M. 2001: Conflicts Unveiled. *The Guardian*, July 7 review section.

Jaye, M. C. and Chalmers Watts, A. (eds.) 1981: *Literature and the American Urban Experiences*. Manchester: Manchester University Press.

Knoepflmacher, C. U. C. 1973: The Novel Between the City. In Dyos, J. and Wolff, M. (eds.), *The Victorian City*, vol. 2. London: Routledge, 537–57.

Massey, D., Allen, J., and Pile, S. (eds.) 1999: *City Worlds*. London: Routledge.

Modjeska, D. 1989: *Inner Cities*. Sydney: Penguin.

Moretti, F. 1983: *Signs Taken for Wonders*. London: Verso.

Oates, J. C. 1981: Imaginary Cities: America. In Jaye, M. C. and Chalmers Watts, A. (eds.), *Literature and the American Urban Experiences*. Manchester: Manchester University Press.

Robins, K. 1995: Collective Emotion and Urban Culture. In Healey, P. S., Cameron, S., Davoudi, S., Graham, S., and Madani-Pour, A. (eds.), *Managing Cities: The New Urban Context*. Chichester: John Wiley and Sons.

Spender, S. 1981: Poetry and the Modern City. In Jaye, M. C. and Chalmers Watts, A. (eds.), *Literature and the American Urban Experiences*. Manchester: Manchester University Press.

Vidler, A. 1992: *The Architectural Uncanny*. Cambridge, MA: MIT Press.

Wade, M. (ed.) 1947: *The Journals of Francis Parkman*, vol. 1. London: Eyre and Spottiswoode.

Williams, R. 1973: *The Country and the City*. Oxford: Oxford University Press.

Chapter 1

The Metropolis and Mental Life

Georg Simmel

The deepest problems of modern life flow from the attempt of the individual to maintain the independence and individuality of his existence against the sovereign powers of society, against the weight of the historical heritage and the external culture and technique of life. This antagonism represents the most modern form of the conflict which primitive man must carry on with nature for his own bodily existence. The eighteenth century may have called for liberation from all the ties which grew up historically in politics, in religion, in morality and in economics in order to permit the original natural virtue of man, which is equal in everyone, to develop without inhibition; the nineteenth century may have sought to promote, in addition to man's freedom, his individuality (which is connected with the division of labour) and his achievements which make him unique and indispensable but which at the same time make him so much the more dependent on the complementary activity of others; Nietzsche may have seen the relentless struggle of the individual as the prerequisite for his full development, while socialism found the same thing in the suppression of all competition – but in each of these the same fundamental motive was at work, namely the resistance of the individual to being levelled, swallowed up in the social-technological mechanism. When one inquires about the products of the specifically modern aspects of contemporary life with reference to their inner meaning – when, so to speak, one examines the body of culture with reference to the soul, as I am to do concerning the metropolis today – the answer will require the investigation of the relationship which such a social structure promotes between the individual aspects of life and those which transcend the existence of single individuals. It will require the investigation of the adaptations made by the personality in its adjustment to the forces that lie outside of it.

The psychological foundation, upon which the metropolitan individuality is erected, is the intensification of emotional life due to the swift and continuous shift of external and internal stimuli. Man is a creature whose existence is dependent on differences, i.e. his mind is stimulated by the difference between present impressions and those which have preceded. Lasting impressions, the slightness in their differences, the habituated regularity of their course and contrasts between them, consume, so to speak, less mental energy than the rapid telescoping of changing images, pronounced differences within what is grasped at a single glance, and the unexpectedness of violent stimuli. To the extent that the metropolis creates these psychological conditions – with every crossing of the street, with the tempo and multiplicity of economic, occupational and social life – it creates in the sensory foundations of mental life, and in the degree of awareness necessitated by our organization as creatures dependent on differences, a deep contrast with the slower, more habitual, more smoothly flowing rhythm of the sensory-mental phase of small town and rural existence. Thereby the essentially intellectualistic character of the mental life of the metropolis becomes intelligible as over against that of the small town which rests more on feelings and emotional relationships. These latter are rooted in the unconscious levels of the mind and develop most readily in the steady equilibrium of unbroken customs. The locus of reason, on the other hand, is in the lucid, conscious upper strata of the mind and it is the most adaptable of our inner forces. In order to adjust itself to the shifts and contradictions in events, it does not require the disturbances and inner upheavals which are the only means whereby more conservative personalities are able to adapt themselves to the same rhythm of events. Thus the metropolitan type – which naturally takes on a thousand individual modifications – creates a protective organ for itself against the profound disruption with which the fluctuations and discontinuities of the external milieu threaten it. Instead of reacting emotionally, the metropolitan type reacts primarily in a rational manner, thus creating a mental predominance through the intensification of consciousness, which in turn is caused by it. Thus the reaction of the metropolitan person to those events is moved to a sphere of mental activity which is least sensitive and which is furthest removed from the depths of the personality.

This intellectualistic quality which is thus recognized as a protection of the inner life against the domination of the metropolis, becomes ramified into numerous specific phenomena. The metropolis has always been the seat of money economy because the many-sidedness and concentration of commercial activity have given the medium of exchange an importance which it could not have acquired in the commercial aspects of rural life. But money economy and the domination of the intellect stand in the closest relationship to one another. They have in common a purely matter-of-fact attitude in the treatment of persons and things in which a formal justice is often combined with an unrelenting hardness. The purely intellectualistic person is indifferent to all things personal because, out of them, relationships and reactions develop which are not to be completely understood by purely rational methods – just as the unique element in events never enters into the principle of money. Money is concerned only with what is common to all, i.e. with the exchange value which reduces all quality and individuality to a purely quantitative level. All emotional relationships between persons rest on their individuality, whereas intellectual relationships deal with persons as with numbers, that is, as with elements which, in themselves, are indifferent, but which are of interest only insofar as they offer something objectively perceivable. It is in this very manner that the inhabitant of the metropolis reckons with his merchant, his customer and with his servant, and frequently with the persons with whom he is thrown into obligatory association. These relationships stand in distinct contrast with the nature of the smaller circle in which the inevitable knowledge of individual characteristics produces, with an equal inevitability, an emotional tone in conduct, a sphere which is beyond the mere objective weighting of tasks performed and payments made. What is essential here as regards the economic-psychological aspect of the problem is that in less advanced cultures production was for the customer who ordered the product so that the producer and the purchaser knew one another. The modern city, however, is supplied almost exclusively by production for the market, that is, for entirely unknown purchasers who never appear in the actual field of vision of the producers themselves. Thereby, the interests of each party acquire a relentless matter-of-factness, and its rationally calculated economic egoism need not fear any divergence from its set path because of the imponderability of personal relationships. This is all the more the case in the money economy which dominates the metropolis in which the last remnants of domestic production and direct barter of goods have been eradicated and in which the amount of production on direct personal order is reduced daily. Furthermore, this psychological intellectualistic attitude and the money economy are in such close integration that no one is able to say whether it was the former that effected the latter or vice versa. What is certain is only that the form of life in the metropolis is the soil which nourishes this interaction most fruitfully, a point which I shall attempt to demonstrate only with the statement of the most outstanding English constitutional historian to the effect that through the entire course of English history London has never acted as the heart of England but often as its intellect and always as its money bag.

In certain apparently insignificant characters or traits of the most external aspects of life are to be found a number of characteristic mental tendencies. The modern mind has become more and more a calculating one. The calculating exactness of practical life which has resulted from a money economy corresponds to the ideal of natural science, namely that of transforming the world into an arithmetical problem and of fixing every one of its parts in a mathematical formula. It has been money economy which has thus filled the daily life of so many people with weighing, calculating, enumerating and the reduction of qualitative values to quantitative terms. Because of the character of calculability which money has there has come into the relationships of the elements of life a precision and a degree of certainty in the definition of the equalities and inequalities and an unambiguousness in agreements and arrangements, just as externally this precision has been brought about through the general diffusion of pocket watches. It is, however, the conditions of the metropolis which are cause as well as effect for this essential characteristic. The relationships and concerns of the typical metropolitan resident are so manifold and complex that, especially as a result of the agglomeration of so many persons with such differentiated interests, their relationships and activities intertwine with one another into a many-membered organism. In view of this fact, the lack of the most exact punctuality in promises and performances would cause the whole to break down into an inextricable chaos. If all the watches in Berlin suddenly went wrong in different ways even only as much as an hour, its entire economic and commercial life would be derailed for some time. Even though this may seem more superficial in its significance, it transpires that the magnitude of distances results in making all waiting and the breaking of appointments an ill-afforded waste of time. For this reason the technique of metropolitan life in general is not conceivable without all of its activities and reciprocal relationships being organized and coordinated in the most punctual way into a firmly fixed framework of time which transcends all subjective elements. But here too there emerge those conclusions which are in general the whole task of this discussion, namely, that every event, however restricted to this superficial level it may appear, comes immediately into contact with the depths of the soul, and that the most banal externalities are, in the last analysis, bound up with the final decisions concerning the meaning and the style of life. Punctuality, calculability and exactness, which are required by the complications and extensiveness of metropolitan life, are not only most intimately connected with its capitalistic and intellectualistic character but also colour the content of life and are conductive to the exclusion of those irrational, instinctive, sovereign human traits and impulses which originally seek to determine the form of life from within instead of receiving it from the outside in a general, schematically precise form. Even though those lives which are autonomous and characterized by these vital impulses are not entirely impossible in the city, they are, none the less, opposed to it *in abstracto*. It is in the light of this that we can explain the passionate hatred of personalities like Ruskin and Nietzsche for the metropolis – personalities who found the value of life only in unschematized individual expressions which cannot be reduced to exact equivalents and in whom, on that account, there flowed from the same source as did that hatred, the hatred of the money economy and of the intellectualism of existence.

The same factors which, in the exactness and the minute precision of the form of life, have coalesced into a structure of the highest impersonality, have on the other hand, an influence in a highly personal direction. There is perhaps no psychic phenomenon which is so unconditionally reserved to the city as the blasé outlook. It is at first the consequence of those rapidly shifting stimulations of the nerves which are thrown together in all their contrasts and from which it seems to us the intensification of metropolitan intellectuality seems to be derived. On that account it is not likely that stupid persons who have been hitherto intellectually dead will be blasé. Just as an immoderately sensuous life makes one blasé because it stimulates the nerves to their utmost reactivity until they finally can no longer produce any reaction at all, so, less harmful stimuli, through the rapidity and the contradictoriness of their shifts, force the nerves to make such violent responses, tear them about so brutally that they exhaust their last reserves of strength and, remaining in the same milieu, do not have time for new reserves to form. This incapacity to react to new stimulations with the required amount of energy constitutes in fact that blasé attitude which every child of a large city evinces when compared with the products of the more peaceful and more stable milieu.

Combined with this physiological source of the blasé metropolitan attitude there is another, which derives from a money economy. The essence of the blasé attitude is an indifference toward the distinctions between things. Not in the sense that they are not perceived, as is the case of mental

dullness, but rather that the meaning and the value of the distinctions between things, and therewith of the things themselves, are experienced as meaningless. They appear to the blasé person in a homogeneous, flat and grey colour with no one of them worthy of being preferred to another. This psychic mood is the correct subjective reflection of a complete money economy to the extent that money takes the place of all the manifoldness of things and expresses all qualitative distinctions between them in the distinction of how much. To the extent that money, with its colourlessness and its indifferent quality, can become a common denominator of all values, it becomes the frightful leveller – it hollows out the core of things, their peculiarities, their specific values and their uniqueness and incomparability in a way which is beyond repair. They all float with the same specific gravity in the constantly moving stream of money. They all rest on the same level and are distinguished only by their amounts. In individual cases this colouring, or rather this de-colouring of things, through their equation with money, may be imperceptibly small. In the relationship, however, which the wealthy person has to objects which can be bought for money, perhaps indeed in the total character which, for this reason, public opinion now recognizes in these objects, it takes on very considerable proportions. This is why the metropolis is the seat of commerce and it is in it that the purchasability of things appears in quite a different aspect than in simpler economies. It is also the peculiar seat of the blasé attitude. In it is brought to a peak, in a certain way, that achievement in the concentration of purchasable things which stimulates the individual to the highest degree of nervous energy. Through the mere quantitative intensification of the same conditions this achievement is transformed into its opposite, into this peculiar adaptive phenomenon – the blasé attitude – in which the nerves reveal their final possibility of adjusting themselves to the content and the form of metropolitan life by renouncing the response to them. We see that the self-preservation of certain types of personalities is obtained at the cost of devaluing the entire objective world, ending inevitably in dragging the personality downward into a feeling of its own valuelessness.

Whereas the subject of this form of existence must come to terms with it for himself, his self-preservation in the face of the great city requires of him a no less negative type of social conduct. The mental attitude of the people of the metropolis to one another may be designated formally as one of reserve. If the unceasing external contact of numbers of persons in the city should be met by the same number of inner reactions as in the small town, in which one knows almost every person he meets and to each of whom he has a positive relationship, one would be completely atomized internally and would fall into an unthinkable mental condition. Partly this psychological circumstance and partly the privilege of suspicion which we have in the face of the elements of metropolitan life (which are constantly touching one another in fleeting contact) necessitates in us that reserve, in consequence of which we do not know by sight neighbours of years standing and which permits us to appear to small-town folk so often as cold and uncongenial. Indeed, if I am not mistaken, the inner side of this external reserve is not only indifference but more frequently than we believe, it is a slight aversion, a mutual strangeness and repulsion which, in a close contact which has arisen any way whatever, can break out into hatred and conflict. The entire inner organization of such a type of extended commercial life rests on an extremely varied structure of sympathies, indifferences and aversions of the briefest as well as of the most enduring sort. This sphere of indifference is, for this reason, not as great as it seems superficially. Our minds respond, with some definite feeling, to almost every impression emanating from another person. The unconsciousness, the transitoriness and the shift of these feelings seem to raise them only into indifference. Actually this latter would be unnatural to us as immersion into a chaos of unwished-for suggestions would be unbearable. From these two typical dangers of metropolitan life we are saved by antipathy which is the latent adumbration of actual antagonism since it brings about the sort of distantiation and deflection without which this type of life could not be carried on at all. Its extent and its mixture, the rhythm of its emergence and disappearance, the forms in which it is adequate – these constitute, with the simplified motives (in the narrower sense) an inseparable totality of the form of metropolitan life. What appears here directly as dissociation is in reality only one of the elementary forms of socialization.

This reserve with its overtone of concealed aversion appears once more, however, as the form or the wrappings of a much more general psychic trait of the metropolis. It assures the individual of a type and degree of personal freedom to which there is no analogy in other circumstances. It has its roots in one of the great developmental tendencies of social life as a whole; in one of the few for which an approximately exhaustive formula can be discovered. The most elementary stage of social organization which is to be found historically, as well as in the present, is this: a relatively small circle almost entirely closed against neighbouring foreign or otherwise antagonistic groups but which has however within itself such a narrow cohesion that the individual member has only a very slight area for the development of his own qualities and for free activity for which he himself is responsible. Political and familial groups began in this way as do political and religious communities; the self-preservation of very young associations requires a rigorous setting of boundaries and a centripetal unity and for that reason it cannot give room to freedom and the peculiarities of inner and external development of the individual. From this stage social evolution proceeds simultaneously in two divergent but none the less corresponding directions. In the measure that the group grows numerically, spatially, and in the meaningful content of life, its immediate inner unity and the definiteness of its original demarcation against others are weakened and rendered mild by reciprocal interactions and interconnections. And at the same time the individual gains a freedom of movement far beyond the first jealous delimitation, and gains also a peculiarity and individuality to which the division of labour in groups, which have become larger, gives both occasion and necessity. However much the particular conditions and forces of the individual situation might modify the general scheme, the state and Christianity, guilds and political parties and innumerable other groups have developed in accord with this formula. This tendency seems to me, however, to be quite clearly recognizable also in the development of individuality within the framework of city life. Small town life in antiquity as well as in the Middle Ages imposed such limits upon the movements of the individual in his relationships with the outside world and on his inner independence and differentiation that the modern person could not even breathe under such conditions. Even today the city dweller who is placed in a small town feels a type of narrowness which is very similar. The smaller the circle which forms our environment and the more limited the relationships which have the possibility of transcending the boundaries, the more anxiously the narrow community watches over the deeds, the conduct of life and the attitudes of the individual and the more will a quantitative and qualitative individuality tend to pass beyond the boundaries of such a community.

The ancient *polis* seems in this regard to have had a character of a small town. The incessant threat against its existence by enemies from near and far brought about that stern cohesion in political and military matters, that supervision of the citizen by other citizens, and that jealousy of the whole toward the individual whose own private life was repressed to such an extent that he could compensate himself only by acting as a despot in his own household. The tremendous agitation and excitement, and the unique colourfulness of Athenian life is perhaps explained by the fact that a

people of incomparably individualized personalities were in constant struggle against the incessant inner and external oppression of a de-individualizing small town. This created an atmosphere of tension in which the weaker were held down and the stronger were impelled to the most passionate type of self-protection. And with this there blossomed in Athens, what, without being able to define it exactly, must be designated as 'the general human character' in the intellectual development of our species. For the correlation, the factual as well as the historical validity of which we are here maintaining, is that the broadest and the most general contents and forms of life are intimately bound up with the most individual ones. Both have a common prehistory and also common enemies in the narrow formations and groupings, whose striving for self-preservation set them in conflict with the broad and general on the outside, as well as the freely mobile and individual on the inside. Just as in feudal times the 'free' man was he who stood under the law of the land, that is, under the law of the largest social unit, but he was unfree who derived his legal rights only from the narrow circle of a feudal community – so today in an intellectualized and refined sense the citizen of the metropolis is 'free' in contrast with the trivialities and prejudices which bind the small town person. The mutual reserve and indifference, and the intellectual conditions of life in large social units are never more sharply appreciated in their significance for the independence of the individual than in the dense crowds of the metropolis, because the bodily closeness and lack of space make intellectual distance really perceivable for the first time. It is obviously only the obverse of this freedom that, under certain circumstances, one never feels as lonely and as deserted as in this metropolitan crush of persons. For here, as elsewhere, it is by no means necessary that the freedom of man reflect itself in his emotional life only as a pleasant experience.

It is not only the immediate size of the area and population which, on the basis of world-historical correlation between the increase in the size of the social unit and the degree of personal inner and outer freedom, makes the metropolis the locus of this condition. It is rather in transcending this purely tangible extensiveness that the metropolis also becomes the seat of cosmopolitanism. Comparable with the form of the development of wealth – (beyond a certain point property increases in ever more rapid progression as out of its own inner being) – the individual's horizon is enlarged. In the same way, economic, personal and intellectual relations in the city (which are its ideal reflection) grow in a geometrical progression as soon as, for the first time, a certain limit has been passed. Every dynamic extension becomes a preparation not only for a similar extension but rather for a larger one, and from every thread which is spun out of it there continue, growing as out of themselves, an endless number of others. This may be illustrated by the fact that within the city the 'unearned increment' of ground rent, through a mere increase in traffic, brings to the owner profits which are self-generating. At this point the quantitative aspects of life are transformed qualitatively. The sphere of life of the small town is, in the main, enclosed within itself. For the metropolis it is decisive that its inner life is extended in a wave-like motion over a broader national or international area. Weimar was no exception because its significance was dependent upon individual personalities and died with them, whereas the metropolis is characterized by its essential independence even of the most significant individual personalities; this is rather its antithesis and it is the price of independence which the individual living in it enjoys. The most significant aspect of the metropolis lies in this functional magnitude beyond its actual physical boundaries and this effectiveness reacts upon the latter and gives to it life, weight, importance and responsibility. A person does not end with the limits of his physical body or with the area to which his physical activity is immediately confined but embraces, rather, the totality of meaningful effects which emanates from him temporally and spatially. In the same way the city exists only in the totality of the effects which transcend their immediate sphere. These really are the actual extent in which their existence is expressed. This is already expressed in the fact that individual freedom, which is the logical historical complement of such extension, is not only to be understood in the negative sense as mere freedom of movement and emancipation from prejudices and philistinism. Its essential characteristic is rather to be found in the fact that the particularity and incomparability which ultimately every person possesses in some way is actually expressed, giving form to life. That we follow the laws of our inner nature – and this is what freedom is – becomes perceptible and convincing to us and to others only when the expressions of this nature distinguish themselves from others; it is our irreplaceability by others which shows that our mode of existence is not imposed upon us from the outside.

Cities are above all the seat of the most advanced economic division of labour. They produce such extreme phenomena as the lucrative vocation of the *quatorzième* in Paris. These are persons who may be recognized by shields on their houses and who hold themselves ready at the dinner hour in appropriate costumes so they can be called upon on short notice in case thirteen persons find themselves at the table. Exactly in the measure of its extension, the city offers to an increasing degree the determining conditions for the division of labour. It is a unit which, because of its large size, is receptive to a highly diversified plurality of achievements while at the same time the agglomeration of individuals and their struggle for the customer forces the individual to a type of specialized accomplishment in which he cannot be so easily exterminated by the other. The decisive fact here is that in the life of a city, struggle with nature for the means of life is transformed into a conflict with human beings, and the gain which is fought for is granted, not by nature, but by man. For here we find not only the previously mentioned source of specialization but rather the deeper one in which the seller must seek to produce in the person to whom he wishes to sell ever new and unique needs. The necessity to specialize one's product in order to find a source of income which is not yet exhausted and also to specialize a function which cannot be easily supplanted is conducive to differentiation, refinement and enrichment of the needs of the public which obviously must lead to increasing personal variation within this public.

All this leads to the narrower type of intellectual individuation of mental qualities to which the city gives rise in proportion to its size. There is a whole series of causes for this. First of all there is the difficulty of giving one's own personality a certain status within the framework of metropolitan life. Where quantitative increase of value and energy has reached its limits, one seizes on qualitative distinctions, so that, through taking advantage of the existing sensitivity to differences, the attention of the social world can, in some way, be won for oneself. This leads ultimately to the strangest eccentricities, to specifically metropolitan extravagances of self-distantiation, of caprice, of fastidiousness, the meaning of which is no longer to be found in the content of such activity itself but rather in its being a form of 'being different' – of making oneself noticeable. For many types of persons these are still the only means of saving for oneself, through the attention gained from others, some sort of self-esteem and the sense of filling a position. In the same sense there operates an apparently insignificant factor which in its effects however is perceptibly cumulative, namely, the brevity and rarity of meetings which are allotted to each individual as compared with social intercourse in a small city. For here we find the attempt to appear to-the-point, clear-cut and individual with extra-ordinarily greater frequency than where frequent and long association assures to each person an unambiguous conception of the other's personality.

This appears to me to be the most profound cause of the fact that the metropolis places emphasis on striving for the most individual forms of personal existence – regardless of whether it is always correct or always successful. The development of modern culture is characterized by the predominance of what one can call the objective spirit over the subjective; that is, in language as well as in law, in the technique of production as well as in art, in science as well as in the objects of domestic environment, there is embodied a sort of spirit (*Geist*), the daily growth of which is followed only imperfectly and with an even greater lag by the intellectual development of the individual. If we survey, for instance, the vast culture which during the last century has been embodied in things and in knowledge, in institutions and in comforts, and if we compare them with the cultural progress of the individual during the same period – at least in the upper classes – we would see a frightful difference in rate of growth between the two which represents, in many points, rather a regression of the culture of the individual with reference to spirituality, delicacy and idealism. This discrepancy is in essence the result of the success of the growing division of labour. For it is this which requires from the individual an ever more one-sided type of achievement which, at its highest point, often permits his personality as a whole to fall into neglect. In any case this over-growth of objective culture has been less and less satisfactory for the individual. Perhaps less conscious than in practical activity and in the obscure complex of feelings which flow from him, he is reduced to a negligible quantity. He becomes a single cog as over against the vast overwhelming organization of things and forces which gradually take out of his hands everything connected with progress, spirituality and value. The operation of these forces results in the transformation of the latter from a subjective form into one of purely objective existence. It need only be pointed out that the metropolis is the proper arena for this type of culture which has outgrown every personal element. Here in buildings and in educational institutions, in the wonders and comforts of space-conquering technique, in the formations of social life and in the concrete institutions of the State is to be found such a tremendous richness of crystalizing, de-personalized cultural accomplishments that the personality can, so to speak, scarcely maintain itself in the fact of it. From one angle life is made infinitely more easy in the sense that stimulations, interests, and the taking up of time and attention, present themselves from all sides and carry it in a stream which scarcely requires any individual efforts for its ongoing. But from another angle, life is composed more and more of these impersonal cultural elements and existing goods and values which seek to suppress peculiar personal interests and incomparabilities. As a result, in order that this most personal element be saved, extremities and peculiarities and individualizations must be produced and they must be over-exaggerated merely to be brought into the awareness even of the individual himself. The atrophy of individual culture through the hypertrophy of objective culture lies at the root of the bitter hatred which the preachers of the most extreme individualism, in the footsteps of Nietzsche, directed against the metropolis. But it is also the explanation of why indeed they are so passionately loved in the metropolis and indeed appear to its residents as the saviours of their unsatisfied yearnings.

When both of these forms of individualism which are nourished by the quantitative relationships of the metropolis, i.e. individual independence and the elaboration of personal peculiarities, are examined with reference to their historical position, the metropolis attains an entirely new value and meaning in the world history of the spirit. The eighteenth century found the individual in the grip of powerful bonds which had become meaningless – bonds of a political, agrarian, guild and religious nature – delimitations which imposed upon the human being at the same time an unnatural form and for a long time an unjust inequality. In this situation arose the cry for freedom and equality – the belief in the full freedom of movement of the individual in all his social and intellectual relationships which would then permit the same noble essence to emerge equally from all individuals as Nature had placed it in them and as it had been distorted by social life and historical development. Alongside of this liberalistic ideal there grew up in the nineteenth century from Goethe and the Romantics, on the one hand, and from the economic division of labour, on the other, the further tendency, namely, that individuals who had been liberated from their historical bonds sought now to distinguish themselves from one another. No longer was it the 'general human quality' in every individual but rather his qualitative uniqueness and irreplaceability that now became the criteria of his value. In the conflict and shifting interpretations of these two ways of defining the position of the individual within the totality is to be found the external as well as the internal history of our time. It is the function of the metropolis to make a place for the conflict and for the attempts at unification of both of these in the sense that its own peculiar conditions have been revealed to us as the occasion and the stimulus for the development of both. Thereby they attain a quite unique place, fruitful with an inexhaustible richness of meaning in the development of the mental life. They reveal themselves as one of those great historical structures in which conflicting life-embracing currents find themselves with equal legitimacy. Because of this, however, regardless of whether we are sympathetic or antipathetic with their individual expressions, they transcend the sphere in which a judge-like attitude on our part is appropriate. To the extent that such forces have been integrated, with the fleeting existence of a single cell, into the root as well as the crown of the totality of historical life to which we belong – it is our task not to complain or to condone but only to understand.

Chapter 2

from *The City of Tomorrow and its Planning*

Le Corbusier

XI. A Contemporary City

The use of technical analysis and architectural synthesis enabled me to draw up my scheme for a contemporary city of three million inhabitants. The result of my work was shown in November 1922 at the Salon d'Automne in Paris. It was greeted with a sort of stupor; the shock of surprise caused rage in some quarters and enthusiasm in others. The solution I put forward was a rough one and completely uncompromising. There were no notes to accompany the plans, and, alas! not everybody can read a plan. I should have had to be constantly on the spot in order to reply to the fundamental questions which spring from the very depths of human feelings. Such questions are of profound interest and cannot remain unanswered. When at a later date it became necessary that this book should be written, a book in which I could formulate the new principles of Town Planning, I resolutely decided *first of all* to find answers to these fundamental questions. I have used two kinds of argument: first, those essentially human ones which start from the mind or the heart or the physiology of our sensations as a basis; secondly, historical and statistical arguments. Thus I could keep in touch with what is fundamental and at the same time be master of the environment in which all this takes place.

In this way I hope I shall have been able to help my reader to take a number of steps by means of which he can reach a sure and certain position. So that when I unroll my plans I can have the happy assurance that his astonishment will no longer be stupefaction nor his fears mere panic.

A contemporary city of three million inhabitants

Proceeding in the manner of the investigator in his laboratory, I have avoided all special cases, and all that may be accidental, and I have assumed an ideal site to begin with. My object was not to overcome the existing state of things, but *by constructing a theoretically water-tight formula to arrive at the fundamental principles of modern town planning*. Such fundamental principles, if they are genuine, can serve as the skeleton of any system of modern town planning; being as it were the *rules* according to which development will take place. We shall then be in a position to take a special case, no matter what: whether it be Paris, London, Berlin, New York or some small town. Then, as a result of what we have learnt, we can take control and decide in what direction the forthcoming battle is to be waged. For the desire to rebuild any great city in a modern way is to engage in a formidable battle. Can you imagine people engaging in a battle without knowing their objectives? Yet that is exactly what is happening. The authorities are compelled to do something, so they give the police white sleeves or set them on horseback, they invent sound signals and light signals, they propose to put bridges over streets or moving pavements under the streets; more garden cities are suggested, or it is decided to suppress the tramways, and so on. And these decisions are reached in a sort of frantic haste in order, as it were, to hold a wild beast at bay. That BEAST is the great city. It is infinitely more powerful than all these devices. And it is just beginning to wake. What will tomorrow bring forth to cope with it?

We must have some rules of conduct.

We must have fundamental principles for modern town planning.

Site

A level site is the ideal site. In all those places where traffic becomes over-intensified the level site gives a chance of a normal solution to the problem. Where there is less traffic, differences in level matter less.

The river flows far away from the city. The river is a kind of liquid railway, a goods station and a sorting house. In a decent house the servants' stairs do not go through the drawing-room – even if the maid is charming (or if the little boats delight the loiterer leaning on a bridge).

Population

This consists of the citizens proper; of suburban dwellers; and of those of a mixed kind.

(*a*) Citizens are of the city: those who work and live in it.

(*b*) Suburban dwellers are those who work in the outer industrial zone and who do not come into the city: they live in garden cities.

(*c*) The mixed sort are those who work in the business parts of the city but bring up their families in garden cities.

To classify these divisions (and so make possible the transmutation of these recognized types) is to attack the most important problem in town planning, for such a classification would define the areas to be allotted to these three sections and the delimitation of their boundaries. This would enable us to formulate and resolve the following problems:

1. The *City*, as a business and residential centre.
2. The *Industrial City* in relation to the *Garden Cities* (*i.e.* the question of transport).
3. The *Garden Cities* and the *daily transport* of the workers.

Our first requirement will be an organ that is compact, rapid, lively and concentrated: this is the City with its well-organized centre. Our second requirement will be another organ, supple, extensive and elastic; this is *the Garden City* on the periphery.

Lying between these two organs, we must *require the legal establishment* of that absolute necessity, a protective zone which allows of extension, *a reserved zone* of woods and fields, a fresh-air reserve.

Density of population

The more dense the population of a city is the less are the distances that have to be covered. The moral, therefore, is that we must *increase the density of the centres of our cities, where business affairs are carried on.*

Lungs

Work in our modern world becomes more intensified day by day, and its demands affect our nervous system in a way that grows more and more dangerous. Modern toil demands quiet and fresh air, not stale air.

The towns of today can only increase in density at the expense of the open spaces which are the lungs of a city.

We must *increase the open spaces and diminish the distances to be covered.*

Therefore the centre of the city must be constructed *vertically*.

The city's residential quarters must no longer be built along "corridor-streets," full of noise and dust and deprived of light.

It is a simple matter to build urban dwellings away from the streets, without small internal courtyards and with the windows looking on to large parks; and this whether our housing schemes are of the type with "set-backs" or built on the "cellular" principle.

The street

The street of today is still the old bare ground which has been paved over, and under which a few tube railways have been run.

The modern street in the true sense of the word is a new type of organism, a sort of stretched-out workshop, a home for many complicated and delicate organs, such as gas, water and electric mains. It is contrary to all economy, to all security, and to all sense to bury these important service mains. They ought to be accessible throughout their length. The various storeys of this stretched-out workshop will each have their own particular functions. If this type of street, which I have called a "workshop," is to be realized, it becomes as much a matter of *construction* as are the houses with which it is customary to flank it, and the bridges which carry it over valleys and across rivers.

The modern street should be a masterpiece of civil engineering and no longer a job for navvies.

The "corridor-street" should be tolerated no longer, for it poisons the houses that border it and leads to the construction of small internal courts or "wells."

Traffic

Traffic can be classified more easily than other things.

Today traffic is not classified – it is like dynamite flung at hazard into the street, killing pedestrians. Even so, *traffic does not fulfill its function*. This sacrifice of the pedestrian leads nowhere.

If we classify traffic we get:

(*a*) Heavy goods traffic.

(*b*) Lighter goods traffic, *i.e.* vans, etc., which make short journeys in all directions.

(*c*) Fast traffic, which covers a large section of the town.

Three kinds of roads are needed, and in superimposed storeys:

(*a*) Below-ground there would be the street for heavy traffic. This storey of the houses would consist merely of concrete piles, and between them large open spaces which would form a sort of clearing-house where heavy goods traffic could load and unload.

(*b*) At the ground floor level of the buildings there would be the complicated and delicate network of the ordinary streets taking traffic in every desired direction.

(*c*) Running north and south, and east and west, and forming the two great axes of the city, there would be great *arterial roads for fast one-way traffic* built on immense reinforced concrete bridges 120 to 180 yards in width and approached every half-mile or so by subsidiary roads from ground level. These arterial roads could therefore be joined at any given point, so that even at the highest speeds the town can be traversed and the suburbs reached without having to negotiate any cross-roads

The number of existing streets *should be diminished by two-thirds*. The number of crossings depends directly on the number of streets; and *cross-roads are an enemy to traffic*. The number of existing streets was fixed at a remote epoch in history. The perpetuation of the boundaries of properties has, almost without exception, preserved even the faintest tracks and footpaths of the old village and made streets of them, and sometimes even an avenue (see Chapter I of *The City of To-morrow*: "The Pack-Donkey's Way and Man's Way").

The result is that we have cross-roads every fifty yards, even every twenty yards or ten yards. And this leads to the ridiculous traffic congestion we all know so well.

The distance between two 'bus stops or two tube stations gives us the necessary unit for the distance between streets, though this unit is conditional on the speed of vehicles and the walking capacity of pedestrians. So an average measure of about 400 yards would give the normal separation between streets, and make a standard for urban distances. My city is conceived on the gridiron system with streets every 400 yards, though occasionally these distances are subdivided to give streets every 200 yards.

This triple system of superimposed levels answers every need of motor traffic (lorries, private cars, taxis, 'buses) because it provides for rapid and *mobile* transit.

Traffic running on fixed rails is only justified if it is in the form of a convoy carrying an immense load; it then becomes a sort of extension of the underground system or of trains dealing with suburban traffic. *The tramway has no right to exist in the heart of the modern city.*

If the city thus consists of plots about 400 yards square, this will give us sections of about 40 acres in area, and the density of population will vary from 50,000 down to 6,000, according as the "lots" are developed for business or for residential purposes. The natural thing, therefore, would be to continue to apply our unit of distance as it exists in the Paris tubes today (namely, 400 yards) and to put a station in the middle of each plot.

Following the two great axes of the city, two "storeys" below the arterial roads for fast traffic, would run the tubes leading to the four furthest points of the garden city suburbs, and linking up with the metropolitan network. At a still lower level, and again following these two main axes, would run the one-way loop systems for suburban traffic, and below these again the four great main lines serving the provinces and running north, south, east and west. These main lines would end at the Central Station, or better still might be connected up by a loop system.

The station

There is only one station. The only place for the station is in the centre of the city. It is the natural place for it, and there is no reason for putting it anywhere else. The railway station is the hub of the wheel.

The station would be an essentially subterranean building. Its roof, which would be two storeys above the natural ground level of the city, would form the aerodrome for aero-taxis. This aerodrome (linked up with the main aerodrome in the protected zone) must be in close contact with the tubes, the suburban lines, the main lines, the main arteries and the administrative services connected with all these.

The plan of the city

The basic principles we must follow are these:

1. We must de-congest the centres of our cities.
2. We must augment their density.
3. We must increase the means for getting about.
4. We must increase parks and open spaces.

At the very centre we have the STATION with its landing stage for aero-taxis.

Running north and south, and east and west, we have the MAIN ARTERIES for fast traffic, forming elevated roadways 120 feet wide.

At the base of the sky-scrapers and all round them we have a great open space 2,400 yards by 1,500 yards, giving an area of 3,600,000 square yards, and occupied by gardens, parks and avenues. In these parks, at the foot of and round the sky-scrapers, would be the restaurants and cafés, the luxury shops, housed in buildings with receding terraces: here too would be the theatres, halls and so on; and here the parking places or garage shelters.

The sky-scrapers are designed purely for business purposes.

On the left we have the great public buildings, the museums, the municipal and administrative offices. Still further on the left we have the "Park" (which is available for further logical development of the heart of the city).

On the right, and traversed by one of the arms of the main arterial roads, we have the warehouses, and the industrial quarters with their goods stations.

All round the city is the *protected zone* of woods and green fields.

Further beyond are the *garden cities*, forming a wide encircling band.

Then, right in the midst of all these, we have the *Central Station*, made up of the following elements:

(*a*) The landing-platform; forming an aerodrome of 200,000 square yards in area.

(*b*) The entresol or mezzanine; at this level are the raised tracks for fast motor traffic: the only crossing being gyratory.

(*c*) The ground floor where are the entrance halls and booking offices for the tubes, suburban, main line and air traffic.

(*d*) The "basement": here are the tubes which serve the city and the main arteries.

(*e*) The "sub-basement": here are the suburban lines running on a one-way loop.

(*f*) The "sub-sub-basement": here are the main lines (going north, south, east and west).

The city
Here we have twenty-four sky-scrapers capable each of housing 10,000 to 50,000 employees; this is the business and hotel section, etc., and accounts for 400,000 to 600,000 inhabitants.

The residential blocks, of the two main types already mentioned, account for a further 600,000 inhabitants.

The garden cities give us a further 2,000,000 inhabitants, or more.

In the great central open space are the cafés, restaurants, luxury shops, halls of various kinds, a magnificent forum descending by stages down to the immense parks surrounding it, the whole arrangement providing a spectacle of order and vitality.

Density of population
(*a*) The sky-scraper: 1,200 inhabitants to the acre.

(*b*) The residential blocks with setbacks: 120 inhabitants to the acre. These are the luxury dwellings.

(*c*) The residential blocks on the "cellular" system, with a similar number of inhabitants.

This great density gives us our necessary shortening of distances and ensures rapid intercommunication.

Note.—The average density to the acre of Paris in the heart of the town is 146, and of London 63; and of the over-crowded quarters of Paris 213, and of London 169.

Open spaces
Of the area (*a*), 95 per cent of the ground is open (squares, restaurants, theatres).

Of the area (*b*), 85 per cent. of the ground is open (gardens, sports grounds).

Of the area (*c*), 48 per cent. of the ground is open (gardens, sports grounds).

*Educational and civic centres,
universities, museums of art and
industry, public services, county
hall*
The "Jardin anglais." (The city can extend here, if necessary.)

Sports grounds: Motor racing track, Racecourse, Stadium, Swimming baths, etc.

*The protected zone (which will be
the property of the city), with its
aerodrome.*
A zone in which all building would be prohibited; reserved for the growth of the city as laid down by the municipality: it would consist of woods, fields, and sports grounds. The forming of a "protected zone" by continual purchase of small properties in the immediate vicinity of the city is one of the most essential and urgent tasks which a municipality can pursue. It would eventually represent a tenfold return on the capital invested.

Industrial quarters[1]
Types of buildings employed
For business: sky-scrapers sixty storeys high with no internal wells or courtyards (see the following chapter).

Residential buildings with "set-backs," of six double storeys; again with no internal wells: the flats looking on either side on to immense parks.

Residential buildings on the "cellular" principle, with "hanging gardens," looking on to immense parks; again no internal wells. These are "service-flats" of the most modern kind.

Garden cities

Their aesthetic, economy,
perfection and modern outlook
A simple phrase suffices to express the necessities of tomorrow: WE MUST BUILD IN THE OPEN. The lay-out must be of a purely geometrical kind, with all its many and delicate implications.

The city of today is a dying thing because it is not geometrical. To build in the open would be to replace our present haphazard arrangements, *which are all we have today,* by a *uniform* lay-out. Unless we do this *there is no salvation.*

The result of a true geometrical lay-out is *repetition.*

The result of repetition is a *standard,* the perfect form (*i.e.* the creation of standard types). A geometrical lay-out means that mathematics play their part. There is no first-rate human production but has geometry at its base. It is of the very essence of Architecture. To introduce uniformity into the building of the city we must *industrialize building.* Building is the one economic activity which has so far resisted industrialization. It has thus escaped the march of progress, with the result that the cost of building is still abnormally high.

The architect, from a professional point of view, has become a twisted sort of creature. He has grown to love irregular sites, claiming that they inspire him with original ideas for getting round them. Of course he is wrong. For nowadays the only building that can be undertaken must be either for the rich or built at a loss (as, for instance, in the case of municipal housing schemes), or else by jerry-building and so robbing the inhabitant of all amenities. A motor-car which is achieved by mass production is a masterpiece of comfort, precision, balance and good taste. A house built to order (on an "interesting" site) is a masterpiece of incongruity – a monstrous thing.

If the builder's yard were reorganized on the lines of standardization and mass production we might have gangs of workmen as keen and intelligent as mechanics.

The mechanic dates back only twenty years, yet already he forms the highest caste of the working world.

The mason dates . . . from time immemorial! He bangs away with feet and hammer. He smashes up everything round him, and the plant entrusted to him falls to pieces in a few months. The spirit of the mason must be disciplined by making him part of the severe and exact machinery of the industrialized builder's yard.

The cost of building would fall in the proportion of 10 to 2.

The wages of the labourers would fall into definite categories; to each according to his merits and service rendered.

The "interesting" or erratic site absorbs every creative faculty of the architect and wears him out. What results is equally erratic: lopsided abortions; a specialist's solution which can only please other specialists.

We must build *in the open*: both within the city and around it.

Then having worked through every necessary technical stage and using absolute ECONOMY, we shall be in a position to experience the intense joys of a creative art which is based on geometry.

The city and its aesthetic

(The plan of a city which is here presented is a direct consequence of purely geometric considerations.)

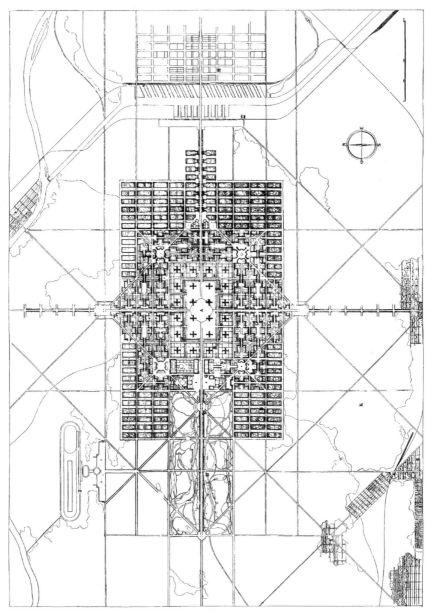

A CONTEMPORARY CITY

The heavy black lines represent the areas built upon. Everything else is either streets or open spaces. Strictly speaking the city is an immense park. Its lay-out furnishes a multitude of architectural aspects of infinitely varying forms. If the reader, for instance, follows out a given route on this map he will be astonished by the variety he encounters. Yet distances are shorter than in the cities of to-day, for there is a greater density of population.

A. *Station.*
B. *Sky-scraper.*
C. *Housing blocks with "set-backs."*
D. *Housing blocks on the "cellular" system.*
E. *Garden cities.*

G. *Public Services.*
H. *Park.*
I. *Sports.*
K. *Protected zone.*
M. *Warehouses, Industrial city, Goods station.*

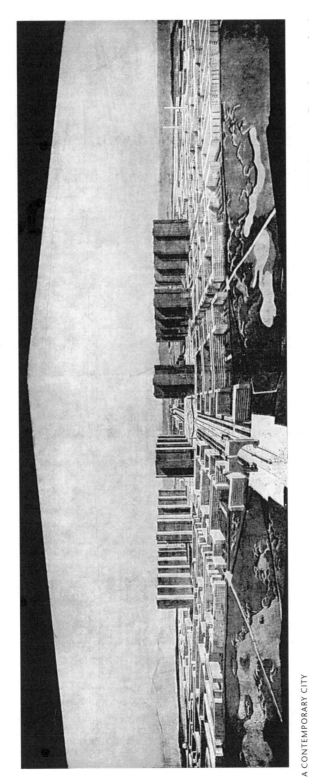

A CONTEMPORARY CITY

Panoramic view of the city. In the foreground are the woods and fields of the protected zone. The Great Central Station can be seen in the centre and the two main tracks for fast motor traffic crossing one another. Among the hills on the horizon and beyond the foliage of the protected zone can just be seen the Garden Cities.

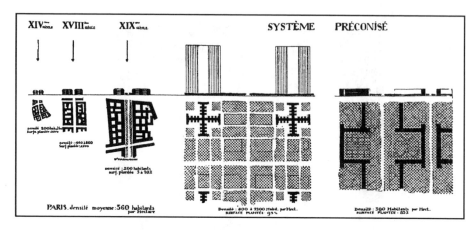

A diagram showing the increase in size of building sites from the fourteenth to the eighteenth and nineteenth centuries. In the nineteenth century the Boulevard Haussmann again offered the "corridor-street" as a solution. But in this plan I allow for sky-scrapers at intervals of 400 yards and for blocks of dwellings with "set-backs." The magnification of the site unit is in proportion to the evolution that has taken place and to the means at our disposal.

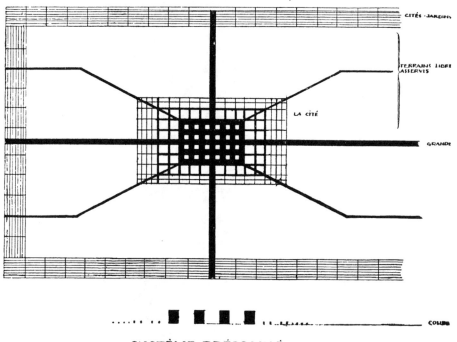

SYSTÈME PRÉCONISÉ
RÉSEAU DES RUES

A diagram showing the relative importance of streets in a great city. The black lines give the width of the streets. This system, which indicates what is needed under the new conditions, is absolutely contrary to the present state of things.

A new unit *on a large scale* (400 yards) inspires everything. Though the gridiron arrangement of the streets every 400 yards (sometimes only 200) is uniform (with a consequent ease in finding one's way about), no two streets are in any way alike. This is where, in a magnificent contrapuntal symphony, the forces of geometry come into play.

Suppose we are entering the city by way of the Great Park. Our fast car takes the special elevated motor track between the majestic sky-scrapers: as we approach nearer there is seen the repetition against the sky of the twenty-four sky-scrapers; to our left and right on the outskirts of each particular area are the municipal and administrative buildings; and enclosing the space are the museums and university buildings.

Then suddenly we find ourselves at the feet of the first sky-scrapers. But here we have, not the meagre shaft of sunlight which so faintly illumines the dismal streets of New York, but an immensity of space. The whole city is a Park. The terraces stretch out over lawns and into groves. Low buildings of a horizontal kind lead the eye on to the foliage of the trees. Where are now the trivial *Procuracies?* Here is the CITY with its crowds living in peace and pure air, where noise is smothered under the foliage of green trees. The chaos of New York is overcome. Here, bathed in light, stands the modern city.

Our car has left the elevated track and has dropped its speed of sixty miles an hour

to run gently through the residential quarters. The "set-backs" permit of vast architectural perspectives. There are gardens, games and sports grounds. And sky everywhere, as far as the eye can see. The square silhouettes of the terraced roofs stand clear against the sky, bordered with the verdure of the hanging gardens. The uniformity of the units that compose the picture throw into relief the firm lines on which the far-flung masses are constructed. Their outlines softened by distance, the sky-scrapers raise immense geometrical façades all of glass, and in them is reflected the blue glory of the sky. An overwhelming sensation. Immense but radiant prisms.

And in every direction we have a varying spectacle: our "gridiron" is based on a unit of 400 yards, but it is strangely modified by architectural devices! (The "set-backs" are in counterpoint, on a unit of 600 × 400.)

The traveller in his airplane, arriving from Constantinople or Peking it may be, suddenly sees appearing through the wavering lines of rivers and patches of forests that clear imprint which marks a city which has grown in accordance with the spirit of man: the mark of the human brain at work.

As twilight falls the glass sky-scrapers seem to flame.

This is no dangerous futurism, a sort of literary dynamite flung violently at the spectator. It is a spectacle organized by an Architecture which uses plastic resources for the modulation of forms seen in light.

NOTES

1   In this section I make new suggestions in regard to the industrial quarters: they have been content to exist too long in disorder, dirt and in a hand-to-mouth way. And this is absurd, for Industry, when it is on a properly ordered basis, should develop in an orderly fashion. A portion of the industrial district could be constructed of ready-made sections by using standard units for the various kinds of buildings needed. Fifty per cent. of the site would be reserved for this purpose. In the event of considerable growth, provision would thus be made for moving them into a different district where there was more space. Bring about "*standardization*" in the building of a works and you would have mobility instead of the crowding which results when factories become impossible congested.

Chapter 3

from *The Image of the City*

Kevin Lynch

III. The City Image and its Elements

There seems to be a public image of any given city which is the overlap of many individual images. Or perhaps there is a series of public images, each held by some significant number of citizens. Such group images are necessary if an individual is to operate successfully within his environment and to cooperate with his fellows. Each individual picture is unique, with some content that is rarely or never communicated, yet it approximates the public image, which, in different environments, is more or less compelling, more or less embracing. . . .

The contents of the city images so far studied, which are referable to physical forms, can conveniently be classified into five types of elements: paths, edges, districts, nodes, and landmarks. . . . These elements may be defined as follows:

1. *Paths.* Paths are the channels along which the observer customarily, occasionally, or potentially moves. They may be streets, walkways, transit lines, canals, railroads. For many people, these are the predominant elements in their image. People observe the city while moving through it, and along these paths the other environmental elements are arranged and related.

2. *Edges.* Edges are the linear elements not used or considered as paths by the ob-

server. They are the boundaries between two phases, linear breaks in continuity: shores, railroad cuts, edges of development, walls. They are lateral references rather than coordinate axes. Such edges may be barriers, more or less penetrable, which close one region off from another; or they may be seams, lines along which two regions are related and joined together. These edge elements, although probably not as dominant as paths, are for many people important organizing features, particularly in the role of holding together generalized areas, as in the outline of a city by water or wall.

3. *Districts.* Districts are the medium-to-large sections of the city, conceived of as having two-dimensional extent, which the observer mentally enters "inside of," and which are recognizable as having some common, identifying character. Always identifiable from the inside, they are also used for exterior reference if visible from the outside. Most people structure their city to some extent in this way, with individual differences as to whether paths or districts are the dominant elements. It seems to depend not only upon the individual but also upon the given city.

4. *Nodes.* Nodes are points, the strategic spots in a city into which an observer can enter, and which are the intensive foci to and from which he is traveling. They may be primarily junctions, places of a break in

transportation, a crossing or convergence of paths, moments of shift from one structure to another. Or the nodes may be simply concentrations, which gain their importance from being the condensation of some use or physical character, as a street-corner hangout or an enclosed square. Some of these concentration nodes are the focus and epitome of a district, over which their influence radiates and of which they stand as a symbol. They may be called cores. Many nodes, of course, partake of the nature of both junctions and concentrations. The concept of node is related to the concept of path, since junctions are typically the convergence of paths, events on the journey. It is similarly related to the concept of district, since cores are typically the intensive foci of districts, their polarizing center. In any event, some nodal points are to be found in almost every image, and in certain cases they may be the dominant feature.

5. *Landmarks*. Landmarks are another type of point-reference, but in this case the observer does not enter within them, they are external. They are usually a rather simply defined physical object: building, sign, store, or mountain. Their use involves the singling out of one element from a host of possibilities. Some landmarks are distant ones, typically seen from many angles and distances, over the tops of smaller elements, and used as radial references. They may be within the city or at such a distance that for all practical purposes they symbolize a constant direction. Such are isolated towers, golden domes, great hills. Even a mobile point, like the sun, whose motion is sufficiently slow and regular, may be employed. Other landmarks are primarily local, being visible only in restricted localities and from certain approaches. These are the innumerable signs, store fronts, trees, doorknobs, and other urban detail, which fill in the image of most observers. They are frequently used clues of identity and even of structure, and seem to be increasingly relied upon as a journey becomes more and more familiar.

The image of a given physical reality may occasionally shift its type with different circumstances of viewing. Thus an expressway may be a path for the driver, and edge for the pedestrian. Or a central area may be a district when a city is organized on a medium scale, and a node when the entire metropolitan area is considered. But the categories seem to have stability for a given observer when he is operating at a given level.

None of the element types isolated above exist in isolation in the real case. Districts are structured with nodes, defined by edges, penetrated by paths, and sprinkled with landmarks. Elements regularly overlap and pierce one another. If this analysis begins with the differentiation of the data into categories, it must end with their reintegration into the whole image ....

Paths

For most people interviewed, paths were the predominant city elements, although their importance varied according to the degree of familiarity with the city. People with least knowledge of Boston tended to think of the city in terms of topography, large regions, generalized characteristics, and broad directional relationships. Subjects who knew the city better had usually mastered part of the path structure; these people thought more in terms of specific paths and their interrelationships. A tendency also appeared for the people who knew the city best of all to rely more upon small landmarks and less upon either regions or paths.

The potential drama and identification in the highway system should not be underestimated. One Jersey City subject, who can find little worth describing in her surroundings, suddenly lit up when she described the Holland Tunnel. Another recounted her pleasure:

> You cross Baldwin Avenue, you see all of New York in front of you, you see the terrific drop of land (the Palisades)...

and here's this open panorama of lower Jersey City in front of you and you're going down hill, and there you know: there's the tunnel, there's the Hudson River and everything... I always look to the right to see if I can see the... Statue of Liberty... Then I always look up to see the Empire State Building, see how the weather is... I have a real feeling of happiness because I'm going someplace, and I love to go places.

....Concentration of special use or activity along a street may give it prominence in the minds of observers. Washington Street is the outstanding Boston example: subjects consistently associated it with shopping and theatres. Some people extended these characteristics to parts of Washington Street that are quite different (e.g., near State Street); many people seemed not to know that Washington extends beyond the entertainment segment, and thought it ended near Essex or Stuart Streets. Los Angeles has many examples—Broadway, Spring Street, Skid Row, 7th Street—where the use concentrations are prominent enough to make linear districts. People seemed to be sensitive to variations in the amount of activity they encountered, and sometimes guided themselves largely by following the main stream of traffic. Los Angeles' Broadway was recognized by its crowds and its street cars; Washington Street in Boston was marked by a torrent of pedestrians. Other kinds of activity at ground level also seemed to make places memorable, such as construction work near South Station, or the bustle of the food markets.

Characteristic spatial qualities were able to strengthen the image of particular paths. In the simplest sense, streets that suggest extremes of either width or narrowness attracted attention... Spatial qualities of width and narrowness derived part of their importance from the common association of main streets with width and side streets with narrowness. Looking for, and trusting to the "main" (i.e., wide) street becomes automatic, and in Boston the real pattern usually supports this assumption....

Proximity to special features of the city could also endow a path with increased importance. In this case the path would be acting secondarily as an edge....

Where major paths lacked identity, or were easily confused one for the other, the entire city image was in difficulty....

That the paths, once identifiable, have continuity as well, is an obvious functional necessity. People regularly depended upon this quality. The fundamental requirement is that the actual track, or bed of the pavement, go through; the continuity of other characteristics is less important. Paths which simply have a satisfactory degree of track continuity were selected as the dependable ones in an environment like Jersey City. They can be followed by the stranger, even if with difficulty. People often generalized that other kinds of characteristics along a continuous track were also continuous, despite actual changes.

...Paths may not only be identifiable and continuous, but have directional quality as well: one direction along the line can easily be distinguished from the reverse. This can be done by a gradient, a regular change in some quality which is cumulative in one direction. Most frequently sensed were the topographic gradients....

A prolonged curve is also a gradient, a steady change in direction of movement. This was not often sensed kinesthetically: the only citations of a bodily sense of curving motion were in the Boston subway, or on portions of the Los Angeles freeways. When street curves are mentioned in the interviews, they seem to relate primarily to visual clues. The turning in Charles Street at Beacon Hill was sensed, for example, because the close building walls heightened the visual perception of curvature.

People tended to think of path destinations and origin points: they liked to know where paths came from and where they led. Paths with clear and well-known origins and destinations had stronger identities, helped tie the city together, and gave the observer a sense of his bearings whenever he crossed them. Some subjects thought of general destinations for paths, to a section of the city, for example, while others thought of specific places. One person, who made rather high demands for intelligibility upon the city environment, was troubled because he saw a set of railroad tracks, and did not know the destination of trains using them. . . .

Once a path has directional quality, it may have the further attribute of being scaled: one may be able to sense one's position along the total length, to grasp the distance traversed or yet to go. Features which facilitate scaling, of course, usually confer a sense of direction as well, except for the simple technique of counting blocks, which is directionless but can be used to compute distances. Many subjects referred to this latter clue, but by no means all. It was most commonly used in the regular pattern of Los Angeles.

Most often, perhaps, scaling was accomplished by a sequence of known landmarks or nodes along the path. The marking of identifiable regions as a path enters and leaves them also constituted a powerful means of giving direction and scaling to a path . . . .

Edges

Edges are the linear elements not considered as paths: they are usually, but not quite always, the boundaries between two kinds of areas. They act as lateral references. They are strong in Boston and Jersey City but weaker in Los Angeles. Those edges seem strongest which are not only visually prominent, but also continuous in form and impenetrable to cross movement. The Charles River in Boston is the best example and has all of these qualities. . . .

It is difficult to think of Chicago without picturing Lake Michigan. It would be interesting to see how many Chicagoans would begin to draw a map of their city by putting down something other than the line of the lake shore. Here is a magnificent example of a visible edge, gigantic in scale, that exposes an entire metropolis to view. Great buildings, parks, and tiny private beaches all come down to the water's edge, which throughout most of its length is accessible and visible to all. The contrast, the differentiation of events along the line, and the lateral breadth are all very strong. The effect is reinforced by the concentration of paths and activities along its extent. The scale is perhaps unrelievedly large and coarse, and too much open space is at times interposed between city and water, as at the Loop. Yet the façade of Chicago on the Lake is an unforgettable sight.

Districts

Districts are the relatively large city areas which the observer can mentally go inside of, and which have some common character. They can be recognized internally, and occasionally can be used as external reference as a person goes by or toward them. Many persons interviewed took care to point out that Boston, while confusing in its path pattern even to the experienced inhabitant, has, in the number and vividness of its differentiated districts, a quality that quite makes up for it. As one person put it:

> Each part of Boston is different from the other. You can tell pretty much what area you're in.

Jersey City has its districts too, but they are primarily ethnic or class districts with little physical distinction. Los Angeles is markedly lacking in strong regions, except for the Civic Center area. The best that can be found are the linear, street-front districts of Skid Row or the financial area. Many Los Angeles subjects referred with some regret to the pleasure of living in a place that has strongly characteristic areas. Said one:

> I like Transportation Row, because it's all there together. That's the main thing; all these other things are spotty. . . There's transportation right there. And all the people have the same thing in common working there. It's very nice.

Subjects, when asked which city they felt to be a well-oriented one, mentioned several, but New York (meaning Manhattan) was unanimously cited. And this city was cited not so much for its grid, which Los Angeles has as well, but because it has a number of well-defined characteristic districts, set in an ordered frame of rivers and streets. Two Los Angeles subjects even referred to Manhattan as being "small" in comparison to their central area! Concepts of size may depend in part on how well a structure can be grasped. . . .

The physical characteristics that determine districts are thematic continuities which may consist of an endless variety of components: texture, space, form, detail, symbol, building type, use, activity, inhabitants, degree of maintenance, topography. In a closely built city such as Boston, homogeneities of façade – material, modeling, ornament, color, skyline, especially fenestration – were all basic clues in identifying major districts. Beacon Hill and Commonwealth Avenue are both examples. The clues were not only visual ones: noise was important as well. At times, indeed, confusion itself might be a clue, as it was for the woman who remarked that she knows she is in the North End as soon as she feels she is getting lost.

Usually, the typical features were imaged and recognized in a characteristic cluster, the thematic unit. The Beacon Hill image, for example, included steep narrow streets; old brick row houses of intimate scale; inset, highly maintained, white doorways; black trim; cobblestones and brick walks; quiet; and upper-class pedestrians. The resulting thematic unit was distinctive by contrast to the rest of the city and could be recognized immediately. . . .

A certain reinforcement of clues is needed to produce a strong image. All too often, there are a few distinctive signs, but not enough for a full thematic unit. Then the region may be recognizable to someone familiar with the city, but it lacks any visual strength or impact. Such, for example, is Little Tokyo in Los Angeles, recognizable by its population and the lettering on its signs but otherwise indistinguishable from the general matrix. Although it is a strong ethnic concentration, probably known to many people, it appeared as only a subsidiary portion of the city image.

Yet social connotations are quite significant in building regions. A series of street interviews indicated the class overtones that many people associate with different districts. Most of the Jersey City regions were class or ethnic areas, discernible only with difficulty for the outsider. Both Jersey City and Boston have shown the exaggerated attention paid to upper-class districts, and the resulting magnification of the importance of elements in those areas. District names also help to give identity to districts even when the thematic unit does not establish a striking contrast with other parts of the city, and traditional associations can play a similar role.

When the main requirement has been satisfied, and a thematic unit that contrasts with the rest of the city has been constituted, the degree of internal homogeneity is less significant, especially if discordant elements occur in a predictable pattern. Small stores on street corners establish a rhythm on Beacon Hill that one subject perceived as part of her image. These stores in no way weakened her non-commercial image of Beacon Hill but merely added to it. Subjects could pass over a surprising amount of local disagreement with the characteristic features of a region. . . .

Nodes

Nodes are the strategic foci into which the observer can enter, typically either junctions of paths, or concentrations of some characteristic. But although conceptually they are small points in the city image, they may in reality be large squares, or somewhat extended linear shapes, or even entire central districts when the city is being considered at a large enough level. Indeed, when conceiving the environment at a national or international level, then the whole city itself may become a node.

The junction, or place of a break in transportation, has compelling importance for the city observer. Because decisions must be made at junctions, people heighten their attention at such places and perceive nearby elements with more than normal clarity. This tendency was confirmed so repeatedly that elements located at junctions may automatically be assumed to derive special prominence from their location. The perceptual importance of such locations shows in another way as well. When subjects were asked where on a habitual trip they first felt a sense of arrival in downtown Boston, a large number of people singled out break-points of transportation as the key places. . . .

The subway stations, strung along their invisible path systems are strategic junction nodes. . . .

Major railroad stations are almost always important city nodes although their importance may be declining. . . .

In theory, even ordinary street intersections are nodes, but generally they are not of sufficient prominence to be imaged as more than the incidental crossing of paths. The image cannot carry too many nodal centers. The other type of node, the thematic concentration, also appeared frequently. Pershing Square in Los Angeles was a strong example, being perhaps the sharpest point of the city image, characterized by highly typical space, planting, and activity. . . .

Many of these qualities may be summed up by the example of a famous Italian node: the Piazza San Marco in Venice. Highly differentiated, rich and intricate, it stands in sharp contrast to the general character of the city and to the narrow, twisting spaces of its immediate approaches. Yet it ties firmly to the major feature of the city, the Grand Canal, and has an oriented shape that clarifies the direction from which one enters. It is within itself highly differentiated and structured: into two spaces (Piazza and Piazzetta) and with many distinctive landmarks (Duomo, Palazzo Ducale, Campanile, Libreria). Inside, one feels always in clear relation to it, precisely micro-located, as it were. So distinctive is this space that many people who have never been to Venice will recognize its photograph immediately.

Landmarks

Landmarks, the point references considered to be external to the observer, are simple physical elements which may vary widely in scale. There seemed to be a tendency for those more familiar with a city to rely increasingly on systems of landmarks for their guides – to enjoy uniqueness and specialization, in place of the continuities used earlier.

Since the use of landmarks involves the singling out of one element from a host of possibilities, the key physical characteristic of this class is singularity, some aspect that is unique or memorable in the context. Landmarks become more easily identifiable, more likely to be chosen as significant, if they have a clear form; if they contrast with their background; and if there is some prominence of spatial location. Figure–background contrast seems to be the principal factor. The background against which an element stands out need not be limited to immediate surroundings: the grasshopper weathervane of Faneuil Hall, the gold dome of the State House, or the peak of the Los Angeles City Hall are landmarks that are unique against the background of the entire city. . . .

Spatial prominence can establish elements as landmarks in either of two ways: by making the element visible from many locations (the John Hancock Building in Boston, the Richfield Oil Building in Los Angeles), or by setting up a local contrast with nearby elements, i.e., a variation in setback and height. In Los Angeles, on 7th Street at the corner of Flower Street, is an old, two-story gray wooden building, set back some ten feet from the building line, containing a few minor shops. This took the attention and fancy of a surprising number of people. One even anthropomorphized it as the "little gray lady." The spatial set-back and the intimate scale is a very noticeable and delightful event, in contrast to the great masses that occupy the rest of the frontage.

Location at a junction involving path decisions strengthens a landmark. The Telephone Building at Boston's Bowdoin Square was used, for example, to help people to stay on Cambridge Street. The activity associated with an element may also make it a landmark: an unusual case of this was the Symphony Hall in Los Angeles. This auditorium is the very antithesis of visual imageability: housed in rented quarters in a nondescript building, whose sign simply says "Baptist Temple," it is completely unrecognizable to the stranger. Its strength as a landmark seemed to derive from the contrast and irritation felt between its cultural status and its physical invisibility. Historical associations, or other meanings, are powerful reinforcements, as they are for Faneuil Hall or the State House in Boston. Once a history, a sign, or a meaning attaches to an object, its value as a landmark rises.

Distant landmarks, prominent points visible from many positions, were often well known, but only people unfamiliar with Boston seemed to use them to any great extent in organizing the city and selecting routes for trips. It is the novice who guides himself by reference to the John Hancock Building and the Custom House.

Few people had an accurate sense of where these distant landmarks were and how to make one's way to the base of either building. Most of Boston's distant landmarks, in fact, were "bottomless"; they had a peculiar floating quality. The John Hancock Building, the Custom House, and the Court House are all dominant on the general skyline, but the location and identity of their base is by no means as significant as that of their top.

The gold dome of Boston's State House seems to be one of the few exceptions to this elusiveness. Its unique shape and function, its location at the hill crest and its exposure to the Common, the visibility from long distances of its bright gold dome, all make it a key sign for central Boston. It has the satisfying qualities of recognizability at many levels of reference, and of coincidence of symbolic with visual importance. . . .

But local landmarks, visible only in restricted localities, were much more frequently employed in the three cities studied. They ran the full range of objects available. The number of local elements that become landmarks appears to depend as much upon how familiar the observer is with his surroundings as upon the elements themselves. Unfamiliar subjects usually mentioned only a few landmarks in office interviews, although they managed to find many more when they went on field trips. Sounds and smells sometimes reinforced visual landmarks, although they did not seem to constitute landmarks by themselves.

Landmarks may be isolated, single events without reinforcement. Except for large or very singular marks, these are weak references, since they are easy to miss and require sustained searching. The single traffic light or street name demands concentration to find. More often, local points were remembered as clusters, in which they reinforced each other by repetition, and were recognizable partly by context.

A sequential series of landmarks, in which one detail calls up anticipation of the next and key details trigger specific moves of the observer, appeared to be a standard way in which these people traveled through the city. In such sequences, there were trigger cues whenever turning decisions must be made and reassuring cues that confirmed the observer in decisions gone by. Additional details often helped to give a sense of nearness to the final destination or to intermediate goals. For emotional security as well as functional efficiency, it is important that such sequences be fairly continuous, with no long gaps, although there may be a thickening of detail at nodes. The sequence facilitates recognition and memorization. Familiar observers can store up a vast quantity of point images in familiar sequences, although recognition may break down when the sequence is reversed or scrambled.

Element interrelations

...Most observers seem to group their elements into intermediate organizations, which might be called complexes. The observer senses the complex as a whole whose parts are interdependent and are relatively fixed in relation to each other.... Outside of this complex there are gaps of identity; the observer must run blind to the next whole, even if only momentarily....

There were indications that the image may be a continuous field, the disturbance of one element in some way affecting all others. Even the recognition of an object is as much dependent on context as on the form of the object itself....

The shifting image

Rather than a single comprehensive image for the entire environment, there seemed to be sets of images, which more or less overlapped and interrelated. They were typically arranged in a series of levels, roughly by the scale of area involved, so that the observer moved as necessary from an image at street level to levels of a neighborhood, a city, or a metropolitan region....

The sequence in which sketch maps were drawn seemed to indicate that the image develops, or grows, in different ways. This may perhaps have some relation to the way in which it first develops as an individual becomes familiar with his environment. Several types were apparent:

a. Quite frequently, images were developed along, and then outward from, familiar lines of movement. Thus a map might be drawn as branching out from a point of entrance, or beginning from some base line such as Massachusetts Avenue.

b. Other maps were begun by the construction of an enclosing outline, such as the Boston peninsula, which was then filled in toward the center.

c. Still others, particularly in Los Angeles, began by laying down a basic repeating pattern (the path gridiron) and then adding detail.

d. Somewhat fewer maps started as a set of adjacent regions, which were then detailed as to connections and interiors.

e. A few Boston examples developed from a familiar kernel, a dense familiar element on which everything was ultimately hung.

The image itself was not a precise, miniaturized model of reality, reduced in scale and consistently abstracted. As a purposive simplification, it was made by reducing, eliminating, or even adding elements to reality, by fusion and distortion, by relating and structuring the parts. It was sufficient, perhaps better, for its purpose if rearranged, distorted, "illogical." It resembled that famous cartoon of the New Yorker's view of the United States.

However distorted, there was a strong element of topological invariance with respect to reality. It was as if the map were drawn on an infinitely flexible rubber sheet; directions were twisted, distances stretched or compressed, large forms so changed from their accurate scale projection as to be at first unrecognizable. But the sequence was usually correct, the map was rarely torn and sewn back together in another order. This continuity is necessary if the image is to be of any value.

Image quality

...Another distinction could be made between concrete, sensuously vivid images, and those which were highly abstract, generalized, and void of sensuous content. Thus the mental picture of a building might be vivid, involving its shape, color, texture, and detail, or be relatively abstract, the structure being identified as "a restaurant" or the "third building from the corner."

Vivid does not necessarily equate with dense, nor thin with abstract. An image might be both dense and abstract, as in the case of the taxicab dispatcher's knowledge of a city street, which related house numbers to uses along block after block, yet could not describe those buildings in any concrete sense.

Images could be further distinguished according to their structural quality: the manner in which their parts were arranged and interrelated. There were four stages along a continuum of increasing structural precision:

a. The various elements were free; there was no structure or interrelation between parts. We found no pure cases of this type, but several images were definitely disjointed, with vast gaps and many unrelated elements. Here rational movement was impossible without outside help, unless a systematic coverage of the entire area were to be resorted to (which meant the building up of a new structure on the spot).

b. In others, the structure became positional; the parts were roughly related in terms of their general direction and perhaps even relative distance from each other, while still remaining disconnected. One subject in particular always related herself to a few elements, without knowing definite connections between them. Movement was accomplished by searching, by moving out in the correct general direction, while weaving back and forth to cover a band and having an estimate of distance to correct overshooting.

c. Most often, perhaps, the structure was flexible; parts were connected one to the other, but in a loose and flexible manner, as if by limp or elastic ties. The sequence of events was known, but the mental map might be quite distorted, and its distortion might shift at different moments. To quote one subject: "I like to think of a few focal points and how

to get from one to another, and the rest I don't bother to learn." With a flexible structure, movement was easier, since it proceeded along known paths, through known sequences. Motion between pairs of elements not habitually connected, or along other than habitual paths, might still be very confusing, however.

d. As connections multiplied, the structure tended to become rigid; parts were firmly interconnected in all dimensions; and any distortions became built in. The possessor of such a map can move much more freely, and can interconnect new points at will. As the density of the image builds up, it begins to take on the characteristics of a total field, in which interaction is possible in any direction and at any distance.

. . .

One might infer from this that the images of greatest value are those which most closely approach a strong total field: dense, rigid, and vivid; which make use of all element types and form characteristics without narrow concentration; and which can be put together either hierarchically or continuously, as occasion demands. We may find, of course, that such an image is rare or impossible, that there are strong individual or cultural types which cannot transcend their basic abilities. In this case, an environment should be geared to the appropriate cultural type, or shaped in many ways so as to satisfy the varying demands of the individuals who inhabit it.

We are continuously engaged in the attempt to organize our surroundings, to structure and identify them. Various environments are more or less amenable to such treatment. When reshaping cities it should be possible to give them a form which facilitates these organizing efforts rather than frustrates them.

Chapter 4

from *Dreaming the Rational City*

M. Christine Boyer

---

13 The City of Collective Memory

Although this book traces the discourse of city planning, it has also been in the end a book considering the crisis of modernism and its impact on physical planning. Industrial development in the nineteenth century, which heedlessly devastated the urban environment physically and socially, produced within planning a reaction to escape from the meanness of this city chaos, to enshroud itself in the promise of technical utilitarianism and functional organization, above all to be liberated from the tyranny of tradition represented by the nineteenth-century metropolis and to build anew a brave, rational city. In the twentieth century modern man and urban life were inseparably and nihilistically joined, for urban life distilled both the alienating man-machine domination as well as the utopian promise of material advancement.

Here the tendency to seek a formal order for the city can be aligned with the modernist gesture to reappropriate a fragmented and compartmentalized modern reality by transforming it into a personal aesthetic style and a private abstract language. This urge to aesthetic abstraction reveals an inability of modern man to establish a rapport with material reality. Thus is created a gap between those concerned with stylistic order and those dependent upon social con-

ditions, as well as a situation that reflects the alienation and separation of modern reality.

This is what Siegfried Kracauer (1975: 67) captured when he claimed that "capitalist thinking can be identified by its abstractness." It is not capable of grasping the actual substance of life. We may gain through science a more rational mode of thought, but this is at the expense of our abilities to depict the material world. The more that material reality is reduced the more removed our consciousness of forming it becomes. Abstraction obstructs a dialogue with images and meanings; we remain above and elusive of physical reality. In the end functional and rational precision exude a cold and sober aesthetic.

In the 1980s the two professions of the built environment, the process planner and the formalist architect, can no longer discuss together the form or future of the American city, a fact we must blame on the antiurban and ahistorical mentality of both of them. Manfredo Tafuri (1980: 60) has suggested that perhaps the disintegration of the concept of form corresponds to the creation of the modern metropolis, for "the secret of form is that it is boundary." Instead an antiurban ideology pervaded the mentality of the architects and planners of the modern movement. Their concept of a global machine city in which spatial organization was fragmented and development abstracted revealed an inherent negativity to the large metropolitan whole. The only way that the city could be experienced was mechanically.

The aesthetics of the machine produced an outburst of abstractions, where the machine city could be understood only in terms of its logic of functional ensembles and technical operations. For this new style, the laws of assemblage and disassemblage became essential. This modern imagination, however, required looking at urban form and texture through a particular set of lenses that occluded the ability to engage in social reality.

In 1903 Georg Simmel wrote, "The deepest problem of modern life arises from the claim of the individual to preserve the independence and identity of his being against the super-powers of society, of his historical inheritance, and of the external culture and technique of life" (Parkinson (1970: 170). This attempt of the individual to make sense of personal existence often leads to a withdrawal from experience. Lukács, following Simmel's lead, wrote that in the theory and practice of modernism, the image of man is by nature solitary and asocial. Man is unable to establish relationships with things or persons outside of himself. So defined he becomes ahistorical; there is neither a reality beyond the self nor a personal history formed through contact with that reality. Thus the unchallenged assumption is the status quo, obscuring political overtones and denying an engagement with social reality. This position saps the vitality of criticism and opposition to the state of existence. In any critique of social conditions, Lukács continued, it is these very conditions that must hold the central place. The modernist position, however, holds no standard against which it can compare the pathological and distorted condition of human existence. Instead technique is isolated from content, its importance amplified in order to avoid significant commentary on social conditions. "The denial of history, of development, and thus of perspective, becomes the mark of

true insight into the nature of reality" (1971: 20–1, 28, 33, 34).

Modernism led to the destruction of traditional modes of physical planning and the abandonment of conventional forms of the American city. Edmund Bacon's comment on the urban process in 1969 can draw our perspective back to the city, for he blamed the failure of cities on the intellectuals' inability to bring about a viable concept of a modern city, as well as their refusal to create a vivid and driving concept toward which we could plan the urban totality. Instead, Bacon claimed, postwar planners were content in devaluing the importance of the traditional urban form and ahistorically were locked into perpetuating the New Deal structure of assumptions. Thus planners still responded to the belief that "one third of the nation was ill-housed, ill-clothed, and ill-fed" and automatically collapsed their vision to focus on the "poor" as an abstract group that never existed. So removed from the contextual situation had the planners become that vast public housing projects sited on open space wastelands were designed to destroy the slums and to eradicate the connective tissue in the historical centers of the American city. Yet another borrowed concept from the 1930s was the demonstration project embedded in such subsidized projects as the greenbelt towns, rural resettlement policies, and slum-clearance programs. Here, Bacon noted, the planner dealt only with a fragment of the urban dilemma and abandoned the old, comforting, but outmoded modes of the familiar "good neighborhoods" and created entirely new ones out of environment and process (1969: 130).

In 1946 Max Horkheimer, considering the domination of nature by rational processes of thought in a different critical context, underlined this failure of modern man to provide a grounding in social reality that would produce a sense of time, history, social change, and perspective:

If reason is declared incapable of determining the ultimate aims of life and must content itself with reducing everything it encounters to a mere tool, its sole remaining goal is simply the perpetuation of its co-ordinating activity.... Yet the more all nature is looked upon as ... mere objects in relation to human subjects, the more is the once supposedly autonomous subject emptied of any content, until it finally becomes a mere name with nothing to denominate. The total transformation of each and every realm of being into a field of means leads to the liquidation of the subject who is supposed to use them. This gives modern industrial society its nihilistic aspect. (1974: 92–3)

Frozen into a rigid position, modern man, without perspective, has no power of decision, no ability to change the social situation.

Richard Bolan's summary of the attack during the 1960s on the classical model of physical planning stressed this nihilistic perpetuation of planning's coordinating activity and the demise, indeed eclipse, of any physical content or formal expression for process planners. Reality, Bolan proclaimed, never measured up to the ideal. An advisory planning commission, with its comprehensive view of the city and the public, capable and responsible for the development of long-range growth goals, was a fragile illusion. A master plan, intended to impose order upon the physical form of the American city, was a chimera on the backs of planners, which the priests of rationality must now exorcise. Political scientists, economists, local politicians, and planners agreed that the urban future could never be accurately predicted, that community goals in a turbulent world remained elusive, that information would always be indeterminate, that a decentralized democratic political system made comprehensive planning from a centralized authority impossible. The ideal of a public interest embodied in a comprehensive plan, moreover, conflicted with the reality that private interests directly influenced public policy formation and that political decision making operated on fragmented choices, not integrated wholes.

Allowing private interests to penetrate the public sphere excused traditional physical planning from engaging in battle over urban space and form. It weakened as well the critical reasonings of planning over state directives and policies as they affected the form of the American city. If planners believed that they were redressing the inequities of the private market by extending the process of planning beyond the physical environment, they did so at the expense of keeping these issues before the gaze of the urban formalists or architects (Friedan 1967). No doubt this split between the architect and the planner goes back to the introduction of the modern movement to America in 1932 when Henry-Russell Hitchcock and Philip Johnson organized an exhibition at the Museum of Modern Art on modern architecture. In their accompanying book (*The International Style*, 1932) they stressed the weaknesses of the European concept of social planning and the new aesthetic directions to be forged from the American experience.

> The Siedlungen [group housing] of the European functionalists generally reach the neutral aesthetic level of good building.... We must not be misled by the idealism of the European functionalists. Functionalism is absolute as an idea rather than as a reality. As an idea it must come to terms with other ideas such as that of aesthetic organization....
>
> The Siedlungen implies preparation not for a given family but for a typical family. This statistical monster... has no personal existence and cannot defend himself against the sociological theories of the architects.... [The] Europeans build for some proletarian superman of the future. Yet in most buildings the expressed desires of a given client are the most explicit and difficult functions. Architects whose discipline is aesthetic as well as functional are usually readier to provide what is actually needed. (1932: 91–3)

While Hitchcock and Johnson pushed the American architect to stress formal style over social function, the planners were left as the sole advocates for social concerns. In consequence architects and planners, each intent on expressing a different set of needs, no longer had a language with which to communicate. As a result the postwar American city suffered an incredible shock for no one paid attention to urban form.

Leon Krier (1977), speaking about the disintegrated form of the European city, claims that zoning, which destroyed the complex urban codes of the nineteenth century, must be the root cause for the broken dialogue between the architect and urban form. In segregated functional cells industry was divorced from cultural centers, offices from residential zones, public from private spaces, and monumental architecture from anonymous buildings. Le Corbusier, Krier states, an unwitting culprit, designed in elegantly artistic forms the contradictions of an industrial society intent on destroying the city. Next Walter Gropius and then the Charter of Athens through their dedication to fresh air, sunlight, health, and recreation devalued still further the memory of the nineteenth-century city. So modern architecture, with its disturbed communication with everyday life and enclosed within a rhetoric of styles, attained complete autonomy from history, urban form, and social concerns.

More recently a new awareness of history in the context of urbanism has been imported from Europe, where the reexamination of the modern movement's betrayal of history is directed toward the creation of a new program for urban form. Manfredo Tafuri, Carlos Aymonino, Aldo Rossi, and Leon Krier are among the members of this dialogue on the postmodern European city. It is to their discourse, but not to their two-dimensional architectural forms, that we turn in order to draw a sharper focus on the city and its morphological form. Now the city is brought once again onto the center stage, for without the city, they claim, architecture would not exist. The city becomes the "ultimate scope of [architecture's] striving for form" (Llorens 1981: 86).

The past failures of the architect-planner to build images of the city reflect the refusal to allow the past to be experienced with the present in a new constellation. In consequence our modern cityscapes show little awareness of their historical past. New architectural structures, spaghetti highway interchanges, and historic preservation projects are seldom integrated with the existing urban texture. Instead the historical centers of the city were dangerous to modern life; they had to be completely removed or reduced to museum pieces (Tafuri 1980: 48–9).

In this manner the modern architect and urban planner failed to allow a clash, a collage of the new with the old. Indeed the dialogue between planning and history was silent, so that the structural elements of the traditional street, district, or public square were not allowed to aid the reshaping and reorganization of the modern order of the American city. A new modern city of functional components negated and emptied its valueless historical centers. Since architects and planners had given up trying to understand the structure and morphology of urban form and the overlaying of historical and interpretive elements, they thus inserted new functional components randomly into the existing fabric.

Tafuri requests that history be allowed to preside over planning, and planning then must become a programmatic guide for architecture and urban design (1980: 40, 45, 57, 58). The entire urban context that configures architecture must be drawn into critical awareness: the regulatory controls, the political and economic conditions, the technical and social means of production, the cultural milieu. To reinterpret the spatial and historical elements of the city in this manner decodes the very meaning of the verb "to plan."

Nevertheless, only after careful consideration will history find its proper place within planning, for the current rescue of "history" from the warehouse of society can be a farce. On one hand we often have historic preservation that looks like a near equivalent to stage designing or an emotional remembrance of a nostalgic past; and on the other hand post-modernism turns toward a past without any idea of how to use it.

The planners for the most part are silent, as if they refuse to create a place for their voices in the historical process and accept instead the sealed empirical world to which they have condemned themselves. When they do find a voice, they attempt to offer a structural analysis of urban form best exemplified in the work of Kevin Lynch. Searching for a way to describe urban form, he isolates landmarks, nodes, paths, edges, and districts in order to offer the user a behavioral image of the city. Thus the sense of a settlement becomes "the clarity with which it can be perceived and identified, and the ease with which its elements can be linked with other events and places and that representation can be connected with nonspatial concepts and values" (1981: 131). Lynch includes in this analysis the sense of identity or place, the sense of how the parts fit together or offer a sense of orientation, the congruence of environmental structures to non-spatial demands, the transparency with which one perceives the operations of various technical functions and social processes. These formal concerns are motivated by behavioral needs, for "sense is an important functional concern, since the ability to identify things, to time behavior, to find one's way and to read the signs, are all requisites of access and effective action" (1981: 144). But in this case the history of place is broken up, and only in fragments as palatable remnants of the past is it allowed to fit into the functional reordering of the city.

An analysis of urban form and a sense of the city must emerge from a dialectical understanding of historical permanence and morphological change. A physical plan of the city would analyze the manner in which the city has been structured, and this would define the method and means for the reorganization of architectural complexes and urban sectors. In a famous essay on James Joyce's *Ulysses*, T. S. Eliot wrote that "one can be 'classical,' in a sense, by turning away from nine-tenths of the material which lies at hand and selecting only mummified stuff from a museum . . . or one can be 'classical' in tendency by doing the best he can with the material at hand" (Poggioli, 1968: 222). What becomes important now is the texture of memories already embedded in the city and how the architect-planner uses these elements to structure and reorder the city with a classical tendency.

John Ruskin too drew our attention to the memory of the city, for he realized in 1849 the modern dilemma: that the vitality of nations was crowding in upon city gates, that modern life would be acted out upon the urban stage. The only influence that could possibly offer the healing inspiration of wood and field from which these urban crowds had fled would be the "power of ancient Architecture." He advised, "We may live without her, and worship without her, but we cannot remember without her," and wisely he warned, "Do not part with it for the sake of the formal square, or of the fenced and planted walk nor of the goodly street nor opened quay. The pride of the city is not in these. Leave them to the crowd" (Ruskin 1849: 187).

More recently Carlos Aymonino has reminded us that to begin to unravel the process where building typology and spatial morphology confront one another and transform urban development, we must return to the economic and political, the cultural and social context that are important to both the spatial morphology and building typology of the city. For example, he points out, when it first became possible to sell land for cash as a good upon the open market, land took on a new form. Privileged zones of development were valued for their high market prices. Thus diverse architectural pastiches and eclectic styles developed, more in response to commercial needs and less as a solution to architectural problems. Uniform block and lot divisions were primarily a response to market exchange, yet they too limited architectural freedom and diversity. As the number of private land investors increased, the allocation of streets, sewers, and railway lines became the only way to control the order of this developing new city. The "readability" of urban form, once grasped through the structural relationships between building types and spatial form, began to decline, and it was only in the ancient quarters of the city where formal completeness remained (Aymonino 1977).

So we must once again look upon these older city centers to draw upon the resources of collective memory. Aldo Rossi claims that the old city is a repository of history where memory becomes the conducting thread of the entire structure. He envisions the city as the finest and most complete expression of architecture, and he places the responsibility upon the architect to explain the form of the city and the principles of architecture governing that form. "In the city there are urban facts that withstand the elements of time... these facts are the monuments that constitute, make up, configurate the city. They give meaning to the life of the city" (Rossi 1976: 31–4). These historical traces are expressed through the city plan, which records the way the city is first impressed upon our minds. Certain features of the city, such as a piazza or an arcade, pass from being instrumental in the development of urban space and become fixed attributes of the city. In consequence Rossi is intent on defining a typology of buildings and urban spaces in their relationship to the city whole, to the division of land, to the motivational forces behind their development. But these must not become frozen attributes outside of the historical context in which they were born, for then these spatial typologies would become memories out of place. Rossi optimistically claims, on the other hand, that these typologies must be seen as a tool not only in the manipulation of aesthetic form but in the critical act of disrobing reality. The act of quoting familiar types then becomes a radical stance, for these categorical types come polluted with political meanings and burdened with cultural memories. Thus it is expected that in the collage effect of the old and the

new parts of the city, a criticism of architecture is offered by referencing these contextual meanings. This can be like walking on a thin tightrope, however, for decorative pastiches do not necessarily arouse our collective memory.

Another approach, with similar intent, is seen in the work of Leon Krier, who focuses on the destruction of the public realm in the modern European city. Again deference is given to the traditional urban elements such as the street, the squares, the colonnades, the arcades and courtyards as the connecting tissue of memory. Building typologies and morphological analyses are then used to reconstruct the city and to reestablish the impoverished public sphere. "The building block," Krier explains, "must be isolated as being dialectically the most important typological element to compare urban space, the key element to any urban pattern." Traced over time the agony of the urban block witnesses its displacement as the keystone of urban form to its complete domination by larger building programs in the modern metropolis. If the future is to allow for a new urban form, then the block must be the basic instrument in forming the public realm of streets and squares (Krier 1978). The re-creation and the design of this public realm take on the vision of a future urbanism: a design program that allows the architect to foresee how to reconstruct the damaged urban form out of old pieces of fabric and new public spaces, recently constructed buildings and a catalog of memories (Krier 1977).

From within architecture and pointing toward the direction of a new physical planning, these European architects preach of a day that the city will be redeemed from the reputation it has suffered since the emergence of modernism. They have, in the manner of Michel Foucault, tried to show "based upon their historical establishment and formation, those systems which are still ours today and within which we are trapped. It is a question, basically, of presenting a critique of our own time, based upon retrospective analyses."

Thus the formation of a humanistic order to the American city still lies in the future, for the characteristic features of the modern city – its alienating abstractions, rational efficiency, fragmented and malign configuration, ruptured tradition and memory – are still very much with us in the present.

REFERENCES

Aymonino, Carlo. "Le role des capitales due XIXe siècle." *Les Cahiers de la recherche architecturale*, no. 1 (Dec. 1977): 57–71.

Bacon, Edmund. "Urban Process: Planning with and for the Community." *Architectural Record* 145, no. 5 (May 1969): 129–34.

Bolan, R. "Emerging Views of Planning" *Journal of the American Institute of Planners* 33 (1967): 233–45.

Frieden, Bernard J. "The Changing Prospects for Social Planning." *Journal of the American Institute of Planners* 33, no. 5 (Sept. 1967): 311–23.

Horkheimer, Max. *Eclipse of Reason.* New York: Seabury, 1974.

Kracauer, Siegfried. "The Mass Ornament." *New German Critique* 5 (Spring 1975): 67–76.

Krier, Leon, ed. "Cities within the City." *Architecture and Urbanisme* 77, no. 11 (Nov. 1977): 69–109.

Krier, Leon. Fourth Lesson: "Analysis and Project for the Traditional Urban Block." *Lotus International* 19 (Jan. 1978): 42–55.

Llorens, Tomas. "Manfredo Tafuri: Neo-Avant-Garde and History." *Architectural Design* 51 (July–Aug. 1981): 83–94.

Lukács, Georg. *Realism in Our Time.* New York: Harper Torch Books, 1971.

Lynch, Kevin. *A Theory of Good City Form.* Cambridge: MIT Press, 1981.

Parkinson, G. H. R., ed. *Georg Lukács: The Man, His Work and His Ideas.* New York: Vintage Books, 1970.

Poggioli, Renato. *The Theory of the Avant-Garde.* Tr. Gerald Fitzgerald. Cambridge: Belknap Press of Harvard University Press, 1968.

Rossi, Aldo. "The Blue of the Sky." *Oppositions* 5 (Summer 1976): 31–4.

Ruskin, John. *The Seven Lamps of Architecture.* 1849.

Sherrill, C. O. and Hoehler, Fred. "How Cincinnati Met the Unemployment Crisis." *National Municipal Review* 19, no. 5 (May 1930): 289–93.

Tafuri, Manfredo. *Theories and History of Architecture.* New York: Harper and Row, 1980.

Chapter 5

Bodies in Space/Subjects in the City

Antony Vidler

Agoraphobia and Abstraction

> The urge to abstraction is the outcome of
> a great inner unrest inspired in man by the
> phenomena of the outside world.... We
> might describe this state as an immense
> spiritual dread of space. (Worringer,
> 1980: 15)

Writing in 1906, following what he described as his "miraculous" encounter
with the sociologist Georg Simmel in the
Trocadero Museum in Paris, the art historian Wilhelm Worringer outlined what for
him lay beneath the universal drive of art
towards abstraction. It was, he argued,
founded on no less than a primitive fear of
nature and a concommittant desire "to
divest the things of the external world of
their caprice and obscurity," to endow
them with a regularity represented in geometric abstraction. Worringer cites "the
fear of space [*raumsheu*] which is clearly
manifested in Egyptian architecture," and
compares what seems to him to be a generalized *geistiger Raumscheu*, or "spiritual
dread of space," to the modern malady of
agoraphobia, or what he terms *platzangst*.
Just as "this physical dread of open places
may be explained as a residue from a
normal phase of man's development, at
which he was not yet able to trust entirely
to visual impression as a means of becoming familiar with a space extended before

him, but was still dependent upon the as-
surances of his sense of touch," so the spiritual dread of open space was a throwback
to a moment of "instinctive fear conditioned by man's feeling of being lost in the
universe" (1980: 15–16). He characterizes
this feeling as "a kind of spiritual agoraphobia in the face of the motley disorder
and caprice of the phenomenal world"
(129). The "sensation of fear [*angst*]," Worringer concludes, was "the root of artistic
creation" (15).

Now while, as Dora Vallier has recently
pointed out, Worringer's observations were
made in strict isolation from Cubist or Ex-
pressionist experiments in abstract art, and,
as Worringer himself claimed, seem to have
been advanced without detailed knowledge
of Georg Simmel's own investigations into
the "mental life" of modernity, his juxtaposition of agoraphobia and abstraction
was nevertheless a calculated reversal of
the turn-of-the-century wisdom that saw
the spaces created by modern abstract
geometry as a direct cause of agoraphobia,
if not the entire psychopathology of
modern urban space (Vallier 1978: 5–7).
Indeed, Camillo Sitte, the Viennese architect and critic, had stressed only eight years
previously the intimate connection of
modern urban spaces – those of the newly
constructed Ringstrasse – to the "fashionable" modern illness of "agoraphobia"
(*platzscheu*). His castigation of the "vast

empty places" of the new Vienna had, by the turn of the century, given fashionable currency to the notion of a psychopathology of space that was distinctly modern (Sitte 1965: 53).

The "metropolis," as Simmel recognized, was the central locus of modern spatial constructions, an amalgam of urban experience and imaginary fear the very scale of which contrasted with its nineteenth-century antecedent, the "Great Town." The nineteenth-century city had been understood to harbor dangerous diseases, epidemics, and equally dangerous social movements; it was the breeding-ground of the all-levelling masses, of frightening crowds, the insanitary home of millions, an asphalt and stone wilderness, the opposite of nature. The metropolis carried forward all these stigmas, but added those newly identified by the mental and social sciences. It rapidly became the privileged territory of George Beard's neurasthenia, of Charcot's hysteria, of Carl Otto Westphal's and Legrand du Saulle's agoraphobia, of Benjamin Ball's claustrophobia. It sheltered a nervous and feverish population, over-excited and enervated, whose mental life as Georg Simmel had noted in 1903 was relentlessly anti-social, driven by money and haunted by the fear of touching (Simmel 1903: 185–206). Already in 1896, Simmel had spoken of the "fear of contact" or *berührungsangst*, a "pathological symptom . . . spread endemically" in turn-of-the-century Berlin, constructing it as a spatial fear, one that stemmed from the too rapid oscillation between closeness and distance in modern life (Simmel 1978: 474).

In this space, all those considered prone to neurasthenic disease – the "weak," the "ennervated," the "over-stimulated," the "degenerated," and the "bored" – were bound to succumb to mental collapse, and first in line, for the psychologists and psychoanalysts, were women and homosexuals. In light of the common belief in what Friedrich Nietzsche called the "feminization" of fin-de-siècle culture (and thereby what he and others, including psychologists like Otto Weininger and Max Nordau saw

as its decadence), it is not surprizing to find that from the outset urban phobias were assigned a definite place in the gendering of metropolitan psychopathology. Despite the predominance of male patients in the samples of agoraphobics and claustrophobics analysed by Carl Westphal and his French colleagues, these disorders were thought of as fundamentally "female" in character; it is no accident that today "agoraphobia" is commonly called "housewives' disease" by doctors.

This ascription was supported by Freud, who found convincing evidence that the causes of agoraphobia in women – their fear of going out into the street – were directly linked to what he called their repressed inner desire to walk the streets – that is to be "streetwalkers." Writing to Wilhelm Fliess in 1896, Freud (1985: 218) announced his theory that the mechanism of agoraphobia in women was connected to "the repression of the intention to take the first man one meets in the street: envy of prostitution and indentification." This observation followed a detailed exposition of the notion of "anxiety" as represented in the formulation "Anxiety about throwing oneself out of the window." Freud constructs this anxiety as "Anxiety+. . . window. . . ," where the *unconscious* idea" of "going to the window to beckon a man to come up, as prostitutes do" leads to sexual release, which, repudiated by the preconscious, is turned into anxiety. The window in this scheme is left as the only conscious motif, associated with anxiety by the idea of "falling out." Hence, Freud argues, anxiety about the window is interpreted in the sense of falling out and the window, opening to the public realm, is avoided. Thus, as he will later claim, "Agoraphobia seems to depend on a romance of prostitution . . . a woman who will not go out by herself asserts her mother's unfaithfulness" (Freud 1985: 248).

By association, and perhaps as a result of Westphal's parallel researches into sexuality, fear of open spaces was equally associated with homosexuality. Thus Marcel Proust (1988: vol. 3) endows the baron de

Charlus, hesitating before entry into Madame Verdurin's salon, with what he describes as the mentality of "the soul of a parent of the feminine sex, auxiliatrice like a goddess or incarnated like a double," that he compares to the feelings of "a young painter, raised by a saintly protestant cousin," as he enters "with inclined and trembling head, eyes to the ceiling, hands plunged into an invisible muff, the evoked form and real guardian presence of which will help the intimidated artist to cross the space, furrowed with abysses, which leads from the antichamber to the small salon, without agoraphobia" (ibid. 299). In a recently published variant, Proust was more explicit:

> M. de Charlus will enter (into the Verdurin's salon) with the movements of bent head, his hands having the air of twisting a small handbag, characteristic of well-brought-up bourgeois women and of those that the Germans call homosexuals with a certain agoraphobia, the agora here being the space of the salon that separates the door from the armchair where the mistress of the salon is seated. (ibid. 1513–14)

Such a pathology of agoraphobia and claustrophobia, joined if not caused by their common site in metropolis, provided ready arguments for modernist architects who were eager to reconstruct the very foundations of urban space. Arguing that urban phobias were precisely the product of urban environments, and that their cure was dependent on the erasure of the old city in its entirety, architects from the early 1920s projected images of a city restored to a natural state, within which the dispersed institutions of the new society would be scattered like pavilions in a landscape garden. Reviving the late eighteenth-century myth of "transparency," both social and spatial, modernists evoked the picture of a glass city, its buildings invisible and society open. The resulting "space" would be open, infinitely extended, and thereby cleansed of all mental disturbance: the site of healthy and presumably aerobically perfect bodies.

Men in Space

> Our period demands a type of man who can restore the lost equilibrium between inner and outer reality. This equilibrium, never static but, like reality itself involved in continuous change, is like that of a tightrope dancer who, by small adjustments, keeps a continuous balance between his being and empty space. (Giedion 1948: 720)

In a recent article, reviewing a number of studies by urban geographers from David Harvey to Edward Soja, Rosalyn Deutsche (1990: 21–3) pointed to the implications of Janet Wolff's 1985 observation that "The literature of modernity describes the experience of men," for the critique of totalizing concepts of vision that fail to recognize the challenge of "feminist theories of visual space" (ibid. 22). Here I want to extend some of the insights provided by the recent gender critique of modernist space to examine further the conditions that on the surface, and from a feminist perspective, endowed modernism with so masculinist a bias. It is obvious that modernist space, and its late twentieth-century extensions, are for the most part constructed by and for men. But this construction, seemingly all too obvious and worthy of little more than curt dismissal, was, and still is, a profoundly problematic one. The apparently serene transparency and all-dominating positivism of modernist urban space was, in fact, founded on extremely shaky bases, and inevitably riddled with the rejection, suppression, anxiety, and phobic fear that its authors were attempting to cure.

Thus, on the surface at least, nothing could be more serene and confident than the mental and spatial state of Ayn Rand's celebrated architect, Howard Roark, in the opening scene of that often cited, but I suspect rarely read architectural novel, *The Fountainhead*, published in 1943. Here Howard Roark is depicted for all intents and purposes as if in a cut from *The Triumph of the Will*, standing on the edge of a cliff and viewed from below. On the edge of a high granite outcrop, his naked body, like some latter-day Prometheus (with whom he later identifies himself at his final trial) or Futurist-cum-Vorticist demi-god, seems as if cut out of the material of the cliff itself – "a body of long straight lines and angles, each curve broken into planes." His face, "like a law of nature," was "gaunt" with high cheekbones betraying pure Aryan ancestry; cold gray eyes steadily betraying iron willpower; contemptuous mouth betraying a position well above the prosaic world – "the mouth of an executioner or a saint," remarks Rand (1971: 15) paraphrasing Hugo on Robespierre.

Roark's very gaze was in the process of building, transforming his surroundings into suitable construction materials and his position into a desirable building site:

> He looked at the granite. To be cut, he thought, and made into walls. He looked at a tree. To be split and made into rafters. He looked at a streak of rust on the stone and thought of iron ore under the ground. ·To be melted and to emerge as girders against the sky. (ibid. 16)

If nature had not rendered the place perfect, surely the architect might be permitted to cut and fill a little: "These rocks, he thought, are here for me; waiting for the drill, the dynamite and my voice; waiting to be split, ripped, pounded, reborn; waiting for the shape my hands will give them" (ibid.) Now while this passionate and violent account of nature-rape by the architect deserves full analysis in the context of modernism's, and subsequently postmodernism's, pretensions to reshape the world, in this context I am more interested in Howard Roark's body, and more precisely in its position in space. For this super-youth was, almost literally, standing in mid-air, an Icarus before the fall:

> He stood naked at the edge of a cliff. The lake lay far below him. A frozen explosion of granite burst in flight to the sky over motionless water. The water seemed immovable, the stone – flowing. The stone

had the stillness of one brief moment in battle when thrust meets thrust and the currents are held in a pause more dynamic than motion.... The rocks went on into the depth unchanged. They ended in the sky. So that the world seemed suspended in space, an island floating on nothing, anchored to the feet of the man on the cliff. (ibid. 15)

Here in a typical reversal, nature is yoked to man's feet, avoiding the Promethean fate.

Roark's space is recognizable enough. Lifted by Rand from the platitudes of the romantic sublime, its philosophical tone heightened, so to speak, by Nietzsche, its characteristics of absolute height, depth and breadth had emerged in the mid-twenties as the lietmotiv of idealistic modernism. Bruno Taut had celebrated it in his attempts to fabricate crystalline cities out of the Alps to form "marble cliffs" as magic as those described by Ernst Jünger; Mies Van der Rohe had envisaged it as gridded and endless – a universal system of three-dimensional graph-paper, to be punctuated (materialized) in the hard steel sections of a new classicism; Le Corbusier, finally, who had first experienced it much like Roark standing on the edge of a cliff during his first visit to the Athenian Acropolis, elevated it into a principle, that of "ineffable space" (*l'espace indicible*).

Ineffable space was, for Le Corbusier, transcendent space. It was, like Roark's, as high as the sky, as deep as the clearest lake, and stretched on all sides to the horizon. Its qualities were those of container and contained; Le Corbusier compared it to a sounding-board, as it resonated and reverberated with the "plastic acoustics" set up by the natural and man-made objects that inhabited it. Objects, if possible freestanding, generated force-fields, took possession of space, orchestrated it and made it sing or cry out with harmony or pain. Such space, Le Corbusier claimed in 1947, was a discovery of modernity – "the fourth dimension" that a number of artists had used to "magnify space" around 1910

(1948: 7–8). "The fourth dimension is the moment of limitless escape evoked by exceptionally just consonance of the plastic means employed" (8). And when correctly employed, this space had a strangely powerful effect on the very buildings that defined it and set it in motion. "In a complete and successful work there are hidden masses of implications, a veritable world which reveals itself to those it may concern," wrote Le Corbusier, adding with a contempt worthy of Roark, "which means: to those who deserve it. Then a boundless depth opens up, effaces the walls, drives away contingent premises, accomplishes the miracle of ineffable space" (8). The feeling – like that described a few years earlier by Freud in a note to Romain Rolland calling it "oceanic" – was virtually religious in nature: "I am not conscious of the miracle of faith, but I often live that of ineffable space, the consummation of plastic emotions" (8).

It is perhaps especially appropriate that both Le Corbusier and Freud first felt this sensation on the same height – that of the Acropolis. Returning to Athens in 1933, Le Corbusier recalled,

> I came to Athens 23 years ago; I spent 21 days on the Acropolis working ceaselessly with the admirable spectacle.... What I know is that I acquired there the

idea of irreducible truth. I left, crushed by the superhuman aspect of the things on the Acropolis, crushed by a truth which is [again echoes of Roark] neither smiling nor light, but which is strong, which is one, which is implacable. (1948: 66)

And, in anticipation of the inner violence of such a scene, a violence later to be unleashed on the cities of Europe, Le Corbusier concluded: "Remember the clear, clean, intense, economical, violent Parthenon – that cry hurled into a landscape made of grace and terror. That monument to strength and purity" (ibid. 66).

Now all this could be put down to the common youthful enthusiasm shared by Rand and Le Corbusier for Nietzsche and Herbert Spencer, for a fin-de-siècle diet of anti-decadence and symbolist aesthetics, motivated by a quasi-religious Wagnerianism fomented by Edouard Schuré, author of *Les grands initiés*, nourished by a good dose of Victor Hugo's *Notre Dame*, which for Le Corbusier, Rand, and notably for Frank Lloyd Wright, had challenged the modern architect to rediscover the authentic roots of cultural and social expression, to fight the increasing hegemony of the printed word, if not the movies, and to return, cutting through the academic undergrowth, to natural forms and forces....

REFERENCES

Deutsche, Rosalyn. "On Men in Space." *Art-forum* (Feb. 1990): 21–3.

Freud, Sigmund. *The Complete Letters of Sigmund Freud to Wilhelm Fliess 1887–1904*. Trans. and ed. Jeffrey Moussaieff Masson. Cambridge: Harvard University Press, 1985.

Giedion, Sigfried. *Mechanization Takes Command: A Contribution to Anonymous History*. New York: Oxford University Press, 1948.

Le Corbusier. "La Rue." *L'Intransigeant* May 1929. Rpt. in *Oeuvre Complée 1910–1929*. Eds. Le Corbusier and Pierre Jeanneret, Zurich: Girsburger-Zurich, 1937. 112–19.

Le Corbusier. *New World of Space*. New York: Reynal and Hitchcock and the Institute of Contemporary Art, Boston, 1948.

Proust, Marcel. *A la recherche du temps perdu*, vol. 3. Paris: Pléiade, 1988.

Rand, Ayn. *The Fountainhead*. New York: Signet, 1971.

Simmel, Georg. "Die Grosstädte und das Geistesleben." *Jahrbuch des Gehestiftung zu Dresden* 9 (1903): 185–206.

Sitte, Camillo. *City Planning According to Artistic Principles*. Trans. George Collins and Christiane Crasemann Collins. New York: Columbia University Press, 1965. Trans. of *Der Städte-Bau nach seinen künstlerischen* grundsätzen. Ein Beitrag zur lösung modernister Fragen des Architecktur und monumentalen Plastik unter Beziehung auf Wien. Vienna: Graeser, 1889.

Vallier, Dora. "Lire Worringer." Intro. to Abstraction et Einfühlung, by Wilhelm Worringer. Trans. Emmanuel Martineau. Paris: Editions Klincksieck, 1978.

Worringer, Wilhelm. Abstraction and Empathy: A Contribution to the Psychology of Style. Trans. Michael Bullock. New York: International University Press, 1980.

Chapter 6

from *City of Bits: Space, Place, and the Infobahn*

W. J. Mitchell

In a world of ubiquitous computation and telecommunication, electronically augmented bodies, postinfobahn architecture, and big-time bit business, the very idea of a city is challenged and must eventually be reconceived. Computer networks become as fundamental to urban life as street systems. Memory and screen space become valuable, sought-after sorts of real estate. Much of the economic, social, political, and cultural action shifts into cyberspace. As a result, familiar urban design issues are up for radical reformulation....

On the Spot/On the Net

Why do some places attract people? Often, it is because being on the spot puts you in the know. The merchants' coffeehouses of eighteenth-century New York, for instance, provided opportunities to get the latest shipping information, to meet potential trading partners, and to exchange other important commercial information.[1] Depending on your trade, you might find the need to locate in the financial district, the garment district, or SoHo, on Harley Street, Fleet Street, or Lincoln's Inn Fields, in Hollywood, Silicon Valley, or Detroit. You might be attracted to the literary salon, the corner saloon, or the Cambridge high table. It's not just a matter of where the jobs are, but of where you can exchange the most up-to-date, specialized information

with the most savvy people; you may be able to do the same work and pursue similar interests if you are out in the sticks, but you are likely to feel cut off and far from the center of things.

In cyberspace, list servers soon evolved to perform some of the same functions. These are programs for broadcasting e-mail messages to all the "subscribers" on specified address lists. They are like electronic Hyde Park Corners – places in which anybody can stand up and speak to the assembled crowd. Lists may assemble formal groups such as the employees of a business, or the students enrolled in a class, or they may be constructed through some informal, self-selection process. As with physical assemblies, some lists are public and some secret, some are open to anybody and some are rigorously exclusive.

Electronic "newsgroups" were also quick to develop. Newsgroup software allows participants to "post" text messages (and sometimes other sorts of files), much as you might pin printed notices to a physical bulletin board. The notices – queries, requests, responses, news items, announcements, tips, warnings, bits of gossip, jokes, or whatever – stay there until they are deleted, and anyone who enters the place can read them. Usually there is a host – a sort of Cyber de Staël or Virtual Gertrude presiding over an online rue de Fleury – who sets topics, coaxes the exchanges along when they flag, and occasionally kicks out an unruly or objectionable participant. By the 1990s there were countless thousands of these places, advertising every interest you might imagine and some that you surely would not. If you wanted to be in touch and up with the latest in your field, it was increasingly important to have ready access to the right newsgroups. And your physical location no longer mattered so much.

When there is a sudden need, ad-hoc newsgroups can spring almost instantly into existence. Within hours of the January 1994 Los Angeles earthquake, there was a Usenet newsgroup called *alt.current-events.la.quake*. Long before the rubble had been swept from Wilshire Boulevard and before telephone service had unjammed, it was providing a place to post damage reports and find news about friends and relatives. It was the best place to be if you wanted to know what was going on.

The virtual communities that networks bring together are often defined by common interests rather than by common location: Unix hackers, Amiga enthusiasts, Trekkies, and Deadheads are scattered everywhere. But the opposite can also be true. When networks and servers are organized to deal with information and issues of local concern to the people of a town or to the students, staff, and faculty of a university, they act to maintain more traditional, site-specific communities. So, for example, the City of Santa Monica's pioneering Public Electronic Network (PEN) is available only to residents of Santa Monica, to people who work in the city, or at thirty-five public-access terminals located within the city boundaries. And the Athena educational network was put in place on MIT's Cambridge campus to serve the MIT community.

Street Networks/World Wide Web

Ever since Ur, urban places have been linked by movement channels of various kinds: doorways and passageways have joined together the rooms of buildings, street grids have connected buildings to each other, and road and rail networks have allowed communication between distant cities. These familiar sorts of physical connections have provided access to the places where people lived, worked, worshipped, and entertained themselves.

Now there is a powerful alternative. Ever since the winter of 1994, I have had a remarkable piece of software called Mosaic on the modest desktop machine that I'm using to write this paragraph (Right now, Mosaic is open in another window.) Mosaic is a "client" program that provides convenient access to World Wide Web (WWW) servers located throughout the Internet. These servers present "pages" of information, which may be in the form of text, graphics, video, or sound. Pages typically have "hyperlinks" pointing to related pages elsewhere in the Web, allowing me to jump from page to page by clicking on highlighted text or images.

The "home page" of any WWW server invites me to step, like Alice through the looking glass, into the vast information flea market of the Web – a cyberspace zone now consisting of countless millions of interconnected pages. The astonishing thing is that a WWW page displayed on my screen may originate from a machine located *anywhere* on the Internet. In fact, as I move from page to page, I am logging into computers scattered around the world.

But as I see it, I jump almost instantaneously from virtual place to virtual place by following the hyperlinks that programmers have established – much as I might trace a path from station to station through the London Underground. If I were to diagram these connections, I would have a kind of subway map of cyberspace.

Neighborhoods/MUDs

MUD crawling is another way to go. Software constructions known as MUDs, Multi-User Dungeons, have burned up countless thousands of log-in hours since the early 1980s. These provide settings – often very large and elaborately detailed ones – for online, interactive, role-playing games, and they often attract vast numbers of participants scattered all over the Internet. They are cyberspace equivalents of urban neighborhoods.

The particular joy of MUDville is the striking way that it foregrounds issues of personal identity and self-representation; as newcomers learn at old MUDders' knees, your first task as a MUD initiate is to construct an online persona for yourself by choosing a name and writing a description that others will see when they encounter you. It's like dressing up for a masked ball, and the irresistible thing is that you can experiment freely with shifts, slippages, and reversals in social and sexual roles and even try on entirely fantastic guises. You can discover how it *really* feels to be a *complete* unknown.

Once you have created your MUD character, you can enter a virtual place populated with other characters and objects. This place has exits – hyperlinks connecting it to other such settings, which have in turn their own exits. Some heavily frequented MUDs are almost incomprehensibly vast, allowing you to wander among thousands of distinct settings, all with their own special characteristics, like Baudelaire strolling through the buzzing complexity of nineteenth-century Paris. You can examine the settings and objects that you encounter, and you can interact with the characters that you meet.

But as you quickly discover, the most interesting and provocative thing about a MUD is its constitution – the programmed-in rules specifying the sorts of interactions that can take place and shaping the culture that evolves. Many are based on popular fantasy narratives such as *Star Trek*, Frank Herbert's *Dune*, C. S. Lewis's *Chronicles of Narnia*, the Japanese animated television series *Speed Racer*, and even more doubtful products of the literary imagination; these are communities held together, as in many traditional societies, by shared myths. Some are set up as hack-'n-slash combat games in which bad MUDders will try to "kill" your character; these, of course, are

violent, Darwinian places in which you have to be aggressive and constantly on your guard. Others, like many of the Tiny-MUDs, stress ideals of constructive social interaction, egalitarianism, and nonviolence – MUDderhood and apple pie. Yet others are organized like high-minded lyceums, with places for serious discussion of different scientific and technical topics. The MIT-based *Cyberion City* encourages young hackers – MUDders of invention – to write MUSE code that adds new settings to the environment and creates new characters and objects. And some are populated by out-of-control, crazy MUDders who will try to engage your character in TinySex – the one-handed keyboard equivalent of phone sex.

Early MUDs – much like text-based adventure video games such as *Zork* – relied entirely on typed descriptions of characters, objects, scenes, and actions. (James Joyce surely would have been impressed; city as text and text as city. Every journey constructs a narrative.) But greater bandwidth, faster computers, and fancier programming can shift them into pictorial and spatial formats. Lucasfilm's *Habitat*, for example, was an early example of a graphic MUD that had its first incarnation, in North America, on the QuantumLink Club Caribe network (a precursor of America Online) and Commodore 64 computers. Later, it spawned a colony, *Populopolis*, that reputedly attracted a lot more paying customers on the NIFtyServe network in Japan.[2]

As a citizen of *Habitat*, you could customize your character, known as your Avatar, by selecting from a menu of body parts and choosing a sex. (That was a one-bit choice, since *Habitat* was marketed as fairly conservative family entertainment.) Players conversed with one another in comic strip speech balloons. A region – one of as many as 20,000 similar ones in the original *Habitat* at its zenith – was a place that you can walk your character around, and it had doors and passages to other regions. These regions were filled with functional objects such as ATM machines to provide cash, bags and boxes to carry things in, books and newspapers to read, weapons, flashlights, and garbage cans. You could walk, take elevators, or teleport to other regions and explore them; you could exchange conversation, buy and sell goods, and even swap body parts. And, if you got tired of your character, you could reconfigure it, give it some drugs, or take it to the Change-o-matic sex-change machine.

As the creators of *Habitat* soon found, their task became one of reinventing architecture and urban design for cyberspace. They commented:

> For 20,000 Avatars we needed 20,000 "houses" organized into towns and cities with associated traffic arteries and shopping and recreational areas. We needed wilderness areas between the towns so that everyone would not be jammed together into the same place. Most of all, we needed things for 20,000 people to do. They needed interesting places to visit – and since they can't all be in the same place at the same time, they needed a *lot* of interesting places to visit – and things to do in those places. Each of those houses, towns, roads, shops, forests, theaters, arenas, and other places is a distinct entity that someone needs to design and create. (ibid.)

Only limitations in bandwidth and processing power inhibit taking the next step – the realization of whizzier World Wide Webs, superMUDs, and other multiparticipant, urban-scale structures consisting of hyperlinked, three-dimensional, sensorily immersive spaces. And these limitations are temporary. The online environments of the future will increasingly resemble traditional cities in their variety of distinct places, in the extent and complexity of the "street networks" and "transportation systems" linking these places, in their capacity to engage our senses, and in their social and cultural richness.

But no matter how extensive a virtual environment or how it is presented, it has an underlying structure of places where you meet people and find things and links connecting those places. This is the organizing framework from which all else grows. In cyberspace, the hyperplan is the generator.

Enclosure/Encryption

You don't get to go just *anywhere* in a city, and the same is true of cyberspace. In both domains, barriers and thresholds play crucial roles.

In the built fabric of a city, the enclosing surfaces of the constituent spaces – walls, floors, ceilings, and roofs – provide not only shelter, but also privacy. Breaches in these surfaces – gates, doors, and windows – incorporate mechanisms to control access and maintain privacy; you can lock your doors or leave them open, lower the window shades or raise them. Spatial divisions and access-control devices are carefully deployed to organize places into hierarchies grading from completely public to utterly private. Sometimes you have to flip your ID to a bouncer, take off your shoes, pay admission, dress to a doorman's taste, slip a bribe, submit to a search, speak into a microphone and wait for the buzzer, smile at a receptionist, placate a watchdog, or act out some other ritual to cross a threshold into a more private space. Traditions and laws recognize these hierarchies and generally take a dim view of illicit boundary crossing by trespassers, intruders, and Peeping Toms.

Different societies have distinguished between public and private domains (and the activities appropriate to them) in differing ways, and urban form has reflected those distinctions. According to Lewis Mumford, domestic privacy was "a luxury of the well-to-do" up until the seventeenth century in the West.[3] The rich were the people who could do pretty much what they wanted, as long as they didn't do it in the street and frighten the horses. As privacy rights trickled down to the less advantaged classes, the modern "private house" emerged, acquired increasingly rigorous protections of constitutional law and public policy, and eventually became the cellular unit of suburban tissue. Within the modern Western house itself – in contrast to some of its ancient and medieval predecessors – there is a staged gradation from relatively public verandahs, entry halls, living rooms, and parlors to more private, enclosed bedrooms and bathrooms, where you can shut and lock the doors and draw down the shades against the outside world.

It doesn't rain in cyberspace, so shelter is not an architectural issue. But privacy certainly is. So the construction technology for virtual cities – just like that of bricks-and-mortar ones – must provide for putting up boundaries and erecting access controls, and it must allow cyberspace architects and urban designers to organize virtual places into public-to-private hierarchies.

Fortunately, some of the necessary technology does exist. Most obviously, in cyberspace construction the rough equivalent of a locked gate or door is an authentication system. This controls access to virtual places (such as your e-mail inbox) by asking for identification and a password from those who request entry. If you give the correct password, you're in. The trouble, of course, is that passwords, like keys, can be stolen and copied. And they can sometimes be guessed, systematically enumerated until one that works is found, or somehow extorted from the system manager who knows them all. So password protection – like putting a lock on a door – discourages illicit entry but does not block the most determined break-in artists....

So the technological *means* to create private places in cyberspace are available, but the *right* to create these places remains a fiercely contested issue. Can you always keep your bits to yourself? Is your home page your castle? These are still open questions.

Public Space/Public Access

Once public and private spaces are distinguished from each other they can begin to play complementary roles in urban life; a well-organized city needs both. And so it is in cyberspace. At the very least, this means that some part of our emerging electronic habitat should be set aside for public uses – just as city planners have traditionally designated land for public squares, parks, and civic institutions. Public pressure for this grew in the 1990s as the importance of cyberspace became increasingly clear. In 1994, for example, Senator Inouye of Hawaii introduced to the US Senate a bill that would reserve 20 percent of all new telecommunication capacity for free, public uses (noncommercial educational and informational services and civic discourse) and would provide funding for those uses.

But urban public space is not merely unprivate – what's left over when everyone walls off their private domains. A space is genuinely public, as Kevin Lynch once pointed out, only to the extent that it really is openly accessible and welcoming to members of the community that it serves.[4] It must also allow users considerable freedom of assembly and action. And there must be some kind of public control of its use and its transformation over time. The same goes for public cyberspace, so creators and maintainers of public, semipublic, and pseudopublic parts of the online world – like the makers of city squares, public parks, office building lobbies, shopping mall atriums, and Disneyland Main Streets – must consider who gets in and who gets excluded, what can and cannot be done there, whose norms are enforced, and who exerts control. These questions, like the complementary ones of privacy and encryption, have become the foci of crucial policy debates.

The Internet and commercial online services like America Online and Compuserve have to date provided only semipublic cyberspace at best, since they are widely but not universally accessible; you have to belong to a subscribing organization or have to pay to get in. This begs the question of how truly public cyberspace – the equivalent, say, of the Piazza San Marco in Venice – might be constructed. The community networks that emerged in the 1980s and 1990s – Santa Monica Public Electronic Network, Blacksburg Electronic Village, Telluride InfoZone, Smart Valley, and Cambridge Civic Network, for example – sought answers by trying to make network access openly available to entire communities in the same way that city hall and the local public parks traditionally have been.

Many of these community networks are structured as so-called free-nets, in which a "city" metaphor is explicitly used to structure information access: you go to the appropriate "building" to find the information or services that you want. Thus the "welcome" screen of the Cleveland Free-Net (one of the oldest and largest, with more than 35,000 registered users and over 10,000 log-ins per day) presents the following quotidian directory:

1   The Administration Building
2   The Post Office
3   Public Square
4   The Courthouse and Government Center
5   The Arts Building
6   Science and Technology Center
7   The Medical Arts Building
8   The Schoolhouse (Academy One)
9   The Community Center and Recreation Area
10 The Business and Industrial Park
11 The Library
12 University Circle
13 The Teleport
14 The Communications Center
15 NPTN / USA Today Headline News

On the free-net model, then, the new, virtual city becomes a kind of electronic shadow of the existing physical one. In many (though not all) cases, a citizen can choose between going to an actual public building or to the corresponding virtual one.

But a free-net's superimposition of the virtual onto the physical, while sensible enough, is not a logical or technical necessity. In fact, one of the most interesting questions for twenty-first-century urban designers to ask is, "How *should* virtual and physical public space relate to one another?"

Consider the obvious options. There is complete dissociation of the two if the electronic public space is accessible only from personal computers in homes and business. Another possibility is to associate access points with civic architecture: put an electronic information kiosk in the lobby of city hall or in the public library, for example. The Berkeley Community Memory and Santa Monica PEN systems have demonstrated a more radical strategy by placing rugged workstations in places like laundromats and at congregation points for the homeless; these workstations thus begin to play a public role much like the traditional one of fountains in the public places of Rome. The artist Krzysztof Wodiczko has gone a step further by suggesting that the physically homeless and displaced might carry electronic "alien staffs" – personal devices that connect them to cyberspace and sometimes construct public representations of self by providing information to others about who they are and where they come from. These are public rather than personal digital assistants.

Since physical distance means little in cyberspace, the possibility also exists to "condense" scattered rural communities by creating public spaces that serve large, thinly populated areas. The Big Sky Telegraph, which has been running in Montana since 1988, successfully pioneered this idea. It began by linking one-room and two-room rural schoolhouses across the state, and it has focused on education, economic opportunity, and economic self-sufficiency.

In economically disadvantaged communities, where adequate public facilities of a traditional kind do not exist, the possibility of providing public cyberspace may become an important community development issue. Increasingly, communities and their planners will have to consider trade-offs between investing scarce resources in creating or upgrading parks and community buildings and putting the money into effective electronic networks.

Whatever approach is taken to deploying network capacity for public purposes, though, simply making computers available and providing some kind of electronic access to civic information and discourse is not enough to create successful public cyberspace. Just as parks and squares must be pleasant and welcoming to a diverse population in order to function effectively, so must the interfaces to public areas of cyberspace; an interface that depends on cryptic commands and arcane knowledge of computer technology is as much a barrier to most people as is a flight of steps to a park user in a wheelchair. People must also feel secure and comfortable – not subject to hostility, abuse, or attack. And more subtly, but just as importantly, the cultural presumptions and cues that are built into an interface must not discourage potential users. Think of important physical public spaces like New York's Central Park and consider the extent to which both their successes and their failures depend on these sorts of things; designers of public cyberspace will have to deal with them as well.

Community Customs/Network Norms

Where public cyberspace exists, how can and should it be used? Do the customs and laws that govern physical public space still make sense in this new context?

As usage of the Internet and commercial online services has grown, there have been increasingly frequent disputes that have tested the limits of acceptable behavior in electronic public places and raised the question of how these limits might reasonably be enforced. In April 1994, for example, some particularly thick-skinned lawyers from Phoenix spammed the Internet by indiscriminately spraying a commercial advertisement for the services of their firm into thousands of newsgroups. This blast of unwanted bits had the same effect as driving a blaring sound truck into a public park. The Internet community reacted with outrage and disdain, and flamed back tens of thousands of complaints. One of the

unrepentant perpetrators proclaimed his right to be a pain and threatened to do it again. Eventually – to cries of "censorship!" from some quarters – a young Norwegian programmer wrote and unleashed an effective piece of "cancelbot" software that sniffed out and automatically removed the offending advertisements wherever they showed up.

In another widely publicized incident that unfolded almost simultaneously, a graduate student at MIT was busted by the FBI for operating an Internet bulletin board that had become a very active site for illegal activity – much like a bar in which drug deals were going down. Copies of commercial software were being posted, then downloaded without payment by users who logged in from all over the world. Was the operator of this openly accessible place responsible for knowing and controlling what was going on there? Or could he rightfully claim that it was just none of his business?

Like the proprietors of shopping malls and Disneylands, the operators of commercial online services must struggle with the inherently contradictory nature of the semipublic places they create. On the one hand, these places need lots of paying customers to support them, so they have to seem as welcoming, open, and inclusive as possible. On the other hand, though, the operators want to stay in firm control of what goes on. (The question is often framed as one of whether these services should be regarded as common carriers, like the telephone companies, and therefore not responsible for any libelous, obscene, or criminal information that they might carry or whether they should be in control and therefore held responsible like book and newspaper publishers and television broadcasters.) The last time I peeked at Prodigy, for example, I found the following notice from the management (a bit like the "Do not spit" signs that used to appear in railway stations): "And please remember that PRODIGY is for people of all ages and backgrounds. Notes containing obscene, profane or sexually explicit language (including descriptions of sexual acts, and whether or not masked with 'x's and the like) are not allowed. A good test is whether the language in your note would be acceptable at a public meeting."

Prodigy explicitly aims at a family audience, so it remorselessly enforces the norms of Middle America. Its competitors Compuserve and Genie have different sorts of constituencies, but their operators also take care to remove messages they consider obscene or illegal. And America Online has shut down some feminist discussion forums because, according to a spokesperson, kids might see the word "girl" in the forum's headline and "go in there looking for information about their Barbies."[5] The excluded feminists might be forgiven for responding in not-for-prime-time language. And forget the 'x's. These places have found a useful role to play, but don't mistake them for genuine, open-to-all, watch-out-for-yourself spaces for unconstrained public discourse....

But then, there will always be a Berkeley! The Berkeley Community Memory system is a radical political invention – a transposition of the Free Speech Movement and People's Park into cyberspace.[6] All information on the system is community generated, postings can be anonymous, and no central authority controls the content of postings. Funding is decentralized as well: there are coin-operated terminals on which postings can be read without charge, but it costs a quarter to post an opinion and a dollar to open up a new forum.

Nolli and the Net

The story of virtual communities, so far, is that of urban history replayed in fast forward – but with computer resource use playing the part of land use, and network navigation systems standing in for streets and transportation systems. The WELL, the World Wide Web, MUDs, and Free Nets are – like Hippodamos's gridded layout for Miletos, Baron Haussmann's radial patterning of Paris, or Daniel Burnham's grand plan for Chicago – large-scale structures of places and connections organized to meet the needs of their inhabitants.

And the parallels don't stop there. As traditional cities have evolved, so have customs, norms, and laws governing rights to privacy, access to public and semipublic places, what can be done where, and exertion of control. The organization of built space into public-to-private hierarchies, with gates and doors to control boundary crossings, has reflected this. Nolli's famous map of Rome vividly depicted it. Now, as cyberspace cities emerge, a similar framework of distinctions and expectations is – with much argument – being constructed, and electronic plazas, forums, lobbies, walls, doors, locks, members-only clubs, and private rooms are being invented and deployed. Perhaps some electronic cartographer of the future will produce an appropriately nuanced Nolli map of the Net.

NOTES

1 Eric H. Monkkonen, *America Becomes Urban: The Development of US Cities and Towns 1780–1880* (Berkeley: University of California Press, 1988).

2 Chip Morningstar and F. Randall Farmer, "The Lessons of Lucasfilm's Habitat," in Michael Benedikt, ed., *Cyberspace: First Steps* (Cambridge, MA: The MIT Press, 1991); Howard Rheingold, "Habitat: Computer-Mediated Play," in *The Virtual Community* (Reading, MA: Addison-Wesley, 1993).

3 Lewis Mumford, *The City in History* (New York: Harcourt Brace and World, 1961).

4 Kevin Lynch, *A Theory of Good City Form* (Cambridge, MA: The MIT Press, 1981).

5 Peter H. Lewis, "Censors Become a Force on Cyberspace Frontier," *The New York Times*, Wed., June 29, 1994, pp. 1, D5.

6 Steven Levy, *Hackers: Heroes of the Computer Revolution* (New York: Dell, 1984).

Chapter 7

Literary Geography: Joyce, Woolf and the City

Jeri Johnson

Why do I dramatise London perpetually?
Virginia Woolf[1]

DEAR DIRTY DUBLIN   James Joyce[2]

Two famous remarks made by two of the most famous modernist writers: Virginia Woolf in her 1905 essay 'Literary Geography': 'A writer's country is a territory within his own brain; and we run the risk of disillusionment if we try to turn such phantom cities into tangible brick and mortar...to insist that [a writer's city] has any counterpart in the cities of the earth is to rob it of half its charm'[3]; and James Joyce to Frank Budgen: 'I want to give a picture of Dublin so complete that if the city one day suddenly disappeared from the earth it could be reconstructed out of my book'.[4] On the one hand, cities as found in literature are imaginative constructions; on the other, at least one literary city aims to reflect the material reality of its original so accurately that from it Dublin could be rebuilt (much as legend has it Warsaw was from the faithfully rendered paintings of Canaletto minor). Of these two positions – which might be recharacterized as 'cities in literature represent something other than themselves' and 'cities in literature represent at least themselves' (or their particular material histories) – the former has had the stronger support from literary critics and theorists. It has become almost a truism of

criticism that within literature, especially the novel, space as represented figures not space per se, but something else.

Most persuasively, it has been argued that space functions in fiction through and as temporality, as a narrative event or events. So for Franco Moretti,

> the city as a physical place – and therefore as a support to descriptions and classifications – becomes the mere backdrop to the city as a network of developing social relationships – and hence as a prop to narrative temporality. The novel reveals that the meaning of the city is not to be found in any particular place, but manifests itself only through a temporal trajectory...the urban novel...seeks to resolve the spatial in terms of the sequential[5]

Similarly, for J. Hillis Miller,

> a novel is a figurative mapping. The story traces out diachronically the movement of the characters...as the crisscross of relationships gradually creates an imaginary space.... The houses, roads, paths, and walls stand...for the dynamic field of relations among [the characters].[6]

For Raymond Williams, whose arguments in *The Country and the City* differ from Moretti's and Miller's less in kind than in degree, whatever material reality may be being represented through presentations of the city (or indeed the country) this is significant only insofar as it communicates an ideology of the individual as s/he exists within a community. So he argues that in *Ulysses*, a novel in which much is narrated as interior monologue,[7]

> the forces of the action have become internal and in a way there is no longer a city, there is only a man walking through it...The substantial reality, the living variety of the city, is in the walker's mind...The history is not in this city but in the loss of a city, the loss of relationships. The only knowable community is in the need, the desire, of the racing and separated forms of consciousness.[8]

Not surprisingly given their avowed Marxian sympathies, Moretti's and Williams's descriptions resemble one another more strongly than do Miller's either, most clearly in the attention the former two pay to the particularities of social history delineated in and through the mapping of human relations across these literary topographies. But all agree that cities in literature stand for something other than themselves, that they represent a network of relationships unfolded (or not) over narrative time. In this, of course, they echo (and give a particularly literary twist to) the well-rehearsed arguments of that social theorist of the urban, George Simmel, for whom the significance of 'the city' lies in the effect it has on the mental life, and by extension the relationships, of those who live there. In such readings, cities never signify themselves: theirs is never a meaning *per se* but always a meaning *for*.

There is something particularly ironic about Williams's remark about *Ulysses* – 'the forces of the action have become internal and in a way there is no longer a city, there is only a man walking through it' – when taken with Joyce's own insistence on the fidelity of his representation to material fact. (What a slippery work is done by that phrase 'in a way': it allows Williams to get away with a great deal.[9]) But perhaps perversely, what I want to argue briefly is that, 'in a way' that Williams never imagines, he

is right about Joyce's *Ulysses* even as he ignores Joyce's faithfulness to the materiality of Dublin. Similarly the Woolf who in the 1930s wrote *The Years* had changed significantly in her attitudes about the meaning of the city in (at least her own) literature from the young woman who wrote in 1905 that 'we run the risk of disillusionment if we try to turn such phantom cities into tangible brick and mortar'. I want to argue that Williams (and the young essayist Woolf) are both right and wrong. Joyce and the novelist Woolf *are* concerned, like their near-contemporary Simmel, to interrogate the effect of the metropolis on the mental life of the individuals who live there.[10] And yet, in their writings, Joyce and (the older) Woolf also insistently figure the cities of Dublin and London in significantly material terms (or terms that signify a particular material history). In this latter, the urban theorist more relevant to their work is their other near-contemporary, the Walter Benjamin of *Charles Baudelaire*.[11] Beyond this, though and perhaps perversely, I want to draw a distinction between that most famous and 'quintessentially metropolitan' modernist text, *Ulysses* (1922), and Woolf's much less well known *The Years* (1937) to suggest that it is in the latter that the effect of the metropolis on mental life is the more fully drawn.

As early as 1905 when he was writing the stories that would finally be published in 1914 as *Dubliners*, Joyce defended the work precisely as being about Dublin, a city worthy of representation: 'When you remember that Dublin has been a capital for thousands of years, that it is the "second" city of the British Empire, that it is nearly three times as big as Venice it seems strange that no artist has given it to the world'.[12] 'The expression "Dubliner" seems to me to have some meaning and I doubt whether the same can be said for such words as "Londoner" and "Parisian" both of which have been used by writers as titles' (*LII*: 122). Because when writing the stories he was not in Dublin, but in Trieste and Rome, he constantly bombarded his brother Stanislaus with questions about the precise particularities of Dublin's fabric: 'Are Aungier St and Wicklow in the Royal Exchange Ward?...Are the police at Sydney Parade of the *D* division? Would the city ambulance be called out to Sydney Parade for an accident? Would an accident be treated at Vincent's Hospital?' (*LII*: 109). Of his Aunt Josephine Murray, he requested that she send an 'Xmas present made up of tramtickets, advts, handbills, posters, papers, programmes &c. I would like to have a map of Dublin on my wall. I suppose I am becoming something of a maniac' (*LII*: 186).

This was a habit he was to continue, of course. When writing *Ulysses*, he wrote to Aunt Josephine again: 'Is it possible for an ordinary person to climb over the area railings of no 7 Eccles street, either from the path or the steps, lower himself from the lowest part of the railings till his feet are within 2 feet or 3 of the ground and drop unhurt. I saw it done myself but by a man of rather athletic build' (*LI*: 175); 'are there trees in Leahy's terrace at the side or near, if so, what, are there steps leading down to the beach?' (*LI*: 136). Aunt Josephine appears to have replied, for Joyce changed the trees in Leahy's terrace from the elms they were in manuscript to the laurel hedges that appear in the final version. That in his composition of the book Joyce relied as well on *Thom's Official Directory of the United Kingdom of Great Britain and Ireland*, Dublin section, 1904 edition, to place with accuracy the shops, museums, libraries, pubs, cemeteries, schools, churches, breweries, tearooms, turkish baths, bookshops through which his fictional (and 'real') characters move is well known. In doing so, he made certain that when he made that very number 7 Eccles Street the residence of Leopold and Molly Bloom on 16 June 1904, the house was otherwise uninhabited by any 'real' person. So accurately are the geographical dimensions of Dublin rendered that one critic could take a stopwatch and walk each of the separate fragments of 'Wandering Rocks', the most 'urban' of

the 18 episodes of *Ulysses*, and discover that each narrative fragment as written would intersect with others so exactly that they could be precisely chronologically charted.[13]

In fact, from the beginning so insistent was Joyce on providing the exact dimensions of Dublin in his work that he refused to change to fictional the real names of actual pubs, restaurants, railway companies when his contracted Irish publisher for *Dubliners* demand that he do so. That publisher, George Roberts, responded:

> I submitted the whole matter to [our legal advisers], and I regret to say that they find the book to abound in risks of action of libel. They advise me that in practically every case where any going concern (e.g. public house, restaurant, railway company or other existing person, firm or body corporate with vested interests) is mentioned by actual name, then having regard to the events described as taking place in connection with them, there is no doubt that actions in libel would lie...That being so, the publication of the book by Maunsell & Co. is out of the question. (*LII*: 313)

Joyce stood firm; *Dubliners* was published two years later by the English publisher Grant Richards.[14]...

Clearly Joyce had a peculiar and particularly obsessional attitude to the facts of geographical Dublin. (These weren't, of course, the only facts about which Joyce was so fastidious. His 'mistakes' seem always to accord with Stephen's statement in *Ulysses*: 'A man of genius makes no mistakes. His errors are volitional and are the portals of discovery'.[15]) The Kildare House example is typical. In making the correction in 1917, Joyce does something more than put Stephen and Lynch on the right track. He adds a fillip from the political history of Ireland. Similarly in *Dubliners*'s 'Two Gallants', Joyce creates not only a story of sexual treachery and betrayal – as critics have frequently remarked – but one which echoes Ireland's history of political betrayals. In their precisely charted walk through the streets of Dublin and in their exploitation thereon of an Irish 'slavey', the story's two central characters, Lenehan and Corley, resemble most obviously the Garrison – those British troops stationed in Ireland to keep the 'wild Irish' under control – and its (even if only passive) supporters among the Irish themselves.[16] (Joyce's political critique in *Dubliners* targets the Irish as well as the British to the extent that they remain, as the narrator of another *Dubliners* story puts it, '*gratefully* oppressed'.[17]) As Donald T. Torchiana succinctly remarks, 'If Lenehan shamelessly exemplifies a slack and indifferent nineteenth-century Irishry that stands by as the nation is defrauded, then Corley is rightly identified as the active force in bringing that nation willingly to her knees and getting paid for it to boot'.[18] But by carefully orchestrating their movements, Joyce adds even greater historical texture to the tale. The two men move through a Dublin redolent not only with the history of the Garrison, but with that of the Ascendancy at its height, through streets and past buildings which bear the names of those who, particularly in the period of the Ascendancy's greatest strength, not only 'oppressed' Ireland but were rewarded for doing so.[19] So, for example, when they 'walk along Nassau Street and then turn into Kildare Street', they pass 'the club' near the porch of which stands a 'harpist . . . playing to a little ring of listeners':

> He plucked at the wires heedlessly, glancing quickly from time to time at the face of each newcomer and from time to time, wearily also, at the sky. His harp too, heedless that her coverings had fallen about her knees, seemed weary alike of the eyes of strangers and of her master's hands. . .

> The two young men walked up the street without speaking, the mournful music following them.[20]

Of course, the harp, always feminized, represents Ireland herself; 'she' invariably comes 'mournful', 'heedless' and 'weary' of being used alike by 'strangers' and by 'her master's hands'. But as Torchiana points out, Joyce increases the irony by situating the scene on the steps of 'the club', from its location clearly identifiable as The Kildare Street Club, founded in 1782 by the Rt. Hon. William Burton Conyngham, Teller of the Exchequer, and his cronies, and 'long the haven of Unionism in Ireland',[21] the very home of the 'stranger' of whose hands the harp has wearied.

The contemporary tale of Lenehan and Corley bears a historical and political significance beyond itself, a significance unfolded through Joyce's precise and obsessive detailing of Dublin's geography. If, as Hillis Miller suggests, 'the houses, roads, paths, and walls' of fiction stand 'for the dynamic field of relations' among characters, in *Joyce's* fiction that 'dynamic field' is opened up through his detailing of Dublin's geography to the sedimented layers of Ireland's political (and social) history. This is that history to which Stephen in *Ulysses* refers when he remarks, 'History is a nightmare from which I am trying to awake'.[22]

Ironically, Joyce's very insistence on fidelity to material history means that *Ulysses*, for all its quintessentially urban character, presents its central characters in situations less metropolitan than provincial. In the main (and I will return to the exception below), it does not demonstrate the effects of the metropolis on mental life, at least as they were being delineated by the likes of Simmel and Benjamin. Both of these urban theorists were keen to stress the effects on the individual of having to cope with a density of population (and therefore of events, of 'stimuli') which rendered one anonymous, alienated (or in Simmel's term, 'blasé', in Benjamin's as the '*flâneur* . . . addicted to the phantasmagoria of space'[23]). If Leopold Bloom, *Ulysses*'s own *flâneur*, is alienated (and this is debatable), it is not because he lives in a metropolis, but because he is *eccentric* or (etymologically) 'out of the centre'.[24] He is a Jew, not a Catholic; his paternal line Hungarian, not Celtic. This means at least that Joyce's text is more cosmopolitan than metropolitan – or at least that Joyce is trying to bring

Dublin, kicking and screaming, into cosmopolitan Europe. Further, Bloom has none of the anonymity suffered by Simmel's blasé type (nor any of the pleasure enjoyed by the Benjaminian *flâneur*): he is not anonymous. Nor for that matter are any of the characters in *Ulysses*. Everyone in this book knows everyone else. The Dublin of *Ulysses* as conveyed through the relationships represented within it resembles most not those of a great metropolis, but those of a large village. And at the level of the material, this can be explained in part by the simple fact of population density. Compare for a moment, the population figures for Dublin in 1901 (*Ulysses* is set in 1904) and 1921 (it was published in 1922) with those of London for the same years: Dublin, 1901: 373,000; 1921: 399,000; London, 1901: 6,586,000; 1921: 7,488,000.[25] These are huge differences; London had nearly 20 times the population of Dublin. This is why, when the *Aeolus* episode of *Ulysses* presents us with a headline announcing that we are 'IN THE HEART OF THE HIBERNIAN METROPOLIS',[26] we recognize it as satire....

It would be perverse to suggest that in her fiction Virginia Woolf displayed anything like Joyce's obsessive insistence on getting the facts of the material city right. But she did repeatedly situate her fictions in the urban space of London. That from at least *Night and Day* (1919) through to *The Years* (1937) Woolf's characters' lives find their meanings delineated against the backdrop of *this* city is self-evident.[27] In addition, her letters and diaries are saturated with accounts of the city's enticements for her – 'London itself perpetually attracts, stimulates, gives me a play & a poem, without any trouble, save that of moving my legs through the streets'[28] – and with her celebrations of it:

> London is enchanting. I step out upon a tawny coloured magic carpet, it seems, and get carried into beauty without raising a finger. The nights are amazing, with all the white porticos and broad silent avenues. And people pop in and out, lightly, divertingly like rabbits; and I look down Southampton Row, wet as a seal's back or red and yellow with sunshine, and watch the omnibuses going and coming and hear the old crazy organs.[29]

But often such celebrations – and this example is typical – eschew the material 'facts' of the city, troping the scene instead into a landscape the metaphors of which are drawn not from an urban but from a rural lexicon: note the rabbits and the seal's back. Woolf repeatedly refigured what other commentators saw as the brutalism, the shocks, the alienating effects of the metropolis in terms more exultant than deprecatory, more lyrical than prosaic: 'the house is ours... with... the view of the square in front & the desolated buildings behind, & Southampton Row, & the whole of London – London thou art a jewel of jewels, & jasper of jocunditie', she writes, jubilantly misquoting William Dunbar *In Honour of the City of London*.[30]...

Woolf had repeatedly expressed her desire to take the novel as a form away from what she perceived as the mere 'materialism' of the fictions of her novelistic predecessors, Galsworthy, Bennett and Wells. They, she insisted, were not interested as was she in 'character' but in 'something outside'.[31] The issue went to the very heart of her creative method. In her novels, from at least *Mrs Dalloway* on, she includes 'externality', the 'facts' of the material world, not as material detail 'objectively' rendered through an omniscient narrator but as perception filtered through the affective response of a narrated subject.[32]...

So how does she include the 'facts' of the material city in *The Years*? And what kind of meanings do they convey? Remember that Woolf's concern was to write 'history' (and to place it precisely in time: the chapters of the novel have as their titles seemingly randomly chosen dates: '1880', '1891', '1907', '1908', '1910', '1911', '1913', '1914', '1917', '1918', 'Present

Day'). Not surprisingly therefore, the London through which her characters move – and they repeatedly move in an alternating rhythm between the private space of the home and the public realm of streets, shops, restaurants, theatres, law courts, parks, bridges, buses – comes freighted with history and with political significance. So, for example, when Eleanor Pargiter and her niece Peggy travel across London in a cab, they reach the theatre district:

> Their own taxi was held up. It stopped dead under a statue: the lights shone on its cadaverous pallor.
>
> 'Always reminds me of an advertisement for sanitary towels,' said Peggy, glancing at the figure of a woman in nurse's uniform holding out her hand . . .
>
> 'The only fine thing that was said in the war,' [Eleanor] said aloud, reading the words cut on the pedestal.
>
> 'It didn't come to much,' said Peggy sharply.[33]

What the statue is is never overtly revealed, nor are the words cut on the pedestal spoken aloud for the reader's elucidation. But the statue is clearly identifiable as that of Edith Cavell which stands on an island between St Martin-in-the-Fields and the National Portrait Gallery. Cavell, an English nurse working in Belgium, helped soldiers escape to neutral Holland after the German occupation of Belgium in 1914; she was arrested by the Germans, sentenced to death and executed on 12 October 1915. The inscription on the pedestal, supposedly her last words, reads: 'I realize that patriotism is not enough. I must have no hatred or bitterness towards anyone.' Knowing the statue means understanding Eleanor's comment, but Woolf will not stoop to 'preaching' by including the inscription itself. Similarly, when, walking through Hyde Park, Martin and Sara pass 'the bald rubbed space where speakers congregate' and stop to listen, Woolf expects not only that the reader will recognize Speaker's Corner but that she will know that it was

here that the right of assembly was finally established in 1872 after repeated public demonstrations.[34] When they pass Colonel Pargiter's 'club' in Piccadilly, she expects a recognition of the Naval and Military Club at 94 Piccadilly (known from the markings on its gates as 'The In and Out') and an understanding of this patriach's place in the history of the British Empire and of his retreat to the safety of a men's club with all that that implies for the history of relations between men and women. When they laugh at the 'splayed out figure at Temple Bar' (Charles Birch's bronze griffin surmounting Horace Jones's memorial), she expects that the reader will know the history of Temple Bar: site of a prison, site of the monarch's ceremonial entry into the City of London, site of the display of the remains (usually the heads) of 'traitors of the populace', site of the pillorying of Titus Oates and Daniel Defoe.[35]

Throughout the novel, Woolf deploys London details to convey indirectly information the direct enunciation of which would pull the book into polemic. So, for example, she frequently remarks social and economic class through allusion to particular parts of London: 'She had always thought he lived at Ealing. So he lived at Westminster, did he?' Eleanor thinks of her fellow committee member, Mr Pickford, the 'clean-shaven, dapper little man, whom she had always seen in her mind's eye running to catch a train with a newspaper under his arm. But he lived at Westminster, did he? That was odd, she thought'.[36] Of course, Woolf also expects that her reader will register the nuances of meaning carried by 'Ealing' and 'Westminster' in 1910, the year of the chapter in which Eleanor makes her observation. Some topographic allusions are easier to read than this one, though not all. The book is riddled with passing comments (either by name or clearly identifiable by careful geographic pointers) on Bermondsey, Hoxton, (Lisson) Grove, Notting Hill Gate, Covent Garden, Fulham, Shoreditch, Lambeth, all of which were deprived areas at the times Woolf's characters make their asides – as indeed were parts of Westminster. When Colonel Pargiter visits his mistress, he must go to Westminster to do so:

> When he came to Westminster he stopped. He did not like this part of the business at all. Every time he approached the little street that lay under the huge bulk of the Abbey, the street of dingy little houses, with yellow curtains and cards in the window, the street where the muffin man seemed always to be ringing his bell, where children screamed and hopped in and out of white chalk-marks on the pavement, he paused, looked to the right, looked to the left; and then walked very sharply to Number Thirty and rang the bell. He gazed straight at the door as he waited with his head rather sunk. He did not wish to be seen standing on that door-step.[37]

Such neighbourhoods are exactly those that his own daughter and nieces will subsequently live in, after their parents have died and the inheritance has gone to the sons. In fact, Woolf puts Pargiter's niece in this same house 37 years later, and subtly makes a point again about gender and the fates of the daughters of sons of the Empire.

But in *The Years*, Woolf goes beyond these nuanced references through London's topography to the material histories of (representative individuals within) this particular culture. As early as 1924, she had confided to her diary, 'One of these days I will write about London, and how it takes up the private life and carries it on, without any effort'.[38] By the 1930s, she had come to realize that, as she claimed in *The Years'* sibling *Three Guineas*, 'the public and the private worlds are inseparably connected; that the tyrannies and servilities of the one are the tyrannies and servilities of the other'.[39] To 'write about London, and how it takes up the private life' now would also of necessity be to write of 'the public', and *vice versa*. Writing the metropolis now became for Woolf a matter of writing about the interlocked, interwoven relationship between private and public worlds. To write the metropolis she would

write mental life as it was configured in, through and as direct confrontation and interaction with the material public sphere. This Woolf accomplishes in *The Years*. But in her configuration of the metropolis and mental (and public) life, Woolf came to be more sanguine, more hopeful and, as she put it, more 'constructive' than Simmel.[40] I stress that she *came to be*, for she was not initially so.

Uncharacteristically for Woolf, very late in the composition process of *The Years* (after the book had been already set in galleys) she cut from it what Leonard Woolf referred to as 'two enormous chunks'.[41] These 'chunks' comprise scenes of interlocked narrative fragments which follow first one character, then another with whom the first has had an encounter, and then a third with whom the second has engaged, and so on, as these individuals move through the public space of London (from Richmond's streets to Kew Gardens, to the tube train, to Piccadilly Circus and Leicester Square, to Trafalgar Square and on to an omnibus, past Hyde Park and so on). The first 'chunk' occurs in 1917; the second begins in 1918 and jumps surreptitiously to 1921 as two individuals spotted by one character in 1918 open the next narrative fragment when the omniscient narrator spies them together again three years later. These scenes typically catch encounters between strangers: Crosby, the Pargiter family servant, sees a young man and woman sitting together on a park bench at Kew, jumps to the conclusion they are married, only to find herself wrong when the two walk off separately without having spoken a word; the young man catches the tube where he is crowded by the soldiers on board and eyes them with admiration; a 'meagre white-haired old lady...screw[s] up her eyes and trie[s] to read the headline on the man's paper who [sits] beside her'.[42] This, we come to learn, is Eleanor Pargiter, perhaps the central character of the novel, a woman we readers know intimately by now, but who here has become anonymous, alien, when narrated from the perspective of the stranger on the train. These fragments repeatedly present the experience of city life as it might have been delineated by Simmel or Benjamin. . . .

Let us examine one final example of the complexity and subtlety with which she unfolds these meanings. When in '1914' Martin Pargiter travels to St Paul's he stands looking at the cathedral, shifting his vantage point to get an adequate perspective on the building. In the paragraphs preceding Martin gazing at St Paul's, the narrative has given a more distanced, aerial view of the same city scene. Here, the omnibuses circle round in a 'perpetual current': 'The statue of Queen Anne seemed to preside over the chaos and to supply it with a centre, like the hub of a wheel.' This figure 'ruled the traffic with her sceptre; directed the activities' of the passers-by. This image of regal power organizing the chaos dissolves when 'a little old man carrying a paper bag' arrives to feed the birds. 'Soon he was haloed by a circle of fluttering wings. Sparrows perched on his head and his hands. Pigeons waddled close to his feet. A little crowd gathered to watch him feeding the sparrows. He tossed his bread round him in a circle' (p. 244). The power of Queen Anne gives way before the greater charisma arising from the humbler occupation of a St Francis. But this configuration too dissolves when, with 'a ripple in the air',

> [T]he great clock, all the clocks of the city, seemed to be gathering their forces together; they seemed to be whirring a preliminary warning. Then the stroke struck. "One" blared out. All the sparrows fluttered up into the air; even the pigeons were frightened; some of them made a little flight round the head of Queen Anne. (p. 244)

When Martin enters the open space in front of the cathedral, he must step back to gain perspective. As he looks up, 'all the weights in his body seemed to shift. He had a curious sense of something moving in his body in harmony with the building; it righted itself: it came to a full stop. It was exciting

– this change of proportion' (p. 244). But Martin finds the passers-by interfere with his attempt to see clearly and thinks the pigeons a nuisance.

The scene corresponds with many of the recurrent patterns that Woolf deploys in *The Years*, but here what concerns us is her drawing out into significance the feelings experienced by this individual city dweller as he enters the public space in front of the monumental cathedral. Woolf figures Martin's response as somatic pleasure: 'all the weights in his body seemed to shift'; 'it was exciting'. He connects the pleasure with his private fantasy–that he might have become an architect instead of living simply on the inheritance his father has left him–but Woolf expands the scene into a political and historical significance beyond Martin's self-indulgence. She precedes his emergence into the open space with the scene of Queen Anne 'ruling' the circling traffic with her sceptre, an image of the ostensibly unifying force of regal power and political domination. This image disperses, supplanted by the suggestion of an alternative arrangement of society as the 'birdman' 'haloed' by 'circling wings' figures the possibility of charitable action as stimulus for social cohesion. But this utopian possibility too breaks apart with the striking of the clocks as actual time and contemporary history intrude upon the brief vision of an alternative social formation. Their intoned 'One' mandates not the unity of society but the dismemberment of it into discrete individuals. When we realize that this is 1914 and that World War I looms on the horizon, the reconfiguration of the pattern around the statue of Queen Anne acquires the political significance Woolf refuses to didactically assert. Of course, as one of those individuals caught within the vortex of history, Martin can experience only 'a curious sense of something moving in his body in harmony with the building.' His somatic response brings pleasure and excitement, and stirs a personal fantasy, but neither recognition of Woolf's diagnosis of the state of contemporary history nor her suggestion of the possibility of alternative modes of living is available to him. That pleasure is reserved for the reader.

Both Joyce and Woolf repeatedly and insistently returned to site their novels in the urban space of the Modern City. Both saw the city as significantly, profoundly, embedded within specific, material, political histories. For both, the sedimented layers of history lay behind and beneath and upon the surfaces of Dublin and London. For both, the meanings of the lives of those who lived therein were produced within and by means of those very material cities. For both – Dublin for the one, London for the other – these cities were both insistently themselves and persistently something other.

NOTES

1 Virginia Woolf to Ethel Smyth (25 September 1940), in *The Letters of Virginia Woolf* (1975–1980), Nigel Nicholson and Joanne Trautmann (eds) (6 volumes), Vol. VI, p. 434, London: Hogarth Press.

2 Actually, James Joyce repeating Lady Sidney Morgan's epithet (*Ulysses*: The 1922 Text, 1993, Jeri Johnson (ed.), p. 139, Oxford: Oxford University Press, Oxford World's Classics.

3 'Literary Geography' in *The Essays of Virginia Woolf* (1986), Andrew McNeillie (ed.) (4 volumes), Vol. 1, p. 35, London: Hogarth Press.

4 Joyce to Frank Budgen, quoted in Frank Budgen, *James Joyce and the Making of 'Ulysses'* (1934, reprinted 1960), pp. 67–8, Bloomington: Indiana University Press.

5 Franco Moretti (1988) *Signs Taken for Wonders: Essays in the Sociology of Literary Forms*, trans. Susan Fischer, David Forgacs and David Miller (rev. edn), p. 112, London: Verso.

6 J. Hillis Miller (1995) *Topographies*, pp. 19–20, Stanford: Stanford University Press.

7 'Interior monologue': the presentation in the first person–and therefore as unmediated by an external, often oversimplistically characterized as 'omniscient' or 'objective' narrator – of the unvocalized and fragmented 'thoughts' of the characters.

8 Raymond Williams (1973) *The Country and the City*, pp. 243–5, London: Chatto & Windus.

9 Because what we are given in *Ulysses* is a representation of a man thinking, Williams argues, we have not a city but (a representation of) his thoughts about a city. But cities in literature are always representations in language of someone's thoughts about cities, even if those thoughts are masked as objective because relayed through an external 'objective' narrator. In what way is George Eliot's Middlemarch a more substantial material space than Joyce's Dublin, as it would be by Williams's reasoning? Carried to its logical conclusion, such a mode of reading would necessarily lead us to say that, 'in a way', there are never cities in literature; there is only language which itself merely represents the thoughts of the writer about cities.

10 See Georg Simmel (1903) 'The Metropolis and Mental Life'.

11 Walter Benjamin, 'The Paris of the Second Empire in Charles Baudelaire' (1938), 'Some Motifs in Baudelaire' (1939) and 'Paris – The Capital of the Nineteenth Century', all in *Charles Baudelaire: A Lyric Poet in the Era of High Capitalism* (1973, 1997), trans. Harry Zohn, London: Verso.

12 James Joyce, letter to Stanislaus Joyce, 24 September 1905 (Letters of James Joyce (1957, 1966), Vol. 1, Stuart Gilbert (ed.); Vols II and III, Richard Ellmann (ed.) (3 volumes), Vol. II, p. 111, New York: Viking. Henceforth cited in the text by volume and page number.

13 Clive Hart (1982) 'Wandering Rocks', in Clive Hart and David Hayman (eds) *James Joyce's 'Ulysses': Critical Essays*, Berkeley: University of California Press.

14 Not that Richards comes off as the defender of 'truth': he had already contracted in 1906 to publish *Dubliners*; it was the withdrawal of his offer – when Joyce refused to emend the text when Richards expressed a fear that a prosecution for obscenity might be launched were it not changed – that occasioned Joyce's attempt

at publication with the Irish Maunsell & Co.

15 Joyce, *Ulysses*, Johnson (ed.), p. 182.

16 See Robert Boyle (1963) '"Two Gallants" and "Ivy Day in the Committee Room"', *James Joyce Quarterly* 1.1 (Fall), pp. 3–6; Florence Walzl (1965) 'Symbolism in Joyce's "Two Gallants"', *James Joyce Quarterly*, 2.2 (Winter), pp. 73–81; and Donald T. Torchiana (1986) '"Two Gallants": A Walk through the Ascendancy', *Backgrounds to Joyce's 'Dubliners'*, pp. 91–108, Boston: Allen and Unwin.

17 James Joyce (2000, forthcoming) *Dubliners*, Jeri Johnson (ed.), p. 30 (emphasis added), Oxford: Oxford University Press, Oxford World's Classics.

18 Torchiana, p. 91.

19 See Torchiana, p. 91–108.

20 Joyce, *Dubliners*, Johnson (ed.), pp. 39–40.

21 Torchiana, pp. 93, 92, and n. 6.

22 *Ulysses*, Johnson (ed.), p. 34.

23 Simmel, 'The Metropolis and Mental Life': 'there is perhaps no psychic phenomenon which is so unconditionally reserved to the city as the blasé outlook' (p. 73); Benjamin, 'Paris – the Capital of the Nineteenth Century', *Charles Baudelaire*, p. 174.

24 'Eccentric': from the Greek 'ἐκ-' ('out [of]') 'κεντρυ´' ('*centre*').

25 Source: B. R. Mitchell (1975) *European Historical Statistics 1750–1970*, London: Macmillan.

26 Joyce, *Ulysses*, Johnson (ed.), p. 112; this is the first 'headline' of the *Aeolus* episode of *Ulysses*; these 'headlines' are inevitably ironic comments on the text which follows.

27 That Woolf also wrote numerous essays detailing life in, and the urban landscape of, London is less well known. She published her first such essay, 'Street Music' when she was just 22, her most significant 'Street Haunting' in 1927, while as late as 1931–1932 she wrote for *Good Housekeeping* a series, *Six Articles on London Life*: Virginia Woolf, 'Street Music' (1905), reprinted in *The Essays of Virginia Woolf*, Andrew McNeillie (ed.), Vol. 1, pp. 27–31; 'Street Haunting: A London Adventure' (1927), reprinted in *The Essays*, McNeillie (ed.), Vol. IV, pp. 480–90; all the *Good Housekeeping* articles–'The Docks of London' (Dec. 1931), 'Oxford Street Tide' (Jan 1932), 'Great Men's Houses' (Mar 1932), 'Abbeys and Cathedrals' (May 1932), 'This is the House of Commons' (Oct 1932) and 'Portrait of a Londoner' (Dec 1932) – except the last were republished as *The London Scene* (1975, reprinted 1982), London: Hogarth.

28 The Diary of Virginia Woolf (1977–84) Anne Olivier Bell and Andrew McNeillie (eds) (5 volumes), Vol. III, p. 186, London: Hogarth Press.

29 Woolf, *Diary*, Vol. II, p. 301.

30 Dunbar's actual lines: 'London, thou are the flour of cities all. Gemme of all joy, jaspre of jocunditie, Most myghty carbuncle of vertue and valour'.

31 Woolf, 'Modern Fiction' (1919), reprinted in Virginia Woolf (1993) *The Crowded Dance of Modern Life*, Rachel Bowlby (ed.), p. 6, London: Penguin; and 'Mr Bennett and Mrs Brown' (1924), reprinted in Virginia Woolf (1993) *A Woman's Essays*, Rachel Bowlby (ed.), p. 77, London: Penguin.

32 Strictly, Woolf most frequently uses the mode of narration known as free indirect discourse, whereby a third-person narrator moves surreptitiously into the thoughts of the character while grammatically retaining the past tense and the third person, so without signalling directly that such a move has happened (e.g. by avoiding direct citation through quotation marks and the tag 'she thought'). So, in *Mrs Dalloway*: 'She could see what she lacked. It was not beauty; it was not mind. It was something central that permeated' ((1923, 1993) Elaine Showalter (ed.), p. 34, London: Penguin.) (Interior monologue, Joyce's device in *Ulysses*, would give something like this – 'Know what I lack. Not beauty; not mind. Something central that permeates' – though one cannot imagine any character in *Ulysses* thinking anything remotely like this.) Her novels typically, therefore, create character at the intersection of exterior (third-person narrator) and interior (individual perception, affective response); characters are neither distinctively integral nor wholly collective. The same is true of the external material world: it does not exist in her novels independently of characterized perceptions of it. Thus, Woolf blurs the ostensible divide between the subject and the object.

33 Woolf, *The Years*, Johnson (ed.), p. 246.

34 Woolf, *The Years*, Johnson (ed.), p. 347; and Ben Weinreib and Christopher Hibbert (eds) (1993) *The London Encyclopedia* (rev. edn), p. 414, London: Papermac.

35 *Woolf*, The Years, Johnson (ed.), p. 171; and *London Encyclopedia*, p. 881.

36 Woolf, *The Years*, Johnson (ed.), p. 130.

37 Woolf, *The Years*, Johnson (ed.), p. 5.

38 Woolf, Diary, Vol. II, p. 301 (May 1924).

39 Woolf, *Three Guineas* (1938), reprinted in '*A Room of One's Own*' and '*Three Guineas*' (1993) Michèle Barrett (ed.), p. 270, London: Penguin; *Three Guineas* was in many ways the offspring of *The Years*: 'lumping the Years & 3 G[uineas]s to-gether as one book – as indeed they are' (Woolf, Diary, Vol. V, p. 148); and see Johnson, 'Introduction', *The Years* (ed.) Johnson, pp. xix–xxi.

40 Woolf in commenting on Basil de Selincourt's review of the novel remarks 'he sees that it is a creative, a constructive book' (Diary, Vol. V, 68).

41 Leonard Woolf (1967) *Downhill All the Way: An Autobiography of the Years 1919–1939*, reprinted (1980) in *An Autobiography*, Vol. II, p. 302, Oxford: Oxford University Press. These 'two enormous chunks' form the 'Appendix' of Woolf, *The Years*, Johnson (ed.), pp. 361–401.

42 Woolf, *The Years*, Johnson (ed.), p. 364.

Chapter 8

The Hem of Manhattan

Djuna Barnes

In July 1917, shortly after the US joined the war in Europe, Barnes wrote this account of a forty-mile boat trip around Manhattan Island for the readers of the Morning Telegraph. Up the East River – that isn't a river at all but a strait separating Manhattan from Long Island – through the narrow channel called Hell Gate, to Spuyten Duyvil Creek where on Manhattan's northern boundary the Harlem River meets the Hudson; south along the sleep cliffs of the Palisades to Battery Park at the island's southern tip, and under the magnificent Brooklyn Bridge; past the first of New York's great skyscrapers, the wedge-shaped Flatiron Building, and the Woolworth Tower, at sixty stories the tallest when completed in 1913, magnificently Gothic and still one of the city's most remarkable buildings.

To take a yacht trip around Manhattan Island is to find yourself in the awkward position of one who must become a stranger in his own house that he may describe it with the necessary color.

How much easier, for instance, to have been sent to Russia to paint a word picture of their afternoon meal and their homes. Or to have gone to France, there to stroll among the ruins of what used to be the descriptive parts of Cousin Milly's letters home; to have walked awhile along the

boulevards or to have coveted hats in a window in a street off from that cafe Jules talked of with me the other night. Or to have watched the smoking of French cigarettes, or to have visited Napoleon's tomb or walked where Bernhardt used to walk, or to have tried to find the cafe where Verlaine and Baudelaire wrote their poems, or any one of the million and ten things that one expects to be seen doing when he takes a trip to a foreign country.

There one would notice how the buttons were made because it would be a strange, new person wearing them in a strange, old land. Here one's buttons are never missed until they fall off.

Here one looks upon things because one has eyes. There one has eyes that he may contemplate. This is the inevitable tragedy of being familiar with one's home. Here we live and go through the usual daily program because we must; but it is only when one travels – be it only to Kansas, providing Kansas is a foreign land – that one comes upon the discovery that to appreciate and to understand one should never be on anything but a friendly footing either with architecture or with people.

It's the saying of "How do you do?" that is the educational part of life. The goodbye is only the sad little period to a no-longer-needed paragraph.

Who was it who said, "My friend, you cannot reach into your home because it is from there you were found reaching out"? And so I am condemned with a thousand million unless I find myself in a lonely place, where I may be profitable in my crying for the echoes I set around me that have never called back since I was born; a place that will be as strange to me as I to it.

It's a pleasant thought, but still I cannot escape my ultimate task: the fact that Manhattan Island has passed before me in review.

I believe this trip is advertised as one of pleasure. Well, perhaps I am melancholy, as I have often been told, but what can one be when to reach the boat one has to cross Death Avenue first? And what is one going to suffer if not despair, when for three hours and a half there pass misery, poverty, death, old age, and insanity?

The two shore lines are separated by a strip of level, uncomplaining water, like two convicts who have between them three links of impassive chain: two terrible positives separated by a negative.

But as the storyteller would say, this is not beginning at the beginning.

I think it was something like two-thirty when I started. The boat was the smallest of its kind I have ever patronized, and as I climbed aboard, the upper deck was already covered with stiff-backed, Middle West school teachers and others, most of whom were bearded gentlemen with gold nuggets mounted and used as tiepins.

They all sat there in uncompromising rows as though they were in a classroom, and off and on they turned their heads just enough to look at the water with determination, because they were there to see, and they would see.

The sun was hot, and you could hear the cordage and the planking creaking. Let me mention that I did not see more than one child on this trip. And after all, this was quite the right thing. Children are taken to Bear Island, or up the Hudson to some camping ground, to some place that resembles at least a definite spot.

Presently, as the yacht pulled out and started moving in a side circle about the Battery, the megaphone man stepped forward and began chanting: "This building to your left is known as the Woolworth Tower, the largest building in the world; it stands so-many-and-so-many feet high," giving the exact number of feet and inches, as though it were growing, and then he turned in the other direction and added casually, "This is a transport steamer to your right, filled, as you see, by our boys in khaki."

Then we heard their voices, hundreds of them, coming to us over the intervening water. A strange cry, a happy cry, an exultant cry, proclaiming doom and death. They all rose up, calling aloud, waving their arms and their handkerchiefs. A few words drifted back to us as we pulled alongside and then moved on. "We'll get the Kaiser," and the often-repeated, "Come on, too." One of them standing a little forward kissed his hand lightly; others thrust their shaggy heads out of the portholes. It made me think of Coney Island and the voice that usually accompanies an outthrust head; "Three shots for a nickel."

I looked around me: everyone was sitting in the same passive manner, stiffly and conventionally and unemotionally.

Looking at the skyline as we rounded the Battery, New York rose out of the water like a great wave that found it impossible to return again and so remained there in horror, peering out of the million windows men had caged it with.

Boats, like pet dogs, were leashed to the docks, and one little tug looking like a spitz growled at our side, sticking its nose out of the green, loose water as though it were trying to bite.

The Brooklyn Bridge, the Manhattan, the Williamsburg, and the Queensboro came into view, stretching away into the distance. The megaphone man came back again, explaining that Steve Brodie was the first man to jump this bridge without loss of life; afterward he kept a cafe and was quite a character.

And then I thought of another trip I had taken once – a cheap excursion trip on a larger and dirtier boat. Somehow I had liked that better; there was something living and careless and human about it. Babies sprawled about the decks in Oriental attitudes crying for the bottle; young people in blouses and open shirts giggled together and sang songs; there was a great disorder about it, dancing, music, fun. Lunches in small uniform boxes, a sandwich, an egg, a piece of cake, and then the mugs of soda water, the bottles of ginger beer, and the occasional splash as one hit the water, thrown from the upper deck by some satiated youth. And I turned in again and looked at this boat's passengers, who sat with folded hands upon gingham and dimity gowns, murmuring to themselves at times that they hoped the educational parts of New York and surrounding country would be visible to the naked eye. Well, they were, but they didn't see it.

The only refuse that cannot be renovated seems to be the human mind. Here at the waterfronts, barges heaped with the city's garbage swayed in the greasy, dark water, great mounds of a city's refuse suspiring in the sun like a glutton lolling after an orgy. One felt that, had one listened sharply enough, one would have caught its thick, throaty breathing; the mounds seemed to move, rising slowly, falling slowly, a great stomach on a couch. Ah, our modern lily maids of Astolat are the unnamed dead from the morgue who are rowed up to potter's field past the hospitals and this great, unending, daily birth of the city's dead food. I never realized before that there are places more terrible than the cemetery. They are the dumping grounds, and like carrion birds that sweep over a battlefield, men move in among this filth and decay, picking out wood for kindling, paper for the mills, and rags for the paper factories, and God knows what else for what, and someone making a million upon this terrible resurrection.

It was from the water's edge that we crawled in the days of our oblivion and first started that slow ascent into the life of man, and it is to the water's edge that we are brought back again in the end, the great, wet tomb that dries all tears, that

gives the raw material and takes back the finished tool and knows neither pleasure nor pain; for "This is the end of all the songs men sing."

And as I said, "Man is the only thing that has no further use after something goes amiss." Look for yourselves and see. Exactly opposite this line of refuse, these heavy-laden barges, is a home for the insane. There is no hand moving in these poor, disordered brains in search of some one thought that could be used again. No man pays the city for the privilege of saving some lost and beautiful thing among this sad refuse; no hired hands thrust their fingers in to save some little kindling from this wrecked house, nor is anything profitable to be found for the decay of the garden.

And side by side, the Old Men's Home. Gray figures bent like hooks move about the splendid lawns and pause beneath the great trees spilling their green bloom to the ground; Old men like futile pollen in a breeze whose scattering will bring no profit to the world.

And you will say, "Enough, enough; this was a pleasure trip! Pass on, and describe its beauties." How can I, when there was nothing beautiful nor pleasant to see, save the ever-lovely sky, the green of the grass and the trees, and an occasional handsome spire?

We progressed, the megaphone man cutting the trip up in two jokes, one to the effect that dogs wagged their tails up and down instead of sideways in the Flatiron Building, and another that no deaf man had been ever condemned – this as we passed a prison – for the simple reason that he must be given "a hearing."

And when I looked at this island with its old men and its prisons, hospitals, and home for incurables, I thought again of that day I had spent on a strip of land just on the other side of Hell Gate with a young boy who had found society too difficult to understand. It was a lonely, flat stretch of marsh, thick with wild, high grass set in water. Planking ran from the brokendown house to the edge of the bank where a boat was anchored. This island, with its broken bits of wreckage and its ooze and salty smell at low tide, made me think of these human beings. Sometimes nature has an ailment: this island was one of them. Across the water, late in the afternoon, came the cries of the mad – a wild, sad scream that was taken up by the others gradually, as though they were playing a game at madness – and a shiver ran through me, and I wanted to cry also, and I asked him how he could bear it. He was smiling, "Sometimes," he said, "I think we are the loony ones. You have songs on which to go to death?" Afterward he said that often they swam across and played together quite amicably.

Well, that has passed – the island lies under the sun and rain now, and the boy has gone – where, no one knows – a tramp perhaps – an inmate of one of the houses on the other side of the island. But I know one thing, that wherever he has gone he has taken with him a little of the freedom of a wild life that no standard insanity can harm.

Presently we passed the last bridge in the Harlem series, where a soldier stood, gun over shoulder – and came out into the half-moon of Spuyten Duyvil Creek. Little naked children ran hither and thither in the wooded banks and dropped, sighing, down upon the leaves like acorns. Others looked at us with small, water-wet, squinting eyes and waved, diving off hastily that we might accord them due praise for their excellent agility.

We took the turn in Spuyten Duyvil Creek well, watching these children until we could see them no more. It was here that I drew my first contented breath. Up on the heights several handsome houses peeped between the trees, and in the coming evening the Palisades stood out no heavier than a puff of smoke.

There was a hint of rain in the air, too. A small motorboat shot past us, a brown-armed boy shouting hello as he steered. A three-oared canoe with a girl up front turned in from the creek behind us, the oars in steady, rhythmic motion dripping fine, silver beads of water.

A boy crying "Ice-cold soda here" came out of the hot cabin. A chocolate vendor stepped on my hat – I smiled.

The pilot, brown and lined of face, turned the wheel slowly, looking away into the distance. The megaphone man told us to pay strict attention to a white house on the drive: "Made possible by cigarettes," he said. We all leaned forward. Then he called attention to the college. All the Middle Western schoolmarms got to their feet.

"I wonder," one of them said, "if they discuss higher mathematics there." And another answered laconically, "Spinoza." They sat down again.

Somewhere, everywhere over there in that world that we had been around, and against which only one voice was raised – that of the megaphone man – actresses were getting their beauty sleep or were at school learning arduously a new dance. Somewhere a man was killing a gnat and somewhere else a man building a bomb. Someone was kissing, and someone was killing, someone was being born, and someone was dying. Some were eating and drinking and laughing, and others were starving. Some were thinking, and others were not. Waiters moved about in the great hotels, dragging their servility with them like trains. Pompous gentlemen in fat rings discussed politics amid spittoons, and handsome women read yellow-backed novels and gave their hands to be kissed by gallants. And there some were walking about, looking over at us as we looked back at them.

The tall buildings threw their shadows down on little buildings, great men on small men, joy on sorrow.

Someone was yawning at my side and buying postal cards, thirty-five views for a quarter, and I had a thousand for nothing!

And yet the city gave out only a faint sound of fabric being rent: one-half of the mass pulling one way and the other half in an opposing direction. Another self-sufficient tugboat hooted at us from the docks, and factory whistles shrieked back at them like masters calling them home. An electric sign stood up against the sky advertising some brand of chewing gum and beside it the steeple of a church. Great warehouses and grain elevators supported flaring advertisements; it looked as though the whole of Manhattan were for sale.

A dark line of boats to the left of us – Holland, German, Italian.

And somewhere in all this tangle of lives and tangle of buildings, inland out of sight of the sea and fog, there was my own particular little studio called home.

And "There's no place like home," chiefly because here we can best forget.

Chapter 9

from *Bleak House*

Charles Dickens

Chapter 1: *In Chancery*

London. Michaelmas term lately over, and the Lord Chancellor sitting in Lincoln's Inn Hall. Implacable November weather. As much mud in the streets, as if the waters had but newly retired from the face of the earth, and it would not be wonderful to meet a Megalosaurus, forty feet long or so, waddling like an elephantine lizard up Holborn Hill. Smoke lowering down from chimney-pots, making a soft black drizzle with flakes of soot in it as big as full-grown snowflakes – gone into mourning, one might imagine, for the death of the sun. Dogs, undistinguishable in mire. Horses, scarcely better; splashed to their very blinkers. Foot passengers, jostling one another's umbrellas, in a general infection of ill temper, and losing their foot-hold at street-corners, where tens of thousands of other foot passengers have been slipping and sliding since the day broke (if this day ever broke), adding new deposits to the crust upon crust of mud, sticking at those points tenaciously to the pavement, and accumulating at compound interest.

Fog everywhere. Fog up the river, where it flows among green aits and meadows; fog down the river, where it rolls defiled among the tiers of shipping, and the waterside pollutions of a great (and dirty) city. Fog on the Essex Marshes, fog on the Kentish heights. Fog creeping into the cabooses of collier-brigs; fog lying out on the yards, and hovering in the rigging of great ships; fog drooping on the gunwales of barges and small boats. Fog in the eyes and throats of ancient Greenwich pensioners, wheezing by the firesides of their wards; fog in the stem and bowl of the afternoon pipe of the wrathful skipper, down in his close cabin; fog cruelly pinching the toes and fingers of his shivering little 'prentice boy on deck. Chance people on the bridges peeping over the parapets into a nether sky of fog, with fog all round them, as if they were up in a balloon, and hanging in the misty clouds.

Gas looming through the fog in divers places in the streets, much as the sun may, from the spongey fields, be seen to loom by husbandman and ploughboy. Most of the shops lighted two hours before their time – as the gas seems to know, for it has a haggard and unwilling look.

The raw afternoon is rawest, and the dense fog is densest, and the muddy streets are muddiest, near that leaden-headed old obstruction, appropriate ornament for the threshold of a leaden-headed old corporation: Temple Bar. And hard by Temple Bar, in Lincoln's Inn Hall, at the very heart of the fog, sits the Lord High Chancellor in his High Court of Chancery.

Never can there come fog too thick, never can there come mud and mire too deep, to assort with the groping and floundering condition which this High Court of Chancery, most pestilent of hoary sinners, holds, this day, in the sight of heaven and earth.

On such an afternoon, if ever, the Lord High Chancellor ought to be sitting here – as here he is – with a foggy glory round his head, softly fenced in with crimson cloth and curtains, addressed by a large advocate with great whiskers, a little voice, and an interminable brief, and outwardly directing his contemplation to the lantern in the roof, where he can see nothing but fog. On such an afternoon, some score of members of the High Court of Chancery bar ought to be – as here they are – mistily engaged in one of the ten thousand stages of an endless cause, tripping one another up on slippery precedents, groping knee-deep in technicalities, running their goat-hair and horsehair warded heads against walls of word and making a pretence of equity with serious faces, as players might. On such an afternoon, the various solicitors in the cause, some two or three of whom have inherited it from their fathers, who made a fortune by it, ought to be – as are they not? –ranged in a line, in a long matted well (but you might look in vain for Truth at the bottom of it), between the registrar's red table and the silk gowns, with bills, cross-bills, answers, rejoinders, injunctions, affidavits, issues, references to masters, masters' reports, mountains of costly nonsense, piled before them. Well may the court be dim, with wasting candles here and there; well may the fog hang heavy in it, as if it would never get out; well may the stained-glass windows lose their colour, and admit no light of day into the place; well may the uninitiated from the streets, who peep in through the glass panes in the door, be deterred from entrance by its owlish aspect, and by the drawl languidly echoing to the roof from the padded dais where the Lord High Chancellor looks into the lantern that has no light in it, and where the attendant wigs are all stuck in a fog-bank! This is the Court of Chancery; which has its decaying houses and its blighted lands in every shire; which has its worn-out lunatic in every madhouse, and its dead in every churchyard; which has its ruined suitor, with his slipshod heels and threadbare dress, borrowing and begging through the round of every man's acquaintance; which gives to monied might the means abundantly of wearying out the right; which so exhausts finances, patience, courage, hope; so overthrows the brain and breaks the heart; that there is not an honourable man among its practitioners who would not give – who does not often give – the warning, 'Suffer any wrong that can be done you, rather than come here!'. . .

My Lady is at present represented, near Sir Leicester, by her portrait. She has flitted away to town, with no intention of remaining there, and will soon flit hither again, to the confusion of the fashionable intelligence. The house in town is not prepared for her reception. It is muffled and dreary. Only one Mercury in powder, gapes disconsolate at the hall-window; and he mentioned last night to another Mercury of his acquaintance, also accustomed to good society, that if that sort of thing was to last – which it couldn't, for a man of his spirits couldn't bear it, and a man of his figure couldn't be expected to bear it – there would be no resource for him, upon his honour, but to cut his throat!

What connexion can there be, between the place in Lincolnshire, the house in town, the Mercury in powder, and the whereabout of Jo the outlaw with the broom, who had that distant ray of light upon him when he swept the churchyard-step? What connexion can there have been between many people in the innumerable histories of this world, who, from opposite sides of great gulfs, have, nevertheless, been very curiously brought together!

Jo sweeps his crossing all day long, unconscious of the link, if any link there be. He sums up his mental condition, when asked a question, by replying that he 'don't know nothink.' He knows that it's hard to keep the mud off the crossing in dirty weather, and harder still to live by doing it. Nobody taught him, even that much; he found it out.

Jo lives – that is to say, Jo has not yet died – in a ruinous place, known to the like of him by the name of Tom-all-Alone's. It is a black, dilapidated street, avoided by all decent people; where the crazy houses were seized upon, when their decay was far advanced, by some bold vagrants, who, after establishing their own possession, took to letting them out in lodgings. Now, these tumbling tenements contain, by night, a swarm of misery. As on the ruined human wretch, vermin parasites appear, so, these ruined shelters have bred a crowd of foul existence that crawls in and out of gaps in walls and boards; and coils itself to sleep, in maggot numbers, where the rain drips in; and comes and goes, fetching and carrying fever, and sowing more evil in its every footprint than Lord Coodle and Sir Thomas Doodle, and the Duke of Foodle, and all the fine gentlemen in office, down to Zoodle, shall set right in five hundred years – though born expressly to do it.

Twice, lately, there has been a crash and a cloud of dust, like the springing of a mine, in Tom-all-Alone's; and, each time, a house has fallen. These accidents have made a paragraph in the newspapers, and have filled a bed or two in the nearest hospital. The gaps remain, and there are not unpopular lodgings among the rubbish. As several more houses are nearly ready to go, the next crash in Tom-all-Alone's may be expected to be a good one.

This desirable property is in Chancery, of course. It would be an insult to the discernment of any man with half an eye, to tell him so. Whether 'Tom' is the popular representative of the original plaintiff or defendant in Jarndyce and Jarndyce; or, whether Tom lived here when the suit had laid the street waste, all alone, until other settlers came to join him; or, whether the traditional title is a comprehensive name for a retreat cut off from honest company and put out of the pale of hope; perhaps nobody knows. Certainly, Jo don't know.

'For *I* don't,' says Jo, 'I don't know nothink.'

It must be a strange state to be like Jo! To shuffle through the streets, unfamiliar with the shapes and in utter darkness as to the meaning, of those mysterious symbols, so abundant over the shops, and the corner of streets, and on the doors, and in the windows. To see people read, and to see people write, and to see the postman deliver letters, and not to have the least idea of all that language – to be, to every scrap of it, stone blind and dumb! It must be very puzzling to see the good company going to the churches on Sundays, with their books in their hands and to think (for perhaps Jo *does* think, at odd times) what does it all mean, and if it means anything to anybody, how comes it that it means nothing to me? To be hustled, and jostled, and moved on; and really to feel that it would appear to be perfectly true that I have no business here, or there, or anywhere; and yet to be perplexed by the consideration that I *am* here somehow, too, and everybody overlooked me until I became the creature that I am! It must be a strange state, not merely to be told that I am scarcely human (as in the case of my offering myself for a witness), but to feel it of my own knowledge all my life! To see the horses, dogs, and cattle, go by me, and to know that in ignorance I belong to them, and not to the superior beings in my shape, whose delicacy I offend! Jo's ideas of a Criminal Trial, or a Judge, or a Bishop, or a Government, or that inestimable jewel to him (if he only knew it) the Constitution, should be strange! His whole material and immaterial life is wonderfully strange; his death, the strangest thing of all.

Jo comes out of Tom-all-Alone's, meeting the tardy morning which is always late in getting down there, and munches his dirty bit of bread as he comes along. His way lying through many streets, and the houses not yet being open, he sits down to breakfast on the door-step of the Society for the Propagation of the Gospel in Foreign Parts, and gives it a brush when he has finished, as an acknowledgement of the accommodation. He admires the size of the edifice, and wonders what it's all about. He has no idea poor wretch, of the spiritual destitution of a coral reef in the

Pacific, or what it costs to look up the precious souls among the cocoanuts and bread-fruit.

He goes to his crossing, and begins to lay it out for the day. The town awakes; the great tee-totum is set up for its daily spin and whirl; all that unaccountable reading and writing, which has been suspended for a few hours, recommences. Jo, and the other lower animals, get on in the unintelligible mess as they can. It is market-day. The blinded oxen, over-goaded, over-driven, never guided, run into wrong places and are beaten out; and plunge, red-eyed and foaming, at stone walls; and often sorely hurt the innocent, and often sorely hurt themselves. Very like Jo and his order; very, very like!

Chapter 10

from *Dubliners*

James Joyce

Two Gallants

The grey warm evening of August had descended upon the city and a mild warm air, a memory of summer, circulated in the streets. The streets, shuttered for the repose of Sunday, swarmed with a gaily coloured crowd. Like illumined pearls the lamps shone from the summits of their tall poles upon the living texture below which, changing shape and hue unceasingly, sent up into the warm grey evening air an unchanging unceasing murmur.

Two young men came down the hill of Rutland Square. One of them was just bringing a long monologue to a close. The other, who walked on the verge of the path and was at times obliged to step on to the road, owing to his companion's rudeness, wore an amused listening face. He was squat and ruddy. A yachting cap was shoved far back from his forehead and the narrative to which he listened made constant waves of expression break forth over his face from the corners of his nose and eyes and mouth. Little jets of wheezing laughter followed one another out of his convulsed body. His eyes, twinkling with cunning enjoyment, glanced at every moment towards his companion's face. Once or twice he rearranged the light waterproof which he had slung over one shoulder in toreador fashion. His breeches, his white rubber shoes and his jauntily slung waterproof expressed youth. But his figure fell into rotundity at the waist, his hair was scant and grey and his face, when the waves of expression had passed over it, had a ravaged look.

When he was quite sure that the narrative had ended he laughed noiselessly for fully half a minute. Then he said:

— Well! . . . That takes the biscuit!

His voice seemed winnowed of vigour; and to enforce his words he added with humour:

— That takes the solitary, unique, and, if I may so call it, *recherché* biscuit!

He became serious and silent when he had said this. His tongue was tired for he had been talking all the afternoon in a public-house in Dorset Street. Most people considered Lenehan a leech but, in spite of this reputation, his adroitness and eloquence had always prevented his friends from forming any general policy against him. He had a brave manner of coming up to a party of them in a bar and of holding himself nimbly at the borders of the company until he was included in a round. He was a sporting vagrant armed with a vast stock of stories, limericks and riddles. He was insensitive to all kinds of discourtesy. No one knew how he achieved the stern task of living, but his name was vaguely associated with racing tissues.

— And where did you pick her up, Corley? he asked.

Corley ran his tongue swiftly along his upper lip.

— One night, man, he said, I was going along Dame Street and I spotted a fine tart under Waterhouse's clock and said goodnight, you know. So we went for a walk round by the canal and she told me she was a slavey in a house in Baggot Street. I put my arm round her and squeezed her a bit that night. Then next Sunday, man, I met her by appointment. We went out to Donnybrook and I brought her into a field there. She told me she used to go with a dairyman.... It was fine, man. Cigarettes every night she'd bring me and paying the tram out and back. And one night she brought me two bloody fine cigars – O, the real cheese, you know, that the old fellow used to smoke.... I was afraid, man, she'd get in the family way. But she's up to the dodge.

— Maybe she thinks you'll marry her, said Lenehan.

— I told her I was out of a job, said Corley. I told her I was in Pim's. She doesn't know my name. I was too hairy to tell her that. But she thinks I'm a bit of class, you know.

Lenehan laughed again, noiselessly.

— Of all the good ones ever I heard, he said, that emphatically takes the biscuit.

Corley's stride acknowledged the compliment. The swing of his burly body made his friend execute a few light skips from the path to the roadway and back again. Corley was the son of an inspector of police and he had inherited his father's frame and gait. He walked with his hands by his sides, holding himself erect and swaying his head from side to side. His head was large, globular and oily; it sweated in all weathers; and his large round hat, set upon it sideways, looked like a bulb which had grown out of another. He always stared straight before him as if he were on parade and, when he wished to gaze after some one in the street, it was necessary for him to move his body from the hips. At present he was about town. Whenever any job was vacant a friend was always ready to give him the hard word. He was often to be seen walking with policemen in plain clothes, talking earnestly. He knew the inner side of all affairs and was fond of delivering final judgments. He spoke without listening to the speech of his companions. His conversation was mainly about himself: what he had said to such a person and what such a person had said to him and what he had said to settle the matter. When he reported these dialogues he aspirated the first letter of his name after the manner of Florentines.

Lenehan offered his friend a cigarette. As the two young men walked on through the crowd Corley occasionally turned to smile at some of the passing girls but Lenehan's gaze was fixed on the large faint moon circled with a double halo. He watched earnestly the passing of the grey web of twilight across its face. At length he said:

— Well... tell me, Corley, I suppose you'll be able to pull it off all right, eh?

Corley closed one eye expressively as an answer.

— Is she game for that? asked Lenehan dubiously. You can never know women.

— She's all right, said Corley. I know the way to get around her, man. She's a bit gone on me.

— You're what I call a gay Lothario, said Lenehan. And the proper kind of a Lothario, too!

A shade of mockery relieved the servility of his manner. To save himself he had the habit of leaving his flattery open to the interpretation of raillery. But Corley had not a subtle mind.

— There's nothing to touch a good slavey, he affirmed. Take my tip for it.

— By one who has tried them all, said Lenehan.

— First I used to go with girls, you know, said Corley, unbosoming; girls off the South Circular. I used to take them out, man, on the tram somewhere and pay the tram or take them to a band or a play at the theatre or buy them chocolate and sweets or something that way. I used to spend money on them right enough, he added, in a convincing tone, as if he were conscious of being disbelieved.

But Lenehan could well believe it; he nodded gravely.

— I know that game, he said, and it's a mug's game.

— And damn the thing I ever got out of it, said Corley.

— Ditto here, said Lenehan.

— Only off of one of them, said Corley.

He moistened his upper lip by running his tongue along it. The recollection brightened his eyes. He too gazed at the pale disc of the moon, now nearly veiled, and seemed to meditate.

— She was . . . a bit of all right, he said regretfully.

He was silent again. Then he added:

— She's on the turf now. I saw her driving down Earl Street one night with two fellows with her on a car.

— I suppose that's your doing, said Lenehan.

— There was others at her before me, said Corley philosophically.

This time Lenehan was inclined to disbelieve. He shook his head to and fro and smiled.

— You know you can't kid me, Corley, he said.

— Honest to God! said Corley. Didn't she tell me herself?

Lenehan made a tragic gesture.

— Base betrayer! he said.

As they passed along the railings of Trinity College, Lenehan skipped out into the road and peered up at the clock.

— Twenty after, he said.

— Time enough, said Corley. She'll be there all right. I always let her wait a bit.

Lenehan laughed quietly.

— Ecod! Corley, you know how to take them, he said.

— I'm up to all their little tricks, Corley confessed.

— But tell me, said Lenehan again, are you sure you can bring it off all right? You know it's a ticklish job. They're damn close on that point. Eh? . . . What?

His bright, small eyes searched his companion's face for reassurance. Corley swung his head to and fro as if to toss aside an insistent insect, and his brows gathered.

— I'll pull it off, he said. Leave it to me, can't you?

Lenehan said no more. He did not wish to ruffle his friend's temper, to be sent to the devil and told that his advice was not wanted. A little tact was necessary. But Corley's brow was soon smooth again. His thoughts were running another way.

— She's a fine decent tart, he said, with appreciation; that's what she is.

They walked along Nassau Street and then turned into Kildare Street. Not far from the porch of the club a harpist stood in the roadway, playing to a little ring of listeners. He plucked at the wires heedlessly, glancing quickly from time to time at the face of each new-comer and from time to time, wearily also, at the sky. His harp too, heedless that her coverings had fallen about her knees, seemed weary alike of the eyes of strangers and of her master's hands. One hand played in the bass the melody of *Silent, O Moyle*, while the other hand careered in the treble after each group of notes. The notes of the air throbbed deep and full.

The two young men walked up the street without speaking, the mournful music following them. When they reached Stephen's Green they crossed the road. Here the noise of trams, the lights and the crowd released them from their silence.

— There she is! said Corley.

At the corner of Hume Street a young woman was standing. She wore a blue dress and a white sailor hat. She stood on the curbstone, swinging a sunshade in one hand. Lenehan grew lively.

— Let's have a squint at her, Corley, he said.

Corley glanced sideways at his friend and an unpleasant grin appeared on his face.

— Are you trying to get inside me? he asked.

— Damn it! said Lenehan boldly, I don't want an introduction. All I want is to have a look at her. I'm not going to eat her.

— O ... A look at her? said Corley, more amiably. Well ... I'll tell you what. I'll go over and talk to her and you can pass by.

— Right! said Lenehan.

Corley had already thrown one leg over the chains when Lenehan called out:

— And after? Where will we meet?

— Half ten, answered Corley, bringing over his other leg.

— Where?

— Corner of Merrion Street. We'll be coming back.

— Work it all right now, said Lenehan in farewell.

Corley did not answer. He sauntered across the road swaying his head from side to side. His bulk, his easy pace, and the solid sound of his boots had something of the conqueror in them. He approached the young woman and, without saluting, began at once to converse with her. She swung her sunshade more quickly and executed half turns on her heels. Once or twice when he spoke to her at close quarters she laughed and bent her head.

Lenehan observed them for a few minutes. Then he walked rapidly along beside the chains to some distance and crossed the road obliquely. As he approached Hume Street corner he found the air heavily scented and his eyes made a swift anxious scrutiny of the young woman's appearance. She had her Sunday finery on. Her blue serge skirt was held at the waist by a belt of black leather. The great silver buckle of her belt seemed to depress the centre of her body, catching the light stuff of her white blouse like a clip. She wore a short black jacket with mother-of-pearl buttons and a ragged black boa. The ends of her tulle collarette had been carefully disordered and a big bunch of red flowers was pinned in her bosom stems upwards. Lenehan's eyes noted approvingly her stout short muscular body. Frank rude health glowed in her face, on her fat red cheeks and in her unabashed blue eyes. Her features were blunt. She had broad nostrils, a straggling mouth which lay open in a contented leer, and two projecting front teeth. As he passed Lenehan took off his cap and, after about ten seconds, Corley returned a salute to the air. This he did by raising his hand vaguely and pensively changing the angle of position of his hat.

Lenehan walked as far as the Shelbourne Hotel where he halted and waited. After waiting for a little time he saw them coming towards him and, when they turned to the right, he followed them, stepping lightly in his white shoes, down one side of Merrion Square. As he walked on slowly, timing his pace to theirs, he watched Corley's head which turned at every moment towards the young woman's face like a big ball revolving on a pivot. He kept the pair in view until he had seen them climbing the stairs of the Donnybrook tram; then he turned about and went back the way he had come.

Now that he was alone his face looked older. His gaiety seemed to forsake him, and, as he came by the railings of the Duke's Lawn, he allowed his hand to run along them. The air which the harpist had played began to control his movements. His softly padded feet played the melody while his fingers swept a scale of variations idly along the railings after each group of notes.

He walked listlessly round Stephen's Green and then down Grafton Street. Though his eyes took note of many elements of the crowd through which he passed they did so morosely. He found trivial all that was meant to charm him and did not answer the glances which invited him to be bold. He knew that he would have to speak a great deal, to invent and to amuse, and his brain and throat were too dry for such a task. The problem of how he could pass the hours till he met Corley again troubled him a little. He could think of no way of passing them but to keep on walking. He turned to the left when he came to the corner of Rutland Square and felt more at ease in the dark quiet street, the sombre look of which suited his mood. He paused at last before the window of a poor-looking shop over which the words *Refreshment Bar* were printed in white letters. On the glass of the window were two flying inscriptions: *Ginger Beer* and *Ginger Ale*. A cut ham was exposed on a great blue dish while near it on a plate lay a segment of very light plum-pudding. He eyed this food earnestly for some time and then, after glancing warily up and down the street, went into the shop quickly.

He was hungry for, except some biscuits which he had asked two grudging curates to bring him, he had eaten nothing since breakfast-time. He sat down at an un-covered wooden table opposite two work-girls and a mechanic. A slatternly girl waited on him.

— How much is a plate of peas? he asked.

— Three halfpence, sir, said the girl.

— Bring me a plate of peas, he said, and a bottle of ginger beer.

He spoke roughly in order to belie his air of gentility for his entry had been followed by a pause of talk. His face was heated. To appear natural he pushed his cap back on his head and planted his elbows on the table. The mechanic and the two work-girls examined him point by point before resuming their conversation in a subdued voice. The girl brought him a plate of hot grocer's peas, seasoned with pepper and vinegar, a fork and his ginger beer. He ate his food greedily and found it so good that he made a note of the shop mentally. When he had eaten all the peas he sipped his ginger beer and sat for some time thinking of Corley's adventure. In his imagination he beheld the pair of lovers walking along some dark road; he heard Corley's voice in deep energetic gallantries and saw again the leer of the young woman's mouth. This vision made him feel keenly his own pov-erty of purse and spirit. He was tired of knocking about, of pulling the devil by the tail, of shifts and intrigues. He would be thirty-one in November. Would he never get a good job? Would he never have a home of his own? He thought how pleasant it would be to have a warm fire to sit by and a good dinner to sit down to. He had walked the streets long enough with friends and with girls. He knew what those friends were worth: he knew the girls too. Experience had embittered his heart against the world. But all hope had not left him. He felt better after having eaten than he had felt before, less weary of his life, less vanquished in spirit. He might yet be able to settle down in some snug corner and live happily if he could only come across some good simple-minded girl with a little of the ready.

He paid twopence halfpenny to the slat-ternly girl and went out of the shop to begin his wandering again. He went into Capel Street and walked along towards the City Hall. Then he turned into Dame Street. At the corner of George's Street he met two friends of his and stopped to converse with them. He was glad that he could rest from all his walking. His friends asked him had he seen Corley and what was the latest. He replied that he had spent the day with Corley. His friends talked very little. They looked vacantly after some figures in the crowd and sometimes made a critical remark. One said that he had seen Mac an hour before in Westmoreland Street. At this Lenehan said that he had been with Mac the night before in Egan's. The young man who had seen Mac in Westmoreland Street asked was it true that Mac had won a bit over a billiard match. Lenehan did not know: he said that Holohan had stood them drinks in Egan's.

He left his friends at a quarter to ten and went up George's Street. He turned to the left at the City Markets and walked on into Grafton Street. The crowd of girls and young men had thinned and on his way up the street he heard many groups and couples bidding one another good-night. He went as far as the clock of the College of Surgeons: it was on the stroke of ten. He set off briskly along the northern side of the Green, hurrying for fear Corley should return too soon. When he reached the corner of Merrion Street he took his stand in the shadow of a lamp and brought out one of the cigarettes which he had re-served and lit it. He leaned against the lamp-post and kept his gaze fixed on the part from which he expected to see Corley and the young woman return.

His mind became active again. He wondered had Corley managed it successfully. He wondered if he had asked her yet or if he would leave it to the last. He suffered all the pangs and thrills of his friend's situation as well as those of his own. But the memory of Corley's slowly revolving head calmed him somewhat: he was sure Corley would pull it off all right. All at once the idea struck him that perhaps Corley had seen her home by another way and given him the slip. His eyes searched the street: there was no sign of them. Yet it was surely half-an-hour since he had seen the clock of the College of Surgeons. Would Corley do a thing like that? He lit his last cigarette and began to smoke it nervously. He strained his eyes as each tram stopped at the far corner of the square. They must have gone home by another way. The paper of his cigarette broke and he flung it into the road with a curse.

Suddenly he saw them coming towards him. He started with delight and, keeping close to his lamp-post, tried to read the result in their walk. They were walking quickly, the young woman taking quick short steps, while Corley kept beside her with his long stride. They did not seem to be speaking. An intimation of the result pricked him like the point of a sharp instrument. He knew Corley would fail; he knew it was no go.

They turned down Baggot Street and he followed them at once, taking the other footpath. When they stopped he stopped too. They talked for a few moments and then the young woman went down the steps into the area of a house. Corley remained standing at the edge of the path, a little distance from the front steps. Some minutes passed. Then the hall-door was opened slowly and cautiously. A woman came running down the front steps and coughed. Corley turned and went towards her. His broad figure hid hers from view for a few seconds and then she reappeared running up the steps. The door closed on her and Corley began to walk swiftly towards Stephen's Green.

Lenehan hurried on in the same direction. Some drops of light rain fell. He took them as a warning and, glancing back towards the house which the young woman had entered to see that he was not observed, he ran eagerly across the road. Anxiety and his swift run made him pant. He called out:

— Hallo, Corley!

Corley turned his head to see who had called him, and then continued walking as before. Lenehan ran after him, settling the waterproof on his shoulders with one hand.

— Hallo, Corley! he cried again.

He came level with his friend and looked keenly in his face. He could see nothing there.

— Well? he said. Did it come off?

They had reached the corner of Ely Place. Still without answering Corley swerved to the left and went up the side street. His features were composed in stern calm. Lenehan kept up with his friend, breathing uneasily. He was baffled and a note of meance pierced through his voice.

— Can't you tell us? he said. Did you try her?

Corley halted at the first lamp and stared grimly before him. Then with a grave gesture he extended a hand towards the light and, smiling, opened it slowly to the gaze of his disciple. A small gold coin shone in the palm.

Chapter 11

from *Mrs Dalloway*

Virginia Woolf

Striding, staring, he glared at the statue of the Duke of Cambridge. He had been sent down from Oxford – true. He had been a Socialist, in some sense a failure – true. Still the future of civilization lies, he thought, in the hands of young men like that; of young men such as he was, thirty years ago; with their love of abstract principles; getting books sent out to them all the way from London to a peak in the Himalayas; reading science; reading philosophy. The future lies in the hands of young men like that, he thought.

A patter like the patter of leaves in a wood came from behind, and with a rustling, regular thudding sound, which as it overtook him drummed his thoughts, strict in step, up Whitehall, without his doing. Boys in uniform, carrying guns, marched with their eyes ahead of them, marched, their arms stiff, and on their faces an expression like the letters of a legend written round the base of a statue praising duty, gratitude, fidelity, love of England.

It is, thought Peter Walsh, beginning to keep step with them, a very fine training. But they did not look robust. They were weedy for the most part, boys of sixteen, who might, tomorrow, stand behind bowls of rice, cakes of soap on counters. Now they wore on them unmixed with sensual pleasure or daily preoccupations the solemnity of the wreath which they had fetched from Finsbury Pavement to the empty tomb. They had taken their vow. The traffic respected it; vans were stopped.

I can't keep up with them, Peter Walsh thought, as they marched up Whitehall, and sure enough, on they marched, past him, past everyone, in their steady way, as if one will worked legs and arms uniformly, and life, with its varieties, its irreticences, had been laid under a pavement of monuments and wreaths and drugged into a stiff yet staring corpse by discipline. One had to respect it; one might laugh; but one had to respect it, he thought. There they go, thought Peter Walsh, pausing at the edge of the pavement; and all the exalted statues, Nelson, Gordon, Havelock, the black, the spectacular images of great soldiers stood looking ahead of them, as if they too had made the same renunciation (Peter Walsh felt he, too, had made it the great renunciation), trampled under the same temptations, and achieved at length a marble stare. But the stare Peter Walsh did not want for himself in the least; though he could respect it in others. He could respect it in boys. They don't know the troubles of the flesh yet, he thought, as the marching boys disappeared in the direction of the Strand – all that I've been through, he thought, crossing the road, and standing under Gordon's statue, Gordon whom as a boy he had worshipped; Gordon standing lonely with one leg raised and his arms crossed, – poor Gordon, he thought.

And just because nobody yet knew he was in London, except Clarissa, and the earth, after the voyage, still seemed an island to him, the strangeness of standing alone, alive, unknown, at half-past eleven in Trafalgar Square overcame him. What is it? Where am I? And why, after all, does one do it? he thought, the divorce seeming all moonshine. And down his mind went flat as a marsh, and three great emotions bowled over him; understanding; a vast philanthropy; and finally, as if the result of the others, an irrepressible, exquisite delight; as if inside his brain, by another hand, strings were pulled, shutters moved, and he, having nothing to do with it, yet stood at the opening of endless avenues down which if he chose he might wander. He had not felt so young for years.

He had escaped! was utterly free – as happens in the downfall of habit when the mind, like an unguarded flame, bows and bends and seems about to blow from its holding. I haven't felt so young for years! thought Peter, escaping (only of course for an hour or so) from being precisely what he was, and feeling like a child who runs out of doors, and sees, as he runs, his old nurse waving at the wrong window. But she's extraordinarily attractive, he thought, as, walking across Trafalgar Square in the direction of the Haymarket, came a young woman who, as she passed Gordon's statue, seemed, Peter Walsh thought (susceptible as he was), to shed veil after veil, until she became the very woman he had always had in mind; young, but stately; merry, but discreet; black, but enchanting.

Straightening himself and stealthily fingering his pocket-knife he started after her to follow this woman, this excitement, which seemed even with its back turned to shed on him a light which connected them, which singled him out, as if the random uproar of the traffic had whispered through hollowed hands his name, not Peter, but his private name which he called himself in his own thoughts. 'You,' she said, only 'you', saying it with her white gloves and her shoulders. Then the thin long cloak which the wind stirred as she walked past Dent's shop in Cockspur Street blew out with an enveloping kindness, a mournful tenderness, as of arms that would open and take the tired –

But she's not married; she's young; quite young, thought Peter, the red carnation he had seen her wear as she came across Trafalgar Square burning again in his eyes and making her lips red. But she waited at the kerbstone. There was a dignity about her. She was not worldly, like Clarissa; not rich, like Clarissa. Was she, he wondered as she moved, respectable? Witty, with a lizard's flickering tongue, he thought (for one must invent, must allow oneself a little diversion), a cool waiting wit, a darting wit; not noisy.

She moved; she crossed; he followed her. To embarrass her was the last thing he wished. Still if she stopped he would say 'Come and have an ice,' he would say, and she would answer, perfectly simply, 'Oh yes'.

But other people got between them in the street, obstructing him, blotting her out. He pursued; she changed. There was colour in her cheeks; mockery in her eyes; he was an adventurer, reckless, he thought, swift, daring, indeed (landed as he was last night from India) a romantic buccaneer, careless of all these damned proprieties, yellow dressing-gowns, pipes, fishing-rods, in the shop windows; and respectability and evening parties and spruce old men wearing white slips beneath their waistcoats. He was a buccaneer. On and on she went, across Piccadilly, and up Regent Street, ahead of him, her cloak, her gloves, her shoulders combining with the fringes and the laces and the feather boas in the windows to make the spirit of finery and whimsy which dwindled out of the shops on to the pavement, as the light of a lamp goes wavering at night over hedges in the darkness.

Laughing and delightful, she had crossed Oxford Street and Great Portland Street and turned down one of the little streets, and now, and now, the great moment was approaching, for now she slackened, opened her bag, and with one look in his direction, but not at him, one look that bade farewell, summed up the whole situation and dismissed it triumphantly, for ever, had fitted her key, opened the door, and gone! Clarissa's voice saying, Remember my party, Remember my party, sang in his ears. The house was one of those flat red houses with hanging flower-baskets of vague impropriety. It was over.

Well, I've had my fun; I've had it, he thought, looking up at the swinging baskets of pale geraniums. And it was smashed to atoms – his fun, for it was half made up, as he knew very well; invented, this escapade with the girl; made up, as one makes up the better part of life, he thought – making oneself up; making her up; creating an exquisite amusement, and something more. But odd it was, and quite true; all this one could never share – it smashed to atoms.

He turned; went up the street, thinking to find somewhere to sit, till it was time for Lincoln's Inn – for Messrs Hooper and Grateley. Where should he go? No matter. Up the street, then, towards Regent's Park. His boots on the pavement struck out 'no matter'; for it was early, still very early.

It was a splendid morning too. Like the pulse of a perfect heart, life struck straight through the streets. There was no fumbling – no hesitation. Sweeping and swerving, accurately, punctually, noiselessly, there, precisely at the right instant, the motor car stopped at the door. The girl, silk-stockinged, feathered, evanescent, but not to him particularly attractive (for he had had his fling), alighted. Admirable butlers, tawny chow dogs, halls laid in black and white lozenges with white blinds blowing, Peter saw through the opened door and approved of. A splendid achievement in its own way, after all, London; the season; civilization. Coming as he did from a respectable Anglo-Indian family which for at least three generations had administered the affairs of a continent (it's strange. he thought. what a sentiment I have about that, disliking India, and empire, and army as he did), there were moments when civilization, even of this sort, seemed dear to him as a personal possession;

moments of pride in England; in butlers; chow dogs; girls in their security. Ridiculous enough, still there it is, he thought. And the doctors and men of business and capable women all going about their business, punctual, alert, robust, seemed to him wholly admirable, good fellows, to whom one would entrust one's life, companions in the art of living, who would see one through. What with one thing and another, the show was really very tolerable; and he would sit down in the shade and smoke.

There was Regent's Park. Yes. As a child he had walked in Regent's Park – odd, he thought, how the thought of childhood keeps coming back to me – the result of seeing Clarissa, perhaps; for women live much more in the past than we do, he thought. They attach themselves to places; and their fathers – a woman's always proud of her father. Bourton was a nice place, a very nice place, but I could never get on with the old man, he thought. There was quite a scene one night – an argument about something or other, what, he could not remember. Politics presumably.

Yes, he remembered Regent's Park; the long straight walk; the little house where one bought air-balls to the left; an absurd statue with an inscription somewhere or other. He looked for an empty seat. He did not want to be bothered (feeling a little drowsy as he did) by people asking him the time. An elderly grey nurse, with a baby asleep in its perambulator – that was the best he could do for himself; sit down at the far end of the seat by that nurse.

She's a queer-looking girl, he thought, suddenly remembering Elizabeth as she came into the room and stood by her mother. Grown big; quite grown-up, not exactly pretty; handsome rather; she can't be more than eighteen. Probably she doesn't get on with Clarissa. 'There's my Elizabeth' – that sort of thing – why not 'Here's Elizabeth' simply? – trying to make out, like most mothers, that things are what they're not. She trusts to her charm too much, he thought. She overdoes it.

The rich benignant cigar smoke eddied coolly down his throat; he puffed it out again in rings which breasted the air bravely for a moment; blue, circular – I shall try and get a word alone with Elizabeth tonight, he thought – then began to wobble into hour-glass shapes and taper away; odd shapes they take, he thought. Suddenly he closed his eyes, raised his hand with an effort, and threw away the heavy end of his cigar. A great brush swept smooth across his mind, sweeping across it moving branches, children's voices, the shuffle of feet, and people passing, and humming traffic, rising and falling traffic. Down, down he sank into the plumes and feathers of sleep, sank, and was muffled over.

Chapter 12

from *The Sea Wall*

Marguerite Duras

It was a large city of one hundred thousand inhabitants, spread out on either side of a wide and beautiful river.

As in all Colonial cities, there were two towns within this one: the white town – and the other. And in the white town there were still other differences. The periphery of the white town was known as the Haut-Quartier – the upper district, comprising villas and apartment buildings. It was the largest and airiest part of the city and was where the secular and official powers had their palaces. The more basic power – the financial – had its palaces in the center of the white town, where, crowded in from all sides by the mass of the city, buildings sprang up, each year higher and higher. The financiers were the true priests of this Mecca.

In that epoch – the early twenties – the white districts of all the Colonial cities of the world were always of an impeccable cleanliness, as were the white inhabitants. As soon as the whites arrived in the Colonies, they learned to take a bath every day, learned to be clean as children do. They also learned to wear the Colonial uniform, suits of spotless white, the color of immunity and innocence. With the assumption of this costume, the first step had been taken. From then on, the distance augmented by that much, the initial difference being multiplied, white on white, making distinctions among themselves and between them-

selves and the others who were not white. The others washed themselves in the rain from heaven and in the muddy water of the streams and rivers. White is, in effect, a color very easily soiled.

Thus, the whites became ever whiter, taking their baths and their siestas in the cool gloom of their villas, behaving much as do great beasts of prey, beasts with sleek and fragile pelts.

In the upper section lived only the whites who had made a fortune. And, still further to mark the superhuman difference between white people and the others, the sidewalks in this fashionable district were immensely wide. An orgiastic space, quite uselessly wide, was provided for the heedless steps of the powerful-in-repose. And through the avenues glided their cushioned cars on cushioned wheels, as if suspended in an impressive semi-stillness.

All this was asphalted, wide, bordered with exotic trees and divided in two by lawns and flowerbeds, along which were parked the shining taxicabs. Sprinkled several times a day, green and flowering, these streets were as well kept as the paths of an immense zoological garden, where rare species of whites watched over themselves. The center of the Haut-Quartier was their true sanctuary. Here only, in the shade of the tamarind trees, were spread out the immense terraces of their cafés. It was on these terraces, in the evenings, that the inhabitants enjoyed themselves in their own congenial company. Only the café waiters were natives, and they were disguised as whites, having been put into dinner jackets. Similarly, the palm trees of the terraces had been put into earthenware pots. And, until late at night, seated in rattan armchairs behind the potted palms and the jacketed waiters, you could see the whites sipping Pernods, whisky and soda or brandy, acquiring a Colonial liver, in harmony with all the rest.

The gleaming of the cars, show-windows and watered asphalt, the dazzling whiteness of the clothes, the shimmering coolness of the flowerbeds, made of the upper district a magic brothel, where the white race could enjoy, in undiluted peace, the sacred spectacle of its own existence. Here, the shops displayed for sale only hats, perfumes, imported blond tobaccos – nothing of utilitarian value. Even money, here, must appear to serve no real purpose. The wealth of the whites must not weigh heavily upon them. In this district everything was noble and aristocratic.

It was the glittering age, the *grande époque*. Hundreds of thousands of native workers bled the trees of hundreds of thousands of hectares of red earth, bled themselves to open the trees that grew in an earth which, by chance, had been called red before being possessed by a few hundred white planters of colossal fortune. Latex flowed. Blood, too. But only the latex was collected as precious, only the latex paid a profit. Blood was wasted. In that epoch the idea was avoided that there might sometime come a day when a great number of people would demand payment for all that blood.

The circuit of the trolley cars scrupulously avoided the fashionable upper district. Indeed, trolleys would have been useless in that part of the city where everyone rode in his own car. Only the natives and the poor white trash of the lower districts used the trolleys. The trolley circuits, in fact, strictly delimited the Eden of the upper district from the rest of the city. They encircled it hygienically, following

concentric lines, of which the stops were all at a distance of two kilometers at least from the center of the city.

And it was only from these crowded trolleys and beyond that you could have any idea of the other city, that one in which no white people lived. White with dust and under an implacable sky, they lumbered along with a moribund slowness and with a thunderous clanking of metal. Old castoffs of the metropolis, built for a temperate climate, these trolleys had been patched up and put back into service by the mother-country for use in the Colonies. The native conductors started out each morning wearing a uniform, but towards ten o'clock they tore it off their bodies, placing it beside them and finishing the day invariably half naked, streaming with a sweat caused partly by the big cups of green tea drunk at every stop. The tea caused perspiration and this, with a draught of air, enabled the conductors to cool off. They had ensured themselves of that current of air by calmly breaking the glass partitions of their driver's section, a thing that had been done during the first days the trolleys were put into service. The passengers likewise, in order to survive, had been obliged to break the car windows. Once these precautions had been taken, the trolley cars functioned satisfactorily. Numerous, and always full to bursting, these trolleys were the most evident symbol of Colonial progress. The incredible success of Colonial management was demonstrated by the development of the native zone and its constantly receding line. Naturally, no white person worthy of the name would ever have ventured to use these trolley cars; to be seen in one would be to lose face – Colonial face.

It was in the district situated between the Haut-Quartier and the native suburbs that were to be found the whites who had made no fortune – the Colonial natives, you might call them. There the streets were without trees, the lawns disappeared. There, the shops of the white people were replaced by "native apartment-houses," those buildings for which Monsieur Jo's father had found the magic formula. The streets in this district were watered once a week only. They swarmed with playful and screaming children and with street peddlers who, in the burning dust, stridently shouted their wares.

The Hotel Central, where Ma, Suzanne, and Joseph put up, was in this zone. It occupied the second floor of a crescent-shaped building overlooking the river on one side, the central trolley line on the other. The main floor of the building was given over to cheap restaurants, half native and half white, opium dens, and Chinese grocery stores.

The people who stopped at that hotel were resident salesmen, two prostitutes in business for themselves, a dressmaker, and a large number of subordinate Post Office and Customs employees. The transient guests of the hotel were minor Civil Service employees about to return to the mother-country, hunters, planters, and, at the arrival of every mail-steamer, sea captains and other officers. But chiefly there were prostitutes of every nationality who had come to stay at the hotel for a more or less extended period before finding a place for themselves either in the brothels of the fashionable district or in the swarming brothels of the harbor, into which poured, in tidal waves, all the crews of the Pacific steamship lines.

Madame Marthe, a sixty-five-year-old Colonial, descendant in a straight line from one of the harbor brothels, was the proprietress of the Hotel Central. She had a daughter, Carmen, of uncertain paternity. Wanting to preserve her from a fate similar to her own, Madame Marthe had put aside, during the twenty years of her career as prostitute, sufficient savings to buy enough stock in the Association of Colonial Hotels to obtain the management of this hotel.

Carmen was now thirty-five years old. She was called Mademoiselle Carmen by everyone except the regular guests of the hotel who called her merely Carmen. She was a good and devoted daughter, full of respect for her mother, from whom she now took over the entire tricky job of managing the Hotel Central. Rather tall, neat and trim, with eyes that were small but of a bright clear blue, Carmen would not have been bad-looking had it not been for the prominent lower jaw with which she had unfortunately been endowed at birth. However, this defect was partly compensated by particularly fine teeth, big and strong, so noticeable that she always seemed to be trying to show them off, which gave to her mouth a likably greedy and carnivorous look. But what made Carmen Carmen, what made her irreplaceable and gave irreplaceable charm to her hotel management, was her legs. For indeed, Carmen had extraordinarily beautiful legs. Had her face been correspondingly beautiful, she would long ago have become the mistress of some bank director or rich northern planter, would have had an apartment of her own in the Haut-Quartier, would have been covered with gold and the glory of scandal – especially that – and she would have known very well how to accommodate herself to these things and still remain herself. Instead of this, Carmen had only her legs. Therefore she would presumably go on managing the Hotel Central for the rest of her life. . . .

from *Beirut Blues*

Hanan al-Shaykh

But then Beirut was plunged into its own war and I found I was pulled down into the abyss with you from the moment I saw you again sitting in a newly opened restaurant in a residential street. Because of its position this restaurant was unlike any other of the city's multitude of restaurants, and strangely out of keeping with its surroundings: the war simply vanished from all our minds as soon as we stepped over the threshold. We piled on to the seats near the window watching the passers-by, convinced we were somewhere safe, inviolable, even when the world outside was rocked by explosions. The circumstances of war coloured the personality of the regulars, whether they were intellectuals who had stayed on in the country, ex-combatants or those still actively engaged in the fighting. Powerful relationships were quickly formed in those circumstances, and disintegrated at the same speed, but the curiosity to find out what lay behind new names and faces remained undiminished as social circles in the city became increasingly restricted.

You rose to your feet as soon as you saw me and reached out your arms to embrace me like a father reunited with his long-lost daughter, but I suspected that the turmoil of this new war had changed you. I could distinguish that special smell, which I must have retained in my memory since the sixty-seven war, accompanying the kiss which I had planned in advance. I expected some

burning emotion to be rekindled between us, but the kiss ended quickly and there was no aftermath.

Another few years have passed and you knock back the whisky as I sit watching you, and seem tense and out of sorts. I wish you would go back to being your old self. I don't mean full of optimism, convincing yourself that the war is bound to take conflicting paths, that those guns are just noises, the fires colours, the black red, the dead merely statistics in newspapers. I just want the old Naser.

I sit watching you, knowing that I am your newspaper and bringer of bad news. I have become your only link with the outside world, an owl screeching with foreboding, looking at you with unblinking eyes. I tell you about the people who have taken refuge on the stretch of beach off the Corniche between the British and American embassies, and about the rifles abandoned on the sands at the knees of a mother or wife in case a fighter comes back from the sea, about the backgammon tables, about how people are scrambling to get food, water, generators and paraffin lamps. When I go on to describe an international football game you explode: "I know. Do you think I'm deaf? What do you think all the radios in the neighbourhood are for?"

I grew to hate this task of mine, and so I didn't tell you how committees and fronts were being formed to administer food supplies, baking, welfare clinics, publications, for you would have taken this as an indication of just how futile your efforts had been. I stopped going into detail about what I'd seen or felt. Your presence was a dead weight: every time I wanted to stay with you, you shocked me by your desire for your own company, and whenever I stayed at home I had the idea you were clutching on to me, even at a distance, so that I'd transmit some of my freedom to you. I wanted to be close to you, my longing for you flowing from me and coming to a halt in my fingertips. But your silence inhibited me from approaching you and I sat dumb and distant, reproaching you inwardly for not accepting me and sticking with me. I saw you as a grasshopper, never still, alighting here and there. I used to take off your shirt, which you hadn't changed for a week, your trousers, your underpants, feeling your breathing on my neck. As you paced up and down like a panther shut up in a birdcage, I felt the weight of your body on mine. The words spilled out of you like foam and I nodded my head and closed my eyes.

I was naïve to think I had become responsible for you. I used to keep quiet about what I'd heard and seen: the crowds out on the streets reminding me of feast days in my childhood; the games of chance people were playing. Are you staying or leaving? Are you going to live or die? Who will be the unlucky one this time? Or is this a lottery everybody loses?

But you seemed to have been blessed with X-ray vision, for I arrived one day and sat on the couch, breathing heavily, closing my eyes, pretending to be tired and instead of asking what had happened, you poured paraffin over your papers in the middle of the room, set light to them and stood back and watched them disappearing in the flames. You remained motionless until the fire began to spread a little. I wanted to tell you about the fire my mother had caused at the time of my father's death. I wanted to make you feel well-disposed towards me so that you

would forgive me for what I had thought on my way to see you. As I raced through Harj Beirut I had been confronted by tree stumps and charred embers instead of the dappled green canopy of pines. Sobbing, I continued on my way over the blackened road, thinking that perhaps the Palestinians ought to go; then the sky would not be full of Israeli aircraft leaving their mark on everything. I know. I know that if they went, you'd go with them. But I didn't want Beirut to change so much that we no longer recognized it. Its skies were being transformed by the coloured leaflets the Israelis dropped, dancing in the air instead of paper aeroplanes and clouds. But were they Israeli planes dropping leaflets from the sky, or "flights of birds striking us with stones of baked clay" as if we were Ethiopians threatening Mecca in the Quran?

The pavement was riddled with holes, big and small, but it was still a Beirut pavement. People still walk in the streets of Beirut; their eyes register the wrecked buildings, the broken glass, the burnt trees. The toy shop has become a roast-chicken takeaway. The barber's is closed for ever, boarded up with sheets of metal. But do they want Beirut to disintegrate completely? . . .

Was this really the same Beirut which has always been like a ball of many colours rolling along? Bronzed faces, immodest bathing costumes, cars bearing splendid names, theatres and cinemas, cafés and sports clubs; women with dark eyes ringed with kohl, world-famous singers, artists, girls on motorbikes. Modern apartments – some shuttered, others with their windows wide open – in tall buildings like capsules, floating in a vacuum, whose inhabitants only ever saw the blue sea. And the old quarters too, where familiar cooking smells hung around the staircases, and from the balconies came the sound of carpets being beaten. The contradictions made the inhabitants of Beirut seem eternal.

I used to watch the high life breathlessly from a distance, not daring to move in close. I was too well aware that I was not comfortable with it. I didn't want to stop being critical, despite my fascination, so I expressed my disapproval of the wealth and at the same time coveted the material which reminded me of pictures of palaces in Venice, and dreamed endlessly of having an emerald-coloured lamp for my dressing table. What stopped me approaching the glittering Beirut was the crush of people around it; women and girls who seemed like princesses with their hairstyles, clothes and haughty calm – a way of moving which betrayed self-confidence and experience – and men who went in for foreign culture whether they lived abroad or stayed in Lebanon. I used to ask myself why I hesitated and didn't plunge in like them and pounce on everything new that came from outside, whether it was to my taste or not.

Was it the same place I discovered through you? With the outbreak of war it was as if the country had announced it was staging an international fair, and representatives of various organizations, fighters and journalists poured in the moment the celebrations began. Their ideas and muscle power flowed over its open borders, and a relationship which began in the heart and mind sometimes extended to the pocket. Also those who thought of Lebanon before the war as a rich tart living off immoral earnings, because of the gleam of money and gold and the luxurious hotels, and thought that she must be heading for ruin, came to see Beirut become more human; no longer sparkling like a jewel, it started to suit the likes of my grand-mother and Zemzem.

My father should come back to life now: the city would understand him better, understand why he used to go around the restaurants and bring back the leftovers. The popular cafés that cling to the mouth of the sea belong to a city with soul. Even the alley cats have become real cats, catching flies, lacking an eye or a leg. You took me around and introduced me to my city which had begun to pulsate with life like cities with long histories, Cairo for example. Characters emerged who seemed eternal and had some kinship with the half-

collapsed walls; apartments which previously dreamt only of the smell of food and the rustle of soft dresses became houses for convictions, ideas, where people could breathe freely and make love. You sat me in front of people peacefully smoking hookahs, or selecting fish and savouring the air, and this great serenity seemed to pass between them and the waves. I was like a bee, discovering the honeycomb city with you. I sat facing the sea, the hookahs bubbling around me, and found I was not distracted by the images of devastation and dead bodies the way I used to be before.

Later that day we descend the stairs from your room eagerly; you introduce me to the porter, asking him about a dog hit in the bombardment. We go into a patisserie and you draw my attention to the colour of a piece of pistachio in a baqlawa, sing "aah" along with Umm Kulthum on the radio, sip sugar-cane juice. You take me to a club in Zaytouna where the singers are tired, the dancers drunk and the band given to surges of enthusiasm interspersed with long interludes of apathy. Each player in the band seems to have settled on a woman to favour with his attentions. He winks at her or licks his lips suggestively or passes a hand over his hair in a sort of greeting.

You loved that club, which was almost deserted, and told me it was real, more real than any other nightclub. There is a constant popping of champagne corks and the girls empty the remains of their drinks under the tables or in among the dead plants, unable to drink any more. You dance the tango with me, your eyes on the sea. In your jacket pocket you have some papers which you take out and study from time to time, while I watch the other customers and the musicians, embarrassed because the sight of us dancing like this must give them the feeling that we don't take them seriously. You dance looking out to sea even though with the darkness outside and the light inside you can't possibly see it, and in any case the glass is dirty and misted over. You close your eyes euphorically, drawing me so close that I am almost swallowed up in your breath before your body envelops me and you are whispering into my ear and my neck that you want to eat me. "You Lebanese want to destroy us. You want to drive us out."

Were you exaggerating? Because it seemed to me at the time that the sea of Lebanon, stretching away for ever, was only for paper boats and the sky was for clouds and the sun; that the snows and the birds of prey were the only spies on the mountain tops; and the hunters watching the little birds skimming over streams and plantations and declaring war on them with small shot, the only observers.

The same sea became your obsession in the final days when accounts of what was happening in Hamra reached you at last: the fighters were preparing to leave and the back streets had been transformed into a vast departure lounge full of luggage; all the shops had started selling bags and cases, and lawyers were everywhere, transferring ownership of cars and apartments from the departing fighters obliged to leave them to those who remained. They were like pupils in the school hall on the last day of the year, saying goodbye after the prizes had been distributed, signing autographs, writing lines like, "Everything passes with the passing of time except the memory which lasts for ever."

Did I tell you that I wrote that once to a boy in the village? I was so proud, mainly of my handwriting, but also of the fact that I knew this line by heart. He struck his head against the wall saying that I didn't love him, and I wept in disbelief. Everyone was exchanging addresses and giving convoluted instructions. "Get in touch with so and so and I'll get in touch with him as soon as I find out where I'm going to end up. Or I'll write to your address in Lebanon. The Lebanese post is bound to start working again soon. In any case I'll definitely write."

Everything was in uproar in the city's damp heat. In one place the departing fighters were covered in flowers; flowers were stuck everywhere: in gun barrels, button holes, jeeps and civilian cars. When you boarded the ship, I was lying in bed

thinking of a way to smuggle you out across the mountains past the houses with red-tiled roofs and green-painted windows, and the pine trees and laurels; I had absolute faith that all these things would stand with us and prevent anyone trying to drag you from your hiding-place. I believed until yesterday that you would never escape by sea. You would continue to trust that the city and its labyrinths would love and protect you. I had thought about getting you a forged passport, or taking your case to the UN, or driving you out in my car. You had shaken your head; perhaps you saw another reality: that this country was no longer open to all who descended on it, with customs officials who stamped passports and didn't look too closely. Your intuition was sounder than mine, even though you had been shut away in that room. My car with us on board, heading for safety, looked about as secure as a cardboard box carrying two feeble wraiths bowling towards the gates of hell. I thought that my struggle to learn to drive despite Zemzem's dream, which my grandmother interpreted as a warning to abandon the idea, had been a waste of time. For when I needed it to escape on to safe roads, it gave up in the face of the roadblocks all along the coast as far as Sidon. You told me that Alexander the Great was never so moved as when he had to take his leave of Sidon, with the colour of its sea and the smell of its orange blossom, and I remember thinking at the time that this no longer meant anything when its asphalt was being pounded by huge Israeli army boots.

When you didn't open the door to me, I started at its blank surface, listening to the hollow sound of my own insistent knocking. I swallowed and it felt as if my tongue had dropped into my guts. I guessed you were on the high seas on one of the ships with hundreds of other fedayeen and I seemed to taste the sea's salty water and choke on it. I rushed to the nearest sea I could find. Its water was colourless. I stared hard at it and looked along the horizon but all I found there was heat and indifference. This is something that irritates me about the war: nature fulfilling its function without missing a beat. The waves continued to crash on to the same rocks, the spray boiled up and subsided. Only the sky was not its usual colour because so many bullets had been sown in its and it still bore the acrid traces of the farewell rounds fired on your behalf. You must have cursed these little hailstorms and ridiculed them, your eyes alighting briefly on the boys eagerly collecting the spent bullets, or a boy alone catching baby fish in a plastic bottle, or another clutching a faded bouquet which he was trying to sell to the departing fighters or their friends and relations. But why do things appear more serious when we read about them in history books: "They were surrounded, so that the sea was the only escape route left to them"?

I rushed to the football stadium, the collecting point. The ululations had stopped and grains of rice and broken flowers strewed the ground. I went home dejectedly. A picture of you sitting fiddling with your papers for ages before you burnt them loomed large in my mind. I was beside you, pretending to read the newspaper, and you said to me, "I'm stupid. Have I really not learnt my lesson yet? Not learnt that things change? There were so many people strangling this place, and suddenly they find other hands at their own throats." . . .

9 My Dear Beirut

I've realized that you have two skies, because I've begun to see you through Jawad's eyes: a sky of telephone wires and electricity cables coming from every direction like a spider-web tent, and another high above where there are stars shining. I don't remember stars like that in your sky before. Is it because the damp weather has cleared, or is it the darkness which hides wrinkles and makes bright stars visible? The moon, bigger and fuller than ever, appears to be doing its job properly for the first time, moving away from the sea to light up the streets. The buildings are in darkness, apart

from the occasional lighted window. Jawad says, "Once upon a time, Clever Hasan saw a glimmer of light in the distance . . ."

The darkness had the effect of making people's voices quieter and deadening the constant blare of televisions. Jawad wanted to go to the Italian restaurant to see if the waiter with arms nearly to his feet was still there. There was a huge pile of rotting garbage at the door but the waiter was inside and a handful of tables was occupied. Much to Jawad's surprise the women had handbags with them, instead of the usual water containers. We went on to the Corniche and sat on two chairs belonging to a mobile café facing Jounieh and the dark mountains. The sound of the waves drowned out the noise of the generator, as we drank tea and watched the mist rising up off the sea and advancing towards us. Jawad gripped the grey chain railing. The mist grew thicker, cocooning us, drawing us close in to you, and Jawad, affected by the surroundings, remarked that cities never die.

He sits, absent-minded and removed from my desire for him. I feel closer to him tonight. The car was different in the dark as we waited at checkpoints. The buildings change at night, the streets are empty of cars and people and at dawn the sound of invisible cats and dogs reaches a crescendo, to be replaced by the shouting of soldiers on their morning exercises.

I realize this night isn't going to go anywhere; Jawad sits silent and distracted, then says he wants to go to bed early. He asks me if I'll drive him around the following day or if he should hire a taxi. Hire a taxi, as if he is going to the seaside or the cafés up the mountain! I laugh, shaking my head and saying nothing.

The next morning I took him "downtown", the word he repeated constantly until he saw the ruins, when he held his breath in case he missed a single detail and looked up into the sky, perhaps to confirm that life went on. I was shocked by what I saw, even though I had visited the ruined markets several years before with Hayat. Silence hung over the long grass and monstrous plants, which would have looked less strange had they been trees with thick roots, growing individually, but they were springing out of the floors and walls and up through the roofs of the melancholy shops and offices.

Jawad closes his eyes, wanting to believe that things are as they were and that he's merely gone deaf or has distorted vision. Images buried in the convolutions of his mind rise to the surface. The top floor of the building like an elephant lying on its side used to house an eye clinic. There his mother had shown him two photographs of his grandmother, displayed to encourage prospective patients, before and after an operation to her right eye. The occasion of the operation had been the old lady's first time in the city and as she went to get in to the lift she had turned to her daughter crossly and said, "For goodness' sake, what have you been giving me to eat if you need to bring me to scales like these to weigh me?"

"Paloma" was the hairdresser's where they put a wig on my mother's head to encourage her to buy it. The smell of hairspray and the beer they used to make the hair lie flat and smooth as paper seems to linger in the air. The narrow lane is still there and the rooms overlooking it where I'd dreamt I was destined to end my days. A taxi had dropped me and Zemzem near here, between a repair garage and a bakery, close to the taxi rank. I clutched Zemzem's hand as she protested loudly to the driver who refused to go on to Sahat Al-Burj. "Lord, what a disaster!" she cried.

Instructing me not to look to right or left, she wrapped her scarf round her face, almost covering her eyes, and shouted to me to hurry; as I ran I was looking about me to try and find out why she was afraid, but all I could see were the garage mechanics covered in oil from head to foot. "Why? What is this place?" I asked, smelling the newly baked bread.

"A market where respectable people work."

I didn't realize that she meant the opposite until I heard her telling my grandmother

about it, trembling, raising her eyes imploringly to the ceiling: "Lord, I hope nobody saw me," she moaned.

"So what if they did? Asma was with you, wasn't she? What's all the fuss about?" my grandmother had replied scornfully.

When I first thought about sex and love, instead of dreaming of a boy of my own age or a movie star, I began to have nightmares about being in a room in the red-light district and not daring to escape in case one of the men of the family killed me. The dream comes back to haunt me and makes me more frightened than ever of approaching Sahat Al-Burj from the direction of the market.

Jawad must realize why I laughed yesterday when he suggested taking a taxi. These ruins are bound to be shocking: you need to be prepared and be with someone you know. They're always shocking, however much you think you're used to their barbarity.

I remember when I was with Hayat a militiaman rising from behind a table in the emptiness and offering us a cup of coffee. Hayat hesitated, but I nodded my head gratefully. I was moved to be confronted by his kind, lonely eyes in the midst of this destruction; the tall plants all around created a sombre, slightly eerie atmosphere and I asked him if he was scared at nights. He laughed and tapped his gun. "How could I be?"

As we stood up to go he whispered in my ear that he was afraid of owls and there were dozens about. "And of crazy dogs," he added, like someone concerned to be as honest as possible.

To my surprise he asked if he could have a lock of my hair. As I was thinking that perhaps he hadn't seen a woman for a long time or was on drugs, he took out a Swiss army knife with a tiny pair of scissors attached to it. I held out my hand to take it but he came close to me and cut off an end of my hair, then tore a piece off an old newspaper serving as a table-cloth under a dish and empty beer glass, wrapped the hair carefully in it and put it away in his shirt pocket. I couldn't erase the scene from my mind for days and had visions of the lock of hair in the torn-off bit of newspaper hidden in his pocket each time I brushed my hair, and thought of that vast high-ceilinged room open to the street where there was a fighter who was afraid of hooting owls.

Now I am bored by these ruins, but I don't want to force Jawad to leave for it takes time to absorb it all. It's impossible not to have vivid memories of the past here, and then the ruins spring to life, with the temporary return of the imported palm trees, hurrying pedestrians, blaring horns, and distinctive smells of coffee, grilled meat, garlic. I remember my first visit to the commercial district after a gap of several years. I woke up one day in Simon's apartment and opened my eyes to see him picking his clothes up off the floor and pulling them on. He kissed me on the forehead and told me to wait for him in the hotel that afternoon. Simon was a press photographer who had a sad look in his green eyes, except when he was working. We had only dared to speak to one another the day before but we'd been exchanging furtive glances for the previous week. Although I was hung over I got up too and dressed hurriedly so that I could go with him to Sahat Al-Burj. Almost overnight this area had become a malign sickness affecting the collective mind. It had been the commercial heart of the city and now the roads had turned in on themselves and were known only as access and exit points. My breathless enthusiasm lasted until I saw a fig tree bearing a single fruit; it was bent double as if groaning with exhaustion, its broad, spreading leaves silent and covered in dust. I felt it was looking at me sadly, without reproach, but I knew I was a traitor because I had shown no aversion to the war.

From the roof of the Azariyya building I saw buildings collapsing like dominoes. The ones that resisted seemed to be waiting their turn, observing the splendid collapse of those around them; it was as if they preserved within them the memory of the past in the colour of their paint, the tiles, the electricity cables and the hoardings. An advertisement for a film surviving as a reminder of the city in the days when it used to swallow lights and spit them out like a fire-breathing dragon. The remains of a neon arrow pointing to Aazar coffee. The collapsing buildings like spotted leopards crashing to the ground. Strange colours for which people had no names, as they stood watching overwhelmed by the spectacle of the dismemberment of what had constituted everyday life. I found myself thinking of our house. Would it be like this one day? Then I rushed into the jaws of death with Simon and ate sandwiches with a group of snipers; a little end of the blue sea showed behind us, very blue. Simon wanted to make me understand that sniping was a military tactic, not a giant in the sky who regarded everything that moved on the ground as fair game.

There were three of them. One was staring intently through a pair of binoculars searching for prey. He said to the others quietly, "See the washing line. That woman pouring coffee. No. Next to the building with green windows. Yes, there."

"Yes, yes. I said from the start above the Pepsi Cola sign."

"That's right. The woman in a stripy dress."

Their sudden silence took me by surprise. I saw the gun recoil violently, then the man who had fired it laid it on the ground. "It was the woman in a blue dress," he said.

What I saw with Simon made me think about the war in a completely different way from those who didn't leave their houses and derived their view of what was happening from the radio, newspapers and the terror of the battles outside their windows. I hadn't simply grown accustomed to the idea of war; life and death had become realities embedded in the space before my eyes and in my throat, thanks to Simon. He was like two different people: one confident that he was protected from death by being in the thick of things, and the other suffering from a fear he couldn't dislodge, a chronic condition which set in as soon as it got dark, making him feel as if he was in a sauna bathed alternately in hot and cold sweat. He lit

large numbers of candles but they only increased his feelings of isolation. His imagination gave birth to spectres and he felt
that he was being watched. The moment
he extinguished his candles his thoughts
rushed in, confused and sick, and the
night became an instrument of torture,
bearing down on his chest with its leaden
blackness so that he had difficulty breathing. He tried to shift it without success, for
the air he breathed in the house was as
heavy as if it was weighed down with tiny
fragments of metal. Any moment now
he was certain a bullet would lodge in
his head, or flying shrapnel would burst
through the walls and blow the place
apart. He went to bed, but couldn't sleep;
he wanted some affection. He wanted sex.
He wanted to forget the violence. But even
these sexual feelings couldn't erase the entrenched fear which had become synonymous with his soul, and which only departed
in the morning, when he got up and light
was flooding the room, and his clothes and
the furniture and everything around him
looked familiar and reminded him of the
orderly routine of life. Out in the street, he
liked the familiar disc of the sun, first red
then yellow, which penetrated the fibres of
his anxiety with a brilliant warmth, making
him forget the night even existed and giving
him the spirit to start the day afresh. The
reality of the war re-established itself gradually and he rushed from place to place,
with his camera slung round his neck,
recording his fear and deferring it till night
time.

Simon became the strength I drew on to
carry me through my day, the news bulletin
which, however unpleasant, was clear and
activated my mind, bringing me closer to
events. But Simon decided to leave. This
didn't bother me at first, because he said
he was leaving all the time. The first time
we talked he told me how he decided to
leave during the massacre of Karantina
when he was certain he was going to be
killed. In Karantina he had seen bodies
piled up at street corners just like garbage.
Bodies stacked in pyramids of assorted
colours with irregular corners because of a
random hand or foot or head sticking out.
When he realized who was guarding one of
these lopsided pyramids, not allowing pho-
tographers anywhere near it, he knew his
luck was in. It was Abu'l-Zooz, the joiner
who did work for his family and made all
the wooden furniture they required. "I said
to Abu'l-Zooz, 'I want to take a photo,'"
Simon told me. "He was delighted for me to
see him in this important position.

"'Certainly. You can take everything
except this,' gesturing at the pile of corpses.

"'Fine. I wouldn't want to anyway. No
one would publish it,' I answered indiffer-
ently, without looking at the human pyra-
mid.

"I started clicking away, and managed to
get a picture of it while he was busy offering
me a glass of champagne and asking after
my family. That picture was published in
the world press and even though my name
didn't appear on it I was terrified of Abu'l-
Zooz. Only when things had settled down
did he go back to his old trade. My mother
invited him to the house to make sure that
he was well-disposed towards me, filling up
his plate each time he emptied it so he
couldn't say anything about me."

But Simon wept, determined to leave the
western sector. He had discovered how misguided he'd been to think the fact he was
a Christian wouldn't stand in the way
of him forming close relationships with
the fighters, be they Palestinians, commun-
ists, Shiites or Druzes. All along he had
remained convinced his name and religion
were matters of chance and had nothing to
do with him personally. He wouldn't even
acknowledge that this could have been
changed by the war. But, on a day when
the desire for revenge reached huge proportions following battles and kidnappings on
both sides, he was taken captive at a check-
point and learnt that his name could be a
matter of life and death.

In the end he hadn't been saved by the
permits he carried nor by mentioning
the names of important people in the resistance, since the militiaman holding him was
impervious to reason and sense. All that
saved him from certain death was the deci-

sion of the high-up official who came to inspect the hostages. Questioning Simon, he found he was wearing a bullet-proof jacket and this convinced him he had tumbled on a foreign spy, not a press photographer as the hostage claimed to be.

I couldn't help wondering, as Simon told me he had finally decided to go, how he would live away from the war, which had become his full-time job. His office was the trenches, the barricades and the empty buildings. I felt then that I didn't know him and hadn't experienced the taste of his lips, the weight of his body on mine, although sometimes we had been content just to hold hands in the darkness which was so powerful and so soft that it drowned out the sound of explosions. We derived warmth and tenderness from the sound of each other's breathing like two old people obliged to be together because they shared the same dentures. As I said goodbye to him I held him close, even though it was broad daylight in the hotel entrance lounge, promising to visit him in the eastern sector and stay with him for a few days every now and then. But as soon as I turned away from the hotel, Simon went right out of my mind; I thought about him from time to time when I wanted some affection, some physical contact, and crossed into the east as if I was walking a tightrope, swinging wildly between wanting to be with him and wishing I hadn't come. Eventually the thread that had joined us wore away and we rarely met because our city was divided in two.

After the duty-free market with its beautiful stone walls, the ruins and the jungle of monster plants, Jawad and I take a road which leads us by women with heads wrapped in black kerchiefs. One of them has a candle in her hand: I guess she must make regular visits to the remains of the church there.

One day I had broken free from my father's hand and gone into this little church. It smelt strongly of candles and incense and was lit by glowing chandeliers and the Virgin Mary's face ringed with gold and silver haloes behind protective glass. If you stuck a twenty-five piastre piece on the glass you knew that your prayers would be answered. I remember rushing outside to my father, who was buying vegetables, and pretending to be nauseous with hunger so that he would give me a quarter lira to stick on the magic glass in the church, then perhaps the glittering gold saint would exchange my father for a new one. But he wouldn't give me a quarter lira and dragged me from one market to another and through a narrow archway into a little place, gloomy as a rat's hole, which opened into another market smelling of roast meat; here we sat down with a lot of men at wooden tables. I heard one of them saying he could eat three camels. I asked my father if I had to eat a whole camel.

My father used to have a shop close by which my uncle had been forced to sell because it became obvious the losses could never be recouped once my father had decided to work for God; he refused to make a profit of one single piastre on his fine quality broadcloth, even though his brother and other members of the family took him to consult a man of religion, who urged him to return to buying and selling as before, limiting his profits in accordance with religious law. But my father renounced everything. He began selling off the Persian rugs in our house and my mother's jewellery, unknown to her, then donated the money to mosques in Iraq, indifferent to her wails of protest: she had been proud that my father's business was in the heart of a commercial area and well known to many people, and tried to make him do his duty again, threatening to leave him or devising ways to catch him out, but my father had moved into a world of his own, far removed from ordinary everyday life. He would have liked to be able to prohibit Isaf the maid and my mother from discussing mundane topics, so that they could spend their time and energy on praying. He stopped shaving his beard regularly, wore the same suit and pair of shoes every day, had his old red tarboosh repaired again and even shaved his head for the sake of cleanliness and purity. His relations gradually stopped visiting us, as all he talked about was repentance and Judgement Day. He advised one of them not to send his son to medical school, since God was the only true doctor, and said that instead he should go to Iraq to study Islamic jurisprudence and law. So it went on, until we found we had even stopped waiting for him at mealtimes. In fact it was a burden to us when he did appear, and my mother started up a flurry of activity in the house whenever he began to pray, hoping he would go to the mosque.

Jawad and I progress from the duty-free zone and Suq Sursuq to Al-Azariyya where the smell of old books still seems to hang in the air. His father had apparently insisted on bringing him secondhand books, in particular from a bookshop here belonging to a relative's family, and was never happy buying a new book, however cheap. Meanwhile I am thinking of the Capitol Hotel and Omar Sharif. I tell Jawad about going to the hotel with Aida who was thirteen, and on her way to take her father his lunch in the cloth market when she saw Omar Sharif going into the hotel. She caught up with him inside and told him about his admirers in her school. He was amused by this bright little girl who offered him some of her father's lunch. "You take care of your father's lunch, my dear," he said, "and we'll see you again some time."

Aida went back that same afternoon with three pretty girls from the top class and led them up to his room. He opened the door and looked embarrassed because he was wearing a hairnet to flatten out his crinkly hair.

Jawad responds to the mood of these memories, but proceeds to tell me of experiences as remote from mine as they could be. His thoughts had always revolved around phrases he couldn't get out of his mind, and feelings which pestered him to let them see themselves on paper. He wrote his first novel and hawked it round the publishing houses, who asked if he was prepared to pay the costs of having it published. As a result he stopped writing and put all his efforts into finding a way of leaving the country and going abroad, explaining to foreign consulates how vital it was for him to study in their countries, how much he longed to go abroad and experience a foreign culture, and describing his situation living in a house which was full of noise from morning till night.

I sit with Jawad in a café overlooking the sea with the ruins behind us. We hear the waves gently lapping against the wooden foundations and they seem to say everything's still the same. It's as if I've never left this chair, as if I'm still sitting in a group of students and we form a single network of thoughts and ambitions. Now I can erase from my mind the vision of myself naked in his arms, grateful to the circumstances which have prevented this idea becoming a reality. I find doing this gives me a feeling of strength which changes to happiness and makes me fly above the café table, at ease and restored to myself after a long separation. I study my fingers and the palm of my hand which seem important again as they did in the past.

As soon as we get up to go, the destruction is there in front of us again in spite of the sea, the sky, the sun, the leaves on the trees, the distant birds. We are uneasy too far from the sight of the war and its trail of refuse. Even the groups of soldiers, whether they are Syrian or Lebanese, arouse vague feelings of affection.

Everyone says "The eastern sector" and "The western sector", and your divisions have become a fact of life.

The eastern sector and the western sector. The old names have faded in importance, names that seemed to have been there for all time: Jounieh, Jbeil, Al-Dawrah. New names have become prominent: Tariq al-Franciscan, Sudeco, the Museum with its mud and water, the smell of urine and the people crossing from one sector to another with sorrow in their faces, a heavy weight on their shoulders, and the sense of frustration which escalates if this route is suddenly closed. People are always uncertain whether to choose the Sudeco route where there is sniping or the route by the Museum which is more difficult and requires advance planning.

Jawad is studying the roads again, no doubt trying to recognize them. His silence, punctuated by deep sighs, speaks clearly to me, his thoughts burn straight into my mind and interfere with my memories. As I look towards Sharia Muhammad al-Hout he shouts, "That's the racecourse! Would you believe it? The main entrance of the racecourse!"

The black iron gates have split right through and are covered in spots of rust like leprous scabs infecting even the gold whorls adorning the top of them. At Jawad's insistence we go into the racecourse. People are dipping through a hole in the wall as if escaping into a green oasis between the trees. Despite the strong smell of urine they pour through in their tens and hundreds, walking silently. They must be calculating the risks to themselves, hoping to reach the other sector without hearing a shot, and so they move as if they are on an urgent mission.

Jawad is thinking, "If they allow people to cross here, why don't they allow them to cross anywhere?"

I'm thinking, "I'm sure these people are wondering if they'll find anyone to give them a lift when they reach the eastern sector."

Jawad says aloud, "They are rushing through a bare landscape, between two sections of a city. Where are they going? Are they escaping from an ogre or congratulating themselves on winning their own personal Battle of Hittin? Or are they thirsty tribesmen who know where there's another oasis with plenty of grass and water?"

I laugh at Jawad's comparisons although I'm irritated at the way he continues to look at everything as if he is turning it into a work of literature.

Some people are going to their jobs in the other sector carrying their papers and food. An elegantly dressed woman bends down and puts on a pair of plastic overshoes. She must have got them from Europe. Two girls strut along unconcerned, in high heels that plunge deep into the mud, on their way to keep a date. One puts a bit more lipstick on and the other rearranges her hair.

Jawad used to go to the racecourse with his family and play in the big gardens. There was nothing to equal the smell of the racecourse gardens: pine, camomile, wild rose. He remembers Ruhiyya lighting a fire of pine twigs when he had whooping cough and making him inhale the smoke.

I have to strain to see the top of Sharia Muhammad al-Hout where I was born. It branches off Sharia al-Sabaq where we are now. I look at it, and at Sharia Hiroshima and see an image of myself walking along the pavement where the restaurant was, following my father. I see my mother wearing a hairband like a twenties hat, right back off her forehead. I see her laughing eyes. She gasps and says to my uncle, "Did the fortune teller really say that?" My uncle is reading her the biography of the singer Asmahan. "You were born in water and in water you will die." . . .

Part II   Reading Urban Economies

Introduction: Reading Urban Economies

Gary Bridge and Sophie Watson

Introduction

In the twentieth century the study of the economy of cities was influenced first by neoclassical economics and then, as an analytical and political critique of this, by Marxist political economy. Most of the pieces included in this section of the *Reader* draw on the Marxist tradition, because of its particular influence in urban studies, or they are in turn a critique of Marxist analysis (from variants of postmodernism and poststructuralism). However, a good deal of research in urban studies is still informed by the neoclassical approach and it is important to point out some of the main elements of this conception of the economy of the city.

Neoclassicism

Neoclassical economics stresses the importance of consumer demand and focuses on the conditions of competition between producers to meet that demand. The conditions in which consumers "meet" producers characterizes the nature of the market. A market is considered to be functioning efficiently if consumer demand is met at the lowest price by a large number of producers who are in competition with each other. There is a wide range of circumstances that can prevent perfect competition from operating (monopoly for instance). If, however, a market does operate "perfectly" it is said to be in equilibrium.

In the study of cities there are a number of significant consequences of these simple assumptions. The first is that analysis of the economy is largely confined to a consideration of the *market*. The city has been conceived of as a market in which various types of consumer demand (for land, housing, and a range of consumer goods and public services) meet producers and providers. The city-as-market idea makes the urban system one that is seen as a self-regulating to achieve an equilibrium of supply and demand. Furthermore, in urban studies the market has been equated with the *marketplace*, in the historical sense of a city being a site of trade in the market square. Attention has focused on the city as market either within the built-up urban area or in the relationship between the city as node and the market as the surrounding region or hinterland. This is why a good deal of the economic analysis of cities has involved urban and *regional* data. The idea of the city as a center of a regional market is seen in Christaller's 1933 central-place model in which the spatial range of consumer demand for different goods helps explain the distribution and size of settlements in a region. Higher order goods (luxuries) had a larger spatial range in terms of the tolerance of consumer demand (measured as distance the consumer was prepared to travel to purchase the good). They would be provided by fewer larger places that also provided lower order goods (such as food) to their own populations, i.e. goods that people would not travel very far to purchase. Between the large settlements there would be a range of smaller settlements providing lower order goods across the region. The city was a market to its own population and to the surrounding region. Thus analysis of the city was largely confined to the internal activities and dynamics of the built-up urban area itself or to the relationship between the city as node and region as market.

A second element of the focus of neoclassical economics on the dynamics of the market was that it emphasized the activity of *exchange*: consumers purchasing goods from consumers. In the exchange relation it is consumer demand, rather than the conditions of production, that is given emphasis. The power of consumer demand is the ability to pay for the good. One of the most significant goods on offer in the city is land. Here the adaption of neoclassical principles indicated not a pure market clearing by the price of the good satisfying consumer demand for it, but a market segmentation based on different abilities to pay for the good, the desirability of which increased the closer to the center of the city and therefore the more accessible to the consumer market the land was. Consumer desires to occupy land were differentiated in a kind of bidding system, with the most expensive central city land being consumed by activities with greatest ability to outbid other functions (in this case it was commerical activities). With increasing distance from the center of the city, other uses could successfully bid for land (first industrial and then residential uses). This bid-rent model is an adaption of the earlier classical land-use model of Von Thunen. But whereas von Thunen's model (Von Thunen 1826) in the classical frame focused on factors of production (especially soil fertility) and transport costs, the neoclassical bid-rent model puts stress on consumer demand. The bid-rent model results in the famous concentric ring banding of land uses around the city (see Alonso 1964). Other variants of this approach have been applied to urban housing markets and especially the rapid suburbanization of many cities in the second half of the twentieth century.

The Marxist Revolution in Urban Studies

One of the critiques of the neoclassical approach is that it naturalizes the market. There is an assumption that market equilibrium is achieved by the hidden hand of market adaption to consumer demand that is somehow the natural, stable, and desirable state of affairs. In the face of large numbers of "consumers" around the world in sustained states of poverty and deprivation, the effectiveness of markets to deliver was increasingly questioned. In the 1960s and 1970s this questioning led many to radical alternatives to the neoclassical view of the economy, and particularly to Marxism. In *Social Justice and the City*, the flagship text that hailed in this new era, David Harvey stated that the aim of his Marxist analysis was to make the bid-rent model of urban land use *not* true. That is, even if the bid-rent model could be considered a true reflection of urban land-use processes, the point of Marxist critique was not just to analyze the world but to change it, such that the conditions that gave rise to the "truth" of the bid-rent model would become untrue. These conditions were of course the operation of a capitalist economy.

Whereas the emphasis in the neoclassical tradition had been on markets and exchange, the view of the economy from a Marxist perspective expanded to take in the workings of capitalism at various spatial scales and over historical periods. Indeed David Harvey's avowed mission over the last 30 years has been to lay out the components of historical, geographical materialism (see Harvey 1982, 1985). Whereas the emphasis of neoclassicism was on exchange, in Marxism the focus is the circulation of capital, value in motion, which is a strategy of accumulation of profit, for accumulation's sake, under the pressure of competition between capitalists. This circulation of value makes use of the means of production (capital equipment, buildings, etc.) and labor power to accumulate more profit. Thus the market is seen as only part of a wider system of capitalist accumulation of profit for capitalists which involves a class relation with workers (who don't own the means of production), that takes profit from part of their work that is done over and above what is required to meet their needs (surplus labour). The focus of analysis has shifted to the conditions of commodity production rather than consumer demand and the "normality" of exchange. The rush for profit often leads capitalist competitors to produce too many goods or through competition to produce them at prices that drive down profits, or at other times to encounter impaired demand given the restricted buying power of workers in conditions of exploitation. Thus rather than seeing capitalist markets as self-equilibrating via the hidden hand, Marxist analysis sees the capitalist economy as inherently contradictory and crisis prone in a cycle of boom and bust.

In the extract included here Harvey argues for the special place of cities – in the circulation of capital, in class relations and in dealing with capitalist economic crises. But note first of all that the title refers not to the city but to the "urban process under capitalism." Cities are not to be seen simply as entities (built-up areas, or particular markets) but rather as encompassing a series of processes of capitalist accumulation and class relations operating at different scales and over different time periods. The processual elements of the urban system are shown in the relationship between urban areas and capitalist accumulation. The circulation of capital moves through different circuits – primary commodity production and consumption, secondary – largely the built form, and tertiary – the knowledge economy and social expenditures to ensure the reproduction of labor. Harvey argues that crisis in one circuit of accumulation can be absorbed by activity in another circuit. Control of these switching crises is one of the functions of major cities (see the discussion of global cities and Sassen's extract). Also there is one particular switching effect that has a lot to do with cities as entities, or built forms. That is, that a crisis of accumulation in the primary commodity sector can be absorbed to some degree transferring investment to infrastructure and built form – and this is mostly concentrated in cities – an urban fix. In terms of class relations, cities were early concentrations of labor in conditions of exploitation in the factory system and now show contrasts across the globe between concentration of exploitation in that original sense (in many Asian cities, for example) and complex contrasts of class relations in many western cities (see the extracts in the Division and Difference section of this volume). Global cities now increasingly coordinate global class processes (see Sassen, this section).

The elements of the tertiary circuit of capital – investment in research and knowledge (that leads to technical innovation and the potential for future accumulation) and social expenditures for the reproduction of labor – bring into focus the work of another key figure, alongside Harvey, in developing a Marxist political economy of cities: Manuel Castells. One of the key insights in his early work, especially in *The Urban Question*, is to argue that what distinguishes cities in a capitalist economy is their function as providers of bundles of collective consumption (such as public services) that allows a workforce to be sustained. These ideas have been the subject of more recent debates over the shift from a Fordist regime of accumulation and mode of regulation (involving mass production of standard commodities and mass provision of standardized welfare services) to a post-Fordist one (involving flexible specialization in production and the niching of predominantly privatized services to different subpopulations). Before discussing the extracts that relate to the Fordism/post-Fordism debate it is important to note that Castells' more recent work has identified information and knowledge not just as a facilitator for commodity production or future accumulation through research and development, but as a regime of accumulation itself and one that crosses all sectors of the economy from agriculture to financial futures speculation. Knowledge production has become directly a value-generating activity. The seedbed for innovation in the knowledge economy is concentrated in cities (see Castells' *The Informational City*). The organization and transaction of knowledge matches the network structure of the firm, and these principles of network organization are, according to Castells, structuring social relations such that we can speak of a network society (see Castells 1996–8). In an extract below Castells summarizes his arguments on the information age.

Fordist to Post-Fordist City?

The increasingly network structure of economic organization is a feature that has been researched in detail and with great care by Allen Scott. Scott draws on neo-Ricardian economics (see Straffa 1960) which critiques both neoclassicism (for its limitation to the market) and Marxism (for its labor theory of value). His form of transaction cost analysis demonstrates the economic advantage of geographical clustering when splitting out the stages of production from the large industrial production unit and subcontracting certain functions (such as component supply) to other firms who must supply their product flexibly in terms of rapid supply over time and space. There are a number of significant consequences of Scott's work for our understanding of the economy of the modern metropolis. One is that there are important historical antecedents of this form of production that are embedded in the built form of many cities (in the extract gun and jewelry manufacture in Birmingham, England, are discussed). With the expansion of this form of commodity production in post-Fordism there is a tendency for the development of densely clustered districts of industrial and service firms who need rapid access to each other to maintain the supply chain in more flexible regimes of product development and supply (and of course more flexible and exploitative forms of employment). Scott's mapping of these nodal clusters, especially in the Los Angeles region, reveals a polynuclear industrial geography of the modern metropolis that challenges both the assumptions of post-industrialism and of accessibility in concentric urban markets (assumed in neoclassical models). Key elements of his approach with historical and contemporary examples are discussed in the extract from his book, *Metropolis: From the Division of Labor to Urban Form*.

Post-Fordism and new modes of regulation was argued to be a leading edge in new forms of capitalist competition in western economies that industrialized early (see

Aglietta 1979, Amin 1995). Myung-Rae Cho's piece offers a summary of the debates over capitalist regulation as well as their inflection through the lens of a rapidly industrializing Asian city. He demonstrates how economic restructuring involving new technologies and post-Fordist networked organization is achieved by a metropolitan spatial fix with positive externalities arising from clusters of hi-tech firms in industrial districts working on dense interlinkages. The aggregate effects of these linkages serve to overcome technical limitations resulting from Korea's hitherto more peripheral location in global capital accumulation. Thus Seoul is a crucible for Korea's wider economic restructuring.

Globalization and the Global City

Wheras cities like Seoul might occupy a key location in a national economic trends, very few cities operate as key nodes in the global economy itself. Most crucially New York, London, and Tokyo are the key hubs of the world's 24-hour stockmarket and have key command and control functions in the operation of the world economy. Here we encounter a broader debate over the question of whether capitalism is now globalized, with potential investments and disinvestments affecting all areas of economic activity in all the regions of the world irrespective of national boundaries and politics. According to Saskia Sassen (1998, 2000) certain global cities hold a key position in this new geography of centrality. The annihilation of space in the global economy is countered by the reassertion of the significance of place. Global cities are key places in the sense that they host the financial districts where global investment decisions are made and the producer services (legal, insurance, accountancy) that support the command functions of transnational corporations. Cities that perform such functions – New York, London, Tokyo, Paris, Frankfurt, Zurich, Amsterdam, Los Angeles, Sydney, Hong Kong, Sao Paulo, Buenos Aires, Bangkok, Taipei, Mumbai, Mexico City – often have greater interlinkages between them than they do with their respective regions or nations. Sassen also stresses that these cities also host the other side of globalization, the transnational migrations often involving poorly paid personal service workers who tend to the needs of the professionals on the other side of the global city/globalization divide. The extract that deals with these issues is from Sassen's book *Globalization and Its Discontents*.

One set of activities concentrated in global cities is various forms of trading in futures. This form of speculative activity makes profits out of options to buy stock and involves calculations of the future state of the market, of commodities, or exchange rates, for instance. The connection to current productive activity in the economy is very weak. These forms of hyperspeculation are becoming more common in capitalism according to Harvey, and are based on fictitious capital (see Harvey 1989). The extract from William Cronon's *Nature's Metropolis* provides a careful historical account of the way that a market in futures developed in the wheat market of nineteenth-century Chicago. It also details how the development of that market enhanced the position of Chicago in the national urban hierarchy and how certain institutions (such as the Chicago Board of Trade) were founded for local pragmatic reasons and once established became key urban functions with international influence. Cronon beautifully chronicles how the confluence of transport routes, communications, and other technical developments in the handling of grain (train and telegraph and grain escalator) necessitated the grading of wheat, i.e. its redefinition as a commodity. This quality grading had to have institutional legitimacy, and that, once established (via the Chicago Board of Trade), meant that information about wheat grades could be traded by telegraph, rather than trading the physical commodity itself. As well as being a good example of the development of a national market (and futures market) the Cronon piece also emphasizes (and this is the point of his book overall) the fact that abstract economic transactions and urban form are deeply natural. The growth of Chicago, its built form and economic and political institutions, was literally a product of nature. This piece anticipates more recent work that seeks to disrupt the city/nature/economy distinctions, through discussions on the urbanization of nature and the "nature" of cities (Harvey 1996; Swyngedouw and Kaika 2000).

Fantasy Economies in the Postmodern City

The sorts of speculative activity that were developing in nineteenth-century Chicago have reached perverse proportions in the Orange County scamscape of Ed Soja's "postmetropolis." This description of Orange County in the greater Los Angeles region is meant to capture its role at the heart of the US Savings and Loan scandal of the 1980s, as well as the largest municipal/county bankruptcy in US history and its landscape of boiler rooms, centers of telemarketing frauds, and scams. Developing themes from postmodern theory, Soja argues this is symptomatic of the blurring of the real and imagined – the real city as simulation, the Simcity of the postmetropolis. Economic activity and fictitious fantasy mingle in the postmetropolis of late capitalism. This relates to other analyses of the strangely fictitous and fantasy element of the modern economy and the role of cities in blurring the real and the imagined. Soja's other discourses of the postmetropolis reinforce and take further the themes that have been established in earlier extracts in this section. *Flexcity* refers to the new forms of industrial organization, the industrial districts of the polynodal post-Fodist city. *Cosmopolis* relates to a city's role in the global economy and the mix of the global and the local (glocalization) in the economic activity of the postmetropolis. Decentralization of new urban forms is captured in the discourse on *exopolis* and the phenomenon of *edge city* (Garreau 1991). The sharper social polarizations (metropolarities) that arise from restructured urban economies are a pervasive theme of the new urbanism (see the Division and Difference section of this *Reader*). These social divisions are held in place by greater state surveillance and policing, making the city more like the panoptican prison (drawing on Foucault's work – see the Public section of the *Reader*). The privileged classes increasingly live in fortress-like enclave behind patrolled walls in gated communities (described so vividly by Mike Davis in *City of Quartz*).

Soja is identifying an important contemporary theme in the analysis of urban economies – that of investment and profit increasingly driven by factors (the economy as fantasy, speculation as information) that seem strangely remote from many of the brutal material consequences of those decisions.

From the globalization debates and the view of the urban process as part of the larger scheme of the circulation of capital it would be easy to see economic processes as distinct from culture and social reproduction in the sense that the economy is dominant over them, in the last instance (to borrow Engels' famous phrase). Yet recent work has noted how social and cultural phenomena are deeply embedded and help shape economic processes (see especially Smelser and Swedberg 1994). The relationship between capital and culture has long been the concern of Sharon

Zukin, especially in the context of the gentrification of Manhattan. In an earlier book, *Loft Living*, Zukin analyzes how the cultural activities of artists that occupied former factory lofts in the lower east side of New York became the catalyst for more corporate gentrification of the area, building on its artistic and Bohemian caché. The extracts included here are from her book *Landscapes of Power: From Detroit to Disney World*, where she develops the culture/capital themes. Zukin argues that certain forms of low-key, *ad hoc* social and cultural practices make downtown space liminal – between the market and place. These practices either get superseded or commodified through economic restructuring. In gentrification, for example, success-ful practices are consolidated by a critical infrastructure consisting of restaurant critics, lifestyle gurus, and local dignitaries. Zukin's wider point about all this is made in the second extract, where the types of imaging and imagining that utilize downtown liminality for economic accumulation parallels the way Disneyland con-structs its landscape of familiarity and fantasy. And exactly the same processes have been used to reimage cities like Los Angeles and Miami at key points in their economic histories.

The imaging of the city is now a common practice as cities vie with each other like entrepreneurs to attract business and tourism (see David Harvey's extract in the Urban Interventions section of this *Reader*). In this form of place marketing (see e.g. Rutheiser 1996) the image of the city is just as important as its more traditional assets of land, buildings, and people. The economic importance of city image is revealed in the extract from Lindsay Bremner's piece on "Reinventing the Johannesburg Inner City." After boom and decline based on gold and apartheid, Johannesburg sought to reposition itself in the 1980s as the "Gateway to Africa" which was "inviting and integrated" rather than racially divided and where downtown was portrayed as a "world city showroom." Bremner notes how local government strategy moved through certain phases, emphasizing first city as spectacle and then environmental concerns. Imaging was used in an attempt to reposition Johannesburg in the global market.

The Aesthetic Economy of the City

Although rediscovered through strategies of "urban regeneration," the idea of city of spectacle has a much longer and more theoretically consequential pedigree, though one only recently acknowledged in urban studies. That intellectual heritage is repre-sented in part by the work of Walter Benjamin. Benjamin's work is both voluminous and fragmented and for that reason we have included an extract by Susan Buck-Morss, a prominent Benjamin scholar. This piece would be more typically at home in the cultural studies section of a reader on the city, but we have deliberately placed it in the economy section because it disrupts and extends our thinking about the nature of the economy of cities in a number of ways. First it makes the point about the key role of the city as a site of spectacle and bedazzlement, as a glittering emporium of commodities that Benjamin conveyed so evocatively about the nineteenth-century Paris Arcades or World Expositions. The emphasis on pleasure and diversion in consumption and the "fairylike" element of the urban economy relates very strongly to the more recent interpretations of Sharon Zukin on Disneyland or David Harvey's (1989) observation that the city of spectacle reduces capital turnover (and the speed of accumulation) to, borrowing Marx's phrase, "the twinkling of an eye." The synesthesia of sights and sounds in urban spectacle (or phantasmagoria) had an effect on class relations in diverting expectations from social solidarity to individualized consumption. Benjamin's work, through Buck-Morss's eyes, makes the point that culture, aesthetics, and the psychoanalytics of desire are not just entrained and commodified by separate economic processes but are right in there at the beginning. Benjamin's work tantalizingly suggests, in ways that are only just being explored (see for example Keith 2000), that the economy and culture are not categories that can be held apart, as they traditionally have been in urban studies. Desire, aesthetic nuance, and fantasy are at the heart of the capitalist economy, and the city provides the space to explore their relations.

Critiques of Marxist Political Economy of Cities

Adapating the work of Walter Benjamin on the city indicates how the traditional ways of conceptualizing the economy (be they neoclassical or neo-Marxist) have come under fire in the last ten years. This critique is taken further by J. K. Gibson-Graham, who, combining elements of traditional Marxism with postmodern, poststructuralist, feminist, and psychoanalytic intellectual influences, round on urban economic theory for establishing the Identity of Capitalism as the ultimate container of all meaning and significance. (They are two authors writing under a combined pseudonym.) Appended to this Identity is the economy as Phallus: active, thrusting, dynamic, and the privileged analytical sites of the male laborer and his body. The effect of this on the economic analysis of the city is that women's work and their bodies are rendered invisible or represented by "lack," passivity, and emptiness. Downtown is the Phallic landscape of skyscrapers where serious male work is done, dynamic decision-making in a global economy conducted in a public (male)space of the city. In this analysis female labor is peripheralized to the suburbs and the private realm. The point of Gibson-Graham's argument is to suggest that there is a danger in traditional Marxist discourse on the economy that can render political action and emancipatory desire powerless against the all encompassing, all-powerful, unavoidable presence of the Identity of Capital. This debate about the political effects of the discourse of the urban economy will surely continue.

Some of the politics of what Gibson-Graham are pointing to is evident in the practices of women in the informal section of nonwestern, nonglobal, underanalyzed cities of the south. As Castells argues, most economic activity in the world's cities is informal, feminized, and impoverished (Castells 1996–8). The extract from Aili Mari Tripp's book *Changing the Rules: The Politics of Liberalization and the Urban Informal Economy in Tanzania* reveals some of the day-to-day reality of this female economic activity. What it also does, and this is very much in the spirit of what Gibson-Graham are suggesting, is to point to how women can to some degree change the rules for themselves through their economic activity. As well as documenting the poverty and sheer hard work involved, Tripp also suggests how involvement in the informal sector can lead to a certain degree of autonomy and independence from other (gender, family) constraints. She also shows how women can create new products and therefore new markets for these goods (purified salt, for example) or can introduce established economic activities to new markets (such as the first African woman to open up a hair salon in Dar es Salaam). Women's greater involvement in the informal sector is giving them more power in other elements of their lives, while being embedded in the daily rhythms of their lives as mothers, wives, family and community members. This is all in stark contrast to the conception of the formal economy –

nondomestic, separate from other arenas of life – that has consumed most of the literature on the economies of cities. One suspects that as informal activity becomes more significant in economic analysis and as the boundaries between the formal and informal sectors blur, these activities, as well as the theoretical developments outlined, will start to reshape the way we think about the complexities of the economies of cities.

REFERENCES

Aglietta, P. 1979: *A Theory of Capitalist Regulation*. London: New Left Books.

Alonso, W. 1964: *Location and Land Use: Toward a General Theory of Land Rent*. Cambridge, MA: Harvard University Press.

Amin, A. (ed.) 1995: *Post-Fordism: A Reader*. Oxford: Blackwell.

Castells, M. 1977: *The Urban Question*. London: Edward Arnold.

Castells, M. 1989: *The Informational City*. Oxford: Blackwell.

Castells, M. 1996–8: *The Information Age: Economy, Society and Culture*, vol. 1 (1996), *The Rise of Network Society*; vol. 2 (1997), *The Power of Identity*; vol. 3, *End of Millennium*. Oxford: Blackwell.

Christaller, W. 1966 [1933]: *Central Places in Southern Germany*, trans. C. W. Baskin. London: Prentice-Hall.

Davis, M. 1992: *City of Quartz: Excavating the Future in Los Angeles*. London: Verso.

Garreau, J. 1991: *Edge City: Life on the New Urban Frontier*. New York: Doubleday.

Harvey, D. 1973: *Social Justice and the City*. Baltimore: Johns Hopkins University Press.

Harvey, D. 1982: *The Limits to Capital*. Oxford: Blackwell.

Harvey, D. 1985: *The Urbanization of Capital*. Oxford: Blackwell.

Harvey, D. 1989: *The Condition of Postmodernity*. Oxford: Blackwell.

Harvey, D. 1996: *Nature, Justice and the Geography of Difference*. Oxford: Blackwell.

Keith, M. 2000: Walter Benjamin, Urban Studies, and the Narratives of City Life. In G. Bridge and S. Watson (eds.), *A Companion to the City*. Oxford: Blackwell.

Rutheiser, C. 1996: *Imagineering Atlanta: The Politics of Place in the City of Dreams*. London: Verso

Sassen, S. 1998: *Globalization and Its Discontents*. New York: New Press.

Sassen, S. 2000: *The Global City: New York, London, Tokyo*. Princeton: Princeton University Press (updated edition).

Smelser, N. and Swedberg, R. (eds.) 1994: *The Handbook of Economic Sociology*. Princeton: Russel Sage Foundation.

Straffa, P. 1960: *The Production of Commodities by Means of Commodities*. Cambridge: Cambridge University Press.

Swyngedouw, E. and Kaika, M. 2000: The Environment of the City. In G. Bridge and S. Watson (eds.), *A Companion to the City*. Oxford: Blackwell, 567–80.

Von Thunen, J. H. 1966 [1826]: *Isolated State: An English Edition of Der isolierte Staat*, trans C. M. Wartenberg and ed. P. G. Hall. Oxford: Pergamon.

Zukin, S. 1982: *Loft Living: Culture and Capital in Urban Change*. Baltimore: Johns Hopkins University Press.

Chapter 14

The Urban Process under Capitalism: A Framework for Analysis

David Harvey

My objective is to understand the urban process under capitalism. I confine myself to the capitalist forms of urbanization because I accept the idea that the 'urban' has a specific meaning under the capitalist mode of production which cannot be carried over without a radical transformation of meaning (and of reality) into other social contexts.

Within the framework of capitalism, I hang my interpretation of the urban process on the twin themes of *accumulation* and *class struggle*. The two themes are integral to each other and have to be regarded as different sides of the same coin – different windows from which to view the totality of capitalist activity. The class character of capitalist society means the domination of labour by capital. Put more concretely, a class of capitalists is in command of the work process and organizes that process for the purposes of producing profit. The labourer, on the other hand, has command only over his or her labour power which must be sold as a commodity on the market. The domination arises because the labourer must yield the capitalist a profit (surplus value) in return for a living wage. All of this is extremely simplistic, of course, and actual class relations (and relations between factions of classes) within an actual system of production (comprising production, services, necessary costs of circulation, distribution, exchange, etc.) are

highly complex. The essential marxian insight, however, is that profit arises out of the domination of labour by capital and that the capitalists as a class must, if they are to reproduce themselves, continuously expand the basis for profit. We thus arrive at a conception of a society founded on the principle of 'accumulation for accumulation's sake, production for production's sake'. The theory of accumulation which Marx constructs in *Capital* amounts to a careful enquiry into the dynamics of accumulation and an exploration of its contradictory character. This may sound rather 'economistic' as a framework for analysis, but we have to recall that accumulation is the means whereby the capitalist class reproduces both itself and its domination over labour. Accumulation cannot, therefore, be isolated from class struggle....

Accumulation and the Urban Process

The understanding I have to offer of the urban process under capitalism comes from seeing it in relation to the theory of accumulation. We must first establish the general points of contact between what seem, at first sight, two rather different ways of looking at the world.

Whatever else it may entail, the urban process implies the creation of a material physical infrastructure for production, circulation, exchange and consumption. The first point of contact, then, is to consider the manner in which this built environment is produced and the way it serves as a resource system – a complex of use values – for the production of value and surplus value. We have, secondly, to consider the consumption aspect. Here we can usefully distinguish between the consumption of revenues by the bourgeoisie and the need to reproduce labour power. The former has a considerable impact upon the urban process, but I shall exclude it from the analysis because consideration of it would lead us into a lengthy discourse on the question of bourgeois culture and its complex significations without revealing very much directly about the specifically capitalist form of the urban process. Bourgeois consumption is, as it were, the icing on top of a cake which has as its prime ingredients capital and labour in dynamic relation to each other. The reproduction of labour power is essential and requires certain kinds of social expenditures and the creation of a consumption fund. The flows we have sketched, in so far as they portray capital movements into the built environment (for both production and consumption) and the laying out of social expenditures for the reproduction of labour power, provide us, then, with the structural links we need to understand the urban process under capitalism....

Overaccumulation and long waves in investment in the built environment

The acid test of any set of theoretical propositions comes when we seek to relate them to the experience of history and to the practices of politics. In a short paper of this kind I cannot hope to demonstrate the relations between the theory of accumulation and its contradictions on the one hand, and the urban process on the other in the kind of detail which would be convincing. I shall therefore confine myself to illustrating some of the more important themes which can be identified. I will focus, first, exclu-

sively on the processes governing investment in the built environment.

The system of production which capital established was founded on a physical separation between a place of work and a place of residence. The growth of the factory system, which created this separation, rested on the organization of cooperation, division of labour and economies of scale in the work process as well as upon the application of machinery. The system also promoted an increasing division of labour between enterprises, and collective economies of scale through the agglomeration of activities in large urban centres. All of this meant the creation of a built environment to serve as a physical infrastructure for production, including an appropriate system for the transport of commodities. There are abundant opportunities for the productive employment of capital through the creation of a built environment for production. The same conclusion applies to investment in the built environment for consumption. The problem is, then, to discover how capital flows into the construction of this built environment and to establish the contradictions inherent in this process.

We should first say something about the concept of the built environment and consider some of its salient attributes. It is a complex composite commodity comprising innumerable different elements – roads, canals, docks and harbours, factories, warehouses, sewers, public offices, schools and hospitals, houses, offices, shops, etc. – each of which is produced under different conditions and according to quite different rules. The 'built environment' is, then, a gross simplification, a concept which requires disaggregation as soon as we probe deeply into the processes of its production and use. Yet we also know that these components have to function together as an ensemble in relation to the aggregative processes of production, exchange and consumption. For purposes of exposition we can afford to remain at this level of generality. We also know that the built environment is long-lived, difficult to alter, spatially immobile and often absorbent of large lumpy investments. A proportion of it will be used in common by capitalists and consumers alike and even those elements which can be privately appropriated (houses, factories, shops, etc.) are used in a context in which the externality effects of private uses are pervasive and often quite strong. All of these characteristics have implications for the investment process.

The analysis of fixed capital formation and the consumption fund in the context of accumulation suggests that investment in the built environment is likely to proceed according to a certain logic. We presume, for the moment, that the state does not take a leading role in promoting vast public works programmes ahead of the demand for them. Individual capitalists, when left to their own devices, tend to under-invest in the built environment relative to their own individual and collective needs at the same time as they tend to overaccumulate. The theory then suggests that the overaccumulation can be syphoned off – via financial and state institutions and the creation of fictional capital within the credit system – and put to work to make up the slack in investment in the built environment. This switch from the primary to the secondary circuit may occur in the course of a crisis or be accomplished relatively smoothly depending upon the efficiency of the mediating institutions. But the theory indicates that there is a limit to such a process and that at some point investments will become unproductive. At such a time the exchange value being put into the built environment has to be written down, diminished, or even totally lost. The fictional capital contained within the credit system is seen to be just that and financial and state institutions may find themselves in serious financial difficulty. The devaluation of capital in the built environment does not necessarily destroy the use value – the physical resource – which the built environment comprises. This physical resource can now be used as 'devalued capital' and as such it functions as a free good which can help to reestablish the basis for renewed accumulation. From

this we can see the logic of Marx's statement that periodical devaluations of fixed capital provide 'one of the means immanent in capitalist production to check the fall of the rate of profit and hasten accumulation of capital-value through formation of new capital'.

Since the impulses deriving from the tendency to overaccumulate and to under-invest are rhythmic rather than constant, we can construct a cyclical 'model' of investment in the built environment. The rhythm is dictated in part by the rhythms of capital accumulation and in part by the physical and economic lifetime of the elements within the built environment – the latter means that change is bound to be relatively slow. The most useful thing we can do at this juncture is to point to the historical evidence for 'long waves' in investment in the built environment. Somewhere in between the short-run movements of the business cycle – the 'Juglar cycles' of approximately ten-year length – and the very long 'Kondratieff's', we can identify movements of an intermediate length (sometimes called Kuznets cycles) which are strongly associated with waves of investment in the built environment. . . .

The flow of investment into the built environment depends upon the existence of surpluses of capital and labour and upon mechanisms for pooling the former and putting it to use. The history of this process is extremely interesting. The eighteenth century in Britain was characterized, for example, by a capital surplus much of which went into the built environment because it had nowhere else to go. Investment in the built environment took place primarily for financial rather than use-value reasons – investors were looking for a steady and secure rate of return on their capital. Investment in property (much of it for conspicuous consumption by the bourgeoisie), in turnpikes, canals and rents (agricultural improvement) as well as in state obligations were about the only options open to rentiers. The various speculative crises which beset investment in the turnpikes and canals as well as urban property markets, indicated very early on that returns were by no means certain and that investments had to be productive if they were to succeed.[1] ...

When, precisely, the tendency towards overaccumulation became the main agent producing surplus capital and when the 'long waves' became explicitly tied to overaccumulation is a moot point. The evidence suggests that by the 1840s the connections had been strongly forged in Britain at least. By then, the functioning of the capital market was strongly bound to the rhythms imposed by the development of industrial capitalism. ...

And what of the devaluation which inevitably results? If the devaluation is to function effectively, according to our theory, then it must leave behind a use value which can be used as the basis for further development. When many of the American states defaulted on their debts in the early 1840s, they failed to meet their obligations on the British capital market but kept the canals and other improvements which they had built. This was, in effect, expropriation without compensation – a prospect which the United States government treats with great moral indignation when some third-world country threatens it today. The great railroad booms of the nineteenth century typically devalued capital while littering the landscape with physical assets which could usually be put to some use. When the urban mass transit systems went bankrupt at the turn of the century because of chronic overcapitalization, the mass transit systems were left behind as physical assets. Somebody had to pay for the devaluation of course. There were the inevitable attempts to foist the costs onto the working class (often through municipal expenditures) or onto small investors. But big capital was not immune either, and the problems of the property companies in Britain or the real estate investment trusts in the United States at the present time are exactly of this sort (although the involvement of pension funds and insurance companies affects individuals). The office

space is still there, however, even though the building that houses it has been devalued and is now judged a non-earning asset. The history of devaluations in the built environment is spectacular enough and fits, in general, with the theoretical argument. ...

Marx's extensive analysis of fixed capital in relation to accumulation reveals a central contradiction. On the one hand, fixed capital enhances the productivity of labour and thereby contributes to the accumulation of capital. But, on the other hand, it functions as a use value and requires the conversion of exchange values into a physical asset which has certain attributes. The exchange value locked up in this physical use value can be recouped only by keeping the use value fully employed over its lifetime, which for simplicity's sake we will call its 'amortization time'. As a use value the fixed capital cannot easily be altered and so it tends to freeze productivity at a certain level until the end of the amortization time. If new and more productive fixed capital comes into being before the old is amortized, then the exchange value still tied up in the old is devalued. Resistance to this devaluation checks the rise in productivity and, thus, restricts accumulation. On the other hand the pursuit of new and more productive forms of fixed capital – dictated by the quest for relative surplus value – accelerates devaluations of the old.

We can identify exactly these same contradictory tendencies in relation to investment in the built environment, although they are even more exaggerated here because of the generally long amortization time involved, the fixity in space of the asset, and the composite nature of the commodity involved. We can demonstrate the argument most easily using the case of investment in transportation.

The cost, speed and capacity of the transport system relate directly to accumulation because of the impacts these have on the turnover time of capital. Investment and innovation in transport are therefore potentially productive for capital in general. Under capitalism, consequently, we see a tendency to 'drive beyond all spatial barriers' and to 'annihilate space with time' (to use Marx's own expressions).[2] This process is, of course, characterized typically by 'long waves' of the sort which we have already identified, uneven development in space and periodic massive devaluations of capital.[3]

We are here concerned, however, with the contradictions implicit in the process of transport development itself. Exchange values are committed to create 'efficient' and 'rational' configurations for spatial movement at a particular historical moment. There is, as it were, a certain striving towards spatial equilibrium, spatial harmony. On the other hand, accumulation for accumulation's sake spawns continuous revolutions in transportation technology as well as a perpetual striving to overcome spatial barriers – all of which is disruptive of any existing spatial configuration.

We thus arrive at a paradorx. In order to overcome spatial barriers and to annihilate space with time, spatial structures are created with themselves act as barriers to further accumulation. These spatial structures are expressed in the form of immobile transport facilities and ancillary facilities implanted in the landscape. We can in fact extended this conception to encompass the formation of the built environment as a whole. Capital represents itself in the form of a physical landscape created in its own image, created as use values to enhance the progressive accumulation of capital. The geographical landscape which results is the crowning glory of past capitalist development. But at the same time it expresses the power of dead labour over living labour and as such it imprisons and inhibits the accumulation process within a set of specific physical constraints. And these can be removed only slowly unless there is a substantial devaluation of the exhange value locked up in the creation of these physical assets.

Capitalist development has therefore to negotiate a knife-edge path between preserving the exchange values of past capital investments in the built enviroment and destroying the value of these investments in order to open up fresh room for accumulation. Under capitalism there is, then, a perpetual struggle in which capital builds a physical landscape appropriate to its own condition at a particular moment in time, only to have to destroy it, usually in the course of a crisis, at a subsequent point in time. The temporal and geographical ebb and flow of investment in the built environment can be understood only in terms of such a process. The effects of the internal contradictions of capitalism, when projected into the specific context of fixed and immobile investment in the built environment, are thus writ large in the historical geography of the landscape which results.

Class Struggle, Accumulation and the Urban Process under Capitalism

What, then, of overt class struggle – the resistance which the working class collectively offers to the violence which the capitalist form of accumulation inevitably inflincts upon it? This resistance, once it becomes more than merely nominal, must surely affect the urban process under capitalism in definite ways...

The central point of tension between capital and labour lies in the workplace and is expressed in struggles over the work process and the wage rate. These struggles take place in a context. The nature of the demands, the capacity of workers to organize and the resolution with which the struggles are waged, depend a great deal upon the contextual conditions. The law (property rights, contract, combination and association, etc.) together with the power of the capitalist class to enforce their will through the use of state power are obviously fundamental as any casual reading of labour history will abundantly illustrate. What specifically interests me here, however, is the process of reproduction of labour power in relation to class struggle in the workplace....

Some remarks on the housing question

The demand for adequate shelter is clearly high on the list of priorities from the standpoint of the working class. Capital is also interested in commodity production for the consumption fund provided this presents sufficient opportunities for accumulation. The broad lines of class struggle around the 'housing question' have had a major impact upon the urban process. We can trace some of the links back to the workplace directly. The agglomeration and concentration of production posed an immediate quantitative problem for housing workers in the right locations – a problem which the capitalist intitially sought to resolve by the production of company housing but which thereafter was left to the market system. The cost of shelter is an important item in the cost of labour power. The more workers have the capacity to press home wage demands, the more capital becomes concerned about the cost of shelter. But housing is more than just shelter. To begin with, the whole structure of consumption in general relates to the form which housing provision takes. The dilemmas of potentional overaccumulation which faced the United States in 1945 were in part resolved by the creation of a whole new life style through the rapid proliferation of the suburbanization process. Furthermore, the social unrest of the 1930s in that country pushed the bourgeoisie to adopt a policy of individual homeownership for the more affluent workers as a means to ensure social stability. This solution had the added advantage of opening up the housing sector as a means for rapid accumulation through commodity production. So successful was this solution that the housing sector became a Keynesian 'contra-cyclical' regulator for the accumulation process as a whole, at least until the *débâcle* of 1973. The lines of class struggle in France were markedly different (see Houdeville, 1969). With a peasant sector to ensure social stability in the form of small-scale private property-ownership, the housing problem was seen politically mainly in terms of costs. The rent control of the inter-war years reduced housing costs but curtailed housing as a field for commodity production with all kinds of subsequent effects on the scarcity and quality of housing provision. Only after 1958 did the housing sector open up as a field for investment and accumulation and this under government stimulus. Much of what has happened in the housing field and the shape of the 'urban' that has resulted can be explained only in terms of these various forms of class struggle.

The 'moral influence' of suburbanization as an antidote to class struggle

The second example I shall take is even more complex. Consider in its broad outlines, the history of the bourgeois response to acute threats of civil strife which are often associated with marked concentrations of the working class and the unemployed in space. The revolutions of 1848 across Europe, the Paris Commune of 1871, the urban violence which accompanied the great railroad strikes of 1877 in the United States and the Haymarket incident in Chicago, clearly demonstrated the revolutionary dangers associated with the high concentration of the 'dangerous classes' in certain areas. The bourgeois response was in part characterized by a policy of dispersal so that the poor and the working class could be subjected to what nineteenth-century urban reformers on both sides of the Atlantic called the 'moral influence' of the suburbs. Cheap suburban land, housing and cheap transportation were all a part of this solution entailing, as a consequence, a certain form and volume of investment in the built environment on the part of the bourgeoisie. To the degree that this policy was necessary, it had an important impact upon the shape of both British and American cities. And what was the bourgeois response to the urban riots of the 1960s in the ghettos of the United States? Open up the suburbs, promote low-income and black homeownership,

improve access via the transport system . . .
the parallels are remarkable.

The doctrine of 'community improvement' and its contradictions

The alternative to dispersal is what we now call 'gilding the ghetto' – but this, too, is a well-tried and persistent bourgeois response to a structural problem which just will not disappear. As early as 1812, the Reverend Thomas Chalmers wrote with horror of the spectre of revolutionary violence engulfing Britain as working-class populations steadily concentrated in large urban areas. Chalmers saw the 'principle of community' as the main bulwark of defence against this revolutionary tide – a principle which, he argued, should be deliberately cultivated to persuade all that harmony could be established around the basic institutions of community, a harmony which could function as an antidote to class war. The principle entailed a commitment to community improvement and a commitment to those institutions, such as the church and civil government, capable of forging community spirit. From Chalmers through Octavia Hill and Jane Addams, through the urban reformers such as Joseph Chamberlin in Britain, the 'moral reformers' in France and the 'progressives' in the United States at the end of the nineteenth century, through to model cities programmes and citizen participation, we have a continuous thread of bourgeois response to the problems of civil strife and social unrest.

But the 'principle of community' is not a bourgeois invention. It has also its authentic working-class counterpart as a defensive and even offensive weapon in class struggle. The conditions of life in the community are of great import to the working class and they can therefore become a focus of struggle which can assume a certain relative autonomy from that waged in the factory. The institutions of community can be captured and put to work for working-class ends. The church in the early years of the industrial revolution was on occasion mobilized at the local level in the interests of

the working class much as it also became a focus for the black liberation movement in the United States in the 1960s and is a mobilization point for class struggle in the Basque country of Spain. The principle of community can then become a springboard for class action rather than an antidote to class struggle. Indeed, we can argue that the definition of community as well as the command of its institutions is one of the stakes in class struggle in capitalist society. This struggle can break open into innumerable dimensions of conflict, pitting one element within the bourgeoisie against another and various fragments of the working class against others as the principles of 'turf' and 'community autonomy' become an essential part of life in capitalist society. The bourgeoisie has frequently sought to divide and rule but just as frequently has found itself caught in the harvest of contradictions it has helped to sow. We find 'bourgeois' suburbanites resisting the further accumulation of capital in the built environment, individual communities in competition for development producing a grossly inefficient and irrational spatial order even from the standpoint of capital at the same time as they incur levels of indebtedness which threaten financial stability (the well-publicized current problems of New York are, for example, typical for the historical experience of the United States). We find also civil disorder within the urban process escalating out of control as ethnic, religious and racial tensions take on their own dynamic in partial response to bourgeois promptings (the use of ethnic and racial differences by the bourgeoisie to split the organization in the workplace has a long and ignoble history in the United States in particular).

Working-class resistance and the circulation of capital

The strategies of dispersal, community improvement and community competition, arising as they do out of the bourgeois response to class antagonisms, are fundamental to understanding the material history of the urban process under capitalism. And they are not without their implications for the circulation of capital either. The direct victories and concessions won by the working class have their impacts. But at this point we come back to the principles of accumulation, because if the capitalist class is to reproduce itself and its domination over labour it must effectively render whatever concessions labour wins from it consistent with the rules governing the productivity of investments under capitalist accumulation. Investments may switch from one sphere to another in response to class struggle to the degree that the rules for the accumulation of capital are observed. Investment in working-class housing or in a national health service can thus be transformed into a vehicle for accumulation via commodity production for these sectors. Class struggle can, then, provoke 'switching crises', the outcome of which can change the structure of investment flows to the advantage of the working class. But those demands which lie within the economic possibilities of accumulation as a whole can in the end be conceded by the capitalist class without loss. Only when class struggle pushes the system beyond its own internal potentialities, is the accumulation of capital and the reproduction of the capitalist class called into question. How the bourgeoisie responds to such a situation depends on the possibilities open to it. For example, if capital can switch geographically to pastures where the working class is more compliant, then it may seek to escape the consequences of heightened class struggle in this way. Otherwise it must invest in economic, political and physical repression or simply fall before the working-class onslaught.

Class struggle thus plays its part in shaping the flows of capital between spheres and regions. The timing of the 'long waves' of investment in the built environment of Paris, for example, is characterized by deep troughs in the years of revolutionary violence – 1830, 1848, 1871. At first sight the rhythm appears to be dictated by purely political events yet the typical 15–25-year rhythm works just as well here as it does in other countries where political agitation was much less remarkable. The dynamics of class struggle are not immune to influences stemming from the rhythms of capitalist accumulation, of course, but it would be too simplistic to interpret the political events in Paris simply in these terms. What seems so extraordinary is that the overall rhythms of accumulation remain broadly intact in spite of the variations in the intensity of working-class struggle.

But if we think it through, this is not, after all, so extraordinary. We still live in a capitalist society. And if that society has survived then it must have done so by imposing those laws of accumulation whereby it reproduces itself. To put it this way is not to diminish working-class resistance, but to show that a struggle to abolish the wages system and the domination of capital over labour must necessarily look to the day when the capitalist laws of accumulation are themselves relegated to the history books. And until that day, the capitalist laws of accumulation, replete with all of their internal contradictions, must necessarily remain the guiding force in our history.

NOTES

1 The whole question of the capital surplus in the eighteenth century was first raised by Postan (1935) and subsequently elaborated on by Deane and Cole (1967). Recent studies on the financing of turnpikes and of canals in Britain by Albert (1972) and Ward (1974) provide some more detailed information.

2 I have attempted a much more extensive treatment of the transport problem in Harvey (1975).

3 See Isard (1942) for some interesting material.

REFERENCES

Albert, W. 1972: *The Turnpike Road System in England*. Cambridge: Cambridge University Press.

Deane, P. and Cole, W. A. 1967: *British Economic Growth, 1688–1959: Trends and Structure*. Cambridge: Cambridge University Press.

Harvey, D. 1975: The geography of capitalist accumulation: a reconstruction of the marxian theory. *Antipode* 7 (2), 9–21.

Houdeville, L. 1969: *Pour une civilisation de l'habitat*. Paris: Editions Ouvrières.

Isard, W. 1942: A neglected cycle: the transport building cycle. *Review of Economics and Statistics* 24, 149–58.

Marx, K. edn. 1967: *Capital* (3 vols), New York: International Publishers.

Postan, M. 1935: Recent trends in the accumulation of capital. *Economic History Review* 6, 1–12.

Ward, J. R. 1974: *The Finance of Canal Building in the Eighteenth Century*. Oxford: Oxford University Press.

Chapter 15

An Introduction to the Information Age

Manuel Castells

In the last decade I was struck, as many have been, by a series of major historical events that have transformed our world/ our lives. Just to mention the most important: the diffusion and deepening of the information technology revolution, including genetic engineering; the collapse of the Soviet Union, with the consequent demise of the international Communist movement, and the end of the Cold War that had marked everything for the last half a century; the restructuring of capitalism; the process of globalization; emergence of the Pacific as the most dynamic area of the global economy; the paradoxical combination of a surge in nationalism and the crisis of the sovereign nation-state; the crisis of democratic politics, shaken by periodic scandals and a crisis of legitimacy; the rise of feminism and the crisis of patriarchalism; the widespread diffusion of ecological consciousness; the rise of communalism as sources of resistance to globalization, taking in many contexts the form of religious fundamentalism; last, but not least, the development of a global criminal economy that is having significant impacts in international economy, national politics, and local everyday life.

I grew increasingly dissatisfied with the interpretations and theories, certainly including my own, that the social sciences were using to make sense of this new world. But I did not give up the rationalist project of understanding all this, in a coherent manner, that could be somewhat empirically grounded and as much as possible theoretically oriented. Thus, for the last 12 years I undertook the task of researching and understanding this wide array of social trends, working in and on the United States, Western Europe, Russia, Asian Pacific, and Latin America. Along the way, I found plenty of company, as researchers from all horizons are converging in this collective endeavour.

My personal contribution to this understanding is the book in three volumes that I have now completed, *The Information Age*, with the first volume already published, and the two others scheduled for publication in 1997. The first volume analyses the new social structure, the network society. The second volume studies social movements and political processes, in the framework of and in interaction with the network society. The third volume attempts an interpretation of macro-social processes, as a result of the interaction between the power of networks and the power of identity, focusing on themes such as the collapse of the Soviet Union, the emergence of the Pacific, or the ongoing process of global social exclusion and polarization. It also proposes a general theoretical synthesis.

I will take this opportunity to share with you the main lines of my argument, hoping that this will help a debate that I see emerging from all directions in the whole world. I see coming a new wave of intellectual innovation in which, by the way, British researchers are at the forefront.

Trying to summarize a considerable amount of material within one hour, I will follow a schematic format. I will focus on identifying the main features of what I consider to be the emerging, dominant social structure, the network society, that I find characteristic of informational capitalism, as constituted throughout the world. I will not indulge in futurology: everything I say is based on what I have perceived, rightly or wrongly, already at work in our societies. I will organize my lecture in one disclaimer, nine hypotheies, and one conclusion.

Disclaimer

I shall focus on the structure/dynamics of the network society, not on its historical genesis, that is how and why it came about, although in my book I propose a few hints about it. For the record: in my view, it resulted from the historical convergence of three **independent** processes, from whose interaction emerged the network society:

- The Information Technology Revolution, constituted as a paradigm in the 1970s.
- The restructuring of capitalism and of statism in the 1980s, aimed at superseding their contradictions, with sharply different outcomes.
- The cultural social movements of the 1960s, and their 1970s aftermath (particularly feminism and ecologism).

The Information Technology Revolution DID NOT create the network society. But without Information Technology, the Network Society would not exist.

Rather than providing an abstract categorization of what this Network Society is, let me summarize its main features and processes, before attempting a synthesis of its embedded logic in the diversity of its cultural/institutional variations. There is no implicit hierarchy in the sequence of presentation of these features. They all interact in, guess what, a network.

1 An Informational Economy

It is an economy in which sources of productivity and competitiveness for firms, regions, countries, depend, more than ever, on knowledge, information, and the technology of their processing, including the technology of management, and the management of technology. This is not the same as a service economy. There is informational agriculture, informational manufacturing, and different types of informational services, while a large number of service activities, e.g. in the developing world, are not informational at all.

The informational economy opens up an extraordinary potential for solving our problems, but, because of its dynamism and creativity, it is potentially more exclusionary than the industrial economy if social controls do not check the forces of unfettered market logic.

2 A Global Economy

This is not the same as a world economy. That has existed, in the West, at least since the sixteenth century. The global economy is a new reality: it is an economy whose core, strategically dominant activities have the potential of working as a unit in real time on a planetary scale. This is so for financial and currency markets, advanced business services, technological innovation, high technology manufacturing, media communication.

Most economic activity in the world, and most employment are not only national but regional or local. But, except for subsistence economies, the fate of these activities, and of their jobs, depend ultimately on the dynamics of the global economy, to which they are connected through networks and markets. Indeed, if labour tends to be local, capital is by and large globalized – not a small detail in a capitalist economy. This globalization has developed as a fully fledged system only in the last two decades, on the basis of information/communication technologies that were previously not available.

The global economy reaches out to the whole planet, but it is not planetary, it does not include the whole planet. In fact, it excludes probably a majority of the population. It is characterized by an extremely uneven geography. It scans the whole world, and links up valuable inputs, markets, and individuals, while switching off unskilled labour and poor markets. For a significant part of people around the world, there is a shift, from the point of view of dominant systemic interests, from exploitation to structural irrelevance.

This is different from the traditional First World/Third World opposition, because the Third World has become increasingly diversified, internally, and the First World has generated social exclusion, albeit in lesser proportion, within its own boundaries. Thus, I propose the notion of the emergence of a Fourth World of exclusion, made up not only of most of Africa, and rural Asia, and of Latin American shanties, but also of the South Bronx, La Courneuve, Kamagasaki, or Tower Hamlets of this world. A fourth world that, as I document extensively in volume three, is predominantly populated by women and children.

3 The Network Enterprise

At the heart of the connectivity of the global economy and of the flexibility of informational capitalism, there is a new form of organization, characteristic of economic activity, but gradually extending its logic to other domains and organizations: the **network enterprise**. This is not the same as a network of enterprises. It is a network made either from firms or segments of firms, or from internal segmentation of firms. Multinational corporations, with their internal decentralization, and their links with a web of subsidiaries and suppliers throughout the world, are but one of the forms of this network enterprise. But others include strategic alliances between corporations, networks of small and medium businesses (such as in northern Italy or Hong Kong), and link-ups between corporations and networks of small businesses through subcontracting and outsourcing.

So, the network enterprise is the specific set of linkages between different firms or segments, organized ad hoc for a specific project, and dissolving/reforming after the task is completed, e.g. IBM, Siemens, Toshiba. This ephemeral unit, The Project, around which a network of partners is built, is the actual operating unit of our economy, the one that generates profits or losses, the one that received rewards or goes bust, and the one that hires and lays off, via its member organizations.

4 The Transformation of Work and Employment: The Flexi-workers

Work is at the heart of all historical transformations. And there is no exception to this. But the coming of the Information Age is full of myths about the fate of work and employment.

With the exception, and an important one, of Western Europe, there is no major surge of unemployment in the world after two decades of diffusion in information technology. Indeed, there is much higher unemployment in technologically laggard countries, regions, and sectors.

All evidence and analysis points to the variable impact of technology on jobs depending on a much broader set of factors, mainly firms' strategies and governments' policies. Indeed, the two most technologically advanced economies, the US and Japan, both display a low rate of unemployment. In the US in the last four years there is a net balance of 10 million new jobs, and their educational content for these new jobs is significantly higher than that of the pre-existing social structure: many more information-intensive jobs than hamburger flippers jobs have been created. Even manufacturing jobs are at an all time high on a global perspective: between 1970 and 1989, manufacturing jobs in the world increased by 72 per cent, even if OECD countries, particularly the US and the UK, have indeed de-industrialized.

There is certainly a major unemployment problem in the European Union, as a result of a combination of rigidities in the institutional environment, strategies of global redeployment by firms and, more importantly, the restrictive macroeconomic policies induced by an insane obsession with fitting in the Maastricht criteria that nobody, and particularly not Germany, will be able to qualify for, in an incredible example of collective alienation in paying respect to gods of economic orthodoxy that have taken existence independently from us.

There is indeed a serious unemployment problem in the inner cities of America, England, or France, among the uneducated and switched off populations, or in low technology countries around the world, particularly in the rural areas.

For the majority of people in America, for instance, unemployment is not a problem. And yet, there is tremendous anxiety and discontent about work. There is a real base for this concern:

(a) There is the transformation of power relationships between capital and labour in favour of capital, through the process of socio-economic restructuring that took place in the 1980s, both in a conservative environment (Reagan, Thatcher), and, to a lesser but real extent, in a less conservative environment (Spain, France). In this sense, new technologies allowed business to either automate or offshore production or outsource supplies or to subcontract to smaller firms or to obtain concessions from labour or all the above.

(b) The development of the network enterprise translates into downsizing, subcontracting, and networking of labour, inducing flexibility of both business and labour, and individualization of contractual arrangements between management and labour. So, instead of layoffs what we often have are layoffs followed by subcontracting of services on an ad hoc, consulting basis, for the time and task to be performed, without job tenure and without social benefits provided by the firm.

This is indeed the general trend, exemplified by the rapid growth in all countries of self-employment, temporary work, and part-time, particularly for women. In England, between 40 and 45 per cent of the labour force seems to be already in these categories, as opposed to full time, regularly salaried employment, and is growing. Some studies in Germany project that in 2015, about 50 per cent of the labour force would be out of stable employment. And in the most dynamic region in the world, Silicon Valley, a recent study we have just completed shows that, in the midst of a job creation explosion, in the last ten years, between 50 per cent at least and 90 per cent of new jobs, most of them highly paid, are of this kind of non-standard labour arrangements.

The most significant change in work in the information age is the reversal of the socialization/salarization of labour that characterized the industrial age. The 'organization man' is out, the 'flexible woman' is in. The individualization of work, and therefore of labour's bargaining power, is the major feature characterizing employment in the network society.

5 Social Polarization and Social Exclusion

The processes of globalization, business networking, and individualization of labour weaken social organizations and institutions that represented/protected workers in the information age, particularly labour unions and the welfare state. Accordingly, workers are increasingly left to themselves in their differential relationship to management, and to the market place.

Skills and education, in a constant redefinition of these skills, become critical in valorizing or devaluing people in their work. But even valuable workers may fall down for reasons of health, age, gender discrimination, or lack of capacity to adapt to a given task or position.

As a result of these trends, most societies in the world, and certainly OECD countries, with the US and the UK at the top of the scale, present powerful trends towards increasing inequality, social polarization and social exclusion. There is increasing accumulation of wealth at the top, and of poverty at the bottom.

In the US inequality has regressed to the pre-1920s period. In the limit, social exclusion creates pockets of dereliction with various entry points, but hardly any exits. It may be long-term unemployment, illness, functional illiteracy, illegal status, poverty, family disruption, psychological crisis, homelessness, drugs, crime, incarceration, etc. Once in this underworld, processes of exclusion reinforce each other, requiring a heroic effort to pull out from what I call the black holes of informational capitalism, that often have a territorial expression. The proportion of people in these black holes are staggering, and rapidly growing. In the US, it may reach above 10 per cent of the population, if you consider that simply the number of adults under the control of the justice system in 1966 was 5.4 million, that is almost 3 per cent of the population, while the proportion of people below the poverty line is 15 per cent.

The Information Age does not have to be the age of stepped-up inequality, polarization and social exclusion. But for the moment it is.

6 The Culture of Real Virtuality

Shifting to the cultural realm, we see the emergence of a similar pattern of networking, flexibility, and ephemeral symbolic communication, in a culture organized around electronic media, including in this communication system the computer-mediated communication networks. Cultural expressions of all kinds are increasingly enclosed in or shaped by this world of electronic media. But the new media system is not characterized by the one-way, undifferentiated messages through a limited number of channels that constituted the world of mass media. And it is not a global village.

Media are extraordinarily diverse, and send targeted messages to specific segments of audiences and to specific moods of the audiences. They are increasingly inclusive, bridging from one to another, from network TV to cable or satellite TV, radio, VCR, musical video, walkman type of devices, connected throughout the globe, and yet diversified by cultures, constituting a hypertext with extraordinary inclusive capacity. Furthermore, slowly but surely, this new media system is moving towards interactivity, particularly if we include CMC networks, and their access to text, images, and sounds, that will eventually link up with the current media system.

Instead of a global village we are moving towards mass production of customized cottages. While there is oligopolistic concentration of multimedia groups around the world, there is at the same time, market segmentation, and increasing interaction by and among the individuals that break up the uniformity of a mass audience. These processes induce the formation of what I call **the culture of real virtuality**. It is so, and not virtual reality, because when our symbolic environment is, by and large, structured in this inclusive, flexible, diversified hypertext, in which we navigate every day, the virtuality of this text is in fact our reality, the symbols from which we live and communicate.

7 Politics

This enclosure of communication in the space of flexible media does not only concern culture. It has a fundamental effect on **politics**. In all countries, the media have become the essential space of politics. Not all politics takes place through the media, and imagemaking still needs to relate to real issues and real conflicts. But without significant presence in the space of media, actors and ideas are reduced to political marginality. This presence does not concern only, or even primarily, the moments of political campaigns, but the day-to-day messages that people receive by and from the media.

I propose the following analysis:

To an overwhelming extent people receive their information, on the basis of which they form their political opinion, and structure their behaviour, through the media, particularly television and radio.

- Media politics needs to simplify the message/proposals.
- The simplest message is an image. The simplest image is a person. Political competition revolves around personalization of politics.
- The most effective political weapons are negative messages. The most effective negative message is character assassination of opponents' personalities. The politics of scandal, in the US, in Europe, in Japan, in Latin America etc. is the predominant form of political struggle.
- Political marketing is the essential means to win political competition in democratic politics. In the information age it involves media advertising, telephone banks, targeted mailing, image making, image unmaking, image control, presence in the media, staging of public appearances etc. This makes it an excessively expensive business, way beyond that of traditional party politics, so that mechanisms of political financing are obsolete, and parties use access to power as a way to generate resources to stay in power or to prepare to return to it. This is the fundamental source of political corruption, to which intermediaries add a little personal twist. This is also at the source of systemic corruption, that feeds scandal politics. The use of scandal as a weapon leads to increased expense and activity in intelligence, damage

control, and access to the media. Once a market is created, intermediaries appear to retrieve, obtain, or fabricate information, offering it to the highest bidder. Politics becomes a horse race, and a soap opera motivated by greed, backstage manoeuvres, betrayals, and, often, sex and violence, becoming hardly distinguishable from TV scripts.

Those who survive in this world become politically successful, for a while. But what certainly does not survive, after a few rounds of these tricks, is political legitimacy, not to speak of citizens' hope.

8 Timeless Time

As with all historical transformations, the emergence of a new social structure is necessarily linked to the redefinition of the material foundations of life, **time and space**. Time and space are related, in society as in nature. Their meaning, and manifestations in social practice, evolve throughout histories and across cultures, as Giddens, Thrift, Harvey, Adams, Lash, and Urry, among others, have shown.

I propose the hypothesis that the network society, as the dominant social structure emerging in the Information Age, is organized around new forms of time and space: timeless time, the space of flows. These are the dominant forms, and not the forms in which most people live, but through their domination, they affect everybody. Let me explain, starting with time, then with some greater detail on space, given the specific interests of many in this conference.

In contrast to the rhythm of biological time of most of human existence, and to the clock time characterizing the industrial age, a new form of time characterizes the dominant logic of the network society: **timeless time**. It is defined by the use of new information/communication technologies in a relentless effort to annihilate time, to compress years in seconds, seconds in split seconds. Furthermore, the most fundamental aim is **to eliminate sequencing of** time, including past, present and future in the same hypertext, thus eliminating the 'succession of things' that, according to Leibniz, characterizes time, so that without things and their sequential ordering there is no longer time in society. We live, as in the recurrent circuits of the computer networks in the encyclopedia of historical experience, all our tenses at the same time, being able to reorder them in a composite created by our fantasy or our interests.

David Harvey has shown the relentless tendency of capitalism to eliminate barriers of time. But I think in the network society, that is indeed a capitalist society, but something else at the same time, all dominant processes tend to be constructed around timeless time. I find such a tendency in the whole realm of human activity. I find it certainly in the split second financial transactions of global financial markets, but I also find it, for instance, in instant wars, built around the notion of a surgical strike that devastates the enemy in a few hours, or minutes, to avoid politically unpopular, costly wars. Or in the blurring of the life cycle by new reproductive techniques, allowing people a wide range of options in the age and conditions of parenting, even storing their embryos to eventually produce babies later either by themselves, or through surrogate mothers, even after their procreators are dead. I find it in the twisting of working life by the variable chronology of labour trajectories and time schedules in increasingly diverse labour markets. And I find it in the vigorous effort to use medical technology, including genetic engineering, and computer-based medical care to exile death from life, to bring a substantial proportion of the population to a high level of life-expectancy, and to diffuse the belief that, after all, we are eternal, at least for some time.

As with space, timeless time characterizes dominant functions and social groups, while most people in the world are still submitted to biological time and to clock time. Thus, while instant wars characterize the technological powers, atrocious, lingering wars go on and on for years, around the planet, in a slow-motion destruction process, quasi-ignored by the world until they are discovered by some television programme.

I propose the notion that a fundamental struggle in our society is around the redefinition of time, between its annihilation or desequencing by networks, on one hand, and, on the other hand, the consciousness of glacial time, the slow-motion, intergenerational evolution of our species in our cosmological environment, a concept suggested by Lash and Urry, and a battle undertaken, in my view, by the environmental movement.

9 The Space of Flows

Many years ago (or at least it seems to me as many) I proposed the concept of Space of Flows to make sense of a body of empirical observation: dominant functions were increasingly operating on the basis of exchanges between electronic circuits linking up information systems in distant locations. Financial markets, global media, advanced business services, technology, information. In addition, electronically based, fast transportation systems reinforced this pattern of distant interaction by following up with movements of people and goods. Furthermore, new location patterns for most activities follow a simultaneous logic of territorial concentration/decentralization, reinstating the unity of their operation by electronic links, e.g. the analysis proposed in the 1980s on location patterns of high tech manufacturing; or the networked articulation of advanced services throughout the world, under the system labelled as 'global city'.

Why keep the term of space under these conditions? Reasons: (1) These electronic circuits do not operate in the territorial vacuum. They link up territorially based complexes of production, management and information, even though the meaning and functions of these complexes depend on their connection in these networks of flows. (2) These technological linkages are material, e.g. depend on specific telecommunication/transportation facilities, and on the existence and quality of information systems, in a highly uneven geography. (3) The meaning of space evolves – as the meaning of time. Thus, instead of indulging in futurological statements such as the vanishing of space, and the end of cities, we should be able to reconceptualize new forms of spatial arrangements under the new technological paradigm.

To proceed with this conceptualization I build on a long intellectual tradition, from Leibniz to Harold Innis, connecting space and time, around the notion of space as coexistence of time. Thus, my definition: space is the material support of time-sharing social practices.[1]

What happens when the time-sharing of practices (be it synchronous or asynchronous) does not imply contiguity? 'Things' still exist together, they share time, but the material arrangements that allow this coexistence are inter-territorial or transterritorial: **the space of flows is the material organization of time-sharing social practices that work through flows.** What concretely this material organization is depends on the goals and characteristics of the networks of flows, for instance I can tell you what it is in the case of high technology manufacturing or in the case of global networks of drug traffic. However, I did propose in my analysis some elements that appear to characterize the space of flows in all kinds of networks: electronic circuits connection information systems; territorial nodes and hubs; locales of support and social cohesion for dominant social actors in the network (e.g. the system of VIP spaces throughout the world).

Dominant functions tend to articulate themselves around the space of flows. But this is not the only space. **The space of places continues to be the predominant space of experience**, of everyday life, and of social and political control. Places root culture and transmit history. (A place is a locale whose form, function, and meaning, from the point of view of the social actor, are contained within the boundaries of physical contiguity.)

In the network society, a fundamental form of social domination is **the prevalence of the logic of the space of flows over the space of places.** The space of flows structures and shapes the space of places, as when the differential fortunes of capital accumulation in global financial markets reward or punish specific regions, or when telecom systems link up CBDs to outlying suburbs in new office development, bypassing/marginalizing poor urban neighbourhoods. The domination of the space of flows over the space of places induces intra-**metropolitan dualism** as a most important form of social/territorial exclusion, that has become as significant as regional uneven development. The simultaneous growth and decline of economies and societies within the same metropolitan area is a most fundamental trend of territorial organization, and a key challenge to urban management nowadays.

But there is still something else in the new spatial dynamics. Beyond the opposition between the space of flows and the space of places. As information/communication networks diffuse in society, and as technology is appropriated by a variety of social actors, segments of the space of flows are penetrated by forces of resistance to domination, and by expressions of personal experience. Examples:

(a) Social movements. Zapatistas and the Internet (but from the Lacandona forest). But also American Militia.

(b) Local governments, key agents of citizen representation in our society, linking up through electronic networks, particularly in Europe (see research by Stephen Graham).

(c) Expressions of experience in the space of flows.

Thus, we do witness an increasing penetration, and subversion, of the space of flows, originally set up for the functions of power, by the power of experience, inducing a set of contradictory power relationships. Yes, it is still an elitist mean of communication, but it is changing rapidly. The problem is to integrate these observations in some theory, but for this we still lack research, in spite of some insightful elaborations, such as the one by Sherry Turkle at MIT.

The new frontier of spatial research is in examining the interaction between the space of flows, the space of places, function, meaning, domination, and challenge to domination, in increasingly complex and contradictory patterns. Homesteading in this frontier is already taking place, as shown in the pioneering research by Graham and Marvin, or in the reflections of Bill Mitchell, but we are clearly at the beginning of a new field of study that should help us to understand **and to change** the currently prevailing logic in the space of flows.

Conclusion: The Network Society

So, what is the Network Society? It is a society that is structured in its dominant functions and processes around networks. In its current manifestation it is a capitalist society. Indeed, we live more than ever in a capitalist world, and thus an analysis in terms of capitalism is necessary and complementary to the theory of the network society. But this particular form of capitalism is very different from industrial capitalism, as I have tried to show.

The Network Society is not produced by information technology. But without the information technology revolution it could not be such a comprehensive, pervasive social form, able to link up, or de-link, the entire realm of human activity.

So, is that all? Just a morphological transformation? Well, historically, transformation of social forms has always been fundamental, both as expressions and sources of major social processes, e.g. standardized mass production in the large factory as characteristic of the so-called fordism, as a major form of capitalist social organization; or the rational bureaucracy

as the foundation of modern society, in the Weberian conception.

But this morphological transformation is even more significant because the network architecture is particularly dynamic, open-ended, flexible, potentially able to expand endlessly, without rupture, bypassing/disconnecting undesirable components following instructions of the networks' dominant nodes. Indeed, the February 1997 Davos meeting titled the general programme of its annual meeting 'Building the Network Society'.

This networking logic is at the roots of major effects in our societies. Using it:

- capital flows can bypass controls
- workers are individualized, outsourced, subcontracted
- communication becomes at the same time global and customized
- valuable people and territories are switched on, devalued ones are switched off.

The dynamics of networks push society towards an endless escape from its own constraints and controls, towards an endless supersession and reconstruction of its values and institutions, towards a meta-social, constant rearrangement of human institutions and organizations.

Networks transform power relationships. Power in the traditional sense still exists: capitalists over workers, men over women, state apparatuses still torture bodies and silence minds around the world.

Yet, there is a higher order of power: the power of flows in the networks prevails over the flows of power. Capitalists are dependent upon uncontrollable financial flows; many workers are at the same time investors (often unwillingly through their pension funds) in this whirlwind of capital; networkers are inter-related in the logic of the network enterprise, so that their jobs and income depend on their positioning rather than on their work. States are bypassed by global flows of wealth, information, and crime. Thus, to survive, they band together in multilateral ventures, such as the European Union. It follows the creation of a web of political institutions: national, supranational, international, regional, and local, that becomes the new operating unit of the information age: the network state.

In this complexity, the communication between networks and social actors depends increasingly on shared CULTURAL CODES. If we accept certain values, certain categories that frame the meaning of experience, then the networks will process them efficiently, and will return to each one of us the outcome of their processing, according to the rules of domination and distribution inscripted in the network.

Thus, the challenges to social domination in the network society revolve around the redefinition of cultural codes, proposing alternative meaning and changing the rules of the game. This is why the affirmation of IDENTITY is so essential, because it fixes meaning autonomously *vis-à-vis* the abstract, instrumental logic of networks. I am, thus I exist. In my empirical investigation I have found identity-based social

movements aimed at changing the cultural foundations of society to be the essential sources of social change in the information age, albeit often in forms and with goals that we do not usually associate with positive social change. Some movements, that appear to be the most fruitful and positive, are proactive, such as feminism and environmentalism. Some are reactive, as in the communal resistances to globalization built around religion, nation, territory, or ethnicity. But in all cases they affirm the preeminence of experience over instrumentality, of meaning over function, and, I would dare to say, of use value of life over exchange value in the networks.

The implicit logic of the Network Society appears to end history, by enclosing it into the circularity of recurrent patterns of flows. Yet, as with any other social form, in fact it opens up a new realm of contradiction and conflict, as people around the world refuse to become shadows of global flows and project their dreams, and sometimes their nightmares, into the light of new history making.

NOTES

1   Leibniz: 'Space is something purely relative, like time; space being an order of coexistences as time is an order of successions. For space denotes in terms of possibility and order of things that exist at the same time, in so far as they exist together. . . . When we see several things together we perceive this order of things among themselves.'

Chapter 16

from *Metropolis: From the Division of Labor to Urban Form*

Allen J. Scott

5 The Internal Production Space of the Metropolis: Some Illustrative Sketches

Industrialization and urbanization

In previous chapters, I have described how *protourban forms* emerge from the prespatial logic of commodity production, and how, through the intermediation of industrial organization processes, they take on definite geographical form. As I demonstrated, agglomerative tendencies will often appear with especial intensity in the vicinity of large propulsive industries. However, and more generally, I have also shown that the same impulse toward agglomeration can appear wherever any complex of interlocking units of production starts to develop and grow through the division of labor. Quite frequently, such units as these will consist only of small-scale, specialized, and highly disintegrated industrial establishments.

Much urbanization in capitalism is in fact posited upon various combinations of both large-scale basic industries and small-scale (often very labor-intensive) industries. The former industries were a notably important element of the landscape of the large metropolis over the period that saw the rise and consolidation of the American Manufacturing Belt and down through the era of Fordist industrialization stretching roughly from the 1920s to the

early 1970s. Many of these industries – above all in the nineteenth century – depended on heavy and bulky input materials such as coal, ore, or agricultural resources. These materials were (then as now) difficult and expensive to convey over long distances, especially in view of the more primitive transport technologies that prevailed in the last century. Thus, industrial plants in these sectors regularly congregated around natural resource sites or at nodal points where basic inputs could be cheaply assembled. Many major cities in the nineteenth century grew up on the basis of this sort of large-scale materials-intensive manufacturing, as, for example, in the cases of Pittsburgh with its steel industries, Minneapolis with its flour milling operations, and New Orleans with its sugar refineries. But Chicago is the nineteenth-century city par excellence whose emergence and growth are founded on this kind of industrialization. Fales and Moses (1972) have painted an elaborate picture of Chicago in the 1870s as a major nodal center with a burgeoning industrial base comprising such materials-intensive industries as meat packing, blast furnaces, foundries, brick making, brewing, glass production, and so on. These industries located for the most part close to central transport terminals in the city so that they could easily gain access to the raw materials of the hinterland and just as easily dispatch final outputs to widely dispersed markets in the northern and eastern United States, and thence to the rest of the world.

Many elementary accounts of urban development have actually attempted to construct paradigmatic explanations of the origins of urbanization in the nineteenth century around processes of locational convergence of this (essentially Weberian) type. As significant as these processes have undoubtedly been in many individual cases, however, they certainly do not capture fully and in all its subtlety the central dynamic of industrialization and urbanization. Indeed, in many respects, they represent no more than a very special case. If urban growth were truly founded only on the locational attraction to cheap transport sites of simple basic industries, actual patterns of urbanization in the nineteenth and twentieth centuries would have taken on a radically different aspect from the one they actually have. They would almost certainly have consisted only of a few large conglomerations of manufacturing industry at major resource locations and nodal centers with a wide scattering of mill towns elsewhere. We would in all probability *not* have observed the large numbers of hyper-enlarged urban areas with extremely variegated economic systems that are scattered across the face of the United States today. Even in the nineteenth century, cities such as Baltimore, Boston, Cincinnati, New York, and Philadelphia were patently very complicated geographical phenomena with highly differentiated industrial and trading activities and with considerable amounts of small-scale labor-intensive manufacturing in addition to basic large-scale materials-intensive forms. In the twentieth century, we can even point to some urban centers (the most dramatic case being, no doubt, Silicon Valley) that are effectively bereft of any pregiven locational advantage other than their own internal dynamic of growth and diversification. What is more, over the twentieth century, a very high proportion of the large-scale materials-intensive forms of manufacturing that formerly flourished near the core of the large metropolis has

effectively been eliminated from the urban environment. Much of this industry has decisively decentralized to suburban and peripheral areas in response to rising land and labor costs in the core and to falling transport costs generally. Notwithstanding the systematic decentralization of this element of the urban economic base, and despite occasional crises of the urban system, cities in the major capitalist countries continue to grow as the division of labor moves forward and as new innovative sectors of production make their historical appearance. The tendency toward massive urbanization of the economy in capitalism will undoubtedly continue to manifest itself so long as the logic of fragmentation, interaction, and agglomeration proceeds within growing segments of the economy.

This same logic leads not just to generalized urban agglomeration but also to the emergence of multiple dense industrial districts *within* the metropolis. The internal production spaces of large cities are composed of mosaics of particular kinds of industrial land use focused on localized nodal clusters comprising activities that range from manufacturing to office and service functions. In what now follows I shall examine in detail . . . gun and jewelry manufacture in Birmingham, England; . . . [and] clothing production in New York City . . .

Gun and jewelry manufacture in Birmingham

From the end of the eighteenth century and over much of the nineteenth and twentieth centuries, Birmingham developed as a unique center of small-scale crafts and trades based above all on various forms of metal-working activity. At the height of Birmingham's prosperity in the mid-nineteenth century, its wealth was founded on four major staple industries, i.e., brass goods, buttons, guns, and jewelry, though a bewildering variety of other kinds of manufactures also flourished in the city: e.g., bedsteads, steel pens, locks and latches, pins, nails, and hardware of all varieties.

Birmingham at this time was a living exemplification of Adam Smith's simple parable of the division of labor in manufacture. Virtually all of the specialized trades in the city were highly localized, and none more so than the gun and jewelry industries, in which the fragmentation of labor processes had proceeded very far indeed (Wise, 1949).

Gun manufacture. In the mid-nineteenth century, the Birmingham gun industry consisted of two major branches devoted to the production of sporting and military guns, respectively. At that time, vertical disintegration in the industry had advanced to a remarkable extent. Few if any guns were actually made from start to finish in one workshop. Instead, as Allen (1929) has indicated, a number of master gun makers organized the production process within two major strata of linkage relations. First, the master gun maker put out orders for various parts:

> He purchased materials from the barrel-makers, lock-makers, sight-stampers, trigger-makers, ramrod-forgers, gun-furniture makers, and, if he were engaged in the military branch, from bayonet-forgers. [Allen, 1929, p. 116]

Second, the parts thus acquired were then sent out to a wide variety of "setters-up," who performed the specialized functions leading to the assembly and the finishing of the gun:

> To name only a few, there were those who prepared the front sight and lump end of the barrels; the jiggers, who attended to the breech end; the stockers, who let in the barrel and lock and shaped the stock; the barrel-strippers, who prepared the gun for rifling and proof; the hardeners, polishers, borers and riflers, engravers, and finally the lock-freers, who adjusted the working parts. Some of these were individual outworkers employed by a particular master; others were shop owners working for several employers. [Allen, 1929, p. 117]

All of this fragmentation and interlinkage of gun making encouraged producers to converge locationally around their own center of gravity. In this manner, a specialized gun quarter came into existence close to the center of the city. Its endogenous transactional activities were visible in the very streetscape, for

> an army of boys was to be seen hurrying to and fro about the gun quarter performing the functions of porters. [Allen, 1929, p. 118]

Workshops accordingly huddled close together in order to expedite the whole process of disintegrated but interconnected production.

After the middle of the nineteenth century, there occurred a technological revolution in the process of gun manufacture. With the encouragement of the British government, capital-intensive, routinized, mass-production methods of gun making were imported from the United States, and these came rapidly to dominate the manufacture of guns for military purposes. Military gun production was now concentrated into a small number of large integrated plants located (significantly) in noncentral areas. The old centralized labor-intensive gun-making complex of Birmingham declined rapidly as a consequence. However, a rump of the old gun quarter has continued even down to the present day, though the workshops that now occupy the quarter produce only sporting guns for a rather restricted market. The geography of the Birmingham gun quarter as it was in 1948 is shown in figure 16.1 – a shadow of its former self, but still giving evidence of considerable vertical disintegration and clustering of functions.

Jewelry manufacture. Like the gun industry, the jewelry trades are located in a specialized district near the core of the city. These trades have been an important sector of the economy of Birmingham ever since the early nineteenth century, and they have remained a strongly identified element of the city's landscape throughout the twentieth century. Over this long period of time, the jewelry industry has experienced many

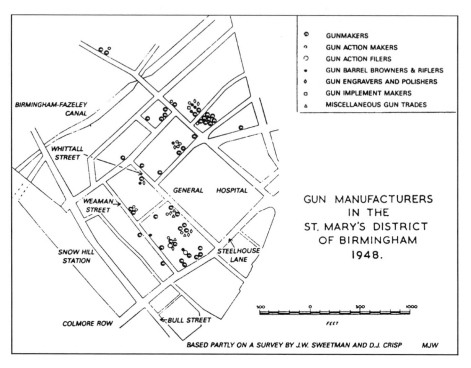

Figure 16.1   Gun manufacturers in the St. Mary's district of Birmingham, 1948.
Source: Wise (1949).

internal mutations as a result of the vagaries of demand and the intensity of competition.

One of the major characteristics of the industry is its proclivity to break up into an extraordinarily elaborate social division of labor. This leads directly to functional diversity and locational agglomeration. These phenomena have been described by Allen (1929, p. 56) in the following terms:

> As the [jewelry] trade grew, processes became more highly specialized and it became necessary for manufacturers who performed complementary operations on some article to be in close proximity to one another. Few makers of finished goods, moreover, were concerned with more than a narrow range of article, and it was an advantage for them to be grouped together since the factors through whom the jewelry was sold, and who required to purchase many different types, were then able to get in touch the more easily with their sources of supply.

Wise (1949) lists the following trades to be found in the central jewelry quarter in 1948: goldsmiths, silversmiths, electroplaters, medalists, gilt and imitation jewelry fabrication, gem sitting, stamping and piercing, engraving, polishing and enameling, die sinkers, jewelry repair, refiners, general outwork, factors and merchants, dealers in bullion and precious stones, jewelers' material suppliers, manufacturers of optical goods, watch-makers, and miscellaneous manufacturers. More than sixty percent of the firms in these trades had ten employees or fewer in 1948, and all were bound together in a dense structure of transactional interrelations. The net geographical result was a closely textured amalgam of workshops and factories huddled together near the core of the city as shown in figure 16.2.

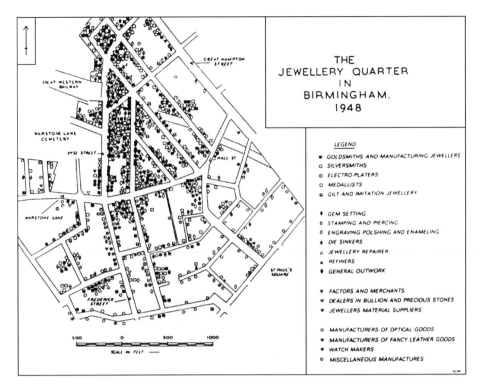

Figure 16.2 The jewelry quarter in Birmingham, 1948.
Source: Wise (1949).

Local labor markets. Through much of their history, both the gun and jewelry quarters of Birmingham have developed in close association with their own specialized local labor markets. Both are defined in part by a series of surrounding residential neighborhoods in which an abundance of workers with locally useful skills and experience could be found. In the nineteenth century, residents of these neighborhoods also engaged massively in homework at reduced rates of pay, and this helped to lower the overall costs of production both by keeping expenditures on labor low and by eliminating the need for various manufacturers' overheads.

These processes seem in general to point in the direction of a spatially recursive determination of intraurban locational patterns. On the one hand, workers gravitate to residential neighborhoods surrounding their places of work. On the other hand, employers have an incentive to locate close to the center of their main sources of labor. In both cases, high levels of mutual accessibility are the result. At the same time, the more any given cluster of producers grows in size, the more it will tend to become locationally focused on the very center of the city in order to maintain accessibility to its total labor force. Conversely, smaller clusters with limited labor demands will be more prone to locate at less accessible locations where land prices are comparatively low. These tendencies will be variously played out in the context of intense competition for land by alternative uses, as described by classical Von Thünen land-use theory. In these ways, specialized and localized territorial complexes of production, work, and local labor market activity are (for a time at least) sustained and reproduced within the fabric of the metropolis....

Clothing production in New York City

The clothing industry is a metropolitan industry first and foremost, and New York City has been the primary center of the industry in the United States throughout the present century.

The clothing industry is typically extremely volatile. Individual producers face uncertain markets, and they are constantly pushed into product differentiation strategies as a means of warding off the market depredations of their competitors. Consequently, the industry is characteristically organized around small labor-intensive plants producing restricted batches of output in limited runs. This, at least, is overwhelmingly the case with the New York industry, which specializes in the more fashion-oriented and competitive end of the market. The New York industry is also much given to fragmentation and subdivision of production processes. Often, manufacturers are only to a minor extent involved directly in the physical production of their own output; rather, they concentrate their efforts on design and marketing and farm out the intermediate stages of manufacture to subcontractors. Such work as cutting, sewing, buttonholing, pleating, hem-stitching, and so on is widely subcontracted out. Indeed, vertical disintegration in the New York clothing industry has proceeded to such an advanced degree that scores of different types of ancillary services form an integral part of the overall complex. Helfgott (1959, p. 63) alludes to the following typical cases of this phenomenon:

> the design, display and selling of textiles, sponging (cloth shrinking); factoring (textile banking); trucking; agencies that provide...models; the supplying of thread and trimming; embroidery; the manufacture of belts; and the repairing of machinery,

and the list could undoubtedly be extended many times over.

All of these different productive activities interpenetrate with one another in a tangled network of linkages. By the same token, they cluster compactly in geographical space, and in this way they form a specialized garment district in the core of the city. This clustering is accentuated both by the small scale of most interactions within the industry and by the need for intense face-to-face contacts in order to negotiate the details of sub-contract work and the precise specifications of needed inputs. It is even further accentuated by the elastic system that ties manufacturers and subcontractors together in mutual symbiosis. In this system, as Haig (1927, p. 81) has indicated, the manufacturer

> expands or reduces his group of contractors with the volume of the business attracted by his offering of garments. Because of the extreme uncertainty of this demand he delays his decisions regarding his models and the quantities until the latest possible moment. When he does arrive at his decision, action must be swift. He must engage sufficient contractors to supply the volume he has decided upon, and he must secure deliveries from them with a minimum loss of time.

This, of course, is precisely an informal verbal transposition of the abstract analysis of the logic of subcontracting under uncertainty.

Figures 16.3 to 16.5 indicate the locations of men's and women's clothing manufacturers in Manhattan in the earlier part of the twentieth century. Notice the extraordinarily dense spatial conflux of plants shown in these figures, and their collective tendency (especially among women's clothing producers) to move steadily uptown with the passage of time away from the financial center of Lower Manhattan and toward the major wholesale and retail market areas that lie north of 34th Street (Hoover and Vernon, 1959). Today, the industry is heavily concentrated in the midtown area of Manhattan within the few blocks that run from 34th Street in the south to 40th Street

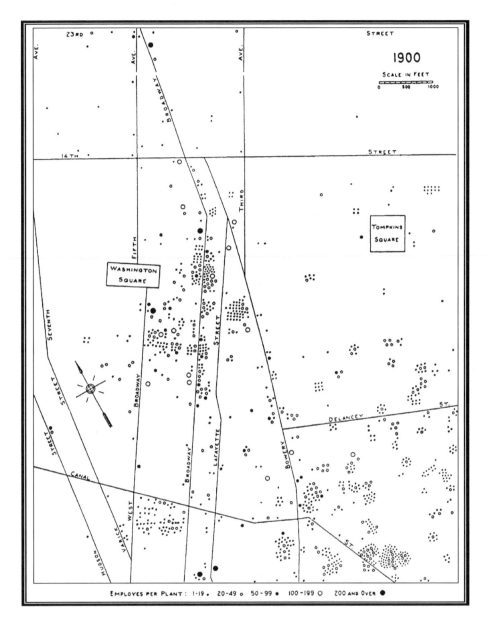

Figure 16.3 Location of plants in men's clothing industry in area of greatest concentration in Manhattan in 1900.

Source: Haig (1927).

in the north, and from Sixth Avenue in the east to Eighth Avenue in the west (see Figure 16.6). This area is a veritable hive of vertically disintegrated production and small-scale transactional activity.

Notwithstanding this very definite spatial nucleation of the New York clothing industry, considerable decentralization of plants has also been evident over the decades, and the industry is, indeed, organized at two different spatial levels. At its core in central Manhattan are those producers who are most directly involved in the high-fashion side of the market, where the

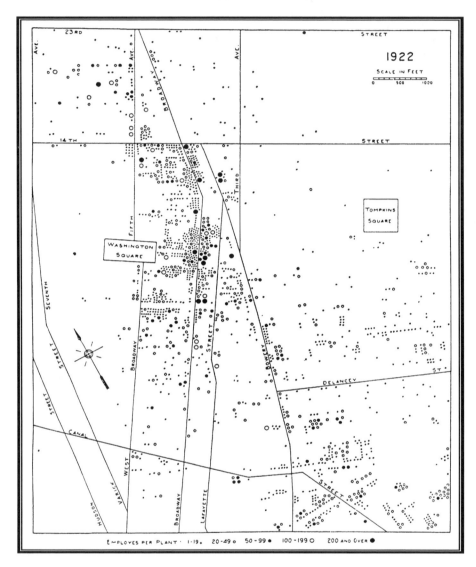

Figure 16.4 Location of plants in men's clothing industry in area of greatest concentration in Manhattan in 1922.

Source: Haig (1927).

style element is important, runs are short, and skilled labor (especially for cutting and sewing) is much in demand. In the periphery, all around the fringes of the Greater New York Region are scattered large numbers of subcontract shops performing more standardized, large-batch low-skilled work (sewing above all) for plants located in the core, (Kenyon, 1964). These geographical relationships are illuminated by the data presented in table 16.1, which shows the spatial distribution of the women's dress industry in the New York metropolitan region in 1946 and 1956 cross-tabulated by a price index of quality. The table reveals two important trends. First, the women's dress industry decentralized systematically from the core to the fringe between 1946 and 1956. Second, however, this decentralization has been

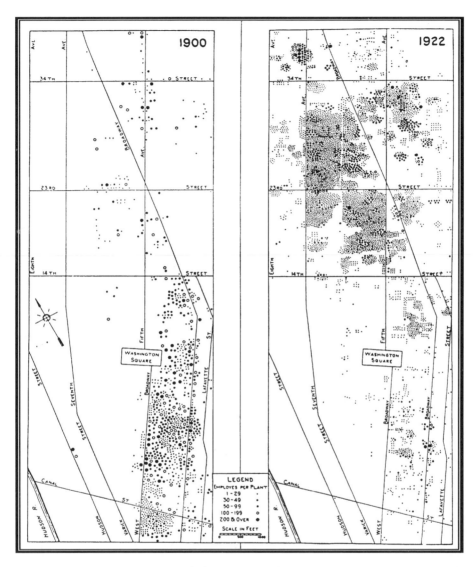

Figure 16.5 Location of plants in women's clothing industry in the area of greatest concentration in Manhattan in 1900 and 1922.

Source: Haig (1927).

most pronounced among shops producing lower-quality and standardized outputs. Shops producing higher-quality, more fashion-oriented outputs scarcely decentralized at all over the specified time period.

In the 1950s, there was particularly active decentralization of large, rapid-turnaround subcontractors to the old textile districts of southern Massachusetts and the anthracite regions of eastern Pennsylva-

nia, where much low-wage female labor could be readily found. These subcontractors were and are functionally connected to the industry of central New York, but by reason of their large scale of operation and their relatively standardized linkages they have been able efficiently to exploit locations in the periphery. Helfgott (1959, p. 105) has observed of this phenomenon:

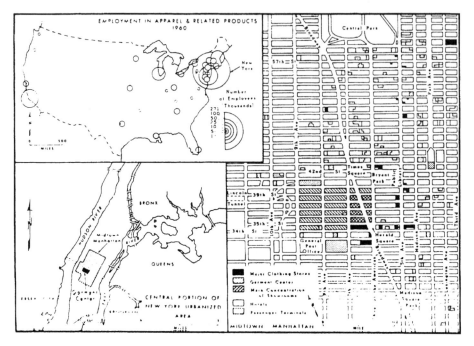

Figure 16.6   Midtown Manhattan garment center.

Source: Kenyon (1964).

Table 16.1:   Geographical distribution of the women's dress industry in the New York metropolitan region

Quality of dress (wholesale price)	1946		1956	
	New York City	Rest of metropolitan region	New York City	Rest of metropolitan region
	(% of total payroll)		(% of total payroll)	
under $5.75	78.1	28.9	40.2	59.8
$5.75–$16.75	81.8	18.2	62.9	37.1
over $16.75	98.7	1.3	94.3	5.7

Source: Helfgott (1959), p. 72.

In the unit priced dress industry the cost of hauling fabrics to points in eastern Pennsylvania and the garments on hangers back to New York ranges from 4 to 11.5 cents per dress, depending on the value of the dress. The slightest labor-cost differential between New York and out-of-town locations clearly compensates for the costs of trucking garments back and forth.

It should also be pointed out that these core/fringe relationships correspond to techno-logical differences between the plants located in the two areas. Central-city shops tend to operate on a making-through basis, (which means that a single operator does the work of making an entire garment). But shops in the periphery are for the most part organized on a section-work basis (which means that each garment is manu-factured by means of deskilled, technically divided labor processes). These differences further accentuate the contrasts between the two areas, and in particular, between the high-quality flexible forms of manufacturing in the core, and the lower-quality routinized forms of manufacturing in the periphery.

In recent years, the New York clothing industry has suffered greatly from continuing rounds of decentralization and from the increasing availability on the market of cheap imported clothing. The midtown section of Manhattan, however, remains the privileged center of the high-fashion garment industry in the United States. Here, conditions of flexible efficiency in the production system via vertical disintegration are still the major underpinning of the continued existence of the industry. These conditions have allowed the industry to survive and prosper even in the very heart of one of the world's largest cities. . . .

Conclusion

The case studies outlined in this chapter have all illustrated important aspects of industrial development in metropolitan areas. We have considered how the organization of production processes can lead under the right conditions of vertical disintegration and external transactional activity to major functional and spatial aggregations of industry in intraurban space. We have also seen how these aggregations can sometimes be dissolved again when technological and organizational change begins to undercut their institutional foundations.

Much of the evidence marshaled above seems to suggest that there is a rough direct correlation between such plant characteristics as size and routinization, and distance from the core of the city. If true, this proposition suggests that technological or organizational changes in industry up or down the scale of plant size and routinization will tend to be associated with decentralization and recentralization, respectively. Certainly, the correlation of plant size and routinization with distance from the city center has often been remarked upon in the literature as a recurrent empirical regularity (Cameron, 1973; Martin, 1969; Scott, 1983, 1984; Vernon, 1960). To the degree that the correlation does indeed exist it can perhaps be seen – crudely – as an expression of (a) decreases in unit transactions costs brought on by increases in plant size and routinization, thus leading to decentralization, combined with (b) the superior accessibility of central-city locations to the total urban labor force, thereby encouraging aggregates of disintegrated (and on balance small) employers to gravitate to the urban core. Obviously, this problem is of considerable complexity, . . .

We really have very limited analytical insights into the logic of these intraurban locational processes. The oversimplified argument that is often recounted in the literature to the effect that large plants need large quantities of land and therefore shift to cheap suburban locations is surely only partially correct. We can no more claim that largeness as such (or, say, horizontal plant layouts) is the cause of decentralization than we can aver that smallness (or, say, multistory building construction) is the cause of the development of central locations. Or rather, these plant size/land use relations must be considered in terms of their intrinsic interdependence with the linkage and labor cost phenomena alluded to above. We should also include in this agenda an analysis of different available production techniques and their input-output and employment effects. The sort of research recently accomplished by theorists such as Barnes and Sheppard (1984) and Huriot (1981) on the spatial switching of production techniques would seem to offer considerable promise in this regard. . . . much of the modern large-scale decentralization of new industrial investment from metropolitan areas to far-flung hinterlands can explicitly be seen as an effect of major technological and organizational changes in the structure of production.

REFERENCES

Allen, G. C. (1929). *The Industrial Development of Birmingham and the Black Country, 1860–1907*. Hemel Hempstead, Herts.: Allen and Unwin.

Barnes, T. and E. Sheppard (1984). "Technical choice and reswitching in space economies." *Regional Science and Urban Economics* 14: 345–62.

Cameron, G. C. (1973). "Intra-urban location and the new plant." *Papers of the Regional Science Association* 31: 125–43.

Fales, R. L. and L. N. Moses (1972). "Land use theory and the spatial structure of the nineteenth century city." *Papers of the Regional Science Association* 28: 49–80.

Haig, R. M. (1927). *Major Economic Factors in Metropolitan Growth and Arrangement*. New York: Regional Plan of New York and its Environs.

Helfgott, R. B. (1959). "Women's and children's apparel," pp. 19–134 in M. Hall, ed., *Made in New York*. Cambridge, Mass.: Harvard University Press.

Hoover, E. M. and R. Vernon (1959). *Anatomy of a Metropolis*. Cambridge, Mass.: Harvard University Press.

Huriot, J. M. (1981). "Rente foncière et modèle de production." *Environment and Planning A* 13: 1125–49.

Kenyon, J. B. (1964). "The industrial structure of the New York garment center," pp. 159–66 in R. S. Thoman and D. J. Patton, eds., *Focus on Geographic Activity*. New York: McGraw-Hill.

Martin, J. E. (1969). "Size of plant and location of industry in Greater London." *Tijdschrift voor Economische en Sociale Geografie* 60: 369–74.

Scott, A. J. (1983). "Industrial organization and the logic of intra-metropolitan location II: a case study of the printed circuits industry in the Greater Los Angeles Region." *Economic Geography* 59: 343–67.

Scott, A. J. (1984). "Industrial organization and the logic of intra-metropolitan location III: a case study of the women's dress industry in the Greater Los Angeles Region." *Economic Geography* 60: 3–27.

Vernon, R. (1960). *Metropolis 1985*. Cambridge, Mass.: Harvard University Press.

Wise, M. J. (1949). "On the evolution of the jewellery and gun quarters in Brimingham." *Transactions of the Institute of British Geographers* 15: 57–72.

Chapter 17

Flexibilization Through Metropolis: The Case of Postfordist Seoul, Korea

Myung-Rae Cho

Clarification of Some Conceptual Issues: A Regulationist Reformulation of Postfordism

. . .

(1) Postfordism is no longer strange jargon in the academic literature (Amin, 1994). Against this tendency, however, some orthodox regulationists like Jessop (1990; 1992) and Leborgne and Lipietz (1992) warn of the vulgarization of the term. What they are worried about is that the debate about postfordism has degenerated into an issue simply of technological and industrial systems which emerge after the supposed crisis of fordism. For them, the theoretical thrust of fordism or postfordism can only be reactivated through a reworking of the concept of regulation in keeping with methodological principles of regulation theories, such as dialectical materialism, realist epistemology and meso-level conceptualization (Cho, 1991; Jessop, 1990; 1992; Jessop and Sum, 1993; Lipietz, 1987; Torfing, 1990).

In regulation theories, what is developed are a series of intermediate or middle-range concepts whose goal is to explain processes of socio-economic development that exhibit significant spatial and historical variations (Dunford, 1990). Key concepts of regulation theories are both a regime of accumulation and a mode of regulation. However, being open-ended research programmes, regulation theories are so extended as to embrace a number of theoretical positions, each with different substantive emphases on key concepts. To run the risk of simplification, one can identify two distinctive schools. As the backbone to the theory, the French School has devoted its efforts to identifying the technological and macro-economic possibilities (i.e. labour processes, industrial organizations) of capital accumulation. Through these efforts the School has developed a distinctive economic-focus approach to capitalist regulation. On the other hand, as regulation theories are becoming more widely researched outside France, new approaches are emerging. These are commonly more loyal to Gramsci's original idea of fordism and interested in specifying the society-wide regulatory processes by which a new regime of accumulation obtains its authenticity as a hegemonic structure. Working with a broad notion of societalization, these non-French schools are as a whole labelled 'the Societalization School' (cf. Bonefeld, Hirsh) or 'the Reformulation School (cf. Torfing). Taken together, regulation theories involve a synthesis of up to four elements: labour processes or industrial paradigm, a regime of accumulation, a mode of regulation and a hegemonic structure (Cho, 1991; Dunford, 1990; Jessop, 1992) (see figure 17.1).

(2) The most significant area of neglect in the regulationist research on postfordism (in Tickell and Peck's words, a missing link) is the mode of regulation which enacts the working of what I call an authentic form of postfordism. An authentic form of postfordism includes or describes more than just economic relations; in other words, it retains a set of traits characteristic of what Hirsh terms a hegemonic structure. A mode of regulation involves a complex ensemble of productive institutions, social and political relations and practices which, in combination, regulate the society-wide processes of accumulation (Schoenberger, 1989). A regime of accumulation, once coupled with society-wide regulatory procedures, becomes durable and reproducible for some time and then allows hegemony to be entrenched throughout a given accumulation system. At this level it appears that regulatory practices have a similarity to 'hegemonic practices' (Torfing, 1990). An integral concept of postfordism therefore refers to a structure of capital accumulation which is articulated through a technological paradigm, industrial organization and societal processes (see figure 17.2).

(3) At stake in postfordism is thus a new mode of regulation. In correspondence with the working of postfordism as a hegemonic structure, there should be a new mode of social regulation geared towards translating social acts – such as new capital-labour relations, industrial interaction, consumption habits – into hegemonic practices. However, postfordist regulatory practices cannot be defined in an institutional formula as clearly as in the case of fordism (Peck and Tickell, 1992; 1994). After the erosion of the nation-state, along with the crisis of fordism, an alternative institutional fix for social regulation has yet to be put in place (Peck and Tickell, 1994). Furthermore, the societal processes of postfordism make its mode of regulation unstable, insecure, transient and globally articulated, due to the flexible nature of technology, labour relations and consumption modes. In such circumstances, the emerging regime appears to be more effectively regulated by non-institutional and discursive means like trust, cooperation and transaction. This means that postfordist regulation is not rigid and form-determined, but, rather, flexible and process-determined. For this reason, flexibilization becomes a key characteristic of the social regulatory processes associated with postfordism. Flexibilization describes the process by which postfordist regulatory practices are carried out in a discursive manner (not stable, not necessarily institutionalized), with the effect of making an accumulation regime durable and then hegemonic.

(4) Compared to fordism on the national scale, the spatialization of postfordism

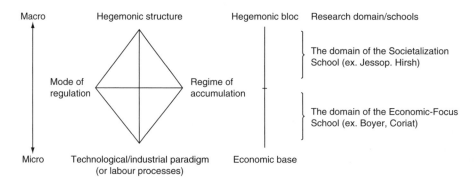

Figure 17.1   The structure of regulation theories

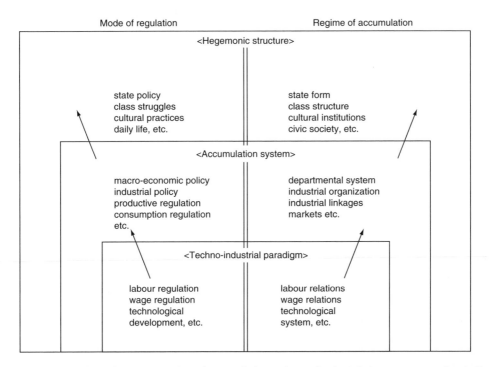

Figure 17.2 Articulation between a regime of accumulation and a mode of regulation: a structure of capitalist accumulation

appears to have two conflicting tendencies: localization (i.e. the spatial scale emphasized by the flexible specialization school: see Piore and Sabel, 1984) and globalization (i.e. the spatial scale stressed by the global-regime school: see Amin, 1994; Dicken *et al.*, 1994; Sassen, 1991). Yet neither of these two tendencies can capture a representative scale of postfordist space. Postfordism operates simultaneously at both distinctive scales of space: for instance, the operation of postfordism requires the locally imbedded social nexus of production as well as the globally networked flow of information and finance (Lipietz, 1993; Swyngedouw, 1989). This simultaneous spatialization creates material postfordist spaces. The new regime may be articulated at different spatial scales, with different functions being dispensed by local, national and supranational states, and different structures of non-state social regulation (Peck and Tickell, 1994). However, among others, metropolitan cities seem to emerge as the most significant socio-spatial nexus in

which a global-local interplay of contemporary capitalist development is not only accommodated with ease, but also discursive regulatory practices are amply pursued (e.g. the economic relationship between urban enterprises is heavily influenced by shared non-economic concerns). The postfordist metropolis now becomes a showcase to display the totality of contemporary change (Harvey, 1989a)....

The Metropolitization of Postfordism

How then can the recent industrial restructuring be focused in Seoul, leading to the ascendancy of postfordism from the metropolis?

New technological processes through a metropolitan spatial fix

Seoul is a mega city with more than 11 million inhabitants and with more than half of the country's productive apparatus and wealth. During the 1970s, Seoul was central to the peripheral fordist division of production. Then, with the advent of the 1980s, it gradually turned into a locus for incubating new innovative industries. As early as 1980 over 80 per cent of hi-tech industries, notably micro-electronics, resided in the Seoul metropolitan area. With this locational precondition, the outbreak of the 1987 nation-wide labour unrest turned this existing hi-tech centre into a postfordist metropolis.

In overcoming the mid-1980 crisis,[1] Korea's leading capital, with the help of the new state, has devoted its efforts to suppressing labour problems, such as the demand for high wages, labour militancy and labour shortages. Major steps have been taken to bring in a new technological system and industrial relations which should be less labour intensive – essentially technology and information based.[2] However, the ways in which industrial restructuring is undertaken vary from region to region. The neotaylorist and neofordist solutions, both lacking profound techno-social interconnections, have been introduced in southern industrial regions, whereas Seoul has been a locus for an in-situ rationalization incorporating a more progressive coupling of new technology and its socialization. If postfordist urban features are to emerge from Seoul, this is not due merely to new technologies or a new industrial system, but to the process by which new technical products and processes are articulated with metropolitan specific social complexity.

New leading production technologies are typified by FA, FMS, CAD, robotics, etc.; most use micro-electronics based information and communication technologies. These technologies are made available by large scale investment: between 1987 and 1992, investment for FA and R&D had increased annually by 41.8 and 35.8 per cent respectively. Geographically, most of this innovation effort is shaped and actualized through the metropolitan technological nexus of Seoul which hosts the bulk of national technological innovation agents and institutes. As a corollary, metropolitan enterprises are always among the earliest introducers of new technologies and production systems. This is indicated by the fact that in 1993 50–60 per cent of enterprises in Seoul ran various forms of FA and other technical equivalents, compared to the national average of 30 per cent or less.

The introduction of new product and process technologies has been led by large conglomerate firms (Samsung, Hyundai and Daewoo, to name a few). Their use of new technologies has had a great effect in stimulating the internal demarcation as well as the intercorporate externalization of production processes along a technical division of labour. As for the internal demarcation of jobs, it takes place as follows: a recomposition of labour deployment between polyvalent core technical workers and the periphery; the organization of internal and external labour markets around different forms of flexibility; a flatter, disintegrated and leaner organization involving teamwork and greater internal autonomy; a flexible organization of production lines geared to changing and differentiated demand, as well as a growing productivity based on economies of scope.

What is more, this reorganization in turn sets in train dense technological linkages and flows across production departments, units, firms and spaces. Quite aptly, new production technologies are characterized as 'system technologies' in that their operation requires a system-wide near integration among different technical units around the production of particular commodities (i.e. microelectronic goods and fashion apparel). It is by virtue of the spatialization of system technologies that the metropolitan space becomes constructed with a complex division of labour among different technical entities. For Seoul, underpinning this technological nexus is its good information and communication infrastructure: 98 per cent of new information industries and their supportive facilities are clustered in Seoul.

Thus, new technologies operate through a metropolitan technological constitution which I call a 'metropolitan spatial fix'. This fix is a nexus through which one technology holder associates with those utilizing other available and adaptable techniques, thus forming a collective technological edifice, or what Pedersen et al. (1994) term a 'metaenterprise', the scope of which goes beyond the individual technical enterprise. Through the fix, technological forces of varying kinds, whether hi-tech or low-tech, global or local, postmodern or traditional, amalgamate into a flexible technological regime to accommodate postfordist (re)production. What is more, through this spatial fix the limitations of technological (or functional) flexibility, which might arise from the technical limits associated with Korea's peripheral accumulation, can be effectively overcome. In fact, Korea's new hi-tech production (notably of micro-electronics) has deep linkages with the traditional, craft, marginal sector.

Our last point, however, is rather depressing. This flexible spatial fix, like in other postfordisms, involves a tendency to bipolarization. This bipolarization is dual, involving a bipolarization between the technical core and the peripheral in new (postfordist) technical and labour organization; and a bipolarization between the large, global, hi-tech firm sector and the small, traditional, labour-intensive firm sector in the wider social organization of production. The latter evolves out of the former. In the dual structure, the cost (e.g. labour cost) incurred by one part (i.e. large technical firms) is transferred via unequal exchange chains to other parts (i.e. small low-tech labour intensive firms). As will be shown later on, technological duality gives rise to the bipolarization of labour markets which is expressed in a new form of uneven technical and social development.

Flexible production organization through metropolitan networks

Veltz characterizes new productive technologies as 'communicative technologies'

by emphasizing their requirement for integrative linkages among fragmented production modules and units in a range from upstream to downstream relations and firms (Veltz, 1991). Thus, the finest crystallization of new technological processes is dense interfirm networks. Korea's dominant corporate networks are woven in such a way that a myriad of small specialized firms are clustered around the nodes of large lead firms. The deepening of interfirm networks is indicated by the rapidly spreading subcontracting relations between large and small firms. In the whole manufacturing sector, the percentage of subcontracting firms increased from 38.0 per cent in 1983 to 73.4 per cent in 1992. For small firms, the proportion of subcontracting in the total output grew from about 20 per cent in 1978–80 to a good 80 per cent in 1990–1. Taken together, 80 per cent of small firms yield 70–80 per cent of their output under subcontracting contract (see Cho, 1995a for more details).

Geographically, the most dense intercorporate networking takes place in the Seoul metropolis. Seoul-based small firms produce almost 80 per cent of their output through subcontracting arrangements with other firms. The proliferation of subcontracting firms has been fastest in Seoul: the percentage of subcontracting firms in Seoul increased from 53.1 per cent in 1987 to 89.4 per cent in 1991 which was 10 per cent higher than the national average. Firms in electronics, electrics and machinery are virtually all in subcontracting relationships with each other. Nowadays, production-via-network practices permeate all industrial branches, including apparel, printing and even producer services like information processing.

The density of industrial linkages (especially in the hi-tech sector) in the Seoul metropolitan region is said to be much higher than in Florida, Scotland, or southeast England, though lower than in the San Francisco Bay area (Park, 1987). Firms in Seoul procure an average of 80.1 per cent of their primary and secondary inputs (including manpower and information) from the

Seoul metropolitan area. Linkage density is much higher among small firms, venture firms and the firms involved in high R&D activities. Partly for this reason, and more importantly because of large firms' networking effects, recently the growth of small firms in Seoul has accelerated. Between 1987 and 1991 about 85 per cent of small scale firms and workshops had been created in the Seoul metropolitan region. In particular the growth of small firms with 5–9 employees has been phenomenal: Seoul's share of this category of small firms in the national total grew from 15.3 per cent to 31.9 per cent over just three years between 1987 and 1990, accounting for more than three quarters of the national total increase. The mushrooming of small firms in Seoul indicates that the metropolitan networks have become more dense and compact.

Recently, Seoul's interfirm relations have become much diversified and multilayered, as illustrated by the fact that the percentage of firms subcontracting with over six firms jumped from 40 per cent in 1987 to 75 per cent in 1991, with the national average increasing from 49 per cent to 59 per cent. What is more, along with the rapid increase in subcontracting, the metropolitan networks tend to deepen vertically. Vertical deepening takes place in two directions. One is the upward ramification of interfirm linkages which results from large firms seeking to form strategic alliances with speciality firms, multinationals (notably Japanese), university or government-run institutes and, in some cases, other conglomerate firms, with the aim of securing innovative inputs for production and maintaining their monopolistic stance in markets. The other direction is the downward ramification of interfirm linkage which occurs in line with subcontracting jobs going along a hierachical interfirm chain down to the second or third tiers of subcontracting small firms in order to exploit their niche skills and productive advantages. Much further down the chain, the limbs of large flexible firms' production reach the workplace where piecework is carried out by hundreds of thousands of housewives or the elderly for low wages.

Seoul's networks are not only very dense, but their structure is also extremely diversified and complex. As regards the latter, Seoul's metropolitan networks are woven by a myriad of production and service activities, ranging from conglomerates' R&D to housewives' piece-wage work. Therefore, the metropolitan networks as a whole function as a flexible production organization which comprises a whole array of innovative technological nuclei, diverse niche skills, segmented labour forces, part/material suppliers and wider outlets. This feature of the Seoul metropolitan region conforms to a model of a system area which Leborgne and Lipietz (1988) define as 'regionally integrated diversified, multisectorial networks, the locus of multiregional firms, incubator of new hi-tech firms, [and] technological innovation'.

The flexibility of metropolitan networks stems chiefly from the complexity and diversity specific to a metropolitan city. The underlying economic logic concerns the economies of scope which occur where it is more efficient to operate two activities in tandem than each in isolation. On the other hand, the economy of scope has some similarity to the cooperation or system economies in which integration of labour processes and regulation of material flows can benefit overall production, such as linking R&D closely with manufacturing, marketing a line of products jointly, or providing a regular supply of inputs.

However, the economies of network flexibility do not equally benefit all participants. This reality echoes the bipolarization of postfordist technological processes. Indeed, though based on mutuality, the metropolitan networks are deeply inscribed by the logic of hierarchy, asymmetrical communication, cost transfer, technical and market dependency, enforced price-fixing and so forth. Therefore it seems that the relationships between large and small firms are still to a great extent governed by this logic. Within the postfordist production system, only a limited number of small firms with special technological capabilities are able to assert their productive sovereignty against 'patriarchical' large lead firms, whereas the majority of small firms, which are technically less competitive, are at the mercy of large firms. In this light, one can rightly argue that the post-1987 upsurge of subcontracting is largely stimulated by the motivation of large firms to transfer labour-intensive jobs, or jobs which are the locus of labour unrest, to small firms, workshops or piecework-producing households, all of which employ a growing number of immigrant labourers, housewives and part-time workers. In fact, Seoul is precisely the place where 60 per cent of all unregistered small-scale enterprises or workshops in the country are concentrated.

A service production regime? A node in glocalized capital circulation

The tendency in the network economy is that the upstream phases (R&D, design, operational management) and the downstream (distribution and sales) constantly increase in importance, whereas by comparison the central phase of production is on the wane (Cooke and Morgan, 1993; Sayer and Walker, 1992; Veltz, 1991). This is true in the case of Seoul. However, Seoul's manufacturing decline exists only in a relative sense, such as the closing down of labour-intensive light industrial firms and the displacement of standardized technical (even hi-tech) firms either to the outskirts of Seoul or remote regions (especially south-west provinces) or overseas (notably China). Out of the recent industrial restructuring new types of industries have arisen, but the ways in which they are produced and consumed has also remarkably changed. Sectorially, Seoul's new industries are specialized in three sectors: (1) traditional craft-based industries, such as apparel, fashion and printing, which have been recently equipped with highly flexible production methods; (2) technology and information intensive industries like machatronics and software; (3) booming

commerce and service industries, bringing with them income increases and industrial expansion. A common characteristic of new industries is that they operate through a complex interfirm division of labour within the Seoul metropolitan region. Such a mode of production is also significantly influenced by a changing mode of demand for new commodities which arises simultaneously from the production and the consumption spheres.

More importantly, these discrete changes in production and consumption combine to give rise to a metropolitan regime of accumulation which centres on the function of linking new production with new consumption. This fusion becomes apparent typically through the rapid growth of service industries. Since 1980, when manufacturing activities reached their highest point (32.6 per cent in employment terms) (Hyung, 1993), the Seoul economy has been led by the service sector. Recently, the fastest growth in the service sector has been marked by the so-called 'producer services': for instance, their share in Seoul's service employment rocketed from 25.9 per cent in 1980 to 40.9 per cent in 1990. Now Seoul's producer services yield more than three-quarters of the national total. Included in the fastest growing producer services are design, advertising, R&D, information-processing, finance, software, real estate, etc. In the 1990s, information processing has been expanding by 60 per cent per annum. The major thrust of demand for these services comes primarily from the globalizing as well as localizing circuit of flexible production under the hold of conglomerate firms. This burgeoning sector is also a generator of the new middle class and a new urban consumption culture. Spatially the bulk of new producer-service business is concentrated in the south-eastern pocket of Seoul, where strong elements of postmodern urban spectacle and consumption culture have come into prominence (Cho, 1993).

On the other hand, consumer services (in other terms, services for reproduction) are also booming due to rapidly rising household income. Over the last five years or so, Seoul's household income has more than doubled, with the effect of bringing about a new consumerist way of life. Some years ago, even symptoms of overconsumption broke out, against which the worried government had to undertake some counter measures. New consumption relates to the consumption of new commodities such as imported luxury goods like furniture, consumer durables like cars, electronic appliances, household equipment, or leisure-forms such as going abroad for holidays, etc. In parallel, the dominant mode of consumption shifts from the using-up of material goods like foods to the squandering of time-goods, image-goods and sensual commodities like video and audio (Cho, 1995b). Changing consumer taste in turn stimulates the expansion of new types of consumer industries. For instance, fast food shops, 24-hour convenience stores, foreign franchised chains, boutiques, department stores, shopping malls and the like are now leading fractions of booming commercial capital.[3] No doubt, the growth of consumer services of this kind is stimulated by the rising income and changing consumption patterns which the new urban middle class, such as polyvalent skilled workers, professionals and new managerial workers, enjoy.

In general, it appears that Seoul's new metropolitan economy is structured around the production of high value-added services which serve, on the production side, the demand for production based on a flexible interfirm division of labour, and, on the consumption side, the demand for differentiated goods and services favoured by the new urban middle class. As demand and supply for new services are met through the dense interplay between local and global networks of the metropolitan economy, Seoul resembles what Veltz (1991) terms a 'networked metropolis' where flows of goods, services and information are articulated not only through integrative global networks, interrelated with the global circuit of capital, but also through communicative local networks, with the trajectories of urban daily-life.

To recapitulate, the metropolitan economy of Seoul has been transformed into a flexible service-production regime. This regime is functional to linking new production with new consumption, a coupling which forms a production-reproduction circulation as the basis of a macro circuit of capital. With this regime, therefore, Seoul plays a renewed role of pumping a 'glocal' circulation of capital into the Korean economy as a whole. But this regime is vulnerable to counter-tendencies with negative effects. Firstly, 'service-centred' means the displacement of manufacturing activities and consequently the loss of a productive basis which holds the entrenched competitiveness of Seoul's economy vis-à-vis other locales in the world city system. Secondly, becoming a node of the glocalized circuit of capital within a context of peripheral accumulation entails the likelihood that Seoul's economy will be fettered by the hegemony of globally mobile financial capital. Thirdly, as the other side of the same coin, local networks of daily life are likely to be either marginalized or colonized by encroaching global forces. Finally, all these could end up in a new form of biopolarization, that is, a widening global-local cleavage in the metropolitan regime of accumulation. This form of cleavage could be said to evolve out of the technological bipolarization of Korean postfordism.

Flexible reproduction through metropolitan labour markets

Metropolitan labour markets are the basis on which new social relations are moulded into a reproducible class configuration.

Recent industrial restructuring has created the need for a new type of technical labourer, capable of new machine operation and flexible job organization. As the new technical core of production comes into operation, it gives rise to a burgeoning upper segment of the labour market, comprising technicians, professionals and managerial workers. Yet, on the other hand, new production stimulates a much greater use of part-time employment, and precarious employment relations as well as marginalized (generally non-unionized) workers and especially foreign workers and women. As stated earlier, this pattern of employment gives shape to a really flexible but dual metropolitan labour market. However, this duality is internally much more complex than the term may imply. Seoul's current labour market has the following characteristics:

1) Flexible industrialization through the metropolis entails a process of reducing the manufacturing workforce, particularly direct production workers. This occurs as a combined effect of, on the one hand, the displacement of labour-intensive manufacturing activities and a process of rationalization deploying labour-saving machines and equipment and, on the other, the growth of service industries. During the 1980s, the proportion of manufacturing in Seoul's employment continued to decline from 32.6 per cent to 29.7 per cent, while service employment expanded from 66.5 per cent to 69.8 per cent.

2) Within the manufacturing sector, however, employment is polarized between core technical, managerial and service workers largely employed in large firms, and peripheral direct-production labourers mostly working with small firms. The ratio between the two strata of workers changed from 31.6:68.4 in 1980 to 40.9:59.1 in 1990. On top of this, Seoul's manufacturing employment is also polarized across sectors, especially between the new technology-intensive sectors such as electronics and machinery and the labour-intensive sectors such as textiles. During the 1980s Seoul's total employment grew by 1.25 million, among which only one-third (about 410,000) were recruited in the manufacturing sector. Within manufacturing, 220,000 were in the technology-intensive sectors such as machinery, electronics and equipment

assembly and 150,000 in the labour-intensive sectors such as chemicals, clothing and textiles.

3) Service industries have become a new source of employment, mainly hoarding a swelling number of part-time and casual workers: a majority of casual workers (about 70 per cent) are now currently employed in the service sector. But within the service sector, casual employment grows faster in the traditional service sectors such as retailing and restaurants, than in the new service sectors such as finance, insurance and information: the share of casual and daily workers in the latter (i.e. new services) increased from 5.0 per cent to 5.3 per cent between 1986 and 1991, but in the former (i.e. traditional services) this grew from 5.5 per cent to 6.8 per cent.

4) With the influx of rural migrants gradually ending and a new phase of industrialization demanding a new type of labour (particularly since 1987), Seoul's industries are suffering from an acute labour shortage: the rate of shortage in manufacturing reached 14.6 per cent in 1991. The lack of labour supply stimulates a rapid expansion of the second labour market composed of marginal labour such as housewives, foreign workers and casual labour like part-time or subcontracting workers. Regular full-time labour in Seoul grew at an annual rate of 8.4 per cent over the last six years, as compared to a national average of 10.8 per cent. The proportion of female labour in all industries remained at 30 per cent between 1980 and 1990, but grew in absolute terms by 5.6 per cent yearly, which was the highest increase amongst all regions, and compares to the national rate of 3.5 per cent Currently the number of foreign workers, mostly illegal, from China, The Philippines and Pakistan, approximates 100,000. A study reports that nearly 10 per cent of manufacturing firms employ foreign workers illegally (Park, 1993).

5) As a result of a flexible mode of employment, Seoul's labour turnover is very high: in 1992 the rate of lay-offs in manufacturing reached 39 per cent. As a corollary, labour union activities have not only become fragmented, but have also lost their previous dynamic momentum which was expressed through the 1987 struggle: in 1993 the rate of labour unionization in Seoul decreased to less than 25 per cent. Nowadays the flexible form of employment tends to spread even further, along with a wave of new machine deployment, resultant job reordering and subcontracting. This no doubt will bring more flexibility into Seoul's labour market.

6) Spatially, the metropolitan labour market is segregated into different reproduction zones, each corresponding to a cluster of sub-metropolitan production networks. The differentiation of reproduction space is caused basically by the factors associated with the dualization of labour relations and markets. In other words, the dualization of labour markets gives rise to new class cleavages which in turn are reflected in the spatially differentiated processes of metropolitan social reproduction. In the course of material wellbeing improving rapidly, class distinction becomes more pronounced in the consumption and reproduction sphere. This class distinction may take the form of consumption classes. In fact Seoul's new class cleavage is drawn between the new affluent 'middle class' in the upper segment of the postfordist labour market and the new deprived 'underclass' (or under-consumption class) in the lower segment. Seoul's new reproduction spaces take new shape as follows: the traditional working class communities, typically the Kuro industrial area in the south-west, are rapidly dissolving; the new service class communities, typically the Kangnam area in the south-east, are becoming widely extended; the new under-class (notably,

subcontracting workers) communities, typically the Kwanak area in the central south, are being scattered around the metropolis. This is a spatial form in which postfordist metropolitan social relations are flexibly reproduced.

Societalization of Metropolitan Postfordism: Reflections on a Flexible Urban Society

. . .

Table 17.1 summarizes the paradoxes derived from the flexibilization of postfordism which proceeds through the space of the Seoul metropolis. This set of paradoxes works to generate new urban stresses which are heavily imposed on, among others, the identity of urban subjects, the meaning of daily life and urban sociability (Knox, 1993; Shields, 1994). In the course of flexible accumulation, most urban residents, regardless of their class status, are situated in a context where their self-identity based on traditional codes (i.e. class) is deeply deconstructed and in its place the new subject, flexibly adaptable to postfordist time-space compression, is formed. Therefore, an individual Seoulite, being a body space into which Korea's compressed societal change from (pre)modern to postmodern life is personally embodied, is apt to experience schizophrenic value-orientations (Cho, 1994). This psychological trait imposes a high sensual overload on the time-spatial trajectory of metropolitan daily life. It is hence not an accident that human relations in Seoul are becoming apparently more dehumanized and permeated by relations based on monetary values (Cho, 1994).

The urban stress deriving from flexibilization is much larger in the lifeworld where capital reproduction is individuated through the consumption of commodities and at the same time individual labour and identity are reproduced through social relationships (i.e. family ties, class relations) and struggles. Where there is minimal state provision for decommodified consumption of, say, houses and education, an indi-

Table 17.1:   Paradoxes of modern postfordism

Areas	Generators of flexibility	Cost of flexibilization
Technology/labour processes	Hi-tech, FA, robotics, communicative tech, conception-execution integration, functional flexibility	Appropriation of traditional skills, technical subordination, externalization of peripheral jobs, increasing use of marginal labour for numerical flexibility
Interfirm relations	Dense large-small firm networks, cooperation, collective efficiency, mutual assistance	Mushrooming small or informal firms/workshops, control linkage, transfer of labour cost, unequal distribution of benefits
Industrial organization	Service-production regime, commending-height, consumption-led economy, globalized circuit of capital	Displacement of manufacturing firms, hegemony of financial capital, consumption-class cleavage, marginalized local network
Labour	Plural, flexible composition, institutionalized wage bargaining	Polarization, dualization, market core-worker centred reward
Class	New middle class on the surface	New underclass underneath
State	Post-BA, local autonomy, workfare-oriented role, entrepreneurialist, cooperation	Neo-conservative state, liberal-productionist intervention, pro-capitalist, coalition
Politics	'Moonmin (civilian)' politics, trans-class consensus, new social movements	Reformist dogma, weakened radical politics, domination of new middle class, new generation politics
Hegemonic norms	Aestheticization, discourse	Commodification, capital imperative
Metropolitan space	Postmodern collage, cultural spectacle, enlarged public space	Repressed (pre)modern spaces, appropriation of space via space exchange value, colonization of reproductive space

vidual's class position in production, from which he/she obtains a basic monetary power for exchange value, determines his/her position in consumption. Therefore, the cleavage of consumption along a class line, in line with increasing consumption, is brought into relief. The differences in consumption capacity between the lower-income group and the upper-income group are, in 1992 figures, 100:479.5 in food consumption, 100:1381 in transportation consumption, 100:2077.5 in housing consumption, 100:4290 in furniture and domestic (cultural) goods consumption, with the difference increasing for cultural consumption.

While Seoul is becoming a theatre of postfordist accumulation, the urban space is fragmenting to accommodate the spatialization of the flexibility of capital circula-

tion. But the spatial fragmentation of the metropolis is a differentiated form of the commodity value of space, so that any access to location, place and land demands a charge of the equivalent of its monetary value. This means that the 'urban collage', constituting a postfordist urban landscape, is nothing more than the fragmented space appropriated by diverse social groups in possession of different exchange values. In other words, the relations installed among fragmented spaces (i.e. different land uses) reflect the social relations through which an individual experiences his/her spatial life given their differentiated levels of social power. In Seoul, increasingly pronounced residential segregation is indicative of the total difference not only in land use and housing value, but also housing type, architectural style, mode of life, amenities, social prestige, etc. Embedded in different reproduction spaces are social relations which institutionalize the differentiation of labour reproduction and new forms of exploitation in production and consumption.

Here, it may be pertinent to remember Harvey's remarks that, behind its postmodern cultural spectacle, '6 faces of social oppression' continue to rampage through the postfordist city: (1) exploitation in the workplace and in the home; (2) marginalization along lines of race, ethnicity, religion, gender, immigration status, age and the like; (3) powerlessness of such social groups as women and homosexuals; (4) cultural imperialism by the white professional class; (5) institutional forms of violence; and (6) ecological exploitation through social projects. It seems that almost all these oppressions are found in the Seoul metropolis, but the degree may be much stronger on account of the additional effect of some social discourses still based on traditional power relations like patriarchism. To one's surprise, however, there seems to be little social awareness of these oppressions. This may be because they are hidden behind the pluri-class cultural spectacle which flexibilization has unleashed. The spectacle is best characterized in Harvey's words: '[In view of] the developed modern complement of money where the totality of the commodity world appears as a whole ... the urban class alliance has consciously used the spectacle ... as a symbol of the supposed unity of a class-divided and radically segregated city' (Harvey, 1989b)....

NOTES

1 Throughout 1987, a total of 3749 labour disputes broke out in all regions and a total of 934,900 workers took part in the disputes.
2 The share of new products, such as microelectronics, transport equipment and machines, in the total manufacturing investment increased from 14.8 per cent in 1987 to 31.9 per cent in 1992. As a corollary, the 1992 index of industrial growth in this new branch has tripled since 1985.
3 During the 1980s, the monthly household income of Seoul's working class families increased by 23.5 per cent annually. As a consequence the pattern of household expenditure has changed. Among other changes, the most striking is that the share of prepared meals in the expenditure of urban households in Seoul increased 10 times between 1980 and 1990. This change is responsible for the explosive expansion of consumer services like restaurants and hotels: in terms of floor acreage they expanded by 266 per cent between 1986 and 1991.

REFERENCES

Amin, A. (1994) Post-fordism: models, fantasies and phantoms of transition. In A. Amin (ed.), *Post-fordism*, Blackwell, Oxford.

Bonefeld, W. and J. Holloway (eds.) (1991) *Postfordism and social form: a marxist debate on the post-fordist state*. Macmillan, London.

Cho, M. R. (1988) *Peripheral fordism, the state and the regional problem: the case of South Korea*. University of Sussex Urban and Regional Studies Working Paper, no. 62.

—— (1991) *Political economy of regional differentiation: the state, accumulation and the regional question*. Hanul Academy Press, Seoul.

—— (ed.) (1993) *Seoul: flexible industrialization, and the new urban society and politics*. Hanul Academy Press, Seoul (in Korean).

—— (1994) New urbanism of Seoul: the urbanization of flexible accumulation and new metropolitan life. *Culture and Science 5* (in Korean).

—— (1995a) *Interfirm network: the foundation of the globalizing economy of South Korea.* Paper presented at the international workshop on 'Poverty Alleviation through International Trade', organized by UNCTAD, Santiago, Chile, 10–13 Jan. 1995.

—— (1995b) Urban industrial restructuring and new emerging urban poverty. *Society and Space 5* (in Korean).

Cooke, P. and K. Morgan (1993) The network paradigm: new departures in corporate and regional development. *Society and Space* 11.5.

Dicken, P., M. Forsgren, and A. Malmberg (1994) The local embeddedness of transnational corporations. In A. Amin and N. Thrift (eds.), *Globalization institutions and regional development in Europe*, Oxford University Press, Oxford.

Dunford, M. (1990) Theories of regulation. *Society and Space 8.*

Harvey, D. (1989a) *The condition of postmodernity.* Oxford: Blackwell.

—— (1989b) *The urban experience.* Oxford: Blackwell.

Hirsh, J. (1991) Fordism and postfordism: the present social crisis and its consequence. In W. Bonefeld and J. Holloway (eds.), *Postfordism and social form: a marxist debate on the postfordist state*, Macmillan, London.

Hyung, K. J. (1993) *Changing pattern of industrial structure and location policy in Seoul.* Proceedings of International Seminar on Changing Structure and Development Policies of Industries for Seoul, Seoul Development Institute, Seoul.

Jessop, B. (1990) Regulation theories in retrospect and prospect. *Economy and Society* 19.

—— (1992) Fordism and postfordism: a critical reformulation. In M. Storper and A. J. Scott (eds.), *Pathways to industrialization and regional development*, Routledge, London.

—— and N. L. Sum (1993) *Integral economics vs. integral politics: the rise of the Schumperterian workfare state in East Asian NICs.* Working paper presented to Franco-British Workshop: Research on Contemporary East and Southeast Asia, School of Oriental and African Studies, London University, 13–14 Nov. 1993.

Knox, P. L. (1993) Capital, material culture and socio-spatial differentiation. In P. Knox (ed.), *The restless urban landscape*, Prentice Hall, New Jersey.

Leborgne, D. and A. Lipietz (1988) New technologies, new modes of regulation: some spatial implications. *Environment and Planning D: Society and Space 6.*

—— and —— (1991) Two social strategies in the production of new industrial spaces. In G. Benko and M. Dunford (eds.), *Industrial change and regional development: the transformation of new industrial spaces*, Belhaven Press, London.

—— and —— (1992) Conceptual fallacies and open questions on postfordism. In M. Storper and A. J. Scott (eds.), *Pathways to industrialization and regional development*, Routledge, London.

Lipietz, A. (1987) *Mirages and miracles.* Verso, London.

—— (1993) The local and the global: regional individuality or interregionalism? *Transactions of the Institutes of British Geographers* 18.

Park, S. O. (1987) *Recent development and linkage of high technology industries in the Seoul metropolitan area.* Paper presented at the 10th Pacific Regional Science Conference, Pusan, Korea, July 1987.

—— (1993) *Firms' strategy on industrial restructuring and future direction of industrial policy: the case of manufacturing industries in Seoul.* Proceedings of International Seminar on Changing Structure and Development Policies of Industries for Seoul, Seoul Development Institute, Seoul.

Peck, J. and Y. Miyamachi (1994) Regulating Japan? Regulation theory versus the Japanese experience. *Environment and Planning D: Society and Space* 12.

—— and A. Tickell (1992) Local modes of social regulation: regulation theory, Thatcherism and uneven development. *Geoforum*, 23.

—— and —— (1994) Searching for a new institutional fix: the after-fordist crisis and global-local order. In A. Amin (ed.), *Post-fordism*, Blackwell, Oxford.

Pedersen, P. O. et al. (eds.) (1994) *Flexible specialization: the dynamics of small-scale industries in the south.* IT Publications, London.

Piore, M. and C. Sabel (1984) *The second industrial divide*, Basic Books, New York.

Sassen, S. (1991) *The global city, New York, London and Tokyo.* Princeton University Press, Princeton.

Sayer, A. and R. Walker (1992) *The social economy: rethinking the division of labour.* Basil Blackwell, Oxford.

Schoenberger, E. (1989) Thinking about flexibility: a response to Gertler. *Transactions of the Institute for British Geographers* 14.

Shields, R. (1994) *Postmodern sociability? An agenda for research on the metropolis.* Paper presented at the Symposium on 'Postfordism and Postmodernism: Reflections on Theory and Practices', Carleton University, Ottawa, 18 February 1994.

Swyngedouw, E. (1989) The heart of the place: the resurrection of locality in an age of hyperspace. *Geografiska Annaler* 71.

Tickell, A. and J. A. Peck (1992) Accumulation, regulation and geographies of postfordism: missing links in regulationist research. *Progress in Human Geography* 16.2.

Torfing, J. (1990) A hegemony approach to capitalist regulation. In R. R. Bertramsen, J. P. F. Thomson and J. Torfing (eds.), *State, economy and society*, Unwin Hyman, London.

Veltz, P. (1991) New models of production organization and trends in spatial development. In G. Benko and M. Dunford (eds.), *Industrial change and regional development: the transformation of new industrial spaces*, Belhaven Press, London.

Chapter 18

from *Globalization and its Discontents*

Saskia Sassen

Introduction: Whose City Is It? Globalization and the Formation of New Claims

One of the organizing themes in this collection is that place is central to many of the circuits through which economic globalization is constituted. One strategic type of place for these developments, and the one focused on here, is the city. Including cities in the analysis of economic globalization is not without conceptual consequences. Economic globalization has mostly been represented in terms of the duality of national–global where the global gains power and advantages at the expense of the national. And it has largely been conceptualized in terms of the internationalization of capital and then only the upper circuits of capital, notably finance. Introducing cities into an analysis of economic globalization allows us to reconceptualize processes of economic globalization as concrete economic complexes situated in specific places. Focus on cities decomposes the national economy into a variety of subnational components, some profoundly articulated with the global economy and others not. It also signals the declining significance of the national economy as a unitary category. To some extent it was only a unitary category in political discourse and policy; the modern nation-state has always had economic actors and prac-

tices that were transnational. Nonetheless, over the last fifteen years we can see a profoundly different phase, one where national economies are less and less a unitary category in the face of the new forms of globalization.

Why does it matter to recover place in analyses of the global economy, particularly place as constituted in major cities? Because it allows us to see the multiplicity of economies and work cultures in which the global information economy is embedded. It also allows us to recover the concrete, localized processes through which globalization exists and to argue that much of the multiculturalism in large cities is as much a part of globalization as is international finance. Finally, focusing on cities allows us to specify a geography of strategic places at the global scale, places bound to each other by the dynamics of economic globalization. I refer to this as a new geography of centrality, and one of the questions it engenders is whether this new transnational geography also is the space for a new transnational politics.

Insofar as an economic analysis of the global city recovers the broad array of jobs and work cultures that are part of the global economy though typically not marked as such, I can examine the possibility of a new politics of traditionally disadvantaged actors operating in this new transnational economic geography – from factory workers in export-processing zones to cleaners on Wall Street. This is a politics that lies at the intersection of 1) the actual economic participation of many disadvantaged workers in the global economy and 2) political systems and rhetorics that can only represent and valorize corporate actors as participants, in this regard a politics of exclusion.

If place, that is, a certain type of place, is central in the global economy, we can posit a transnational economic and political opening in the formation of new claims and hence in the constitution of entitlements, notably rights to place, and more radically, in the constitution of "citizenship." The city has indeed emerged as a site for new claims: by global capital which uses the city as an "organizational commodity," but also by disadvantaged sectors of the urban population, which in large cities are frequently as internationalized a presence as is capital. The denationalizing of urban space and the formation of new claims by transnational actors and involving contestation, raise the question – whose city is it?

I see this as a type of political opening with unifying capacities across national boundaries and sharpening conflicts within such boundaries. Global capital and the new immigrant workforce are two major instances of transnational categories/actors that have unifying properties across borders and find themselves in contestation with each other inside global cities. Global cities are the sites of the over-valorization of corporate capital and the further devalorization of disadvantaged economic actors, both firms and workers. The leading sectors of corporate capital are now global in their organization and operations. And many of the disadvantaged workers in global cities are women, immigrants, and people of color, whose political sense of self and whose identities are not necessarily embedded in the "nation" or the "national community." Both find in the global city a strategic site for their economic and political operations.

The analysis presented here grounds its interpretation of the new politics made possible by globalization in a detailed understanding of the economics of globalization, and specifically in the centrality of place against a rhetorical and policy context where place is seen as neutralized by global communications and the hypermobility of capital. We need to dissect the economics of globalization to understand whether a new transnational politics can be centered in the new transnational economic geography. Second, I think that dissecting the economics of place in the global economy allows us to recover noncorporate components of economic globalization and to inquire about the possibility of a new type of transnational politics, a politics of those who lack power but now have "presence." ...

Immigration is one major process through which a new transnational political economy is being constituted, one which is largely embedded in major cities insofar as most immigrants, whether in the United States, Japan, or Western Europe, are concentrated in major cities. Immigration is, in my reading, one of the constitutive processes of globalization today, even though not recognized or represented as such in mainstream accounts of the global economy.

The global city is a strategic site for disempowered actors because it enables them to gain presence, to emerge as subjects, even when they do not gain direct power. Immigrants, women, African Americans in US cities, people of color, oppressed minorities emerge as significant subjects in a way they are unlikely to do in a suburban context or small town. ...

One of the links between the new corporate world of power and the disadvantaged in large cities is the labor market, or, more pointedly the market for labor. ...

A whole new arena of politics has emerged with the ascendance of subnational units, especially global cities and high-tech industrial districts, as direct actors in the international stage. Digitalization and the growing importance of electronic space for private and public activities have further relocated various components of politics away from national governments....

Place and production in the global economy

Alongside the well-documented spatial dispersal of economic activities have appeared new forms of territorial centralization of top-level management and control operations. National and global markets as well as globally integrated operations require central places where the work of globalization gets done. Further, information industries require a vast physical infrastructure containing strategic nodes with hyperconcentrations of facilities. Finally, even the most advanced information industries have a work process – that is, a complex of workers, machines, and buildings that are more placebound than the imagery of the information economy suggests.

Centralized control and management over a geographically dispersed array of economic operations does not come about inevitably as part of a "world system." It requires the production of a vast range of highly specialized services, telecommunications infrastructure, and industrial services. These are crucial for the valorization of what are today leading components of capital. Rather than simply invoking the power of multinational corporations as the explanatory key of economic globalization, a focus on place and production takes us to the range of activities and organizational arrangements necessary for the implementation and maintenance of a global network of factories, service operations, and markets; these are all processes only partly encompassed by the activities of transnational corporations and banks.

One of the central concerns in my work has been to look at cities as production sites for the leading service industries of our time, and hence to uncover the infrastructure of activities, firms, and jobs, that are necessary to run the advanced corporate economy. I want to focus on the *practice* of global control. Global cities are centers for the servicing and financing of international trade, investment, and headquarter operations. That is to say, the multiplicity of specialized activities present in global cities are crucial for the valorization, indeed overvalorization of leading sectors of capital today. And in this sense such cities are strategic production sites for today's leading economic sectors. This function is also reflected in the ascendance of these activities in developed economies.

The extremely high densities evident in the downtown districts of these cities are one spatial expression of this logic; another one is the recentralization of many of these activities in broader metropolitan areas, rather than universal dispersal. The widely accepted notion that agglomeration has become obsolete now that global telecommunication advances are allowing for maximum dispersal, is only partly correct. It is precisely because of the territorial dispersal facilitated by telecommunication advances that agglomeration of centralizing activities has expanded immensely. This is not a mere continuation of old patterns of agglomeration but, one could posit, a new logic for agglomeration. Information technologies are yet another factor contributing to this new logic for agglomeration. The distinct conditions under which such facilities are available have promoted centralization of the most advanced users in the most advanced telecommunications centers (Castells 1989).

A focus on the work behind command functions, on the actual production process in the finance and services complex, and on global market*places* has the effect of incorporating the material facilities underlying globalization and the whole infrastructure of jobs typically not marked as belonging to the corporate sector of the economy. An economic configuration emerges that is very different from that suggested by the concept of information economy. We recover the material conditions, production sites, and placeboundedness that are also part of globalization and the information economy (*Competition and Change* 1995).

That is to say, we recover a broad range of types of firms, types of workers, types of work cultures, types of residential milieux, never marked, recognized, or represented as being part of globalization processes. Nor are they valorized as such. In this regard, the new urban economy is highly problematic, a fact particularly evident in global cities and their regional counterparts. It sets in motion a whole series of new dynamics of inequality (Sassen 1994, chap. 5; King 1996). The new growth sectors – specialized services and finance – contain profit-making capabilities vastly superior to those of more traditional economic sectors. While the latter may be essential to the operation of the urban economy and the daily needs of residents, their survival is threatened in a situation where finance and specialized services can earn superprofits. Going informal or subcontracting to informal enterprises is often one solution.

Unequal profit-making capabilities among different economic sectors and firms have long been a basic feature of market economies. But what we see today takes place on another order of magnitude and is engendering massive distortions in the operations of various markets, from housing to labor. For example, we can see this effect in the unusually sharp increase in the starting salaries of business and law school graduates who succeed in entering the top firms, and in the precipitous fall in the wages of low-skilled manual workers and clerical workers. We can see the same effect in the retreat of many real estate developers from the low- and medium-income housing market in the wake of the rapidly expanding housing demand by the new highly paid professionals and the possibility for vast overpricing of this housing supply.

These developments are associated with a dynamic of valorization which has sharply increased the disparity between the valorized, indeed overvalorized, sectors of the economy and devalorized sectors even when the latter are part of leading global industries. This devalorization of growing sectors of the economy has been embedded in a massive demographic transition toward a growing presence of women, African Americans, and Third World immigrants in the urban workforce.

We see here an interesting correspondence between great concentrations of corporate power and large concentrations of "others." Major cities in the highly developed world are the terrain where a multiplicity of globalization processes assume concrete, localized forms. These localized forms are, in good part, what globalization is about. We can then think of cities also as one of the sites for the contradictions of the internationalization of capital, and, more generally, as a strategic terrain for a whole series of conflicts and contradictions.

A new geography of centrality and marginality

The global economy materializes in a worldwide grid of strategic places, from export-processing zones to major international business and financial centers. We can think of this global grid as constituting a new economic geography of centrality, one that cuts across national boundaries and across the old North–South divide. It signals the emergence of a parallel political geography of power, a transnational space for the formation of new claims by global capital (See Sassen 1996, chap. 2). This new economic geography of centrality partly reproduces existing inequalities but also is the outcome of a dynamic specific to current types of economic growth. It assumes many forms and operates in many terrains, from the distribution of telecommunications facilities to the structure of the economy and of employment.

The most powerful of these new geographies of centrality at the interurban level binds the major international financial and business centers: New York, London, Tokyo, Paris, Frankfurt, Zurich,

Amsterdam, Los Angeles, Sydney, Hong Kong, among others. But this geography now also includes cities such as São Paulo, Buenos Aires, Bangkok, Taipei, Bombay, and Mexico City. The intensity of transactions among these cities, particularly through the financial markets, trade in services, and investment, has increased sharply, and so have the orders of magnitude involved. At the same time, there has been a sharpening inequality in the concentration of strategic resources and activities between each of these cities and others in the same country. Global cities are sites for immense concentrations of economic power and command centers in a global economy, while traditional manufacturing centers have suffered inordinate declines.

One might have expected that the growing number of financial centers now integrated into the global markets would have reduced the extent of concentration of financial activity in the top centers. But it has not. One would also expect this given the immense increases in the global volume of transactions. Yet the levels of concentration remain unchanged in the face of massive transformations in the financial industry and in the technological infrastructure this industry depends on.

The growth of global markets for finance and specialized services, the need for transnational servicing networks because of sharp increases in international investment, the reduced role of the government in the regulation of international economic activity and the corresponding ascendance of other institutional arenas, notably global markets and corporate headquarters – all these point to the existence of a series of economic processes, each characterized by locations in more than one country and in this regard transnational. We can see here the formation, at least incipient, of a transnational urban system (Sassen 1991, chap. 7; 1994, chap. 3; Knox and Taylor 1995).

The pronounced orientation to the world markets evident in such cities raises questions about the articulation with their nation-states, their regions, and the larger economic and social structure in such cities.

Cities have typically been deeply embedded in the economies of their region, indeed often reflecting the characteristics of the latter; and generally they still do. But cities that are strategic sites in the global economy tend, in part, to become disconnected from their region and even nation. This conflicts with a key proposition in conventional scholarship about urban systems, namely, that these systems promote the territorial integration of regional and national economies.

Alongside these new global and regional hierarchies of cities and high-tech industrial districts lies a vast territory that has become increasingly peripheral, increasingly excluded from the major economic processes that fuel economic growth in the new global economy. A multiplicity of formerly important manufacturing centers and port cities have lost functions and are in decline, not only in the less developed countries but also in the most advanced economies. This is yet another meaning of economic globalization.

But also inside global cities we see a new geography of centrality and marginality. The downtowns of global cities and metropolitan business centers receive massive investments in real estate and telecommunications while low-income city areas are starved for resources. Highly educated workers employed in leading sectors see their incomes rise to unusually high levels while low- or medium-skilled workers in those same sectors see theirs sink. Financial services produce superprofits while industrial services barely survive. These trends are evident, with different levels of intensity, in a growing number of major cities in the developed world and increasingly in major cities of some of the developing countries that have been integrated into the global economy.

The rights of capital in the new global grid

A basic proposition in discussions about the global economy concerns the declining sovereignty of states over their economies.

Economic globalization does indeed extend the economy beyond the boundaries of the nation-state. This is particularly evident in the leading economic sectors. Existing systems of governance and accountability for transnational activities and actors leave much ungoverned when it comes to these industries. Global markets in finance and advanced services partly operate through a "regulatory" umbrella that is not state centered but market centered. More generally, the new geography of centrality is transnational and operates in good part in electronic spaces that override all jurisdiction.

Yet, this proposition fails to underline a key component in the transformation of the last fifteen years: the formation of new claims on national states to guarantee the domestic and global rights of capital. What matters for our purposes here is that global capital made these claims and that national states responded through the production of new forms of legality. The new geography of centrality had to be produced, both in terms of the practices of corporate actors and in terms of the work of the state in producing new legal regimes. Representations that characterize the national state as simply losing significance fail to capture this very important dimension, and reduce what is happening to a function of the global/national duality – what one wins, the other loses.

There are two distinct issues here. One is the ascendance of this new legal regime that negotiates between national sovereignty and the transnational practices of corporate economic actors. The second issue concerns the particular content of this new regime, which strengthens the advantages of certain types of economic actors and weakens those of others. The hegemony of neoliberal concepts of economic relations with its strong emphasis on markets, deregulation, and free international trade has influenced policy in the 1980s in the United States and Great Britain and now increasingly also in continental Europe. This has contributed to the formation of transnational legal regimes that are centered in Western economic concepts of contract and property rights. Through the International Monetary Fund (IMF) and the International Bank for Reconstruction and Development (IBRD), as well as the General Agreement on Tariffs and Trade (GATT) (the World Trade Organization since January 1995), this regime has spread to the developing world (Mittelman 1996). It is a regime associated with increased levels of concentrated wealth, poverty, and inequality worldwide. This occurs under specific modalities in the case of global cities, as discussed earlier.

Deregulation has been a crucial mechanism to negotiate the juxtaposition of the global and the national. Rather than simply seeing it as freeing up markets and reducing the sovereignty of the state, we might underline a much less noted aspect of deregulation: it has had the effect, particularly in the case of the leading economic sectors, of partly denationalizing national territory (see Sassen 1996). In other words, it is not simply a matter of a space economy extending beyond a national realm. It is also that globalization – as illustrated by the space economy of advanced information industries – denationalizes national territory. This denationalization, which to a large extent materializes in global cities, has become legitimate for capital and has indeed been imbued with positive value by many government elites and their economic advisers. It is the opposite when it comes to people, as is perhaps most sharply illustrated in the rise of anti-immigrant feeling and the renationalizing of politics.

The emphasis on the transnational and hypermobile character of capital has contributed to a sense of powerlessness among local actors, a sense of the futility of resistance. But the analysis in the preceding sections, with its emphasis on place, suggest that the new global grid of strategic sites is a terrain for politics and engagement. Further, the state, both national and local, can be engaged. Although certain agencies within the state have contributed to the formation and strengthening of global capital, the state is far from being a unitary institution. The state itself has been transformed by its role in implementing the global economic system, a transformation captured in the ascendance of agencies linked to the domestic and international financial markets in most governments of highly developed countries and many governments of developing countries, and the loss of power and prestige of agencies associated with issues of domestic equity. These different agencies are now at times in open conflict.

The focus on place helps us elaborate and specify the meaning of key concepts in the discourse about globalization, notably the loss of sovereignty. It brings to the fore that important components of globalization are embedded in particular institutional locations within national territories. A strategic subnational unit such as the global city is emblematic of these conditions – conditions not well captured in the more conventional duality of national/global.

A focus on the leading industries in global cities introduces into the discussion of governance the possibility of capacities for local governmental regulation derived from the concentration of significant resources in strategic places. These resources include fixed capital and are essential for participation in the global economy. The considerable placeboundedness of many of these resources contrasts with the hypermobility of the outputs of many of these same industries, particularly finance. The regulatory capacity of the state stands in a different relation to hypermobile outputs than to the infrastructure of facilities, from office buildings equipped with fiber optic cables to specialized workforces.

The specific issues raised by focusing on the placeboundedness of key components of economic globalization are quite distinct from those typically raised in the context of the national/global duality. A focus on this duality leads to rather straightforward propositions about the declining significance of the state *vis-à-vis* global economic actors. The overarching tendency in economic analyses of globalization and of the leading information industries has been to

emphasize certain aspects: industry outputs rather than the production process involved; the capacity for instantaneous transmission around the world rather than the infrastructure necessary for this capacity; the impossibility for the state to regulate those outputs and that capacity insofar as they extend beyond the nation-state. And the emphasis is by itself quite correct; but it is a partial account about the implications of globalization for governance.

The transformation in the composition of the world economy, especially the rise of finance and advanced services as leading industries, is contributing to a new international economic order, one dominated by financial centers, global markets, and transnational firms. Cities that function as international business and financial centers are sites for direct transactions with world markets that take place without government inspection, as for instance the euromarkets or New York City's international financial zone (i.e., International Banking Facilities). These cities and the globally oriented markets and firms they contain mediate in the relation of the world economy to nation-states and in the relations among nation-states. Correspondingly, we may see a growing significance of sub- and supranational political categories and actors.

Unmooring identities and a new transnational politics

The preceding section argues that the production of new forms of legality and of a new transnational legal regime privilege the reconstitution of capital as a global actor and the denationalized spaces necessary for its operation. At the same time there is a lack of new legal forms and regimes to encompass another crucial element of this transnationalization, one that some, including myself, see as the counterpart to that of capital: the transnationalization of labor. However, we are still using the language of immigration to describe the process. Nor are there new forms and regimes to encompass the transnationalization in the formation of identities and loyalties among various population segments which do not regard the nation as the sole or principal source of identification, and the associated new solidarities and notions of membership. Major cities have emerged as a strategic site not only for global capital but also for the transnationalization of labor and the formation of transnational identities. In this regard they are a site for new types of political operations.

Cities are the terrain where people from many different countries are most likely to meet and a multiplicity of cultures come together. The international character of major cities lies not only in their telecommunication infrastructure and international firms, but also in the many different cultural environments they contain. One can no longer think of centers for international business and finance simply in terms of the corporate towers and corporate culture at their center. Today's global cities are in part the spaces of postcolonialism and indeed contain conditions for the formation of a postcolonialist discourse (Hall 1991; King 1996).

The large Western city of today concentrates diversity. Its spaces are inscribed with the dominant corporate culture but also with a multiplicity of other cultures and identities. The slippage is evident: the dominant culture can encompass only part of the city. And while corporate power inscribes these cultures and identifies them with "otherness" thereby devaluing them, they are present everywhere. For instance, through immigration a proliferation of originally highly localized cultures now have become presences in many large cities, cities whose elites think of themselves as cosmopolitan, as transcending any locality. Members of these "localized" cultures can in fact come from places with great cultural diversity and be as cosmopolitan as elites. An immense array of cultures from around the world, each rooted in a particular country, town, or village, now are reterritorialized in a few single places, places such as New York, Los Angeles, Paris, London, and most recently Tokyo.

I think that there are representations of globality which have not been recognized as such or are contested representations. Such representations include immigration and its associated multiplicity of cultural environments, often subsumed under the notion of ethnicity. What we still narrate in the language of immigration and ethnicity, I would argue, is actually a series of processes having to do with the globalization of economic activity, of cultural activity, of identity formation. Too often immigration and ethnicity are constituted as otherness. Understanding them as a set of processes whereby global elements are localized, international labor markets are constituted, and cultures from all over the world are de- and reterritorialized, puts them right there at the center along with the internationalization of capital as a fundamental aspect of globalization. This way of narrating the large migrations of the post-war era captures the ongoing weight of colonialism and postcolonial forms of empire on major processes of globalization today, and specifically those processes binding countries of emigration and immigration. Although the specific genesis and contents of their responsibility will vary from case to case and period to period, none of the major immigration countries are passive bystanders in their immigration histories.

Making claims on the city

These processes signal that there has been a change in the linkages that bind people and places and in the corresponding formation of claims on the city. It is true that throughout history people have moved and through these movements constituted places. But today the articulation of territory and people is being constituted in a radically different way at least in one regard, and that is the speed with which that articulation can change. Martinotti (1993) notes that one consequence of this speed is the expansion of the space within which actual and possible linkages can occur. The shrinking of distance and the speed of movement that characterize the current era find one of its most extreme forms in electronically based communities of individuals or organizations from all around the globe interacting in real time and simultaneously, as is possible through the Internet and kindred electronic networks.

I would argue that another radical form assumed today by the linkage of people to territory is the unmooring of identities from what have been traditional sources of identity, such as the nation or the village. This unmooring in the process of identity formation engenders new notions of community, of membership, and of entitlement.

The space constituted by the global grid of cities, a space with new economic and political potentialities, is perhaps one of the most strategic spaces for the formation of transnational identities and communities. This is a space that is both place centered in that it is embedded in particular and strategic locations; and it is transterritorial because it connects sites that are not geographically proximate yet are intensely connected to each other. As I argued earlier, it is not only the transmigration of capital that takes place in this global grid, but also that of people, both rich (i.e., the new transnational professional workforce) and poor (i.e., most migrant workers) and it is a space for the transmigration of cultural forms, for the reterritorialization of "local" subcultures. An important question is whether it is also a space for a new politics, one going beyond the politics of culture and identity, though at least partly likely to be embedded in it.

Yet another way of thinking about the political implications of this strategic transnational space anchored in cities is the formation of new claims on that space. As was discussed earlier, there are indeed new major actors making claims on these cities over the last decade, notably foreign firms that have been increasingly entitled through the deregulation of national economies, and the increasing number of international businesspeople. These are among the new "city users." They have profoundly marked the urban landscape. Their claim to the city is not contested, even though the

costs and benefits to cities have barely been examined.

The new city users have made an often immense claim on the city and have reconstituted strategic spaces of the city in their image: their claim is rarely examined or challenged. They contribute to changing the social morphology of the city and to constituting what Martinotti (1993) calls the metropolis of second generation, the city of late modernism. The new city of these city users is a fragile one, whose survival and successes are centered on an economy of high productivity, advanced technologies, and intensified exchanges.

On the one hand, this raises a question of what the city is for international businesspeople: it is a city whose space consists of airports, top-level business districts, top of the line hotels and restaurants – a sort of urban glamor zone, the new hyperspace of international business. On the other hand, there is the difficult task of establishing whether a city that functions as an international business center does in fact recover the costs for being such a center: the costs involved in maintaining a state-of-the-art business district, and all it requires, from advanced communications facilities to top-level security and "world-class culture."

Perhaps at the other extreme of legitimacy are those who use urban political violence to make their claims on the city, claims that lack the de facto legitimacy enjoyed by the new business city users. These are claims made by actors struggling for recognition and entitlement, claiming their rights to the city (Body-Gendrot 1993). These claims have, of course, a long history; every new epoch brings specific conditions to the manner in which the claims are made. The growing weight of "delinquency," for example, smashing cars and shop windows, robbing and burning stores, in some of these uprisings during the last decade in major cities of the developed world, is perhaps an indication of the sharpened inequality. The disparities, as seen and as lived, between the urban glamor zone and the urban war zone have become enormous. The extreme visibility of the difference is likely to contribute to further brutalization of the conflict: the indifference and greed of the new elites versus the hopelessness and rage of the poor.

There are then two aspects of this formation of new claims that have implications for transnational politics. One is these sharp and perhaps intensifying differences in the representation of claims by different sectors, notably international business and the vast population of low-income "others" – African Americans, immigrants, and women. The second aspect is the increasingly transnational element in both types of claims and claimants. It signals a politics of contestation embedded in specific places but transnational in character.

Globalization is a process that generates contradictory spaces, characterized by contestation, internal differentiation, continuous border crossings. The global city is emblematic of this condition. Global cities concentrate a disproportionate share of global corporate power and are one of the key sites for its valorization. But they also concentrate a disproportionate share of the disadvantaged and are one of the key sites for their devalorization. This joint presence happens in a context where the globalization of the economy has grown sharply and cities have become increasingly strategic for global capital; and marginalized people have found their voice and are making claims on the city. This joint presence is further brought into focus by the increasing disparities between the two. The center now concentrates immense economic and political power, power that rests on the capability for global control and the capability to produce superprofits. And actors with little economic and traditional political power have become an increasingly strong presence through the new politics of culture and identity, and an emergent transnational politics embedded in the new geography of economic globalization. Both actors, increasingly transnational and in contestation, find in the city the strategic terrain for their operations. But it is hardly the terrain of a balanced playing field.

REFERENCES

Body-Gendrot, Sophie. 1993. *Ville et violence: L'irruption de nouveaux acteurs*. Paris: PUF (Presses Universitaires de France).

Castells, Manuel. 1989. *The Informational City*. Oxford: Blackwell.

Competition and Change: The Journal of Global Business and Political Economy. 1995. vol. 1, no. 1. Harwood Academic Publishers.

Hall, S. 1991. "The Local and the Global: Globalization and Ethnicity." In Anthony D. King, ed., *Culture, Globalization and the World System: Contemporary Conditions for the Representation of Identity. Current Debates in Art History 3*. Department of Art and Art History, State University of New York at Binghamton.

King, Anthony, ed. 1996. *Representing the City: Ethnicity, Capital and Culture in the 21st Century*. London: Macmillan.

Knox, Paul, and Peter J. Taylor, eds. 1995. *World Cities in a World-System*. Cambridge: Cambridge University Press.

Martinotti, Guido. 1993. *Metropoli: La nuova morfologìa sociale della città*. Bologna: Il Mulino.

Mittelman, James, ed. 1996. *Globalization: Critical Reflections. International Political Economy Yearbook*, vol. 9. Boulder, Colo.: Lynne Reinner.

Sassen, Saskia. 1996. *Losing Control? Sovereignty in an Age of Globalization*. New York: Columbia University Press.

——. 1994. *Cities in a World Economy*. Thousand Oaks, Calif.: Pine Forge/Sage Press.

——. 1991. *The Global City: New York, London, Tokyo*. Princeton, NJ: Princeton University Press.

Chapter 19

from *Nature's Metropolis: Chicago and the Great West*

William Cronon

3 Pricing the Future: Grain

Prairie into farm

The train did not create the city by itself. Stripped of the rhetoric that made it seem a mechanical deity, the railroad was simply a go-between whose chief task was to cross the boundary between city and country. Its effects had less to do with some miraculous power in the scream of a locomotive's whistle than with opening a corridor between two worlds that would remake each other. Goods and people rode the rails to get to market, where together buyers and sellers from city and country priced the products of the earth. In this sense, Chicago was just the site of a country fair, albeit the grandest, most spectacular country fair the world had ever seen. The towns and farms that seemed to spring magically into being when railroads appeared in their vicinity were actually responding to the call of that fair. But so was Chicago itself. Its unprecedented growth in the second half of the nineteenth century was in no small measure the creation of people in its hinterland, who in sending the fruits of their labor to its markets brought great change to city and country alike. "The cities have not made the country," reflected one long-time resident of Chicago in 1893; "on the contrary, the country has compelled the cities.... Without the former the latter could not exist. Without farmers there

could be no cities."[1] Nowhere was this more true than in Chicago.

Farmers brought a new human order to the country west of the Great Lakes, as revolutionary in its own way as the train or the city itself. Potawatomis and other Indian peoples had been raising corn on small plots of land around Lake Michigan for generations, but always on a limited scale. The new Euroamerican farmers, on the other hand, raised corn with an eye to the market, and so grew much greater quantities on much larger plots of land, especially once they could ship their harvest by rail. In addition to eating some of the grain themselves, they did things no Indians had ever done with it: turned it into whisky or fed it to hogs and other livestock, in both cases so that they could transport it more easily to market. They also began to raise crops that had never before been part of the regional landscape: old-world grains, especially wheat, as well as a wealth of fruit and vegetable species....

Starting in the second decade of the nineteenth century, when the government first began selling land in southern parts of Illinois, arriving settlers purchased their property in arbitrary units of sections, half sections, and 160-acre quarter sections. An apparently uniform terrain whose natural boundaries were so subtle as to seem almost invisible meant that the survey's checkerboard pattern caused few obvious problems: the grid gave shape to the pastures, meadows, and cornfields of a new agricultural order.[2] From that order would come a cornucopia of wheat and corn, livestock and poultry, all held within neatly rectilinear frames. Rectangular fields meant that farmers and horses could cut long, straight swaths whether they pulled plows, harrows, or newfangled tools like reapers. Because farm fields were large, uniform, and relatively free of rocks or other obstructions, prairie farmers enjoyed economies of scale which left them better able to adopt new agricultural machinery than many of their eastern counterparts – once they could afford to do so....

Watercourses offered another advantage as well. Given the poor state of frontier roads, the rivers of the prairie were its highways. Farmers often sought to float their goods to market, for the land's flatness meant that prairie rivers had few rapids and were easily navigable when they held enough water.

To go to market, farmers had either to build a raft or flatboat themselves or, as happened more often, to sell crops to a local merchant who combined them with other farmers' produce for shipment up or downstream....

For all these reasons, Euroamericans' initial agricultural occupation of the prairie country took place mainly along the spines of the chief watersheds.[3]...

The settlers came from many places. Before the 1833 land rush, the major influx of population came via the Ohio and Mississippi rivers, with southern states – Kentucky, Tennessee, and Virginia as well as southern Ohio and Indiana – accounting for a disproportionate share of settlers. At the same time, a number of British families began to arrive either individually or in colonies.[4] By 1850, as the Great Lakes started to carry more passenger traffic, increased numbers of settlers from New York, Pennsylvania, and New England were joining the stream of new arrivals. In their midst were more and more foreign-born migrants, with Great Britain, Ireland, and Germany contributing the greatest

shares. Foreign migrants settled disproportionately in cities: although Illinois as a whole was only 12.5 percent foreign-born in 1850, fully half of Cook County's inhabitants (most of them living in Chicago) had been born outside the United States.[5] The relative "foreignness" of cities like Chicago, Milwaukee, and St. Louis continued throughout the century, but rural settlements also had their share of immigrant farm families.

A sack's journey

... Settlers did not solve the problem of selling [their] crops simply by hauling them to the banks of the nearest river. They also had to find customers for them, which was not always easy to do in a sparsely settled landscape with few towns and even fewer cities. Farmers sold much of what they grew to merchants and storekeepers in their immediate vicinity, acting out one of the key market relationships in the emerging agricultural economy....

Merchants could earn greater profits than farmers, but they also faced the prospect of considerably greater losses. Given the problems of water transport and the poor quality of information about prices in distant markets, wholesaling farm crops in pretelegraph, prerailroad days could be risky indeed. "No one can realize," wrote the merchant John Burrows of Davenport, Iowa, "the difficulties of doing a produce business in those days. We had no railroads. Everything had to be moved by water, and, of course, had to be held all winter."[6] It was all too easy to buy wheat and other crops in the fall and then find little or no market for them the following spring....

Farmers bartered their produce because they were cash poor. In an economy short of cash, where credit was essential to making exchange possible, merchants served as translators between the world of rural barter and the world of urban money. Because storekeepers sold almost anything farmers needed, the general store became the outpost of a market economy whether it was located in a town, in a village, or in the middle of a prairie. By buying, storing, shipping, and reselling farm produce, merchants linked farm communities to the trade of a wider world.

The gateways to that trade were almost invariably located in cities, which acted as funnels for the increasing flood of grain and other farm products being sent out of the countryside. . . .

Most of [Chicago's] grain merchants conducted their business in the vicinity of South Water Street, immediately adjacent to the south bank of the Chicago River.[7] Warehouses fronted directly on the water, rising three or four stories above it and leaving little room for wagons to maneuver. Ships were equally crowded in the narrow waterway. So hemmed in was the river that it did not figure very prominently in people's mental image of the city. Visitors to Chicago often mentioned the crowded bustle of its streets and the long traffic jams that occurred when drawbridges over the river were open, but they scarcely seemed to notice the river's wharves and piers. . . .

Whether on St. Louis's levee or Chicago's South Water Street, selling grain in the 1840s was a fairly straightforward business. A merchant like Burrows in Davenport would sack up the grain he had purchased from farmers in his vicinity, load it onto a flatboat or steamship, and float downstream to the docks at St. Louis. To reach Chicago during the 1840s, he would have made a similar trip by wagon. Once he arrived, he would unload his grain and try to sell it for cash to dealers who needed it to meet local demand. Much of the street and levee activity that struck visitors in Chicago and St. Louis consisted of sellers trying to find buyers and buyers trying to find sellers for the sacks of grain lying on the ground around them. One Chicago reporter said the buyers reminded him of nothing so much as "bees in a clover field."[8] As often as not, local dealers had all the grain they needed for home use, and so the would-be seller next turned to a commission merchant. Commission merchants made money not by buying grain on their own account but by arranging for

its transportation to a larger city – New Orleans or New York being the two most obvious choices – where it might find a more welcoming market. The country merchant or farmer paid a commission for this service and took whatever profits or losses resulted from the final transaction.

To grasp the changes in grain marketing that occurred in Chicago during the 1850s, one must understand several key features of this early waterborne trading system. All hinged on the seemingly unremarkable fact that shippers, whether farmers or merchants, loaded their grain into sacks before sending it on its journey to the mill that finally ground it into flour. As the sack of grain moved away from the farm – whether pulled in wagons, floated on flatboats, or lofted on stevedores' backs – its contents remained intact, unmixed with grain from other farms. Nothing adulterated the characteristic weight, bulk, cleanliness, purity, and flavor that marked it as the product of a particular tract of land and a particular farmer's labor. When distant urban millers or wholesalers decided to buy the grain, they did so after examining a "representative sample" and then offering a price based on their judgement of its quality. Within any given level of market demand, price reflected how plump, clean, and pure a farm family had managed to make its grain.[9]

Intrinsic to this system of sack-based shipments was the fact that ownership rights to grain remained with its original shipper until it reached the point of final sale. The farmer or storekeeper who sold grain to a Chicago or St. Louis commission merchant continued to own it as it traveled the hundreds of miles to New Orleans or New York. This meant that the shipper bore all risks for damage that might occur during transit. If the grain became waterlogged, if it began to spoil in warm weather, if prices collapsed before it reached market, or if its ship sank, the resulting losses accrued not to the commission merchant or the transport company but to the original shipper.

Because these risks remained in the hands of farmers and merchants who were often of small means, insurance was a key service sold in large cities such as St. Louis or Chicago. Sellers of fire, marine, and commercial insurance, many of them agents of eastern companies, were among the largest businesses in Chicago by the 1840s, when at least one of them outranked city banks in financial resources.[10] Without the services of such firms, small shippers could all too easily face bankruptcy if some disaster happened before they could sell their goods....

Sacks were the key to the whole water-based transportation system. Since grain originated in farms and villages that had only small quantities to sell, it had to start its journey on a modest scale, ideally suited to small groups of sacks. Once embarked on the river passage, sacks offered a convenient solution to the problem of loading the irregular holds of flatboats, keelboats, and steamboats. Moving goods by water almost always meant transferring them several times along the way, from pier to flatboat, from flatboat to levee, from levee to steamboat, from steamboat to sailing craft. Such transfers worked best if shipments were small enough that their weight and bulk did not prevent an individual worker from handling them. Moving grain on and off a ship usually meant negotiating tortuous passageways – across gangways, down stairs, through corridors, into storage bins – and the more complicated the path, the more critical the need to keep down the size of the unit being moved. Beyond these purely physical problems of water-based grain handling, the prevailing apparatus for transferring ownership rights also worked in favor of the sack system. Shippers and their customers wanted to know exactly what they were selling and buying, so it made sense not to break up individual shipments or mix them with others. In all these ways, marketing and transportation systems reflected each other. Sacks and ships seemed an ideal combination.

The water-based grain-marketing system at midcentury was thus designed to move wheat, corn, and other cereal crops without disrupting the link between grain as physical object and grain as saleable commodity.

At every point where grain moved from one form of transportation to another, it did so in individual bags on the backs of individual workers. Wherever it had to wait at transfer points, it did so in warehouses that kept individual lots carefully separated from each other. When shippers completed their final sales, they sold the rights to actual sacks of physical grain. A farm family sending a load of wheat from Illinois to New York could still have recovered that same wheat, packed with a bill of lading inside its original sacks, in a Manhattan warehouse several weeks later. The market had as yet devised few ways of separating grain as a priced commodity from the grain that had so recently clung to yellow stalks on the windy hillsides of former prairies.

The golden stream

The railroads changed all this. By giving rural shippers an alternative way to reach urban markets, they rerouted the flow of farm produce and encouraged new settlement patterns in the areas they serviced. Migrants to Illinois and Iowa had previously settled mainly in the river valleys nearest St. Louis; after 1848, they moved most quickly into the railroad corridors west of Chicago.[11] As they arrived, new settlers increased agricultural production on upland prairies which had heretofore seen little farming: the route of the Illinois Central, for instance, gave new access to the previously unsettled countries of the Grand Prairie in central Illinois.[12] Equally important were the grain shipments out of already settled areas which had formerly had no alternative to rivers for bringing crops to market.[13] By lowering land transportation costs, the railroad allowed farmers to sell more grain and heightened their expectations about the scale of their own production.

The predictable result was an explosion in Chicago's receipts of grain. As late as 1850, St. Louis was still handling over twice as much wheat and flour as Chicago, but within five years the younger city had far surpassed its older rival. The same shift occurred in the waterborne corn trade after 1848 when the Illinois and Michigan Canal began to bring corn north toward Lake Michigan.[14] As the canal and railroads increased the flow of grain into Chicago's warehouses, they simultaneously encouraged an expansion of shipping out of its harbor, contributing to a general reorientation of western trade toward the east and away from the south. Between 1850 and 1854, the net eastward movement of freight shipments via the Great Lakes finally surpassed shipments out of New Orleans.[15] No place was more important than Chicago to this redirection of agricultural trade. The city and its merchants changed forever the way prairie farmers could sell their crops. At the same time, the farmers and their crops fundamentally altered Chicago's markets.

The immense amounts of grain pouring into Chicago expanded the city's markets, but quantity alone was not the whole story. Compared with other modes of transportation, railroad cars moved grain more quickly and in standardized carloads of medium size. With whole freight cars, for instance, carrying nothing but wheat, shippers and railroad managers soon came to think of grain shipments not as individual "sacks" but as "carloads" consisting of about 325 bushels each.[16] The railroad brought grain into the city through the narrow gateways represented by tracks, sidings, and stations. As more and more trains passed more and more frequently through those gateways, adding their grain to the loads that farmers were still hauling in their wagons, freight traffic congestion became more of a problem. As the *Chicago Democratic Press* reported during the harvest season of 1854, "The piles of grain now lying uncovered in our streets, the choked and crowded thoroughfares, the overloaded teams, the bursting bags, ... all testify to a wide-felt want of room.... We want more warehouses.... We want more cars and locomotives."[17]

Geography and the logic of capital meant that congestion *felt* different in Chicago than in St. Louis. The 2.1 million bushels

of wheat that passed across the St. Louis levee in 1854 moved among hundreds of boats and ships scattered along hundreds of yards of waterfront.[18] Hundreds of individuals, many of whom possessed only small amounts of capital, shared responsibility for making sure that grain continued safely on its journey. Although the 3.0 million bushels of wheat that passed through Chicago during that same year was only moderately larger than St. Louis's shipments in total size, well over a million of those bushels entered the city via the tracks of just one railroad, the Galena and Chicago Union.[19] In Chicago, a small group of railroad managers bore the heavy financial responsibility of moving millions of bushels of grain. Given the large capital investment represented by a railroad's cars, sidings, and other equipment, managers had a strong incentive to accelerate the speed with which employees emptied grain cars and returned them to active service. Rapid turnaround was imperative if managers were to maximize their use of capital equipment and prevent congestion.

Achieving these goals meant getting grain out of its sacks, off the backs of individual workers, and into automatic machinery that would move it more rapidly and efficiently. The invention that made this possible was among the most important yet least acknowledged in the history of American agriculture: the steam-powered grain elevator.[20] First introduced in 1842 by a Buffalo warehouseman named Joseph Dart, it was soon adopted by grain dealers in Chicago as well. By the end of the 1850s, Chicagoans had refined their elevator system beyond that of any other city, leading the way toward a transformation of grain marketing worldwide.[21]

Structurally, the elevator was a multistoried warehouse divided into numbered vertical bins containing different lots of grain. But as Anthony Trollope observed of his visit to a Chicago elevator in 1861, "it was not as a storehouse that this great building was so remarkable, but as a channel or a river course for the flooding freshets of corn."[22] What distinguished an elevator from earlier warehouses was its use of machinery instead of human workers to move grain into and out of the building. Grain entered the structure on an endless steam-powered conveyor belt to which large scoops or buckets were attached. After riding the buckets to the top of the building, the grain was weighed on a set of scales – a technique that soon encouraged Chicago dealers to define their standard bushels according to weight rather than volume.[23] Grain dropped out the bottom of the scale into a rotating chute mechanism, which elevator operators could direct into any of the numbered bins inside the warehouse. Once it was inside the bins, workers could deliver grain to a waiting ship or railroad car simply by opening a chute at the bottom of the building and letting gravity do the rest of the work.[24] ...

When all twelve of the city's elevators were operating at full capacity, Chicago could receive and ship nearly half a million bushels of grain every ten hours. The economic benefits of such efficient handling were so great that moving a bushel of grain from railroad car to lake vessel cost only half a cent, giving Chicago a more than tenfold advantage over St. Louis.[25]

These were great benefits to derive from the simple expedient of doing away with grain sacks, but they quickly raised a serious new problem that called into question the entire legal apparatus of the earlier grain-marketing system. Formerly, the transportation network had assiduously maintained the bond of ownership between shippers and the physical grain they shipped. Farmer Smith's wheat from Iowa would never be mixed with Farmer Jones's wheat from Illinois until some final customer purchased both. Now this started to change. As the scale of Chicago's grain trade grew, elevator operators began objecting to keeping small quantities of different owners' grain in separate bins that were only partially filled – for an unfilled bin represented underutilized capital. To avoid that disagreeable condition, they sought to mix grain in common bins. Crops from dozens of different farms

could then mingle, and the reduced cost of handling would earn the elevator operator higher profits. The only obstacle to achieving this greater efficiency was the small matter of a shipper's traditional legal ownership of physical grain.

The organization that eventually solved this problem – albeit after several years of frustrated efforts and false starts – was the Chicago Board of Trade. Founded as a private membership organization in March 1848, the Board initially had eighty-two members drawn from a wide range of commercial occupations.[26] ...

Elevators, with their automatic mechanisms for handling large quantities of grain in continuously moving streams, made the old measure of grain volume – a bushel of standard size – obsolete. Starting in 1854, therefore, the Board pressed city merchants to replace the old, volume-based bushel with a new, weight-based bushel that could be used to calibrate elevator scales.[27] ...

Not until European demand for grain expanded during the Crimean War did the fortunes of the Board begin to change. American wheat exports doubled in volume and tripled in value during 1853 and 1854, while domestic prices rose by more than 50 percent.[28] The surge of foreign buying had impressive effects in Chicago. Between 1853 and 1856, the total amount of grain shipped from Chicago more than tripled, with 21 million bushels leaving the city in 1856 alone.[29] As volume increased and traders found it more convenient to do their business centrally, attendance at daily Board meetings rose. Rather than argue over prices amid heaps of grain in streets and warehouses, traders – usually working on commission for real owners and purchasers – brought samples to the Board's meeting rooms, dickered over prices, and arranged contracts among buyers and sellers. The greater the number of traders who gathered in a single market, the more efficient and attractive that market became. By 1856, Board leaders felt confident enough of their organization's importance that they stopped serving cheese, crackers, and ale to encourage attendance. The advantages of the central-ized market were soon so great that no serious grain merchant could afford not to belong, and so the Board began to issue membership cards that traders had to show to a doorkeeper before entering the meeting rooms. Daily meetings on the floor of what was beginning to be called 'Change (short for "Exchange") soon became so crowded that the Board moved to new quarters on the corner of LaSalle and South Water streets.[30]

Its membership now numbering in the hundreds, the Board finally had sufficient influence to seek a new role: increasingly, its members would take it upon themselves to regulate the city's grain trade. By pro-mulgating rules which all traders using its market agreed to follow, the Board in effect set uniform standards for the city as a whole, and for its grain-raising hinterland as well. Its system of regulations, proposed for the first time in 1856, restructured Chi-cago's market in a way that would forever transform the grain trade of the world. In that year, the Board made the momentous decision to designate three categories of wheat in the city – white winter wheat, red winter wheat, and spring wheat – and to set standards of quality for each.[31]

In this seemingly trivial action lay the solution to the elevator operators' dilemma about mixing different owners' grain in single bins. As long as one treated a ship-ment of wheat or corn as if it possessed unique characteristics that distinguished it from all other lots of grain, mixing was impossible. But if instead a shipment repre-sented a particular "grade" of grain, then there was no harm in mixing it with other grain of the same grade. Farmers and ship-pers delivered grain to a warehouse and got in return a receipt that they or anyone else could redeem at will. Anyone who gave the receipt back to the elevator got in return not the *original* lot of grain but an equal quantity of *equally graded* grain. A person who owned grain could conveniently sell it to a buyer simply by selling the elevator receipt, and as long as both agreed that they were exchanging equivalent quantities

of *like* grain – rather than the physical grain that the seller had originally deposited in the elevator – both left happy at the end of the transaction. It was a momentous change: as one visitor to Chicago later remarked after a tour of one of the eleva-tors, "It dawns on the observer's mind that one man's property is by no means kept separate from another man's."[32] The grading system allowed elevators to sever the link between ownership rights and physical grain, with a host of unanticipated consequences.[33]

[A] key step was to make formal distinc-tions between grains of different quality. Starting in 1857, the Board no longer rec-ognized "spring wheat" as a single category, but instead broke it into three grades ranked from high quality to low: "Club Spring," "No. 1 spring," and "No. 2 spring."[34] Even these proved inadequate, for in 1858 a Board committee announced that "to improve the character of our grain it will be necessary hereafter to reject en-tirely much of the grain that has heretofore passed as standard in this market."[35] Board members therefore added a fourth category – "Rejected" – to define the bottom of the scale. . . .

Over the next several years, grading scales became ever more elaborate; by 1860, there were no fewer than ten differ-ent grades for wheat alone. . . .

[The] Board got the city's elevator oper-ators to agree (not altogether enthusiastic-ally) that they would allow inspectors to enter warehouses to make sure that the grain in individual bins was actually of the grade that the elevator claimed it to be. This last step was crucial, for only thus could the Board guarantee that people pur-chasing elevator receipts in its meeting rooms would receive grain of the desig-nated quality when they went to reclaim their shipments. Inspection underpinned the integrity of the grading system, which underpinned the integrity of the elevators, which underpinned the integrity of the Board's own markets. . . .

The Board's right to impose standardized grades and inspection rules on its members

– and hence on the Chicago market as a whole – was written into Illinois law in 1859, when the state legislature granted the organization a special charter as "a body politic and corporate."[36] ...

Futures

By 1859, then, Chicago had acquired the three key institutions that defined the future of its grain trade: the elevator warehouse, the grading system, and, linking them, the privately regulated central market governed by the Board of Trade. Together, they constituted a revolution. As Henry Crosby Emery, one of the nineteenth century's leading scholars of commodity markets, wrote in 1896, "the development of the system of grading and of elevator receipts is the most important step in the history of the grain trade."[37] The changes in Chicago's markets suddenly made it possible for people to buy and sell grain not as the physical product of human labor on a particular tract of prairie earth but as an abstract claim on the golden stream flowing through the city's elevators.

Chicagoans began to discover that a grain elevator had much in common with a bank – albeit a bank that paid no interest to its depositors. Farmers or shippers took their wheat or corn to an elevator operator as if they were taking gold or silver to a banker. After depositing the grain in a bin, the original owner accepted a receipt that could be redeemed for grain in much the same way that a check or banknote could be redeemed for precious metal. Again as with a bank, as long as people were confident that the elevator contained plenty of grain, they did not need to cash the receipt to make it useful. Because the flow of grain through the Chicago elevators was enormous, one could almost always count on them to contain enough grain to "back up" one's receipt: the volume of the city's trade in effect made receipts interchangeable. Instead of completing a sale by redeeming the receipt and turning over the physical grain to a purchaser, the original owner could simply turn over the receipt

itself. The entire transaction could be completed – and repeated dozens of times – without a single kernel of wheat or corn moving so much as an inch. The elevators effectively created a new form of money, secured not by gold but by grain. Elevator receipts, as traded on the floor of 'Change, accomplished the transmutation of one of humanity's oldest foods, obscuring its physical identity and displacing it into the symbolic world of capital.[38]

The elevator helped turn grain into capital by obscuring and distancing its link with physical nature, while another new technology extended that process by weakening its link with geography. In 1848, the same year that Chicago merchants founded the Board of Trade, the first telegraph lines reached the city. The earliest messages from New York had to be relayed through Detroit and took some eighteen hours to arrive, but that seemed nearly instantaneous compared with the days or weeks such messages had taken before[39] As the telegraph system expanded across the nation and became more efficient, hours became seconds. By the Civil War, there were 56,000 miles of telegraph wire throughout the country, annually carrying some five million messages with lightning speed.[40]

Because commodity prices were among the most important bits of information that traveled the wires, the coming of the telegraph meant that eastern and western markets began to move in tandem much more than before.[41] As a result, those with the best access to telegraph news were often in the best position to gauge future movements of prices. The *Chicago Democrat* in September 1848 related the story of a Chicagoan who had raced down to the docks after receiving word from the telegraph office that wheat prices were rising on the East Coast. "Seeking among the holders of Illinois wheat, whom he might make a meal of," he

> soon came across his man, and immediately struck a bargain for a cargo at eighty

cents per bushel, the seller chuckling over his trade. In less than fifteen minutes, however, the market rose to eighty-five, and the fortunate possessor of the news by the last flash pocketed the cool five hundred.[42]

Although telegraphic information created speculative opportunities of this sort, it also increased the efficiency of regional markets by giving traders throughout the country speedier access to the same news . . . the telegraph brought prices in distant places closer together by reducing the chance that people would act on bad information. In the wake of the telegraph, news of western harvests brought instant shifts in New York markets, while news of European wars or grain shortages just as rapidly changed prices in Chicago. Local events – a drought, say, or an early frost – ceased to be so important in setting prices for grain or other crops. If local circumstances forced up prices at one place, the telegraph allowed knowledgeable buyers to go elsewhere, driving local prices back down. As markets became more efficient, their prices discounted local conditions and converged with regional, national, and even international price levels. The wider the telegraph's net became, the more it unified previously isolated economies. The result was a new market geography that had less to do with the soils or climate of a given locality than with the prices and information flows of the economy as a whole.[43]

As part of its new landscape of information, the telegraph helped focus attention on cities that already had large trade volumes. A farmer in Iowa inevitably wanted to know wheat prices in Chicago, just as a banker in Chicago wanted to know interest rates in New York. Although the telegraph dispersed price information across an ever widening geographical field, it also concentrated the sources of such information in a few key markets. The dense flow of news in cities like Chicago and New York allowed their prices to reflect trade conditions not just for the local economy but for the national and even the global

economy. Once such central markets had become established, people in other places looked to New York and Chicago prices before all others, enhancing the significance and geographical reach of those two cities in a kind of self-fulfilling prophecy.

The new communication technology had much to do with making the Chicago Board of Trade one of the key grain markets in the world by the late 1850s. The Board began regularly posting telegraph messages from New York in 1858, and the Chicago newspapers started carrying daily market reports from New York, Buffalo, Oswego, and Montreal shortly thereafter. When Board members moved into their new Exchange Hall in 1860, they made sure that a telegraph office occupied the western end of the trading room.[44] The same new emphasis on telegraphic information occurred in New York as well, where the New York Stock Exchange rose to prominence as the national market for securities during the same period and in much the same way.[45] News of events in these emerging central markets flashed outward along the wires and helped set prices wherever it went. One eastern traveler in 1851 remarked after seeing a telegraph line crossing the Mississippi River,

> It seemed like the nervous system of the nation, conveying, quick as thought, the least sensation from extremity to head, the least volition from head to extremity. . . . Or, like a vast arterial system, it carries the pulsations of the heart to the farthest extremity; and by these wires stretched across the Mississippi, I could hear the sharp, quick beating of the great heart of New York.[46]

But the very speed of that heartbeat's spreading rhythm created a problem: although prices might travel from New York to Chicago and back again in a matter of minutes or seconds, grain could hardly do the same. Bushels of wheat or corn still took days or weeks to complete their eastward journey. Since everything depended on buyers' being able to examine grain before they offered a price for it, at least part of the shipment had to reach its destination before parties to the sale could reach an agreement. The old grain-marketing system had solved this difficulty by sending forward a small express sample of the larger shipment, allowing eastern buyers to make their purchases before the bulk of the grain arrived. But there was no way in which even small samples could move quickly enough to lock in the prices coming over telegraph wires. By the time a sample or shipment reached its eastern destination so that buyers could make an offer after examining it, prices might already have changed drastically. Neither buyers nor sellers were happy about the risks such delayed transactions entailed.

Fortunately for both parties, there was a way around this dilemma. If buyers and sellers could complete their grain transactions by telegraph, they could escape the risk and uncertainty of a fluctuating market. However much prices might change in the future, merchants and millers could know that they would receive their grain at the price they expected. The means to this happy end were already available from the same institution that had resolved the elevators' problem of mixing grain in common bins. When the Board of Trade adopted a standard grading system, it made grain interchangeable not just between elevator bins but between cities and continents as well. Once people inside and outside Chicago began to know and trust the Board's new grades, a New York grain dealer could purchase five thousand bushels of Chicago No. 2 spring wheat solely on the basis of prices quoted over the telegraph lines. No longer was it necessary to see a sample of any particular shipment, for all grain of a given grade was for practical purposes identical. A New Yorker could simply check telegraph quotations from the floor of 'Change and wire back an order when the price seemed right, without having to examine a sample of the grain in advance.

Telegraphic orders of this sort encouraged a sharp rise in what traders called "to arrive" contracts for grain. Under these contracts, a seller promised to deliver grain to its buyer by some specified date in the future. Like the telegraph, "to arrive" contracts significantly diminished the risks of trading grain. With the advent of standard grades, it became possible to sell grain to its final customer before it actually began its journey east. A western seller could sign a contract agreeing to deliver grain to an eastern buyer at a specified price within thirty days or some other period of time. With the sale thus guaranteed, most of the *time*-related risks of grain storage or transportation disappeared. . . . Moreover, banks were willing to offer loans to farmers and shippers on the basis of such contracts, so commission merchants found their credit requirements significantly reduced. Customers no longer needed to borrow from commission merchants, but could get immediate cash by using their "to arrive" contracts and elevator receipts as security for bank loans.[47] . . .

"To arrive" contracts in combination with standardized elevator receipts made possible Chicago's greatest innovation in the grain trade: the futures market.[48] "To arrive" contracts solved a problem for grain shippers by ending their uncertainty about future price changes; at the same time, they opened up new opportunities for speculators who were willing to absorb the risk of price uncertainty themselves. If one was willing to gamble on the direction of future price movements, one could make a "to arrive" contract for grain one did not yet own, since one could always buy grain from an elevator to meet the contract just before it fell due. This is exactly what speculators did. Contracting to sell grain one didn't yet own – "selling short" – enabled one to gamble that the price of grain when the contract fell due would be lower than the contract's purchaser was legally bound to pay. By promising to deliver ten thousand bushels of wheat at seventy cents a bushel by the end of June, for instance, one could make $500 if the price of wheat was actually only sixty-five cents at that time, since the buyer had contracted to pay seventy cents whatever the market price. When June came to an end, one had only to buy the necessary number of elevator receipts at their current price on the Chicago Board of Trade, and use them to fulfill the terms of the contract. Given the enormous volume of elevator receipts in circulation, there was little reason to fear that grain would not be available when the "to arrive" contract fell due. . . .

At whatever point we choose to locate its origins, a new sort of grain market had emerged at the Chicago Board of Trade by the second half of the 1860s. Alongside the older, more familiar market, in which traders bought and sold elevator receipts for grain actually present in the city, there was a growing market in contracts for the *future* delivery of grain that perhaps did not even exist yet. These new contracts represented a departure from the older grain market in several key ways. As defined by the Board's bylaws, they referred not to actual physical grain but to fixed quantities of standardized *grades* of grain. They called for delivery not at the moment the contract was struck but at a future date and time that was also standardized by the Board's rules. The contract, in other words, followed a rigidly predefined form, so that, as Henry Emery noted, "only the determination of the total amount and the price is left open to the contracting parties."[49] This meant that futures contracts – like the elevator receipts on which they depended – were essentially interchangeable, and could be bought and sold quite independently of the physical grain that might or might not be moving through the city. . . .

The futures market was a market not in grain but in the *price* of grain. By entering into futures contracts, one bought and sold not wheat or corn or oats but the *prices* of those goods as they would exist at a future time. Speculators made and lost money by selling each other legally binding forecasts of how much grain prices would rise or fall.

As the futures market emerged in the years following the Civil War, speculative interests dominated more and more of the trading on the floor of 'Change. On either side of any given futures contract stood two figures, metaphorically known to traders and the public alike as the bull and the bear.[50] Bulls, believing that the trend of grain prices was upward, tended to *buy* futures contracts in the hope that they would be cheaper than the market price of grain by the time they fell due. Bears, on the other hand, believing that the trend of prices was downward, tended to *sell* futures contracts in the hope that they would be more expensive than the market price of grain when they expired. Except under certain special circumstances, neither bulls nor bears cared much about actually owning grain.[51] One was "long" while the other was "short," and each needed the other to make the market in future prices possible. Since both were gambling that the predictions of the other were wrong, the gains of one always matched the losses of the other. From the point of view of the traders, it mattered little whether the actual price of grain rose or fell, whether farm crops were good or bad, except insofar as these things corroborated price predictions and thereby determined which speculative animal won or lost.

Grain elevators and grading systems had helped transmute wheat and corn into monetary abstractions, but the futures contract extended the abstraction by liberating the grain trade itself from the very process which had once defined it: the exchange of physical grain. In theory, one could buy, sell, and settle up price differences without ever worrying about whether anything really existed to back up contracts which purported to be promises for future delivery of grain. One proof of this was the speed with which futures trading surpassed cash trading – the buying and selling of actual grain – at the Chicago Board of Trade. Although no one kept accurate statistics comparing the two markets, the *Chicago Tribune* estimated in 1875 that the city's cash grain business amounted to about $200 million; the trade in futures, on the other hand, was ten times greater, with a volume of $2 *billion*.[52] A decade later, the Chicago futures market had grown to the point that its volume was probably fifteen to twenty times greater than the city's trade in physical grain.[53] That the trade in not-yet-existing future grain far surpassed the number of bushels actually passing through the city's elevators was strong evidence that Chicago speculators were buying and selling not wheat or corn but pieces of paper whose symbolic relationship to wheat or corn was tenuous at best.

And yet however tenuous that relationship might have become, it could never finally disappear, for one simple reason. No futures contract ever overtly stated that it could be canceled by settling the difference between its price and the market price for grain on a given day. Although

the practice of "settling differences" became exceedingly common, written contracts – which after all were enforceable in a court of law – stated that grain would be delivered on the day they expired. Since futures contracts rapidly came to have standardized expiration dates – usually the last day of certain months – the market in future prices and the market in real grain had to intersect each other at regular intervals. On the day a futures contract expired, prices in the cash grain market determined its value. Because they did so, the activities of speculators working the floor of 'Change sooner or later circled back to those of farmers working the black prairie soil of the western countryside. Remote as the two groups often seemed from each other, they were linked by the forces of a single market....

NOTES

1   Caton, "Sixty Years," 590. Cf. Caton, "Address Delivered to the Settlers," 165.

2   Hildegard Binder Johnson, *Order upon the Land: The U. S. Rectangular Land Survey and the Upper Mississippi Country* (1976); Norman J. Thrower, *Original Survey and Land Subdivision: A Comparative Study of the Form and Effect of Contrasting Cadastral Surveys* (1966). Johnson rightly points out that the grid pattern is not so exact as the word "checker-board" suggests, but it certainly biased landowners toward rectilinear property boundaries.

3   Bogue, *Prairie to Cornbelt*, 8–13; see also the very sophisticated analyses of settlement dynamics in Michael J. O'Brien, ed., *Grassland, Forest, and Historical Settlement: An Analysis of Dynamics in Northeast Missouri* (1984). For contemporary descriptions, see the examples in Quaife, ed., *Pictures of Illinois*; Daniel Harmon Brush, *Growing Up with Southern Illinois, 1820 to 1861*, ed. Milo Milton Quaife (1944).

4   The best general survey of early immigration to the upper Mississippi Valley is Mark Wyman, *Immigrants in the Valley: Irish, Germans, and Americans in the Upper Mississippi Country, 1830–1860*

(1984); for a case study of German ethnicity in an urban setting, see Kathleen Neils Conzen, *Immigrant Milwaukee, 1836–1860: Accommodation and Community in a Frontier City* (1976).

5   US Census, 1850.

6   J. M. D. Burrows, *Fifty Years in Iowa* (1888), in Milo Milton Quaife, ed., *The Early Day of Rock Island and Davenport: The Narratives of J. W. Spencer and J. M. D. Burrows* (1942), 162.

7   J. W. Norris, *Norris' Business Directory and Statistics of the City of Chicago for 1846*, ed. Robert Fergus, Fergus Historical Series, no. 25 (1883), 36, 40.

8   Anonymous, quoted by Taylor, ed., *Chicago Board of Trade*, 1:155.

9   Percy Tracy Dondlinger, *The Book of Wheat: An Economic History and Practical Manual of the Wheat Industry* (1919): 221–2.

10 *Norris' Business Directory for 1846*, 44–5; Alice E. Smith, *George Smith's Money: A Scottish Investor in America* (1966). George Smith's famous Chicago Marine and Fire Insurance Company was so successful that it supplied a sizable portion of Chicago's circulating currency during the 1840s and early 1850s, behaving as much

like a bank as an insurance company. It was able to do this partly because the state legislature had imposed steep restrictions on the ability of Illinois banks to issue notes.

11 ICPSR, "Historical Demographic, Economic and Social Data: The United States, 1790–1970" (machine-readable dataset of census statistics). Statistical work for this book is based on an eleven-state subset of the master series, containing economic and demographic statistics for Michigan, Indiana, Illinois, Wisconsin, Minnesota, Iowa, Missouri, Kansas, Nebraska, North Dakota, and South Dakota between 1840 and 1900. I shall refer to it hereafter as ICPSR Census Series. The argument here is based on a simple comparison of z-scores for decennial county growth rates between 1840 and 1860. For less geographically oriented versions of this same argument, see Douglass C. North, *The Economic Growth of the United States, 1790–1860* (1961; reprint, 1966), 146–53; and Fishlow, *American Railroads*, 207–15.

12 Gates, *Illinois Central Railroad*; Corliss, *Main Line of Mid-America*, 81–9.

13 ICPSR Census Series; Fishlow, *American Railroads*, 211–12.

14 Bureau of Statistics, Treasury Department, "The Grain Trade of the United States, and the World's Wheat Supply and Trade," in *Monthly Summary of Commerce and Finance of the United States* (Jan. 1900), 1958–60; CBT, *Annual Reports*.

15 Haites et al., *Western River Transportation*, 8. The northern route had already surpassed New Orleans in shipments of flour at a much earlier date. See Thomas D. Odle, "The American Grain Trade of the Great Lakes, 1825–1873," *Inland Seas* 8 (1952): 103.

16 Guy A. Lee, "History of the Chicago Grain Elevator Industry, 1840–1890" (Ph.D. thesis, Harvard Univ., 1938), 62. A railroad car was small compared with a canalboat or steamboat that might carry four to ten thousand bushels of grain. Chicago's problem was to combine many small loads into the much larger quantities that could be stored in a warehouse or transported on a ship.

17 *Chicago Democratic Press*, Sept. 13, 1854, as quoted in Taylor, *Chicago Board of Trade*, 1: 190–1.

18 U.S. Treasury Department, "Grain Trade of U.S.," 1958.

19 CBT, *Annual Reports;* Annual Review for 1854, *Chicago Daily Democratic Press*.

20 The classic work on Chicago's grain elevators is Guy A. Lee's "History of the Chicago Grain Elevator Industry, 1840–1890," to which I am indebted for several of the central arguments of this chapter. Lee summarized his main points in "The Historical Significance of the Chicago Grain Elevator System," *Ag. Hist.* 11 (Jan. 1937): 16–32.

21 Joseph Dart, "The Grain Elevators of Buffalo," *Publications of the Buffalo Historical Society* 1 (1879): 391–404. Thomas Odle traces the spread of grain elevators around the Great Lakes basin in his "American Grain Trade," 8 (1952): 189–92.

22 Anthony Trollope, *North America* (1862), ed. Donald Smalley and Bradford Allen Booth (1951), 164. Trollope uses "corn" in the English sense, referring to wheat or to grain generally.

23 Taylor, *Chicago Board of Trade*, 1:189. The shift from volume to weight was one step among many toward perceiving grain not as traditional human-scaled *units* but as interchangeable, abstract, and infinitely divisible *flows*.

24 Although elevators grew enormously in size during the second half of the nineteenth century, their essential organization remained relatively unchanged. For illustrations and an excellent technical description of a Chicago grain elevator in the early 1890s, see *Scientific American* 65, no. 17 (Oct. 24, 1891): cover.

25 Annual Review for 1857, *Chicago Daily Press*, 7–8.

26 Colbert, *Chicago*, 48. Given the destruction of pre-1871 records in the fire, Taylor regards Colbert's brief account as one of the most reliable available for the Board's early history. Taylor, *Chicago Board of Trade*, 1: 139–41.

27 Colbert, *Chicago*, 50; Taylor, *Chicago Board of Trade*, 1: 189–91. The Board urged merchants in Buffalo, Toledo, Milwaukee, and other cities to adopt similar standards for weight-based bushels – all soon did – and also suggested that they join in lobbying against New York's continued use of a half-bushel volume measure

for grain transactions. Important as weight-based measures were becoming, New York ignored the appeal and did not use grain elevators until the 1870s. To anticipate my own argument, New York's intransigence about grain elevators resulted only in part from a conservatism encouraged by its preeminent position in the national economy. Because most of the city's grain arrived in the relatively large units represented by canalboats and ocean-going vessels, there was less need for the break-in-bulk capabilities offered by elevators. New Yorkers also faced the special problem of matching their own business practices with those of traders in the British Empire, who strongly favored sale by sample rather than by grade. New York's growing acceptance of the new elevator and grading technologies after 1870 corresponded with the increasing amount of grain entering the city in railroad cars.

28 U. S. Bureau of the Census, *Historical Statistics*, ser. U279–80, 899, ser. E123–4, 209. The growth of Chicago's grain markets was strongly linked to international exports, about which there is a large literature. For important discussions, see R. F. Crawford, "An Inquiry into Wheat Prices and Wheat Supply," *Journal of the Royal Statistical Society* 58 (1895): 75–120; Egerton R. Williams, "Thirty Years in the Grain Trade," *No. Am. Rev.* 161 (1895): 25–33; William Trimble, "Historical Aspects of the Surplus Food Production of the United States, 1862–1902," *American Historical Association Annual Report for 1918* (1921), 223–39; Wilfred Malenbaum, *The World Wheat Economy, 1885–1839* (1953); Morton Rothstein, "America in the International Rivalry for the British Wheat Market, 1860–1914," *MVHR* 47 (1960): 401–18; Rothstein, "The International Market for Agricultural Commodities, 1850–1873," in David T. Gilchrist and W. David Lewis, eds., *Economic Change in the Civil War Era* (1965), 62–82; Rothstein, "Antebellum Wheat and Cotton Exports: A Contrast in Marketing Organization and Economic Development," *Ag. Hist.* 40 (1966): 91–100; Harry Fornari, *Bread upon the Waters: A History of United States Grain Exports* (1973); C. Knick Harley, "Transportation, the World Wheat Trade, and the Kuznets Cycle, 1850–1913," *Explorations in Economic History* 17 (1980): 218–50; and Jeffrey G. Williamson, "Greasing the Wheels of Sputtering Export Engines: Midwestern Grains and American Growth," ibid., 189–217.

29 CBT, *Annual Reports*. For the effect of the war on Chicago prices, see James E. Boyle, *Chicago Wheat Prices for Eighty-one Years* (1922), 14.

30 Colbert, *Chicago*, 50–1.

31 Ibid., 51; Taylor, *Chicago Board of Trade*, 1:220–1.

32 "The Metropolis of the Prairies," *Harper's New Monthly Magazine* 61 (1880): 726.

33 On grading systems generally, see Dondlinger, *Book of Wheat*, 221–6. So complete was this severing process by the 1860s that Chicago elevators began to issue general receipts for whole trainloads of grain, irrespective of who owned which particular lot; see Henry Crosby Emery, *Speculation on the Stock and Produce Exchanges of the United States* (1896), 38. For a discussion of grain grading in the modern world, see Lowell D. Hill, *Grain Grades and Standards: Historical Issues Shaping the Future* (1990).

34 Taylor, *Chicago Board of Trade*, 1:227.

35 CBT, *Annual Report for 1858*, 11.

36 The 1859 charter is reprinted in an appendix to the Board's *Annual Report for 1877*, pp. v–ix, and can also be found in Andreas, *History of Chicago*, 2: 326.

37 Emery, *Speculation on Stock and Produce Exchanges*, 38. Emery's book remains a classic on the origins of futures markets in the United States, and his chief arguments about this subject appear in the work of most historians who have followed him.

38 F. H. West, a Milwaukee representative at the National Board of Trade meeting in Buffalo in 1870, addressed "the subject of issuing grain receipts by warehouses and elevators" as follows: "That is a new feature in the commerce of the West.... The managers of these elevators have adopted the practice of issuing receipts, and those receipts now enter largely into the commerce of our section of the country. They are in some respects analogous to bank-bills, and pass like bank-bills from hand to hand. In our Western States they are a favorite collateral security with banks; in fact they are nearly all the securities we have to offer for demand loans...." *Proceedings of the Third Annual Meeting of*

the National Board of Trade, Held in Buffalo, December, 1870 (1871), 44. The commercial institution I describe in the text is more precisely known as a negotiable instrument, or a mercantile instrument of credit; for a survey of its history and development, see Joseph J. Klein, "The Development of Mercantile Instruments of Credit in the United States," *Journal of Accountancy* 12 (1911): 321–45, 422–49, 526–37, 594–607; 13 (1912): 44–50, 122–32, 207–17.

39 Taylor, *Chicago Board of Trade*, 1: 135.

40 Richard B. DuBoff, "Business Demand and the Development of the Telegraph in the United States, 1844–1860," *Bus. Hist. Rev.* 54 (1980): 459–79; DuBoff, "The Telegraph and the Structure of Markets in the United States, 1845–1890," *Research in Economic History* 8 (1983): 256.

41 This effect had first been apparent at Buffalo, where the arrival of the telegraph in early 1847 reduced the traveling time of New York market reports from more than four days to just under one. See John Langdale, "The Impact of the Telegraph on the Buffalo Agricultural Commodity Market: 1846–1848," *Professional Geographer* 31 (1979): 165–9. On other effects of the telegraph, see DuBoff, "Telegraph and Structure of US Markets," 253–77; and Allan Pred, *Urban Growth and City-Systems in the United States, 1840–1860* (1980), 151–6.

42 *Chicago Democrat*, Sept. 12, 1848, as quoted by Taylor, *Chicago Board of Trade*, 1:147.

43 On general trends in wheat prices after 1867, see Veblen, "Price of Wheat since 1867," 68–103; and Helen C. Farnsworth, "Decline and Recovery of Wheat Prices in the 'Nineties," *Wheat Studies* 10 (1933–4): 289–352.

44 Andreas, *History of Chicago*, 2:325, 333; Taylor, *Chicago Board of Trade*, 1:241, 260, 267.

45 Robert Sobel, *The Big Board: A History of the New York Stock Market* (1965), 52–3; DuBoff, "Telegraph and Structure of US Markets," 262.

46 Reverend J. P. Thompson, in Curtiss, *Western Portraiture*, 334.

47 Odle, "Entrepreneurial Cooperation," 451–3; Odle, "American Grain Trade," 9 (1953): 54–8, 105–9, 162–6.

48 Small futures markets of one sort or another had existed in the past – a few European cities had been conducting them sicne at least the 1830s – and other American cities were experimenting with them at the same time as Chicago. But none had become so large and institutionalized as the Chicago Board of Trade by the end of the Civil War. As with the railroads, the shifting scale of the Chicago market made its grain trade look radically different from its predecessors. See CBT, *Futures Trading Seminar*, 12–16; Emery, *Speculation on Stock and Produce Exchanges*, 40–1.

49 Emery, *Speculation on Stock and Produce Exchanges*, 46. For an excellent summary of the preconditions necessary for futures trading, see FTC, *Grain Trade*, 5:23–7.

50 The origin of these two terms is uncertain. The *Oxford English Dictionary* dates them back to at least early-eighteenth-century England, when those who sold short were sometimes called "bearskin jobbers," suggesting an allusion to the old proverb "To sell the bear's skin before one has caught the bear." "Bull" appeared somewhat later, and is more obscure in its origins.

51 Individual traders might be either bulls or bears at any given moment, though the logic and strategies of the two positions were different enough that many traders tended to specialize in one or the other.

52 *Chicago Tribune*, April 17, 1875.

53 Stevens, "'Futures' in the Wheat Market," 51–5. Stevens gathered weekly statistics on spot and futures sales in wheat at the New York Produce Exchange during the first half of 1887, and found that the dollar volume of futures contracts amounted to about twenty times the volume of spot sales. Although he gathered no such statistics for Chicago, he did assemble them for St. Louis, where the ratio was better than 24 to 1. It seems reasonable to believe that Chicago was in the same ballpark. Indeed, Stevens thought it "well within the limits of probability" that the combined futures trading at St. Louis, Chicago, Toledo, and the major Atlantic ports of the United States during the first half of 1887 "more than equalled the total production of wheat in the world in 1886."

REFERENCES

Andreas, Alfred T. *History of Chicago from the Earliest Period to the Present Time.* 3 vols. Chicago: Alfred T. Andreas, 1884–6.

Annual Reviews of Commerce. *Chicago Tribune* and *Chicago Daily Democratic Press.* 1850–60.

Bogue, Allan G. *From Prairie to Cornbelt: Farming on the Illinois and Iowa Prairies in the Nineteenth Century.* Chicago: Univ. of Chicago Press, 1963.

Boyle, James E. *Chicago Wheat Prices For Eight-one Years,* 1922.

Brush, Daniel Harmon. *Growing Up with Southern Illinois, 1820 to 1861.* Edited by Milo Milton Quaife. Chicago: Lakeside Press, 1944.

Bureau of Statistics, US Treasury Department. "The Grain Trade of the United States, and the World's Wheat Supply and Trade." In *Monthly Summary of Commerce and Finance of the United States.* Washington, DC: GPO, Jan. 1900.

Burrows, J. M. D. *Fifty Years in Iowa.* 1888. Reprint. *The Early Day of Rock Island and Davenport: The Narratives of J. W. Spencer and J. M. D. Burrows.* Edited by Milo Milton Quaife. Chicago: Lakeside Press, 1942.

Caton, John Dean. "An Address Delivered at the Reception to the Settlers of Chicago prior to 1840, by the Calumet Club of Chicago, May 27, 1879." In *Reminiscences of Early Chicago,* edited by Mabel McIlvaine. Chicago: Lakeside Press, 1912.

——. "'Tis Sixty Years Since' in Chicago," *Atlantic Monthly* 71 (May 1893): 588–97.

Chicago Board of Trade. *Annual Reports,* 1858–1901.

Colbert, E[lias]. *Chicago: Historical and Statistical Sketch of the Garden City.* Chicago: P. T. Sherlock, 1868.

Conzen, Kathleen Neils. *Immigrant Milwaukee, 1836–1860: Accommodation and Community in a Frontier City.* Cambridge: Harvard Univ. Press, 1976.

Corliss, Carlton J. *The Day of Two Noons.* Washington, D.C.: Association of American Railroads, 1941.

——. *Main Line of Mid-America. The Story of the Illinoss Central.* New York: Creative Age Press, 1950.

Crawford, R. F. "An Inquiry into Wheat Prices and Wheat Supply." *Journal of the Royal Statistical Society* 58 (1895): 75–120.

Curtiss, Daniel S. *Western Portraiture, and Emigrants' Guide.* New York: J. H. Colton, 1852.

Dart, Joseph. "The Grain Elevators of Buffalo." *Publications of the Buffalo Historical Society* 1 (1879): 391–404.

Dondlinger, Percy Tracy. *The Book of Wheat: An Economic History and Practical Manual of the Wheat Industry.* New York: Orange Judd, 1919.

DuBoff, Richard B. "Business Demand and the Development of the Telegraph in the United States, 1844–1860." *Bus. Hist. Rev.* 54 (1980): 459–79.

——. "The Telegraph and the Structure of Markets in the United States, 1845–1890." *Research in Economic History* 8 (1983): 253–77.

Emery, Henry Crosby. *Speculation on the Stock and Produce Exchanges of the United States.* New York: Columbia Univ. Press, 1896.

Farnsworth, Helen C. "Decline and Recovery of Wheat Prices in the 'Nineties." *Wheat Studies* 10 (1933–4): 289–352.

Federal Trade Commission, *Report on the Grain Trade.* Washington, DC: GPO, 1919.

Fishlow, Albert. *American Railroads and the Transformation of the Ante-Bellum Economy.* Cambridge: Harvard Univ. Press, 1965.

Fornari, Harry. *Bread upon the Waters: A History of United States Grain Exports.* Nashville: Aurora, 1973.

Gates, Paul Wallace. *The Illinois Central Railroad and Its Colonization Work.* Cambridge: Harvard Univ. Press, 1934.

Haites, Erik F., James Mak, and Gary M. Walton. *Western River Transportation: The Era of Early Internal Development, 1810–1860.* Baltimore: Johns Hopkins Univ. Press, 1975.

Harley, C. Knick. "Transportation, the World Wheat Trade, and the Kuznets Cycle, 1850–1913." *Explorations in Economic History* 17 (1980): 218–50.

Hill, Lowell D. *Grain Grades and Standards: Historical Issues Shaping the Future.* Urbana: Univ. of Illinois Press, 1990.

Johnson, Hildegard Binder. *Order upon the Land: The U.S. Rectangular Land Survey and the Upper Mississippi Country.* New York: Oxford Univ. Press, 1976.

Klein, Joseph J. "The Development of Mercantile Instruments of Credit in the United States." *Journal of Accountancy* 12 (1911): 321–45, 422–49, 526–37, 594–607; 13 (1912): 44–50, 122–32, 207–17.

Langdale, John. "The Impact of the Telegraph on the Buffalo Agricultural Commodity Market: 1846–1848." *Professional Geographer* 31 (1979): 165–9.

Lee, Guy A. "History of the Chicago Grain Elevator Industry, 1840–1890." Ph.D. thesis, Harvard Univ., 1938.

Lee, Guy A. "The Historical Significance of the Chicago Grain Elevator System." *Ag. Hist.* 11 (1937): 16–32.

Malenbaum, Wilfred. *The World Wheat Economy, 1885–1939.* Cambridge: Harvard Univ. Press, 1953.

Norris, J. W. *Norris' Business Directory and Statistics of the City of Chicago for 1846.* Edited by Robert Fergus. Fergus Historical Series, no. 25. Chicago, 1883.

North, Douglass, C. *The Economic Growth of the United States, 1790–1860.* 1961. Reprint. New York: W. W. Norton, 1966.

O'Brien, Michael J., ed. *Grassland, Forest, and Historical Settlement: An Analysis of Dynamics in Northeast Missouri.* Lincoln: Univ. of Nebraska Press, 1984.

Odle, Thomas D. "The American Grain Trade of the Great Lakes, 1825–1873." *Inland Seas* 7 (1951): 237–45; 8 (1952): 23–8, 99–104, 177–8, 187–92, 248–54; 9 (1953): 52–8, 105–9, 162–8, 256–62.

——. "Entrepreneurial Cooperation on the Great Lakes: The Origin of the Methods of American Grain Marketing." *Bus. Hist. Rev.* 38 (1964): 439–55.

Pred Allan R. *Urban Growth and City-Systems in the United States, 1840–1860.* Cambridge: Harvard Univ. Press, 1980.

Quaife, Milo Milton., ed. *Pictures of Illinois One Hundred Years Ago.* Chicago: Lakeside Press, 1918.

Rothstein, Morton. "America in the International Rivalry for the British Wheat Market, 1860–1914." *MVHR* 47 (1960): 401–18.

——. "Antebellum Wheat and Cotton Exports: A Contrast in Marketing Organization and Economic Development." *Ag. Hist.* 40 (1966): 91–100.

——."The International Market for Agricultural Commodities, 1850–1873." In *Economic Change in the Civil War Era,* edited by David T. Gilchrist and W. David Lewis. Greenville, Del.: Eleutherian Mills–Hagley Foundation, 1965.

Smith, Alice E. *George Smith's Money: A Scottish Investor in America.* Madison: SHSW, 1966.

Sobel, Robert. *The Big Board: A History of the New York Stock Market.* New York: Free Press, 1965.

Stevens, Albert Clark. "'Futures' in the Wheat Market." *Quarterly Journal of Economics* 2 (1888): 37–63.

Taylor, Charles H., ed. *History of the Board of Trade of the City of Chicago.* Chicago: Robert O. Law, 1917.

Thrower, Norman J. *Original Survey and Land Subdivision: A Comparative Study of the Form and Effect of Contrasting Cadastral Surveys.* Chicago: Association of American Geographers, 1966.

Trimble, William. "Historical Aspects of the Surplus Food Production of the United States, 1862–1902." *American Historical Association Annual Report for 1918.* (Washington, DC: GPO, 1921), 223–39.

Trollope, Anthony. *North America.* 1862. Edited by Donald Smalley and Bradford Allen Booth. New York: Alfred A. Knopf, 1951.

US Bureau of the Census. *Historical Statistics of the United States: Colonial Times to 1970.* Washington, DC: GPO, 1975.

Veblen, Thorstein B. "The Price of Wheat since 1867." *J. Pol. Econ.* 1 (1892–93): 68–103.

Williams, Egerton R. "Thirty Years in the Grain Trade." *No. Am. Rev.* 161 (1895): 25–33.

Williamson, Jeffrey G. "Greasing the Wheels of Sputtering Export Engines: Midwestern Grains and American Growth." *Explorations in Economic History* 17 (1980): 189–217.

Wyman, Mark. *Immigrants in the Valley: Irish, Germans, and Americans in the Upper Mississippi Country, 1830–1860.* Chicago: Nelson-Hall, 1984.

Chapter 20

Six Discourses on the Postmetropolis

Edward W. Soja

... I have recently chosen to use *postmetropolis* as a general term to accentuate the differences between contemporary urban regions and those that consolidated in the middle decades of the twentieth century. The prefix 'post' thus signals the transition from what has conventionally been called the modern metropolis to something significantly different, to new postmodern forms and patternings of urban life that are increasingly challenging well-established modes of urban analysis. As will become clearer in my discussion of the six discourses, there are other post-prefixed terms and concepts packed into the postmetropolis, from the notion of post-industrial society so familiar to sociologists to the more recent discussions of post-Fordist and post-Keynesian political economies and post-structuralist and post-colonial modes of critical analysis. Before turning to these discourses, however, I want to make a few more general introductory observations.

First, as I have already suggested, the changes that are being described or represented by these six discourses are happening not only in Los Angeles but, in varying degrees and, to be sure, unevenly developed over space and time, all over the world. Although they take specific forms in specific places, they are general processes. Furthermore, these processes are not entirely new. Their origins can be traced back well

before the last quarter of this century. It is their intensification, interrelatedness, and increasing scope that makes their present expression different from the past. I also want to emphasise that when I use the term postmetropolis as opposed to the late modern metropolis, I am not saying that the latter has disappeared or been completely displaced, even in Los Angeles. What has been happening is that the new urbanisation processes and patternings are being overlain on the old and articulated with them in increasingly complex ways. The overlays and articulations are becoming thicker and denser in many parts of the world, but nowhere has the modern metropolis been completely erased.

What this means is that we must understand the new urbanisation and urbanism without discarding our older understanding. At the same time, however, we must recognise that the contested cities of today and their complex relations between social process and spatial form, as well as spatial process and social form – what I once called the socio-spatial dialectic – are increasingly becoming significantly different from what they were in the 1960s. While we must not ignore the past, we must nevertheless foreground what is new and different about the present. Looking at contemporary urban sociology, this suggests that we can no longer depend so heavily on the 'new' approaches that flowered so brilliantly in the

1970s with such classic works as Manuel Castells's *The Urban Question* (1977; French ed. 1972), David Harvey's *Social Justice and the City* (1973) and the pioneering world systems sociology of Immanuel Wallerstein. These were, and remain, powerful and incisive interpretations of the late modern metropololis, Castells's *monopolville* and *ville sauvage*, the 'wild cities' that consolidated during the postwar boom and exploded in the urban crises of the 1960s. But the late modern metropolis, to coin a phrase, is not what it used to be.

Many of the insights developed by these theorists and analysts are still applicable and, I must add, the radical politics they encouraged is still possible. My argument, however, is basically that the changes have been so dramatic that we can no longer simply add our new knowledge to the old. There are too many incompatabilities, contradictions, disruptions. We must instead radically rethink and perhaps deeply restructure – that is, deconstruct and reconstitute – our inherited forms of urban analysis to meet the practical, political and theoretical challenges presented by the post-metropolis.

Another preliminary observation complicates things even further. While urbanists continue to debate just how different the new metropolis is from the old and precisely how much we must deconstruct and reconstitute our traditional modes of urban analysis, the postmetropolis itself has begun to change in significant ways. Beginning in the eventful year of 1989 in Berlin, Beijing and other major world cities, and punctuated in Southern California by the Spring uprisings in 1992 and the postmodern fiscal crisis of Orange County in 1994, the postmetropolis seems to be entering a new era of instability and crisis. There are growing signs of a shift from what we have all recognised as a period of crisis-generated restructuring originating in the urban uprisings of the 1960s to what might now be called a *restructuring generated crisis*. That is, what we see in the 1990s may be an emerging breakdown

in the restructured postmetropolis itself, in postmodern and post-Fordist urbanism, and also perhaps in the explanatory power of the six discourses I will be discussing.

My last introductory comment refers to some recent developments in critical urban studies, an exciting new field that has grown from the injection of critical cultural studies into the more traditionally social scientific analysis of urbanism and the urban process. While I consider my own work to be part of this increasingly transdisciplinary field, I have recently become uneasy over what I perceive to be a growing over-privileging of what has been called, often with reference to the work of Michel de Certeau, the 'view from below' – studies of the local, the body, the streetscape, psycho-geographies of intimacy, erotic subjectivities, the micro-worlds of everyday life – at the expense of understanding the structuring of the city as a whole, the more macro-view of urbanism, the political economy of the urban process.

The six discourses I will be presenting are aimed at making sense of the whole urban region, the spatiality and sociality of the urban fabric writ large. They are precisely the kinds of discourses being hammered at by those micro-urban critics who see in them only the distorting, if not repressive, gaze of authoritative masculinist power, the masterful 'view from above'. A primary tactic in fostering these often reductionist critiques of macro-level theorizing has been a kind of epistemological privileging of the experience of the *flâneur*, the street-wandering free agent of everyday life, the ultimate progenitor of the view from below. There is undoubtedly much to be gained from this ground-level view of the city and, indeed, many of those who focus on more macro-spatial perspectives too often overlook the darker corners of everyday life and the less visible oppressions of 'race', gender, class and sexuality. What I am most concerned with, however, is the degree to which such micro-level critiques have been unproductively polarizing critical urban studies, romancing agency and the view from below to the point of labelling all macro-level perspectives taboo, off-limits, politically incorrect.

The six discourses I will now turn to are, in part, an attempt to recapture and reassert the importance of a macro-urban tradition, not in opposition to the local view from below but drawing on insights that come directly from the significant work that has been done on the microgeographies of the city by a variety of critical urban scholars. Understanding the postmetropolis requires a creative recombination of micro and macro perspectives, views from above and from below, a new critical synthesis that rejects the rigidities of either/or choices for the radical openness of the both/and also. With this little plug for an explicitly post-modern critical perspective and after a more extensive introduction than I had originally planned, we are ready to begin examining the six discourses. . . .

1   FLEXCITY: on the restructuring of the political economy of urbanization and the formation of the more flexibly specialised post-Fordist industrial metropolis.
  • the primacy of production
  • crisis-formation and the Great U-Turn
  • the ascendance of post-Fordism
  • the empowerment of flexibility
  • getting lean and mean
2   COSMOPOLIS: on the globalisation of urban capital, labour and culture and the formation of a new hierarchy of global cities.
  • the primacy of globalisation
  • the 'glocalisation' process
  • the glocalisation of discourse in New York and London
  • the vanity of the bonFIRES
  • reworlding Los Angeles
3   EXOPOLIS: on the restructuring of urban form and the growth of edge cities, outer cities and postsuburbia: the metropolis turned inside-out and outside-in.
  • paradigmatic Los Angeles

  • deconstructing the discourse on urban form
  • rosy reconstitutions of the post-metropolis: the New Urbanism
  • exploring the darker side of the Outer and Inner City
4   METROPOLARITIES: on the restructured social mosaic and the emergence of new polarisations and inequalities.
  • a new sociologism?
  • widening gaps and new polarities
  • the 'truly disadvantaged' and the 'underclass' debate
  • the new ethnic mosaic of Los Angeles
5   CARCERAL ARCHIPELAGOS: on the rise of fortress cities, surveillant technologies and the substitution of police for *polis*.
  • cities of quartz: Mike Davis's Los Angeles
  • further elaborations: interdictory spaces in the built environment
  • taking an Other look at *The City of Quartz*
6   SIMCITIES: on the restructured urban imaginary and the increasing hyperreality of everyday life.
  • the irruption of hyperreality and the society of simulacra
  • cyberspace: the electronic generation of hyperreality
  • simulating urbanism as a way of life
  • variations on a theme park
  • scamscapes in crisis: the Orange County bankruptcy

Rather than going over these discourses in detail, I will use what I have just outlined to select a few issues that I think may be of particular interest to a gathering of urban sociologists. Given the challenge of brevity, the critical observations will be blunt and stripped of appropriate (and necessary) qualifications. My intent is not to offer a well-rounded critical presentation of the discourses but to use them to stimulate debate and discussion about how best to make sense of the contemporary urban scene.

The first discourse, on the post-Fordist industrial metropolis, rests essentially on the continued intimate relation between industrialisation and urbanisation processes. In Los Angeles and in many other urban regions as well, it has become perhaps the hegemonic academic discourse in attempting to explain the differences between the late modern (Fordist) metropolis and the post (Fordist) metropolis. It has also entered deeply into the recent literature in urban sociology as a theoretical framework for understanding the social order (and disorder) of the contemporary city. In Savage and Warde's (1993) book on British sociology, for example, there is a clear attempt to redefine and reposition urban sociology around this post-Fordist industrial restructuring.

In some ways, this has been a peculiar embrace, for urban sociologists have contributed relatively little to the industrial restructuring literature and to the conceptual and theoretical debates that have shaped the first discourse. They have instead been content primarily with detailed empirical studies of the new capitalist city, leaving its theorisation and explanatory discourse to geographers, political economists and other non-sociologists. How can we explain sociology's apparent retreat from playing a leading role in conceptualising the new urbanisation processes and the post-metropolis, especially given its pre-eminence in explaining the development of the late modern metropolis in the post-war decades?

Part of the answer may lie in a persistent if not growing 'sociologism', a retreat back into tried-and-true disciplinary traditions of both theoretical and empirical sociology. Even when seeming to reach beyond disciplinary boundaries for theoretical and practical inspiration, such sociologism tends to seek ways to make what is new and challenging old and familiar, that is, absorbable without major paradigmatic disruption or radical rethinking. I think something like this has been happening in sociology with respect to the new discourse on post-Fordist urban-industrial restructuring in particular, and more generally with many other post-prefixed discourses. One vehicle for this retreat back into the disciplinary fold in the face of new challenges has been the continued appeal, especially in the US, of one form or another of the post-industrial society thesis developed within sociology decades ago. Continued use of the term post-industrial is jolting to a discourse built upon the persistent importance of industrialisation and the production process. What has been happening to the industrial capitalist city is much more than the decay of manufacturing industry and a shift to a services economy. De-industrialisation has been occurring alongside a potent re-industrialisation process built not just on high-technology electronics production but also on cheap labour-intensive forms of craft production and the expansion of producer-oriented services and technology. These shifts, often to more flexible production systems and denser transaction-intensive networks of information flow, are creating new industrial spaces that have significantly reshaped the industrial geography of the late modern or Fordist metropolis. Continuing to see the new urban restructuring processes through the eyes of the post-industrial thesis makes it difficult to comprehend the more complex and still production-centered discourse on post-Fordist urbanisation.

Similar problems arise from continued attachment to the politically more radical traditions of urban sociology that developed in the 1970s and early 1980s, especially reflecting the pioneering work of Castells and others on urban social movements and the politics of collective consumption. Here too a lingering consumptionist emphasis makes it difficult to comprehend the production-centred discourse on post-Fordist urbanisation and industrial restructuring. That much of this post-Fordist discourse also centres around explicitly spatial concepts and analyses complicates matters still further, given the recent attempts by such British sociologists as Peter Saunders to de-emphasise space and spatial analysis in the conceptual frameworks of urban sociology. Such efforts have been particularly constraining with regard to the participation of sociologists in the wider debates on postmodernism and critical cultural studies, both of which have experienced a pronounced spatial turn since the late 1980s. But this takes me into another discussion that I cannot expand upon here.

Sociologists have played a much more important role in the second discourse, on globalisation and world city formation. In some ways, despite their interrelatedness and complementarity, the first and second discourses have often developed in competition, each seeing itself as the most powerful explanation for the new urbanisation and urbanism. This constrains both discourses, but I will comment here only on how the discourse on global cities has been weakened by an inadequate understanding of the industrial restructuring process as well as by a touch of the sociologism mentioned above. I can summarise my comments around a playful phrase I once used to express my discontent with the approaches being taken to the study of New York as a 'dual city' standing at the apex of the world hierarchy of the global 'capitals of capital' (Soja 1991: 361–76). The phrase was 'the vanity of the bonFIRES' and it referred to what I saw as an overconcentration on the command and control functions of the FIRE sector (finance, insurance, real estate) in the global cities literature and a closely related overemphasis on two tiny sites where these commanding bonFIRES appear to be burning most brightly, Wall Street in Manhattan and The City in London, along with their tributary yuppified offshoots (Battery Park City, the World Trade Center, South Street Seaport, Canary Wharf, the Docklands).

There are several weaknesses I see arising when the discourse is narrowed so tightly. First, there is a tendency to see world city formation as creating an increasing sectoral and geographical detachment from manufacturing industries on the one hand and the productive base of the regional economy on the other. This may fit well to the post-industrial and de-industrialisation models of urban change and accurately describe some of what has been happening internally within New York City and London. But it distorts the general debate on globalisation and world city formation, especially with regard to such postmetropolises and major manufacturing regions as Tokyo and Los Angeles (and, I might add, the re-industrialising regional hinterlands of Greater New York and London).

I do not want to deny the importance of these research and interpretive emphases, but rather to note the dangers of a sort of Manhattanised or Londonised myopia. In addition to oversimplifying the connections between the financial and industrial sectors, and between the central city and the larger metropolitan region, such myopia also tends to inhibit more comprehensive and sophisticated understanding of the spatiality of globalisation and the new cultural politics of identity and difference being spawned in global cities. This, in turn, widens the breach between more sociological studies of globalisation and the increasingly spatialised cultural studies approaches to interpreting the postmetropolis.

The third discourse focuses on what I have described as the formation of Exopolis, a process that, on the one hand, points to the growth of Outer Cities and Edge Cities and other manifestations of the rather oxymoronic urbanization of suburbia and, on the other, to a dramatic reconstitution of the Inner City brought about both by an outmigration of domestic populations and the inmigration of 'Third World' workers and cultures. The social and spatial organisation of the postmetropolis seems as a result to be turning inside-out and outside-in at the same time, creating havoc with our traditional ways of defining what is urban, suburban, exurban, not urban, etc. Perhaps no other discourse is raising such profound challenges, not only for urban sociology but for all of urban studies as it has been conventionally constituted.

A few examples from Los Angeles can be used to illustrate this deconstruction and reconstitution of urban form, and of the traditional vocabulary developed to describe it. Such classic examples of American suburbia as the San Fernando Valley and Orange County now meet almost all definitions of being urbanised. They are highly heterogeneous agglomerations of industrial production, employment, commerce, cultural and entertainment facilities, and other characteristically 'urban' qualities such as gangs, crime, drug-dealing and street violence. To continue to label these areas 'suburban' is to misrepresent their contemporary reality. Similarly, most of what we continue to label the Inner City of Los Angeles – including the urban ghettoes and barrios of South Central and East Los Angeles – would appear, especially to those familiar with cities in the eastern US, Europe and Asia as characteristically suburban.

I have used the term Exopolis to describe this discourse because of its provocative double meaning: exo-referring both to the city growing 'outside' the traditional urban nucleus and to the city 'without', the city that no longer conveys the traditional qualities of cityness. This radical deconstruction/reconstitution of the urban fabric has stimulated many other neologisms for the new forms emerging in the postmetropolis. In addition to those already mentioned, including Exopolis, there are post-suburbia, metroplex, technopoles, technoburbs, urban villages, countycities, regional cities, the 100-mile city. It has also spawned self-consciously 'new' approaches to urban design, such as the New Urbanism in the US and, in Britain, the related neo-traditionalist town planning so favoured by Prince Charles; and, at the same time, much darker interpretations of the social and environmental consequences of the restructuring of urban form, exemplified with noir-like brilliance in the work of Mike Davis. Here too,

then, the discourse has begun to polarise in potentially unproductive ways, creating the need for more balanced and flexible, yet still critical and politically conscious, approaches to interpreting the changing built environment and social geography of the postmetropolis.

The fourth discourse explores the restructured social mosaic and is probably the discourse that has attracted the largest number of urban sociologists. It is especially attuned to the intensification of what I describe as Metropolarities: increasing social inequalities, widening income gaps, new kinds of social polarization and stratification that fit uncomfortably within traditional dualisms based on class (capital–labour) or race (white–black) as well as conventional upper-middle-lower class models of urban society. As with the discourse on urban spatial form, the discourse on the changing social forms and formations in the postmetropolis has instigated a new vocabulary. Yuppies (including such extensions as yuppification and 'guppies', or groups of yuppies) and the permanent urban underclass (or 'the truly disadvantaged') head the list, but there are many other related terms: dinks (double-income/ no kids families), upper professionals, the new technocracy, the working poor, the new orphans (both youth growing up fatherless and motherless and the elderly abandoned by their children), welfaredependent ghettoes, hyperghettoes, and so on.

Whereas the first two discourses tend to present themselves as capturing (and effectively theorising) the most powerful processes causing the restructuring of the late modern metropolis, the second pair concern themselves primarily with the empirical consequences of these processes. A more explicitly spatial emphasis is infused within the discourse on Exopolis and this, I would argue, creates closer ties to the practical and theoretical insights of the discourses on post-Fordist industrialisation and globalisation. The discourse on metropolarities, while certainly not aspatial, seems to be developing with a relatively simplistic perspective on the complex spatiality of the postmetropolis and, in part because of this, with an inadequate understanding of the links between cause and effect or, more specifically, the restructuring process and its empirical consequences.

Perhaps the best example of this conceptual gap has been the work of American sociologist William Julius Wilson and his associates, which today dominates the contemporary representation of the Chicago School of urban studies. While there is much to be praised in this work on the permanent urban underclass and the truly disadvantaged, it is filled with oversimplified notions of post-Fordist industrial restructuring, location theory and the relations between urban spatiality and the urban social order. Much of what I noted earlier about the constraining effects of sociologism is relevant here, as are my comments on the growing disjunction between theoretical and empirical work in sociological studies of the postmetropolis. Not all of urban sociology suffers from these constraints, to be sure, but I suspect they are more widespread than most of you think.

If the first pair of discourses on the postmetropolis emphasises the causes of urban restructuring and the second pair its empirical spatial and social effects, the third pair explores what might be described as the societal response to the effects of urban restructuring in the postmetropolis. In Los Angeles as well as in many other urban regions, the fifth discourse, on what I call the emergence of a Carceral Archipelago, has been dominated by the work of Mike Davis. In *City of Quartz* (1990) and other writings, Davis depicts Los Angeles as a fortified city with bulging prisons, sadistic street environments, housing projects that have become strategic hamlets, gated and armed-guarded communities where signs say 'trespassers will be shot', and where the city is surveilled and patrolled by a high-tech space police. What his work suggests is that the globalized post-Fordist industrial metropolis, with its extraordinary

cultural heterogeneity, growing social polarities and explosive potential, is being held together largely by 'carceral' technologies of violence and social control, fostered by capital and the state.

What I want to question here is not the validity of Davis's depictions of Los Angeles but the degree to which his work has been 'romanced' by other urbanists, especially on the left, to the point of narrowing all the discourses on the postmetropolis to his politically appealing radical view. I once described *City of Quartz* as the best anti-theoretical, anti-postmodernist, historicist, nativist and masculinist book written about a city. For those who eschew abstract theorization because it takes away from good empirical work and radical political action, who find the whole debate on postmodernism and postmetropolises inherently conservative and politically numbing, who feel much more comfortable with the good old historical materialism of Marx rather than this new-fangled spatial and geographical stuff, who appreciate the gritty streetwise pluck of the truck driver-*flâneur* operating on his home ground, and who recoil from the presumed excesses of postmodern feminist critiques, Mike Davis has become a heroic figure. I can only add here that such romancing seriously constrains our efforts to make practical, political and theoretical sense of contemporary world, and weakens our ability to translate this knowledge into effective radical action.

Finally, we arrive at the sixth discourse, on the postmetropolis as Simcity, a place where simulations of a presumably real world increasingly capture and activate our urban imaginary and infiltrate everyday urban life. A key concept here is that of the simulacrum, roughly defined as an exact copy of something that may never have existed. Stated bluntly and with a nod to the work of Jean Baudrillard, the argument is that such simulations and simulacra, and the hyper-real worlds they define, are more than ever before shaping every aspect of our lives, from who and what we vote for to how we feed, clothe, mate and define our bodies. With this expansive blurring of the difference between the real and the imagined, there is what Baudrillard defines as a 'precession of simulacra', a situation in which simulations increasingly take precedence over the realities they are simulating. Our lives have always been shaped by these hyper-realities and by the specialized manufactories that produce them, from religious institutions to Hollywood and Disneyland. Most of the time, however, one chose to go to these manufactories, usually passing through some gate and paying for admission. Today, again more than ever before, hyper-reality visits you, in your homes, in your daily lives.

At the very least, this Simcity discourse needs to be addressed seriously in contemporary urban studies, not just at the micro-scale of everyday life but also in macro-scale analyses of urbanisation and the social production of urban space. My own work has increasingly focused on this precession of simulacra and the growing hyper-reality of urban life in the postmetropolis, in part because I suspect that this restructuring of the urban imaginary is playing a key role in the emerging mode of social regulation associated with what the French regulation theorists define as the new regimes of capitalist accumulation (arising, I might add, primarily from the processes described in the first two discourses). There is so much to be discussed here, but too little time and space to do so. I offer instead some telling vignettes on what I call the 'scamscapes' of Orange County.

Orange County is one of the richest, best-educated, and most staunchly right-wing and Republican counties in the US. It has been a focal point for the local discourse on post-Fordist industrial restructuring and an exemplary case for my own discussions of the formation of Exopolis and the increasing hyper-reality of urban life (Soja 1992: 277–98). In the hyper-real worlds of Orange County there has developed a particularly effluent scamscape, my term for an environment in which the real and the imagined are so blurred that it encourages fraud and deceit as appropriate if not routine forms of behaviour. Orange County was one of the centres for the notorious Savings and Loans scandal that is costing the US untold billions of dollars to resolve; and it has been the most active area in the country for defence industry frauds. In one recent case, it was discovered that a plant making 'fuzes', switching devices that control whether or not nuclear missiles would explode, failed to test their products primarily because everyone genuinely believed the sign posted on the factory's walls: 'We make the best damned fuzes in the United States'. If so, why bother to test? Just confidently tick 'excellent' after every government query. Also representative of the scamscape are the 'boiler rooms', sort of high-tech sweatshops that are centres for all kinds of telemarketing frauds and scams. Nowhere are there more of these boiler rooms than in Orange County, and they are reputed to make higher profits than the drug dealers. In one of these busy hives of hyperfraud, a sign was found that captures the core of the scamscape's deceitful honesty. It said: 'we cheat the other guy and pass the savings on to you!'

In late 1994, the Orange County scamscape exploded in the largest municipal/county bankruptcy in US history. Exposed in the aftermath of this stunning declaration was a system of county and municipal governance that routinely ran the county's public economy as if it were a form of the popular computer game, *SimCity*, with a *sim*government serving *sim*citizens in what was essentially a *sim*county. Making the bankruptcy even more hyper-real was that the key figure, the county tax collector who was gambling the *sim*county's money in the financial cyberspace of exotic derivatives and leveraged synthetics, had a more than appropriate Orange County name: Citron! In this bastion of the new fiscal populism and small government is better government, this fountainhead of entrepreneurial unregulated capitalism, home of both Disneyland and the Richard M. Nixon Library and Birthplace, the proud centre for the foundational achievements of an ultra-conservative postmodern politics that cheats the other guy and passes the savings on to you, the simulation game broke down – and there was no button to push to reboot.

Also revealed by these events is the extraordinary degree to which government, politics and civil society in the US are being shaped by the precession of simulacra and a spin-doctored game of simulations. And from what I know of Thatcher's legacy, Britain today cannot be too far behind. This leads me to some brief conclusions. Like it or not, we are all living in an increasingly postmodern world that is creating new contexts and new challenges that cannot be effectively responded to by clinging to older ways of thinking and acting politically. The city and the urban still remain sites of contestation and struggle, but the social processes and spatial forms, and the spatial processes and social forms that define these struggles are now significantly different from what they were even ten years ago. Moreover, there are now some ample signs that the predominantly neo-conservative and neo-liberal forms of postmodern society and the postmetropolis that have consolidated from three decades of global and local restructuring are beginning to explode from their own success/excess. Such events as the Los Angeles Justice riots of 1992 and the Orange County bankruptcy of 1994 are not just local, isolated disturbances, but part of what may be emerging as a restructuring-generated global crisis. This makes it even more urgent for the Left and all other progressive thinkers and actors to resolve their internal divisions and act together to create an effective and emancipatory postmodern politics and a conceptual framework for an also explicitly postmodern critical urban studies that is appropriately and effectively attuned to the realities and hyper-realities of the contemporary moment.

REFERENCES

Savage, Mike and Alan Warde, *Urban Sociology, Capitalism and Modernity*, New York: Continuum, 1993.

Soja, Edward W., 'Poles Apart: New York and Los Angeles', in J. Mollenkopf and M. Castells (eds.), *Dual City: The Restructuring of New York*, New York: Russell Sage Foundation, 1991, pp. 361–76.

Soja, Edward W., 'Inside Exopolis: Scenes from Orange County', in M. Sorkin (ed.), *Variations on a Theme Park: The New American City and the End of Public Space*, New York: Hill and Wang/Noonday Press, 1992, pp. 277–98.

Chapter 21

from *Landscapes of Power: From Detroit to Disney World*

Sharon Zukin

Downtown as Liminal Space

In the new era of capital reinvestment in the center, downtown emerges as a key liminal space. Institutionally, its redevelopment straddles public and private power. Visually, the redevelopment process eliminates or incorporates the segmented vernacular into a landscape of power. Since the 1970s, downtown has graphically mapped the forms of social control that we have identified as part of the inner landscape of creative destruction. These include both entrapment and fragmentation, as well as a sense of unlimited power. Downtown mediates the social transformation initiated by capital flows and public policy.

The reassertion of power in the center is shaped by the narrowness of streets and the historic gathering functions of the core, the jigsaw of social uses that reflect uneven economic values, and over all, the density of the built environment that permits markets to generalize the products of a highly specialized place – and to communicate them through a larger market culture. Downtown ironically recapitulates the destiny described by urban ecology, but it does so in a changing economy.

Experience with gentrification shows that new downtown markets are formed in stages. We first find a change in the uses of space: from manufacturers and a working class who are absorbed in material production to a professional, managerial, and service class that spends considerable energy on cultural production and consumption. We then find a change in perspective, or people's relation to the space. The way they view it re-forms the urban vernacular – with its diversity of low-rent quarters – into an aesthetically or historically homogeneous landscape. Finally, we find a change in the nature of space itself. Downtown becomes larger and more expensive, its old structures are joined by new construction, and its social meaning is transformed from "in" to accessible, and therefore "out" of fashion. At that point of liminality between "in" and "out," downtown space becomes too expensive for some of the initial gentrifiers.

We clearly see the effects of this sociospatial restructuring in the demise and reshaping of vernacular landmarks, including the death of the cafeteria and the birth – in all its guises – of the downtown club.

The death in 1986 of Philip Siegel, 85-year-old owner of the Belmore Cafeteria in Manhattan, marked the definitive end of downtown's cafeteria era. For most of Siegel's lifetime, cafeterias were not only a restaurant genre where a cup of coffee was served in heavy china and still cost less than a newspaper. More important, cafeterias were a cheap public space downtown.

Mr. Siegel bought the cafeteria, on Park Avenue South at 28th Street, in 1929. Over the years, he expanded the dining area from 100 to 500 seats and, in the late 1970s, he installed fashionable track lighting and put potted plants in the front windows.

He never dropped the Belmore's slogan – "New York's most fabulous restaurant" – and he never disposed of the turnstile that discharged a little ticket to each customer who entered.

Until Mr. Siegel closed the Belmore and sold the building for a condominium complex in 1981, it was serving about 5,000 people a day on weekdays. It was particularly popular with cab-drivers, students and elderly people on fixed incomes. Scenes for the movie "Taxi Driver" were filmed there.[1]

From the 1960s, however, the downtown cafeteria became as socially obsolete as most downtown manufacturers. Its disappearance did not reflect lack of demand for cheap food served quickly and without ostentation. Far from it: Bickford's and Horn and Hardart's were only replaced by McDonald's and pizza stands. But in contrast to cafeteria habitués, as Isaac Bashevis Singer has often described them, dawdling, dreaming, and arguing over their trays, the clients of fast-food outlets are trained to regard restaurants as a market for eating rather than a place. These are high-rent, high-volume outlets that sell highly standardized food. They are as different from the automat as the lack of formality and absence of novelty that surround them. Familiarity is provided by institutional context rather than social interaction: the form of consuming is vital, not the cultural activity of consumption.

New economic values make it too expensive to preserve the cafeteria's cultural values. Who at any rate is left to mourn the loss? Just as condominium conversion has removed many habitués from their apartments and places of work, so Philip Siegel's survivors have dispersed throughout the metropolitan region or retired to Florida. As downtown expands its landscape of economic power, vernacular landmarks lose meaning and vanish.[2]

This change in the material landscape parallels a change in the way downtown is viewed. From a messy space sporadically supervised by institutions of the public sector – jails, courthouses, and public housing projects – rises a renewed grassroots perspective on downtown as the incubator of cultural innovation. The new symbolic landscape is marked not only by art galleries, but also by downtown nightclubs and central railroad stations. Liminal spaces in themselves, they cross night and day, *haut monde* and underworld, cultural monuments and commerce. They also represent the landmarks of a downtown liminal zone.

Michael Musto, a *Village Voice* reporter, has chronicled the birth and death of this downtown liminality during the 1980s.[3] The East Village, the clubs, and the underground network really worked at the beginning of the decade, when they "attracted a vivid bunch of Euros, downtowners, and rich kids who really mixed amid the Busby Berkeley-style theme changes." Once the whole varied ensemble was perceived "as a stepping stone to bigger things," however, the vernacular scene was finished. Certainly the conspicuous idleness and illegal drug consumption of downtown club denizens "and the snobbery of some doormen" had made this scene far from "idyllic." Yet for little economic cost, downtown offered "glitter, innovation, and raw talent." This downtown was inhabited by those who lived off government grants for the arts, inherited wealth, the new service industries, the informal sector (including drugs), and the wages of celebrity.

Of "three hot clubs" in the 1980s – Area, Limelight, and Danceteria – one "[died] a natural death," the second survived with a less artistic clientele, and the third "[gave] way to expensive office space." "The biggest factor in downtown's demise is,"

Musto decides, "the high cost of living in Manhattan."* "Parasites who happen to be real estate developers" exploit and explode the downtown scene. Yet it is the change of perspective focusing on cultural values that makes downtown accessible to potential investors. And this in turn enhances property values. "Now you have uptown coming downtown and Wall Street coming uptown," the owner-designer of a new "surf-theme" restaurant says to Musto, "but that's what makes the city grow."

The life cycle of clubs suggests how property investments re-forms the urban vernacular away from liminality toward a landscape of power. Instead of artists, rich kids, and literary emigrants who comment with an air of detachment on market culture, downtown is taken over by another kind of market culture, one made by real estate speculators, institutional investors, and big-time international consumers. From Musto's perspective, this real estate market destroys the neighborhood, the artist's community, the *place* that he sees downtown.[4] What Michael Musto regards as "the death of downtown" keynotes, however, the expanding organizational field of central power. By standardizing and replicating cultural forms that originate in the center, and attracting new, often international investment, downtown's liminal space mediates the dialectical tension between centrality and power. Downtown works "best" in this role when new capital, uses, and urban forms subvert and bury the unique vernacular of the downtown scene. By contrast, this dynamic works "worst" where old industrial structures are most entrenched, where shopping cannot replace the jobs and income lost in corporate reorganization, where the urban vernacular remains both structurally and institutionally embedded in the downtown core.[5]

The expansion of both artists' communities and business services since 1975 has made downtown Manhattan an avatar of liminality between commerce and culture. Yet the reassertion of a landscape of central power is constantly tested by resurgence of the urban vernacular, especially by the presence of homeless men and women. Homelessness is a recurrent problem for makers of landscape. Before Central Park was formed at the end of the 1860s, squatters had to be removed from shacks in the middle of the swamp. Years later, during the Great Depression, homeless people built shantytowns in Riverside Park. Again, after 1980, the expansion of the homeless population spilled over from the Bowery downtown to midtown's Port Authority Bus Terminal. Parks, streets, subway stations, and nearly all public space downtown brought the ambivalent nature of liminality in a market economy to the fore: could public space be appropriated by *everyone* and *anyone*, or should its use be defined solely by private development?

Grand Central Terminal during most of the 1980s continuously remapped the boundary between respectability and homelessness, landscape and vernacular. Under the bright blue, gold-starred dome of the arrivals and departures hall, commuters and office workers shared a reasonable landscape of power. Ticket booths, stores, newspaper kiosks, and food stands filled the white marble expanse, where music students performed chamber pieces at lunchtime. The homeless slept downstairs, next to the tracks and in the labyrinth of tunnels. They also filled the waiting and rest rooms. An uneasy truce over these territorial divisions was policed by the city administration and the New York Civil Liberties Union. One compromise involved locking the doors of the terminal every

---

*Despite the later recognition that AIDS had ravaged downtown art and design communities, Musto eventually claimed that the sex scene in downtown clubs had been reborn ("Wild in the Clubs," *Village Voice*, Dec. 20, 1988). The following year, another local newspaper declared that New York nightclubs were more diffuse and less exciting, both too expensive and too tightly regulated by the city administration ("For Night Crawlers, Are City's Glamour, Excitement Fading?" *New York Observer*, Dec. 11, 1989).

night at 1 A.M. so that more homeless men and women wouldn't pour in through the night. By 1987 a clearer division between commercial public space and areas where the homeless slept was desired. The Metro-North Commuter Railroad, the quasi-public authority that owns Grand Central Terminal, developed an architectural plan to renovate the station. As the president of Metro-North said, "We want to put the grand back in Grand Central."

Later that year, the New York City government intensified its efforts to remove the homeless from desirable commercial and residential areas. The most infirm among them were to be removed from public streets, for their own safety, to public hospitals and shelters. But the key to removal was geographical: the homeless were only to be removed from public spaces in the downtown area. The way the downtown was defined, moreover, made it significantly larger than was commonly perceived. Not only did the homeless sweep affect the traditional landscape of downtown power – Wall Street, midtown, and the Upper East Side – but it also expanded the locus of centrality to those areas of Manhattan that had recently been reclaimed by gentrification. Thus the organizational field of central power now extended from West 110th Street and East 96th Street down to the southern tip of the island. The issue of the homeless dramatized the fact that "public space" was no longer open to the public without conditions.[6]

The return of business investment downtown during the 1980s not only changed the face of the center; it made the center larger. In Chicago, the map the Chicago School described around 1920 no longer holds true. The Loop, as the historic central business district is known, has multiplied four-fold in size. The new "super Loop" contains luxury apartments, office lofts, nightclubs, chic restaurants, art galleries, and a continuation of the upscale shopping district for which Michigan Avenue is known.[7] As a result of this expansion, the concept "downtown" no longer has geographical limits.[8] When a reporter asks the singer Madonna to name her favorite downtown store in Manhattan, she mentions one on the Upper West Side. Branching and replication of stores have in fact eliminated the need to "go downtown" in search of a special product. And mass distribution – as with "Fior di Latte" – makes the point of consumption equally convenient to everyone. Downtown now becomes a fluid space, whose abstraction of cultural values into consumer goods makes shopping a significant social experience. As New York magazine put it in a special double issue on downtown Manhattan, "Downtown is a style, a sensibility, a state of mind reflected in the art world, fiction, restaurants, fashion, and the way people live."[9]

While gentrification and downtown expansion have not "integrated" the center of the city, they have overcome its traditional segmentation. On the one hand, mixed uses have rendered obsolete the old barriers of space and time – skid row and the manufacturing districts that most people avoided after nightfall, the entertainment districts of gay bars and secret lives, and tawdry streets of low-price shops – and made downtown a high-profile, night-and-day landscape of consumption. On the other hand, the sensual opportunities densely produced in downtown space – Musto's clubs, avant-garde art, the smell of fresh bread being delivered in Bright Lights, Big City – have shifted downtown's social meaning from production to consumption.*

---

*The novel Bright Lights, Big City offers an object lesson in this sort of transformation. The poor and the misfits intrude on the narrator only as objects of consumption – the peddler who sells him a fake Rolex on the street, the mother in the outer boroughs who exists in front-page tabloid headlines. Similarly, he gets the fresh bread that offers him new life at the end of the novel from a trucker who is unloading a bakery delivery, "a man with a family," he thinks, "somewhere outside the city." In most cases, the bakery that produces this bread is also located outside the city, especially outside Manhattan.

"In a sense, we are redefining the function of the central city," the city planning director of Chicago says. "It was always the center for banking, government, education and health care, but that is becoming even more the case. And now we are adding housing, too, which puts people back on the streets and gives us the possibility of a city that is open 18 hours a day." Recreating downtown as a liminal space enhances economic values. When Moody's Investor Service upgraded Chicago's bond rating to A, it cited fiscal retrenchment on the part of the city administration and "also downtown development and the gentrification of a number of neighborhoods." There is no clearer indication of the synergy between economic and cultural values.[10]

Yet Michael Musto has already declared in print that "downtown" is dead.[11] What he means by this is nothing other than the hallmarks of current structural transformation: the internationalization of investment, a shift in social meaning from production to consumption, and an abstraction – in this case – from cultural to economic values. The "death of downtown" also highlights differences in spatial organization between production and consumption. Production units function best in clusters of customers and suppliers. Historically these clusters gave downtown its specialized aura of variety and innovation. But consumption units are increasingly spread out, diffused, standardized, and reproduced. Decentralization reduces the power of consumption spaces; it requires conscious action to restore their specific meaning.

Under these conditions, mediating the dialectic of power and centrality depends on a critical infrastructure for cultural production and consumption. Here I am thinking of men and women who produce and consume, and also evaluate, new market-based cultural products. Like artists, they both comment critically on, and constitute, a new kind of market culture. Their "inside" view opens up new spaces for consumption. They enhance market values even when they desperately want to conserve the values of place.

The Critical Infrastructure

Gentrification takes older cities into a new organization of consumption based on cultural capital. One of the interesting aspects of this organization of consumption is that it is spatially specific: consumption markets (clubs, housing) are attached to places that claim to be unique. It also provides extensive variety and 24-hour-a-day availability of goods and services. So it strengthens spatial concentration and generates part-time work. New products, and new practices of consumption, require a labor force that can deal with cultural capital. Artists, actors, and graduate students are often mobilized to fill these roles. Neither servile nor professional, restaurant waiters and boutique sales clerks interpret cultural goods to potential consumers. They help constitute the experience of consumption.

For a college-educated generation, the wide array of goods now available requires more carefully considered, *reflexive* consumption. . . . this is mediated in some fields by architects and designers. But increasingly selective consumption is more broadly mediated by those who communicate information about new consumer goods and services. These men and women perform several important social roles. They form a highly visible wedge of gentrification in specific cities. They staff the new service careers in publishing, restaurants, advertising, and cultural institutions on which downtown's economy depends. And by means of their creative products – especially their reviews – they provide an aesthetic critique that facilitates upscale consumption. They supply the critical infrastructure for downtown's transformation.[12]

The critical infrastructure undeniably rests on a wider base of consumer demand. Outside the nexus of food stamps, unemployment, and the minimum wage lies another world where people eat to read and read to eat. While it becomes harder to feed a low-income family a nutritious diet, more affluent, choice-ridden consumers are increasingly preoccupied by new means of consumption – and new anxieties about how to choose between them. . . .

Not just a shift in taste, but a shift in the way taste is produced accounts for the rise of reflexive consumption. The aesthetic and sensual side of gentrification reflects the "Orwellian" norms of redemption, critical distance, and astonishment,[13] but it also requires a shift in mediation from personal protocols to impersonal arbitration.

In Edith Wharton's novel *The House of Mirth*, for example, the character Selden "learned with amusement [from his upper-class New York friends in Monte Carlo] that there were several places where one might miss something by not lunching, or forfeit something by lunching; so that eating actually became a minor consideration on the very spot consecrated to its rites." The quality of food, at the end of the Gilded Age, is clearly secondary to the social space of consumption. "'Of course one gets the best things at the *Terrasse* – but that looks as if one hadn't any other reason for being there: the Americans who don't know any one always rush for the best food. And the Duchess of Beltshire has taken up Bécassin's lately,' Mrs. Bry earnestly summed up."[14]

While a taste "for the best food" doesn't compensate for "whom one knows," it nonetheless substitutes today for hierarchies based on personal networks and social position. In a mass-produced and mass-distributed culture, a taste for "the real thing" becomes a strategy of social differentiation. Yet the real thing refers to two quite different sorts of goods. It refers to goods that offer the authenticity of the past and those that suggest the uniqueness of new design.

Today cultural consumption follows the lead of several mediators: the artist, the primary consumer, and the designer, who interpret desire and direct the consumer to equate awareness of consuming with awareness of life; and the line producer in new service industries, catering to a jaded

consumer "who yearns for homespun to ease the chintz."[15] This yearning is satisfied by a juxtaposition of very old ("historic") and very modern ("state-of-the-art") products. Just as a gentrified neighborhood is a repository of collective memory, so it is also a site of individualized, high-technology household consumption. . . .

The modern city's image of centrality is turned inside out by the landscape of power at the bicoastal extremities of the Sunbelt. Without a traditional center or downtown, cities like Los Angeles and Miami can only be seen in fragments. Intensive real estate development does not produce the usual vertical skyline. Seashore, freeways, and canals erupt, instead, in dense clusters of suburban-style housing like the ranch house, beach house, villa, and bungalow, isolated office buildings, and low-lying industrial parks. There is little difference between "city" and "country" in this clustered diffusion.

Under pressure from investment in the built environment, space both expands and contracts. Collective spatial forms expand to include relatively unstructured cities like Los Angeles and Miami as well as increasingly structured exurban areas (Orange County in southern California and Fort Lauderdale–Palm Beach in Florida). But the same forms are also individualized and collapsed into specific journeys: no one would claim to appropriate the entire experience of LA or Miami. The automobility that flows through these cities makes some people excited or uneasy, for there is little connection – according to modernist expectations – between built form and urban identity. In Miami, in the architect Michael Sorkin's view, "the pattern of settlement [is] obviously in total thrall to the landscape. Clearly, this [is] a zone to be grasped not through the familiar repertoire of urban categories but through a far broader sense of territory."[16]

Beginning in the 1920s, and with greater force since the recognition of a "power shift" to the Sunbelt in the 1970s, the material landscape of contemporary cities has indeed demanded a broader set of categories than modernism offers. The dynamic interplay between nature and artifice in the built environment of Los Angeles or Miami has forced us to visualize urban development as a set of multiple, decentered processes, and to acknowledge the strong force of derivation over originality in architecture. Furthermore, the forging of a metropolis out of many private jurisdictions has challenged the primacy of public space as an organizing principle of social life. From the outset, moreover, Los Angeles and Miami have grown from service rather than manufacturing economies, wrenching the landscape of power from its nineteenth-century roots. This must be our image of postmodern urbanity. Yet it has been a long time building. Palm trees, fast cars on freeways, hot flamingo pinks and dazzling white villas: the symbols of post-World War II choice and alienation stretch continuously from *Play It as It Lays* to *Less than Zero*. This is the world of Raymond Chandler colonized by Walt Disney's world, where the fantasies of the powerless are magically projected onto landscape developed by the powerful. . . .

The entire landscape of cities like Miami and Los Angeles visually projects the liminality between *market* and *place*. The usual forms of social control – by police, employers, corporate elites – are embedded in an amusing architecture and individualized means of consumption like automobiles. Although LA and Miami are real cities, they are built on the power of dreamscape, collective fantasy, and facade. This landscape is explicitly produced for visual consumption. Moreover, it is *self-consciously* produced. As James suspected, the best place to view such a landscape is at the very tips of the Sunbelt, where regional identity is least "southern" and "western" and thus most socially constructed.

Miami was, after all, invented three times in this century. Developed out of swampland as a socially, ethnically, and racially exclusive southern resort in the 1920s, Miami differed little in intention

from its more exclusive neighbor, Palm Beach. After World War II, a second Miami, monopolized by Miami Beach, developed as a cheaper vacation land for middle-class northerners, mainly ethnic and eventually Jewish; Miami offered a more exotic and more individualized consumption of leisure than social camps in the Catskills. From 1960, following Castro's revolution, a new wave of Cuban exiles and other Central Americans swelled the racially and ethnically segregated population in the inner city. By 1980, bypassing the native black population in business and political organization, they made the Miami area a Latin metropolis, an adjunct to Caracas and Rio and an alternative to Havana. Ethnic recruits and Latin capital created in the third Miami a microcosm of global exchange. While the city always had a service economy, hotels became less important than foreign investment in banks, weapons traffic, and the illegal drug trade.[17]

Los Angeles has also been invented three times in this century. Visualized by celluloid fantasy, Los Angeles first figured as backdrop and back lot in countless silent Westerns. The prewar dream capital was created as production space for the manufacture of films, which was, like tourism, a mass leisure industry. But Los Angeles was also created by making desert and hills habitable for immigrant labor, both skilled and unskilled, outside the film industry, in oil and gas refineries, car making, and light manufacturing. The first Los Angeles was an amalgam of East European Jews, Asians, Chicanos, African-Americans, Okies, and most of all, midwesterners. Invention of the second Los Angeles, which dates from 1940, reflected the new labor force required for military and industrial activities in the port and airport and large, unionized plants. This is the Los Angeles of middle-class affluence and social mobility, an American dream. As in Miami, however, much of the population that was drawn to the city in this period has been passed over in the growth of the third Los Angeles.

Both decentralized and recentralized, the new Los Angeles has a coherent landscape downtown, built by new Asian immigrants and mainly foreign investment in banking and financial services. But it also has inner suburbs where manufacturing branch plants of US firms have rapidly shut down, displacing and cheapening union labor, and other industrial suburbs where electronics and garment plants have continued to grow even during economic recessions. These suburbs are integrated by clusters of high-tech industries, yet they are segregated at work by race and gender and segregated in residential communities by race and class.[18]

The constant reinvention of landscape furnishes a narrative for "footloose" capital. It provides a social geography for the shifting landscapes of the global economy. Yet while the real history of Los Angeles and Miami illustrates the processes of structural change in the US economy, these cities are more interesting as spatial metaphors. We are fascinated by Los Angeles and Miami because we think they show us the future. Their freeways, their "decentering," their "Mondo Condo" pursuit of private leisure: this is the way the future looks. These cities stun because of their unique ability to abstract an image of desire from the landscape and reflect it back through the vernacular. Just as they show the power of facade to lure the imagination, so they also represent the facade of global corporate power.

No single image symbolizes a postmodern city like Los Angeles or Miami the way the steel mill symbolizes the company town or downtown symbolizes the modern city. "Ain't no skyline," an ironic song-writer says about LA. We see these landscapes, instead, by modes of visual consumption that play with image and reality. Visual consumption of landscape rests on an interplay of nature and artifice that goes back many years. Toward the end of the eighteenth century, the "Eidophusikon" – a construction of pasteboard cut-outs, lights, and sound – created scenes of London, the countryside, and the seashore. In the nineteenth

century, dioramas and panoramas manipulated light to make translucent images – often images of city streets – on a screen. Their twentieth-century descendants, Hollywood films, widened spectators' power over darkness while strengthening the hold of the image over its viewers. After the reign of still photography during the Depression and World War II, electronic media completed the transformation of image into power. Broadcast television broke all existing barriers between public and private, local and global, the living room and the world, until the viewers rather than the image became the product.[19]

The domestication of fantasy in visual consumption is inseparable from centralized structures of economic power. Just as the earlier power of the state illuminated public space – the streets – by artificial lamplight, so the economic power of CBS, Sony, and the Disney Company illuminates private space at home by electronic images. With the means of production so concentrated and the means of consumption so diffused, communication of these images becomes a way of controlling both knowledge and imagination, a form of corporate social control over technology and symbolic expressions of power.

Fantasy as a Landscape of Power

While Walt Disney won fame as a founder of Hollywood's animation industry, his real genius was to transform an old form of collective entertainment – the amusement park – into a landscape of power. All his life Disney wanted to create his own amusement park. But to construct this playground, he wanted no mere thrill rides or country fair: he wanted to project the vernacular of the American small town as an image of social harmony. "The idea of Disneyland is a simple one. It will be a place for people to find happiness and knowledge," Disney said. But "in fact," a recent essay on Disney points out, "it was the appearance of Disneyland, not the idea, that was simple."[20]

Appearance nonetheless caused the great animator some concern when he began to plan Disneyland, the archetypal theme park, which was finally built in Orange County, California, in 1955. Disney hired two architects whose plans didn't quite capture what he had in mind, and giving up on them, used an animator from his studio to draw up architectural designs to his own specifications. Disney's peculiar vision was based on a highly selective consumption of the American landscape. Anchored by a castle and a railroad station, Disneyland evoked the fantasies of domesticity and illicit mobility that were found in the vernacular architecture of southern California. The castle and station were joined on an axis by "Main Street USA," an ensemble of archaic commercial facades. This mock-up in fact idealized the vernacular architecture Disney remembered from his childhood in Marceline, Missouri, before World War I. But Disney had not had a happy childhood. The son of a disappointed utopian who drifted between factory jobs and small business ventures that always failed, Disney designed Disneyland by abstracting a promise of security from the vernacular.

Disney's fantasy both restored and invented collective memory. "This is what the real Main Street should have been like," one of Disneyland's planners or "imagineers" says. "What we create," according to another, "is a 'Disney realism,' sort of Utopian in nature, where we carefully program out all the negative, unwanted elements and program in the positive elements."[21] And Disneyland succeeded on the basis of this totalitarian image-making, projecting the collective desires of the powerless into a corporate landscape of power. In this way it paralleled the creation of a mass consumption society. Disney's designs also included an element of play that was pure Hollywood construction, for Disneyland featured five different stage-set amusement parks, organized around separate themes: Adventureland, Lilliputian Land, Fantasyland, Frontier Land, and Holiday Land. The unique combination borrowed motifs from carnivals, children's literature, and US history.

That Disneyland significantly departed from the dominant fantasy landscape of the time was dramatized when Disney failed to arouse enthusiasm in a convention of amusement park owners that previewed plans for the park in 1953. They criticized the small number of rides, the large amount of open space that wouldn't generate revenue, and the need for constant, expensive maintenance in the theme parks.[22] In their view, Disneyland would never succeed as a business venture. They objected – had they used the now-fashionable word *concept* in those days – that Disneyland was too self-conscious and unrealistic a concept to be an amusement park. But from our point of view, they failed to understand that Disneyland was an ideal object for visual consumption, a landscape of social power. Despite their criticism, Disneyland was commercially successful from the day it opened.

Disneyland offered a multidimensional collage of the American landscape. The playgrounds organized around a theme provided consumers with their first opportunity to view several different landscapes – some imaginative historical recreations and others purely imaginary – simultaneously. With this variety for individual visitors to choose from, Disneyland differed from historical dioramas and reconstructions like Greenfield Village and Colonial Williamsburg, where costumed actors re-created the routines of daily life in an earlier age. Disneyland, moreover, had no educational veneer. It merely told a story, offering the selective consumption of space and time as entertainment. This was the "wienie," as Walt Disney and amusement park owners alike called the lure that attracted customers to a paying event.

Visitors to Disneyland paid for a variety of entertainment experiences linked by the narrative of the different themes. These in turn provided a narrative for different program segments on the Disney Studio's

weekly television series. Combining narrative with serial expectations, each visual
product of the Disney Company fed into
the others. Although commercial spin-offs
were not a new creation, this commercial-
ization was the most extensive to take place
under a single corporate sponsor. Disney's
business growth also related to important
processes of change in the larger society:
notably, the demographic growth of the
baby boom, the spread of television, and
the increase in domestic consumption.
Moreover, it contributed to the development of both Orange County and the tourist industry. Disney's success coincided with
the expansion of the suburbs and a population shift to the Southwest, the growth of
the service sector, and a boom in leisure-
time activities, including sales of recreational land and travel. Just as the real
landscape reflected the intensive, unplanned development of the country by
subdivision and mass construction, so the
imaginary landscape of Disneyland reflected the growth of mass communications
built on visual consumption.

While this kind of entertainment invited
escape from the modern world, it also
relied upon the centralization of economic
power typical of modern society. Consumption at Disneyland was part of a
service-sector complex relating automobiles and airplanes, highways, standardized
hotels, movies, and television. Furthermore, the social production of Disneyland
related a major corporate presence – the
Disney Company – to entertainment "creation," real estate development and construction, and product franchising. In all
these senses, Disneyland suggested the
social and economic potential of liminality
in the modern American marketplace....

NOTES

1   Obituary notice in *New York Times*, Sept. 5,
    1986.
2   An organization called "City Lore, a center
    for urban folk culture on the Lower East
    Side, [has] set out to capture some of New
    York City's neighborhood institutions on
    film and on tape before they go the way of
    Steeplechase Park *and the Belmore Cafe-
    teria*" (Elizabeth Kolbert, "Street Life: Keep-
    ing 'Beloved Places,'" *New York Times*,
    March 28, 1988; emphasis added.
3   Michael Musto, "The Death of Down-
    town," *Village Voice*, April 28, 1987, pp.
    15–20.
4   Cf. Rosalyn Deutsche and Cara Gendel
    Ryan, "The Fine Art of Gentrification," *Oc-
    tober* 31 (Winter 1984): 91–111.
5   On the lack of profitability of waterfront
    shopping centers in Flint, Michigan, and
    Toledo, Ohio, in contrast to Baltimore and
    Boston, see "Jim Rouse May Be Losing His
    Touch," *Business Week*, April 4, 1988, pp.
    33–4. By the same token, the apparent suc-
    cess of South Street Seaport in downtown
    Manhattan is really questionable. Some
    stores that aimed at an affluent tourist cli-
    entele have failed, giving rise to talk about
    revamping them as service stores for a local
    population: a transformation from new
    urban landscape to new urban vernacular.
    See Mark McCain, "Commercial Property:
    A Troubled Urban Mall; Rouse Makes Plans
    for the South Street Seaport; Among Pro-
    spects, Shops to Serve the Community,"
    New York Times, March 13, 1988.
6   In subsequent years, partly responding to
    local and paying users' complaints, city
    authorities made more stringent rules to
    bar the homeless from the subways, Penn
    Station, the bus terminals, and other public
    spaces, while ignoring private owners'
    attempts to bar the public – especially the
    homeless public – from such "public spaces"
    as plazas and galleries that enjoyed a zon-
    ing bonus. Richard Levine, "Plan Urges
    New Look at Terminal," *New York Times*,
    Jan. 11, 1987; Bob Fitch, "Put 'Em Where
    We Ain't," *Nation*, April 2, 1988, p. 466;
    New York Times, April 11, 1988; Oct. 1 and
    25, 1989; Helen Thorpe, "Open to the
    Public?" *New York Observer*, March 12,
    1990. For a contrasting historical survey
    of downtown Manhattan, cf. Emanuel
    Tobier, "Gentrification: The Manhattan
    Story," *New York Affairs* 5, no. 4 (1979):
    13–25.

7 William E. Schmidt, "Riding a Boom. Downtowns Are No Longer Downtrodden," *New York Times*, Oct. 11, 1987.

8 Michael Musto, *Downtown* (New York: Vintage Books, 1986), p. 5.

9 *New York*, Dec. 25, 1989–Jan. 1, 1990, p. 3. For acknowledgment of the significance to restructuring of shopping and consumption in general, cf. Beauregard, "Chaos and Complexity," pp. 44–5, and Smith, "Of Yuppies and Housing," pp. 165–70.

10 Schmidt, "Riding a Boom."

11 Musto, "Death of Downtown."

12 Cf. William Leiss, "Icons of the Marketplace," *Theory, Culture and Society* 1, no. 3 (1983): 10–21, and Smith, "Of Yuppies and Housing."

13 Wright, "The Ghosting of the Inner City," in *On Living in an Old Country: The National Past in Contemporary Britain* (London: Verso, 1985), p. 230.

14 Edith Wharton, *The House of Mirth* [1905] (New York: Bantam, 1984), p. 175. Cf. Pierre Bourdieu's version of the same pursuit of positional goods: "The sense of good investment which dictates a withdrawal from outmoded, or simply devalued, objects, places or practices and a move into ever newer objects in an endless drive for novelty, and which operates in every area, sport and cooking, holiday resorts and restaurants, is guided by countless different indices and indications, from explicit warnings ('Saint-Tropez' – or the Buffet de la gare in Lyon, or anywhere else – 'has become impossible') to the barely conscious intuitions, which . . . insidiously arouse horror or disgust for objects or practices that have become common" (*Distinction*, p. 249).

15 Quotation from Francis X. Clines, "The Simple Life, with Lobster, in Wales," *New York Times*, September 20, 1987; on the use of marketed objects to create an awareness of consuming and hence an awareness of life, see "Interview with Ettore Sottsass," *Industrial Design*, Jan.–Feb. 1988, p. 31.

16 Michael Sorkin, "Travel: Miami Virtues: Sun, Sea and Dazzling Urban Design," *Vogue*, January 1986, p. 140; lack of correlation between urban form and social form

from Reyner Banham, *Los Angeles: The Architecture of Four Ecologies* (London: Allen Lane, Penguin Press, 1971), p. 237. Also see E. W. Soja, "Taking Los Angeles Apart: Some Fragments of a Critical Human Geography," *Environment and Planning D: Society and Space* 4 (1986): 255–72 and James J. Flink, *The Automobile Age* (Cambridge, Mass.: MIT Press, 1988), pp. 140–8.

17 See Raymond A. Mohl, "Miami: The Ethnic Cauldron," in *Sunbelt Cities: Politics and Growth since World War II*, ed. Richard M. Bernard and Bradley R. Rice (Austin: University of Texas Press, 1983), pp. 58–99; Penny Lernoux, "The Miami Connection," *Nation*, Feb. 18, 1984, pp. 186–98; Joan Didion, *Miami* (New York: Simon & Schuster, 1987).

18 See Edward W. Soja, "Economic Restructuring and the Internationalization of the Los Angeles Region," in *The Capitalist City*, ed. Michael Peter Smith and Joe R. Feagin (New York: Blackwell, 1987), pp. 178–98; Allen J. Scott, *Metropolis: From the Division of Labor to Urban Form* (Berkeley and Los Angeles: University of California Press, 1988), pp. 91–202; Mike Davis, *City of Quartz: Excavating the Future in Los Angeles* (London: Verso, 1990).

19 Eidophusikon, dioramas, and panoramas described in Wolfgang Schievelbusch, *Disenchanted Night: The Industrialization of Light in the Nineteenth Century*, trans. Angela Davies (Berkeley and Los Angeles: University of California Press, 1988); also see Francis D. Klingender, *Art and the Industrial Revolution* (London: Paladin, 1972), pp. 86–7; Joshua Meyerowitz, *No Sense of Place: The Impact of Electronic Media on Social Behavior* (New York: Oxford University Press, 1985), p. 73.

20 Martin Pawley, "Tourism: The Last Resort," *Blueprint*, Oct. 1988, p. 38.

21 Cleaning the past of its contradictions is developed in Mike Wallace, "Mickey Mouse History: Portraying the Past at Disney World," *Radical History Review* 32 (1985): 33–57; imagineers quoted on pp. 35–6.

22 Pawley, "Tourism: The Last Resort," p. 39.

Chapter 22

Reinventing the Johannesburg Inner City

Lindsay Bremner

Introduction

Since 1990, Johannesburg's local authority has spearheaded two local economic development initiatives to reinvent, re-image and reformulate its inner city landscape. These have been driven by the twin objectives of positioning the city advantageously in the global economy and averting the urban economic decline experienced from the 1970s onwards. To do this, images have been constructed of the city's future, around which investment, public opinion and social accord have been mobilized. . . .

The Changing Character of the Johannesburg Inner City

After the discovery of the Witwatersrand gold reef in 1886, the city of Johannesburg became, within a very short period of time, the financial and commercial hub of sub-Saharan Africa. Within the first 10 years of its existence, banks, finance houses and mining company headquarters lined its streets (Chipkin, 1993). Successive waves of economic activity, corresponding largely to the booms and slumps of the gold mining industry, produced, by 1990, a city housing the headquarters of 65 out of the 100 largest public companies listed on the Johannesburg Stock Exchange, 13 of South Africa's 30 largest companies, 6 of the 8 mining conglomerates and 9 of the 18

leading life assurance companies. In addition, it functioned as the national banking center, housing 11 of the leading 16 banking institutions, the Johannesburg Stock Exchange and the National Reserve Bank (Tomlinson et al., 1995). Its adjoining high density residential suburbs, developed speculatively in the 1960s (Chipkin, 1993), served as a point of arrival for new European immigrants to the city. The black working class, set apart by apartheid legislation, lived and commuted from Soweto, the sprawling township to the south west of the city.[1]

From its inception, the city was constructed to conform to images of Western modernity. Its building boom prior to the turn of the century drew on the Fin de Siecle European style, while the boom following the Boer War (1889–1902) produced monumental imperial buildings, consolidating the gold mining industry and the financial district in the appearance of British Edwardianism (Chipkin, 1993). The depression of the 1930s, which saw the abandoning of the gold standard in 1932, resulted in foreign capital flooding into the country and transformed Johannesburg into a little New York, or if not New York, then at least Chicago or Saint Louis (De Kiewiet, 1966, in Chipkin, 1993). By 1936, at the time of the British Empire Exhibition, Johannesburg was described as the "largest and most densely populated

European city in Africa" with "fascinating shops and smartly dressed shoppers" (*Times Weekly Edition*, 1936, in Chipkin, 1993: 105) and claimed for itself the status of "the Empire's great gold center" (Rogerson, 1996: 141).

This image began to be tarnished by the 1970s, as growing opposition to apartheid revealed the city's racial segregations and political divisions (Rogerson, 1996). The city's image was an exclusive one that "celebrated white dominance and brushed aside the alternative black experience of the city" (Rogerson, 1996: 141). By 1986, at the time of the city's centenary celebrations, black opposition to the image of the "city-with-a-golden-heart" reached its peak and rendered the celebrations meaningless. The authorities realized that the city needed reinventing.

Over this period, a gradual movement of black people from the township areas into inner city suburbs picked up momentum. The lifting of influx control and escalating repression and violence in the townships under the apartheid government's State of Emergency contributed to this. By 1986, at the time of the city's centenary celebrations, approximately 20000 black people, of a population of 120000, lived in the inner city suburb of Hillbrow (Morris, 1996). Migration into inner city suburbs accelerated rapidly. By 1993, 85 per cent of the inner city residential population were black (Morris, 1996) and by 1996, only 5 per cent were white (Crankshaw, 1997). Unlike in United States inner city neighborhoods, the bulk of this population did not constitute an underclass or ghetto poor (Wilson, 1987 and Wilson, 1991). The majority (ICHUT, 1996; Crankshaw, 1997; Morris, 1996) were more affluent than their counterparts, who remained in the segregated "ghetto" of the black township.

This rapid "greying" of the inner city was accompanied by physical decline and racial stereotyping of new residents (Morris, 1996). In many cases, the exodus of white residents had been aided and abetted by landlords, who saw the "illegal" status of black tenants as an opportunity for raising rents and reducing building maintenance (Zack et al., 1989, in Morris, 1996). In many buildings, rents were increased, apartments overcrowded and services not maintained. These conditions fueled the racial prejudice of white inner city residents who had left and who romanticized life before the arrival of black residents (Morris, 1996).

Further demographic shifts have occurred during the second half of the 1990s as Africans from countries further north, mainly Nigeria and the Democratic Republic of Congo, have arrived in the inner city. In 1995, 23000 Congolese were estimated to be living in Johannesburg (Kadima and Kalombo, 1995), while Morris (1996) estimated 3000 Nigerians to be living in the inner city. These population groups have been subjected to high levels of persecution from South Africans (Dhlomo, 1997). They are blamed for the overcrowded informal trading sector, the growth of the narcotics trade and deterioration of the physical environment (Simone, 1998). Increasing xenophobia, assaults and conflicts over space and access have led to the construction of a defensive, ethnically defined spatiality. Immigrant communities can, in many ways, be compared to immigrant minorities in the United States (Morris, 1996; Ogbu, 1993).

Turning to the economy of the inner city – in ways typical of similar cities across the world, Johannesburg's economy has declined since 1980. Its traditional manufacturing base (clothing, printing, textiles, food, fabricated metals) lost activity across all sectors, declining from R3.4 billion in 1980 to R2.5 billion in 1994 (Pienaar, 1994).[2] At the same time, its financial and government sectors increased (finance from R3.2 to 4.8 billion, government from R0.8 to 1.2 billion), while commercial activity on the other hand, remained stagnant at R3 billion (Pienaar, 1994).

Between 1982 and 1994, 17 of the 65 top 100 national public companies located in Johannesburg moved from the Central Business District (CBD)[3] to decentralized locations (Tomlinson et al., 1995).

Similarly, of a total of 104 top national business enterprises located in Johannesburg, in 1994, only 27 per cent were located in the CBD. Of the top 10 retail companies in the country having their head offices in Johannesburg, only two remain in the CBD. In the area of accounting, all leading accounting firms in the country have retained their head offices in Johannesburg, but, whereas in 1982, all seven were located in the CBD, by 1994, only three remained. In the advertising industry, of the top 15 firms in the country, 14 are based in Johannesburg. In 1994, these were all located in decentralized areas, whereas in 1991, seven were located in the CBD. While these relocations can be attributed to many factors (infrastructure requirements, convenience factors, corporate restructuring, prestige factors etc; Tomlinson et al., 1995), a clear picture emerges of capital flight from the CBD (*Business Day Property Supplement*, 1996; Muyanda, 1996). While the Johannesburg area has maintained its national head office function, the central city has weakened for nearly all sectors, with the exception of retail.[4]

Remaining in the Central Business District are the major financial institutions which have sunk considerable investments into property over the last 90 years. Of these, life assurance companies (Old Mutual, Sage and Sanlam), national banking institutions (ABSA, who announced a R400 million four-city block development in 1996, Standard, First National and Nedcor), mining houses, Anglo American and the Johannesburg Chamber of Industry are dominant. With approximately 13 other owner occupiers, this group own and control the major landholdings in the CBD (Tomlinson et al., 1995).

By far the most rapid transformation of the inner city area from the early 1990s onwards, however, was the growth of the informal commerce and catering sector (Biller, 1997). Informal trading became one of the most "spectacular expressions" of the desegregation of urban space associated with the end of apartheid (Tomlinson et al.,

1995: 123). This growth can be attributed to an official policy change, from repression to tolerance or promotion, a downturn in the formal economy, repeal of influx control and an increase in international migration (Tomlinson et al., 1995). By 1993, it was estimated that there were 15000 people earning their living on the streets of Greater Johannesburg, mostly at a survivalist level (Johannesburg, 1993b). Four thousand of these were located in the inner city, and 45 per cent of them were foreign (*Star*, 1993; *Citizen*, 1993). By 1999, the number of traders in the inner city was estimated to be 10,000, with 300,000–400,000 "tourist shoppers" passing through its streets each month (Greater Johannesburg, 1999a: 2).

In response to these changing conditions, the Johannesburg City Council (1991–3) and later the Greater Johannesburg Metropolitan Council (1995 onwards) developed an evolving set of local economic development initiatives to reinvent, re-image and re-market the Johannesburg inner city.

The City's Response 1: Gateway to Africa

The first of these (Rogerson, 1996) was based on models of urban entrepreneuralism (Harvey, 1989) and urban regeneration (Imrie and Thomas, 1993) drawn from North America and Western Europe, centered on physical regeneration and investment in buildings and infrastructure. It falls squarely into what Beauregard (1993: 26) called the "mainstream" approach to urban economic revival. It had very little to do with the economic, social and physical changes which had taken place in the city over time, instead seeking to capitalize on South Africa's imminent re-entry into the world as an opportunity for re-imaging and regenerating the city. Typically, this approach involved "glossy plan preparation; public sector infrastructure investment; partnership development of flagship schemes in retailing, leisure and commercial development; an emphasis on arts and culture; and strong marketing to reverse or alter existing poor images of the city"

(Fitzsimons, 1995: 7–8, in Rogerson, 1996: 139). Imrie and Thomas (1993), Boyle (1988) and Ettlinger (1994) elaborate the emphasis on the shift to public-private partnerships for development inherent in this approach. The role of the local state shifts in emphasis from one of provider of social services and goods to the promotion of local growth and the reversal of economic decline (Bingham and Mier, 1993).

Johannesburg's late-apartheid vision and strategies for regeneration were based upon an aspiration towards "world city" status, as a goal to be achieved through urban policy making (Shachar, 1994). Johannesburg's authorities began to portray it as the "Tokyo or New York of Africa" (Wright, 1992: 13). The city began positioning itself in the new economic geography of global capitalism through styling itself as the "Gateway to Africa" (Rogerson, 1996: 141).

> We are looking forward to Johannesburg resuming its rightful place as the economic and social powerhouse of South Africa's most prosperous region. It will become the Gateway to Africa (Anon, 1994, in Tomlinson et al., 1995: 57).

Strategies were devised to achieve this, involving a typical property-led development programme, an aggressive marketing campaign and a particular emphasis on sport and culture as vehicles for investment, drawn from the experience of a number of British cities (Glasgow, Sheffield and Birmingham) (Tomlinson et al., 1995). Johannesburg was marketed to the world through its locational advantages, communications infrastructure, and mature financial dominance, as a launch pad into the hinterland of Africa (Rogerson, 1996). This assumption of the position of frontier town displays a characteristic colonial ambivalence to Africa (Rostron, 1999). Johannesburg lies on the edge of Africa, beyond the frontier of the civilized world. At the same time, it presents vast, untapped resources for exploitation. Executive directors of commerce and industry, sport and culture were

appointed by the City Council in 1991 for the first time and Johannesburg was proclaimed the fourth of the top ten growth cities in the world. International business delegations were hosted by the city and a number of corporate business partnerships designed to promote business and partnership arrangements between Johannesburg and other cities such as Atlanta, New York and Birmingham.

At the same time, the city authorities attempted to overcome negative perceptions of the city's racial exclusivity by ironically (and unsubstantiatedly) proclaiming it as South Africa's most "integrated city" (Johannesburg, 1993a, in Rogerson, 1996: 143). Attempts were made to style the city as "inviting and integrated" (Rice, 1993: 15), not through investment in social or service infrastructure, but through an emphasis on the importance of culture and urban design (Rogerson, 1996). A "Civic Spine" was created by tying together existing public buildings in the central business district into a cohesive designed precinct, and a neglected council-owned tract of land on the western edge of the city was transformed into the "Newtown Cultural Precinct" through substantial public sector investment and cultural events. The annual "Arts Alive Festival" and the bi-annual Johannesburg Biennial were inaugurated. These hoped to capture local and international cultural imaginations and establish the area as a recreational and cultural theme park, emulating waterfront developments in Baltimore, Boston, San Francisco or Cape Town (Horak, 1994).

Through these initiatives, the inner city was portrayed as a "world city showroom", able to "assert itself unequivocally as the key economic center of a subcontinental region" (Johannesburg, 1993b, in Rogerson, 1996: 148). In 1991, ten top strategic projects were identified to involve the private sector in rebuilding the local economy and enhance Johannesburg's chance at world city status. The choice of the projects was based on a "boosterist" strategy (Tomlinson et al., 1995: 10), aimed at attracting and keeping investors in the city and on the basis of apparent research into the characteristics of world cities (Rogerson, 1996). They included: inner city housing; a R200 million light rail link between the high rise inner city suburbs and the central business district; the "Bara-link" project, involving the development of the area around the Baragwanath Hospital in Soweto to integrate Soweto with the city; the establishment of markets for inner city street trading; a R200–300 million convention center in the inner city; the development of a R100 million commercial theme park, known as "Jewel City" in the eastern sector of the central business district; and a series of projects using culture and sport as vehicles for local economic development. The Newtown Cultural Precinct and the Ellis Park Sports Precinct on the opposite eastern side of town were initiated. A world class 35,000-seater athletics stadium was completed in 1995. Johannesburg was ambitiously billed as the "premier cultural center of the country" (Francis, 1992: 53, in Rogerson, 1996: 152) and the "premier sports and entertainment venue in Africa" (*Engineering News*, 1995, in Rogerson, 1996: 152). A handful of small scale projects were initiated to improve sporting facilities in the high density inner city suburbs.

This reinvention of the city had some impact. In 1994, Johannesburg was voted as one of the world's top 50 cities by *Fortune* business magazine (Rogerson, 1996). In 1994, bidding against 20 other cities in the new province of Gauteng, Johannesburg won the vote of the newly formed provincial legislature, which relocated from neighboring Pretoria to the Johannesburg central business district, thereby showing confidence in and throwing its weight behind the city's regenerative efforts.

Nevertheless, it failed to impress the new metropolitan and local councillors elected in 1995 to supercede those of the former racially-based local councils. In a very short time, the key architects of the old new Johannesburg – the executive directors of trade and industry, culture and sport were demoted or fired, budgets were cut to the top ten strategic projects and a new more inclusive process devised to reinvent the inner city more in line with local imperatives.

The City's Response 2: Golden Heartbeat

The new re-imaging initiative was based, not on a speculative gamble for world city status, but on stabilizing decline and promoting neighborhood organization as a precursor to growth (Roysten, 1997). It was developed through an inclusive partnership between government, civil society, labor and the private sector, known as the Johannesburg Inner City Development Forum (JICDF). Its vision, adopted in 1996, aspired towards an inner city which was:

The Golden Heartbeat of Africa.
A dynamic city that works.
Liveable, safe, well managed and welcoming.
People centered, accessible and celebrating cultural diversity
A vibrant 24 hour city.
A city for residents, workers, tourists, entrepreneurs and learners.
Focused on the 21st Century, respecting its heritage and capitalizing on its position in South Africa, Africa and the world, a truly global city.
The trading hub of Africa thriving through participation, partnerships and the spirit of ubuntu. (Roysten, 1997: 5)

This implied a substantial change in emphasis and approach from that which had preceded it. Johannesburg is still portrayed as the city with a heart of gold, staking its inherent identity on its founding and most popularly identifiable feature. However, it is no longer located at the edge of Africa, as its gateway, but as its center, its life-force, its heartbeat. For the first time, Johannesburg acknowledges its location *in* Africa, rather than on its margins, and seeks to incorporate its African-ness into its image of itself. The focus of development is not primarily directed at the attraction of foreign investment, but rather at local upliftment ("livable, safe, well managed and welcoming ... a city for residents, workers, tourists, entrepreneurs and learners") while the aspiration to global status is maintained ("focused on the 21st Century ... capitalizing on its position in South Africa, Africa and the world, a truly global city"). The driving force of economic development is trade rather than sport or culture.

This vision was launched with great fanfare in 1997 at an event on the library gardens in the central business district, opened by then Deputy Present Thabo Mbeki (Reeves, 1997). It was accompanied by statements of support by all sectors and a general mood of optimism that the inner city was about to be "turned around" (Alfreds, 1997: 1).

Its strategy focused on developing environmental and infrastructural programs targeting crime, grime, congestion, homelessness and deteriorating public sector services through public-private partnerships (*Sunday Times Metro*, 1996; Russell, 1996). Legislation (Gauteng Provincial Government, 1997) legalized the existence of Business Improvement Districts (BIDs), facilitating private sector supplementation to local authority service provision. Soon the management of these districts claimed great success in the reduction of crime, improved cleanliness, reduction in office vacancies and increase in office rentals, with the Johannesburg project winning the international Downtown Association award in New York (*Citizen*, 1996). By 1999, muggings in Improvement Districts were down 90 per cent from 1994 figures, a retail survey indicated that 42 per cent of the formal retail sector in BIDs was optimistic about staying in the inner city and employment had been created for 250 cleansing and security staff in the areas affected (*City Vibe*, 1999).

Key urban renewal projects in this new reinvention of the city demonstrate the shift from "spectacle" to "environment" as the cornerstone of urban regeneration. While limited resources have been allocated by

the city to maintaining the investments previously made into sport and culture, major public/private investment has gone into infrastructure for the relief of environmental or social problems – taxi-ranks, informal trading markets or homeless people's shelters. These include a R160 million upgrade of the Johannesburg central station (Radebe, 1996), three taxi management facilities catering for 6000 taxis (Greater Johannesburg, 1999a: 6), the re-imaging of squares and parks in the inner city (*City Vibe*, 1999) and the provision of six housing facilities for homeless people, two of which are already operational (Greater Johannesburg, 1999a: 6).

Management and development of street trading, the taxi industry and other forms of micro-business activity are seen as high priorities for confidence building and stabilizing the inner city's economic environment. A progressive and accommodative stance towards informal economic activity was adopted and a quasi-government development agency, the Informal Trade Management Company created (Urban Market Joint Venture, 1999). This is responsible for restructuring informal trade within the inner city. Its current initiative will build six market places which combine trading stalls, productive and housing units and give 2400 traders a more permanent stake in the inner city economy (Urban Market Joint Venture, 1999).

One of the major thrusts of the new vision is to stabilize the inner city residential environment (Chalmers, 1996; Du Venage, 1996; Mantjiu, 1997). The public media has recorded some success in this regard (*Star Business Report*, 1996; *Star*, 1996). Existing housing stock has been upgraded for ownership through joint ventures between public and private sectors and by promoting the maintenance and proper management of buildings through incentives and public relations exercises. By 1999, 18 upgrading projects involving 2000 housing units were in progress (Greater Johannesburg, 1999a: 6). A bad buildings programme is facilitating the transfer of buildings to new owners prepared to invest in management, maintenance and refurbishment (Greater Johannesburg, 1999a: 5).

Many of these ideas have been tested in a pilot project around the largest inner city park, Joubert Park. The project covers seven city blocks, where congestion of streets and overcrowding of apartments are particularly serious. Strategies have been developed and are being implemented to improve the public environment and upgrade the private residential environment through, eg, the creation of refurbishment funds, incentives for the external maintenance and management of buildings, better local authority management procedures and employment creation for residents of the area (Roysten, 1997: 15).

This project exemplifies the shift from a high-profile, leisure-industry driven public/private regeneration strategy to one focusing on people's living and working environments, employment creation and social equity. It too has had some impact. The media have announced that the city is "winning the battle against crime and grime" (Lund, 1996: 3), that home ownership will "halt inner city rot" (Mantjiu, 1997: 6) and that the Station upgrade will "save the decaying CBD" (Radebe, 1996: 19). Swart (1996: 3) goes so far as to claim that "crime is no longer the prime concern in the scruffy CBD," focusing rather on the aesthetics of "scruffiness" as its major detraction. The inner city is no longer a frightening place, just a messy one.

Conclusion

This recent and ongoing history of development in the Johannesburg inner city tells of the transformation, reformulation and re-imagining of an urban landscape. The decline of its industrial base, loss of relative strength in the national economy, the flight of corporate capital, changing racial demography of its residential suburbs and burgeoning informal sector transformed a business district which could rightfully claim its position as the financial and commercial hub of sub-Saharan Africa into one

which, in the latest formulations of the city authorities, is identified as a Priority Intervention Zone (PIZ) (Greater Johannesburg, 1999b).

This chapter has traced the responses of the city authorities to this transformation by examining the two local economic development initiatives formulated since 1990, one before and one after the democratic elections. The first was expansionist and buoyant. It relied on an aesthetic, property-led development programme to regenerate a declining economy, re-image a city tarnished by its oppressive, racist past and position Johannesburg as a "world city" as it entered the global economy. The second was more cautious and less speculative, advocating an environmentally-led programme of stabilization and neighborhood development to address immediate problems of inner city decay, as a precursor to growth.

This is in line with most discussions of the future of cities post-1980 (Davies and Champion, 1983; Williams and Smith, 1986), which argue that the world economic crisis of 1973 and the subsequent restructuring of the global economy have rendered speculative extrapolation impossible and linked national and local economies into complex, integrated, interdependent unpredictable networks (Williams and Smith, 1986; Castells, 1996). However, it is this complexity and interdependency, and the substantive forces involved, which are not yet fully acknowledged or embraced in Johannesburg (Tomlinson, 1998). City authorities are still fixated on the image of Johannesburg as a "world class, globally competitive city" (Greater Johannesburg, 1999b: 10). This mantra has justified political and economic programs of urban restructuring (the most recent being the iGoli 2002 plan (Greater Johannesburg, 1999b)) in the interests of corporate capital. Amongst other things, these are characterized by somewhat naive understandings of the wider processes of global restructuring taking place and of Johannesburg's position within them.

Integration of regions and cities into the world economy is uneven and contingent upon multiple contradictory tendencies. Castells (1996: 135) ominously predicts the "structural irrelevance" of most of Africa in the newest international division of labor.[5] However, within the internal differentiation of Africa, South Africa is most likely to attract certain of the productive and managerial functions of the global economy. In doing so, it will also become a depository of large segments of the population around it who have been marginalized and who perceive the opportunities it offers as their only chance of survival. The large cities of South Africa – Johannesburg, Durban and Cape Town – are the places where this marginality will most likely make itself visible.

This is what has been witnessed recently in the inner city of Johannesburg. Capital disinvestment has created a space for those excluded from formal economic activity to gain a foothold in the urban system. Micro-enterprise, survivalist trade, illicit economic activity (Jennings et al., 1995a and Jennings et al., 1995b; Rogerson, 1995; Tomlinson et al., 1995) and, more particularly, migratory economic activity, cross-border trade and the presence in the city of immigrant entrepreneurs (Crush, 1997; Simone, 1998; Reitzes et al., 1997; Rogerson, 1997; and Rogerson, 1998), are becoming significant and possibly structural features of the inner city economy as in other parts of the world (Castells and Portes, 1989). In addition, the increasing occupancy by small African enterprises of the lower grade office space in the inner city has changed the complexion of inner city commerce (Tomlinson et al., 1995). These new presences are, however, largely absent from official policy making (Haffajee, 1998a and Haffajee, 1998b).

These new residents have been well-used by the popular media to construct new urban imagery of the inner city as diseased, crime riddled, dangerous and disordered (*City Press*, 1997; Warren, 1996; Robertson, 1997). They are less than social; they are part of the physical environment to be sanitized, relocated and rendered invisible (Ramothata, 1996). Reactionary protectionism against foreigners demands their restriction into enclaves of exclusion or repatriation (Simone, 1998; Paton, 1999; Masunda, 1999). Frontier imagery, reminiscent of that in American literature and popular media (Smith, 1986), portrays the inner city as the new "meeting point between savagery and civilization" (Turner, 1958, in Smith, 1986: 15). Images of nature ("Hillbrow tenants conquering their own Everest", Prabhakaran, 1997: 6) and conquest ("Send task force to save Hillbrow", Madondo, 1997: 26) connote a place beyond the limits of civilization. It is black, threatening, untamed and barbaric. Urban regeneration has, to date, aimed at its conquest and re-incorporation into the civilized white world of corporate respectability.

Until this image of the future is superceded by one which incorporates the multitude of contradictory presences and dynamics at play in the new global city, Johannesburg's present will continue to be defined along modernist lines as defective, degenerative and decayed. While new efforts to consolidate an African identity and position in the global economy through the image of an African Renaissance are currently emerging (Mangcu, 1998), these have only provisionally touched upon the issue of a contemporary African spatiality. Simone (1998) suggests the recovery of the original function of most African cities as points of crossing – entry, exit, crossroads, railheads, etc. – as a means of making sense of current translocations, while Tomlinson (1998) premises a vision for the future on the principles of economic and social inclusion. This means finding appropriate institutions to manage the co-existence of transience and stasis, of global and local, corporate and provisional, in any political or economic programme of urban restructuring. It requires adopting critical relations to current institutions, urbanism and practice and defining new ways of working, thinking and representing the city....

NOTES

1 Urban residents were spatially segregated on the basis of race in terms of the Group Areas Act, No. 40 of 1950. Each racial group was allocated to areas reserved exclusively for them. The movement and residence of Africans in particular was further controlled by an array of legislation, including the Blacks (Urban Areas) Consolidation Act of 1945. This legislation meant that the vast majority of Johannesburg's estimated 3 million black residents were confined to townships on the periphery of the city, while its approximately 1 million white residents were located close to the city center.

2 Rogerson and Rogerson's (1996) research on Johannesburg's inner city manufacturing activity indicates that its overall downturn arose from the high death of inner city enterprises in relation to the birth rate of new enterprises (237 as opposed to 182) and short-distance relocations to adjacent areas. The inner city has lost its competitive advantage to new industrial sites favoring smaller, cleaner locations along main road and rail routes (Tomlinson et al., 1995: 90).

3 The CBD is an area of approximately 2 km², comprising the commercial and financial districts of the former city of Johannesburg.

Surrounding it is an area of similar size made up of high density residential and manufacturing suburbs. The entire area constitutes what is known as the Johannesburg inner city.

4 The inner city has retained its importance as a retail center, though the nature of this activity has adjusted to the changing racial complexion of its residents and the increasing buying power of Soweto residents for whom the inner city is the closest and most accessible shopping precinct (Cox, 1996). While this has appeared to result in a general "downgrading" of the inner city retail economy, it has also resulted in a number of major national retailers opening flagship stores in the inner city and reporting massive turnovers (Rowley, 1996; Moya, 1996). Furniture and household appliance stores, men's outfitters, shoe stores and jewelers, catering for the tastes of the new black consumer, have seen considerable growth over the last decade (Tomlinson et al, 1995: 125).

5 "The systematic logic of the new global economy does not have a role for the majority of the African people in the newest international division of labor" (Castells, 1996: 135).

REFERENCES

Alfreds, L. (1997) R2-billion kickstart for Jo'burg CBD revamp. *Star*, 14 July, 1.

Anon (1994) Preserving our past in the present for the future. *Contact: Newsletter of the Central Johannesburg partnership*, 7 July, 5.

Beauregard, R. A. (1993) Constituting economic development: a theoretical perspective. In *Theories of Local Economic Development*, ed. R. D. Bingham and R. Mier. Sage, Newbury Park.

Biller, H. (1997) Eating out – on the streets of Johannesburg and New York. *Star*, 10 July, 13.

Bingham, R. D. and Mier, R. (1993) Preface. In *Theories of Local Economic Development*, ed. R. D. Bingham and R. Mier. Sage, Newbury Park.

Boyle, R. (1988) Private sector urban regeneration: the Scottish experience. In *Regenerating the Cities: the UK Crisis and the US Experience*, eds. M. Parkinson, B. Foley and

D. Judd. Manchester University Press, Manchester.

Business Day Property Supplement (1996) Decentralisation hits CBD's, 18 Oct., 9.

Castells, M. (1996) *The Rise of the Networked Society (1)*. Blackwell, Oxford.

Castells, M. and Portes, A. (1989) World underneath: the origins, dynamics and effects of the informal economy. In *The Informal Economy*, eds. A. Portes, M. Castells and L. A. Benton. Johns Hopkins, Baltimore.

Chalmers, R (1996) Inner city tenants in landmark deal. *Business Day*, 5 March, 19.

Chipkin, C. (1993) *Johannesburg Style Architecture and Society 1880's–1960's*. David Philip, Cape Town.

Citizen (1993) 29 Sept.

Citizen (1996) Downtown, Johannesburg project wins NY award, 23 Sept., 20.

City Press (1997) Crime hot spots to avoid in CBD, 13 July, 6.

City Vibe (1999) Sept.

Crankshaw, O. (1997) *Challenging the Myths. Johannesburg: Inner City Residents Housing Usage and Attitudes.* Survey commissioned by the Inner City Housing Upgrading Trust.

Crush, J. (1997) *Covert Operations: Clandestine Migration, Temporary Work and Immigration Policy in South Africa.* Migration Policy Series No. 1, South Africa Migration Project, Cape Town.

Davies, R. L. and Champion, A. G. (eds.) (1983) *The Future for the City Center.* Academic Press, London.

De Kiewiet, C. W. (1996) *A History of South Africa, Social and Economic.* Oxford University Press, Oxford.

Dhlomo, M. (1997) Attacking foreign hawkers not solution. *Sowetan*, 18 Sept., 9.

Du Venage, G. (1996) End in sight for Gauteng slumlords. *Saturday Star*, 9 March, 9.

Engineering News (1995) 24 March.

Ettlinger, N. (1994) The localization of development in comparative perspective. *Economic Geography* 70, pp. 144–66; EconLit GEOBASE.

Fitzsimons, D. S. (1995) Planning and promotion: city re-imaging in the 1980's and 1990's. In *Re-imaging the Pariah City: Urban Development in Belfast and Detroit*, eds. W. J. V. Neill, D. S. Fitzsimons and B. Murtagh. Avebury, Aldershot.

Francis, B. (1992) Cultural transformation and renewal through popular participation in the city of Johannesburg. In *Background Material: Strategic Initiative for Central Johannesburg*, pp. 50–3. City Council, Johannesburg.

Gauteng Provincial Government (1997) *City Improvement Districts Bill.* Johannesburg.

Greater Johannesburg (1999a) Johannesburg inner city briefing document. Unpublished report, Metropolitan Council Inner City Office, Johannesburg.

Greater Johannesburg (1999b) *Igoli 2002.* Metropolitan Council, Johannesburg.

Haffajee, F. (1998a) City streets: where South Africa's economy is changing. *Mail and Guardian*, 7–13 July, 12.

Haffajee, F. (1998b) The road to a changing economy. *Mail and Guardian*, 30 Oct.–5 Nov., 13.

Harvey, D., 1989. From managerialism to entrepreneuralism: the transformation in urban governance in late capitalism. *Geografiska Annaler* 71B, pp. 3–17

Horak, E. (1994) Jo'burg gets ready to shape up. *Engineering News*, 21 Jan.

ICHUT (1996) *Inner-city Housing Research Report.* Johannesburg.

Imrie, R. and Thomas, H. (1993) Urban policy and urban development corporations. In *British Urban Policy and the Urban Development Corporations*, eds. R. Imrie and H. Thomas. Paul Chapman, London.

Jennings, R., Hirschowitz, R., Tshandu, Z. and Orkin, M. (1995a) *Our Daily Bread: Earning a Living on the Pavements of Johannesburg. Part 1: The Census.* Community Agency for Social Enquiry, Johannesburg.

Jennings, R., Segal, K., Hirschowitz, R. and Orkin, M. (1995b) *Our Daily Bread: Earning a Living on the Pavements of Johannesburg. Part 2: the Survey.* Community Agency for Social Enquiry, Johannesburg.

Johannesburg (1993a) *Johannesburg 2004 for Africa: the Case for Johannesburg.* City Council, Johannesburg.

Johannesburg (1993b) Towards a development framework for the inner city. Unpublished paper, City Council, Johannesburg.

Kadima, D. and Kalombo, G. (1995) *The Motivation for Emigration and Problems of Integration of the Zairean Community in South Africa.* University of the Witwatersrand, Johannesburg.

Lund, T. (1996) CBD initiative winning crime-and-grime battle. *Star*, 11 April, 3.

Madondo, B. (1997) Send task force to save Hillbrow. *City Press*, 20 April, 26.

Mangcu, X. (1998) Seeking common national values. *Mail and Guardian*, 5 June, 28.

Mantjiu, M. (1997) Plan to halt inner city rot by making homes. *Star Business Report*, 14 July, 6.

Masunda, D. (1999) An express train to the border. *Mail and Guardian*, 19–25 Nov., 47.

Morris, A. (1996) *Bleakness and Light. Inner City Transition in Hillbrow, Johannesburg.* Witwatersrand University Press, Johannesburg.

Moya, F. (1996) Shoppers flock to new Woolworths store, which aims to help revitalize the inner city. *Star*, 21 Nov., 2.

Muyanda, L. (1996) UAL joins list of firms moving from city center. *Business Day*, 6 Nov., 29.

Ogbu, J. (1993) Minority status and schooling in plural societies. *Comparative Education Review* June, pp. 168–90

Paton, C. (1999) The rainbow alienation. *Sunday Times*, 18 April, 17.

Pienaar, H. (1994) Economic study: Johannesburg/central wits. Unpublished memo, Johannesburg City Council Urban Strategies Division, Johannesburg.

Prabhakaran, S. (1997) Hillbrow tenants conquer their own Everest. *Mail and Guardian*, 29 Aug., 6.

Radebe, H. (1996) Park Station project to save decaying CBD. *Star*, 27 Nov., 19.

Ramothata, W. (1996) Hawkers "must go." *Sowetan Business*, 20 June, 2.

Reeves, J. (1997) Broken promises. *Saturday Star*, 13 July, 1–2.

Reitzes, M., Tamela, Z. and Thulare, P. (1997) *Strangers Truer than Fiction: The Social and Economic Impact of Migrants on the Johannesburg City*. Center for Policy Studies, Johannesburg.

Rice, R. (1993) Imaging Johannesburg: reflections of change 1986–1993. Unpublished paper, Department of Geography, University of the Witwatersrand, Johannesburg.

Robertson, D. (1997) Sanlam joins the lane heading out of violent, dirty CBD's. *Saturday Star*, 13 July, 1–2.

Rogerson, C. M. (1996) Image enhancement and local economic development in Johannesburg. *Urban Forum* 7, 2, pp. 139–58

Rogerson, C. M. (1997) *International Migration, Immigrant Entrepreneurs and South Africa's Small Enterprise Economy*. Migration Policy Series No. 3, South Africa Migration Project, Cape Town.

Rogerson, C. M. (1998) "Formidable entrepreneurs" the role of foreigners in the Gauteng SMME economy. *Urban Forum* 9, 1, pp. 143–53

Rogerson, J. M. (1995) The changing face of retailing in the South African city: the case of inner city Johannesburg. *Africa Insight* 25, pp. 163–71.

Rostron, B. (1999) Africa's otherness lingers deeply in European minds. *Mail and Guardian*, 17–22 Sept., 24.

Roysten, L. (1997) *The Golden Heartbeat of Africa*. Greater Johannesburg Metropolitan Council, Johannesburg.

Russell, S. (1996) Partnership slashes CBD crime figures. *Star Business Report*, 23 Aug., 6.

Shachar, A. (1994) Randstad Holland: a "world city." *Urban Studies* 31, pp. 381–400.

Simone, A. M. (1998) Globalization and the identity of African urban practices. In *Blank___Architecture, Apartheid and After*,

ed. H. Judin and I. Vladislavic. NAi, Rotterdam.

Smith, N. (1986) Gentrification, the frontier, and the restructuring of urban space. In *Gentrification of the City*, eds. N. Smith and P. Williams. Allen & Unwin, Boston.

Star (1993) 31 Aug.

Star (1996) Living in Hell-brow – and loving it, 1 March, 7.

Star Business Report (1996) Inner city alive and well in Johannesburg, 27 Aug., 10.

Sunday Times Metro (1996) Working together to make the CBD safe, 3 March, 19.

Swart, K (1996) Crime no longer prime concern in scruffy CBD. *Saturday Star*, 9 March, 3.

Times Weekly Edition (1936) Jan.

Tomlinson, R., Hunter, R., Jonker, M., Rogerson, C. and Rogerson, J. (1995) *Johannesburg Inner City Strategic Development Framework: Economic Analysis*. Greater Johannesburg Transitional Metropolitan Council City Planning Department, Johannesburg.

Tomlinson, R. (1998) Jo'burg's dynamo will hum in 2010. *Mail and Guardian*, 26 June–2 July, 41.

Turner, F. J. (1958) *The Frontier in American History*. Holt, Rinehart & Winston, New York.

Urban Market Joint Venture (1999) *Inner City Street Trading Management Strategy*. Greater Johannesburg Metropolitan Council, Johannesburg.

Warren, G. (1996) City. *Sunday Independent – Sunday Life*, 29 Sept., 6–10.

Williams, P. and Smith, N (1986) From "renaissance" to restructuring: the dynamics of contemporary urban development. In *Gentrification of the City*, eds. N. Smith and P. Williams, pp. 204–6. Allen & Unwin, Boston.

Wilson, W. J. (1987) *The Truly Disadvantaged: The Inner City, The Underclass, and Public Policy*. University of Chicago Press, Chicago.

Wilson, W. J. (1991) Studying inner-city social dislocations: the challenge of public agenda research. *American Sociological Review* 56, pp. 1–14.

Wright, C. (1992) Improving the economy and attracting investment. In *Background Material: Strategic Initiative for Central Johannesburg*. City Council of Johannesburg.

Zack, T., Segal, A., Padayachee, N. and Hurwitz, H. (1989) The changing face of Hillbrow. Unpublished paper presented to the 9th Biennial National Housing Congress, Johannesburg, 5–8 June.

Chapter 23

from *The Dialectics of Seeing: Walter Benjamin and the Arcades Project*

Susan Buck-Morss

Arcades

The arcades were "the original temple of commodity capitalism".[1] "Arcades – they beamed out onto the Paris of the Second Empire like fairy grottoes."[2] Constructed like a church in the shape of a cross (in order, pragmatically, to connect with all four surrounding streets), these privately owned, publicly traversed passages displayed commodities in window showcases like icons in niches. The very profane pleasure houses found there tempted passersby with gastronomical perfections, intoxicating drinks, wealth without labor at the roulette wheel, gaiety in the vaudeville theaters, and, in the first-floor galleries, transports of sexual pleasure sold by a heavenly host of fashionably dressed ladies of the night: "The windows in the upper floor of the Passages are galleries in which angels are nesting; they are called swallows."[3]

> Angela
> one flight up on the right[4]

During the Second Empire of Napoleon III, the urban phantasmagoria burst out of the narrow confines of the original arcades, disseminating throughout Paris, where commodity displays achieved ever grander, ever more pretentious forms. The Passages "are the precursors of the department stores."[5] The phantasmagoria of display reached its apogee in the international expositions.

World Expositions

The first world exposition was held in London in 1851. Its famous Crystal Palace was constructed out of the same iron and glass that originally had been used in the Passages, but more daringly, in monumental proportions.[6] Entire trees were covered over by the 112-foot roof. Industrial products were displayed like artworks, vying with ornamental gardens, statues, and fountains for the public's attention. The exposition was described by contemporaries as "'incomparably fairylike.'"[7] The Crystal Palace blended together old nature and new nature – palms as well as pumps and pistons – in a fantasy world that entered the imagination of an entire generation of Europeans. In 1900, Julius Lessing wrote:

> I remember from my own childhood years how the news of the Crystal Palace reached over into Germany, how, in remote provincial towns, pictures of it were hung on the walls of bourgeois rooms. All that we imagined from old fairy tales of princesses in a glass casket, of queens and elves who lived in crystal houses, seemed to us to be embodied in it [...].[8]

While not the place of the first international exposition, Paris was host to some of the grandest. Its earliest[9] took place in 1855 under a "'monstrous glass roof,'"[10] and "'all Europe was on the move to view the wares'."[11] The structure built for the next Paris fair in 1867 was compared to the Colosseum: "'It looked as if there were before you a monument built on another planet, Jupiter or Saturn, in a taste we do not know, and in colors to which our eyes are not yet accustomed.'"[12] Subsequent fairs in 1889 and 1900 left permanent traces on the city landscape: the Grand Palais, Trocadero, and Paris' hallmark, the Eiffel Tower.[13] The expositions' displays were compared by Sigfried Giedion to *Gesamtkunstwerke*[14] (total works of art). The reason was precisely their phantasmagoric quality, a blend of machine technologies and art galleries, military cannons and fashion costumes, business and pleasure, synthesized into one dazzling visual experience.

The international fairs were the origins of the "pleasure industry [*Vergnugungsindustrie*]," which

> [...] refined and multiplied the varieties of reactive behavior of the masses. It thereby prepares the masses for adapting to advertisements. The connection between the advertising industry and world expositions is thus well-founded.[15]

At the fairs the crowds were conditioned to the principle of advertisements: "Look, but don't touch,"[16] and taught to derive pleasure from the spectacle alone.

Wide spans of glass windows originated in the arcades, as did window shopping as the activity of the flâneur. But here display was not a financial end in itself. The shops full of "novelties" and the pleasure establishments depended on a public clientele of the well-to-do. At world's fairs, in contrast, the commerce in commodities was not more significant than their phantasmagoric function as "folk festivals" of capitalism[17] whereby mass entertainment itself became big business.[18] There were eighty thousand exhibitors at Paris' 1855 fair[19] In

1867, the fair's fifteen million visitors[20] included four hundred thousand French workers to whom free tickets had been distributed, while foreign workers were housed at French government expense.[21] Proletarians were encouraged by the authorities to make the "pilgrimage" to these shrines of industry, to view on display the wonders that their own class had produced but could not afford to own, or to marvel at machines that would displace them.[22]

Phantasmagoria of Politics

The *Passagen-Werk* is fundamentally concerned with the effect of the fairs on workers and working-class organization: Three different workers' delegations were sent to London in 1851: "None of them accomplished anything of significance. Two were official [sent by the French and Paris governments]; the private one came with subsidizing from the press [...]. The workers had no influence on putting these delegations together."[23]

It has been claimed that the world expositions were the birthplace of the International Workingman's Association, because they provided the opportunity for workers from different nations to meet and discuss common interests.[24] But despite the initial fears of those in power,[25] the fairs proved to have quite the contrary effect. A phantasmagoria of politics had its source in the world expositions no less than a phantasmagoria of merchandise, wherein industry and technology were presented as mythic powers capable of producing out of themselves a future world of peace, class harmony, and abundance. The message of the world exhibitions as fairylands was the promise of social progress for the masses without revolution. Indeed, the fairs denied the very existence of class antagonisms.[26] Even when workers were permitted to elect their own delegation to them[27] any potentially revolutionary consequences of such a proletarian assembly was co-opted. Benjamin cites David Riazanov, Soviet editor of the complete works of

Marx and Engels (in which Marx's early writings first appeared):

> "The interests of industry... were placed in the foreground, and the necessity of an understanding between the workers and industrialists was heavily emphasized as the only means whereby the bad situation of the workers could be improved... We cannot consider... this congregation as the birthplace of the IWA [International Workingman's Association]. This is a legend...."[28]

The Russian Marxist George Plekhanov believed that world expositions could teach a very different lesson. Writing after the 1889 Parisian Exposition that, significantly, celebrated the centennial of the French Revolution, he expressed optimism as to its progressive effect:

> [... "I]t was as if the French bourgeoisie had been out to prove intentionally to the proletariat, before its very eyes, the economic possibility and necessity of a social revolution. The world exposition gave this class an excellent idea of the previously unheard of levels of development of the means of production that have been attained by all civilized countries, and that have far transcended the wildest fantasies of utopians of the past century... This same exposition demonstrated further that the modern development of productive powers, given the anarchy presently reigning in production, must necessarily lead to industrial crises that are evermore intensive and thus evermore destructive in their effects on the workings of the world economy."[29]

Such a view was more wishful thinking than fact, as the historical logic of world expositions was the reverse: The wider the gap between progress in developing the means of production and "anarchy" (crisis and unemployment) in the world economy, the more these capitalist folk festivals were needed to perpetuate the myth of automatic historical progress in order to prevent the proletariat from deriving just such a revolutionary lesson.

National Progress on Display

In the late nineteenth century, the world expositions thus took on an additional meaning. Not only did they provide a utopian fairyland that evoked the wonder of the masses. Each successive exposition was called upon to give visible "proof" of historical progress toward the realization of these utopian goals, by being more monumental, more spectacular than the last. The original exposition was purely a business venture, committed to laissez-faire principles of trade. But by 1900, governments had gotten involved to the point where they were hardly distinguishable from entrepreneurs themselves.[30] As part of the new imperialism, "national" pavilions promoted national grandeur, transforming patriotism itself into a commodity-on-display. And the state became a customer: World fairs claimed to promote world peace, while displaying for government purchase the latest weapons of war.[31]

Urbanism

The role of the state in constructing the modern phantasmagoria was not limited to world fairs. Benjamin deals centrally with the new urbanism financed by the state, which was contemporaneous with the fairs,[32] and which in Paris was the obsessive occupation of Napoleon III's minister, Baron Haussmann.[33] The phantasmagoric illusions fostered by this "artist of demolition"[34] figured heavily in the mythic imagery of historical progress, and functioned as a monument to the state's role in achieving it. As a classic example of reification, urban "renewal" projects attempted to create social utopia by changing the arrangement of buildings and streets – objects in space – while leaving social relationships intact. Under Haussmann, schools and hospitals were built, and air and light were brought into the city,[35] but class antagonisms were thereby covered up, not eliminated.

Haussmann's slum "clearance" simply broke up working-class neighborhoods and moved the eyesores and health hazards of poverty out of central Paris and into the suburbs.[36] His system of public parks and "pleasure grounds" provided the illusion of social equality,[37] while behind the scenes his building projects initiated a boom of real estate speculation whereby the government expanded the private coffers of capitalists with public funds.[38] Railways penetrated to the heart of Paris, and railroad stations took over the function of city gates.[39] The demolition of Paris occurred on a massive scale, as destructive to the old Paris as any invading army might have been.[40] The urban "perspectives"[41] which Haussmann created from wide boulevards, lined with uniform building facades that seemed to stretch to infinity and punctuated by national monuments, were intended to give the fragmented city an appearance of coherence. In fact the plan, based on a politics of imperial centralization, was a totalitarian aesthetics, in that it caused "'the repression of every individualistic part, every autonomous development'" of the city,[42] creating an artificial city where the Parisian [. . .] no longer feels at home.'"[43]

As with the world fairs, the *Passagen-Werk*'s concern is with the political effects of urbanism in undermining the revolutionary potential of the working class:

> The true goal of Haussmann's works was the securing of the city against civil war [. . .]. The width of the avenues was to prohibit the erection [of street barricades], and new streets were to provide the shortest routes between the barracks and the working-class sections. Contemporaries christened the undertaking "strategic beautification."[44]

Haussmann's "strategic beautification" is the ur-form of the culture of modern statism.

Progress Deified

In 1855, the year of the first Paris Exposition, Victor Hugo, "'the man of the nineteenth century as Voltaire had been man of the eighteenth',"[45] announced: "'Progress is the footstep of God himself'."[46] Progress became a religion in the nineteenth century, world expositions its holy shrines, commodities its cult objects, and Haussmann's "new" Paris its Vatican City. The Saint-Simonians were the self-proclaimed, secular priests of this new religion, writing poems of praise to industry's advances, and distributing their tracts by the millions (18,000,000 printed pages between 1830 and 1832).[47] In these mass-produced, low-cost publications, the great entreprenurial enterprises, including world expositions, received their sanctification. They imbued railroad construction with a sense of mission. Benjamin cited the Saint-Simonian Michel Chevalier:

> "One can compare the zeal and enthusiasm which civilized nations today give to the construction of railroads with that which occurred some centuries ago with the erection of churches . . . Indeed, it can be demonstrated that the word religion comes from *religare* [to bind together] . . ., the railroads have more affinity than one would have thought with the spirit of religion. There has never existed an instrument with so much power for. . . uniting peoples separated from one another."[48]

Such "uniting" of peoples contributed to the illusion that industrialism on its own was capable of eliminating class divisions, achieving the common brother- and sisterhood that had traditionally been religion's goal. Indeed, the most decisive political characteristic of Saint-Simon's theory was his conception of workers and capitalists united in a single "industrial class,"[49] and he considered entrepreneurs exploited "because they paid interest."[50] Benjamin observed: "The Saint-Simonians had only very limited sympathies for democracy";[51] according to them: "All social antagonisms dissolve in the fairy tale that *progrés* is the prospect of the very near future."[52] . . .

NOTES

1 V, p. 86 (A2, 2; also L°, 28).

2 V, p. 700 (T1a, 8).

3 V, p. 614 (O1a, 2; also c°, 2).

4 V, p. 90 (A3, 3).

5 V, p. 45 (1935 exposé).

6 Cf. V, p. 239 (G2a, 7; G2a, 8). The length of the Crystal Palace measured 560 meters (G8, 5).

7 Lothar Bacher (n.d.), cited by Julius Lessing, cited V, p. 248 (G6–6a).

8 Julius Lessing (1900), cited V, pp. 248–9 (G6–6a).

9 Already beginning in 1798 there had been national industrial expositions in Paris "'to amuse the working class'" (Sigmund Engländer [1864], cited V, p. 243 [G4, 7]); after 1834 these were held every five years (cf. V, pp. 242–3 [G4, 2–G4, 4]).

10 (1855), cited V, p. 257 (G11, 1).

11 Paul Morand (1900), cited V, p. 243 (G4, 5).

12 Théophile Gautier (1867), cited V, pp. 253–4 (G9, 2).

13 Cf. V, p. 243 (G4, 4) and p. 268 (G16a, 3).

14 V, p. 238 (G2, 3).

15 V, p. 267 (G16, 7).

16 V, p. 267 (G16, 6; again m4, 7). Other aspects of the pleasure industry were spawned by the fairs – the first amusement parks, and perhaps the first form of international mass tourism as well, as foreign pavilions provided cultures-on-display for visual consumption: "In 1867 the 'Oriental quarter' was the center of attraction" (V, p. 253 [G8a, 3]); the Egyptian exhibition was in a building modelled after an Egyptian temple (V, p. 255 [G9a, 6]).

17 "'These expositions are the first actually modern festivals'" (Hermann Lotze [1864], cited V, p. 267 [G16, 5]).

18 The Eiffel Tower cost six million francs to build, and in less than a year, it had earned 6,459,581 francs from the sale of entry tickets (V, p. 253 [G9, 1]). Fittingly, given the stress on spectacle over commerce, the task of organizing the first world exposition in New York City, 1853, fell to Phineas Barnum, whose business was circuses (V, p. 249 [G6a, 2]).

19 V, p. 255 (G9a, 5).

20 V, p. 253 (G8a, 4).

21 V, p. 250 (G7, 5).

22 Cf. Walpole's description of the exhibition of machines in London's Crystal Palace: "'In this hall of machines there were automated spinning machines [...,] machines that made envelopes, steam looms, models of locomotives, centrifugal pumps and a locomobile; all of these were laboring like crazy, whereas the thousands of people who were beside them in top hats and workers' caps sat quietly and passively, and without suspecting that the age of human beings on this planet was at an end'" (Hugh Walpole [1933], cited V, p. 255 [G10, 2]).

23 V, p. 252 (G8, 4).

24 Cf. the "myth" of the proletariat as the "child born in the workshops of Paris [...] and brought to London [during the exposition] for nursing" (S. Ch. Benoist [1914], cited V, p. 261 [G13, 3]).

25 The King of Prussia protested against the London exposition of 1851, refusing to send a royal delegation. Prince Albert who, in fact, had endorsed the project (which was financed and organized by private entrepreneurs) related to his mother the spring before the fair opened that opponents of the exposition believed "'foreign visitors will begin a radical revolution here, will kill Victoria and myself, and proclaim the red republic. A breakout of the plague [they believe] will certainly result from the concourse of such a huge multitude, and devour those whom the accumulated costs of everything have not driven away" (cited V, p. 254 [G9, 3]). During the fair there was continuous police surveillance of the crowd (V, p. 255 [G10, 1]). At the 1855 Paris exposition: "Workers' delegations this time were totally barred. It was feared that it [the exposition] would provide the workers with a chance for mobilizing" (V, p. 246 [G5a, 1]).

26 Cf. V, p. 256 (G10a, 2).

27 Cf. V, p. 252 (G8a, 1).

28 David Riazanov (1928), cited V, pp. 245–6 (G5, 2).

29 Plekhanov (1891), cited V, p. 244 (G4a, 1).

30 "'1851 was the time of free trade ... Now for decades we find ourselves in a time of ever-increasing tariffs [...] and whereas in

1850 the highest maxim was no government interference in these affairs, now
the government of every country has
come to be viewed as itself an entrepreneur'" (Julius Lessing [1900], cited V, p.
247 [G5a, 5]).

31   V, p. 247 (G5a, 6).

32   Cf. V, p. 1219 (note 19).

33   Cf. ed. note, V, p. 1218: "The second stage
of work on the *Passagen* began in early
1934 with plans for an article in French
on Haussmann...for *Le Monde*." Some
notes for this never completed article have
been preserved (see V, pp. 1218–19, 1935
exposé, note 19). Benjamin wrote to Gretel
Adorno in 1934 of plans for the Haussmann article, mentioning that Brecht considered it an important theme, and that it
was "in the immediate proximity of my
Passagenarbeit" (V, p. 1098).

34   V, p. 188 (E3, 6).

35   Cf. V, p. 187 (E3, 2).

36   Benjamin cites Engels: "'I understand
under 'Haussmann' the now general practice of turning the workers' districts into
rubble, particularly those lying at the
center of our great cities....The result is
everywhere the same...their disappearance with the great self-congratulations of
the bourgeoisie..., but they spring up
again at once somewhere else [...].'" (V,
p. 206 [E12, 1]).

37   "'The great ladies are out for a stroll; behind them play the little ladies'" (Nguyen
Trong Hiep [1897], cited V, p. 45 [1935
exposé]).

38   Cf. V, p. 182 (E1a, 4).

39   V, p. 182 (E2a, 5).

40   Benjamin notes: "For the architectonic
image of Paris the [Franco-Prussian] war
of the 70s was perhaps a blessing, as Napoleon III intended further to redesign
whole areas of the city" (V, p. 1016 [K°,
5, again; E1, 6]).

41   Benjamin notes: "Illusionism settles into
the image of the city: perspectives" (V,
p. 1211 [1935 exposé, note no. 5]).

42   J. J. Honegger (1874), cited V, p. 181
(E1a, 1).

43   Dubech-D'Espezel (1926), cited V, p. 189
(E3a, 6).

44   V, p. 57 (1935 exposé); cf. V, p. 190 (E4, 4,
also E8, 1).

45   Newspaper obituary of Hugo, cited V,
p. 905 (d2, 3).

46   V, p. 905 (d2, 2). Benjamin notes elsewhere:
"A telltale vision of progress in Hugo:
Paris incendié (L'année terrible): 'What?
scarifice everything? Even the granary of
bread? What? The library, this ark where
the dawn arises, this unfathomable ABC of
ideals, where Progress, eternal reader, leans
on its elbows and dreams...'" (V, p. 604
[N15a, 2]).

47   V, p. 736 (U14, 3).

48   Michel Chevalier (1853), cited V, p. 739
(U15a, 1). "Chevalier was the disciple
of [the Saint-Simonian] Enfantin [...and]
Editor of the *Globe*" (V, p. 244 [G4a,
4]).

49   Cf. V, pp. 717–18 (U5, 2).

50   V, p. 716 (U4, 2).

51   V, p. 733 (U13, 2).

52   V, p. 716 (U4a, 1).

Chapter 24

from *The End of Capitalism (As We Knew It): A Feminist Critique of Political Economy*

J. K. Gibson-Graham

A parallel construction of woman's body and female sexuality may be found in certain (feminist) knowledges of the city. Again, these knowledges are often based upon both the experience of women in the city and on contemporary theories of urban structure. From behavioral geographic research into gendered activity patterns and social networks a picture has been developed of women inhabiting certain spaces of the city – domestic space, neighborhood space, local commercial space, while men are more prevalent inhabitants of the central city, industrial zones and commercial areas. In urban studies women are often situated within the theoretical spaces of consumption, reproduction and the private, all of which are mapped onto the suburb (Wilson 1991, Saegert 1980, England 1991). As vacuous spaces of desire that must be satisfied by consumption, women are positioned in one discourse as shoppers, legitimately entering the economic space of the city in order to be filled before returning to residential space where new and ultimately insatiable consumer desires will be aroused (Swanson 1995). As hallowed spaces of biological reproduction, women's bodies are represented in another urban discourse as empty, needful of pro-

tection in the residential cocoon where they wait, always ready to be filled by the function of motherhood (Saegert 1980). Vacant and vulnerable, female sexuality is something to be guarded within the space of the home. Confined there, as passive guardians of the womb-like oasis that offers succor to active public (male) civilians, women are rightfully out of the public gaze (Marcus 1993).

In this type of urban theory the spatiality of women's bodies is constituted in relation to two different but perhaps connected Forms or Identities, that of the Phallus and that of Capital. These discourses of gender difference and capitalist development associate "woman" with lack, emptiness, ineffectiveness, the determined. As we have already seen in the rape script which is articulated within the broader hegemonic discourse of gender, woman is differentiated from man by her passivity, her vulnerability, ultimately her vacuousness. She is indeed the symbol of "absolute space," a homogeneous inert void, a container, something that can only be spoken of in terms of the object(s) that exist(s) within it. Inevitably, the object that exists within/invades/penetrates the inert void – bringing woman into existence – is the Phallus. Woman is necessarily rape space in the phallocentric discourse of gender.

In the urban script which is articulated within the broader hegemonic discourse of Capitalism, woman is constituted as an economic actor allocated to the subordinate functions of the capitalist system. As consumer she is seen to participate in the realization of capitalist commodities, putting them to their final, unproductive uses; under the influence of capitalist advertising and mood manipulation she translates her sexual desires into needs which must be satisfied by consumption. This transfiguration of private into public desire is enacted in consumption spaces – the shopping mall, the high street, the department store – horizontal, sometimes cavernous, "feminized" places within the urban landscape. Represented as maker and socializer of the future capitalist workforce, woman plays a part in the dynamic of social reproduction. In her role of bearing children, ministering to their needs and assisting the state in their education and social training, woman is portrayed as an unpaid service worker attending to the requirements of capital accumulation. Within her limited field of action in the sphere of reproduction, resistance is possible – she may organize around local community and consumption issues – but the rules are made by Capital.

In this urban discourse woman is represented as an active player rather than a passive container; she is a crucial constituent of capitalist social relations, though not situated at the center of accumulation, nor cast as the subject of history. The discourse of Capitalism renders the space of woman no longer homogeneous and void. Instead woman–space is "relative space," given form by multiple (subordinated) roles, each situated in relation to capitalist production. Women's economic bodies are portrayed as complements to men's economic bodies, adjuncts with important reproductive, nurturing and consumption functions. Indeed, woman becomes "positive negative space," a background that "itself is a positive element, of equal im-portance with all others" (Kern 1983: 152). Like the structured backgrounds of cubist painting, woman–space as relative space is more visible, less empty, more functional than is absolute space. But woman–space is still defined in terms of a positivity that is not its own. Whether as absolute or relative space, woman is presented as fixed by, or in relation to, an Identity/Form/Being – the Phallus or Capital.

In an attempt to address women's oppression, feminists may celebrate shopping, birth, homemaking, the fecund emptiness of woman's body, the shopping mall, the suburban home, the caring and nurturing functions, the woman–space. But in doing so they accept the boundaries of difference and separation designated by the discourses of capitalism and binary gender. Another feminist strategy has been to attempt to ignore or even reverse the spatialized binary by claiming back men's economic and urban space as rightfully women's. Women (particularly white female-headed households) have begun to desert the suburbs and, as one of the main groups involved in gentrification, have reasserted their right to a central location in the city (Rose 1989). Women have successfully fought for child-care centers, vacation programs for school-age children, better community care for the elderly and disabled so that they can temporarily free themselves from the role of carer and claim a rightful place in the capitalist paid workforce (Fincher 1988). Indeed, the fact that such services are better provided for in cities contributes to the feminization of households in central urban areas. Significant though all these changes have been for women in the city, these strategies rest upon the assumption that women remain the carers, the supplementary workers in a capitalist system, who, if they undertake labor in the "productive" spheres of the economy must also provide the "reproductive" labor. The central city is one space that allows the (exhausted) middle-class superwoman to function – it has become the site of a new "problem that has no name."

Similar strategies of reversal are represented in "Take back the night" rallies and other urban actions where women have claimed their right to the city streets, pressing for better lighting, better policing of public transport, guarded parking stations, and other mechanisms of public surveillance of men's behavior (Worpole 1992). As the geography of women's fear has been made visible, so has the "reality" of male sexuality and the "inevitability" of violence against women been accepted. While greater public surveillance is advocated, women are simultaneously warned not to trespass into public space where, on the streets at night or on public transport after work hours, they are most certainly "asking" to become players in a rape script.

Feminist strategies of celebration and reversal are all contributing to changes in the liveability of urban space for women. But what might be the cost of these changes if they rest upon the acceptance of both the Phallus and Capital as the "Identities" which define women–space, if they force women–space into the victim role that the sexual rape script allocates and the subordinate role that the economic urban script confers? What potentialities are suppressed by such a figuring of women and space? Perhaps we can only answer these questions by looking to alternative notions of Identity to see how they might differently configure women–space, as well as other possibilities they might entail. . . .

How might this respatialization of the body contribute to new geographies for women in the city? It might lead us to identity the multiple urban spaces that women claim, but not solely in the name of consumer desire or reproductive/biological function. Here one could think of the heterotopias of lesbian space, prostitution space, bingo space, club space, health spa, body building and aerobics space, nursing home space, hobby space – all terrains of public life in which women's agency is enacted in an effective, if indeterminate manner. One could identify the ways in which such spaces are regulated and ordered by dominant discourses of hetero-

sexuality, health, youth, beauty, and respectability and influenced by discourses of transgression. One could explore and map an urban performance space of women that is defined in terms of positivity, fullness, surface and power. But in order for such a reinscription not to fall back into simply celebrating woman–space in the city, theoretical work must continually and repeatedly displace (rather than only reverse) the binary hierarchy of gender.

One strategy of displacement might lead us to deconstruct and redefine those consumption and reproductive spaces/spheres that are the designated woman–space in the discourse of urban capitalism. Within geography, for example, the urban restructuring literature points to the massive involvement of women in the paid workforce where they are active in a variety of economic roles apart from that of final consumer or reproducer of the capitalist labor force. Feminist geographers and sociologists are researching women in office space (Pringle 1988), in finance space (McDowell 1994), in retail space (Dowling 1993), in ethnic small business (Alcorso 1993), in industrial space (Phizacklea 1990) – again all public arenas in which women's agency is enacted. In some texts we may even see glimmers of spaces beyond or outside capitalism, where women operate in noncapitalist spaces of production and contribute to the reproduction of noncapitalist economic forms.

Despite these glimmers, what characterizes much of the restructuring literature is an overriding sense of "capitalocentrism" in that women's entry into the paid labor force is understood largely in terms of the procurement by capital of cheaper, more manipulable labor. Capital has positioned the superexploited female worker just as it has produced women's roles as reproducers (of the capitalist workforce) and consumers (of capitalist commodities). Any attempt to destabilize woman's position and spatiality within urban discourse must dispense with the Identity of Capitalism as the ultimate container and constituter of women's social and economic life/space.

It would seem that the rethinking of female sexuality and the creation of alternate discourses of sexuality and bodily spatiality are well in advance of the rethinking of economic identity and social spatiality (Grosz 1994)....

REFERENCES

Alcorso, C. 1993 "And I'd like to thank my wife": gender dynamics and the ethnic "family business." *Australian Feminist Studies* 17: 93–108.

Dowling, R. 1993 Feminity, place and commodities: a retail case study. *Antipode* 25(4): 295–319.

England, K. 1991 Gender relations and the spatial structure of the city. *Geoforum* 22(2): 135–47.

Fincher, R. 1988 Class and gender relations in the local labour market and the local state. In J. Wolch and M. Dear (eds.), *The Power of Geography*, London: Unwin Hyman, 93–117.

Grosz, E. 1990 Contemporary theories of power and subjectivity. In S. Gunew (ed.), *Feminist Knowledge: critique and construct*, London and New York: Routledge, 59–120.

—— 1994 *Volatile Bodies: toward a corporeal feminism*. Bloomington, IN: Indiana University Press.

Kern, S. 1983 *The Culture of Time and Space 1880–1918*. Cambridge, MA: Harvard University Press.

Marcus, S. 1992 Fighting bodies, fighting words: a theory and politics of rape prevention. In J. Butler and J. Scott (eds.), *Feminists*

Theorize the Political, London and New York: Routledge, 385–403.

—— 1993 Placing *Rosemary's Baby*. *Differences: A Journal of Feminist Cultural Studies* 5(3): 121–53.

Phizacklea, A. 1990 *Unpacking the Fashion Industry*. London: Routledge.

Pringle, R. 1988 *Secretaries Talk: sexuality, power and work*. Sydney: Allen & Unwin.

Rose, D. 1989 A feminist perspective on employment and gentrification: the case of Montreal. In J. Wolch and M. Dear (eds.), *The Power of Geography: how territory shapes social life*, Boston: Unwin Hyman, 118–38.

Saegert, S. 1980 Masculine cities and feminine suburbs. *Signs* 5 (3): 96–111.

Swanson, G. 1995 "Drunk with glitter": consuming spaces and sexual geographies. In S. Watson and K. Gibson (eds.), *Postmodern Cities and Spaces*, Oxford: Blackwell, 80–98.

Wilson, E. 1991 *The Sphinx in the City: urban life, the control of disorder, and women*. London: Virago Press.

Worpole, K. 1992 *Towns for People: transforming urban life*. Buckingham: Open University Press.

from *Changing the Rules: The Politics of Liberalization and the Urban Informal Economy in Tanzania*

Aili Mari Tripp

Women and Changing Household Dependencies

Urban women's social and economic isolation and dependence on men is a theme that is often repeated in the literature on African women (Little 1973, 29; Pellow 1977, 26). In Tanzania the evidence pointed in this direction until the 1980s (Sabot 1979, 92; M. -L. Swantz 1985, 130). With the deepening of the crisis and the increased economic role of women in the household, many scholars continued to emphasize the dependence of women and exhibited a tendency to overlook the measure of autonomy they had gained in the process. These authors argued correctly that for the urban poor these were difficult times that had placed new burdens on women to engage in small businesses. But they left the argument at that, describing women as simply caught between the dictates of a relentless economic situation and the demands of their husbands. Although it is true that women have borne more responsibility for feeding their families than they did in the past, their involvement in income-generating activities also has given them greater control and autonomy within the household. They have not been merely passive victims of the hardships wrought by the economic disintegration of the formal economy; they have been actively pursuing solutions to their individual difficulties – solutions that have had a collective impact at the societal level.

Autonomy within the context of the household economy involves women's ability to decide freely whether to pursue an income-generating activity, to determine what kind of activity it should be, and to make all of the major decisions relating to the operation of the project. It involves a woman's prerogative to do as she pleases with her returns; that is, to decide whether her income should go toward the daily consumption of the household, for major family expenses like the building of a house, toward reinvestment in the business, or into savings. Although autonomy in one sphere does not necessarily replicate itself in other spheres of life, it is nevertheless important to recognize those areas in which women do exert a measure of control. Even in situations where real limitations constrain women, it is important to recognize the ways in which women assert their power. As Annette B. Weiner aptly put it (1976, 228–9):

> Whether women are publicly valued or privately secluded, whether they control politics, a range of economic commodities, or merely magic spells, they function

within that society, not as objects but as individuals with some measure of control. We cannot begin to understand either in evolutionary terms or in current and historical situations why and how women in so many cases have been relegated to secondary status until we first reckon with the power women do have, even if this power appears limited and seems outside the political field.

Women generally sought revenue from projects that were considered within the sphere of female work: making and selling pastries, frying and selling fish, or braiding hair, for example. In a nationwide survey of informal-sector activity, women predominated as stall sellers, pottery workers, and street food vendors (Planning Commission and Ministry of Labour and Youth Development 1991, 1–77). For the most part, the production of these goods and services took place at home. Goods could be marketed by children. Even if a woman did the selling herself, it usually involved only a brief excursion outside the home; that is, a woman who made *maandazi* pastries sold them for an hour or two in the morning to people on their way to work. If a woman kept her finances separate, her husband did not have to openly acknowledge the importance of her work to the financial well-being of the family. The projects often appeared benign to men, who might otherwise have been threatened by such real assertions of economic independence.

Women's income-generating activities

Women's increased involvement in income-generating activities is by far one of the most significant changes in urban households in the 1980s. As far back as the 1940s and 1950s, when women first began to migrate to the cities, they had been involved in small, income-generating projects (Leslie 1963, 168–69, 226; Mbilinyi 1989, 116–22). Although it is difficult to gauge the prevalence of these activities in the past, the few quantitative studies available indicate that they never reached the proportions seen in the late 1980s. In his survey, R. H. Sabot found 66 percent of women in 1970–1 with no source of income (1979, 92). A survey conducted by the Department of Sociology at the University of Dar es Salaam in 1970 found 4 percent of the wives in Dar es Salaam self-employed and 9 percent wage employed (Westergaard 1970, 7). Another 1974 survey showed 2 to 3 percent of the wives of low-income civil servants engaged in self-employment (Lindberg 1974). Anders Sporrek's 1976 survey of market sellers found that only 3 percent of 3,223 sellers were women (1985, 181).

The situation could not have been more different in the late 1980s, with the majority of women (69 percent) in Dar es Salaam self-employed and 9 percent wage employed, according to my survey. Half of the wives were self-employed; only 3 percent had wage employment. Similarly, another survey of 134 women conducted in Dar es Salaam in 1987 indicated that 70 percent of all women had projects and that only 5 percent were employed (Tibaijuka 1988). Women began their projects more recently than men, with 86 percent starting their businesses between 1980 and 1987, compared with only 66 percent of men in the same period. For most with small projects this was their first.

The paradox of the situation in the late 1980s was that women who might have once unsuccessfully sought employment and coveted a wage-earning job were now in a better position to increase their earning power outside the workplace. Whereas in the 1950s and 1960s one could talk about "unemployment" among women in the city, the 1980s saw a dramatic rise in women leaving the workforce to pursue projects on a full-time basis.

Wage earners in general made up 48 percent of the adult urban population in Dar es Salaam in 1984; women wage earners constituted only 9 percent of this same population. One of the reasons for the disparity between the numbers of male and female workers has to do with the fact that women have been discriminated against in the workforce. They faced employers' rigid notions of what women could and could not do in industrial production. Employers' beliefs that women were not as productive as men due to childbearing and menstruation acted as another constraint on the hiring of women, as did the low educational levels of women in general. Furthermore, the problem of childcare and the lack of daycare facilities mitigated against women's participation in the workforce (Bryceson 1980, 20–1; M. -L. Swantz 1985, 150–1). From 1967 to 1978 women's wage employment declined from 44 percent to 24 percent, compared with a decline from 74 percent to 70 percent for men during the same period. In 1971 women had a 20 percent unemployment rate (in contrast to 6 percent unemployment for men) (Sabot 1974, 8). This had largely to do with increasing rates of rural–urban migration for women at that time.

In the late 1980s, however, with the decline in migration, the lack of wage employment among women could be directly attributed to individual decisions to leave the workplace. My survey, for example, showed that although few women left their jobs from 1953 to 1980, between 1980 and 1987 the numbers leaving employment more than doubled. As I mentioned earlier, the most common reason men and women gave for leaving their jobs was low pay.

The choice to leave employment, however, was mainly an option for married women, whose husbands generally remained at work. A woman who was employed and single, divorced, or widowed needed her job for the same reasons a husband tended to stay on the job if his wife had a project: wages often served as backup capital if one's project took a temporary downturn. Although employment may have been inadequate as a source of income, it nevertheless remained a source of status, of access to people, and of resources that could be useful in one's project.

Finding niches in the market

Because large numbers of women were starting income-generating projects much later than were men, they faced additional market constraints. In overcoming these they had to employ a number of innovative and imaginative strategies.

One strategy women employed was to find an uncaptured niche in the market. In the early 1980s a Haya woman became one of the first women sellers in one of Dar es Salaam's largest markets. She found her niche catering to the appetites of people from her home area of Bukoba by selling *matoke* cooking bananas. Another woman had been inspired to purify and whiten salt, which is usually gray in color. She then took the salt to the market to sell. Another made small paper bags from larger, discarded cement bags.

In order to open up new areas of entrepreneurship women often needed to create a demand for their products or services. One woman reported having been the first African to open up a hair salon in Dar es Salaam in 1984 that did permanent waves. Since then dozens of similar hair salons have sprung up throughout the city. In the past, African women had done each other's hair, and until recently hairdressing was noncommercialized. Because of this, the hairdresser initially encountered resistance to the idea. As she explained, "The Asian and European women who had salons told me that an African hair salon won't work because people won't pay to have their hair done. But now look at how well I have done."

Most women preferred to enter businesses that in the past had been considered female enterprises. One of the most common income-generating activities among women was making buns and pastries known by their Swahili names as *maandazi, vitumbua* (rice cakes), *chapati, mkate wa kumimina* and *bagia*. Women also make confections like *visheti, vibata, vijogoo,* and *kalimati.*

All of the 61 women we interviewed who made these pastries operated independently, but children frequently helped sell the goods. They would prepare the mixture at 9 P.M. before going to bed and would get up to fry the pastries from 3 A.M. to 6 P.M. They would then go out and sell them until around 10 A.M.. Some sold near garages and factories or along the street near bus stops, hoping to catch workers on their way to work in the morning. Others would give a dish of pastries to a shopkeeper or the owner of a restaurant or teahouse to sell. A few simply placed them in a dish on a stool in front of their home, hoping to entice passersby. Still others sold near school grounds to children on their way to school or during breaks. Women were also found selling pastries at outdoor eating places that served food to workers on their lunch breaks.

On average, women pastry sellers had been in business for six years. Women making maandazi brought home a daily profit of around TSh 190 ($1.90 at 1988 exchange rates), whereas those making *chapati* took in TSh 144, and those making *vitumbua* earned only TSh 70. Nevertheless, they were still making considerably more than they would have if they had been employed. The average monthly income from making *maandazi* was still 4.5 times the minimum salary. The main difficulties they reported included shortages of flour, rice and sugar, along with illegally hiked prices for these and other inputs....

Women's Economic Activity as Embedded Activity

Women's increased involvement in the informal economy has not only changed household dependencies and enhanced women's autonomy. The way women invest and save capital, how they go about setting prices, how they select the kinds of activities they choose to engage in, how they establish clients and customers, how they form support networks, and how they contribute to the larger community all challenge notions of self-interest, decision making based on individual gain, competition, profit maximization, the separation of market and nonmarket activities, and so forth that are so prevalent in neoclassical economic thinking. Government and donor economic policies rarely have taken into consideration the particular ways in which women (also poor people more generally) engage in economic activity as producers of capital, as investors and savers, and as members of the labor force. Policies tend to be based on underlying assumptions that women's economic activities are discrete activities, separate from the rest of their responsibilities.

Women's entrepreneurial activities are heavily embedded in their daily lives and are part of a whole array of day-to-day activities. Women's involvement in the market takes place within the context of all of these life-sustaining activities and is not separate from the many other dimensions of life. These activities include childcare, family care, buying and cooking food, housecleaning, keeping the home and its surroundings tidy, physically building houses, clothing the children, fetching fuel wood and water, taking care of the health of the family, taking care of the disabled, elderly, and sick, cultivating, tending cows and goats, helping neighbors with needs, taking care of the poor in the community, organizing celebrations, helping raise funds for the community, helping with extended family needs, assisting other women in childbirth, assisting in funeral preparations, helping in the husband's business, and many other such activities. These alternative logics are revealed in a number of ways....

REFERENCES

Bryceson, Deborah F. 1980. "The Proletarianization of Women in Tanzania." *Review of African Political Economy* 17: 4–27.

Leslie, J. A. K. 1963. *A Survey of Dar es Salaam*. Oxford: Oxford University Press.

Lindberg, Olof. 1974. "Survey of Civil Servants' Wives Economic and Occupational Activities." Dar es Salaam: BRALUP, University of Dar es Salaam.

Little, Kenneth. 1973. *African Women in Towns: An Aspect of Africa's Social Revolution*. Cambridge, England: Cambridge University Press.

Mbilinyi, Marjorie. 1989. "'This Is an Unforgettable Business': Colonial State Intervention in Urban Tanzania." pp. 111–29 in *Women and the State in Africa*, eds. Jane L. Parpart and Kathleen A. Staudt. Boulder, Colo.: Lynne Rienner Publishers.

Pellow, Deborah. 1977. *Women in Accra: Options for Autonomy*. Algonac, Mich.: Reference Publications Inc.

Planning Commission and Ministry of Labour and Youth Development. 1991. *Tanzania: The Informal Sector 1991*. Dar es Salaam: Government Printer.

Sabot, R. H. 1974. "Open Unemployment and the Employed Compound of Urban Surplus Labour." Dar es Salaam: Economic Research Bureau, University of Dar es Salaam.

—— 1979. *Economic Development and Urban Migration: Tanzania 1900–1971*. Oxford: Clarendon Press.

Sporrek, Anders. 1985. *Food Marketing and Urban Growth in Dar es Salaam*. Lund Studies in Geography, Series B, Human Geography, vol. 51. Malmö: Gleerup.

Swantz, Marja-Liisa. 1985. *Women in Development: A Creative Role Denied?* London: C. Hurst and Co.

Tibaijuka, Anna K. 1988. "The Impact of Structural Adjustment Programmes on Women: The Case of Tanzania's Economic Recovery Programme." Report prepared for the Canadian International Development Agency. Dar es Salaam: Economic Research Bureau, University of Dar es Salaam.

Weiner, Annette. 1976. *Women of Value, Men of Renown*. Austin: University of Texas Press.

Westergaard, Margaret. 1970. "Women and Work in Dar es Salaam." Dar es Salaam: Department of Sociology, University of Dar es Salaam.

Part III   Reading Division and Difference

Introduction: Reading Division and Difference

Gary Bridge and Sophie Watson

Sociospatial divisions in the city have long fascinated urban analysts and urban reformers. Though many cities have grown haphazardly with little or no regulation and planning, in most cities different localities can be characterized according to land use, wealth and poverty, housing type, social mix, economic activity, and so on. This is not to suggest that city areas are homogenous entities encompassing little complexity within their borders, far from it. But it is to say that there are patterns, concentrations, segregations, and exclusions in most cities which shape urban form. Sometimes these are visible and easy to read, such as the central business district with its gleaming high office blocks, or the deprived urban ghetto with its rundown housing and infrastructure, and sometimes the articulation of difference remains hidden, performed and lived in the domestic spaces or interstitial spaces of the urban fabric. This section of the reader charts some of the key trends in the exploration of division and difference and residential segregation in the city.

Divided Cities

The University of Chicago School of Sociology during the first half of the twentieth century is well known for developing the new field of urban sociology taking Chicago and its streets as a site for studying urban society and dynamics. In particular the work of Robert Park, Louis Wirth, and Ernest Burgess influenced urban debates over several decades. In the extract included here, drawing on analogies from the natural sciences and plant ecology, Burgess develops what is sometimes referred to as an ecological model of urban growth. This is a concentric-zone model which sees the expansion of the city as a process whereby groups and individuals are sifted through competition for space according to their residence and occupation which gives a particular "form and character to the city." In this model the city is divided into five zones expanding radially from the central business district out through a zone of transition, a zone of worker's residences, a residential zone, and finally a commuters' zone. This model was further developed by other urbanists, as well as critiqued, and influenced a considerable range of later work: for example, William Julius Wilson's study of the urban underclass also extracted here. It was not until the rise of Marxist/

political economy approaches within urban studies, from the late 1960s, that the dominance of the Chicago paradigms began to subside.

The new Marxist urban studies, drawing on and developing the early work of Marx and Engels, brought new forms of analyses of social/spatial divisions in the city, though these too mapped urban divisions spatially in a relatively undifferentiated way. In these texts the capitalist city, with its role in the accumulation of profit and circulation of capital, produces sociospatial cleavages which are predicated on class. In a seminal work "The Great Towns" from *The Condition of the Working Class*, Engels (1845) describes the misery, degradation, congestion, and urban poverty of the industrial working classes in Manchester which is rooted in the rise of industrial capitalism. Based on a walking tour of Manchester's poorer districts, this powerful description of a class-divided city is echoed in many other social realist texts which followed, from Henry Mayhew's *London Labour and the London Poor* (1851–62) to George Orwell's (1933) *Down and Out in Paris and London* and Beatrix Campbell's (1984) *Wigan Pier Revisited*. David Harvey, in *Social Justice and the City* (1972), and Manuel Castells in *The Urban Question* (1977), explore the marginalization and exclusions of the working class through the processes of capitalist production and reproduction. While for Harvey the relations of production underpin social/ spatial cleavages in the city, Castells draws greater attention to the processes of collective consumption (of public services and resources) and their role in producing social divisions.

The divided city in Marxist terms is thus predominantly an economic one where social divisions derive from labor market position and are mapped onto cities. In this divided city over the latter part of the twentieth century the rich have got richer and the poor poorer, as the middle class has gradually declined (Fainstein, Gordon, and Harloe 1992). This sociospatial polarization and new forms of social exclusion posits the resulting divisions as an inevitable consequence of global capitalist restructuring and processes of uneven development. As the old manufacturing sector in cities has fallen into decline with the concomitant rise of the services sector, new spaces of marginalization and exclusion have emerged, entrenching the unemployed, low paid, and homeless at the bottom of the spiral.

The dual city approach has had its problems in constructing divisions in terms that tend to be too homogenizing and which fail to draw attention to the heterogeneity and complexities inherent within social classes and groups. Peter Marcuse attempts to solve the problem by arguing that it may be more helpful to talk in terms of quarters or parts of cities (Marcuse 1989, 1995). In his view cities are increasingly fragmented and chaotic, yet behind the chaos he suggests there are patterns. Rather than think in terms of divisions it is useful to think in terms of quartered cities or five-parted ones where the parts are intricately linked, walled in and walled out, hierarchical in power, and dependent on outside social forces. In the technologically developed cities of today Marcuse defines five types of city which form independent cities in an ordered and interdependent pattern: the residential city, the gentrified city, the suburban city, the tenement city, and the abandoned city. The economic city is similarly divided into five or more parts: the controlling city, the city of advanced services, the city of direct production, the city of unskilled work and informal production, and the residual city. Marcuse takes the argument further, considering how these quarters or parts are differentiated by walls.

With a more precise focus on employment, Mollenkopf and Castells's (1991) study of New York argues for a six-fold division of the occupational structure, since in their view "the complexity of New York's social structure cannot be reduced to a dichotomy between the two extremes of the income distribution" (p. 401). In their formulation there is an upper stratum of executives, managers, and professionals, clerical workers, service sector workers, manufacturing workers, public sector employees, and those outside of the labor force, and each of these interrelate in a multiplicity of ways. On the basis of their work Fainstein, Gordon, and Harloe (1992, pp. 257–61) also conclude by modifying the dualistic account to a tripartite division of the social structure. At the top are the upper class which expanded in the 1980s as a result of the expansion in financial and allied services, who are mainly white and male, and the new service class which is frequently tied to international as well as local labor markets and is also usually white and male. The second group comprises the middle and lower levels of the service class – many of whom are women and /or from ethnic minorities, as well as the contracting skilled working class. The third group is comprised of the unskilled working class, whose positions are often very insecure and low waged, combined with what they call the underclass – those excluded from participation in the formal labor market, who tend to be women, immigrants, elderly, and young unqualified men. In this formulation the social divisions are mapped in relation to labor markets rather than in terms of their spatial distribution in the city.

Each of these different approaches represents a start in unpacking simple divisions and dichotomies and analyses of a growing polarization between the rich and the poor. Saskia Sassen in her recent work (1996, pp. 183–97; 2000) argues for a more complex way of understanding global forces and their impact on the city and its residents. It is less and less possible, she suggests, to accept the notion of a hierarchical ordering which has created the semblance of a unitary economic system in which individuals are clearly located. Though "the centre concentrates immense power, a power that rests on the capability for global control" at the same time marginality, notwithstanding weak economic and political power, has become in Hall's words a "powerful space" (p. 197). The devalued sectors which rest largely on the labor of women, immigrants, and African-Americans in the cities of the US represent a terrain where battles are fought on many fronts and in many sites and these battles lack clear boundaries.

In this reader there are several pieces which focus on sociospatial divisions in a range of ways. Katznelson's *City Trenches* charts the impacts of industrial capitalism on the social structure of American cities, which he argues became increasingly segregated into distinctive functional spaces – notably work and home. This, he suggests, produced a clear separation between the politics of work – which was class and union based – and the politics of community, where ethnic and territorial identifications cut through and disrupted class alliances. This emphasis on the place of ethnic divisions in constructing new political allegiances and consciousness takes on greater force as the play of differences – other than class – enters center stage in urban analysis of the 1980s and 1990s, as we discuss shortly.

The combination of the growing power of the Civil Rights movements during the 1960s, race riots in a number of cities – notably Los Angeles and Notting Hill in London – and a growing concern with the problems of Black inner-city ghettos in the US and the UK, brought the question of race came forcefully onto the urban agenda. That Black people were concentrated in areas of high unemployment, poverty, crime, and drugs was not disputed. More contentious were the explanations as to the cause. Conservatives traditionally have blamed the victim for their own problems or the importance of different group values and competitive resources. Liberal urban analysts in contrast have tended to link disadvantage with broader social problems including discrimination and social-class subordination, and have argued for social reform and policies, including antidiscrimination and affirmative action legislation, to open up the opportunity structure. In many liberal accounts there has been a reluctance to consider the significance of class. Willam Julius Wilson's *The Truly Disadvantaged* represents the major text in the US which reclaims class and poverty as central to the racialization of urban society. Asserting the importance of the notion of underclass, his argument is that the poverty and disadvantage of urban Blacks, though once a product of racial discrimination, can now be located in the workings of the US economy. Though US Black people could once find work, albeit low-paid, unpleasant, and segregated, by 1984 these unskilled manual jobs had largely disappeared, leaving Black people unemployed, welfare dependent, and vulnerable to drugs and crime. This is not a problem to be addressed by race-specific affirmative action policies, but rather is one that needs to address the lack of skills and training amongst all poor people – that is, those of the underclass.

This is one view of race and the city, others (e.g. Cohen, 2000; Keith and Pile, 1993; Gilroy, 1987; Anderson, 1990) see race and ethnicity as operating as an independent structure, register, or identity. Here the racialization of urban space, albeit also through mechanisms of poverty, is a key frame in understanding segregated city spaces and the construction of identity and new urban imaginaries. While contributors to Hesse's (2000) anthology on multiculturalisms foreground the irrepressible issues which unsettle the racialized meanings of social norms and the cultural habits of national politics. In the US context there is now a considerable literature on the Latinization of American cities and the new marginalizations as well as new identity formations of Latino populations, who now in several cities, particularly in California and the south, outnumber the black populations (Davis, 2000).

The spatial concentration of the urban poor in squatter or fringe settlements is a key feature of cities in many non-Western, and indeed some Western (e.g. Aboriginal settlements on the edge of Alice Springs), cities (King). For many migrants moving from impoverished rural areas to the city to find work, there is no chance of finding affordable, secure, or well-maintained housing. Millions of poor urban dwellers are consigned to insecure shelter, be it the pavements of Bombay, the shacks on the edge of Sao Paolo, the tin sheds by the river in Bangkok, or the shanty towns of Johannesburg. These urban dwellers are subject to violence, ill health, poor sanitary conditions, and eviction. This represents one of the most serious and neglected housing issues in the world which, despite United Nations directives, in many countries is barely addressed. In the extract selected here Rahman illustrates the plight of one such group of marginalized urban dwellers – the basteebashees in Bangladesh. Rahman forcefully argues for the housing rights of the poor to be recognized in government housing policies and program where security of land is key to any such development.

A consistent theme running through the urban literature on city divisions has been the role of housing, in particular the processes of gentrification. Identified first by Ruth Glass (1963) in the early 1960s in London, the terms denotes the complex processes by which the housing stock is transferred from renting to owner occupation and physically improved, thereby displacing the working-class population from inner-city areas. Explanations for the phenomenon have varied. Neil Smith (1979) has posited gentrification as a product of the urban land and property market, in particular, what he saw as the growing "rent gap" between the current value of the property and the underlying land value. Hamnett (1991; 2000) has emphasized the shift from industrial to postindustrial society and the associated changes in the class structure, notably the rise of the middle classes with different cultural tastes and consumption practices. Bridge (1994, 2001) has suggested how conscious class practices in the neighborhood relate to broader sociospatial changes (via social networks) in the city as a whole. In the extract here, Neil Smith challenges the rise of anti-urbanism in US cities and arguments suggesting gentrification's demise – coined "degentrification" (Beauregard, 1993). Linking the iconic struggle between the homeless of Tompkins Square Park in Manhattan and the forces of gentrification, with the globalization of the national economy, he reasserts the importance of patterns of investment and disinvestment in creating the opportunity and possibility for gentrification.

Embodied Differences

The dominance of class as the crucial source of sociospatial divisions in the city came under growing critique from the 1970s from a number of different quarters. Feminists, theorists of race and ethnicity, gay theorists, and theorists working around disability draw on different theoretical frameworks to argue forcefully for other exclusions, marginalities, and identities to be taken into account in urban theory. Some tried to relate these to class (as discussed earlier in relation to William Julius Wilson), others saw gender or age questions, for example, cross-cutting class, while others developed highly complex and interconnected accounts. The "cultural turn" in social theory further developed the idea of difference, celebrating different identities and voices from the margins and connecting different marginalities to power relations both symbolic and real. Differences were argued to be constructed across a whole range of symbolic and cultural terrains, as well as political/economic ones. New cultural geographies mapped how different spaces in the city came to have different meanings and attachments for different groups (Bridge and Watson, 2000, Part 3; Fincher and Jacobs, 1998). The body, which had remained remarkably absent from more material analysis, was increasingly inserted into the frame, disrupting earlier analyses of social construction and the sex/gender distinction which had underpinned much of the early feminist work (Butler, 1993; Gatens, 1992). Given the breadth of work in the field, and the impossibility of including an extract on every category of difference here, there are many notable absences. Readers wishing to pursue the field further should turn to Fincher and Jacobs' (1998) volume for some excellent contributions to the debate, Part 3 of the *Companion to the City* (Bridge and Watson, 2000), and McDowell (1999).

Watson in the extract here looks at feminist debates on the significance of city spaces in constructing gender relations, both symbolically and materially. This piece charts feminist urban theory from its inception in the 1970s to contemporary accounts which draw on poststructuralist ideas and questions of subjectivity and corporeality. Watson suggests that though early paradigms which focused on gendered forms of exclusion and marginality in the city are still important, more recent perspectives have shifted the simple binaries of public and private and home and work and opened up a new terrain which brings a fresh light on old problems. Elizabeth Grosz's extract offers an illustration of such an approach. Her concern in "Bodies-Cities" is to explore the mutually defining relation between bodies and cities. Her argument here is that the city is one of the crucial factors in the social production of sexed corporeality. The relation between bodies and cities, she suggests is neither causal nor representational, but combines elements from each; the body and the city are mutually defining. In *Geographies of Disability* Gleeson also stresses embodiment but returns to a more material account of how the physical layout and design of cites discriminate against disabled people and, in this sense, construct the disabled body. As a result people with disabilities are excluded from public urban spaces, from employment, and often from their preferred living environment. Gleeson looks at how disabled people have resisted this discrimination and marginalization and considers what more enabling environments might be.

The segregation and exclusion of bodies inscribed as "other" or different has a very long history, as Sennett illustrates in his discussion of the Jewish Ghetto in Renaissance Venice. In "Fear of Touching" Sennett describes how the Venetians justified enclosing Jews in the Ghetto through a belief that they were isolating a disease that had infected the Christian community, since they identified the Jews with corrupting bodily vices. The Jewish body, as in Nazi Germany, as also the homosexual body, is seen as unclean, alien, but also seductive. In Venetian discourse, where touch itself seemed fatal, there is some resonance with modern rhetoric about AIDS, where seduction and infection appear almost inseparable. But this is not simply a story of the victimization of an "othered" and excluded race. The formation of the Jewish Ghetto is also a narrative of a people who made new forms of life and community out of their segregation. While the Ghetto increased the Jew's daily Otherness, it also increased their self-determination and the bonds between themselves.

Surveilling Difference

The surveillance and monitoring of minorities constructed and perceived as a threat likely to disrupt urban order and civic peace is also not new. The panoptic gaze conceived by Bentham and developed in Foucault's writings (for example, *Discipline and Punish*) instilled forms of self-regulation among urban citizens, which minimized the need for drastic and punitive measures to control and monitor unruly behavior, and individuals and groups constructed as a threat. The growing sociospatial divisions, and a widening gulf between the rich and the poor, combined with new surveillance technologies, have produced what Davis describes as the fortress city. In this seminal piece from his *City of Quartz* Davis gives a graphic account of the destruction of public space in Los Angeles and the forced removal of the homeless and poor from the streets of that city. This is a story, though perhaps sometimes less brutal in form, that can be told in cities across the world, where the imperatives of tourism and strategies for inward investment and property development, have swept out of sight the "undesirables" of the city.

REFERENCES

Anderson, E. 1990: *Streetwise: Race, Class and Change in an Urban Community*. Chicago: University of Chicago Press.
Beauregard, R. A. 1993: *Voices of Decline*. Oxford: Blackwell.
Bridge, G. 1994: Gentrification, class and residence: a reappraisal. *Environment and Planning D: Society and Space* 12: 31–51.
Bridge, G. 2001: Estate agents as interpreters of economic and cultural capital: the gentrification premium in the Sydney housing market. *International Journal of Urban and Regional Research* 25: 87–101.

Bridge, G. and Watson, S. 2000: *A Companion to the City*. Oxford: Blackwell.

Butler, J. 1993: *Bodies That Matter*. London: Routledge.

Cohen, P. 2000: From the other side of the tracks: dual cities, third spaces, and the urban uncanny in contemporary discourses of "race" and class. In Bridge and Watson (eds.), *A Companion to the City*. Oxford: Blackwell.

Davis, M. 2000: Magical urbanism: Latinos reinvent the US big city. *New Left Review* 234: 3–43.

Fainstein S., Gordon, I., and Harloe, M. 1992: *Divided Cities*. Oxford: Blackwell.

Fincher, R. and Jacobs, J. (eds.) 1998: *Cities of Difference*. New York: Guilford.

Gatens, M. 1992: Power, bodies, difference. In Phillps, A. and Barrett, M. (eds.), *Destabilising Theory*. Cambridge: Polity.

Gilroy, P. 1987: *There Ain't No Black in the Union Jack*. London: Unwin Hyman.

Glass, R. 1963: *London: Aspects of Change*. Centre for Urban Studies, London: University College London.

Hamnett, C. 1991: The blind man and the elephant: the explanation for gentrification. *Transactions of the Institute of British Geographers* 16: 173–89.

Hamnett, C. 2000: Gentrification, postindustrialism, and restructuring. In Bridge and Watson (eds.), *A Companion to the City*. Oxford: Blackwell.

Hesse, B (ed) 2000: *Unsettled Multiculturalisms*. London: Zed Books.

Keith, M. and Pile, S. (eds.) 1993: *Place and the Politics of Identity*. London: Routledge.

Marcuse, P. 1989: Dual city: a muddy metaphor for a quartered city. *International Journal of Urban and Regional Research* 13(4): 697–708.

Marcuse, P. 1995: Not chaos but walls: postmodernism and the partitioned city. In Watson, S. and Gibson, K. (eds.), *Postmodern Cities and Spaces*. Oxford: Blackwell.

McDowell, L. 1999: City life and differences: negotiating diversity. In Allen, J., Masey, D., and Pryke, M. (eds.), *Unsettling Cities*. London: Routledge, 95–136.

Mollenkopf, J. and Castells, M. (eds.) 1991: *Dual City: Restructuring New York*. New York: Russell Sage Foundation.

Orwell, G. 1997 [1933]: *Down and Out in Paris and London*, ed. P. Davidson. London: Secker and Warburg.

Sassen, S. 1996: Rebuilding the global city: economy, ethnicity and space. In King, A. (ed.), *Re-Presenting the City*. London: Macmillan.

Sassen, S. 2000: *Cities in a World Economy*. Thousand Oaks, CA: Pine Forge Press.

Smith, N. 1979: Toward a theory of gentrification: a back to the city movement by capital not people. *Environment and Planning D: Society and Space* 5: 151–72.

Chapter 26

The Growth of the City

Ernest W. Burgess

The outstanding fact of modern society is the growth of great cities. Nowhere else have the enormous changes which the machine industry has made in our social life registered themselves with such obviousness as in the cities. In the United States the transition from a rural to an urban civilization, though beginning later than in Europe, has taken place, if not more rapidly and completely, at any rate more logically in its most characteristic forms.

All the manifestations of modern life which are peculiarly urban – the skyscraper, the subway, the department store, the daily newspaper, and social work – are characteristically American. The more subtle changes in our social life, which in their cruder manifestations are termed "social problems," problems that alarm and bewilder us, as divorce, delinquency, and social unrest, are to be found in their most acute forms in our largest American cities. The profound and "subversive" forces which have wrought these changes are measured in the physical growth and expansion of cities. . . .

Expansion as Physical Growth

The expansion of the city from the standpoint of the city plan, zoning, and regional surveys is thought of almost wholly in terms of its physical growth. Traction studies have dealt with the development of transportation in its relation to the distribution of population throughout the city. The surveys made by the Bell Telephone Company and other public utilities have attempted to forecast the direction and the rate of growth of the city in order to anticipate the future demands for the extension of their services. In the city plan the location of parks and boulevards, the widening of traffic streets, the provision for a civic center, are all in the interest of the future control of the physical development of the city. . . .

In Europe and America the tendency of the great city to expand has been recognized in the term "the metropolitan area of the city," which far overruns its political limits, and in the case of New York and Chicago, even state lines. The metropolitan area may be taken to include urban territory that is physically contiguous, but it is coming to be defined by that facility of transportation that enables a business man to live in a suburb of Chicago and to work in the loop, and his wife to shop at Marshall Field's and attend grand opera in the Auditorium.

Expansion as a Process

No study of expansion as a process has yet been made, although the materials for such a study and intimations of different aspects of the process are contained in city planning, zoning, and regional surveys. The typical processes of the expansion of the city can best be illustrated, perhaps, by a series of concentric circles, which may be numbered to designate both the successive zones of urban extension and the types of areas differentiated in the process of expansion.

Figure 26.1 represents an ideal construction of the tendencies of any town or city to expand radially from its central business district – on the map "The Loop" (I). Encircling the downtown area there is normally an area in transition, which is being invaded by business and light manufacture (II). A third area (III) is inhabited by the workers in industries who have escaped from the area of deterioration (II) but who desire to live within easy access of their work. Beyond this zone is the "residential area" (IV) of high-class apartment buildings or of exclusive "restricted" districts of single family dwellings. Still farther, out beyond the city limits, is the commuters' zone – suburban areas, or satellite cities – within a thirty- to sixty-minute ride of the central business district.

This chart brings out clearly the main fact of expansion, namely, the tendency of each inner zone to extend its area by the invasion of the next outer zone. This aspect of expansion may be called *succession*, a process which has been studied in detail in plant ecology. If this chart is applied to Chicago, all four of these zones were in its early history included in the circumference of the inner zone, the present business district. The present boundaries of the area of deterioration were not many years ago those of the zone now inhabited by independent wage-earners, and within the memories of thousands of Chicagoans contained the residences of the "best families." It hardly needs to be added that

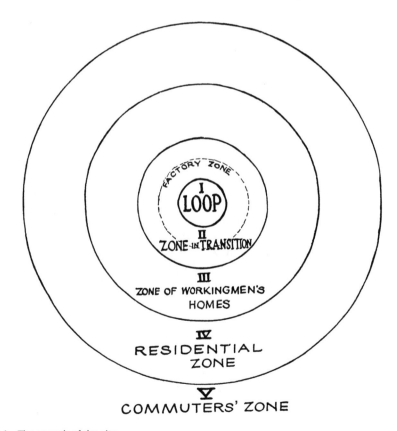

Figure 26.1 The growth of the city

neither Chicago nor any other city fits perfectly into this ideal scheme. Complications are introduced by the lake front, the Chicago River, railroad lines, historical factors in the location of industry, the relative degree of the resistance of communities to invasion, etc.

Besides extension and succession, the general process of expansion in urban growth involves the antagonistic and yet complementary processes of concentration and decentralization. In all cities there is the natural tendency for local and outside transportation to converge in the central business district. In the downtown section of every large city we expect to find the department stores, the skyscraper office buildings, the railroad stations, the great hotels, the theaters, the art museum, and the city hall. Quite naturally, almost inevitably, the economic, cultural, and political life centers here. The relation of centralization to the other processes of city life may be roughly gauged by the fact that over half a million people daily enter and leave Chicago's "loop." More recently sub-business centers have grown up in outlying zones. These "satellite loops" do not, it seems, represent the "hoped for" revival of the neighborhood, but rather a telescoping of several local communities into a larger economic unity. The Chicago of yesterday, an agglomeration of country towns and immigrant colonies, is undergoing a process of reorganization into a centralized decentralized system of local communities coalescing into sub-business areas visibly or invisibly dominated by the central business district. The actual processes of what may be called centralized decentralization are now being studied in the developement of the chain store, which is only one illustration of the change in the basis of the urban organization.

Expansion, as we have seen, deals with the physical growth of the city, and with the extension of the technical services that have made city life not only livable, but comfortable, even luxurious. Certain of these basic necessities of urban life are possible only through a tremendous development of communal existence. Three millions of people in Chicago are dependent upon one unified water system, one giant gas company, and one huge electric light plant. Yet, like most of the other aspects of our communal urban life, this economic co-operation is an example of co-operation without a shred of what the "spirit of co-operation" is commonly thought to signify. The great public utilities are a part of the mechanization of life in great cities, and have little or no other meaning for social organization.

Yet the processes of expansion, and especially the rate of expansion, may be studied not only in the physical growth and business development, but also in the consequent changes in the social organization and in personality types. How far is the growth of the city, in its physical and technical aspects, matched by a natural but adequate readjustment in the social organization? What, for a city, is a normal rate of expansion, a rate of expansion with which controlled changes in the social organization might successfully keep pace?

Social Organization and Disorganization as Processes of Metabolism

These questions may best be answered, perhaps, by thinking of urban growth as a resultant of organization and disorganization analogous to the anabolic and katabolic processes of metabolism in the body. In what way are individuals incorporated into the life of a city? By what process does a person become an organic part of his society? The natural process of acquiring culture is by birth. A person is born into a family already adjusted to a social environment – in this case the modern city. The natural rate of increase of population most favorable for assimilation may then be taken as the excess of the birth-rate over the death-rate, but is this the normal rate of city growth? Certainly, modern cities have increased and are increasing in population at a far higher rate. However, the natural rate of growth may be used to measure the disturbances of metabolism caused by any excessive increase, as those which followed the great influx of southern Negroes into northern cities since the war. In a similar way all cities show deviations in composition by age and sex from a standard population such as that of Sweden, unaffected in recent years by any great emigration or immigration. Here again, marked variations, as any great excess of males over females, or of females over males, or in the proportion of children, or of grown men or women, are symptomatic of abnormalities in social metabolism.

Normally the processes of disorganization and organization may be thought of as in reciprocal relationship to each other, and as co-operating in a moving equilibrium of social order toward an end vaguely or definitely regarded as progressive. So far as disorganization points to reorganization and makes for more efficient adjustment, disorganization must be conceived not as pathological, but as normal. Disorganization as preliminary to reorganization of attitudes and conduct is almost invariably the lot of the newcomer to the city, and the discarding of the habitual, and often of what has been to him the moral, is not infrequently accompanied by sharp mental conflict and sense of personal loss. Oftener, perhaps, the change gives sooner or later a feeling of emancipation and an urge toward new goals.

In the expansion of the city a process of distribution takes place which sifts and sorts and relocates individuals and groups by residence and occupation. The resulting differentiation of the cosmopolitan American city into areas is typically all from one pattern, with only interesting minor modifications. (See figure 26.2.) Within the central business district or on an adjoining street is the "main stem" of "hobohemia," the teeming Rialto of the homeless migratory man of the Middle West. In the zone of deterioration encircling the central business section are always to be found the so-called "slums" and "bad lands," with their submerged regions of poverty, degradation, and disease, and their underworlds of crime and vice. Within a deteriorating area are rooming-house districts, the purgatory of "lost souls." Near by is the Latin Quarter, where creative and rebellious spirits resort. The slums are also crowded to over-flowing with immigrant colonies – the Ghetto, Little Sicily. Greek-town, Chinatown – fascinatingly combining old world heritages and American adaptations. Wedging out from here is the Black Belt, with its free and disorderly life. The area of deterioration, while essentially one of decay, of stationary or declining population, is also one of regeneration, as witness the mission, the settlement, the artists' colony, radical centers – all obsessed with the vision of a new and better world.

The next zone is also inhabited predominatingly by factory and shop workers, but skilled and thrifty. This is an area of second immigrant settlement, generally of the second generation. It is the region of escape from the slum, the *Deutschland* of the aspiring Ghetto family. For *Deutschland* (literally "Germany") is the name given, half in envy, half in derision, to that region beyond the Ghetto where successful neighbors appear to be imitating German Jewish standards of living. But the inhabitant of this area in turn looks to the "Promised Land" beyond, to its residential hotels, its apartment-house region, its "satellite loops," and its "bright light" areas.

This differentiation into natural economic and cultural groupings gives form and character to the city. For segregation offers the group, and thereby the individuals who compose the group, a place and a rôle in the total organization of city life. Segregation limits development in certain directions, but releases it in others. These areas tend to accentuate certain traits, to attract and develop their kind of individuals, and so to become further differentiated.

The division of labor in the city likewise illustrates disorganization, reorganization, and increasing differentiation. The immigrant from rural communities in Europe and America seldom brings with him economic skill of any great value in our

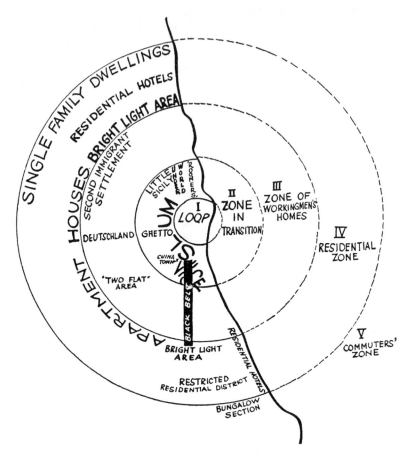

Figure 26.2 Urban areas

industrial, commercial, or professional life. Yet interesting occupational selection has taken place by nationality, explainable more by racial temperament or circumstance than by old-world economic background, as Irish policemen, Greek ice-cream parlors, Chinese laundries, Negro porters, Belgian janitors, etc.

The facts that in Chicago one million (996,589) individuals gainfully employed reported 509 occupations, and that over 1,000 men and women in *Who's Who* gave 116 different vocations, give some notion of how in the city the minute differentiation of occupation "analyzes and sifts the population, separating and classifying the diverse elements." These figures also afford some intimation of the complexity and complication of the modern industrial mechanism and the intricate segregation and isolation of divergent economic groups. Interrelated with this economic division of labor is a corresponding division into social classes and into cultural and recreational groups. From this multiplicity of groups, with their different patterns of life, the person finds his congenial social world and – what is not feasible in the narrow confines of a village – may move and live in widely separated, and perchance conflicting, worlds. Personal disorganization may be but the failure to harmonize the canons of conduct of two divergent groups.

If the phenomena of expansion and metabolism indicate that a moderate degree of disorganization may and does facilitate social organization, they indicate as well that rapid urban expansion is accompanied by excessive increases in disease, crime, disorder, vice, insanity, and suicide, rough indexes of social disorganization. But what are the indexes of the causes, rather than of the effects, of the disordered social metabolism of the city? The excess of the actual over the natural increase of population has already been suggested as a criterion. The significance of this increase consists in the immigration into a metropolitan city like New York and Chicago of tens of thousands of persons annually. Their invasion of the city has the effect of a tidal wave inundating first the immigrant colonies, the ports of first entry, dislodging thousands of inhabitants who overflow into the next zone, and so on and on until the momentum of the wave has spent its force on the last urban zone. The whole effect is to speed up expansion, to speed up industry, to speed up the "junking" process in the area of deterioration (II). These internal movements of the population become the more significant for study. What movement is going on in the city, and how may this movement be measured? It is easier, of course, to classify movement within the city than to measure it. There is the movement from residence to residence, change of occupation, labor turnover, movement to and from work, movement for recreation and adventure. This leads to the question: What is the significant aspect of movement for the study of the changes in city life? The answer to this question leads directly to the important distinction between movement and mobility.

Mobility as the Pulse of the Community

Movement, per se, is not an evidence of change or of growth. In fact, movement may be a fixed and unchanging order of motion, designed to control a constant situation, as in routine movement. Movement that is significant for growth implies a change of movement in response to a new stimulus or situation. Change of movement of this type is called *mobility*. Movement of

the nature of routine finds its typical expression in work. Change of movement, or mobility, is characteristically expressed in adventure. The great city, with its "bright lights," its emporiums of novelties and bargains, its palaces of amusement, its underworld of vice and crime, its risks of life and property from accident, robbery, and homicide, has become the region of the most intense degree of adventure and danger, excitement and thrill.

Mobility, it is evident, involves change, new experience, stimulation. Stimulation induces a response of the person to those objects in his environment which afford expression for his wishes. For the person, as for the physical organism, stimulation is essential to growth. Response to stimulation is wholesome so long as it is a correlated *integral* reaction of the entire personality. When the reaction is *segmental*, that is, detached from, and uncontrolled by, the organization of personality, it tends to become disorganizing or pathological. That is why stimulation for the sake of stimulation, as in the restless pursuit of pleasure, partakes of the nature of vice.

The mobility of city life, with its increase in the number and intensity of stimulations, tends inevitably to confuse and to demoralize the person. For an essential element in the mores and in personal morality is consistency, consistency of the type that is natural in the social control of the primary group. Where mobility is the greatest, and where in consequence primary controls break down completely, as in the zone of deterioration in the modern city, there develop areas of demoralization, of promiscuity, and of vice.

In our studies of the city it is found that areas of mobility are also the regions in which are found juvenile delinquency, boy's gangs, crime, poverty, wife desertion, divorce, abandoned infants, vice.

These concrete situations show why mobility is perhaps the best index of the state of metabolism of the city. Mobility may be thought of in more than a fanciful sense, as the "pulse of the community." Like the pulse of the human body, it is a process which reflects and is indicative of all the changes that are taking place in the community, and which is susceptible of analysis into elements which may be stated numerically.

The elements entering into mobility may be classified under two main heads: (1) the state of mutability of the person, and (2) the number and kind of contacts or stimulations in his environment. The mutability of city populations varies with sex and age composition, the degree of detachment of the person from the family and from other groups. All these factors may be expressed numerically. The new stimulations to which a population responds can be measured in terms of change of movement or of increasing contacts. Statistics on the movement of urban population may only measure routine, but an increase at a higher ratio than the increase of population measures mobility. In 1860 the horse-car lines of New York City carried about 50,000,000 passengers; in 1890 the trolley-cars (and a few surviving horse-cars) transported about 500,000,000; in 1921, the elevated, subway, surface, and electric and steam suburban lines carried a total of more than 2,500,000,000 passengers. In Chicago the total annual rides per capita on the surface and elevated lines were 164 in 1890; 215 in 1900; 320 in 1910; and 338 in 1921. In addition, the rides per capita on steam and electric suburban lines almost doubled between 1916 (23) and 1921 (41), and the increasing use of the automobile must not be overlooked. For example, the number of automobiles in Illinois increased from 131,140 in 1915 to 833,920 in 1923.

Mobility may be measured not only by these changes of movement, but also by increase of contacts. While the increase of population of Chicago in 1912–22 was less than 25 per cent (23.6 per cent), the increase of letters delivered to Chicagoans was double that (49.6 per cent) – (from 693,084,196 to 1,038,007,854). In 1912 New York had 8.8 telephones; in 1922, 16.9 per 100 inhabitants. Boston had, in 1912, 10.1 telephones; ten years later, 19.5 telephones per 100 inhabitants. In the same decade the figures for Chicago increased from 12.3 to 21.6 per 100 population. But increase of the use of the telephone is probably more significant than increase in the number of telephones. The number of telephone calls in Chicago increased from 606,131,928 in 1914 to 944,010,586 in 1922 an increase of 55.7 per cent, while the population increased only 13.4 per cent.

Land values, since they reflect movement, afford one of the most sensitive indexes of mobility. The highest land values in Chicago are at the point of greatest mobility in the city, at the corner of State and Madison streets, in the Loop. A traffic count showed that at the rush period 31,000 people an hour, or 210,000 men and women in sixteen and one-half hours, passed the southwest corner. For over ten years land values in the Loop have been stationary but in the same time they have doubled, quadrupled, and even sextupled in the strategic corners of the "satellite loops," an accurate index of the changes which have occurred. Our investigations so far seem to indicate that variations in land values, especially where correlated with differences in rents, offer perhaps the best single measure of mobility, and so of all the changes taking place in the expansion and growth of the city.

In general outline, I have attempted to present the point of view and methods of investigation which the department of sociology is employing in its studies in the growth of the city, namely, to describe urban expansion in terms of extension, succession, and concentration; to determine how expansion disturbs metabolism when disorganization is in excess of organization; and, finally, to define mobility and to propose it as a measure both of expansion and metabolism, susceptible to precise quantitative formulation, so that it may be regarded almost literally as the pulse of the community. . . .

Chapter 27

from *City Trenches: Urban Politics and the Patterning of Class in the US*

Ira Katznelson

City Trenches

It is hard to find the right words to discuss politics and the American working class without reaching for the clinical language of schizophrenia. The main element of what Raymond Williams calls the "select-ive tradition" of the working class in the United States has been a stark split between the ways workers in the major industrial cities think, talk, and act when they are at work and when they are away from work in their communities. When was this dis-connected pattern first formed? How did it differ from the ways working classes developed in other Western societies at comparable moments? What were the main causes of the political dissociation between work and home?[1] ...

In his study of New York, Carl Abbott argues that the mercantile city was not an integrated jumble of work and resid-ence with little differentiation of neighbor-hoods. Rather, a new built form was being created in which different kinds of func-tional spaces could be distinguished:

> Proceeding on the basis of economic func-tion, one can discover a commercial dis-trict along the lower East River, a sector devoted to light manufacturing and retailing in the middle part of town, and a heavier manufacturing sector on its northern edge. The city was similarly split into residential neighborhoods of dif-ferent status and characteristics. Its upper classes lived within the commercial dis-trict and adjacent to it west of Broad Street. Artisans and tradesmen ... lived as well as worked in a broad band across the center of the city. Areas with the poorest housing, worst physical condi-tions, and most undesirable and transient population were found on the fringes. (Abbott 1974: 51)

Nevertheless, in spite of these emerging divisions in space, the mercantile cities in the Revolutionary era stood, from the vant-age point of 1860, rather closer to the level of differentiation characteristic of medieval cities than to that typical of the modern commercial-industrial city. The incipient divisions – which Abbott, among others, rightly emphasizes and sets against overro-manticized notions of the mercantile city – were more in the nature of a combination of emerging tendencies and traditional pat-terns. The cities were very compact and crowded. A complete, or even a terribly well-defined, separation of land uses and activities was virtually impossible, given the ecology and topography of the cities. The latter developed close to their shores (their "hinge" to the world market) and hugged the coast. Philadelphia in 1780 was nine blocks square and had a popula-tion of 16,500. New York's 22,000 resi-dents lived and worked in a triangle only four thousand feet wide and six thousand feet from apex to base (Abbott 1974). This crowding expressed and helped reproduce the ideology and reality of an integrated community. Thus, Warner has insisted that late-eighteenth-century Philadelphia

> was a community. Graded by wealth and divided by distinctions of class though it was, it functioned as a single community. The community had been created out of a remarkably inclusive network of business and economic relationships and it was maintained by the daily interactions of trade and sociability... every man and occupation lived jumbled together in a narrow compass. (Warner 1968: 11)

By the time of Civil War, the ambiguous status of "community" in the older port cities had been resolved, by the impact of capitalist development. Between 1800 and 1850 Philadelphia grew in population from 69,000 to 340,000; and New York City from 60,000 to 516,000 (Rosenwaike 1972: 16). The cities were becoming unmistakably divided into distinctive districts of work and home.[2] The "unity of everyday life, from tavern to street, to workplace, to housing," of the late-eighteenth-century city shattered; Philadelphia was by 1860 "a city of closed social cells." One manufacturing worker in four labored in the principal downtown ward (the sixth) in a city of twenty-four wards:

> The garment industry in all its branches, boot and shoe makers, bookbinders, printers, and paper box fabricators, glass manufacturers, machinists, coopers, sugar refiners, brewers, and cigar makers especially concentrated here. Thousands of workers walked to the downtown every day, while omnibuses, and just before the Civil War, horse-drawn streetcars brought shopkeepers and customers. No tall office buildings yet outlined the downtown, no manufacturing lofts filled entire blocks, but the basic manufacturing-wholesale-retail-financial elements had already been assembled by 1860 for the future metropolis. (Warner 1968: 58–9)

New manufacturing clusters radiated "out from the original urban core like a crude

spiderweb spun through the blocks of little houses." Although the incompleteness of street directories and census data makes it very difficult to know precisely how many workers left their homes to labor, documented commutation patterns for Philadelphia and New York indicate unmistakably that "work began to be separated from home neighborhood"(ibid.:59). Even before the rapid industrial development of the 1840s, there were "significant alterations in the propensity to commute and in the average length of commutation that did occur." Pred very conservatively estimates that in New York City in 1840 approximately one-fourth of the *industrial* workers were already working outside their homes (Pred 1966: 208). The increasing separation of work and home was matched by the growing segregation of residence communities by class, ethnicity, and race....

This organization of the city's social landscape altered the class composition of local associations and clubs. The membership of lodges, benefit associations, parish churches, gangs, athletic clubs, fire companies, and political clubs no longer cut across the class divisions of the social structure. The new working classes of the antebellum city borrowed many of the organizational forms of the mercantile city. But in their increasingly segregated communities, separated not only from their workplaces but also from merchants and industrial capitalists, workers controlled these institutions. They were free to develop new organizations as they saw fit, and those they did create belonged exclusively to them. Together with the labor organizations that workers were beginning to devise at work, these neighborhood institutions provided the possibility for the development of an independent working-class culture. Paradoxically, just at the moment when the development of industrial capitalism undercut the skill levels and control over work that artisans had exercised, the working class became capable of developing and controlling the institutions of daily neighborhood life.

For this reason, many social historians see this period of the history of the working class, not only in the United States, but also in England, France, Prussia, and other industrializing areas of western Europe, as the era of the development of an autonomous working-class culture.[3] This period's structural developments – the split between work and residence and the growth of workingmen's social clubs, gangs, and other institutions – were not unique to the United States. What was different, and what therefore requires explanation, was the distinctive response of American workers to the separation of work and home, and the social and political use that they made of the local institutions they controlled.

By the Civil War the connections between conflicts at work and conflicts in residence communities became increasingly tenuous. This separation between the politics of work and the politics of community was much more stark in the United States than elsewhere. The patterns of consciousness, speech, and organization at work and away from work grew increasingly distinctive. Away from work, ethnic and territorial identifications became dominant. They were acted out through community groups and through local political parties, churches, and secondary associations. At work, workers were class conscious, but with a difference, for the awareness narrowed down to labor concerns and to unions that established few ties to political parties.

These essential elements of the early system of American "city trenches" continue to define the idiom of U.S. politics to such an extent that we forget how special they were. In England a modern working class, although sharing the structural attributes of the American working class, was "made" in a very different way. The English drew from a similar experience of industrialization and urbanization to arrive at a coherent presocialist interpretation of class that saw the new society divided along a single class cleavage at work, in politics, and in community life (Briggs

1959; Foster 1975; Tholfsen 1977; Thompson 1968). In other societies, including those of Belgium and Holland, ethnicity rather than class came to frame political conflicts both at work and in residential areas (Zolberg 1978). The rigid separation of the American pattern was thus by no means inevitably dictated by capitalist industrialization....

This new urban system of "city trenches" had three main elements: trade unions at the workplace; a quite separate decentralized party system; and an array of new government services that were delivered to citizens in their residential communities.

The trade unions that developed at the workplace in the antebellum period sought to protect the traditional prerogatives of skilled workers, struggled for better working conditions, and, above all, fought for higher wages. These unions were prepared to be quite militant, especially in periods of prosperity and labor scarcity. Urban unions called many strikes, which were notably successful in raising pay scales. Between 1850 and 1857 skilled unionized workers in New York secured a 25 percent increase in wages. The unions of the 1850s collected dues systematically and accumulated strike funds. Their most important progressive achievement was their ability "to apply the principles of collective bargaining to the whole trade in order to establish a uniform wage scale for all workers" (Foner 1972: 221, 223 see also Commons *et al.* 1918, ch. 7). More than any other institution of the period, the trade unions overcame the differences between native and immigrant workers to forge a common consciousness of class....

Although most of these unions were shattered by the economic crisis of 1857, they left a legacy of a class-conscious labor movement and of the familiar paraphernalia of the union shop, strike funds, and collective bargaining. They also left the legacy of restricting their attention to immediate trade-union demands and eschewing party activity and political action outside the workplace.

The antebellum party system complemented the limited focus of the unions because it was grounded exclusively in the residence community. The main political parties in the three decades before the Civil War were less interested in ideology than in mobilizing voters. Their attempts to garner votes in the big cities were organized on the geographical basis of the ward by professional politicians who used new kinds of patronage to woo supporters.

Although the parties competed in national presidential elections, party organizations were intensely *local* territorial institutions. Seen from the bottom of party hierarchies, party life in this period, especially with respect to local offices, gave the overwhelming impression of factional fluidity, individual initiative, clientalistic ties between leaders and followers, and the isolation of organizations in one ward from those in other parts of the large cities. The centralized urban machines date from the 1870s and beyond. In the antebellum years the urban party structures especially were decentralized and enmeshed in the organizational life of neighborhoods – their gangs, firehouses, secret societies, saloons. The ward, as community and as the juridical unit of politics, was the core of the political community.

In these wards, indeed at all levels of the political system, the professional politician (whose prototype can be found in the Albany Regency of the 1820s) (Foner 1972: 224) superseded the older governing elite of patrician merchants. The sheer number of elections and the organizational skills and time required "put a premium on the efforts of men who were willing to devote all, or almost all, of their time to politics, and who did not expect leadership to fall to them as a matter of deference, celebrity, or wealth" (Hofstadter 1965: 211). For these new organizers the perpetuation of the party took precedence over ideological commitments. They sought to prosper by organizing political life. And they reflected in their diverse social backgrounds and ties to neighborhood institutions the increasingly heterogeneous class

and ethnic character of the urban mosaic. Not all these politicians, of course, came from working-class wards. But those who did were, from the vantage point of working-class neighborhoods, a part of "us," not "them."[4] ...

The party system's decentralized and intensely community-based character reflected the necessary parallelism between government structure and party organization. Its distributive character hinged on the development of political control over public bureaucracies. In important recent treatments of administrative developments at the national level, Crenson and Shefter stress how the Jacksonians created the rudiments of modern bureaucratic structures by divorcing job descriptions and duties from the characteristics of individual persons (Crenson 1975; Shefter 1979). ...

These national changes were paralleled and reinforced by patronage developments at the local level. In the antebellum years a new kind of political system was created there; at its center were municipal *services*. The systematic organization of disciplined professional policemen at the city level was unknown in the West before the creation of a police force in London in 1829. The London system was introduced in the major cities of the United States in the three decades before the Civil War. This period is also characterized by the bureaucratization of municipal charity and poor relief and by the establishment of modern mass public school systems. These organizations, together with the massive expansion in the budgets and the capacities of local governments to license, award contracts, and shape the tempo and spatial direction of city growth, put unprecedented distributive resources in the hands of local government and party officials (Ravitch 1974; Rothman 1971; Miller 1977; Goodnow 1909; Holden 1966). These tangible resources provided the largesse needed to organize the world's first mass urban political parties that were working-class based. By the 1850s, it is important to stress, local political parties at the community level were genuinely working-class institutions, rooted deeply in the local institutions and cultural life made possible by the development of class-homogeneous neighborhoods separate from workplaces.

Significantly, however, these parties at the neighborhood-ward level organized workers not as workers, but as residents of this or that ward, as members of this or that ethnic group; and they did not intrude on workplace concerns. Although throughout the antebellum period such class-related economic issues as banking, tariffs, internal improvements, and slavery dominated the national and state political agendas, votes were increasingly solicited on the basis of ethnic and religious affiliations. It is striking that in a society undergoing very rapid change, and offering many possible points of conflict between groups and classes, the party system exploited locality-based ethnic divisions in the older cities more than anything else....

The political groupings that were created by party activity were based exclusively in the residence community. They had no direct organizational ties to the period's trade unions, and they did not discuss politics in terms of class. As a result, politics in the antebellum city came to be defined in the main, not as a politics of capital and labor, but as a politics of competition between ethnic-territorial communities from which capital was absent.[5]

These developments quite clearly reflected the material realities associated with the separation of work from home and with the demographic distribution of the population. Capitalist industrialization was experienced directly as conflict over the use of scarce space at the community level. German and Irish immigrants became the tangible symbols (some thought the cause) of the ascendancy of industrial capital. Native-born Protestant artisans who had the most to lose expressed their rebellion against the new order in their neighborhoods by resisting residential incursions. The result was many bloody clashes – between nativists and immigrants, between Protestants and Catholics, and in some cases between blacks and whites.

These conflicts heightened the importance of territorial identities and of such institutions as gangs and fire companies that gave expression to them; and these institutions provided the organizational base for party organization. From the immigrants' perspective the integrity of their religion and cultural practices was at stake in their communities. Bitter conflicts over local control of the new public schools reflected these intensely felt concerns (Ravitch 1974; Tyack 1974)....

The withdrawal of the traditional governing elite from city politics, in short, was doubly self-interested. The rewards of money lay with private capital, and social cohesion depended on new political relationships they were incapable of creating. One consequence may well have been, as Robert Dahl has stressed (Dahl 1961), the democratization of local leadership, but the substantive result was a new system of urban politics, city trenches that protected capital.

III

On the eve of the Civil War, all the elements of this system were in place, but just barely. The depression of 1857 decimated urban trade unions. Political machines were still largely neighborhood affairs that lacked coordination. Local services were crude and limited. Many neighborhoods continued to function as integrated worlds of work and home, and some still contained a multiplicity of classes. From the vantage point of 1860, the newly constructed city trenches could not have looked too secure. By the last two decades of the century, however, the uncertainties had been resolved, and as the century turned, the new urban system dominated the political landscape.

Labor unions resumed their path of separate development. Both the short-lived Knights of Labor and the American Federation of Labor (AFL), as their names imply, conceived of workers as "labor" and had virtually no connections of a regular electoral sort with local mainstream or insurgent party organizations. With only rare exceptions, subsequent labor organizations have maintained this tradition.

The residence community became the political forum managed by parties and bureaucracies that were divorced from workplace concerns. These urban working-class neighborhoods were neighborhoods of immigrants who came increasingly from southern and eastern Europe. Like the mercantile cities of the eighteenth century, they were walking neighborhoods; yet unlike the older port cities, these neighborhoods constituted only a part of the ethnic worker's universe. Caroline Golab's sensitive portrait of Poles in Philadelphia in the late-nineteenth century captures the intense localism and provinciality of these residence spaces:

> They walked ... to the grocery store, to the butcher shop and bakery. They walked to church and to school. They walked to visit friends and relatives (unless they lived in another Polish neighborhood, in which case they took the trolley). Their children were born at home, and when they died in Nicetown, Bridgesburg, Richmond, or Manaynuk, they were not too far from the cemetery. Because all their needs could be satisfied within their immediate environment, they had little reason to venture outside. The beauty of the neighborhood was its self-sufficiency.... *The city remained an abstraction, the neighborhood was a reality. It was the neighborhood, not the city, which provided immigrants with their identity, security, and stimulation.* (Golab 1977: 154, 156)

In these neighborhoods, residents were policed by newly organized police forces, assisted by new welfare agencies, and taught by new public common schools. The prototype of the modern police force was the constabulary established in London in 1829. Before that date the propertied classes had protected their own property by themselves or by hiring watchmen and guards. When public order had been threatened beyond their capacity to main-

tain social peace, military force had generally been used to quell the "dangerous classes." By contrast, in a policed society, government authorities exercise "potentially violent supervision over the population by bureaucratic means widely diffused throughout civil society in small and discretionary operations that are capable of rapid concentration." It was the job of the police to penetrate the new class-homogeneous neighborhoods of the older cities to maintain order and prevent crime, and in so doing to represent the "continual presence of central political authority throughout daily life" (Silver 1967: 8, 12–13). The policeman, often a resident of the policed community, became the instrument of joining local residents to state authority. These relationships, from the start, were often themselves sources of major conflicts between residents and local government, as the police, especially in areas where the policeman came from a different (usually Irish) ethnic group, embodied all undesirable intrusions and traits of "them" or of all who were not "us."

Similar patterns prevailed with respect to welfare and educational services. In the late-eighteenth and early-nineteenth centuries, private individual and associational charity paralleled private police and private schools. As late as the 1830s and 1840s, it often made little sense to distinguish between private and public benevolent associations. In New York City the Humane Society built a soup house for the poor with public funds; the Society for New York Hospital was funded by legislative grants; the "Society for the Prevention of Pauperism formalized the relationship between public and private bodies by providing that five of its managers be appointed by the common council." The patrician officials who ran city government were often the same people, or at least members of the same families, who directed the city's welfare establishments. By the late 1840s, however, city government came increasingly under the control of professional politicians and had to administer a growing welfare burden. Approximately 57,000 people received public outdoor relief in 1848, compared to about 8,000 four decades earlier. Benevolent societies also expanded their activities, but apart from those of local government. Politics and benevolence had become separate realms of activity; the old ruling class dominated the latter. But in both public and private spheres, paid employees with specialized skills came to take over the delivery of welfare benefits and services to working-class ethnic neighborhoods. The creation of a profession of social work later in the century helped crystallize these patterns, as it also reinforced an emerging set of conflicts between the producers and consumers of welfare services (Heale 1976: 25, 29).

Educational issues provided still another new arena for tension between communities and local government. As in the case of the police, the schools were key instruments in visibly linking class and ethnically specific neighborhoods to the larger political and social system. "In almost every city where the population was heterogeneous," David Tyack writes about the late-nineteenth century, "contests erupted in educational politics. Although there were sometimes overtones of class assertion or resentment in such conflicts, the issues were not normally phrased in class terms, but in the cross-cutting cultural categories of race, religion, ethnicity, neighborhood loyalties, and partisan politics" (Tyack 1974: 78).

This language of city affairs was predominantly determined by the increasingly centralized party organizations of the post–Civil War era. Dominant citywide machines came to control the ward organizations, and to impose discipline on neighborhood political actors. In New York City, for example, an era of "rapacious individualism" ... was followed by a period of organization building under the leadership of John Kelly that culminated in Tammany's triumph over its potential party rivals and in the establishment of a network of district political clubs throughout the city (Shefter 1976: 34).

The new citywide machines established centralized control on the basis of standardized community organizations. Each of these party clubs – like its pre – Civil War precursors – was enmeshed in the ethnic and territorial culture of the ward or precinct. Ostrogorski well understood the communitarian basis of the machine. He wrote in 1910,

> The small politician has no need to create the political following which he forms around him; he finds it ready to hand in social life, in which neighbourly ties, and above all common tastes and mutual sympathies, give rise to small sets, groups of people who meet regularly to enjoy the pleasures of sociability and friendship. The street corner serves them as a rendezvous as long as they are in the youthful stage. Then, when they grow older and have a few cents to spend, they meet in a drinking-saloon or in a room hired for the purpose with their modest contributions. Several "gangs" unite to found a sort of club, in which they give small parties, balls, or simply smoke, drink, and amuse themselves. This merry crew is a latent political force; when the elections come round it may furnish a compact band of voters. The small politician therefore has but to lay his hand on it. (Ostrogorski 1964: 180)

The centralized machine's political clubs organized this social impulse and made it the cornerstone of an electoral politics through patronage and services. The potency of the community as the locus of political identities lay not merely in the existence of community networks nor in their being promoted by party organizations. Rather, the interaction of the organization and the community base strengthened both, as it gave new impetus to communal ties, and in so doing solidified the prospects of the political party. As a consequence, workers were regularly integrated into the political process on the basis of communally bounded affiliations. The machines, for workers, were "us," yet the machine also limited the content of "us."

Werner Sombart's most acute observations spoke directly to this point. He observed that this kind of party system "makes it extremely easy for the proletariat to belong to the traditional parties. In attaching himself to one of the two parties, even the class-conscious worker need never go against the dictates of his intellect, because these parties do not have to be seen as class organizations and as advocates of a specific class interest." In turn, this situation "also influences the position they take towards the proletariat." By stressing particularistic rewards and nonclass affiliations, "the traditionally good relationship is maintained intact" (Sombart 1976: 50).

Every election reinforced the split consciousness of the American working class. As a consequence of the mosaic pattern of ethnic settlement and the ward organization of electoral competition, urban political parties, I have noted elsewhere, "to win elections, had to put together electoral majorities composed of blocs of ethnic groups. . . . the opportunity for ethnic communities to enter the political process acted to solidify group consciousness and to perpetuate the division of the city, demographically and politically, into ethnic components" (Katznelson 1973: 87). Indeed, the very rules of electoral politics reinforced this system of ethnicity, community, and party. Douglas Rae has stressed how the single-member district system, such as we have in the United States, "strengthens already strong parties by making small party challenges difficult." And he has made the more important point that the system of territorial districts puts a premium on the identities that are to be found where people live rather than where they work (Rae 1967; Casper 1976).

As most standard treatments of urban politics have stressed, the urban system has been essentially a system of ethnic bargaining and accommodation. Drawing on the political, organizational, and cultural resources of their communities, ethnic groups have been joined in a complex game whose prizes are patronage and city services. I have stressed that the urban system is more than this. By constricting the politics of class to the workplace, the urban system made challenges to the larger social order very difficult indeed. Over a long period of time, the stark division in people's consciousness, language, and action between the politics of work and the politics of community became a tacit mechanism in the selection of alternatives. As Raymond Williams has observed, "in certain social-historical circumstances, there are things which could not be said, and therefore, in any connecting way, not thought" (Williams 1979: 182). Social control in the United States has depended on just such an imposition of silence. The system of city trenches has produced a working class unique in the West: militant as labor, and virtually nonexistent as a collectivity outside the workplace. Workers have thus tended "to oppose capitalists rather than capitalism."

It is not surprising that there have been attempts to challenge this urban class system through working-class socialist or laborist parties that would appeal to workers *as workers* both in the community and in the laboring portions of their lives. American urban history is in part the story of such attempts: socialist campaigns in the late 1870s in Chicago; the United Labor party candidacy of Henry George for mayor of New York that utilized trade-union organizations for electoral purposes; socialist strength on the Lower East Side of Manhattan at the turn of the century; and the election of socialist councilmen in many cities, and mayors in a few, most notably in Milwaukee. Taken as a whole, however, these challenges were hardly successful. Indeed, American socialists achieved most when one of two very special conditions obtained: when workplaces and residence communities were tightly bound together as in the Finnish mining communities of northern Michigan; or when the voting public consisted principally of first-generation immigrants from Europe who brought a socialist tradition with them.[6] In almost all other cases, the city trenches held against socialist incursions.

NOTES

1 Remarkably, with the exception of Susan Hirsch, in her first-rate study of Newark, New Jersey, scholars have left these issues unexamined. Hirsch's work, moreover, for all its merits, is rather more descriptive of the split between work and community than analytical. Susan G. Hirsch, *Roots of the American Working Class* (Philadelphia: University of Pennsylvania Press, 1978).

2 It is tempting to overstate the extent of change in the internal organization of city space that economic change entailed. As late as 1860, Warner cautions, most areas of Philadelphia were still "a jumble of occupations and classes, shops, homes, immigrants and native Americans." Yet the direction of change was unmistakable, and its degree quite dramatic. Warner, *Private City*, p. 50.

3 For a brief comparative and theoretical discussion, see my "Working Class Formation in Europe and the United States: CES Research Group Report," *European Studies Newsletter* 9 (June 1980). See also the special issue on "Culture and Class," *Radical History Review*, no. 18 (fall 1978).

4 For a rich, if flawed, Beardian discussion of these issues, see Gabriel Almond, "Plutocracy and Politics in New York City" (Ph.D. diss., University of Chicago, Department of Political Science, 1938), esp. chap. 4.

5 The pioneering study of voting behavior in this period is Lee Benson, *The Concept of Jacksonian Democracy* (Princeton, NJ.

Princeton University Press, 1961). For a critique of this volume and for subsequent accounts in this tradition, see Richard B. Latner and Peter Levine, "Perspectives on Antebellum Pietistic Politics," *Reviews in American History* 4 (March 1976). Two important case studies are Kathleen Neils Conzen, *Immigrant Milwaukee, 1836–1860* (Cambridge, Mass.: Harvard University Press, 1976); and Oscar Handlin, *Boston's Immigrants* (New York: Atheneum, 1974).

6 Cf. James Weinsten, *The Decline of Socialism in America* (New York, Vintage Books, 1969); Al Gedicks, "Ethnicity, Class Solidarity, and Labor Radicalism among Finnish Immigrants in Michigan Copper Country," *Politics and Society* 7, no. 2 (1977); Melvyn Dubofsky, "Success and Failure of Socialism in New York City, 1900–1918: A Case Study," *Labor History* 9 (fall 1968); Seymour Martin Lipset, "Why No Socialism in the United States," in Seweryn Bialer and Sophia Sluzar, eds., *Sources of Contemporary Radicalism* (New York: Westview Press, 1977); Charles Leineweber, "The American Socialist Party and 'New' Immigrants," *Science and Society* 32 (winter 1968); Henry F. Bedford, *Socialism and the Workers in Massachusetts, 1886–1912* (Amherst, Mass.: University of Massachusetts Press, 1966); and Stanley Buder, *Pullman* (New York: Oxford University Press, 1967).

REFERENCES

Abbott, C. 1974: The Neighbourhoods of New York, 1760–1775. *New York History* 55: Jan.

Briggs, A. (ed.) 1959: *Chartist Studies*. London: Macmillan.

Casper, G. 1976: Social Differences and the Franchise. *Daedalus*, fall.

Commons, J. et al. 1918: *History of Labor in the United States*, vol. 1. New York: Macmillan.

Crenson, M. 1975: *The Federal Machine: Beginnings of Bureaucracy in Jacksonian America*. Baltimore: Johns Hopkins University Press.

Dahl, R. 1961: *Who Governs?* New Haven, CT: Yale University Press.

Foner, P. 1972: *History of the Labor Movement in the United States*, vol. 1. New York: International Publishers.

Foster, J. 1975: *Class Struggle and the Industrial Revolution*. London: Methuen.

Golab, C. 1977 *Immigrant Destinations*. Philadelphia: Temple University Press.

Goodnow, F. 1909: *Municipal Government*. New York: Century.

Heale, M. 1976: From City Fathers to Social Critics: Humanitarianism and Government in New York, 1790–1860. *Journal of American History* 63, June.

Hofstadter, R. 1965: *The Idea of a Party System*. Berkeley and Los Angeles: University of California Press.

Holden, M. 1966: Ethnic Accommodation in a Historical Case. *Comparative Studies in Society and History* 8, Jan.

Katznelson, I. 1973: *Black Men, White Cities: Race, Politics and Migration in the United States, 1900–1930, and Britain, 1948–68.* New York: Oxford University Press.

Miller, W. 1977: *Cops and Bobbies: Police Authority in New York and London, 1830–1870.* Chicago: University of Chicago Press.

Ostrogorski, M. 1964: Democracy and the Organisation of Political Parties, vol. 2. New York: Doubleday Anchor.

Pred, A. 1966: *The Spatial Dynamics of US Urban-Industrial Growth, 1800–1914.* Cambridge, MA: MIT Press.

Rae, D. 1967: *The Political Consequences of Electoral Laws.* New Haven, CT: Yale University Press.

Ravitch, D. 1974: *The Great School Wars.* New York: Basic Books

Rosenwaike, I. 1972: *Population History of New York City.* Syracuse, NY: Syracuse University Press.

Rothman, D. 1971: *The Discovery of the Asylum.* Boston: Little Brown.

Shefter, M. 1976: The Emergence of the Political Machine: An Alternative View. In W. Hawley, M. Lipsky, et al. (eds.), *Theoretical Perspectives on Urban Politics.* Englewood Cliffs, NJ: Prentice-Hall.

Shefter, M. 1979: Party Bureaucracy and Political Change in the United States. In L. Maisel and J. Cooper (eds.), *The Development of Political Parties: Patterns of Evolution and Decay.* Sage Electoral Studies Yearbook, vol. 4. Beverly Hills: Sage Publications.

Silver, A. 1967: The Demand for Order in Civil Society: A Review of Some Themes in the History of Urban Crime, Police and Riot. In D. Bordua (ed.), *The Police.* New York: Wiley.

Sombart, W. 1976: *Why Is There No Socialism in the United States?* White Plains, NY: Sharpe.

Tholfsen, T. 1977: *Working Class Radicalism in Mid Victorian England.* New York: Columbia University Press.

Thompson, E. P. 1968: *The Making of the English Working Class.* London: Penguin Books.

Tyack, D. 1974: *The One Best System.* Cambridge, MA: Harvard University Press.

Warner, S. B. 1968: *The Private City: Philadelphia in Three Periods of Its Growth.* Philadelphia: University of Philadelphia Press.

Williams, R. 1979: *Politics and Letters.* London: New Left Books.

Zolberg, A. 1978: Belgium. In R. Grew (ed.), *Crises of Political Development in Europe and the United States.* Princeton, NJ: Princeton University Press.

Chapter 28

from *The Truly Disadvantaged: The Inner City, the Underclass, and Public Policy*

William Julius Wilson

Cycles of Deprivation and the Ghetto Underclass Debate

In the mid-1960s, urban analysts began to speak of a new dimension to the urban crisis in the form of a large subpopulation of low-income families and individuals whose behavior contrasted sharply with the behavior of the general population.[1] Despite a high rate of poverty in ghetto neighborhoods throughout the first half of the twentieth century, rates of inner-city joblessness, teenage pregnancies, out-of-wedlock births, female-headed families, welfare dependency, and serious crime were significantly lower than in later years and did not reach catastrophic proportions until the mid-1970s.

These increasing rates of social dislocation signified changes in the social organization of inner-city areas. Blacks in Harlem and in other ghetto neighborhoods did not hesitate to sleep in parks, on fire escapes, and on rooftops during hot summer nights in the 1940s and 1950s, and whites frequently visited inner-city taverns and nightclubs.[2] There was crime, to be sure, but it had not reached the point where people were fearful of walking the streets at night, despite the overwhelming poverty in the area. There was joblessness, but it was nowhere near the proportions of unemployment and labor-force nonparticipation that have gripped ghetto communities since 1970. There were single-parent families, but they were a small minority of all black families and tended to be incorporated within extended family networks and to be headed not by unwed teenagers and young adult women but by middle-aged women who usually were widowed, separated, or divorced. There were welfare recipients, but only a very small percentage of the families could be said to be welfare-dependent. In short, unlike the present period. Inner-city communities prior to 1960 exhibited the features of social organization – including a sense of community, positive neighborhood identification, and explicit norms and sanctions against aberrant behavior.[3]

Although liberal urban analysts in the mid-1960s hardly provided a definitive explanation of changes in the social organization of inner-city neighborhoods, they forcefully and candidly discussed the rise of social dislocations among the ghetto underclass....

...the debate over the problems of the ghetto underclass has been dominated in recent years by conservative spokespersons as the views of liberals have gradually become more diffused and ambiguous. Liberals have traditionally emphasized how the plight of disadvantaged groups can be related to the problems of the broader society, including problems of discrimination and social-class subordination. They have also emphasized the need for progressive social change, particularly through governmental programs, to open the opportunity structure. Conservatives, in contrast, have traditionally stressed the importance of different group values and competitive resources in accounting for the experiences of the disadvantaged; if reference is made to the larger society, it is in terms of the assumed adverse effects of various government programs on individual or group behavior and initiative....

The declining influence of the liberal perspective on the ghetto underclass

The liberal perspective on the ghetto underclass has become less persuasive and convincing in public discourse principally because many of those who represent traditional liberal views on social issues have been reluctant to discuss openly or, in some instances, even to acknowledge the sharp increase in social pathologies in ghetto communities. This is seen in the four principal ways in which liberals have recently addressed the subject....

One approach is to avoid describing any behavior that might be construed as unflattering or stigmatizing to ghetto residents, either because of a fear of providing fuel for racist arguments or because of a concern of being charged with "racism" or with "blaming the victim."... liberal social scientists, social workers, journalists, policy-makers, and civil rights leaders have been, until very recently, reluctant to make any reference to race at all when discussing issues such as the increase of violent crime, teenage pregnancy, and out-of-wedlock births. The more liberals have avoided writing about or researching these problems, the more conservatives have rushed headlong to fill the void with popular explanations of inner-city social dislocations that much of the public finds exceedingly compelling.

A second liberal approach to the subject of underclass and urban social problems is to refuse even to use terms such as *under-*

class. As one spokesman put it: "'Underclass' is a destructive and misleading label that lumps together different people who have different problems. And that it is the latest of a series of popular labels (such as the 'lumpen proletariat,' 'undeserving poor,' and the 'culture of poverty') that focuses on individual characteristics and thereby stigmatizes the poor for their poverty."[4] However, the real problem is not the term *underclass* or some similar designation but the fact that the term has received more systematic treatment from conservatives, who tend to focus almost exclusively on individual characteristics, than from liberals, who would more likely relate these characteristics to the broader problems of society. While some liberals debate whether terms such as *underclass* should even be used, conservatives have made great use of them in developing popular arguments about life and behavior in the inner city.[5]...

Today's ghetto neighborhoods are populated almost exclusively by the most disadvantaged segments of the black urban community, that heterogeneous grouping of families and individuals who are outside the mainstream of the American occupational system. Included in this group are individuals who lack training and skills and either experience long-term unemployment or are not members of the labor force, individuals who are engaged in street crime and other forms of aberrant behavior, and families that experience long-term spells of poverty and/or welfare dependency. These are the populations to which I refer when I speak of the *underclass*. I use this term to depict a reality not captured in the more standard designation *lower class*.

In my conception, the term *underclass* suggests that changes have taken place in ghetto neighborhoods, and the groups that have been left behind are collectively different from those that lived in these neighborhoods in earlier years. It is true that long-term welfare families and street criminals are distinct groups, but they live and interact in the same depressed community and they are part of the population that has, with the exodus of the more stable work-ing-and middle-class segments, become increasingly isolated socially from main-stream patterns and norms of behavior. It is also true that certain groups are stigma-tized by the label *underclass*, just as some people who live in depressed central-city communities are stigmatized by the term *ghetto* or *inner city*, but it would be far worse to obscure the profound changes in the class structure and social behavior of ghetto neighborhoods by avoiding the use of the term *underclass*. Indeed, the real challenge is to describe and explain these developments accurately so that liberal pol-icymakers can appropriately address them. And it is difficult for me to see how this can be accomplished by rejecting a term that aids in the description of ghetto social transformations.

A third liberal approach to the subject of problems in the inner city and the ghetto underclass is to emphasize or embrace se-lective evidence that denies the very exist-ence of an urban underclass. We have seen this approach in two principal ways. First, . . . a number of liberals, particularly black liberals, began in the late 1960s and early 1970s to emphasize the positive aspects of the black experience.[6] Thus earlier arguments, which asserted that some aspects of ghetto life were patho-logical,[7] were rejected and replaced with those that accented the strengths of the black community. Arguments extolling the strengths and virtues of black families re-placed those that described the breakup of black families. In fact, aspects of ghetto behavior described as pathological in the studies of the mid-1960s were reinterpreted or redefined as functional because, it was argued, blacks were demonstrating their ability to survive and even flourish in an economically depressed and racist environ-ment. Ghetto families were portrayed as resilient and capable of adapting creatively to an oppressive society. These revisionist arguments purporting to "liberate" the social sciences from the influence of racism helped shift the focus of social scientists away from discussions of the consequences

of racial isolation and economic class sub-ordination to discussions of black achieve-ment. Since the focus was solely on black achievement, little attention was paid to internal differences within the black com-munity. Moreover, since the problems were defined in racial terms, very little discussion was devoted either to problems created by economic shifts and their impact on the poor black community or to the need for economic reform. In short, such arguments effectively diverted attention from the ap-propriate solutions to the dreadful eco-nomic condition of poor blacks and made it difficult for blacks to see, in the words of one perceptive observer, "how their fate is inextricably tied up with the structure of the American economy."[8]

More recently, in response to arguments by conservatives that a growing number of inner-city residents get locked into a culture of poverty and a culture of welfare, some liberals have been quick to cite research indicating that only a small proportion of Americans in poverty and on welfare are persistently poor and persistently on wel-fare. The problem of long-term poverty and welfare dependency began to receive detailed and systematic empirical attention when it became possible to track the actual experiences of the poor and those who re-ceive welfare with adequate longitudinal data provided by the Michigan Panel Study of Income Dynamics (PSID). A series of initial studies based on the PSID revealed that only a very small percentage of those in poverty and on welfare were long-term cases. For example, one study found that only 3 percent of the population was poor throughout a ten-year time span;[9] another study reported that only 2.2 percent of the population was poor eight of the ten years (1968–78) covered in the research.[10] These studies have been widely cited and have been said to provide powerful evidence against the notion of an underclass.[11]

However, more recent studies based on the PSID data seriously challenge interpret-ations based on these findings.[12] Specific-ally, these studies revealed that the previous PSID research on spells of poverty and welfare dependency observed over a fixed time frame – say, eight or ten years – under-estimated the length of spells because some individuals who appear to have short spells of poverty or welfare receipt are actually beginning or ending long spells. To correct for this problem, the more recent studies first identified spells of poverty and welfare receipt, then calculated exit probabilities by year to estimate the duration of spells. With this revised methodology it was found that, although most people who become poor during some point in their lives experience poverty for only one or two years, a substantial subpopulation remains in poverty for a very long time. Indeed, these long-term poor constitute about 60 percent of those in poverty at any given point in time and are in a poverty spell that will last eight or more years. Furthermore, families headed by women are likely to have longer spells of poverty – at a given point in time, the average child who became poor when the family makeup changed from married-couple to female-headed is in the midst of a poverty spell lasting almost twelve years. It was reported that "some 20 percent of poverty spells of children begin with birth. When they do, they tend to last ten years. The average poor black child today appears to be in the midst of a poverty spell which will last for almost two decades."[13] Similar findings were reported on spells of welfare receipt. Long-term welfare mothers tend to belong to racial minorities, were never married, and are high school dropouts.

Thus, despite the findings and interpret-ations of earlier PSID reports on long-term poverty and welfare dependency, there is still a firm basis for accepting the argument that a ghetto underclass has emerged and exhibits the problems of long-term poverty and welfare dependency. Accordingly, lib-eral attempts to deny the existence of an underclass on the basis of the earlier opti-mistic Michigan panel studies now seem especially questionable.

Finally, a fourth liberal approach to the subject of the ghetto underclass and urban social problems is to acknowledge the rise in inner-city social dislocations while em-phasizing racism as the explanation of these changes. There are two basic themes associated with this thesis. The more popu-lar theme is that the cycle of pathology characterizing the ghetto can only be com-prehended in terms of racial oppression and that "the racial dehumanization Americans permit is a symptom of the deep-seated, systematic and most dangerous social dis-ease of racism."[14] In response to this argu-ment, I should like to emphasize that no serious student of American race relations can deny the relationship between the dis-proportionate concentration of blacks in impoverished urban ghettos and historic racial subjugation in American society. But to suggest that the recent rise of social dislocations among the ghetto underclass is due mainly to contemporary racism, which in this context refers to the "conscious re-fusal of whites to accept blacks as equal human beings and their willful, systematic effort to deny blacks equal opportunity,"[15] is to ignore a set of complex issues that are difficult to explain with a race-specific thesis. More specifically, it is not readily apparent how the deepening economic class divisions between the haves and have-nots in the black community can be accounted for when this thesis is invoked,[16] especially when it is argued that this same racism is directed with equal force across class boundaries in the black community.[17] Nor is it apparent how racism can result in a more rapid social and economic deterior-ation in the inner city in the post-civil rights period than in the period that immediately preceded the notable civil rights victories. To put the question more pointedly, even if racism continues to be a factor in the social and economic progress of some blacks, can it be used to explain the sharp increase in inner-city social dislocations since 1970? Unfortunately, no one who supports the contemporary racism thesis has provided adequate or convincing answers to this question.

The problem is that the proponents of the contemporary racism thesis fail to distinguish between the past and the present effects of racism on the lives of different segments of the black population. This is unfortunate because once the effects of historic racism are recognized it becomes easier to assess the importance of current racism in relation to nonracial factors such as economic-class position and modern economic trends. Moreover, once this distinction is made it clears the way for appropriate policy recommendations. Policy programs based on the premise that the recent rise of social dislocations, such as joblessness, in the inner city is due to current racism will be significantly different from policy programs based on the premise that the growth of these problems is due more to nonracial factors. . . .

In sum, the liberal perspective on the ghetto underclass and inner-city social dislocations is less persuasive and influential in public discourse today because many of those who represent the traditional liberal views on social issues have failed to address straightforwardly the rise of social pathologies in the ghetto. As I have attempted to show, some liberals completely avoid any discussion of these problems, some eschew terms such as *underclass*, and others embrace selective evidence that denies the very existence of an underclass and behavior associated with the underclass or rely on the convenient term *racism* to account for the sharp rise in the rates of social dislocation in the inner city. The combined effect of these tendencies is to render liberal arguments ineffective and to enhance conservative arguments on the underclass, even though the conservative thesis is plagued with serious problems of interpretation and analysis. It is to the conservative perspective that I now turn.

The increasing influence of the conservative perspective on the underclass

If the most forceful and influential arguments on the ghetto underclass in the 1960s were put forth by liberals, conservative arguments have moved to the forefront

in the 1980s, even though they have undergone only slight modification since the 1960s. Indeed, many students of social behavior recognize that the conservative thesis represents little more than the application of the late Oscar Lewis's culture-of-poverty arguments to the ghetto underclass.[18] Relying on participant observation and life-history data to analyze Latin American poverty, Lewis described the culture of poverty as "both an adaptation and a reaction of the poor to their marginal position in a class stratified, highly individuated, capitalistic society."[19] However, he also noted that once the culture of poverty comes into existence, "it tends to perpetuate itself from generation to generation because of its effect on the children. By the time slum children are age six or seven," argued Lewis, "they have usually absorbed the basic values and attitudes of their subculture and are not psychologically geared to take full advantage of changing conditions or increased opportunities which may occur in their life-time."[20]

Although Lewis was careful to point out that basic structural changes in society may alter some of the cultural characteristics of the poor, conservative students of inner-city poverty who have built on his thesis have focused almost exclusively on the interconnection between cultural traditions, family history, and individual character. For example, they have argued that a ghetto family that has had a history of welfare dependency will tend to bear offspring who lack ambition, a work ethic, and a sense of self-reliance.[21] Some even suggest that ghetto underclass individuals have to be rehabilitated culturally before they can advance in society.[22] . . .

. . . liberal scholars in the 1960s argued that cultural values do not ultimately determine behavior or success. Rather, cultural values emerge from specific social circumstances and life chances and reflect one's class and racial position. Thus, if underclass blacks have limited aspirations or fail to plan for the future, it is not ultimately the product of different cultural norms but the consequence of restricted opportunities, a bleak future, and feelings of resignation resulting from bitter personal experiences. Accordingly, behavior described as socially pathological and associated with the ghetto underclass should be analyzed not as a cultural aberration but as a symptom of class and racial inequality.[23] As economic and social opportunities change, new behavioral solutions originate and develop into patterns, later to be complemented and upheld by norms. If new situations appear, both the patterns of behavior and the norms eventually undergo change. "Some behavioral norms are more persistent than others," wrote Herbert Gans in 1968, "but over the long run, all of the norms and aspirations by which people live are nonpersistent: they rise and fall with changes in situations."[24] ...

By 1980, however, the problems of inner-city social dislocations had reached such catastrophic proportions that liberals were forced to readdress the question of the ghetto underclass, but this time their reactions were confused and defensive. The extraordinary rise in inner-city social dislocations following the passage of the most sweeping antidiscrimination and antipoverty legislation in the nation's history could not be explained by the 1960 explanations of ghetto-specific behavior. Moreover, because liberals had ignored these problems throughout most of the 1970s, they had no alternative explanations to advance and were therefore ill prepared to confront a new and forceful challenge from conservative thinkers. The result was a diffused and confused reaction typified by the four responses to the subject that I discussed above.

The new conservative challenge does not represent a change in the basic premise of the interplay among cultural tradition, family biography, and individual character; rather, it builds on this premise with the argument that the growth of liberal social policies has exacerbated, not alleviated, ghetto-specific cultural tendencies and problems of inner-city social dislocations. Widely read neoconservative books such as *Thinking about Crime, Wealth and*

Poverty, Civil Rights: Rhetoric or Reality, and *Losing Ground* present a range of arguments on the negative effects of liberal social policy on the behavior and values of the ghetto underclass.[25] Thus liberal changes in the criminal justice system are said to have decreased the sanctions against aberrant behavior and thereby contributed to the rise of serious inner-city crime since 1965; affirmative action pressures are linked with the deteriorating plight of the underclass because, while they increase the demand for highly qualified minority members, they decrease the demand for the less qualified due to the cost, particularly at times of discharge and promotion; and the Great Society and other social welfare programs have been self-defeating because they have made people less self-reliant, promoted joblessness, and contributed to the rise of out-of-wedlock births and female-headed families. Thus, unlike their liberal counterparts, conservatives have attempted to explain the sharp rise in the rates of social dislocation among the ghetto underclass, and their arguments, which strike many as new and refreshing, have dominated public discourse on this subject for the last several years. But there are signs that this is beginning to change. There are signs of a liberal revival. And the spark for this revival, I believe, is Charles Murray's provocative book, *Losing Ground.*

Probably no work has done more to promote the view that federal programs are harmful to the poor....Indeed, *Losing Ground* not only attributes increasing poverty to programs such as those of the Great Society, it also explains increasing rates of joblessness, crime, out-of-wedlock births, female-headed families, and welfare dependency, especially among the ghetto underclass, in terms of such programs as well. Murray argues that recent changes in social policy have effectively changed the rewards and penalities that govern human behavior....

Whereas Murray contends that despite substantial increases in spending on social programs, from 1968 to 1980 the poverty rate failed to drop – thus indicating that these programs were not successful – liberal critics argue that Murray "neglects the key facts that contradict his message," namely, that the unemployment rate in 1980 was twice that of 1968.[26] When unemployment increases, poverty also rises. What Murray fails to consider, they argue, is that many people slipped into poverty because of the economic downturn and were lifted out by the broadening of benefits. According to Robert Greenstein, director of the Center on Budget and Policy Priorities in Washington, DC, "The two trends roughly balanced each other and the poverty rate remained about the same" from 1968 to 1980.[27]

Murray, on the other hand, maintains that the slowing of the economy had nothing at all to do with the failure of the poverty rate to decline in the 1970s. He argues that the economy, according to the Gross National Product (GNP), grew more in the 1970s than in the 1950s, when the poverty rate dropped. Liberal critics have responded with the argument that, although growth in the GNP does create jobs, in the 1970s the growth was insufficient to handle the "unusually large numbers of women and young people (from the baby boom generation) who were entering the job market," resulting in an increase in unemployment. Moreover, real wages, which had risen steadily in the 1950s and 1960s, stopped growing in the 1970s. Greenstein states that "when unemployment rises and real wages fall, poverty increases – and low income groups (especially black males) are affected the most." Thus, liberal critics maintain that far from being unimportant, the economy was the major cause of the failure of poverty to decline in the 1970s. If it had not been for the benefit programs that Murray attacks, the poverty rate would have risen further still.[28]

Murray's book has indeed "lit a fire" under liberals; if these and other responses are any indication, we could be seeing the beginnings of a major revival in the liberal approach to the ghetto underclass phenomenon. . . .

NOTES

1   Kenneth B. Clark, *Dark Ghetto: Dilemmas of Social Power* (New York: Harper and Row, 1965); Lee Rainwater, "Crucible of Identity: The Negro Lower-Class Family," *Daedalus* 95 (Winter 1966): 176–216; Daniel P. Moynihan, *The Negro Family: The Case for National Action* (Washington, DC: Office of Policy Planning and Research, US Department of Labor, 1965); and idem, "Employment, Income and the Ordeal of the Negro Family," in *The Negro American*, ed. Talcott Parsons and Kenneth B. Clark (Boston: Beacon Press, 1965), pp. 134–59.

2   David L. Lewis, *When Harlem Was in Vogue* (New York: Alfred A. Knopf, 1981); Clark, *Dark Ghetto*; and Thomas Sowell, *Civil Rights: Rhetoric or Reality?* (New York: William Morrow, 1984).

3   See St. Clair Drake and Horace R. Cayton, *Black Metropolis: A Study of Negro Life in a Northern City*, vol. 2 (New York: Harper and Row, 1945).

4   Richard McGahey, "Poverty's Voguish Stigma," *New York Times*, March 12, 1982, p. 29. Also see, Michael B. Katz, *In the Shadow of the Poorhouse: A Social History of Welfare in America* (New York: Basic Books, 1986), esp. pp. 274–5.

5   For a discussion of recent conservative analyses of the underclass, see Ken Auletta, *The Underclass* (New York: Random House, 1982).

6   Moynihan, *Negro Family*. See, e.g., Joyce Ladner, ed., *The Death of White Sociology* (New York: Random House, 1973); Robert B. Hill, *The Strength of Black Families* (New York: Emerson Hall, 1972); Nathan Hare, "The Challenge of a Black Scholar," *Black Scholar* 1 (1969): 58–63; Abdul Hakim Ibn Alkalimat [Gerald McWorter], "The Ideology of Black Social Science," *Black Scholar* 1 (1969): 28–35; and Robert Staples, "The Myth of the Black Matriarchy," *Black Scholar* 2 (1970): 9–16.

7   Clark, *Dark Ghetto*; E. Franklin Frazier, *The Negro Family in the United States* (Chicago: University of Chicago Press, 1939); Moynihan, *Negro Family*; Rainwater, "Crucible of Identity."

8   Orlando Patterson, *Ethnic Chauvinism: The Reactionary Impulse* (New York: Stein and Day, 1977), p. 155. Also see Martin Kilson, "Black Social Classes and Intergenerational Poverty," *Public Interest* 64 (Summer 1981): 58–78.

9   Martha S. Hill, "Some Dynamic Aspects of Poverty," in *Five Thousand American Families: Patterns of Economic Progress*, eds. M. S. Hill, D. H. Hill, and J. N. Morgan, vol. 19 (Ann Arbor: Institute for Social Research, University of Michigan Press, 1981).

10 Mary Corcoran and Greg J. Duncan, "Demographic Aspects of the Underclass," paper presented at the Annual Meeting of the Population Association of America, Pittsburgh, PA 1983.

11 See, e.g., Katz, *Shadow of the Poorhouse*.

12 Mary Jo Bane and David T. Ellwood, "Slipping into and out of Poverty: The Dynamics of Spells," working paper no. 1199, National Bureau of Economic Research, Cambridge, Mass., 1983; idem, *The Dynamics of Dependence: The Routes to Self-Sufficiency* (Washington, DC: US Department of Health and Human Services, 1983).

13 Bane and Ellwood, *Slipping into and out of Poverty*, p. 36.

14 Kenneth B. Clark, "The Role of Race," *New York Times Magazine*, Oct. 5, 1980, p. 109.

15 Carl Gershman, "Carl Gershman Responds," *New York Times Magazine*, Oct. 5, 1980, p. 33.

16 See William Julius Wilson, *The Declining Significance of Race: Blacks and Changing American Institutions*, 2nd ed. (Chicago: University of Chicago Press, 1980).

17 See, e.g., Clark, "Role of Race"; Alphonoso Pinkney, *The Myth of Black Progress* (Boston: Cambridge University Press, 1984); and Charles V. Willie, "The Inclining Significance of Race," *Society* 15 (July/Aug. 1978): 10, 12–15.

18 Oscar Lewis, "The Culture of Poverty," in *On Understanding Poverty: Perspectives from the Social Sciences*, ed. Daniel Patrick Moynihan (New York: Basic Books,

1968), pp. 187–200. Also see *idem, Five Families: Mexican Case Studies in the Culture of Poverty* (New York: Basic Books, 1959); *idem, The Children of Sanchez* (New York: Random House, 1961); and idem, *La Vida: A Puerto Rican Family in the Culture of Poverty – San Juan and New York* (New York: Random House, 1966).

19 Lewis, "Culture of Poverty," p. 188.

20 Ibid.

21 For a good discussion of these points, see Auletta, *Underclass*, esp. chap. 2.

22 See, e.g., Edward Banfield, *The Unheavenly City*, 2nd ed. (Boston: Little, Brown, 1970).

23 See Herbert J. Gans, "Culture and Class in the Study of Poverty: An Approach to Anti-Poverty Research," in Moynihan, *On Understanding Poverty*, pp. 201–8; Lee Rainwater, "The Problem of Lower-Class Culture and Poverty-War Strategy," in Moynihan, *Understanding Poverty*, pp. 229–59; Hylan Lewis, "Culture, Class and the Behavior of Low-Income Families," paper prepared for Conference on Views of Lower-Class Culture, New York, NY, June 1963; and Stephen Steinberg, *The Ethnic Myth: Race, Ethnicity and Class in America* (New York: Atheneum, 1981). Steinberg's analysis is a succinct restatement of points made by liberal critics in the 1960s.

24 Gans, "Culture and Class," p. 211.

25 James Q. Wilson, *Thinking about Crime* (New York: Basic Books, 1975); George Gilder, *Wealth and Poverty* (New York: Basic Books, 1981); Sowell, *Civil Rights*; Charles Murray, *Losing Ground: American Social Policy, 1950–1980* (New York: Basic Books, 1984).

26 See, e.g., Robert Greenstein, "Losing Faith in 'Losing Ground,'" *New Republic*, March 25, 1985, pp. 12–17; Christopher Jencks, "How Poor Are the Poor?" *New York Review of Books*, May 9, 1985, pp. 41–9; and Sheldon Danziger and Peter Gottschalk, "Social Programs – A Partial Solution to, But Not a Cause of Poverty: An Alternative to Charles Murray's View," *Challenge Magazine*, May/June 1985.

27 Greenstein, "Losing Faith," p. 14.

28 Ibid., p. 15; Danziger and Gottschalk, "Social Programs"; Jencks, "How Poor Are the Poor"; Robert Kuttner, "A Flawed

Case for Scrapping What's Left of the Great Society," *Washington Post Book World*, Dec. 17, 1984, pp. 34–5; David Ellwood and Lawrence Summers, "Poverty in America: Is Welfare the Answer or the Problem?" paper presented at a conference on Poverty and Policy. Retrospect and Prospects, Williamsburg, Va., Dec. 6, 1984.

Chapter 29

Bastee Eviction and Housing Rights: A Case of Dhaka, Bangladesh

Mohammed Mahbubur Rahman

1 Introduction

The existence of *bastees*[1] is very common in the urban areas of Bangladesh. The National Housing Policy (NHP) recognises the rights of the poor *basteebashees* to proper housing. The government and various other authorities have, however, ignored the policy provisions, and practiced forced eviction. There have been many such incidents, which show the government's unwillingness to solve the bastee problem more humanely. Public housing schemes hardly cater for the poor, and its limited provisions are grossly inadequate.

Many international declarations and charters have opposed forced eviction of squatters without relocation. However, Bangladesh has not observed these resolutions. Though many developing countries have started to look sympathetically towards squatters, Bangladesh has not shown any inclination towards improving their environment. Several options are available through which the poor urban dwellers can obtain housing land with secured tenure.

Presently, awareness of the positive role of the *bastees* is growing in Bangladesh. Several NGOs are working to establish the housing rights of the urban poor. Nevertheless, this requires a change of attitude by the authority towards the issues of urban poor, their housing rights, migration and their *bastee* status, the abandonment of the government's traditional role as 'provider', and a concerted effort by the government, NGOs and communities to solve the problem.

2 Bastees in Dhaka

A high rate of urbanisation is a typical phenomenon in many Third World countries. Most of this is the result of unabated migration by impoverished migrants from rural areas. Due to their inability to break into the formal economic sectors of the cities to which they have migrated, 30–50% of the urban populations are either homeless or inadequately housed in informal settlement areas (Sinha, 1994a). The growth of these informal settlements has shown no sign of retarding despite the efforts of the governments, international agencies and institutions.

The present rate of urbanisation in Bangladesh, for example, is above 5%, making it one of the highest in the world. Dhaka, the capital city with an estimated present population of 10 million, receives most of this increased population. Of the population growth, 55% is accounted by migration (McDonald, Culpin Associates, & EPS, 1997). According to Rahman & Seraj (1994), the equivalent of 10 busloads of migrants arrive in the city every day. Most of them resort to squatting.

Bastee settlements were initially formed because of the transfer of the capital out of East Bengal in the early-18th century and later during the period of colonisation. The rate of *bastee* formation accelerated with independence in 1971. In the early-1970s, landlessness and unemployment in the rural areas increased along with natural calamities and oppression by the new socio-political elite. As a result, urban migration increased and growth of new *bastee* areas took place all over Dhaka. The 1974–5 famine and flood pushed a large number of the rural poor who needed jobs, food and shelter into Dhaka. In early 1975, all *basteebashees* were resettled on three unutilised government-acquired sites at the outskirts of the city in a large-scale eviction. However, they soon started to form new bastees in the main city as the resettlement camps had no jobs or commuting facilities (Hasnath, 1977; Ullah, 1994). Fresh *bastees* were formed in Dhaka in the first 15 years of Independence at a rate of 20 settlements per year (CUS, 1988) and then at a rate of 100 settlements per year (IDSS-BCL-Prashika, 1996).

It is not easy to estimate the total number of either *bastees* or *basteebashees*. Many *bastees* are mobile in character and some may disappear over time (Mumtaz, 1993; IDSS, 1996). The shacks housing the *basteebashees* are not recognised as dwelling units, and hence are not covered in the national census. Estimates in several studies show that in 1990 there were 1 million *basteebashees* in 2156 clusters (defined as consisting of at least 10 shelters) within the Dhaka metropolitan area (BSNC, 1990). The number increased over the next 6 years to 1.5 million in over 2800 clusters (IDSS, 1996). The present *bastee* population in Dhaka exceeds 40% of the city's population, or makes up about one-sixth of the population of the Statistical Metropolitan Area.

More than half of the urban population in Bangladesh lives below the poverty line (IDSS, 1996; Islam, 1996), and the majority of these live in the *bastees*. The situation of Dhaka's *bastees* is similar in many ways to those of other cities in developing countries. These are characterised by high-density living, unsanitary situation, unhygienic environment lacking basic services and amenities, high rate of illiteracy, unemployment and crime, environmental and psychological degradation, and precarious health situation (BIDS, 1988; Rahman, 1990; Mizanuddin, 1994; Paul-Majumder, 1994; IDSS, 1996). The *basteebashees* find employment mainly in the informal sector, which is typified by low wages, long working hours and insecurity (Paul-Majumder & Choudhury-Zahir, 1994). The poor only just fulfil the basic needs for survival as resources are mostly controlled by the rich (Islam, 1978; Siddiqui, Qadir, Alamgir, & Haq, 1990; Ghafur, 1999).

3 Bastee Eviction

There have been numerous cases in which the *bastees'* shacks have been demolished in the process of evicting the *basteebashees* in the urban areas of Bangladesh, particularly from Dhaka. At the beginning of the Bangladesh War of Liberation in 1971, the Pakistani army demolished the *bastees* formed before the independence; and thousands of *basteebashees* were either killed or made refugees. Another major incident that occurred after Independence was the eviction of about 173,000 *basteebashees* in the first week of January 1975, carried out by the police and paramilitary forces. In this instance, not even the people's representatives or the relevant government officials were consulted before the decision to remove them was made and executed. A one-party government was in power at that time that ignored the rights of the *basteebashees*. This was in part because the *basteebashees* neither had voting rights, nor was their participation in political rallies required anymore (Rahman, 1990; Mizanuddin, 1994).

In November 1983, fences made of metal sheets were erected along the 15 km long road leading to the President's house from the airport. This was done to hide the views of the bastees from foreign dignitaries.

In April 1990, several inmates of Kalyanpur bastee died in an arson attack that was used by the hired *mastaans* as a means of evicting them from their homes. In fact, arson has been used in other bastees in many parts of the City to clear the squatters; such as in Kamalapur, Mohammedpur, Tejgaon, Maghbazaar, Babupura and Kazipara. In August of the same year, one child fell under a bulldozer and died in Agargaon *bastee* while an eviction operation was being carried out. On that day, 20,000 shelters were demolished.

The largest *bastee* before the Independence was formed along an old railway track that had not been used since 1967. This *bastee* was demolished, but was re-formed only to be demolished again in 1971 and 1975. Since 1979, however, a new *bastee* started to form in Palashi on part of the old track that has now been converted into a poorly utilised avenue. On a rainy day in October 1992, it was demolished again on the initiative of Dhaka's Mayor. A subsequent study has shown that this *bastee* could have been relocated on only 2% of the adjacent government land that had remained unused for 50 years (Zia, 1992). New *bastees* have grown in nearby areas, but are under a constant fear of eviction (Murshed, 1994).

In February 1994, the Public Works Department asked the Agargaon *basteebashees* to remove their shelters within a week. This was done to please the Prime Minister, who was due to be in the vicinity of this largest *bastee* of the city to initiate the National Science and Technology Week. Ironically the *bastee*, a stronghold of the ruling party, was named after it.

Three months later in May 1994, the Railway Minister ordered part of the *bastees* along the railway track to be evicted within 72 h, citing accident risk. This was duly complied with. Both of these incidents ignored the provisions of the just adopted NHP, and nearly 10,000 families were affected, and their housing situation further aggravated.

The students of the Dhaka Medical College boycotted classes for a couple of months in late 1994. They were demanding the eviction of employees living in a nearby *bastee* so that an auditorium could be constructed there. This was supported by the college doctors. The ensuing impasse was resolved temporarily by the Health Minister who promised an alternative location for resettling the threatened families; this was never followed up.

Petty businessmen on footpaths have been evicted several times, which has affected the livelihoods of nearly a million people, including their dependants. The evictees were promised relocation to planned government shopping complexes, which was never materialised. On the Labour Day of 1996, which coincided with a Muslim holy festival, the Azimpore *basteebashees* got engaged in a fight with police who came to evict them.

There were several incidents of eviction, court cases, and announcements of government programs to 'rehabilitate' the *basteebashees* during the month of August 1999. In these incidents, at least 50,000 people were evicted by the police after one of their constables was killed by petty narcotics traders who had allegedly taken refuge in the *bastees*. In the end, the Court expressed its concern with the incidents, along with similar reactions from the NGOs and IFAs, and most other sections of the civil society.

The government authorities have shown no qualms about regularly evicting bastees, which have been located on government land (Rabinson, 1995). An estimated 200,000 people have been affected and US$ 2.5 million worth of properties were destroyed in 30 cases of major forced eviction in Dhaka from 1990 to 1992 (Sinha, 1994b). The actual number of evictions could have been much higher as not all cases are reported either to the relevant authority, by police, by the poor individuals, their organisations or the media. The authorities adopt cruel and brutal means in the evictions. The most frequently used technique, which is both cheap and effective, is to cordon off the *bastees*, ignite them and beat the *basteebashees* to ensure that they leave (Rabinson, 1995; Sinha, 1994a,b). In every summer for the last several years, women and children have been killed and many small plastic and moulding industries destroyed by arson in the Shahidnagar-Islambag-Rasulpur *bastee*.

The Government and Local Authority Land and Building (Recovery of Possession) Ordinance 1970 requires a 30 days notice to be given by the District Commissioner (DC) to legally evict unauthorised occupants. The order can also be obtained from a court of law, which however may allow a longer time. In reality, however, neither organisations nor individuals follow this regulation in carrying out evictions. In most cases, less than 48 hours is given to the *basteebashees* to abandon their shelters (Rabinson, 1995; Ferozuddin, 1999). Sometime, the immediate eviction is announced over a microphone and *mastaans* take advantage of the confusing situation. At other times, false stories about a pending eviction are spread and tolls collected from the *basteebashees* for so-called negotiation with the absent-authorities.

4 Housing rights

The rights of the urban poor, *basteebashees*, homeless and destitute have been recognised variously and repeatedly in international and national declarations and charters. Awareness to the need to intensify national and international efforts to produce, deliver and improve shelter for all was confirmed in the International Year of Shelter for the Homeless (1987). In view of this, the UN General Assembly endorsed the proposal of the Commission on Human Settlements (Resolution 43/18; 20.12.88) to undertake a global strategy for 'shelter for all by the year 2000'. The Assembly recognised that adequate and secure shelter is a basic human right and is vital for the fulfilment of human aspirations. The reso-

lution aims at the delivery of shelter for all income groups, particularly to those residing in slums and squatter settlements, which can only be successful if framed within a comprehensive shelter strategy that lists priorities, identifies affordable approaches and makes provisions for the proper allocation of resources.

Further resolutions state (No. 1992/14; 27.8.92):

1) Affirming that the practice of forced evictions constitutes a gross violation of human rights, in particular the right to adequate housing.
2) Urges Government to take immediate measures at all levels aimed at eliminating the practice of forced evictions.
3) Also urges Governments to confer legal security of tenure to all persons currently threatened with forced eviction and to adopt all necessary measures giving full protection against forced evictions based upon effective participation, consultation and negotiation with affected persons or groups.
4) Recommends that all Governments provide immediate restitution, compensation and/or appropriate and sufficient alternative accommodation or land consistent with their wishes or needs, to persons and communities which have been forcibly evicted following mutually satisfactory negotiations with the affected persons or groups.

The issue of eviction is also covered by other UN resolutions on forced migration and refugees. In August, 1991, an UN subcommittee on the prevention of discrimination and protection of minorities termed forced eviction "a gross violation of human rights". Governments were urged in the resolution to undertake policy and legislative measures to stop forced evictions. UN Commission on Human Rights resolution 1993/77 about eviction states that "every woman, man and child has the right to a secure place to live in peace and dignity"....

7 Seeking a Solution

Poor people migrate to the city to derive socio-economic benefits. They fail to meet their objectives primarily because of the inherent class system, and already low economic base and limited opportunities that exist. Various urban administrations, through alliance with the vested interest groups, serve the cause of the elite to appropriate all benefits, where there is a conscious attempt to exclude the *basteebashees*. In the context of the eviction-rehabilitation debate, the questions relative to the city and to 'urban reality' are not fully recognised. Neither is it confronted in a culture of 'power–project–profit', and is usually subject to a conspiracy of silence. When it is addressed, the discussion ranges from a sterile discussion of socially unresponsive policy prescriptions to a display of dubious technical solutions (Ghafur, 1999).

Two major impediments to addressing the housing rights of the urban poor in Bangladesh are the authority's hostile attitude to the *bastees* and lack of land ownership among the *basteebashees* (Rahman, 1994). The authority sees the *bastees* as overcrowded, ugly, full of anti-social elements, which cannot be allowed to exist. It follows that the 'problem' could be 'solved' by evicting the bastees (Amirul, 1999).

The Government gave five main justifications for the recent *bastee* eviction, which have been rejected by Ghafur (1999). The premise that the general public will be benefited with an improvement in the overall crime situation is highly disputed, as there is no data showing that most *basteesbashees* are involved in criminal activities. The premise that eviction will put an end to the illegal consumption of public utilities is not true given that there are more significant defaulters and the *basteebashees* are actually paying for their services. There is no substantation that eviction will result in the recovery of government land, as there is considerable under-utilised government land and government land that is occupied by influential bodies. The government also blamed the *bastees* for the overall reduction of the aesthetic environment of the city, which is only marginally true. After all, given the situation, they do not have any other option. The argument that relocation projects will boost the construction sector is acceptable, but it will be at the cost of the urban poor losing access to those housing and infrastructure developments (Ghafur, 1999).

Migration is both a consequence and a cause of urbanisation. In the underdeveloped world, one result of it is frequently a deteriorating housing situation. Yet it is very difficult to retard the migration process, as only the most radical of steps can slow down the process (Todaro, 1989). Therefore, approaches are needed to keep it within a manageable level, which will allow proper provision for the *basteebashees* who form the majority of the migrants. There are many things that the informal-based *basteebashees* can do better and more efficiently than the formal sector. They form a large labour force which is essential to the city's economy, and are found particularly in such sectors as rickshaw-pullers, garments workers and domestic servants, about 100,000 members in each occupation group (authors estimate). *Bastees* already hold all the expertise that goes into building cities. The building skill of the *basteebashees* could be channelled into improving their own living environments (Rahman, 1999). CUS (1983), Satter (1987), Hafiz (1987) and Miah et al. (1989) have all suggested that the *bastees* could be upgraded at half the relocation cost.

Widespread eviction is a threat to both the housing rights of the poor and the ingenious solutions they devise to the problems they face. Many countries have approached squatting problems through methods other than eviction. There has been an international change of attitude toward the squatters since the late 1960s, led by international financing agencies, such as the World Bank. *In situ* upgrading is seen as one of the most feasible solutions (Choguill, 1987). Many upgrading schemes have been successfully implemented in the cities of Asia and Africa. Context-sensitive innovative means have been applied to address the eviction issue in many cities. Most common of these, widely used in South-east Asian cities, is negotiated land buying with the help of saving and bank loans and resettlement through land-sharing. These are evidences of an increasingly positive recognition of squatters' rights in the developing countries.

For example, the Vacant Land Act in India prohibits landlords from evicting poor inhabitants. In Calcutta, regular squatters cannot be evicted, pavement sleepers can be evicted but must be relocated. In Bombay, pavement sleepers have been provided with night sleeping sheds and potable water. Similar strategies have been included in the Bangladesh NHP, but have not yet been implemented. In Thailand, the government does not assist a landowner in the eviction of settlers unless he negotiates land sharing. In Columbia, squatters are given a form of land title after 30 years of occupation. In Mexico, Korea and Pakistan, irregular settlements are regularised. Eviction is discouraged in Philippines; instead the country has various low-income housing programs, such as the Community Mortgage Program (CMP) and PHASE.

Land ownership is a critical issue in giving legitimacy to the squatter settlements. Without a secured tenure, no authority, service agency or lending institution feels confident in catering for squatters' needs. Without ownership, no squatter, who is always under the threat of eviction no matter how remote, wants to upgrade the shelter even if it is possible. Agricultural land which is near the city and which is likely to be taken over for unplanned urban uses, can be made available for the urban poor on a temporary basis, along the lines used in the tripartite arrangements in SIP. Government organisations frequently occupy more land than they would need which itself often encourage squatting (Islam & Choudhury, 1990). Therefore, the urban poor could be given security of

tenure on the areas where they are living if there is no acceptable relocation site and if no development program is imminent, by separating titles, development rights and use rights, or through long-term lease.

Scarcity of suitably placed developed and serviced land for housing in required amounts at an affordable price restricts the squatters' proper access to land. The solution to this problem is basic to the solution of the housing problem in general and squatting in particular. The major urban centres of many countries would benefit from an effective land policy and management program. Few cities would benefit as much as Dhaka, which is an unfairly structured city where the rich enjoy greater opportunities and public subsidies than the poor (Wilcox, 1983; Ghafur, 1999). Extensive intervention by the government in urban land markets was advocated in the 1976 Habitat Conference in Vancouver. Many techniques are available in this regard....

All housing developments in the Philippines and Indonesia allocate 20–40% of the housing provision to low-income groups. In Malaysia, the Philippines and Colombia the government sells serviced sites at subsidised prices to developers. This sale carries the condition that the developer would partly build non-profit social housing. A similar project was proposed in Bangladesh in Panchabati of the DND area in 1992. The proposed project faced stiff resistance from vested quarters that Rajuk could not overcome.

The plot reconstitution method has been popularly exploited to increase the supply of developed and serviced plots cheaply in most of the East and South-East Asian countries. Several attempts have been made to use techniques like guided land development, land pooling and plot reconstitution in Dhaka. None of these could be implemented due to the vehement opposition of the landowners and lack of commitment and willpower of the implementing agencies and the government (Haque, 1982; Rahman, 1991; McDonald, 1997; Muhit, 1996).

The spare plot mechanism, as tried in Mexico where double the required amount is allocated to low-income households to reap the enhanced value in future to cross-subsidise the cost..., is another technique that can be adopted in Dhaka's buoyant land market.

One impediment to innovative solutions is the general belief that any provision for the poor *basteebashees* in Bangladesh would result in huge subsidies to this group (Ferozuddin, 1999). Most *basteeba-shees* pay dearly to the mastaans for illegal service connections, and proportionately higher percentage of income on housing (Haque, 1982; Rahman, 1991; Paul-Majumder, 1994; Khalid, 1994; IDSS, 1996; Matin, 1998, Ferozuddin, 1999). This suggests that they can afford the cost, and therefore cost recovery from service provisions to the *bastees* is possible. One study has shown that the *basteebashees* have available resources to pay for housing (Rahman, 1991, 1993)....

Another problem in enhancing the housing rights of the poor seems to be the lack of responsibility and co-ordination among various efforts. This could be alleviated through the establishment of a National Housing Authority (NHA)...

A final impediment is the lack of social awareness and resulting little legislative support. Without them, eviction seems to be acceptable and inevitable to most people. Though some NGOs are changing the scenario through their advocacy schemes, legal education programs and legal battles, these events are neither well-publicised nor do they attract participation from a wider section of the society. Moreover, very few legal experts are willing to challenge evictions and provide free support to poor *basteebashees*. More appropriate laws need to be enacted on illegal occupation, forced eviction, use rights and development rights, second mortgage, temporary transfer of title and other rights, so that these can give adequate protection to the destitute and facilitate land development and sharing schemes.

8 Conclusion

The government in Bangladesh should recognise the housing rights of the poor in both its policies and programs to serve the needs of the majority of the population (Sinha, 1994a). Strong people's organisations can provoke and create an environment conducive to accomplish this. Co-operation among the policy making machinery, civil society and community organisations will facilitate this and overcome the situation where policies are rarely implemented due to the lack of political commitment and stability (Rahman, 1996). The present situation has made the policymakers largely impotent in finding a solution to the unabated urban housing crisis. Yet at the same time, the poor have demonstrated capabilities to build houses that are affordable and suitable to their socio-cultural needs. Given legitimacy and impetus, they can take up to solve their own problems. Eviction is not a pragmatic solution in a country with severe resource constraints. The state should protect both housing rights and property rights but must never negate one to protect the other (Sinha, 1994a). A change of attitude towards the *bastees* is urgently required at all levels. It should be made a political issue and included in manifestos of the political parties, who should have clear vision regarding the ways to face the situation.

The government in Bangladesh cannot solve the housing problem of the *basteeba-shees* on its own by acting as a provider. It should create an atmosphere conducive to the development of appropriate and affordable housing. Operated within a framework; The NGOs and CBOs can participate in social housing (Dunham, 1994; Rahman, 1999). The contention of this paper is that *in situ* upgrading along with provisions of land; materials and capital for house building can meet the housing need of the urban poor. Security of land tenure is a key to such development. The following aspects may be considered to recognise the housing rights of the *basteebashees*; and to improve their housing situation:

i) Accept the *basteebashees'* rights to decent living; evict only with relocation when the land is required for public-interest development projects.
ii) Strengthen the informal housing system already serving the poor, and encourage and improve these with proper new legislation.

iii) Invest in *bastees* upgrading in a way that leads to positive return; encourage domestic saving through appropriate tools; introduce micro-credit through CBOs for income generation informal sector entrepreneurship, environmental upgrading with self-help, and self-sustaining utility services.
iv) Develop unutilised land for the poor through schemes based on interim ownership, separate development right and cross-subsidy.

NOTES

1 The indigenous term, derived from *basati* meaning settlement, is used for the slums and squatter settlements in Bangladesh and part of India and Pakistan: the dwellers are termed *basteebashees* in Bengali.

REFERENCES

Amirul, A. (1999). Drug abuse and crime. *The Daily Star*, May 04, p. 4.

Bastee Samashya Nirasan Committee (BSNC, 1990). *Report of the slum problem eradication committee*. Ministry of Land Reform & Land Administration, Govt. of Bangladesh, Dhaka (in Bengali).

BIDS (1988). *A survey of the socio-economic condition of the squatter dwellers of Agargaon bastee*. Bangladesh Institute of Development Studies, Dhaka.

Choguill, C. L. (1987). *New communities for urban squatters – lessons from the plan that failed in Dhaka, Bangladesh*. New York: Plenum Press.

CUS (1983). *Slums in Dhaka City – a socio-economic survey for the feasibility of slum clearance and urban renewal programme in Dhaka City*. Centre for Urban Studies, Dhaka.

CUS (1988). *Slums and Squatters in Dhaka City*. Centre for Urban Studies, Dhaka.

Dunham, K. (1994). *Appropriate housing system for low-income working women*. Fulbright Research Report, USIS Dhaka.

Ferozuddin, M. (1999). Urban low-income housing – reality and need for change. *IAB seminar on occasion of the World Habitat Day*, Dhaka, Oct. 29.

Ghafur, S. (1999). For whom are our cities. *The Daily Star*, Oct. 4, p. 4.

Hafiz, R. (1987). *Sites and Services Schemes – a strategy for housing lower-income people in the Dhaka Metropolis*. unpublished MURP thesis, Dept. of URP, BUET, Bangladesh.

Haque, A. (1982). *The myth of self-help housing*. Stockholm: Royal Institute of Technology.

Hasnath, S. A. (1977). Re-squatting in Dhaka city – some policy proposals and techniques. *International conference on low-income housing technique and policy*. June, AIT, Bankok.

IDSS-BCL-Prashika (1996). *Report of the Urban Poverty Reduction Project*. ADB-GOB-LGED, Dhaka.

Islam, N. (1978). Urbanisation in Bangladesh-patterns, problems and policies. *South Asian regional seminar on small and medium sized towns in regional development*, Kathmandu, April 9–16.

Islam, N. (1996). *The urban poor in Bangladesh*. Dhaka: CUS.

Islam, N., & Choudhury, A. I. (1990). *Urban land management in Bangladesh*. Ministry of Land & Ministry of Works, GOB-UNESCAP, Dhaka.

Khalid, M. (1994). Ganaktuli Sweepers Colony – lessons in self building. *Earth (special issue on the Housing for the Urban Poor*), 01(1), 22–3.

Matin, N. (1998). *Social inter-mediation: Towards gaining access to water for squatter communities in Dhaka*. Dhaka; World Bank Working Paper.

McDonald, M., Culpin Associates & EPC (1997). *Dhaka metropolitan development program*. GOB.

Miah, A. K., Weber, K. E., & Islam, N. (1989). *Upgrading an urban settlement in Dhaka*. Human Settlement Division, AIT, Bangkok.

Mizanuddin, M. (1994). Community life in bastee – a study in Dhaka. *Earth (special issue on the Housing for the Urban Poor)*, 01(1), 10–11.

Muhit, M. A. (1996). *Public community partnership in urban land development at fringe areas of Dhaka megacity*. World Habitat Day Souvenir. Dhaka: RAJUK.

Mumtaz, S. (1993). *Low income housing delivery system with emphasis on rental housing*. unpublished M.Ing. thesis, Katholieke Universiteit Leuven, Leuven.

Murshed, M. (1994). Down to earth. *Earth (special issue on the Housing for the Urban Poor)*, 01(1), 26–7.

Paul-Majumder, P. (1994). Housing for the bastee dwellers. *Earth (special issue on the Housing for the Urban Poor)*, 01(1), 4–5.

Paul-Majumder, P., & Choudhury-Zahir, S. (1994). *Socio-economic condition of the female workers employed in the garments industry of Bangladesh*. Dhaka: Ekata Publication.

Rabinson, I. (1995). The safety of a slum; in *The Daily Star*, Dhaka, 15 Feb. 1995.

Rahman, M. M. (1990). Seventeen Facts on Dhaka's Bastees. *Ekistics*, *57*(342/343), 172–80.

Rahman, M. M. (1991). *Urban lower-middle- and middle-income housing in Dhaka, Bangladesh – an investigation into affordability and options*. unpublished Ph.D. thesis, University of Nottingham, UK.

Rahman, M. M. (1993) Housing attainability – a concept in solving the housing crisis in Bangladesh. *Planning for better living envir-*

onment, 2nd Congress of Asian planning schools, University of Hong Kong, Aug. 25–8.

Rahman, M. M. (1994). Urban poor's housing – an attitudinal problem. *Earth (special issue on the Housing for the Urban Poor)*, 01(1), 20–1.

Rahman, M. M. (1996). Housing policies in Bangladesh – the gap between strategies and programmes. XXIV IAHS World Housing Congress, Ankara, May 27th – June 01.

Rahman, M. M. (1999). *Role of NGOs in urban housing for the poor in Dhaka, Bangladesh*. Robert McNamara Fellowship Program, Economic Development Institute, The World Bank, Washington, DC.

Rahman, G. & Seraj, T. M. (1994). Housing problems in Dhaka metropolitan area; *International workshop on housing development & management*, Calcutta, Dec. 9–11, 1994.

Satter, Q. G. (1987). An approach of upgrading low-income urban settlements – a case study of Shahidnagar area in Dhaka city. unpublished MURP thesis, Dept. of URP, BUET, Bangladesh.

Siddiqui, K., Qadir, S., Alamgir, R., & Haq, S. (1990). *Social formation in Dhaka city*. Dhaka: University Press Ltd.

Sinha, D. (1994a). Urbanisation, eviction and housing right. *Earth (special issue on the Housing for the Urban Poor)*, 01(1), 1.

Sinha, D. (1994b). Stopping evictions in Asia – report from Bangladesh. *Housing by people in Asia*, Asian Coalition for Housing Rights, July, Bankok.

Todare, M. P. (1989). *Economic development in the third world*. New York: Longman.

Ullah, S. (1994). Two decades of basthuhara resettlement. *Earth (special issue on the Housing for the Urban Poor)*, 01(1), 6–7.

Wilcox, D. L. (1983). Urban land policy where the population bombs have already exploded. *HABITAT International*, *7*(5/6), 33–46.

Zia, A. H. (1992). *Resettlement of Palashi bastee*. Mimeo, M.Arch. term paper, Dept. of Architecture, BUET, Dhaka.

Chapter 30

After Tompkins Square Park: Degentrification and the Revanchist City

Neil Smith

The Revanchist City

After the stretch-limo optimism of the 1980s was rear-ended in the financial crash of 1987, then totalled by the onset of economic depression two years later, real estate agents and urban commentators quickly began deploying the language of 'de-gentrification' to represent the apparent reversal of urban change in the 1990s. 'With the realty boom gone bust in once gentrifying neighborhoods', writes one newspaper reporter, 'co-op converters and speculators who worked the streets and avenues...have fallen on hard times. That, in turn, has left some residents complaining of poor security and shoddy maintenance, while others are unable to sell their once-pricey apartments in buildings where a bank foreclosed on a converter.' 'Degentrification', explains one New York realtor, 'is a reversal of the gentrification process': in the 1990s, unlike the 1980s, 'there is no demand for pioneering, transitional, recently discovered locations'. Those few real estate deals that are transacted, he suggests, have retrenched to 'prime areas'.[1] 'In the 1970s, the theory was that a few gentrified areas would have a contagious effect and pull up neighboring districts' but 'that didn't happen', says another commentator. Most bluntly, in the words of census bureau demographer Larry Long, 'gentrification has come and gone'.[2]

Such media proclamations of the end of gentrification have begun to find broader support in the academic literature, where commentators were in any case usually more bromidic in their rhetoric about gentrification. In a clearly argued essay drawing on a Canadian case study, Larry Bourne anticipates 'the demise of gentrification' in those few cities where, he suggests, it had even a minor significance in the 1980s. Gentrification 'will be of less importance as a spatial expression of social change during the 1990s than it has been in the recent past'.[3] The last decade and a half, he suggests, were:

> a unique period in post-war urban development in North America – a period that combined the baby boom, rising educational levels, a rapid growth in service employment and real income, high rates of household formation, housing stock appreciation, public sector largesse, widespread (and speculative) private investment in the built environment, and high levels of foreign immigration. This set of circumstances, except for the latter, no longer prevails.[4]

The 'post-gentrification era' will experience a much reduced 'rate and impact of gentrification' in favor of a more unevenly developed, polarized and segregated city.

The coining of 'degentrification' and the prediction of gentrification's demise are part of a wider 'discourse of urban decline'[5] that has repossessed the public representation of urbanism in the 1990s, especially in the US. Historically, according to Beauregard, this discourse of decline has been 'more than the objective reporting of an uncontestable reality'; rather the discourse 'functions ideologically to shape our attention, provide reasons for how we should react in response, and convey a comprehensible, compelling, and reassuring story of the fate of the twentieth-century city in the United States'.[6] The recrudescence of this discourse in the 1990s has been dramatic. Gone is the white, upper-middle-class optimism of gentrification which was supposed to reclaim the 'new urban frontier' in the name of largely white 'pioneers',[7,8,9] an optimism that significantly modulated the discourse of decline during the 1980s. In its place, an unabated litany of crime and violence, drugs and unemployment, immigration and depravity – all laced through with terror – now script an unabashed recidivism of the city. The revanchism of contemporary urban management is a visceral component of the new anti-urbanism, a reaction against the 'theft' of the city by variously defined 'others', and in large part a defence of a traditionally white, middle-class world view. This revanchist anti-urbanism of the 1990s portends an occasionally vicious reaction against minorities, the working class, homeless people, the unemployed, women, gays and lesbians, immigrants.

The 'revanchist city' is becoming a powerful reality. More than anything it expresses a race/class/gender terror felt by middle and ruling-class whites who are suddenly stuck in place by a ravaged property market, the threat and reality of unemployment, the decimation of even minimal social services, and the emergence of minority and immigrant groups as well as women as powerful urban actors. The revanchist city is justified by the recidivism

of prime time – the local news, 'Cops', 'Hard Copy', 'NYPD Blue'; it represents a reaction to an urbanism defined by recurrent waves of unremitting danger and brutality fuelled by venal and uncontrolled passion. It is a place, in fact, where the reproduction of social relations has gone stupifyingly wrong,[10] but where the response is a virulent reassertion of many of the same oppressions and prescriptions that created the problem in the first place. 'In the US', says Ruth Gilmore, quoting Amiri Baraka, 'where real and imagined social relations are expressed most rigidly in race/gender hierarchies, the "reproduction" is really a *production* and its by-products, fear and fury, are in service of a "changing same": the apartheid local of American nationalism'.[11]

Two separate events on different coasts, equally coded by race and nationalism entwined with class and gender, have crystallized the revanchism of the so-called post-gentrification city. In Los Angeles, widely heralded in the 1980s as the new, raw, Pacific urbanism for a new century, the 1992 uprising following the acquittal of four police officers in the vicious beating of Rodney King, defied habitual media efforts to explain the 'riot' as a simple black assault on whites. The flood of racial stereotypes as a means to explain the uprising was deafening and in the end unsuccessful, for it was, as Mike Davis put it, 'an extremely hybrid uprising, possibly the first multi-ethnic rioting in modern American uprising'.[12,13] Likewise, the bombing less than a year later of New York City's World Trade Center – simultaneously a symbol of 1970s downtown renewal (and the massive displacement this involved) and the 1980s global urbanism – evoked vivid images of a real life *Towering Inferno*, and unleashed a xenophobic media hunt for 'foreign Arab terrorists'.[14] While the complete failure of the building's security systems led to its depiction as a 'sick building' in a 'sick city', the Trade Center bombing cemented the connection between American urban life and apparently arbitrary but brutal violence (terror) on the international scene.

The xenophobic hysteria that followed enlisted even the *New York Times* whose language of blithe exaggeration passed for uncontested fact as they documented the search for foreign conspirators – 'a ring accused of plotting to blow up New York City'.[15] No mere Manhattan Project that.

These are not new themes, of course. Anti-urbanism runs deep in US public culture,[16] and the postwar portrayal of the city as jungle and wilderness was never entirely absent through the 1980s, accompanying as much as contradicting the redemptive gentrification narrative. What *is* new is the extent to which this panoply of 'fear and fury'[17] has again come to monopolize public media visions of urban life, and the extent to which the revanchist American city is now recognized as an inherently international artefact. The safety of US borders, real and imagined, has dissolved. Not since the villainization of the city in the teens and early twenties of this century, when European immigrant socialists were identified as attacking the fabric of urban democracy, has US anti-urbanism involved such an explicitly international recognition. Neither the seeming *deus ex machina* of nuclear attack nor the McCarthyism of the cold war produced comparable visions of a US urbanism vulnerable to foreign attack from within; and for their part, the civil rights uprisings of the 1960s which had a sufficient effect on urban structure to provoke the racist term, 'white flight', was represented as a largely domestic question, connections to the anti-Vietnam War movement notwithstanding.

What *is* surprising, perhaps, is not so much that a new anti-urbanism incorporates a reluctant acknowledgement of the internationalization of local social economies in the last two decades. Rather what is surprising is that media self-representations of US cities – ostensibly among the most cosmopolitan of cities, at least in terms of the flow of capital and culture, commodities and information – were so systematically able to insulate and indeed isolate the triumphs and crises of American urban life from international events in general, but especially from the results of US military, political and economic policy abroad. It is hardly an exaggeration to say that the internationalism of the US city was largely restricted on the one hand to recognizing the connections of capital and the market and on the other to the recognition of nostalgic if palpably real Little Italies, Little Taiwans, Little Jamaicas, Little San Juans that dotted the urban landscape, as if to allow a tokenist internationalism at the neighborhood (working-class) scale while insisting on the Americanism of the city as a whole. The scripting of the revanchist city, however, is viscerally local *and* global, no longer so isolated or insulated, if indeed it ever was.

Tompkins Square Park and Beyond

Shortly after 5.00 a.m. on 3 June 1991, 350 police officers dressed in full riot gear moved into Tompkins Square Park in New York City's Lower East Side, woke more than 200 sleeping residents, and evicted them. Remaining clothes, tents, shanties, other structures and private belongings were bulldozed into several waiting sanitation trucks, and seven protestors were arrested. The 10.5 acre park was then cordoned off with an 8 foot-high chain link fence, and most of the 350 officers were left to patrol its perimeter. Access was allowed to only two parts of the park: to the playgrounds, children and their guardians were allowed to pass the police guard; and to the dog run, dogs and their owners were permitted to pass.

Tompkins Square Park became a national symbol[18] of the struggle against gentrification and homelessness on 6 August 1988 when a force of 400 police, ostensibly attempting to re-enforce a nineteenth century curfew in the park, initiated a police riot against homeless residents, protestors, punks and other park users. As a result of that riot, 121 complaints against the police were filed with the Civilian Review Board, but none resulted in a civil conviction. For the next three years, until the final eviction in June 1991, the park became a focal point of resistance in the city, drawing in homeless people and squatters, some housing and anti-gentrification activists, as well as local anarchists. As many as 100 structures were erected in the park at any one time, and nearly 300 people slept there on its busiest nights; squatters took over as many as 50 buildings in the neighborhood, housing as many as a thousand people. Meanwhile the city's homeless population swelled to between 70,000 and 100,000.

Only gingerly at first did the police return to the 'liberated zone' of the park, then more brazenly with three attempted 'sweeps' of Tompkins Square and a series of pitched battles between December 1989 and May 1991. Many of these battles occurred around May Day or Memorial Day celebrations, organized around such demands as 'Housing is a Human Right' and slogans like 'Gentrification is Genocide' and 'Eat the Elite', as well as the original 1988 slogan: 'Whose park is it, it's our fucking park'.

'This park is a park . . . It is not a place to live', explained Mayor David Dinkins, heralding the park's final closure in June 1991.[19] Dinkins, a Liberal Democratic and sometime member of Democratic Socialists of America, was elected with strong support from New York City's housing and anti-homelessness movement, but quickly sanctioned the first evictions of homeless people from the park in December 1989 only weeks after his election, initiating a four-year corrosion of Dinkins' connections with the mass support that had elected him. As the Village Voice noted of the evictions, for 'the homeless residents, many of them now scattered in abandoned lots around the park, the closing of the park was just one more betrayal for an administration they thought would stand up for the rights of the poor'.[20] In finally closing the park, Dinkins borrowed a script not from housing or homeless advocates but from the editorial pages of the New York Times, which quoted the Webster's dictionary definition of 'park' then judged that Tompkins Square was no park at all:

'A park is not a shantytown. It is not a campground, a homeless shelter, a shooting gallery for drug addicts or a political problem. Unless it is Tompkins Square Park in Manhattan's East Village'. Homeless residents of the park, according to the Times, had 'stolen it from the public' and the park would have to be 'reclaimed'. Just three days before the closure, the newspaper inveighed against further partial solutions, preferring instead a 'clean sweep' as 'the wiser course though riskier politically'. There were, it seems, 'some legitimately homeless people' who 'live in the park', and therefore 'misplaced sympathy abounds'.[21] In an interview for National Public Radio, Parks Commissioner Betsy Gotbaum borrowed from the same script, adding her own racial coding of the urban frontier: 'It was filled with tents, even a teepee at one point . . . It was really disgusting'.

Following the police offensive to close the park in 1991, the historic bandshell – symbolic not just as a cultural icon from the 1960s music scene but as the park's only shelter for homeless residents against the rain – was bulldozed, and a hasty, comprehensive, if unpublicized and probably therefore illegal 'park reconstruction plan' was enacted by the City. Meanwhile the locus of political action spread out from the park as the entire neighborhood became the contested zone and the neighboring streets became a shifting DMZ. In the immediate surrounds of the park, a nightly ritual of 'walk the pig' ensued. It is worth quoting at length from an eyewitness report by Sarah Ferguson of just one incident, which offers a visceral portrait of the agency behind the revanchist city:

> Since the police takeover 3 June, there have been nightly gatherings on the steps of St. Brigid's Church on Avenue B [on the southeast side of the park], a focal point of community resistance. On Friday, a dozen parents with their children gathered among the punks and anarchists and tried to march against the line of riot police blocking their way, chanting 'Open the park!' When they were forced back

onto the sidewalks, some 800 residents took to the streets, banging on drums and garbage can lids, and leading the police cordon [protecting the park] that dutifully followed them from Loisaida through the West Village and back through the projects off Avenue D – what locals call the nightly 'walk the pig' routine.

They were confronted on the steps of St. Brigid's by at least 100 cops, who beamed blinding high-intensity lights into the crowd. The protesters remained peaceful until two undercover cops shoved their way into the church entrance on Avenue B, claiming they wanted to inspect the roof for bottle throwers. One parishioner, Maria Tornin, was struck in the face and knocked against the stairs by one of the cops, and Father Pat Maloney of Lazaru Community was shoved against the wall. Backed by his parishioners, St. Brigid's Father Kuhn pushed the undercover cops out the door.

'When the law ends, tyranny begins, and these guys are tyrants', shouted Father Maloney, leading an angry mob to the paddy wagon where the undercovers had fled...

Last Saturday, as bulldozers rumbled past the ripped-up benches and shattered chess tables [in the cordoned-off park], a second demonstration of over 1000 Lower East Side residents linked arms around the park. As the church bells of St. Brigid's rang out, dreadlocked anarchists in combat boots and nose rings held hands with Jewish grandmothers in print dresses and plastic pearls in a peaceful show of unity not seen since the 1988 police riot.[22]

The closure of Tompkins Square Park marked the onset of a stern anti-homeless and anti-squatter policy throughout the city that betokened the coming of the revanchist city. Spearheaded by 'Operation Restore' in the Lower East Side, this new policy for the 1990s was intended to 'take back' the parks, streets and neighborhoods from those who had supposedly 'stolen' them from 'the public'. With 500 to 700 squatters still in nearly 40 buildings in the Lower East Side at the beginning of 1992, the attack on squatters actually proved too

difficult for the City although several buildings in the neighborhood as well as in the Bronx were cleared. The major effort came with what the *New York Times* called a 'crackdown on homeless'.[23] Homeless people had responded to the park closure by immediately establishing shanties and tent-cities on several empty lots in the neighborhood, generally in the poorer, still largely Puerto Rican neighborhood to the east of the park. Several sites, mostly between Avenues B and D, were colonized and were quickly dubbed 'Dinkinsville',[24] adapting the mayor's name to the Hoovervilles of the Depression. Not so much a discrete place, Dinkinsville comprised as many as ten separate encampments and shanty settlements linked by the political history of repeated eviction, the determination to colonize the interstices of private and public space, and resistance to enforced homelessness.

As Dinkinsville grew, the new sites were also subjected to surveillance and eventually bulldozing, beginning in October 1991 with a sweep of three vacant lots and the re-eviction of 200 people.[25] These sites too were fenced in to prevent public squatting by homeless people on empty space. Once again the evictees were moved further east, setting up or joining encampments under the Brooklyn, Manhattan and Williamsburg Bridges, under the FDR Drive, or in any available space defensible from public view, police attack, and bad weather. Fire destroyed the Williamsburg Bridge encampment, killing one resident, and a year later in August 1993, the City bulldozed 'the Hill' beneath the Manhattan Bridge, a well-established shantytown of 50 to 70 residents described as 'one of the most visible symbols of homelessness in Manhattan'.[26] Squeezed further east again, many evictees scattered up and down the waterfront of the East River, into Sara Delano Roosevelt Park, and to sites throughout Manhattan.

Elsewhere in the city, shantytowns under the West Side Highway, at Columbus Circle and in Penn Station were simultaneously razed beginning in the autumn of 1991.

And to match emerging hardline policies concerning outdoor public space, the Transit Authority instituted new anti-homeless policies for its major hubs, aimed at beginning to deny homeless people access to indoor public space. At Grand Central Station, a more novel approach was tried. Formed in the wake of Mobil Oil's departure from Manhattan and their parting movie, which depicted the tribulations of a white male Executive trying to commute to work through mobs of harassing homeless people, the 'Grand Central Partnership' was formed to privatize public functions. Funded by levies from local businesses, the Partnership instigated private security patrols, and offered food and shelter to homeless people in a nearby church. The overall object was to 'clean up' the station even if the eviction of homeless people was done with a lighter hand.

Eviction, in fact, represented the only true homeless policy of the Dinkins administration; it was, more appropriately, an anti-homeless policy. As the 'crackdown' began in late 1991, a frustrated Director of the Mayor's Office on Homelessness resigned, and by 1993, with hundreds of homeless people sleeping overnight in City offices, the city administration and several bureaucrats were found in contempt of court for their lack of a homeless policy and failure to provide court-ordered shelter.

Back in the early 1980s, just at the beginning of the gentrification boom, a Lower East Side developer speculated somewhat whimsically that as gentrification swept east through the neighborhood, homeless people would 'all be forced out. They'll be pushed east to the river and given life preservers'.[27] In retrospect, one has to wince at the acuity of his urban political geography. A *New York Times* editorial, sounding not a little like Frederick Engels a century and a half ago, perceived the City's anti-homeless policy with equal clarity:

> Last June, police in riot gear tore down a shantytown in New York's Tompkins Square Park and evicted the homeless.

> Then they swept through vacant lots to tear down a new shantytown and evict the homeless again. Can't the city do better than chase the homeless from one block to another?[28]

In Engels' words:

> The bourgeoisie has only one method of settling the housing question.... The breeding places of disease, the infamous holes and cellars in which the capitalist mode of production confines our workers night after night are not abolished; they are merely *shifted elsewhere*.[29]

Meanwhile back at the park, despite a major City budget crisis, retaking Tompkins Square Park from its homeless residents cost an estimated $14 million dollars – $4 million for the actual renovation and nearly $10 million in police costs.[30,31] Rebuilt over 14 months with railings that kept park users on the concrete paths and with benches sporting wrought iron dividers to prevent anyone from sleeping or even lying on them, the park was reopened in August 1992. Demonstrations met the park reopening; there were several bouts of arrests in the following days and weeks, and protestors and occasional homeless people cautiously began to reuse the renovated park, but a heavy police presence prevented impromptu political gatherings and musical events and prevented the park from again becoming a home for homeless people.

Local Places, International Spaces

An immediate pressing question after Tompkins Square Park is how a nominally progressive political administration, strongly supported by the City's housing movement, found itself presiding over a more vicious anti-homelessness than even its predecessor. And how such a seemingly progressive government, headed by an African-American, could become the most accomplished practitioner of the revanchist city.

In the wake of the police riot in 1988, there was broad sympathy in the neighborhood for the homeless residents of the park, and this endured for at least two years despite the lack of effective organization in and around the park. For most people the Park was far from ideal as a solution to homelessness, but surely it was better than forcing people to sleep on grates and in doorways scattered throughout the city. St. Brigid's Church was a central focus of support, as was the Church more broadly. This, for example, from the Episcopal Archdeacon of New York, the Reverend Michael S. Kendall:

> When I was in South Africa last year, I saw much the same tactics used against squatters in Soweto and other townships. To close Tompkins Square Park and squatter camps without providing adequate homes for those who have none is immoral.[32]

Another more colorful story suggests the broad civic distrust of official authority. During a May Day celebration in the Park in 1990 which devolved into a melee, six protestors were arrested and when they came to trial, most of the charges, including riot, were either dropped or reduced by an obviously sympathetic jury. The jury did not at all 'believe the prosecutor's contention that the cops were beneficient public servants' and the protestors 'a crazed mob of political extremists'. Confronted with the prosecutors' defense of a supposedly 'restrained' police force, 'one female juror said, 'Gimme a break, where does he think we live?' The trial lasted 11 days, and the jury deliberations were contentious, but according to one report, the jurors were sufficiently sympathetic that, during their daily bus ride from courthouse to sequestered hotel and back, they echoed the Park defendants' slogan with their own chant: 'Whose bus is it, it's our fucking bus!'[33]

But it was the opposition that won out. The local Community Board 3 had opposed the curfew in 1988, but several of its members colluded with the police to 'authorize' just such a curfew that led to the police riot. Several community organizations, most notably the innocuous sounding Tompkins Square Neighborhood Association, emerged after the riot to argue vociferously against the presence of homeless people in the park, and they began to organize a broad campaign. These organizations formed what could be described as a 'restoration coalition', and were variously composed of recent immigrants into the neighborhood, gentrifiers, homeowners and developers as well as some longer term residents. While often decrying homeless residents of the park as drug addicts, they successfully opposed City plans to build a drug rehabilitation facility and an AIDS treatment center for addicts in the Lower East Side. They contested elections for the Community Board, eventually achieving a sympathetic majority, worked with the local police precinct against the homeless residents of the park, and applied steady pressure on the City administration to 'clean up' the park.

Community support for those living in the park clearly eroded as the encampment became more entrenched. The park was workplace and playspace, living room and bathroom, for hundreds of people daily, and the result was hardly a salubrious solution to emergency housing and other social needs. Even a sympathetic observer had to conclude when the park was closed that 'the situation had reached a crisis point that even the tolerant Lower East Side milieu could no longer sustain...Most residents are too fed up with the homeless and the park to put up another fight. And the community surrounding the park has already changed'.[34] This erosion of sympathetic support and action came in the context of a broad media discovery that in liberal as much as not-so-liberal neighborhoods, 'a growing national ambivalence about the homeless' had become pervasive.[35] Beginning in more conservative cities from Miami to Atlanta, but quickly adopted in bastions of liberal administration such as Seattle and San Francisco, cities around the US began enacting harsh measures against sleeping and camping in public, pavement sitting, panhandling and windscreen washing.[36] The revanchist city was a national phenomenon. The national press, in the meantime, was running out of new angles on the visceral reality of homelessness, and they either continued to run increasingly anaemic, predictable stories of the streets or else eschewed the issue altogether.

Much less ambivalent was the public embrace of New York as a 'global city'. The unprecedented globalization of finance in Wall Street and the Downtown Financial District was accompanied by the equally unprecedented internationalization of the population as nationally defined immigrant communities emerged in the outer boroughs and suburbs. Indians, Jamaicans, El Salvadorans, Mexicans, Chinese, Polish, Koreans, Barbadians, Russians, Thais, Colombians and many other groups established new communities in the metropolitan area. These immigrant groups are variously employed in service and retail jobs that can be traced directly to the globalization of the financial sector, expansion of middle-class consumption, and indeed gentrification.[37] The gentrification of the Lower East Side is equally bound up with the globalization of the city economy. Beginning a mile to the north-east of the downtown Financial District, the area's gentrification provided housing for, among others, young professionals employed downtown. The area was also affected by the continued northward encroachment of Chinatown into the Lower East Side, fueled by massive financial flows and immigration from Hongkong, Taiwan and China. Culturally, the art market that flourished in the 1980s was not just the progenitor of internationally celebrated styles and artists but the object of several international exhibitions, while the club and music scenes are still on the international circuit.

That the restoration coalition in the Lower East Side found their symbolic leader in Antonio Pagan is therefore symptomatic. Pagan's political career in the Lower East Side symbolizes both the rise to power of a more established immigrant group and, anticipating the electoral defeat of David Dinkins, the erosion and transformation of a long time liberal tradition in New York City. Antonio Pagan is no stereotype. A Latino community organizer who moved to the area in the early 1980s, Pagan became a housing developer concerned with housing for the poor and elderly as well as market-rate apartments. He is openly gay yet he also helped to form a pressure group called BASTA (Before Another Shelter Tears US Apart) which successfully blocked a homeless shelter in the neighborhood for people with AIDS. A zealous neo-conservative Democrat who led the crusade to close Tompkins Square, he is virulently opposed to squatters in the neighborhood. At one point, he even attempted to persuade Cardinal O'Connor to dismiss Father Kuhn of St Brigid's Church because of the latter's support for squatters, but was rebuffed. Pagan capitalized on the closure of the Park in 1991 with a political campaign for the local seat on the City Council. Heavily financed by real estate and contracting interests, and endorsed by the *New York Times*, he blamed liberals and liberal guilt for the destruction of the institutions of social reproduction, and cast the eviction of homeless people from Tompkins Square Park as a victory for poor Lower East Siders who now had their park back. Pagan's rise, concluded the *Voice*, 'has all the standard '90s earmarks of the ambitious ethnic pol who pulls the ladder up behind him'.[38]

Opposed by many gays, by 'a coalition of progressive Latinos' who 'protested his support of gentrification', and by AIDS activists as well as housing activists, who began referring to him as the 'Clarence Thomas of the Lower East Side' – say one thing do the other – Pagan succeeded in fashioning a conservative coalition of property owners, gentrifiers, conservative Jews, and enough old time residents and Puerto Ricans to defeat very narrowly the long-term liberal incumbent, Miriam Friedlander.[39]

If Pagan's political victory in the Lower East Side is in part the result of a changed citizenry due to gentrification, he was also significantly assisted by a dubious re-districting of council seats that brought cries of gerrymandering. Approved by the Dinkins administration on the same day that they closed the Park, this plan split the Lower East Side between two districts, the northern one (Pagan's) app-ended to the well-off Gramercy Park neigh-borhood, and the southern one attached to Chinatown and the new corporate condo and co-op neighborhood around Wall Street and Battery Park. Pagan consolidated his victory in the 1993 elec-tion.

But more than anything, Pagan's ascent to power in the Lower East Side, comple-mented by Dinkins' citywide defeat in 1993 by Giuliani (the city's first Republican mayor in a quarter century) corroborated the abject failure of liberal housing and anti-homeless policies. Further, it portends the advent of a more ruthless urbanism, an entrenched revanchism. That Dinkins, the failed liberal, and Pagan, the rising conservative moralist, are respectively Af-rican-American and Latino is precisely the point of the revanchist city in which the reassertion of power by the white ruling class takes numerous forms. Pagan wins with the help of Gramercy Park, but Din-kins is ousted by Giuliani. Days after taking power as mayor, and in the midst of a record cold spell, Giuliani was questioned by a reporter about his homeless policies given the severe weather. What did the mayor intend to do, he was asked. 'We're working on the weather', responded the mayor.

Conclusion: Degentrification?

The reopening of the park in 1992 was accompanied by a predictable naturaliza-tion of Tompkins Square's history, geog-raphy and culture in the press. Noting the parallels with Central Park in the 1930s – read: Tompkins Square Park is an old story – the *New York Times* immedi-ately heralded the reconstructed Tompkins Square as a 'shining emerald'.[40] Within a

year, the aestheticization of the neighbor-hood was in full swing with photographs in the press of young, white middle-class families enjoying the park once again. A fashion article in the *Times* celebrated the neighborhood as virtually an inner city, 'serendipitous, ad hoc mall', noting without any mention of the preceding con-flicts, that the rehabilitation of the park was followed by a thorough-going 'fashion rehab'. Despite the lingering depression affecting the region, more than 25 new shops opened in the year after the park's reopening, readying themselves 'for the neighborhood's inevitable onset of young professionals'. 'Since the renovation of Tompkins Square Park… the area from Seventh Street to Ninth Street between Second Avenue and Avenue B has become extremely desirable from a commercial point of view… With rents from $20 to $30 a square foot (and climbing), there is sudden interest "from successful businesses in the West Village and SoHo who want to relocate",' observes one local broker.[41]

In this context, the argument for 'degen-trification' seems at best, premature. Pre-dictions of the demise of gentrification are premised on essentially consumption side explanations of the process, and indeed the conditions of consumption have altered with the maturation of the baby boom generation. But if, as I have suggested, the patterns of capital investment and disin-vestment are at least as important in creat-ing the opportunity and possibility for gentrification, then a rather different vision emerges. The decline in housing and land prices since 1989 has been accompanied by a disinvestment from older housing stock – repairs and maintenance unper-formed, building abandonment – and these are precisely the conditions which led in the first place to the availability of a comparatively cheap housing stock in cen-tral locations. Far from ending gentrifica-tion, the depression of the late 1980s and early 1990s may well enhance the possibil-ities for reinvestment. Whether gentrifica-tion resurges following the economic depression now appears to be a significant test of production-side versus consumption-side theories.

The language of degentrification, of course, not only justifies the political momentum behind the revanchist city, but feeds the self-interest of real estate developers and contractors. 'Gentrification' has become a 'dirty word' that expresses well the class dimensions of recent inner urban change, and it is hardly surprising that real estate professionals have taken advantage of a very real slow down in gentrification to attempt to expunge the word and the memory of the word's politics from the popular discourse. But neither the memory nor the profits of gentrification are likely to be erased so quickly. Indeed it may not be too much of an exaggeration to surmise that proclaiming the end of gentrification today may be akin to anticipating the end of suburbanization in 1933.

The continuance of gentrification, possibly at a more intense rate than in the past, will not mean the end of the revanchist city and the return of a kinder, gentler urbanism. The more likely scenario is of a sharpened bipolarity of the city in which white middle class assumptions about civil society retrench as a narrow set of social norms against which the recidivism of the city is found dangerously wanting; and, by way of corollary, we can expect a deepening villainization of working-class, minority, homeless and many immigrant residents of the city, through interlocking scripts of violence, drugs and crime. Gentrification and reactions to it will play a central role in this revanchist city. Now, however, the 'apartheid local of the American national', as Ruth Gilmore[42] so lucidly puts it, is increasingly also an apartheid local of American *internationalism*.

NOTES

I would like to thank Sharon Zukin for alerting me to some of the initial press reports on 'degentrification'.

1 C. V. Bagli, '"De-gentrification" Can Hit When Boom Goes Bust', *New York Observer*, 5–12 Aug. 1991, p. 1.
2 E. Uzelac, '"Out of Choices": Urban Pioneers Abandon Inner Cities', *The Sun*, 18 Sept. 1991, pp. 1, 4A.
3 L. S. Bourne, 'The Demise of Gentrification? A Commentary and Prospective View', *Urban Geography*, 14 (1993), pp. 95–107.
4 Ibid, pp. 105–6.
5 R. A. Beauregard, *Voices of Decline* (Blackwell, Oxford, 1993).
6 Ibid., p. xi.
7 N. Smith, 'From Renaissance to Restructuring: Gentrification, the Frontier and Urban Change', in N. Smith and P. Williams (eds), *Gentrification of the City* (Allen & Unwin, London, 1986)
8 N. Smith, 'Tompkins Square: Riots, Rents and Redskins', *Portable Lower East Side*, 6 (1989), pp. 1–36.
9 N. Smith, 'New City, New Frontier: The Lower East Side as Wild West', in M. Sorkin (ed.), *Variations on a Theme Park. The New*

American City and the End of Public Space (Hill and Wang, New York, 1992), pp. 61–93.
10 C. Katz, 'A Cable to Cross a Curse', unpublished paper, 1991.
11 R. Gilmore, 'Terror Austerity Race Gender Excess Theater', in Gooding-Williams (ed.), *Reading Rodney King/Reading Urban Uprising* (Routledge, New York, 1993), pp. 23–37.
12 C. Katz and N. Smith, 'LA Intifada: Interview with Mike Davis', *Social Text*, 33, 1992, p. 19.
13 R. Gooding-Williams (ed.), *Reading Rodney King/Reading Urban Uprising* (Routledge, New York, 1993).
14 A. Ross, 'Bombing the Big Apple', in *The Chicago Gangster Theory of Life* (Verso, London, forthcoming).
15 R. Blumenthal, 'Tangled Ties and tales of FBI Messenger', *New York Times*, 9 Jan. 1994.
16 M. White and L. White, *Intellectuals Versus the City* (Oxford University Press, New York, 1977.)
17 R. Gilmore, p. 26 (see note 11).
18 Insofar as Lou Reed's 'New York' album included a song entitled 'Meet you in

Tompkins Square', the park gained international as well as national notoriety.

19 J. Kifner, 'New York Closes Park to Homeless', *New York Times*, 4 June 1991.

20 S. Ferguson, 'Should Tompkins Square be like Gramercy', *Village Voice*, 11 June 1991 p. 20.

21 Anon., 'Make Tompkins Square a Park Again', *New York Times* 31 May 1991.

22 S. Ferguson, 'The Park is Gone', *Village Voice*, 18 June 1991, p. 25.

23 S. Roberts, 'Crackdown on homeless and what led to shift', *New York Times*, 28 Oct. 1991.

24 S. Ferguson, 'Tompkins Squares Everywhere', *Village Voice*, 24 Sept. 1991.

25 T. Morgan, 'New York City bulldozes squatters' shantytowns', *New York Times*, 16 Oct. 1991.

26 I. Fisher, 'For Homeless, A Last Haven is Demolished', *New York Times*, 18 Aug. 1993.

27 C. Unger, 'The Lower East Side: There Goes the Neighborhood', *New York*, 28 May 1984.

28 Anon., 'Hide the Homeless?' *New York Times*, 11 Nov. 1991.

29 F. Engels, *The Housing Question* (Progress, Moscow, 1975).

30 J. Kifner (see note 19).

31 S. Ferguson, 'Bucking for Realtors. Antonio Pagan: the Clarence Thomas of the Lower East Side?' *Village Voice*, 14 Sept. 1993.

32 M. S. Kendall, 'Military Style Evictions', Letter to *New York Times*, 6 Nov. 1991.

33 S. Ferguson, 'Riot Jury Riots', *Village Voice*, 25 Feb. 1992.

34 S. Ferguson (see note 24).

35 S. Roberts, 'Evicting the Homeless', *New York Times*, 22 June 1991.

36 T. Egan, 'In 3 Progressive Cities, Stern Homeless Policies', *New York Times*, 12 Dec. 1993.

37 S. Sassen, *The Global City* (Princeton University Press, 1991).

38 S. Ferguson (see note 31).

39 Ibid.

40 J. Bennet, 'One Emerald Shines, Others Go Unpolished', *New York Times*, 30 Aug. 1992.

41 J. Servin, 'Mall Evolution', *New York Times*, 10 Oct. 1993.

42 R. Gilmore, p. 26 (see note 11).

Chapter 31

City A/genders

Sophie Watson

Gendered Cities

How does space matter to the construction of gender in material and symbolic ways? At the macro level how cities are organized has real effects on women's lives. Urban development and planning have tended to reflect, and also reinforce, traditional assumptions about gender. Traditionally, employment has been concentrated in the centre of cities separated out from residence in the suburbs. The transport system is constructed to support the needs of the worker leaving home in the morning and returning in the evening on a radial system which links centres with peripheries but rarely links suburbs to each other. Services and facilities are dispersed throughout the suburbs and the taking of children to school or the doctor, doing the shopping and other household chores operate on different temporal and spatial scales such that the complexity of running a home and bringing up children militates against participation in the labour force, at least on a full-time basis.

Transport links seldom connect schools, shops, services, employment and shopping centres and many women do not have the use of a car during the day. The assumption underpinning this spatial organization is that the man of the household goes out to work while the woman stays at home and looks after the children. This kind of city form, combined with the lack of childcare facilities, in part explains the concentration of women in part-time or home-based work. As the Marxist urban theorist Manuel Castells wrote as early as 1977, the city could not function without the unpaid labour of women to oil its wheels.

The lack of safety associated with the public spaces of the city, the lack of street lighting and the imagined and real dangers of public transport, particularly at night, curtail women's easy movement, particularly older and younger women and migrants from rural areas, who may have little experience of city life. Urban design and built forms, though implicitly imbued with gendered assumptions, at the same time are rarely sensitive to the needs of women with children. Roads are difficult to cross with prams, safe play areas are few and far between, and designated public spaces are often more suited to the needs of young adolescent men than women with young children. Studies of the central business districts of cities have shown that the majority of women are afraid to walk through them at night.

The home, while seen as the domain of women, particularly in middle-class homes, offers each member of the household their own space except the woman. Children often have a playroom, men have the study, garage, shed or workshop. The women's space is a site of labour – the kitchen, while the 'master' bedroom suggests a sexual sleeping area where men have control. Virginia Woolf was an early advocate of the need for autonomous space in *A Room of One's Own* (1929).

The suburbs are not simply gendered in the sense that women spend more time at home and its locality, they are also gendered in a symbolic sense. With the increasing separation of home and work associated with industrialization, femininity was mapped onto the home, the local, and a sense of place. The suburban home came to represent the 'haven in the heartless world', the warm and cosy space to which men returned after a hard day at work in the hurly burly of the city. Thus women were constituted in the home as nurturing, passive, subordinate mothers, while men were powerful, public, active and even aggressive. At the same time this haven has been unpacked to reveal the suburban home as a site of violence, isolation and work for women, but its gendered symbolic force remains.

Feminist Urban Theory

The early feminist interest in space developed out of geography and related disciplines. In the UK, a geography and gender group was initiated in the early 1980s (McDowell 1983). Initially feminists sought to address women's absence from urban planning literature and policy and attempted to reinsert them into the frame. The emphasis was on the ways in which women were marginalized within urban systems either via constraints or lack of access to goods and services. A central argument was that city forms and structures and urban institutions created and reinforced women's dependence, consigned them to the domestic arena and disabled them from fully entering public life and spaces. Theoretically the work was underpinned by different forms of analysis each of which had very different implications for policy and change.

The most pragmatic approach derived from Weberian or institutional approaches

which saw women's exclusion or marginalization in terms of institutional failures and regulatory systems (e.g. Brion and Tinker 1980; Coles 1980). On the one hand policies were seen to favour masculine patterns of responsibility and work, such as the public transport system being organized around the needs of suburban dwellers travelling to the city centres for work, rather than the mobility requirements and patterns of women at home trying to combine domestic and paid employment. Over the following decade these arguments seeped into policy discussions in radical local and metropolitan authorities like the Greater London Council which had its own women and planning group (Hamilton and Jenkins 1989). But changing the physical structure of cities proved to be more difficult and expensive than changing the regulations or procedures that marginalize women.

Alternatively the problem was seen to lie with the 'gatekeepers' in the urban system who allocated public goods, such as housing or finance, according to prejudice or discriminatory practices. Thus single parents were allocated poorer quality housing than nuclear families, or single women had difficulty gaining access to mortgage finance when lenders made assumptions about their repayment potential. In 1983 lone women borrowers accounted for 8 per cent of all borrowers compared to an equivalent figure of 17 per cent for men (CML 1983). In British cities many single parents were housed in the poorer quality public housing (DHSS 1974). The political and policy solutions suggested by these kinds of analyses lay in legal or institutional reforms or in education or training of the actors involved, and there was no fundamental challenge to the status quo.

A more radical critique came from Marxist feminists who saw the source of women's spatial marginality or exclusion as patriarchal capitalism where the city was structured to reinforce the place of women as domestic labourers and men as waged labourers (McDowell 1983; Watson 1988). Keeping women in the home meant cities could run more smoothly as women carried out the necessary reproductive activities and wages could be kept lower since these activities were being performed for free. The argument's weaknesses lay in its sometimes conspiratorial flavour and its rather functionalist analysis. These debates were more oriented to critique than to reform. The policy implications were unclear and the political solution was ultimately to overthrow capitalism, which was constructed at this time as a monolithic unified system. In a similar vein radical feminists posed the problem as patriarchy (Wekerle et al., 1980). The city, they suggested, worked in men's interests, men controlled space, they were the gatekeepers of resources and they had a lot to lose if things changed. The solution implied here lay in more women entering the policy-making arenas and the professions of architecture and planning, or in subverting the gatekeepers of the system – those who controlled the resources.

Through the 1980s a growing number of women entered planning and architecture schools and the professions. Others took the route of the manual trades, challenging one of the more gendered labour forces and skills. These women, who mostly took advantage of government training schemes to become carpenters and builders, formed the 'women in manual trades' collective. There were strong parallels with the early utopian feminists and communitarians excavated by Dolores Hayden (1981) in *The Grand Domestic Revolution*, who saw the reorganization of space as a route to the freedom of women and the subversion of gender divisions. A group of women architects and builders set up a collective 'Matrix'. The aim was to examine how spatial forms limited, defined or constrained women's lives: underpasses with no ramps, poorly lit streets, poorly designed kitchens. There was a tension between short-term goals trying to facilitate women's lives as carers, and a recognition that focusing on women's needs as such could ossify them in a domestic role. In some senses the analysis was deterministic in that it assumed a changed built environment would mean changed social relations, and space was treated as a homogeneous category which had visible and clear-cut effects. The goal of getting more women into the design professions and the building trades was predicated on an assumption that women would understand their own needs better.

In the less specifically spatial disciplines feminist sociologists, cultural and social historians and anthropologists from the 1970s (e.g. Davidoff 1979; Pringle 1983) continued to develop analyses of how different meanings were produced spatially, and this was a precursor to contemporary postmodern accounts. Suburbs were analysed in terms of discourses of 'female', 'safe', 'haven', 'sexual', etc. versus the urban as 'male' 'aggressive' and 'assertive' and these were mapped onto a consumption/production binary. Other work deconstructed notions of home and homelessness and its sexed differentiation (Watson 1986). Though framed also by earlier Marxist ideas, the ideological underpinning of the production of space was 'foregrounded': that is, space was not simply seen as a blank undifferentiated surface which has no effects. The terrain of political intervention implied was thus also at the level of subverting and challenging meaning and discursive practices. A related body of work came out of geography and allied disciplines which looked at the spatialization of gender relations. Feminist geographers used techniques such as local empirical studies to explore, for example, how capital shifted to localities where women's supposed docile and cheap labour could be exploited (McDowell and Massey 1984). The potential political dimension to these analyses lay in developing links with the trade union movement and in strategic interventions in arenas like the local economic development strategies initiated by authorities such as the radical Greater London Council.

Feminist perspectives over the first ten years or so came from different quarters and had different strategic potential. One area where the analysis was limited was in developing links between gender, race and space. By the late 1980s, the impact of new theory and an interest in space across a range of disciplines (notably cultural studies and philosophy) brought new ways of thinking about space. These have enabled a different form of politics which takes account of the imaginary and the importance of meaning, on the one hand, and which brings together diverse players, for example community artists with planners, on the other. These shifts offer exciting possibilities for rethinking and reshaping space. Though the early debates were important for raising issues of inequality and marginalization, which still need to be addressed, feminists need also to think about what kind of cities and spaces might offer new ways of living which accommodate the diversity of women's and men's lives on the one hand, and the huge social and economic shifts on the other. Taking the urban system as given and trying to accommodate it to women, or dismantling it entirely – as was suggested by some analyses – have proved limited routes.

More recent feminist urban theory draws on post-structuralist or postmodernist ideas and theories of subjectivity, identity and meaning. In these new discourses earlier notions of space have come under scrutiny for constructions of space which were too homogenized, continuous, objective, Cartesian and knowable. In postmodern versions space is seen as fragmented, imploding, imaginative, subjective, unknowable and fantastic. Space is linked with power and difference. These feminist approaches to space have opened up possibilities of a new politics and way of thinking about gender and the city which earlier approaches foreclosed.

One path takes the construction of meaning in the sexed and gendered spaces and places of the city as its starting point for rethinking the urban, planning and housing. This kind of work draws on qualitative research methodologies. Thus, Susan Thompson (1994), for example, showed how the home for migrant women repre-

sents a site of power, or atonement for loss or a sign of success. Challenging earlier feminist urban analysis which viewed the process of suburbanization as controlling and subjugating women, and locking them into domestic roles, she suggests that suburban discourse is fractured. Thompson thus explores how stereotypical representations of suburbia tell only half the story. Other work (Duruz 1994; Mee 1994) has looked at how women now redraw the post-war suburbs in memory and imagination and what meanings are encoded. What this allows for politically are possibilities for a rethinking of the 'private' domain and constructing suburbs of the future. It offers a more textured way of intervening into urban policy debates around the compact city versus the suburban city, or development on greenfield versus brownfield sites. Instead of crude caricatures of what constitutes suburban or inner-city life, different meanings are examined. Australian feminist activists have drawn on these ideas to develop new models of local planning which acknowledge different cultural practices.

Foucault's notion of the Panopticon whereby conditions of uncertainty and invisibility of surveillance produce selfsocialization, surveillance and regulation, has also influenced feminist work. As Margo Huxley (1994) has shown, the zoning of cities can be read in terms of strategies of social control which are resisted by multiple intersecting practices such as the setting up of gay and lesbian households or legal appeals through the planning system. These resistances challenge dominant forms of divisions and the regulation of space, and can contribute to strategies to create a more participatory, less discriminatory planning system and alternative uses and development of social space.

Sexuality, which has long been central to feminist thought and analysis and, indeed, present in the early debates around the home and suburbia, has re-emerged in a contemporary guise. Elizabeth Wilson (1995) highlights the crucial influence of sexuality on spatial structure, regulation and behaviour, and explores how the male gaze in the late nineteenth century eroticized city life and sexualized the spaces it viewed. Designating prostitutes as the public face of woman in the city, the respectable woman's movements in urban space became a subject for regulation. Such work is helpful in illustrating the ways in which women have been denied an urban sociality and civic subjectivity. Further shifts in the debate have questioned the ways in which queer sexualities are located in specific geographical sites (Probyn 1996). These approaches take us away from the earlier feminist analyses which see the state as the solution to women's exclusion from the city and suggest new and transgressive ways of inhabiting postmodern spaces.

Contemporary feminist interest in the body has also been mapped onto space. In *Space, Time, and Perversion* Elizabeth Grosz (1995) considers questions of spatiality, space and the design professions of architecture and planning, and their relationship to subjectivity, corporeality and thought. Grosz argues that an understanding of the ways in which women occupy space is predicated on an exploration of the appropriation and disenfranchisement of femininity within dominant knowledge systems. New ways of dwelling must acknowledge the invaded nature of bodies and spaces as we know them. She sees bodies as formed by the city spaces they inhabit. The model is based on a productive notion of bodies and cities defining each other. Again a new politics of space is suggested by her work. In this there is no ideal environment for the body or perfect city in terms of the potential it offers for wellbeing. The question then becomes how to distinguish conductive and unconducive environments – physical and socio-cultural – and how these produce different bodies. The city is the locus for the production and circulation of power and the city leaves traces on the subject's corporeality; the dramatic information revolution will thus have its corporeal effects. This way of

thinking shifts the focus of the lens and suggests new struggles and possibilities.

Kathie Gibson and Sophie Watson, drawing out some of the implications of these debates (Gibson and Watson 1994; Watson and Gibson 1995), have suggested that postmodern feminist theory has much to offer conventional notions of planning and urban policy. The heroic visions of modernist politics and mass mobilization of the exploited masses have eclipsed other strategic possibilities, especially for women. Modernist planning was underpinned by the notion of a rational and clear solution to city chaos and inequality which was predicated on gendered social relations and patterns of movement. It assumed a linearity of progress and reform that was fixed and not easily open to change and fluidity. A recognition of difference and embodiment challenges the universalist and normative assumptions and principles of planners acting in the public good. This notion of planning for difference is compatible with new theories of the state which see the state as a set of discursive arenas where different interests are constructed and contested (Pringle and Watson 1992). In this formulation ebbs and flows of power are embedded in the planning system and are not fixed.

New possibilities for feminist strategies, both theoretically and practically, are thus beginning to emerge. Planning in this frame can take account of the local and the specific, and can be flexible and allow for change, recognizing that there is no one solution for all time, and that any so-called solution will itself later represent a node of power and be contested. Postmodern urban politics suggests a shift from the old class politics around space to an assertion of multiple forms of resistances and alliances articulated at different sites and at different times (Gibson-Graham 1996). This is important since it allows for a politics of difference across race, gender and sexuality and recognizes that there is no one strategy which will provide the solution. It means taking account of identities and how these are formed in urban spaces and in the interstices of the city. It implies rethinking public and private and recognizing that these too are shifting and not fixed.

Feminist perspectives on space have moved a long way from their early preoccupation with gendered forms of exclusion and marginality in the city. Over time these have become less and less located in the simple binaries of public and private and home and work, and less and less analysed in terms of a simple functionalism. Important new directions are opened up as feminists like J. K. Gibson-Graham (1996) start to dismantle the monolithic categories of class and capitalism. By

attacking these shibboleths, spaces are freed up in which to move. In this new terrain subjectivity, sexuality, corporeality and the place of the imaginary come to the fore. The reforms sought have also shifted. Though feminists are still keen to campaign for a greater provision of urban services which are sensitive to women's lived experiences in the city and also for an end to discriminatory practices, there is a greater complexity in forms of analysis and outcomes sought. My argument here is not that earlier forms of analysis are no longer important, rather that new perspectives bring a fresh light to old problems....

REFERENCES

Brion, M. and Tinker, A. (1980) *Women in Housing*. London: Housing Centre Trust.

Castells, M. (1977) *The Urban Question*. London: Edward Arnold.

Coles, L. (1980) Women and leisure: a critical perspective, in D. Mercer and E. Hamilton-Smith (eds.) *Recreational Planning and Social Change in Australia*. Melbourne: Sorrett Publishing.

Council of Mortgage Lenders (1983) *CML Year Book*. London: CML.

Davidoff, L. (1979) The separation of home and work? Landladies and lodgers in nineteenth-century England, in S. Burman (ed.) *Fit Work for Women*. London: Croom Helm.

DHSS (1974) *Report of the Committee on One Parent Families* (The Finer Report), Cmnd. 4728. London: HMSO.

Duruz, J. (1994) Romancing the suburbs, in K. Gibson and S. Watson (eds) *Metropolis Now*. London: Pluto Press.

Gibson, K. and Watson, S. (eds.) (1994) *Metropolis Now*. London: Pluto Press.

Gibson-Graham, J. K. (1996) *The End of Capitalism (as we knew it)*. Oxford: Blackwell.

Grosz, E. (1995) *Space, Time, and Perversion*. Sydney: Allen & Unwin.

Hamilton, K. and Jenkins, L. (1989) Why women and travel? in M. Grieco and L. Pickup (eds.) *Gender, Transport and Employment: the Impact of Travel Constraints*. Aldershot: Avebury.

Hayden, D. (1981) *The Grand Domestic Revolution*. Boston: MIT Press.

Huxley, M. (1994) Panoptica: Utilitarianism and land use control, in K. Gibson and S. Watson (eds.) *Metropolis Now*. London: Pluto Press.

McDowell, L. (1983) Towards an understanding of the gender division of urban space. *Society and Space: Environment and Planning D*, 1(1): 59–72.

McDowell, L. and Massey, D. (1984) A woman's place, in D. Massey and J. Allen (eds.) *Geography Matters*. Cambridge: Cambridge University Press.

Mee, K. (1994) Dressing up the suburbs: representations of Western Sydney, in K. Gibson and S. Watson (eds.) *Metropolis Now*. London: Pluto Press.

Pringle, R. (1983) Women and consumer capital, in C. Baldock and B. Cass (eds.) *Women, Social Welfare and the State*. Sydney: Allen & Unwin.

Pringle, R. and Watson S. (1992) Women's interests and the post-structural State, in M. Barrett and A. Phillips (eds.) *Destabilising Theory*. Cambridge: Polity Press.

Probyn, E. (1996) *Outside Belongings*. Sydney: Allen & Unwin.

Thompson, S. (1994) Suburbs of opportunity: the power of home for migrant women, in K. Gibson and S. Watson (eds.) *Metropolis Now*. London: Pluto Press.

Watson, S. (1986) *Housing and Homelessness: A Feminist Perspective*. London: Routledge & Kegan Paul.

Watson, S. (1988) *Accommodating Inequality*. Sydney: Allen & Unwin.

Watson, S. and Gibson, K. (eds.) (1995) *Post-modern Cities and Spaces*. Oxford: Blackwell.

Wekerle, G., Peterson, R. and Morley, D. (eds.) (1980) *New Space for Women*. Boulder, CO: Westview Press.

Wilson, E. (1995) The invisible flaneur, in S. Watson and K. Gibson (eds.) *Post-modern Cities and Spaces*. Oxford: Blackwell.

Woolf, V. (1929) *A Room of One's Own*. London: Hogarth Press.

Chapter 32

Bodies-Cities

Elizabeth Grosz

I Congruent Counterparts

For a number of years I have been involved in research on the body as sociocultural artifact. I have been interested in challenging traditional notions of the body so that we can abandon the oppositions by which the body has usually been understood – mind and body, inside and outside, experience and social context, subject and object, self and other, and underlying these, the opposition between male and female. Thus "stripped," corporeality in its sexual specificity may be seen as the material condition of subjectivity, that is, the body itself may be regarded as the locus and site of inscription for specific modes of subjectivity. In a "deconstructive turn," the subordinated terms of these oppositions take their rightful place at the very heart of the dominant ones.

Among other things, my recent work has involved a kind of turning *inside out* and *outside in* of the sexed body, questioning how the subject's exteriority is psychically constructed, and conversely, how the processes of social inscription of the body's surface construct for it a psychical interior. In other words, I have attempted to problematize the opposition between the inside and the outside by looking at the outside of the body from the point of view of the inside, and looking at the inside of the body from the point of view of the outside, thus

reexamining and questioning the distinction between biology and culture, exploring the way in which culture constructs the biological order in its own image, the way in which the psychosocial simulates and produces the body as such. Thus I am interested in exploring the ways in which the body is psychically, socially, sexually, and discursively or representationally produced, and the ways, in turn, bodies reinscribe and project themselves onto their sociocultural environment so that this environment both produces and reflects the form and interests of the body. This relation of introjections and projections involves a complex feedback relation in which neither the body nor its environment can be assumed to form an organically unified ecosystem. (The very notion of an ecosystem implies a kind of higher-order unity or encompassing totality that I will try to problematize in this paper.) The body and its environment, rather, produce each other as forms of the hyperreal, as modes of simulation which have overtaken and transformed whatever reality each may have had into the image of the other: the city is made and made over into the simulacrum of the body, and the body, in its turn, is transformed, "citified," urbanized as a distinctively metropolitan body.

One area that I have neglected for too long – and I am delighted to have the opportunity here to begin to rectify this – is the constitutive and mutually defining relation between bodies and cities. The city is one of the crucial factors in the social production of (sexed) corporeality: the built environment provides the context and coordinates for most contemporary Western and, today, Eastern forms of the body, even for rural bodies insofar as the twentieth century defines the countryside, "the rural," as the underside or raw material of urban development. The city has become the defining term in constructing the image of the land and the landscape, as well as the point of reference, the centerpiece of a notion of economic/social/political/cultural exchange and a concept of a "natural ecosystem." The ecosystem notion of exchange and "natural balance" is itself a counterpart to the notion of a global economic and informational exchange system (which emerged with the computerization of the stock exchange in the 1970s).

The city provides the order and organization that automatically links otherwise unrelated bodies. For example, it links the affluent lifestyle of the banker or professional to the squalor of the vagrant, the homeless, or the impoverished without necessarily positing a conscious or intentional will-to-exploit. It is the condition and milieu in which corporeality is socially, sexually, and discursively produced. But if the city is a significant context and frame for the body, the relations between bodies and cities are more complex than may have been realized. My aim here will be to explore the constitutive and mutually defining relations between corporeality and the metropolis, if only in a rather sketchy but I hope suggestive fashion. I would also like to project into the not-too-distant future some of the effects of the technologization and the technocratization of the city on the forms of the body, speculating about the enormous and so far undecidable prosthetic and organic changes this may effect for or in the lived body. A deeper exploration would of course be required to elaborate the historico-geographic specificity of bodies, their production as determinate

types of subject with distinctive modes of corporeality.

Before going into any detail, it may be useful to define the two key terms I will examine today, *body* and *city*.

By *body* I understand a concrete, material, animate organization of flesh, organs, nerves, muscles, and skeletal structure which are given a unity, cohesiveness, and organization only through their psychical and social inscription as the surface and raw materials of an integrated and cohesive totality. The body is, so to speak, organically/biologically/naturally "incomplete"; it is indeterminate, amorphous, a seires of uncoordinated potentialities which require social triggering, ordering, and long-term "administration," regulated in each culture and epoch by what Foucault has called "the micro-technologies of power." The body becomes a *human* body, a body which coincides with the "shape" and space of a psyche, a body whose epidermic surface bounds a psychical unity, a body which thereby defines the limits of experience and subjectivity, in psychoanalytic terms, through the intervention of the (m)other, and, ultimately, the Other or Symbolic order (language and rule-governed social order). Among the key structuring principles of this produced body is its inscription and coding by (familially ordered) sexual desires (the desire of the other), which produce (and ultimately repress) the infant's bodily zones, orifices, and organs as libidinal sources; its inscription by a set of socially coded meanings and significances (both for the subject and for others), making the body a meaningful, "readable," depth-entity; and its production and development through various regimes of discipline and training, including the coordination and integration of its bodily functions so that not only can it undertake the general social tasks required of it, but so that it becomes an integral part of or position within a social network, linked to other bodies and objects.

By *city*, I understand a complex and interactive network which links together, often in an unintegrated and de facto way, a number of disparate social activities, processes, and relations, with a number of imaginary and real, projected or actual architectural, geographic, civic, and public relations. The city brings together economic and informational flows, power networks, forms of displacement, management, and political organization, interpersonal, familial, and extra-familial social relations, and an aesthetic/economic organization of space and place to create a semipermanent but ever-changing built environment or milieu. In this sense, the city can be seen, as it were, as midway between the village and the state, sharing the interpersonal interrelations of the village (on a neighborhood scale) and the administrative concerns of the state (hence the need for local government, the preeminence of questions of transportation, and the relativity of location).

II Body Politic and Political Bodies

I will look at two pervasive models of the interrelation of bodies and cities, and, in outlining their problems, I hope to suggest alternatives that may account for future urban developments and their corporeal consequences.

In the first model, the body and the city have merely a de facto or external, contingent rather than constitutive relation. The city is a reflection, projection, or product of bodies. Bodies are conceived in naturalistic terms, predating the city, the cause and motivation for their design and construction. This model often assumes an ethnological and historical character: the city develops according to human needs and design, developing from nomadism to sedentary agrarianism to the structure of the localized village, the form of the polis through industrialization to the technological modern city and beyond. More recently, we have heard an inverted form of this presumed relation: cities have become (or may have always been) alienating environments, environments which do not allow the body a "natural," "healthy," or "conducive" context.

Underlying this view of the city as a product or projection of the body (in all its variations) is a form of humanism: the human subject is conceived as a sovereign and self-given agent which, individually or collectively, is responsible for all social and historical production. Humans *make* cities. Moreover, in such formulations the body is usually subordinated to and seen merely as a "tool" of subjectivity, of self-given consciousness. The city is a product not simply of the muscles and energy of the body, but the conceptual and reflective possibilities of consciousness itself: the capacity to design, to plan ahead, to function as an intentionality and thereby be transformed in the process. This view is reflected in the separation or binarism of design, on the one hand, and construction, on the other, the division of mind from hand (or art from craft). Both Enlightenment humanism and marxism share this view, the distinction being whether the relation is conceived as a one-way relation (from subjectivity to the environment), or a dialectic (from subjectivity to environment and back again). Nonetheless, both positions consider the active agent in social production (whether the production of commodities or in the production of cities) to be the subject, a rational or potentially rational consciousness clothed in a body, the "captain of the ship," the "ghost in the machine."

In my opinion, this view has at least two serious problems. First, it subordinates the body to the mind while retaining a structure of binary opposites. Body is merely a tool or bridge linking a nonspatial (i.e., Cartesian) consciousness to the materiality and coordinates of the built environment, a kind of mediating term between mind on the one hand and inorganic matter on the other, a term that has no agency or productivity of its own. It is presumed to be a machine, animated by a consciousness. Second, at best, such a view only posits a one-way relation between the body or the subject and the city, linking them through a causal relation in which body or subjectivity is conceived as the cause, and the city its effect. In more sophisticated versions of this view, the city can have a negative feedback relation with the bodies that produce it, thereby alienating them. Implicit in this position is the active causal power of the subject in the design and construction of cities.

Another equally popular formulation proposes a kind of parallelism or isomorphism between the body and the city. The two are understood as analogues, congruent counterparts, in which the features, organization, and characteristics of one are reflected in the other. This notion of the parallelism between the body and social order (usually identified with the state) finds its clearest formulations in the seventeenth century, when liberal political philosophers justified their various allegiances (the divine right of kings, for Hobbes; parliamentary representation, for Locke; direct representation, for Rousseau, etc.) through the metaphor of the body-politic. The state parallels the body; artifice mirrors nature. The correspondence between the body and the body-politic is more or less exact and codified: the King usually represented as the head of the body-politic, the populace as the body. The law has been compared to the body's nerves, the military to its arms, commerce to its legs or stomach, and so on. The exact correspondences vary from text to text, and from one political regime to another. However, if there is a morphological correspondence or parallelism between the artificial commonwealth (the "Leviathan") and the human body in this pervasive metaphor of the body-politic (see Feher 1989), the body is rarely attributed a sex. If one presses this metaphor just a little, we must ask: if the state or the structure of the polis/city mirrors the body, what takes on the metaphoric function of the genitals in the body-politic? What kind of genitals are they? In other words, does the body-politic have a sex?

Here once again, I have serious reservations. The first regards the implicitly phallocentric coding of the body-politic, which, while claiming it models itself on the *human* body, uses the male to represent the human. Phallocentrism is, in my understanding, not so much the dominance of the phallus as the pervasive unacknowledged use of the male or masculine to represent the human. The problem, then, is not so much to eliminate as to reveal the masculinity inherent in the notion of the universal, the generic human, or the unspecified subject. The second reservation concerns the political function of this analogy: it serves to provide a justification for various forms of "ideal" government and social organization through a process of "naturalization": the human body is a natural form of organization which functions not only for the good of each organ but primarily for the good of the whole. Similarly, the body politic, whatever form it may take, justifies and naturalizes itself with reference to some form of hierarchical organization modeled on the (presumed and projected) structure of the body. A third problem: this conception of the body-politic relies on a fundamental opposition between nature and culture, in which nature dictates the ideal forms of culture. Culture is a supercession and perfection of nature. The body-politic is an artificial construct which replaces the primacy of the natural body. Culture is molded according to the dictates of nature, but transforms nature's limits. In this sense, nature is a passivity on which culture works as male (cultural) productivity supercedes and overtakes female (natural) reproduction.

But if the relation between bodies and cities is neither causal (the first view) nor representational (the second view), then what kind of relation exists between them? These two models are inadequate insofar as they give precedence to one term or the other in the body/city pair. A more appropriate model combines elements from each. Like the causal view, the body (and not simply a disembodied consciousness) must be considered active in the production and transformation of the city. But bodies and cities are not causally linked. Every cause must be logically distinct from its effect. The body, however, is not distinct, does not have an existence separate from the city, for they are mutually defining. Like the representational model, there may be an isomorphism between the body and the city. But it is not a mirroring of nature in artifice. Rather, there is a two-way linkage which could be defined as an *interface*, perhaps even a cobuilding. What I am suggesting is a model of the relations between bodies and cities which sees them, not as megalithic total entities, distinct identities, but as assemblages or collections of parts, capable of crossing the thresholds between substances to form linkages, machines, provisional and often temporary sub- or microgroupings. This model is a practical one, based on the practical productivity bodies and cities have in defining and establishing each other. It is not a holistic view, one that stresses the unity and integration of city and body, their "ecological balance." Instead, I am suggesting a fundamentally disunified series of systems and interconnections, a series of disparate flows, energies, events or entities, and spaces, brought together or drawn apart in more or less temporary alignments.

The city in its particular geographical, architectural, spatializing, municipal arrangements is one particular ingredient in the social constitution of the body. It is by no means the most significant. The structure and particularity of, say, the family is more directly and visibly influential, although this in itself is to some extent a function of the social geography of cities. But nonetheless, the form, structure, and norms of the city seep into and effect all the other elements that go into the constitution of corporeality and/as subjectivity. It effects the way the subject sees others (domestic architecture and the division of the home into the conjugal bedroom, separated off from other living and sleeping spaces, and the specialization of rooms are as significant in this regard as smaller family size), as well as the subject's understanding of, alignment with, and positioning in space. Different forms of lived spatiality (the verticality of the city, as opposed to the horizontality of the landscape – at least our own) effect the ways we live space, and thus our comportment and cor-poreal orientations and the subject's forms of corporeal exertion – the kind of terrain it must negotiate day by day, the effect this has on its muscular structure, its nutritional context, providing the most elementary forms of material support and sustenance for the body. Moreover, the city is, of course, also the site for the body's cultural saturation, its takeover and transformation by images, representational systems, the mass media, and the arts – the place where the body is representationally reexplored, transformed, contested, reinscribed. In turn, the body (as cultural product) transforms, reinscribes the urban landscape according to its changing (demographic, economic, and psychological) needs, extending the limits of the city, of the suburban, ever towards the countryside which borders it. As a hinge between the population and the individual, the body, its distribution, habits, alignments, pleasures, norms, and ideals are the ostensible object of governmental regulation, and the city is a key tool (see Foucault 1978 on the notion of biopower).

III Body Spaces

Some general implications:

First, there is no natural or ideal environment for the body, no "perfect" city, judged in terms of the body's health and well-being. If bodies are not culturally pregiven, built environments cannot alienate the very bodies they produce. However, what may prove unconductive is the rapid transformation of an environment, such that a body inscribed by one cultural milieu finds itself in another involuntarily. This is not to say that there are not *un*conducive city environments, but rather there is nothing intrinsically alienating or unnatural about the city. The question is not simply how to distinguish conducive from unconducive environments, but to examine how different cities, different sociocultural environments actively produce the bodies of their inhabitants as particular and distinctive types of bodies, as bodies with particular physiologies, affective lives, and concrete behaviors. For example, the slum is not inherently alienating, although for those used to a rural or even a suburban environment, it produces extreme feelings of alienation. However, the same is true for the slum dweller who moves to the country or the suburbs. It is a question of negotiation of urban spaces by individuals/groups more or less densely packed, who inhabit or traverse them: each environment or context contains its own powers, perils, dangers, and advantages.

Second, there are a number of general effects induced by city-spaces, which can only be concretely specified in particular cases. The city helps to orient sensory and perceptual information, insofar as it helps to produce specific conceptions of spatiality, the vectorization and setting for our earliest and most ongoing perceptions. The city orients and organizes family, sexual, and social relations insofar as the city divides cultural life into public and private domains, geographically dividing and defining the particular social positions and locations occupied by individuals and groups. Cities establish lateral, contingent, short- or long-term connections between individuals and social groups, and more or less stable divisions, such as those constituting domestic and generational distinctions. These spaces, divisions, and interconnections are the roles and means by which bodies are individuated to become subjects. The structure and layout of the city also provide and organize the circulation of information, and structure social and regional access to goods and services. Finally, the city's form and structure provide the context in which social rules and expectations are internalized or habituated in order to ensure social conformity, or position social marginality at a safe or insulated and bounded distance (ghettoization). This means that the city must be seen as the most immediately concrete locus for the production and circulation of power.

I have suggested that the city is an active force in constituting bodies, and always leaves its traces on the subject's corporeality. It follows that, corresponding to the dramatic transformation of the city as a result of the information revolution will be a transformation in the inscription of bodies. In his paper, "The Overexposed City," Paul Virilio makes clear the tendency toward hyperreality in cities today: the replacement of geographical space with the screen interface, the transformation of distance and depth into pure surface, the reduction of space to time, of the face-to-face encounter to the terminal screen:

> On the terminal's screen, a span of time becomes both the surface and the support of inscription; time literally... surfaces. Due to the cathode-ray tube's imperceptible substance, the dimensions of space become inseparable from their speed of transmission. Unity of place without unity of time makes the city disappear into the heterogeneity of advanced technology's temporal regime (Virilio, 1986: 19).

The implosion of space into time, the transmutation of distance into speed, the instantaneousness of communication, the collapsing of the workspace into the home computer system, will clearly have major effects on specifically sexual and racial bodies of the city's inhabitants as well as on the form and structure of the city. The increased coordination and integration of microfunctions in the urban space creates the city not as a body-politic but as a political machine – no longer a machine modeled on the engine but now represented by the computer, facsimile machine, and modem, a machine that reduces distance and speed to immediate, instantaneous gratification,. The abolition of the distance between home and work, the diminution of interaction between face-to-face subjects, the continuing mediation of interpersonal relations by terminals, screens, and keyboards, will increasingly affect/infect the minutiae of everyday life and corporeal existence.

With the advent of instantaneous communications (satellite, TV, fiber optics, telematics) arrival supplants departure: everything arrives without neccessarily having to depart....Contributing to the creation of a permanent present whose intense pace knows no tomorrow, the latter type of time span is destroying the rhythms of a society which has become more and more debased. And "monument," no longer the elaborately constructed portico, the monumental passageway punctuated by sumptuous edifices, but idleness, the monumental wait for service in front of machinery: everyone bustling about while waiting for communication and telecommunication machines, the lines at highway tollbooths, the pilot's checklist, night tables as computer consoles. Ultimately, the door is what monitors vehicles and various vectors whose breaks of continuity compose less a space than a kind of countdown in which the urgency of work time plays the part of a *time center*, while unemployment and vacation time play the part of the periphery – *the suburb of time*: a clearing away of activity whereby everyone is exiled to a life of both privacy and deprivation (Virilio, 1986: 19–20).

The subject's body will no longer be disjointedly connected to random others and objects according to the city's spatiotemporal layout. The city network – now vertical more than horizontal in layout – will be modeled on and ordered by telecommunications. The city and body will interface with the computer, forming part of an information machine in which the body's limbs and organs will become interchangeable parts with the computer and with the technologization of production. The computerization of labor is intimately implicated in material transformations, including those which pose as merely conceptual. Whether this results in the "cross-breeding" of the body and machine – that is, whether the machine will take on the characteristics attributed to the human body ("artificial intelligence," automatons) or whether the body will take on the characteristics of the machine (the cyborg, bionics, computer prosthesis) remains unclear. Yet it is certain that this will fundamentally transform the ways in which we conceive both cities and bodies, and their interrelations.

REFERENCES

Sue Clifford. "Common Ground." *Meanjin* 47, no. 4 (Summer 1988): 625–36.

Philip Cook. "Modernity, Postmodernity and the City." *Theory, Culture and Society* 5 (1988): 475–93.

Manuel De Landa. "Policing the Spectrum." *Zone* 1/2 (1986): 176–93.

Gilles Deleuze and Félix Guattari. "City/State." *Zone* 1/2 (1986): 194–9.

Michael Feher, ed., *Fragments of a History of the Human Body*, vol. 1. New York: Zone Books.

Jon Jerde. "A Philosophy for City Development." *Meanjin* 47, no. 4 (Summer 1988): 609–14.

Michel Foucault. *Discipline and Punish: The Birth of the Prison*. Trans. Alan Sheridan. New York: Vintage, 1979.

Michel Foucault. *The History of Sexuality*, Vol. I: *An Introduction*. Trans. Robert Hurley. New York: Pantheon, 1978.

Sanford Kwinter. "La Città Nuova: Modernity and Continuity." *Zone* 1/2 (1986): 80–127.

Alison Sky. "On Site." *Meanjin* 47, no. 4 (Summer 1988): 614–25.

Paul Virilio. "The Overexposed City." *Zone* 1/2 (1986): 14–39.

David Yencken. "The Creative City." *Meanjin* 47, no. 4 (Summer 1988): 597–609.

Chapter 33

from *Geographies of Disability*

Brendan Gleeson

The Disabling City

Urban oppression

Disability oppression takes a distinctive form in cities. Certain general urban characteristics – notably city design, urban employment patterns and the distribution of land uses – entrench social discrimination against disabled people. Disabled people, their advocates, and occasionally governments, have identified two main urban dimensions of disability oppression: physical inaccessibility and socio-spatial exclusion in institutionalised forms of social care.[1] While these aspects of oppression take specific socio-spatial forms in different cities, they none the less have a common genesis in the economic and cultural devalorisation of disabled people in capitalist societies. As new geographies of rural and regional experiences of disability emerge, it will be possible to better elaborate how these broad structures of oppression condition the production of space in distinct contexts....

Physical inaccessibility

A powerfully disabling feature of capitalist cities is their inaccessible design (Imrie, 1996). This means that the physical layout of cities – including both macro land use patterns and the internal design of buildings – discriminates against disabled people

by not taking account of their mobility requirements. Practically speaking, this discrimination takes the form of:

- physical barriers to movement for disabled people, including broken surfaces on thoroughfares (streets, guttering, paving) which reduce or annul the effectiveness of mobility aids (e.g., wheelchairs, walking frames),
- building architecture which excludes the entry of anyone unable to use stairs and hand-opened doors,
- public and private transport modes which assume that drivers and passengers are non-impaired, and
- public information (e.g., signage) presented in forms that assume a common level of visual and aural ability.

The above list is not exhaustive but does point to some of the more common discriminatory aspects of the built environments of contemporary Western cities.

Even allowing for the distinctive morphologies, economies, cultures, and planning policies of Western cities, the international breadth of concern raised by disabled people concerning inaccessibility demonstrates that this is a pervasive feature of urban life. As Hahn observes: 'In terms of ease or comfort, most cities have been designed not merely for the nondisabled but for a physical ideal that few human beings can ever hope to approximate' (1986: 273).

For disabled people, these pervasive mobility handicaps are more than simply the quotidian urban frictions which irritate non-disabled people (e.g., public transport delays, road blockages, freak weather, periodic crowding). Rather, discriminatory design is a critical manifestation, and cause, of *social oppression* because it reduces the ability of disabled people to participate fully in urban life. More particularly, mobility constraints in the contemporary capitalist city are serious impediments to one's chances of gaining meaningful employment, and hence are linked to heightened poverty risk. In addition, an inaccessible built environment reduces disabled people's capacity to both engage in political activities and establish and maintain affective ties. It is not surprising therefore that Hahn (1986: 274) sees inaccessibility as a threat to 'principles of democratic freedom and equality for citizens with disabilities'.

Both Liachowitz (1988) and Alcock (1993) argue that contemporary capitalist cities both reflect and entrench disablement through their physical inaccessibility and discriminatory labour markets. Alcock (1993) draws particular attention to the link between inaccessibility and poverty, arguing that there are many 'additional costs of coping with a disability in the able-bodied world' (Alcock, 1993: 188). Inaccessibility also often means that disabled people are unable to engage in mainstream consumption activities, thereby reducing their capacity to purchase goods and services at optimal prices. These goods and services include major urban consumption items, such as housing, education, transport and finance (Oliver, 1991).

Most Western governments now have in place forms of planning and building regulations which aim to prevent or at least reduce the production of inaccessible built environments and transport systems. However, as Imrie (1996) has shown for Britain, these regulations are often poorly enforced. Human rights legislation has been another regulatory avenue used by states in attempts to guarantee inclusive environmental design. In recent years, a number of Western states have enacted various forms of national disability rights legislation with the aim of improving disabled people's access to built environments, and to social life in general. Again, however, there is evidence to show that the rights-based approach to combating discriminatory design has serious political and institutional limitations....

Socio-spatial exclusion

In addition to the problem of inaccessibility within public urban spaces, disabled people also experience barriers to choice in their preferred living environment in the contemporary Western city (Dear, 1992; Steinman, 1987). These two areas of socio-spatial injustice present difficult policy challenges, to say the least, for Western governments, most of whom have struggled to lessen the constraints experienced by disabled people in obtaining both employment and a preferred living setting. Not surprisingly, the exclusion of disabled people from employment realms is mirrored in the housing sector. Oliver (1991) argues that disabled people in contemporary British cities suffer housing poverty due both to income deprivation and the discriminatory effects of housing markets that ignore needs for non-standard forms of accommodation. A similar problem has been recognised in Australia (Campbell, 1994; Le Breton, 1985) and in the United States (Dorn, 1994; Harrison and Gilbert, 1992). In 1993, for example, it was estimated that 13,500 disabled Australians had unmet needs for accommodation and respite services (*Canberra Times*, 21 Nov. 1997: 3).

The combined effect of poverty, inaccessibility and inappropriate accommodation is to reduce the ability of disabled people to participate in the mainstreams of urban social life. Gilderbloom and Rosentraub (1990: 271) argue that in many United States cities disabled people 'are often trapped in restrictive living units and are unable to gain access to a city's resources by transportation systems not adapted for them'. For these authors, such cities were no less than 'invisible gaols' for disabled people. Moreover, the powerful gender norms that govern women's embodiment in the mainstreams of city life can mean that disabled women are 'doubly handicapped' in public space (Butler and Bowlby, 1997, Parr, 1997).

In the late 1980s the United States National Council on Disability undertook a survey of disabled people's lifestyles and came to the following disturbing conclusion:

> The survey results dealing with social life and leisure experiences paint a sobering picture of an *isolated and secluded population of individuals with disabilities*. The large majority of people with disabilities do not go to movies, do not go to the theater, do not go to see musical performances, and do not go to sports events. A substantial minority of persons with disabilities never go to a restaurant, never go to a church or synagogue. The extent of non-participation of individuals with disabilities in social and recreational activities is alarming. (cited in Harrison and Gilbert, 1992: 18) (emphasis added)

Historically, state support services have been a major cause of the socio-spatial isolation of disabled people. Large institutions have provided both residential 'care' and 'sheltered' employment for disabled people for much of the twentieth century. The oppressive experience of institutionalisation by disabled people was frequently characterised by, *inter alia*, material privation, brutalising and depersonalised forms of 'care', a lack of privacy and individual freedom, and separation from friends and family (Horner, 1994; Shannon and Hovell, 1993).

The failure of institutions as socialised forms of care for disabled people exposes, among other things, the inadequacy of the welfarism which broadly framed the urban social policies of Western states since the Second World War. Institutions may have distributed a very minimal level of material

support to disabled people (which admittedly improved in many countries over time), but they also ensured the socio-spatial exclusion of disabled people from the mainstreams of social life, thus entrenching the political invisibility and powerlessness of this social group. . . .

Recognising the inadequacies of welfarist forms of care, Western governments have sought to deinstitutionalise support for disabled people. This has usually involved both the closure of large-scale residential centres and their replacement with small, dispersed community care units. I will address more fully the limits of this set of policy reforms in the next chapter. Suffice it to say now that many disabled people in most Western countries remain in poor-quality and inappropriate forms of accommodation. In the United States, for example, Dorn reports that 'over two and a half million people with disabilities are warehoused in nursing homes and other institutions at a national cost of approximately [US]$140 billion' (1994: 211).

The social geography of deinstitutionalisation has been thoroughly documented for North America in a set of landmark studies by Michael Dear and Jennifer Wolch. *Landscapes of Despair* (Dear and Wolch, 1987) traced the construction of new urban 'zones of dependence', being clusters of service-dependent groups and facilities designed to support them, usually located in declining inner city areas (see also Dear, 1980, and Joseph and Hall's (1985) examination of clustering in Toronto). Both this, and a follow-up study, *Malign Neglect* (Wolch and Dear, 1993) emphasised how poor public funding and community opposition had forced many deinstitutionalised people into homelessness and 'ghettoisation' in the emerging zones of dependence. Milligan's recent (1996) analysis examined the applicability of these North American findings to Scotland. Milligan concluded that while deinstitutionalised people suffer socio-spatial exclusion in Scotland, this marginalisation departs from the common North American experience due to the mediation of different legislative mechanisms, policy structures and service provision forms.

One major weakness of deinstitutionalisation initiatives has been their lack of congruence with urban planning policies and regulations. In many Western countries, the process of creating community care networks has been slowed, or in some instances actually halted, by planning and building regulations. . . .

Spaces of Resistance

In countries such as the United States, Canada, Britain and Australia, resistance against disability oppression has been rising over the past few decades. Much of this resistance has occurred in cities, and has included frequent and dramatic demonstrations of disabled people's anger and frustration with oppressive structures and institutions. Disabled people have targeted large urban areas in their resistance campaigns, recognising that the city hosts both the mainstreams of public political life in Western countries and also the centrepoints of many of the institutions that have contributed to their oppression. Moreover, disabled people have focused their activism on the political city – regional and national capitals – in order to maximise the profile and impact of their campaigns. As Dorn (1994) explains, a common feature of disability activism in the United States has been dramatic seizures of public spaces in and around places such as courthouses, government buildings and public transport systems.

One group in particular, the American Disabled for Accessible Public Transportation (ADAPT), has favoured this spatial politics of resistance, including actions where 'ADAPT' activists throw themselves out of their wheelchairs and crawl up the massive stone steps in front of the Capitol Building in Washington (Dorn, 1994: 160). A recent instance of this strategy was the ADAPT protest in early November 1997 outside the White House gates. This action in favour of a national attendant care policy resulted in the arrest of 92 activists.

Around the same time, ADAPT protesters shut down the Federal Department of Transportation building in Washington for five hours in a dramatic escalation of their struggle for accessibility on inter-city coaches.[2]

Australian disability activists used a similar tactic in July 1997 when they besieged the Prime Minister's Sydney office, protesting against cuts to the budget of the national Human Rights and Equal Opportunities Commission. The protest gained a high profile in the national media, and was described dramatically in one national radio report as 'a stand-off between protesters in wheelchairs and armed guards outside the Prime Minister's office' (ABC Radio News Report, 4 July 1997). In the next month, disabled people in Melbourne staged a protest outside the State Premier's office using their wheelchairs to run over and demolish computers. The demonstration was aimed at new public policies that emphasised the provision of technological aids – especially personal computers – as the answer to disabled people's social needs. As a protest spokesperson argued, the neo-liberal State Government's cuts to basic support services had created a social crisis for disabled people that technological aids could not solve: 'The Internet cannot respond to crisis and people need crisis response because many people out there are in crisis' (ABC Radio News Report, 18 Aug. 1997).

This is not to imply, however, that disability activism has taken the form only of dramatic actions in public space. As a set of (largely urban) social movements, disabled people's organised resistance against oppression has worked at many political levels, including within major political parties. However, the marginalisation of disabled people from mainstreams of power, including formal political spheres, has encouraged the practice of direct action in public spaces. To use Fraser's (1997) terminology, the disability movements of various Western countries have constituted themselves as 'subaltern counterpublics' that have opposed hegemonic and discriminatory constructions of 'the public sphere'. However, these counterpublics have varied significantly across and within countries – in particular, the tactics used by various national and regional advocacy groups have differed, reflecting specific cultural, institutional and legal contexts.

It is not my intention here to provide a history or detailed contemporary profile of the various national disability movements. Historical accounts of disability social movements have already been written – for example, in the chronicles on the United States by Shapiro (1993) and Britain by Campbell and Oliver (1996). I do, however, think it important here to point briefly to some broad character differences between the national disability movements in the English-speaking world. These differences, both in political approach and in the social gains achieved, reveal the limits of some strategies of resistance to disability oppression. In particular, I believe that the different experiences of disability movements expose the limitations of a rights-based model of resistance . . .

As Dorn (1994) and Imire and Wells (1993) point out, the disability movements of the United States and Britain have tended to pursue quite different advocacy strategies. In the United States, the disability movement has long followed a militant rights-based course, traceable to the broader eruption of civil rights struggles in the 1960s. By contrast, the British 'disabled people's movement', to use Campbell and Oliver's term, has focused less on the pursuit of individual rights and more on the achievement of social policy gains. The absence of a written constitution laying out individual rights in Britain has lessened the appeal of the rights-based advocacy model in that country (Imrie and Wells, 1993). Moreover, in Britain, organised charities have played a far greater role in the struggle for progressive disability legislation than has been the case in the United States where advocacy groups have been at the forefront of anti-discrimination struggles (Dorn, 1994).

Imrie and Wells (1993) claim that in contrast to the United States experience, the British movement has been characterised by political conservatism and social conformism. Some key members of the British disabled people's movement would dispute this depiction – Oliver, for example, is critical of the political-economic cast of the United States movement.[3] In particular, he criticises the latter's focus on the pursuit of individual rights and 'independent living' (IL) for disabled people, which he sees as inferior to a more collectivist approach aimed at changing basic social structures.

> there has always been a distinction between what we mean by IL in Britain and what they meant in the States. IL in America is organised around self-empowerment, individual rights and the idea that in the land of the free and the home of the brave – all that crap – individuals, if they are given access under the law and the constitution, can be independent. In contrast in Britain . . . IL entailed collective responsibilities for each other and a collective organisation. IL wasn't about individual self-empowerment; it was about individuals helping one another. Once you accept that notion . . . you are beginning to question the foundations of the society in which we live. It is bizarre for people to think that we, as disabled people can live in Britain with full civil rights and all the services we need without fundamental changes. We are not actually talking about tinkering around at the edges of society to let people in. *For disabled people to play a full part in British society, this society will have to change fundamentally.* (cited in Campbell and Oliver, 1996: 204) (emphasis added)

In Australia and New Zealand, disability movements have pursued a 'hybrid strategy' that has aimed to secure both improved civil rights and also social structural change, mainly through initiatives in state policy regimes. In Australia, the latter strategy was partly successful during the 1980s, measured in a series of legislative and programmatic initiatives by

State and Federal governments that sought to address the employment and income dimensions of disability poverty (Gleeson, 1998). However, at the time of writing (early 1998), these policy gains appeared vulnerable to the cost-cutting agendas of new conservative State and Federal governments.

In most English-speaking countries, there now exists some form of national civil rights legislation protecting disabled people from discrimination, although the strength and effectiveness of these laws varies considerably. The United States Americans with Disabilities Act (1990) is probably the strongest rights legislation. By contrast, the hard-won British Disability Discrimination Act (1995) provides a considerably weaker set of protections for disabled people (Butler and Bowlby, 1997). Australia passed a national Disability Discrimination Act in 1992 (Yeatman, 1996), while in New Zealand disability discrimination was dealt with through the enactment of a Human Rights Act in 1993 (Stewart, 1993) ...

Urban social movements need, I would argue, a set of political-ethical principles that can guide resistance struggles by supplying both a theory of injustice specific to the group in question and also the criteria for emancipation. This requires both a broad and inclusive ethical ideal, such as an end to all forms of disability oppression, and also a set of subsidiary principles that can be applied to the various spatio-temporal contexts, affinity groups and individual struggles that together constitute the broad phenomenon we denote as a 'social movement'. . . .

Towards Enabling Environments

Radical geography and justice

During the 1970s, advocates of the (now largely dormant) welfare perspective applied the question of social justice to geographical analysis (e.g., Smith, 1977). This new emphasis on social equity represented an important break from the prevailing positivism of Human Geography (Johnston et al., 1994). In this sense, Welfare Geography represented an important early 'radical' impulse in Social Geography. However, there were significant conceptual and political limits to Welfare Geography and the perspective has been criticised for its tendency to focus only upon the *distributional consequences* of the material and ideological structures that condition the production of space (Badcock, 1984; Johnston et al., 1994). This is to echo the criticisms of Fraser (1995) and Young (1990) of the conceptual and political limits of welfarist notions of equity.

By contrast, the subsequent tradition of radical Social Geography – in particular, historical-geographical materialism – provides a more promising conceptual basis from which to formulate a spatial notion of enabling justice. The key insight of radical social geographical analysis in this respect is the view that oppression and exclusion arise from the socio-cultural production of space. . . . this ontology sees society and space as mutually constitutive dynamics. Importantly, 'environment', as the physical and social context of life, is assumed to be an artefact of human society, rather than merely a surface upon which materialities are rearranged. This spatial ontology thus problematises the justice (or otherwise) of structures which *produce* space in capitalist societies. As Young (1990) points out, the capitalist city is an environment where injustice has been produced in multiple, interdependent forms. A radical enabling justice would thus presuppose the broad ethical and political goal of producing environments which liberate the social capacities of all people. Put differently, enabling justice requires the production of spaces and places which guarantee the capacity of all to participate in social life in meaningful ways, such that each individual's material and non-material needs are satisfied (e.g., inclusion, affectivity, liberty).

While the ethic of care cannot replace the need for meta-ethical formulations, the criticisms which many feminists have levelled against de-contextualised notions of justice should be borne in mind. An enabling justice would recognise that the universal need for material welfare, social participation and cultural respect must be realised at a variety of socio-spatial scales, each defined by unique sets of affective and social ties, group affiliations, and environmental conditions. In this sense, an ethic of care complements rather than contradicts justice by stressing the need for contextually appropriate, rather than uniform, mechanisms for material distribution and social participation.

Ethical contextualisation has also been an important theme of communitarian theorists, several of whom are implacably opposed to universalist notions of justice (Smith, 1994). Communitarians such as Sandel (1982) and Walzer (1983) have stressed the 'community' (defined at a variety of socio-spatial scales) both as the source of unique, context-bound moral frameworks and as the most appropriate sphere for ethical practice. In recent years, a diluted form of communitarian thinking has played an influential role in political discourses within a range of Western (mostly English-speaking) countries. For example, parties and thinkers from both the Right and the Left have promoted versions of 'welfare pluralism' which, while differing on some key political-economic grounds (e.g., the extent of marketisation of the public sphere), none the less share an emphasis on the community as a vehicle for decentralised, participatory structures of social service delivery (Clapham and Kintrea, 1992; Jary and Jary, 1991).

Neo-liberals, in particular, have championed 'the community' as a fulcrum of moral responsibility and efficient social adaptability in contradistinction to the supposed inflexibility and unaccountability of state institutions. However, it can be argued that the real agenda of neo-liberal communitarianism is to shift the costs of morally based action, such as the provision of social support services, from the state to local communities and individuals (espe-

cially women) (Jary and Jary, 1991). Given the uneven capacity of communities and individuals to resource social support, this reallocation of costs and service responsibilities inevitably worsens distributional injustice. Although speaking the language of contextualised ethics, this form of communitarianism is clearly antithetical to enabling justice.

Transforming the environment of disability

What would enabling justice mean for disabled people? At the minimum, the goal of enablement demands the creation of new social spaces that 'accommodate a broader range of human capabilities than the present environment' (Hahn, 1987: 188). Thus, disability scholars and activists have called for the creation of *enabling environments* in capitalist societies which emphasise the capabilities rather than the impairments of disabled people (see, for example, the collections edited by Hales, 1996 and Swain et al., 1993). For Corker (1993), the 'enabling environment' would aim to establish social independence for all inhabitants, meaning that disabled people, in particular, would be empowered to meet their own needs within a network of mutual obligations rather than within a hierarchy of dependency relationships (e.g., care giver/care receiver). Finkelstein and Stuart echo this theme, envisaging the socio-cultural emancipation of disabled people through a wholesale transformation of public policies:

> In [this] new world...services for disabled people should be conceived in terms of 'support' and would acquire an *enabling* role in the same way that public utilities (for example, postal services, railways, water and electricity supplies, and so on) are created by able-bodied for able-bodied people to enable more satisfying life-styles. As such, they form part of the necessary public support network which *enables* both full participation in society and citizenship rights. (1996: 171) (emphasis added)

The complementary ideals of full citizenship rights and social independence would require the integration of disabled people within both mainstream political settings and principal economic spheres, especially labour markets (cf. Kavka, 1992).

As Harvey (1996) argues, broad social change is realised through the multiple forms of spatial struggle that attempt to create material, representational and symbolic places of emancipation. Thus, the 'enabling environment' might range in scale from the level of a local policy sphere which empowers disabled people to meet specific needs (e.g., accommodation, education, work) to that of a whole society which has ceased to oppress and exclude people on the basis of any social difference. Although possessing shifting, indeed contested, geographies, the disabled people's movements are good examples of the specific enabling environments – or 'subaltern counterpublics' – that have arisen within cities in opposition to structures of oppression. If generalised to the level of society as a whole, the enabling environment ideal would restore to disabled people the material needs, cultural respect and political voice that many are at present denied.

Thus the broad definition of enabling justice offered earlier can be re-stated in more specific terms for disabled people as:

- the satisfaction of material needs, as socially defined in the relevant regional or national context;
- socio-political participation and cultural respect; and
- socio-spatial inclusion.

It may be objected that these conditions for justice are utterly quixotic given that a defining feature of capitalism – commodity relations – has been implicated in the economic devalorisation, and therefore social oppression, of disabled people. The first response to this criticism – versions of which are commonly directed at all 'radical' political movements – is that many disabled people themselves have insisted that nothing less than profound socio-spatial change will remedy the oppression they endure. Finger, for example, insists that the realisation of enabling work environments requires a fundamental transformation of capitalist labour markets, involving, *inter alia*, replacing the law of value with a new social measurement of economic usefulness:

> we need to argue against 'productivity' and 'bringing home a paycheck' as a measure of human value. We need to work for a society that values a range of kinds of labor and ways of working – everything from raising children to working for disability rights. (1995: 15)

The justice criteria listed above reflect the emancipatory demands levelled by disabled people in Western countries through both advocacy fora (e.g., Disability Alliance, 1987a, 1987b; Eastern Bay of Plenty People First Committee, 1993; Ronalds, 1990; UPIAS, 1976) and theoretical discourses (e.g., Abberley, 1991a, 1991b; Morris, 1991; Oliver, 1990, 1996; Swain et al., 1993).

However, this answer does not respond adequately to the charge of utopianism that conventional critics always level at transformative principles, such as enabling justice. Indeed, given the obvious difficulties of removing key sources of disability oppression in an era of 'market triumphalism', what practical political purpose can the principle offer to radical social scientists and activists?

My argument is that enabling justice – and the subsidiary ideal of an enabling environment – can provide the basis for progressive political practice in state policy spheres. Obviously, these broad ideals have implications outside public policy realms – however, the emphases on material distributions, spatial inclusion and citizenship have a particularly strong resonance in the state arena. Moreover, some commentators have argued that the state must take a lead role in countering disability oppression through the enactment of enabling policies and legislation. Oliver and Barnes (1993: 275), for example, argue that the state must 'cease its current discriminatory welfare provision and move towards forms of provision which are truly enabling'. Importantly, the enabling principle problematises the attempts of conventional public policy frameworks to address the causes and outcomes of social oppression. In particular, the principle of enabling justice can be used to interrogate, and – it is to be hoped – exact policy concessions from, state institutional practices which affect the well-being of socially oppressed people. . . .

NOTES

1 There is a voluminous literature which both supports these assertions, and highlights the pervasiveness of these discriminations in Western cities generally. This literature cannot be surveyed in entirety here; however, useful starting sources are Swain et al., (1993) (UK), Minister for Health, Housing and Community Services (1991) (Australia) and Eastern Bay of Plenty People First Committee (1993) (New Zealand). Lunt and Thornton (1994) also provide an authoritative overview of employment and disability in fifteen Western countries.

2 My information comes from ADAPT press releases posted on the GEOGABLE listserv on 15 Nov. 1997.

3 Dorn (1994) also correctly observes that the United States disability movement lacks the critical social theoretical appreciation of its British counterpart.

REFERENCES

Abberley, P. (1991a) *Disabled People: Three Theories of Disability*. Occasional Papers in Sociology, no. 10, Bristol: Department of Economics and Social Science, Bristol Polytechnic.

Abberley, P. (1991b) *Handicapped by Numbers: A Critique of the OPCS Disability Surveys*. Occasional Papers in Sociology, no. 9, Bristol: Department of Economics and Social Science, Bristol Polytechnic.

Alcock, P. (1993) *Understanding Poverty*, London: Macmillan.

Badcock, B. (1984) *Unfairly Structured Cities*, Oxford: Blackwell.

Butler, R. E. and Bowlby, S. (1997) 'Bodies and Spaces: an Exploration of Disabled People's Experiences of Public Space', *Environment and Planning D: Society and Space*, 15, 4, 411–33.

Campbell, J. and Oliver, M. (1996) *Disability Politics: Understanding Our Past, Changing Our Future*, London: Routledge.

Campbell, S. (1994) 'The Valued Norm: Supported Accommodation for People with Disabilities: A Discussion Paper', Sydney: New South Wales. Department of Community Services, Ageing and Disability Services Directorate.

Clapham, D. and Kintrea, K. (1992) *Housing Co-Operatives in Britain: Achievements and Prospects*, Harlow: Longman.

Corker, M. (1993) 'Integration and Deaf People: the Policy and Power of Enabling Environments', in Swain, J., Finkelstein, V., French, S. and Oliver, M. (eds.), *Disabling Barriers – Enabling Environments*, London: Sage.

Dear, M. (1980) 'The Public City', in Clark, W. A. V. and Moon, E. G. (eds.), *Residential Mobility and Public Policy*, Beverly Hills: Sage.

Dear, M. (1992) 'Understanding and Overcoming the NIMBY Syndrome', *Journal of the American Planning Association*, 58, 3, 288–99.

Dear, M. and Wolch, J. (1987) *Landscapes of Despair: From Deinstitutionalization to Homelessness*, Cambridge: Polity.

Disability Alliance (1987a) *Disability Rights Bulletin*, London: Disability Alliance.

Disability Alliance (1987b) *Poverty and Disability: Breaking the Link*, London: Disability Alliance.

Dorn, M. (1994) 'Disability as Spatial Dissidence: A Cultural Geography of the Stigmatized Body', unpublished M.Sc. thesis, The Pennsylvania State University.

Eastern Bay of Plenty People First Committee (1993) 'People First Conference Report 1993', Copy available from People First, PO Box 3017, Ohope Eastern Bay of Plenty, New Zealand.

Finger, A. (1995) '"Welfare Reform" and Us', *Ragged Edge*, Nov./Dec., 15 and 36.

Finkelstein, V. and Stuart, O. (1996) 'Developing New Services', in Hales, G. (ed.), *Beyond Disability: Toward an Enabling Society*, London: Sage.

Fraser, N. (1995) 'From Redistribution to Recognition? Dilemmas of Justice in a "Post-Socialist" Age', *New Left Review*, 212, 68–73.

Fraser, N. (1997) *Justice Interruptus: Reflections on the 'Postsocialist' Condition*, New York: Routledge.

Gilderbloom, J. I. and Rosentraub, M. S. (1990) 'Creating the Accessible City: Proposals for Providing Housing and Transportation for Low Income, Elderly and Disabled People', *American Journal of Economics and Sociology*, 49, 3, 271–82.

Gleeson, B. J. (1998) 'Disability and Poverty', in Fincher, R. and Nieuwenhuysen, J. (eds.), *Australian Poverty: Then and Now*, Melbourne: Melbourne University Press.

Hahn, H. (1986) 'Disability and the Urban Environment: a Perspective on Los Angeles', *Environment and Planning D: Society and Space*, 4, 273–88.

Hahn, H. (1987) 'Civil Rights for Disabled Americans: the Foundation of a Political Agenda', in Gartner, A. and Joe, T. (eds.), *Images of the Disabled/Disabling Images*, New York: Praeger.

Hales, G. (ed.) (1996) *Beyond Disability: Toward an Enabling Society*, London: Sage.

Harrison, M. and Gilbert, S. (eds.) (1992) *The Americans with Disabilities Handbook*, Beverly Hills, CA: Excellent Books.

Harvey, D. (1996) *Justice, Nature and the Politics of Difference*, Oxford: Blackwell.

Horner, A. (1994) 'Leaving the Institution', in Ballard, K. (ed.), *Disability, Family, Whanau and Society*, Hamilton North: Dunmore.

Imrie, R.F. (1996) *Disability and the City: International Perspectives*, London: Paul Chapman.

Imrie, R. F. and Wells, P. E. (1993) 'Disablism, Planning and the Built Environment', *Environment and Planning C: Government and Policy*, 11, 2, 213–31.

Jary, D. and Jary, J. (1991) *Dictionary of Sociology*, London: Harper-Collins.

Johnston, R. J., Gregory, D. and Smith, D. (eds.) (1994) *The Dictionary of Human Geography*, 3rd edn, Oxford: Blackwell.

Joseph, A. E. and Hall, G. B. (1985) 'The Locational Concentration of Group Homes in Toronto', *The Professional Geographer*, 37, 2, 143–54.

Kavka, G. S. (1992) 'Disability and the Right to Work', *Social Philosophy and Policy*, 9, 1, 262–90.

Le Breton, J. (1985) *Residential Services and People with a Disability*, Canberra: Australian Government Publishing Service.

Liachowitz, C. H. (1988) *Disability as Social Construct: Legislative Roots*, Philadelphia: University of Pennsylvania Press.

Lunt, N. and Thornton, P. (1994) 'Disability and Employment: Towards an Understanding of Discours and Employment', *Disability and Society*, 9(2), 223–8.

Milligan, C. (1996) 'Service Dependent Ghetto Formation – a Transferable Concept?', *Health and Place*, 2, 4, 199–211.

Minister for Health, Housing and Community Services (Australia) (1991) *Social Justice for People with Disabilities*, Canberra: Australian Government Publishing Service.

Morris, J. (1991) *Pride against Prejudice: Transforming Attitudes to Disability*, London: The Women's Press.

Oliver, M. (1990) *The Politics of Disablement*, London: Macmillan.

Oliver, M. (1991) 'Disability and Participation in the Labour Market', in Brown, P. and Scase, R. (eds.), *Poor Work: Disadvantage and the Division of Labour*, Milton Keynes: Open University Press.

Oliver, M. (1996) *Understanding Disability: From Theory to Practice*, London: Macmillan.

Oliver, M. and Barnes, C. (1993) 'Discrimination, Disability and Welfare: From Needs to Rights', in Swain, J., Finkelstein, V., French, S. and Oliver, M. (eds.), *Disabling Barriers – Enabling Environments*, London: Sage.

Parr, H. (1997) 'Mental Health, Public Space, and the City: Questions of Individual and Collective Access', *Environment and Planning D: Society and Space*, 15, 4, 35–54.

Ronalds, C. (1990) *National Employment Initiatives for People with Disabilities – a Discussion Paper*, Canberra: Australian Government Publishing Service.

Sandel, M. (1982) *Liberalism and the Limits of Justice*, Cambridge: Cambridge University Press.

Shannon, P. T. and Hovell, K. J. (1993) *Community Care Facilities: Experience and Effects*, Report prepared for Dunedin City Council and the Otago Area Health Board, Dunedin, New Zealand.

Shapiro, J. P. (1993) *No Pity: People with Disabilities Forging a New Civil Rights Movement*, New York: Times.

Smith, D. M. (1977) *Human Geography: a Welfare Approach*, London: Edward Arnold.

Smith, D. M. (1994) *Geography and Social Justice*, Oxford: Blackwell.

Steinman, L. D. (1987) 'The Effect of Land-Use Restrictions on the Establishment of Community Residences for the Disabled: a National Study', *The Urban Lawyer*, 19, 1–37.

Stewart, B. (1993) 'New Human Rights Bill is a Big Advance', *New Zealand Disabled*, July, 8–10.

Swain, J., Finkelstein, V., French, S. and Oliver, M. (1993) 'Introduction' in Swain, J., Finkelstein, V., French, S. and Oliver, M. (eds.) *Disabling Barriers – Enabling Environments*, London: Sage, 1–7.

Union of Physically Impaired Against Segregation (UPIAS) (1976) *Fundamental Principles of Disability*, London: UPIAS.

Walzer, M. (1983) *Spheres of Justice, A Defence of Pluralism and Equality*, New York: Basic Books.

Wolch, J. and Dear, N. (1993) *Malign Neglect: Homelessness in an American City*, San Francisco: Jossey-Bass.

Yeatman, A. (1996) *Getting Real: the Interim Report of the Review of the Commonwealth/State Disability Agreement*, Canberra: Australian Government Publishing Service.

Young, I. M. (1990) *Justice and the Politics of Difference*, Princeton, NJ: Princeton University Press.

Chapter 34

from *Flesh and Stone: The Body and the City in Western Civilization*

Richard Sennett

Fear of Touching: The Jewish Ghetto in Renaissance Venice

The plot of Shakespeare's *Merchant of Venice* (1596–97) turns on a circumstance which seems odd the moment we think about it. Shylock, the rich Jewish moneylender of Venice, has lent Bassanio 3,000 ducats for three months, and Bassanio's friend Antonio has pledged to repay the loan to Shylock. If Antonio fails, Shylock, who hates the aristocratic Christian Antonio and all the stands for, wants a pound of Antonio's flesh as a forfeit. As things tend to happen in plays, fortune goes against Antonio; ships carrying all his wealth are ruined in a storm. The odd thing is that Antonio and the Christian authorities who enter the play should feel obliged to keep their word to a Jew.

Outside the theatre, Shakespeare's audience treated Jews as half-human animals due little respect at law. Just a few years before Shakespeare wrote *The Merchant of Venice*, the most prominent Jew in England had been denied legal protection. Elizabeth I's physician Dr. Lopez was accused of having been in a plot to poison her; even though the Queen insisted Dr. Lopez should be tried, the public needed no other proof than his Jewish race, and Dr. Lopez was lynched. In his play, Shakespeare compounds these prejudices by making the Jewish moneylender into a cannibal.

Thus one might expect the Duke (*Doge*) of Venice to enter, a powerful *deus ex machina*, and throw the cannibal into prison, or at least declare the contract immoral and therefore void. Yet when one of the minor characters in *The Merchant of Venice* says he is sure the Duke is going to solve things exactly in this way, Antonio responds that "The Duke cannot deny the course of law."[1] The power Shylock holds over Antonio is the right of contract; once both parties have "freely entered into it," nothing else matters. The Duke acknowledges this when he meets Shylock, for all the Duke can do is plead with Shylock, who, safe in his rights, turns a deaf ear to the supreme power in the city. Portia, the woman who will eventually cut this Gordian knot, declares, "There is no power in Venice can alter a decree established."[2]

The plot of *The Merchant of Venice* seems to display the power of the economic forces first formed in the medieval university and other corporations. Shylock's money rights rule, the state cannot resist them. The play shows indeed a new extension of economic might as well in the binding power of a contract once, like Antonio and Shylock, the parties have agreed to it.

The Jew's economic force attacks, moreover, Christian community among Shakespeare's beleaguered Venetians. Antonio has generously agreed to help his friend Bassanio. Unlike Shylock, Antonio asks

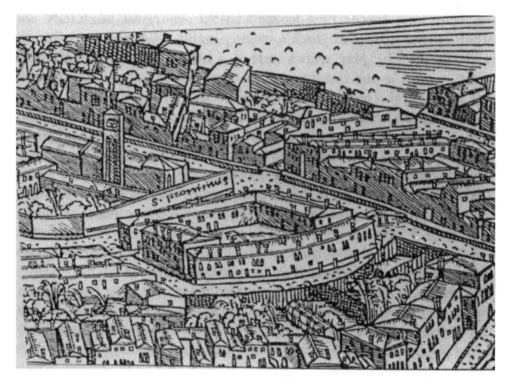

Figure 34.1   Jacopo dei Barbari's woodcut drawing of the Venetian Ghetto, 1500

for nothing in return; he feels compassion for Bassanio's plight. Shakespeare's Venetians are English gentlemen in business. These dream Venetians reappear in many guises in other plays of Shakespeare, in *A Midsummer Night's Dream* for instance, when Christian compassion sets things right in the end. But Venice had a special significance for Shakespeare and his contemporaries.

Venice was undoubtedly the most international city of the Renaissance, thanks to its trade, the gatepost between Europe and the East and between Europe and Africa. Englishmen and continental Europeans hoped they could develop navies like the great Venetian fleet, and thus profit from this international trade. Although by the 1590s, when Shakespeare wrote *The Merchant of Venice*, the wealth of Venice was in fact beginning to fade, its image in Europe was of a golden and luxuriant port. This image of the city Shakespeare could have gleaned from books like the expatriate Italian John Florio's *A World of Words*, or through the music of another expatriate, Alfonso Ferrabosco; a little later Shakespeare's audience would have seen the influences of the great Venetian architect Palladio on the architecture of Inigo Jones.

Venetian society appeared as a city of strangers, vast numbers of foreigners who came and went. The Venice which Elizabethans saw in their imagination was a place of enormous riches earned by contact with these heathens and infidels, wealth flowing from dealings with the Other. But unlike ancient Rome, Venice was not a territorial power; the foreigners who came and went in Venice were not members of a common empire or nation-state. Resident foreigners in the city – Germans, Greeks, Turks, Dalmatians, as well as Jews – were barred from official citizenship and lived as permanent immigrants. Contract was the key to opening the doors of wealth in this city of strangers. As Antonio declared,

For the commodity that strangers have
With us in Venice, if it be denied,
Will much impeach the justice of the state,
Since that the trade and profit of the city
Consisteth of all nations.[3]

In the real Venice where Shakespeare set his play, much of the action of the story would have been impossible. At one point Antonio invites Shylock to dinner. In the play, the Jew declines; in the real Venice, he would have had no choice. A real Jewish money-lender lived in the Ghetto the Venetians built for Jews in the course of the sixteenth century. A real moneylender was let out of the Ghetto, situated at the edge of the city, at dawn, where he made his way to the financial district around the Rialto wooden drawbridge near the city's center. By dusk the Jew was obliged to return to the cramped Ghetto; at nightfall its gates were locked, the shutters of its houses that looked outward closed; police patrolled the exterior. The medieval adage "*Stadt Luft macht frei*" would leave a bitter taste in the Jew's mouth, for the right to do business in the city did not bring a more general freedom. The Jew who contracted as an equal lived as a segregated man.

In that real Venice, the desire for Christian community lay somewhere between a dream and an anxiety. The impurities of difference haunted the Venetians: Albanians, Turks, and Greeks, Western Christians like the Germans, all were segregated in guarded buildings or clusters of buildings. Difference haunted the Venetians, yet exerted a seductive power.

When they shut the Jews inside the Ghetto, the Venetians claimed and believed they were isolating a disease that had infected the Christian community, for they identified the Jews in particular with corrupting bodily vices. Christians were afraid of touching Jews: Jewish bodies were thought to carry venereal diseases as well as to contain more mysterious polluting powers. The Jewish body was unclean. A little detail of ritual in business illuminated this unease of touch; whereas among Christians a contract was sealed with a kiss or with a handshake, contracts with Jews were sealed with a bow, so that the bodies of the parties need not touch. The very contract Shylock draws with Antonio, the payment in flesh, conveyed the fear the Jew would defile a Christian's body by using his power of money.

In the medieval era, the Imitation of Christ made people more sympathetically aware of the body, especially the suffering body. The fear of touching Jews represents the frontier of that conception of a common body; beyond the frontier lay a threat – a threat redoubled because the impurity of the alien body was associated with sensuality, with the lure of the Oriental, a body cut free from Christian constraints. The touch of the Jew defiles, yet seduces. The segregated space of the Ghetto represented a compromise between the economic need of Jews and these aversions to them, between practical necessity and physical fear.

The making of the Ghetto occurred at a crucial moment for Venice. The city leaders had lost a great advantage in trade, and suffered a crushing military defeat, a few years before. They blamed these losses largely on the state of the city's morals, bodily vices provoked by the very wealth now slipping from its grasp; from this moral campaign to reform the city came the plan for the Ghetto. By segregating those who were different, by no longer having to touch and see them, the city fathers hoped peace and dignity would return to their city. This was the Venetian version of Brueghel's tranquil dreamscape in *Landscape with the Fall of Icarus*.

It is easy to imagine today that Jews had always lived in Europe isolated in ghetto space. Indeed, from the Lateran Council of 1179 forward, Christian Europe had sought to prevent Jews living in the midst of Christians. In all European cities which harbored colonies of Jews, such as London, Frankfurt, and Rome, they were forced to live apart. Rome typified the problem of enforcing the edict of the Lateran Council. Rome had what is now called its Ghetto from early medieval times; a few streets in the Jewish quarter of medieval Rome were gated, but the urban fabric was too disordered for the Jews to be totally sealed in. In Venice, the physical character of the city made it possible finally to realize the rule prescribed by the Lateran Council – Venice a city built on water, water the city's roads which separated clusters of buildings into a vast archipelago of islands. In the making of the Jewish Ghetto, the city fathers put the water to use to create segregation: the Ghetto was a group of islands around which the canals became like a moat.

If the Venetian Jews suffered from the struggle to impose a Christian community on the economic mosaic, they did not suffer as passive victims. The formation of the Jewish Ghetto tells the story of a people who were segregated but who then made new forms of community life out of their very segregation; indeed, the Jews of Renaissance Venice gained a certain degree of self-determination in the Ghettos. Moreover, the city protected a Jew or a Turk against Christian mobs at Lent or at other times of high religious passion, so long as the non-Christian was in the space reserved for the outsider.

Segregation increased the Jew's daily Otherness, non-Christian lives ever more enigmatic to the dominant powers beyond Ghetto walls. For the Jews themselves, the Ghetto raised the stakes of contact with the outside world: their own Jewishness seemed at risk when they ventured outside the Ghetto. For over three thousand years the Jews had survived in small cells mixed among their oppressors, a people sustained in their faith no matter where they lived. Now the bonds of faith among these People of the Word began to depend more upon having a place of their own, where they could be Jewish.

Community and repression: Venetian Christians sought to create a Christian community by segregating those who were different, drawing on the fear of touching alien, seductive bodies. Jewish identity became entangled in that same geography of repression. . . .

The urban condom

The Jews were not the first group of outsiders that the Venetians shut away in a prophylactic space; Greeks, Turks, and other ethnic groups were also segregated. Perhaps the least controversial of the outsiders segregated before were the Germans, who were, after all, fellow Christians. The link between Germany and Venice was apparent to Shakespeare in England, who has Shylock burst out at one point in *The Merchant of Venice*, "A diamond gone [that] cost me two thousand ducats in Frankfurt."[4]

By Shakespeare's time, trade with Germans had become of great importance to Venice. The Germans came to Venice to sell, as well as to buy. In 1314, the Venetians decided they would make sure that the Germans paid their taxes by concentrating them all in one building; here the Germans registered themselves and their goods, and were meant both to live and work. This building was the *Fondaco dei Tedeschi* – the "Factory of the Germans." The original Fondaco dei Tedeschi was a medieval house writ large, with the further condition that all its inhabitants be German. As a building, it provided the model for later, more repressive spatial forms of segregation.

In its early form, the Fondaco served as a reception center for distinguished foreigners in addition to resident Germans. But in principle no one was supposed to leave it after dark; in fact nighttime proved the busiest part of the day for the Germans, who smuggled goods in and out under cover of darkness to avoid paying customs. In 1479, the government therefore took steps to ensure that this place of segregation became a building of isolation; it was decreed that at dusk the windows were to be shut and the doors to the Fondaco locked – from the outside.

Within, the building also became a repressive space, the Germans constantly under the watchful eyes of the Venetians. "Everything was arranged for them," says the historian Hugh Honour. "All the servants and higher functionaries were appointed by the State. The merchants were allowed to transact business only with born Venetians and only through the brokers who were allotted to them and who took a percentage on every deal."[5] The German Fondaco that exists today in Venice was built in 1505. It is an enormous building, and testified to the wealth of the Germans, yet in its very form refined the principles of concentration and isolation which had shaped the use of the older Fondaco. The new Fondaco dei Tedeschi, which today serves Venice as a post office, is a squat, uniform building built around a central court; open galleries ran around this courtyard at each story, and were policed by the Venetians, who could thus practice surveillance day and night of their northern "guests."

These Germans, of course, were Christian. Their surveillance began as a matter of pure economics. In the decades after the disaster of the League of Cambrai wars, however, the Venetians as good Catholics were first becoming aware of the great tide of Reformation taking place in Germany and in other lands to the north; and so the city's control over its German merchants began to shift from a purely commercial basis to a cultural one as well. At this point, images of the body intruded. The authorities wanted to halt the "infection" of the Reformation, its heresies perceived as forms of self-indulgence, free of the priests, leading to sins like sloth and luxury. The Reformed German moved closer in the Catholic imagination to the Jew.[6] Until 1531 some few Germans, usually the very wealthiest, could buy their way out of the Fondaco dei Tedeschi. In 1531 the city ordered all Germans to live together in the Fondaco, once and for all, and added spies to the guards in their midst to detect signs of religious heresy.

As a consequence of segregation, herded together, isolated, these foreigners began to feel a bond amongst themselves. They acted cohesively in their dealings with the Italians, even though in fact there were sharp divisions between the Protestants and the Catholics in the building. The space of repression became incorporated into their own sense of community. This was the future which awaited the Jews.

In 1515 the Venetians started to explore the possibility of using the Ghetto Nuovo as a site for segregating Jews. *Ghetto* originally meant "foundry" in Italian (from *gettare*, "to pour"). The Ghetto Vecchio and Ghetto Nuovo served as the old foundry districts of Venice, far from the ceremonial center of the city; their manufacturing functions had shifted by 1500 to the Arsenal. The Ghetto Nuovo was a rhomboid piece of land surrounded on all sides by water; buildings created a wall all around its edges with an open space in the center. Only two bridges connected it to the rest of the urban fabric. With these bridges closed, the Ghetto Nuovo could be sealed up.

At the time the Ghetto Nuovo was transformed, the city's "streets, squares, and courtyards were not covered, as they are now, with the uniform paving of rectangular blocks of volcanic trachyte. Many streets and courtyards had no hard surface at all.... Often only the parts of squares adjoining particular buildings were paved."[7] During the century before the Ghetto Nuovo enclosed the Jews, the city began to form steep banks to line the sides of the canals. These banks encouraged the rapid flow of water, and so kept the canals from silting up. The built-up banks then made it possible to place paths alongside the canals, a water-and-land form called a *fondamente*. The Cannaregio area of Venice was regularized in such a way, and it was near this area that the Ghetto Nuovo and Ghetto Vecchio were located. The two Ghettos, abandoned for industry and lightly populated, were not part of this renovation; they were both physical and economic islands within the city. The few bridges that connected these inner islands to other landmasses debouched in an ancient Venetian urban form, the *sottoportegho*. The sottoportegho was a passageway made under a building, low and dank, since the passageway lay at the same level as the pilings and foundation stones which supported the buildings above. At the end of the *sottoporti* were locked doors. It was a scene far, far removed from rich boys dressed only in jewels gliding past the Ca D'Oro on the Grand Canal.

The proposal to make use of the Ghetto Nuovo came from Zacaria Dolfin in 1515. His plan for the segregation of the Jews was to

> Send all of them to live in the Ghetto Nuovo which is like a castle, and to make drawbridges and close it with a wall; they should have only one gate, which would enclose them there and they would stay there, and two boats of the Council of Ten would go and stay there at night, at their expense, for their greater security.[8]

This proposal contains one key difference from the conception of segregation built into the Fondaco dei Tedeschi: in the Jewish Ghetto there was to be no *internal* surveillance. External surveillance would take place from the boats, circling the Ghetto throughout the night. Imprisoned inside, the Jews were to be left to themselves, an abandoned people.

Dolfin's proposal was put into practice beginning in 1516. Jews were moved into the Ghetto Nuovo from all sections of the city, but particularly from the Giudecca, where Jews had congregated since 1090. Not all Jews, however. When the Sephardic Jews were expelled from Spain in 1492, a group came to live in a little colony in Venice near a burial ground for executed criminals. There they remained, as did Levantine Jews in other parts of the city, who passed in and out of Venice from the Adriatic coast and the Middle East. Moreover, an important part of the story of the Ghetto is that many Venetian Jews, when faced with the prospect of living in the Ghetto, left the city instead.

About seven hundred Jews, mostly Ashkenazim, were first sent into the Ghetto in 1516. The original annexation in the Ghetto was twenty houses only. These were owned by Christians, since Jews in Venice, as elsewhere, were denied the right to own land or buildings; they could only rent from year to year. As more houses were renovated, rents sky-rocketed; Brian Pullan says that rent on "the narrow houses in the Ghetto was three times as high as it would have been on similar cramped accommodation in the Christian city."[9] The buildings were gradually added to, reaching six or seven stories in height, listing to the sides since their weight was not well supported by piles in the substrate.

The drawbridges opened in the morning and some Jews fanned out into the city, mostly around the area of the Rialto where they circulated with the ordinary crowd. Christians came into the Ghetto to borrow money or to sell food and do business. At dusk, all the Jews were obliged to be back in the Ghetto, the Christians to be out; the draw bridges were raised. Moreover, the windows fronting the exterior were shut every evening and all balconies removed from them, so that the buildings facing the canals outside became like the sheer walls of a castle.

This was the first stage of segregating the Jews. The second stage involved expanding the Jewish quarter to the Ghetto Vecchio, the old foundry district. This occurred in 1541. By this time, the Venetians were hurting even more financially; their customs tariffs had become higher than other cities and they were losing trade. The long twilight of the Venetian Republic, so feared since the discovery of another route to the Far East, had begun. The Venetian authorities decided in the 1520s to lower their customs barriers, and one result was that Levantine Jews, mostly from what is now Romania and Syria, stayed longer in the city. They were slightly more than travelling peddlers and slightly less than bourgeois businessmen; they hawked whatever they could lay their hands on. Sanuto put crisply the attitude of his fellow Venetians toward such Jewish dealers: "Our countrymen have never wanted Jews to keep shops and to trade in this city, but to buy and sell and go away again."[10] But now these Jews did not go away; they wanted to stay and were willing to pay a price for it.

To house them, the old Ghetto was transformed into a Jewish space, its outer walls sealed, its balconies removed. Unlike the first, this second Ghetto had a small open square and many small streets, a squalid turf entirely unpaved, the piles so carelessly driven into the substrate that the buildings of the Old Ghetto began to sink the moment they were constructed. A century later, a third Ghetto space, the Ghetto Nuovissimo, was opened in 1633, a smaller plot of land with somewhat better housing stock, which was again treated to the castle-and-moat process of walling in. When the third Ghetto was filled with people, the population densities were about triple those of Venice as a whole. Because of these physical conditions, plague found a welcome home in the Ghetto. The Jews sought to protect themselves by recourse to their own doctors, but medical knowledge could not combat the condition of soil and buildings, as well as the ever-mounting density of population. When plague struck in the Ghetto, the gates of the Ghetto were instead locked for most of the day as well as night.

No attempt was made to alter the behavior of Jews after forcing them into the Venetian Ghettos, for there was no desire to reclaim the Jew for the city. In this, the Ghetto of Venice embodied a different ethos of isolation from the ethos practiced shortly afterward in Renaissance Rome, in the Roman Ghetto Pope Paul IV began to build in 1555. The Roman Ghetto was indeed meant to be a space to transform the Jews. Paul IV proposed closing up all the Jews together in one place in order that Christian priests could systematically convert them, house by house, forcing the Jews to listen to Christ's word. The Roman Ghetto was a miserable failure in this, only twenty or so Jews a year out of a population of four thousand inhabitants succumbing to conversion.

Moreover, the Roman Ghetto differed from the Venetian in that it occupied a highly visible place in the center of the city. Its walls cut into two a commercial zone previously controlled by prominent Roman commercial families, who in turn traded with the resident community of Jews. In taking over the space of the Roman Ghetto for conversion, the Pope sought to weaken the spatial grip of this old Christian merchant class on Roman affairs. To be sure, Rome at this time was more insular than Venice, despite the presence of the papacy; it contained many fewer foreigners, and the strangers who came to the Papal Court were clerics, ambassadors, or other diplomats. Venice was a different kind of international city, suffused with dubious foreigners.

A moralizing force sure of itself will challenge and transform moral "filth," as did the Roman papacy. A society profoundly uncertain of itself, as at this moment Venice was, fears that it lacks powers of *resistance*. It fears it may succumb when it mixes physically with the Other. Infection and seduction are inseparable. The Venetian moralists after Agnadello feared that a city of many thousand would succumb by contact with a few hundred; the moralists spoke of the Jews with their bags of money and the boys gliding naked on the canals in the same breath, or of usury as tinged with the allures of prostitution. The Venetian language in which touch seems fatal resonates with some of the same moral undertow as modern rhetoric about AIDS, in which seduction and infection also seem inseparable. In turn, the Ghetto represented something like an urban condom. . . .

NOTES

1 William Shakespeare, *The Merchant of Venice*, ed. W. Moelwyn Merchant (London: Penguin, 1967), III.3.26.

2 Ibid., IV. 1.215–16.
3 Ibid., III.3.27–31.
4 Ibid., III. 1.76–7.

5   Hugh Honour, *Venice* (London: Collins, 1990), 189.

6   See Mary Douglas, *Purity and Danger: An Analysis of Concepts of Pollution and Taboo* (London: Routledge & Kegan Paul, 1978), for an entirely convincing, general account of how asceticism can "migrate" into sensuality in the eyes of those it threatens.

7   Norbert Huse and Wolfgang Wolters, *The Art of Renaissance Venice: Architecture, Sculpture, and Painting, 1460–1590*, trans. Edmund Jephcott (Chicago: University of Chicago Press, 1990), 8.

8   Zacaria Dolfin; quoted in Benjamin Ravid, "The Religious, Economic, and Social Background and Context of the Establishment of the Ghetti of Venice" (1983), *Gli Ebrei e Venezia*, ed. Gaetano Cozzi (Milano: Edizioni di Communità, 1987), 215.

9   Brian S. Pullan, *The Jews of Europe and the Inquisition of Venice, 1550–1670* (Totowa, NJ: Barnes & Noble, 1983), 157–8.

10 Quoted in ibid., 158.

Chapter 35

from *City of Quartz: Excavating the Future in Los Angeles*

Mike Davis

The carefully manicured lawns of Los Angeles's Westside sprout forests of ominous little signs warning: 'Armed Response!' Even richer neighborhoods in the canyons and hillsides isolate themselves behind walls guarded by guntoting private police and state-of-the-art electronic surveillance. Downtown, a publicly-subsidized 'urban renaissance' has raised the nation's largest corporate citadel, segregated from the poor neighborhoods around it by a monumental architectural glacis. In Hollywood, celebrity architect Frank Gehry, renowned for his 'humanism', apotheosizes the siege look in a library designed to resemble a foreign-legion fort. In the Westlake district and the San Fernando Valley the Los Angeles Police barricade streets and seal off poor neighborhoods as part of their 'war on drugs'. In Watts, developer Alexander Haagen demonstrates his strategy for recolonizing inner-city retail markets: a panoptican shopping mall surrounded by staked metal fences and a substation of the LAPD in a central surveillance tower. Finally on the horizon of the next millennium, an ex-chief of police crusades for an anti-crime 'giant eye' – a geo-synchronous law enforcement satellite – while other cops discreetly tend versions of 'Garden Plot', a hoary but still viable 1960s plan for a law-and-order armageddon.

Welcome to post-liberal Los Angeles, where the defense of luxury lifestyles is translated into a proliferation of new repressions in space and movement, undergirded by the ubiquitous 'armed response'. This obsession with physical security systems, and, collaterally, with the architectural policing of social boundaries, has become a zeitgeist of urban restructuring, a master narrative in the emerging built environment of the 1990s. Yet contemporary urban theory, whether debating the role of electronic technologies in precipitating 'postmodern space', or discussing the dispersion of urban functions across polycentered metropolitan 'galaxies', has been strangely silent about the militarization of city life so grimly visible at the street level. Hollywood's pop apocalypses and pulp science fiction have been more realistic, and politically perceptive, in representing the programmed hardening of the urban surface in the wake of the social polarizations of the Reagan era. Images of carceral inner cities (*Escape from New York, Running Man*), high-tech police death squads (*Blade Runner*), sentient buildings (*Die Hard*), urban bantustans (*They Live!*), Vietnam-like street wars (*Colors*), and so on, only extrapolate from actually existing trends.

Such dystopian visions grasp the extent to which today's pharaonic scales of residential and commercial security supplant residual hopes for urban reform and social integration. The dire predictions of

Richard Nixon's 1969 National Commission on the Causes and Prevention of Violence have been tragically fulfilled: we live in 'fortress cities' brutally divided between 'fortified cells' of affluent society and 'places of terror' where the police battle the criminalized poor.[1] The 'Second Civil War' that began in the long hot summers of the 1960s has been institutionalized into the very structure of urban space. The old liberal paradigm of social control, attempting to balance repression with reform, has long been superseded by a rhetoric of social warfare that calculates the interests of the urban poor and the middle classes as a zero-sum game. In cities like Los Angeles, on the bad edge of postmodernity, one observes an unprecedented tendency to merge urban design, architecture and the police apparatus into a single, comprehensive security effort.

This epochal coalescence has far-reaching consequences for the social relations of the built environment. In the first place, the market provision of 'security' generates its own paranoid demand. 'Security' becomes a positional good defined by income access to private 'protective services' and membership in some hardened residential enclave or restricted suburb. As a prestige symbol – and sometimes as the decisive borderline between the merely well-off and the 'truly rich' – 'security' has less to do with personal safety than with the degree of personal insulation, in residential, work, consumption and travel environments, from 'unsavory' groups and individuals, even crowds in general.

Secondly, as William Whyte has observed of social intercourse in New York, 'fear proves itself'. The social perception of threat becomes a function of the security mobilization itself, not crime rates. Where there is an actual rising arc of street violence, as in Southcentral Los Angeles or Downtown Washington DC, most of the carnage is self-contained within ethnic or class boundaries. Yet white middle-class imagination, absent from any first-hand knowledge of inner-city conditions, magnifies the perceived threat through a demonological lens. Surveys show that Milwaukee suburbanites are just as worried about violent crime as inner-city Washingtonians, despite a twenty-fold difference in relative levels of mayhem. The media, whose function in this arena is to bury and obscure the daily economic violence of the city, ceaselessly throw up spectres of criminal underclasses and psychotic stalkers. Sensationalized accounts of killer youth gangs high on crack and shrilly racist evocations of marauding Willie Hortons foment the moral panics that reinforce and justify urban apartheid.

Moreover, the neo-military syntax of contemporary architecture insinuates violence and conjures imaginary dangers. In many instances the semiotics of so-called 'defensible space' are just about as subtle as a swaggering white cop. Today's upscale, pseudo-public spaces – sumptuary malls, office centers, culture acropolises, and so on – are full of invisible signs warning off the underclass 'Other'. Although architectural critics are usually oblivious to how the built environment contributes to segregation, pariah groups – whether poor Latino families, young Black men, or elderly homeless white females – read the meaning immediately.

The Destruction of Public Space

The universal and ineluctable consequence of this crusade to secure the city is the destruction of accessible public space. The contemporary opprobrium attached to the term 'street person' is in itself a harrowing index of the devaluation of public spaces. To reduce contact with untouchables, urban redevelopment has converted once vital pedestrian streets into traffic sewers and transformed public parks into temporary receptacles for the homeless and wretched. The American city, as many critics have recognized, is being systematically turned inside out – or, rather, outside in. The valorized spaces of the new megastructures and super-malls are concentrated in the center, street frontage is denuded, public activity is sorted into strictly functional compartments, and circulation is internalized in corridors under the gaze of private police.[2]

The privatization of the architectural public realm, moreover, is shadowed by parallel restructurings of electronic space, as heavily policed, pay-access 'information orders', elite data-bases and subscription cable services appropriate parts of the invisible agora. Both processes, of course, mirror the deregulation of the economy and the recession of non-market entitlements. The decline of urban liberalism has been accompanied by the death of what might be called the 'Olmstedian vision' of public space. Frederick Law Olmsted, it will be recalled, was North America's Haussmann, as well as the Father of Central Park. In the wake of Manhattan's 'Commune' of 1863, the great Draft Riot, he conceived public landscapes and parks as social safety-valves, *mixing* classes and ethnicities in common (bourgeois) recreations and enjoyments. As Manfredo Tafuri has shown in his well-known study of Rockefeller Center, the same principle animated the construction of the canonical urban spaces of the La Guardia – Roosevelt era.[3]

This reformist vision of public space – as the emollient of class struggle, if not the bedrock of the American *polis* – is now as obsolete as Keynesian nostrums of full employment. In regard to the 'mixing' of classes, contemporary urban America is more like Victorian England than Walt Whitman's or La Guardia's New York. In Los Angeles, once-upon-a-time a demi-paradise of free beaches, luxurious parks, and 'cruising strips', genuinely democratic space is all but extinct. The Oz-like archipelago of Westside pleasure domes – a continuum of tony malls, arts centers and gourmet strips – is reciprocally dependent upon the social imprisonment of the third-world service proletariat who live in increasingly repressive ghettoes and barrios. In a city of several million yearning immigrants, public amenities are radically shrinking, parks are becoming derelict and beaches more segregated, libraries and playgrounds are closing, youth congregations of ordinary kinds are banned, and the streets are becoming more desolate and dangerous.

Unsurprisingly, as in other American cities, municipal policy has taken its lead from the security offensive and the middle-class demand for increased spatial and social insulation. De facto disinvestment in traditional public space and recreation has supported the shift of fiscal resources to corporate-defined redevelopment priorities. A pliant city government – in this case ironically professing to represent a bi-racial coalition of liberal whites and Blacks – has collaborated in the massive privatization of public space and the subsidization of new, racist enclaves (benignly described as 'urban villages'). Yet most current, giddy discussions of the 'postmodern' scene in Los Angeles neglect entirely these overbearing aspects of counter-urbanization and counter-insurgency. A triumphal gloss – 'urban renaissance', 'city of the future', and so on – is laid over the brutalization of inner-city neighborhoods and the increasing South Africanization of its spatial relations. Even as the walls have come down in Eastern Europe, they are being erected all over Los Angeles.

The observations that follow take as their thesis the existence of this new class war (sometimes a continuation of the race war of the 1960s) at the level of the built environment. Although this is not a comprehensive account, which would require a thorough analysis of economic and political dynamics, these images and instances are meant to convince the reader that urban form is indeed following a repressive function in the political furrows of the Reagan–Bush era. Los Angeles, in its usual prefigurative mode, offers an especially disquieting catalogue of the emergent liaisons between architecture and the American police state.

The Forbidden City

The first militarist of space in Los Angeles was General Otis of the *Times*. Declaring himself at war with labor, he infused his surroundings with an unrelentingly belli-cose air:

> He called his home in Los Angeles the Bivouac. Another house was known as the Outpost. The *Times* was known as the Fortress. The staff of the paper was the Phalanx. The *Times* building itself was more fortress than newspaper plant, there were turrets, battlements, sentry boxes. Inside he stored fifty rifles.[4]

A great, menacing bronze eagle was the *Times*'s crown; a small, functional cannon was installed on the hood of Otis's touring car to intimidate onlookers. Not surpris-ingly, this overwrought display of aggres-sion produced a response in kind. On 1 October 1910 the heavily fortified *Times* headquarters – citadel of the open shop on the West Coast – was destroyed in a catastrophic explosion blamed on union saboteurs.

Eighty years later, the spirit of General Otis has returned to subtly pervade Los Angeles's new 'postmodern' Downtown: the emerging Pacific Rim financial complex which cascades, in rows of skyscrapers, from Bunker Hill southward along the Fig-ueroa corridor. Redeveloped with public tax increments under the aegis of the powerful and largely unaccountable Com-munity Redevelopment Agency, the Down-town project is one of the largest postwar urban designs in North America. Site as-semblage and clearing on a vast scale, with little mobilized opposition, have res-urrected land values, upon which big devel-opers and off-shore capital (increasingly Japanese) have planted a series of billion-dollar, block-square mega-structures: Crocker Center, the Bonaventure Hotel and Shopping Mall, the World Trade Center, the Broadway Plaza, Arco Center, CitiCorp Plaza, California Plaza, and so on. With historical landscapes erased, with megastructures and superblocks as primary components, and with an increas-ingly dense and self-contained circulation system, the new financial district is best conceived as a single, demonically self-referential hyper-structure, a Miesian sky-scape raised to dementia.

Like similar megalomaniac complexes, tethered to fragmented and desolated Downtowns (for instance, the Renaissance Center in Detroit, the Peachtree and Omni Centers in Atlanta, and so on), Bunker Hill and the Figueroa corridor have provoked a storm of liberal objections against their abuse of scale and composition, their deni-gration of street landscape, and their con-fiscation of so much of the vital life activity of the center, now sequestered within sub-terranean concourses or privatized malls. Sam Hall Kaplan, the crusty urban critic of the *Times*, has been indefatigable in de-nouncing the anti-pedestrian bias of the new corporate citadel, with its fascist oblit-eration of street frontage. In his view the superimposition of 'hermetically sealed fortresses' and air-dropped 'pieces of sub-urbia' has 'dammed the rivers of life' Downtown.[5]

Yet Kaplan's vigorous defense of pedes-trian democracy remains grounded in hack-neyed liberal complaints about 'bland design' and 'elitist planning practices'. Like most architectural critics, he rails against the oversights of urban design with-out recognizing the dimension of foresight, of explicit repressive intention, which has its roots in Los Angeles's ancient history of class and race warfare. Indeed, when Downtown's new 'Gold Coast' is viewed en bloc from the standpoint of its inter-actions with other social areas and land-scapes in the central city, the 'fortress effect' emerges, not as an inadvertent fail-ure of design, but as deliberate socio-spatial strategy.

The goals of this strategy may be sum-marized as a double repression: to raze all association with Downtown's past and to prevent any articulation with the non-Anglo urbanity of its future. Everywhere on the perimeter of redevelopment this strategy takes the form of a brutal architec-tural edge or glacis that defines the new Downtown as a citadel vis-à-vis the rest of the central city. Los Angeles is unusual amongst major urban renewal centers in preserving, however, negligently, most of its circa 1900–30 Beaux Arts commercial core. At immense public cost, the corporate headquarters and financial district was shifted from the old Broadway-Spring corridor six blocks west to the greenfield site created by destroying the Bunker Hill residential neighborhood. To emphasize the 'security' of the new Downtown, virtually all the traditional pedestrian links to the old center, including the famous Angels' Flight funicular railroad, were removed.

The logic of this entire operation is revealing. In order cities developers might have attempted to articulate the new skyscape and the old, exploiting the latter's extraordinary inventory of theaters and historic buildings to create a gentrified history – a gaslight district, Faneuil Market or Ghirardelli Square – as a support to middle-class residential colonization. But Los Angeles's redevelopers viewed property values in the old Broadway core as irreversibly eroded by the area's very centrality to public transport, and especially by its heavy use by Black and Mexican poor. In the wake of the Watts Rebellion, and the perceived Black threat to crucial nodes of white power (spelled out in lurid detail in the McCone Commission Report), resegregated spatial security became the paramount concern.[6] The Los Angeles Police Department abetted the flight of business from Broadway to the fortified redoubts of Bunker Hill by spreading scare literature typifying Black teenagers as dangerous gang members.[7]

As a result, redevelopment massively reproduced spatial apartheid. The moat of the Harbor Freeway and the regraded palisades of Bunker Hill cut off the new financial core from the poor immigrant neighborhoods that surround it on every side. Along the base of California Plaza, Hill Street became a local Berlin Wall separating the publicly subsidized luxury of Bunker Hill from the lifeworld of Broadway, now reclaimed by Latino immigrants as their primary shopping and entertainment street. Because politically connected

speculators are now redeveloping the northern end of the Broadway corridor (sometimes known as 'Bunker Hill East'), the CRA is promising to restore pedestrian linkages to the Hill in the 1990s, including the Angels' Flight incline railroad. This, of course, only dramatizes the current bias against accessibility – that is to say, against *any* spatial interaction between old and new, poor and rich, except in the framework of gentrification or recolonization.[8] Although a few white-collars venture into the Grand Central Market – a popular emporium of tropical produce and fresh foods – Latino shoppers or Saturday strollers never circulate in the Gucci precincts above Hill Street. The occasional appearance of a destitute street nomad in Broadway Plaza or in front of the Museum of Contemporary Art sets off a quiet panic; video cameras turn on their mounts and security guards adjust their belts.

Photographs of the old Downtown in its prime show mixed crowds of Anglo, Black and Latino pedestrians of different ages and classes. The contemporary Downtown 'renaissance' is designed to make such heterogeneity virtually impossible. It is intended not just to 'kill the street' as Kaplan fears, but to 'kill the crowd', to eliminate that democratic admixture on the pavements and in the parks that Olmsted believed was America's antidote to European class polarizations. The Downtown hyperstructure – like some Buckminster Fuller post-Holocaust fantasy – is programmed to ensure a seamless continuum of middle-class work, consumption and recreation, without unwonted exposure to Downtown's working-class street environments.[9] Indeed the totalitarian semiotics of ramparts and battlements, reflective glass and elevated pedways, rebukes any affinity or sympathy between different architectural or human orders. As in Otis's fortress *Times* building, this is the archisemiotics of class war.

Lest this seem too extreme, consider *Urban Land* magazine's recent description of the profit-driven formula that across the United States has linked together clustered development, social homogeneity, and a secure 'Downtown image':

HOW TO OVERCOME FEAR OF CRIME
IN DOWNTOWNS
Create a Dense, Compact, Multifunctional Core Area. A downtown can be designed and developed to make visitors feel that it – or a significant portion of it – is attractive and the type of place that 'respectable people' like themselves tend to frequent.... A core downtown area that is compact, densely developed and multifunctional will concentrate people, giving them more activities.... The activities offered in this core area will determine what 'type' of people will be strolling its sidewalks; locating offices and housing for middle-and upper-income residents in or near the core area can assure a high percentage of 'respectable', law-abiding pedestrians. Such an attractive redeveloped core area would also be large enough to affect the downtown's overall image.[10]

Sadistic Street Environments

This conscious 'hardening' of the city surface against the poor is especially brazen in the Manichaean treatment of Downtown microcosms. In his famous study of the 'social life of small urban spaces', William Whyte makes the point that the quality of any urban environment can be measured, first of all, by whether there are convenient, comfortable places for pedestrains to sit.[11] This maxim has been warmly taken to heart by designers of the high-corporate precincts of Bunker Hill and the emerging 'urban village' of South Park. As part of the city's policy of subsidizing white-collar residential colonization in Downtown, it has spent, or plans to spend, tens of millions of dollars of diverted tax revenue on enticing, 'soft' environments in these areas. Planners envision an opulent complex of squares, fountains, world-class public art, exotic shubbery, and avant-garde street furniture along a Hope Street pedestrian corridor. In the propaganda of official boosters, nothing is taken as a better index of Downtown's 'liveability' than the idyll of office

workers and upscale tourists lounging or napping in the terraced gardens of California Plaza, the 'Spanish Steps' or Grand Hope Park.

In stark contrast, a few blocks away, the city is engaged in a merciless struggle to make public facilities and spaces as 'unliveable' as possible for the homeless and the poor. The persistence of thousands of street people on the fringes of Bunker Hill and the Civic Center sours the image of designer Downtown living and betrays the laboriously constructed illusion of a Downtown 'renaissance'. City Hall then retaliates with its own variant of low-intensity warfare.[12]

Although city leaders periodically essay schemes for removing indigents *en masse* – deporting them to a poor farm on the edge of the desert, confining them in camps in the mountains, or, memorably, interning them on a derelict ferry at the Harbor – such 'final solutions' have been blocked by council members fearful of the displacement of the homeless into their districts. Instead the city, self-consciously adopting the idiom of urban cold war, promotes the 'containment' (official term) of the homeless in Skid Row along Fifth Street east of the Broadway, systematically transforming the neighborhood into an outdoor poorhouse. But this containment strategy breeds its own vicious circle of contradiction. By condensing the mass of the desperate and helpless together in such a small space, and denying adequate housing, official policy has transformed Skid Row into probably the most dangerous ten square blocks in the world – ruled by a grisly succession of 'Slashers', 'Night Stalkers' and more ordinary predators.[13] Every night on Skid Row is Friday the 13th, and, unsurprisingly, many of the homeless seek to escape the 'Nickle' during the night at all costs, searching safer niches in other parts of Downtown. The city in turn tightens the noose with increased police harassment and ingenious design deterrents.

One of the most common, but mind-numbing, of these deterrents is the Rapid Transit District's new barrelshaped bus bench that offers a minimal surface for uncomfortable sitting, while making sleeping utterly impossible. Such 'bumproof' benches are being widely introduced on the periphery of Skid Row. Another invention, worthy of the Grand Guignol, is the aggressive deployment of outdoor sprinklers. Several years ago the city opened a 'Skid Row Park' along lower Fifth Street, on a corner of Hell. To ensure that the park was not used for sleeping – that is to say, to guarantee that it was mainly utilized for drug dealing and prostitution – the city installed an elaborate overhead sprinkler system programmed to drench unsuspecting sleepers at random times during the night. The system was immediately copied by some local businessmen in order to drive the homeless away from adjacent public sidewalks. Meanwhile restaurants and markets have responded to the homeless by building ornate enclosures to protect their refuse. Although no one in Los Angeles has yet proposed adding cyanide to the garbage, as happened in Phoenix a few years back, one popular seafood restaurant has spent $12,000 to build the ultimate bag-lady-proof trash cage: made of three-quarter inch steel rod with alloy locks and vicious outturned spikes to safeguard priceless moldering fishheads and stale french fries.

Public toilets, however, are the real Eastern Front of the Downtown war on the poor. Los Angeles, as a matter of deliberate policy, has fewer available public lavatories than any major North American city. On the advice of the LAPD (who actually sit on the design board of at least one major Downtown redevelopment project),[14] the Community Redevelopment Agency bulldozed the remaining public toilet in Skid Row. Agency planners then agonized for months over whether to include a 'freestanding public toilet' in their design for South Park. As CRA Chairman Jim Wood later admitted, the decision not to include the toilet was a 'policy decision and not a design decision'. The CRA Downtown prefers the solution of 'quasi-public restrooms' – meaning toilets in restaurants, art galleries and office buildings – which can be made available to tourists and office workers while being denied to vagrants and other unsuitables.[15] The toiletless no-man's-land east of Hill Street in Downtown is also barren of outside water sources for drinking or washing. A common and troubling sight these days are the homeless men – many of them young Salvadorean refugees – washing in and even drinking from the sewer effluent which flows down the concrete channel of the Los Angeles River on the eastern edge of Downtown.

Where the itineraries of Downtown powerbrokers unavoidably intersect with the habitats of the homeless or the working poor, as in the previously mentioned zone of gentrification along the northern Broadway corridor, extraordinary design precautions are being taken to ensure the physical separation of the different humanities. For instance, the CRA brought in the Los Angeles Police to design '24-hour, state-of-the-art security' for the two new parking structures that serve the Los Angeles *Times* and Ronald Reagan State Office buildings. In contrast to the mean streets outside, the parking structures contain beautifully landscaped lawns or 'microparks', and in one case, a food court and a historical exhibit. Moreover, both structures are designed as 'confidence-building' circulation systems – miniature paradigms of privatization – which allow white-collar workers to walk from car to office, or from car to boutique, with minimum exposure to the public street. The Broadway Spring Center, in particular, which links the Ronald Reagan Building to the proposed 'Grand Central Square' at Third and Broadway, has been warmly praised by architectural critics for adding greenery and art (a banal bas relief) to parking. It also adds a huge dose of menace – armed guards, locked gates, and security cameras – to scare away the homeless and poor.

The cold war on the streets of Downtown is ever escalating. The police, lobbied by Downtown merchants and developers, have broken up every attempt by the homeless and their allies to create safe havens or self-organized encampments. 'Justiceville', founded by homeless activist Ted Hayes, was roughly dispersed; when its inhabitants attempted to find refuge at Venice Beach, they were arrested at the behest of the local councilperson (a renowned environmentalist) and sent back to the inferno of Skid Row. The city's own brief experiment with legalized camping – a grudging response to a series of exposure deaths in the cold winter of 1987[16] – was ended abruptly after only four months to make way for construction of a transit repair yard. Current policy seems to involve a perverse play upon Zola's famous irony about the 'equal rights' of the rich and the poor to sleep out rough. As the head of the city planning

commission explained the official line to incredulous reporters, it is not against the law to sleep on the street per se, 'only to erect any sort of protective shelter'. To enforce this prescription against 'cardboard condos', the LAPD periodically sweep the Nickle, confiscating shelters and other possessions, and arresting resisters. Such cynical repression has turned the majority of the homeless into urban bedouins. They are visible all over Downtown, pushing a few pathetic possessions in purloined shopping carts, always fugitive and in motion, pressed between the official policy of containment and the increasing sadism of Downtown streets.[17] . . .

NOTES

1   See National Committee on the Causes and Prevention of Violence, *To Establish Justice, To Ensure Domestic Tranquility (Final Report)*, Washington DC 1969.

2   'The problems of inversion and introversion in development patterns, and ambiguity in the character of public space created within them, are not unique to new shopping center developments. It is commonplace that the modern city as a whole exhibits a tendency to break down into specialised, single-use precincts – the university campus, the industrial estate, the leisure complex, the housing scheme . . . each governed by internal, esoteric rules of development and implemented by specialist agencies whose terms of reference guarantee that they are familiar with other similar developments across the country, but know almost nothing of the dissimilar precincts which abut their own.' (Barry Maitland, *Shopping Malls: Planning and Design*, London 1985, p. 109.)

3   Cf. Geoffrey Blodgett, 'Frederick Law Olmsted: Landscape Architecture as Conservative Reform', *Journal of American History* 62: 4 (March 1976); and Manfredo Tafuri, 'The Disenchanted Mountain: The Skyscraper and the City', in Giorgio Ciucci, et al., *The American City*, Cambridge, Mass., 1979.

4   David Halberstam, *The Powers That Be*, New York 1979, p. 102.

5   Los Angeles *Times*, 4 November 1978, X, p. 13. See also Sam Hall Kaplan, *L. A. Follies: A Critical Look at Growth, Politics and Architecture*, Santa Monica 1989.

6   Governor's Commission on the Los Angeles Riots. *Violence in the City – An End or Beginning?*, Los Angeles 1965.

7   In the early 1970s the police circularized members of the Central City Association about an 'imminent gang invasion'. They urged businessmen 'to report to the police the presence of any groups of young Blacks in the area. These are young people between the ages of twelve and eighteen, both boys and girls. One gang wears earrings and the other wears hats. When encountered in groups of more than two they are very dangerous and armed.' (Los Angeles *Times*, 24 Dec. 1972, I, p. 7.)

8   Gentrification in this case is 'Reaganization'. In a complex deal aimed at making the north end of the Broadway corridor an upscaled 'bridge' linking Bunker Hill, the Civic Center and Little Tokyo, the CRA has spent more than $20 million inducing the State to build the 'Ronald Reagan Office Building' a block away from the corner of Third and Broadway, while simultaneously bribing the Union Rescue Mission $6 million to move its homeless clientele out of the neighborhood. The 3,000 civil servants from the Reagan Building are intended as shock troops to gentrify the strategic corner

of Third and Broadway, where developer Ira Yellin has received further millions in subsidies from the CRA to transform the three historic structures he owns (the Bradbury Building, Million Dollar Theater and Grand Central Market) into 'Grand Central Square'. The 'Broadway-Spring Center' – discussed in the text – provides 'security in circulation' between the Reagan Building and the Square.

9   In reflecting on the problem of the increasing social distance between the white middle classes and the Black poor, Oscar Newman, the renowned theorist of 'defensible space', argues for the federally ordered dispersion of the poor in the suburban residential landscape. He insists, however, that 'bringing the poor and the black into the fold' (*sic*) must be conducted 'on a tightly controlled quota basis' that is non-threatening to the middle class and ensures their continuing social dominance. (*Community of Interest*, Garden City 1981, pp. 19–25.) Such 'tightly controlled quotas', of course, are precisely the strategy favored by redevelopment agencies like Los Angeles's as they have been forced to include a small portion of low or very-low income housing in their projected 'urban villages'. It seems inconceivable to Newman, or to these agencies, that the urban working class is capable of sustaining their own decent neighborhoods or having any voice in the definition of public interest. That is why the working poor are always the 'problem', the 'blight' in redevelopment, while the gilded middle classes always represent 'revitalization'.

10   N. David Milder, 'Crime and Downtown Revitalization', in *Urban Land*, Sept. 1987, p. 18.

11   *The Social Life of Small Spaces*, New York 1985.

12   The descriptions that follow draw heavily on the extraordinary photographs of Diego Cardoso, who has spent years document-

ing Downtown's various street scenes and human habitats.

13   Since crack began to replace cheap wine on Skid Row in the mid 1980s, the homicide rate has jumped to almost 1 per week. A recent backpage *Times* story – 'Well, That's Skid Row' (15 Nov. 1989) – claimed that the homeless have become so 'inured to street violence' that 'the brutal slayings of two people within two blocks of each other the night before drew far less attention than the taping of an episode of the television show, "Beauty and the Beast"'. The article noted, however, the homeless have resorted to a 'buddy system' whereby one sleeps and the other acts as 'spotter' to warn of potential assailants.

14   For example, the LAPD sits on the Design Advisory Board of 'Miracle on Broadway', the publicly funded body attempting to initiate the gentrification of part of the Downtown historic core. (*Downtown News*, 2 Jan. 1989.)

15   Interviews with Skid Row residents; see also Tom Chorneau, 'Quandary Over a Park Restroom', *Downtown News*, 25 Aug. 1986, pp. 1, 4. In other Southern California communities the very hygiene of the poor is being criminalized. New ordinances specifically directed against the homeless outlaw washing oneself in public 'above the elbow'.

16   See 'Cold Snap's Toll at 5 as Its Iciest Night Arrives', *Times*, 29 Dec. 1988.

17   See my '*Chinatown*, Part Two? The Internationalization of Downtown Los Angeles', *New Left Review*, July–Aug. 1987. It is also important to note that, despite the crack epidemic on Skid Row (which has attracted a much younger population of homeless men), there is no drug treatment center or rehabilitation program in the area. Indeed within the city as a whole narcotic therapy funding is being cut while police and prison budgets are soaring.

Part IV   Reading City Publics

Introduction: Reading City Publics

Gary Bridge and Sophie Watson

The public life of the city has fascinated novelists, film-makers, visitors, and inhabitants. Ideas of the city as a political space were a critical question in ancient Greece and Renaissance Italy as much as they are in contemporary urbanism. The quality of urban public space has concerned planners and architects to a greater and lesser extent in the design and redevelopment of urban space. But what exactly constitutes "the public" and is that realized in the social and spatial setting of the city? This section of the reader deals with these questions. It looks at how the public is constituted as an intellectual idea and political ideal, and how those constructions are themselves politicized. Different understandings of the relationship between constructions of the public realm as a political space, or a space for politics, and the public space of cities are discussed. This brings in the changing relationship between notions of the private and the public and how these are mapped across gender, race, and class, as well as other identity constructions (particularly the homeless). The way that the idea of the public relates to conceptions of time and space is an underlying theme.

The Decline of the Public

The strongest contribution to an understanding of the public life of western cities has been made by Richard Sennett (see Sennett 1970, 1974, 1990, 1994). Overall he sees the loss of a public realm in the city over the last 200 years. This is because the idea of the public has been built on a series of oppositions out of which the public is defined but also destroyed. The public realm for Sennett is characterized by an idea (from Hannah Arendt, 1958, particularly) of the richer types of relationships that are possible among strangers who are different to each other. It is a self-constituting political sphere. Rather than being seen as this open, fuller type of relationship, the public realm of the city has been opposed and defined by ideas of the private realm as "natural," the refuge of assumed fuller relations shared in families against the anonymity of the city (families against the city). If an idea of the complexity and richness of impartial relations in public is lost, then the realm of politics becomes that of assumed intimacy and the cult of personality. Equally if the open, unconstrained spaces of the city are lost, then urban dwellers have no space and distance to be able to feel sociable. Sennett's extract describes the loss of public space or creation of public space that is merely a space between buildings (dead public space). This means a loss of opportunity for unpredictable but unpressured encounters in public between unlike strangers. The retreat of the more affluent into socially homogeneous suburbs, a flight from the city, is a larger sociospatial loss of the public diversity of the city. With the decline of fully urban, civil relationships and the rise of secularism and consumer capitalism comes an emphasis on appearances in public. Experience of the public becomes the cult of personality constructed through appearances, rather than a more impersonal development of the social order.

Sennett's argument is that architecture and urban planning are in part responsible for the creation of dead public space and a depleted public realm. Jane Jacobs' concern in her classic *The Death and Life of Great American Cities* was to register how urban planning was creating public space that was not dead but threatening and prone to crime. In the extract here she argues how busy and constant pedestrian traffic makes for more secure urban environment because of the informal surveillance of "eyes on the street." This is facilitated by a mix of land uses (especially houses and shops) that keeps the street active with different types of people throughout the day and night. It is the tendency of modern land-use planning to split up these land uses into separate districts that has resulted in zones of the city with little activity or informal surveillance and therefore greater risk of crime. The significance of the Jacobs piece for the conceptions of the public is to suggest how informal practices of cooperative behaviour amongst neighbours and strangers can be built up from the mutual security of actively used public space. More political norms of civility can emerge from everyday practices in public space.

One of the important issues in discussions of the public and the city has been how the formal design and maintenance of public space has sought to influence the types of activity that go on in this space and the types of people that participate. The everyday activities of homeless people are often not part of the urban authorities' vision of the "successful" city. This situation suggests a critical link between urban public space and the constitution of a political public realm that explains why the homeless person has become an iconic figure in the politics of public space. Examples of this include Neil Smith's (1996) analysis of the battle for Tomkins Square Park in New York (see the extract in Part III above), or Don Mitchell (1995) on the struggle for People's Park in Berkeley, or Mike Davis's (1992 – see the extract in Part III) descriptions of the aggressive street architecture to deter the homeless in Los Angeles. Homeless people invert the relationship between the public/private, city space/domestic space divisions that Sennett has argued are crucial to contemporary conceptions of the public. Homeless people occupy public space but have to carry out private, everyday activities there. They occupy public space but have no private realm which is implicitly necessary in this conception in order to count as a public political subject. To "be" in public is to emerge from the private realm.

The treatment of who counts and who doesn't in public space and its implications for the public realm are also evident in Low's comparison of two public parks in San José, Costa Rica. Here too is the blend of colonial influence as well as contemporary planning in the intention for the use of public space. Low notes the attempts to control the space in certain ways, usually to protect the middle-class ideals of leisure and consumption and to protect the space for the tourist gaze. She remarks how the everyday practices of different groups (the hawkers, the pensioners, the teenagers) appropriate the space in ways that subvert the intentions of the city authorities to some degree.

The Constitution of the Public as the Appropriation of Space

The idea of appropriation of space comes from Lefebvre (1991). Representations of space (through planning and architecture) seek to designate the use of space, whereas representational space is space that is appropriated by daily uses that in some cases can resist or adapt representations of space. Lefebvre was important in providing a Marxist critique of a positivist view that treats space as a container of activity that changes with the nature of that activity. According to Lefebvre space is socially produced in certain ways, some of which appear neutral and abstract, but in fact are partial and political. The specialization of activity in spaces of the city is symptomatic of this objectification of space. For Lefebvre space has to be seen as a dialectical relation. This dialectical urbanism suggests that a right to the city is not the right to be in certain spaces in the city but (as argued in the extract) the right to urban life itself. The power relations of different spatial imaginations and how they are inscribed on the city is a necessary precursor to any consideration of what constitutes the public in any particular urban space. He emphasizes a conception of the whole city, rather than the specialisms of scientific urbanism. Against the abstract rationality of the capitalist, scientific city Lefebvre stresses the importance of play and creativity as well as the capacity of the working class to "inhabit" the city, to be fully immersed in its rhythms such that they might be creatively re-cast.

The power of certain representations of space to control the social life of cities seems to be immense. The disciplinary effects of social administration are at the heart of Foucault's influential poststructurlist work. The audits of social data and the process of bureaucratic administration are seen in some senses to produce the subjectivities of the citizens to which they are meant to administer. The ideas of surveillance, capillary power, and disciplinary practices in space have been adapted to the analysis of the city. The extract included from *Discipline and Punish* starts with the direct urban example serving as larger social metaphor of the crisis administration of the plague town. Here movement was curtailed and the minutiae of life prised open to inspection by the state. The freezing and separation of space (intonations of rationalist urban planning) is a disciplinary mechanism. The specialization and surveillance of urban space is obvious in the increasing use of CCTV cameras to patrol urban space (in a militaristic fashion in the fortress space of Los Angeles, for example – Davis, 1992). The idea of the panoptican is a broader metaphor for the city, in which public space is increasingly privatized and policed and in which public administration and governance are increasingly routinized. This has an effect on its citizens of self-disciplining quiescence. In this sense the "public" is a produced effect of disciplinary power.

If in this vision, disciplinary power goes all the way down to microprocesses, then the city may indeed come to resemble modern society in being, as Foucault claims, totally administered. Yet it is at the level of microspatial practices that resistance to the public as power effect can start to take place. This is de Certeau's argument that simple everyday spatial practices such as walking can work against the quotidian discipline of the rationalist model. Just as speech acts have the capacity to make new meaning within the disciplinary confines of language, so walking in the city has a rhetorical function in that it can weave together different elements of the city, can take shortcuts or be deliberately circuitous. The capacity for unplanned movement can give an expressive character to walking in the city, and like speech acts can make new meaning. Walking, like speech acts, has an enunciative function; its mobility and paths through the city cannot be fully constrained by disciplinary power. De Certeau's work is symptomatic of a literature on the public spaces of the city being the site of everyday practices that have the capacity for resistance by building on the heterogeneity of the city (in a way reminiscent of Sennett's early work [1970] on anarchist space in the city).

The End of Public Space?

Sorkin (1992) and others have argued that public space is more and more being controlled by private interests and is the site of privatized consumption practices. Thus the malling of America has meant the death of the street and the presentation of thematic fantasy consumption landscapes (see especially Zukin, 1995). The Disneyfication of urban landscapes means the death of public space. This is a sense of public space not emptied-out as a site of surveillance, but filled up with commodities and consumption spectacles in ways that stupify and individuate the urban dweller. This is not a new theme in understanding the public spaces of cities. The work of Walter Benjamin has become increasingly influential because of the way that he captures the aesthetic and cultural practices of commodification (see the extract from Susan Buck-Morss in Part II of this *Reader*). Benjamin also evokes the significance of the city as the shop window of these social processes. Thus he describes how one is drawn into the Arcades (precursors of contemporary shopping malls) of mid-nineteenth-century Paris, there to find a heady mix of commodities and spectacles that transform the covered walkways into another world, another city. The cornucopia of commodities fills up the senses at the same time that the sense of others in the city is being flattened, becoming more about surface appearances. Both commodities and people merge in an atmosphere of surface and deception: of mystification. A key metaphor that appears in the extract here is mirror reflections, both for the sparkle of the spectacle of commodities and the deceptive masks of passers-by whose eyes are like "veiled mirrors." So here we have public spaces in the city, but ones in which consumerism and spectacle bedazzle the walkers and prevent any kind of human connection between people that might lead towards a richer public realm.

Disrupting the Public

Representations of space may reach back in more profound ways to produce the idea of the public. For Rosalyn Deutsche power is the ability to define what is public, for example as urban space and not "public" education. She mobilizes her argument with the example of questions about what defines public art. The constitution of the public here lies behind even what is normally argued over as being public. Thus the debates over the end of public space necessarily assume a certain conception of what is public in the first place, that there was a prior, more public era in the city. In fact the very constitution of the public, from ancient Greece onwards, has relied on certain exclusions (full participation of Greek citizens in the agora required the exclusion of women and slaves to service the free citizens). For Deutsche it rests on the fantasy of a unified urban space, whereas she argues that space is necessarily conflictual and should be acknowledged to be so. This echoes a set of debates around the possibility that a unified public realm in fact merely supports dominant conceptions of the public (white, male, and middle class, usually), and that to enable less powerful groups to establish a sense of the public there has to be a range of publics, including those that may be in conflict with, or critical of, the dominant public realm: what Nancy Fraser (1990) has called "subaltern counter publics."

The dominant imaginings of the public are disturbed when the established binary hierarchies are upset. As well as the homeless person in the contemporary city there is one other iconic figure that historically challenged the established public realm: that of the prostitute, or more particularly the streetwalker. The presence of an unaccompanied woman in public, operating on the cash nexus, upset Victorian male bourgeois constructions of both the public realm of men and female domesticity. At the same time the prostitute aroused base desires that were in contrast to rational self-conduct in public. The extracts by both Judith Walkowitz and Elizabeth Wilson draw our attention to the significance of prostitutes in relation to the public realm, and the ambiguity of identity that was reflected in literature and various acts of public administration and policing in the nineteenth-century metropolis (particularly in London and Paris). These challenges to the constitution of the public were particularly important at a time when the white male bourgeois was making the whole of the public realm in his image. The establishment of a public realm that assumed the values of male bourgeois life truly was a bourgeois revolution as Habermas (1989) has argued.

The visibility of the prostitute as a potential source of disorder to the careful respectability of the bourgeois public realm contrasts with the invisibility of that iconic figure of male bourgeois identity in public – the *flâneur*. Both Walkowitz and Wilson note the way in which the bourgeois male is able to move through the city, observing the diversity of the city without having to connect to it. His affluence and position in a gendered society quite literally gave him the space in the city to move freely and be untouched by the events that he witnessed. In this sense the male *flâneur* in the metropolis was the personification of the establishment of the male bourgeois order in the public realm more widely. Yet the way he was able to move through the city, to make unusual juxtapositions, created an individualized sense of mystery and fantasy. It represented the set of expectations against which the bourgeois as *flâneur* and other identities and ways of being in the city had to respond, a point that Wilson makes in relation to bohemian and lesbian identities.

In the same way that the notion of the public has been socially constituted in response to power, so the ideal of community has a logic of identity which, argues Iris Marion Young, is partial and political. Using Derrida's ideas of deconstruction, she argues idea of community is used as a fully present meaning. Yet the politics of community can be exclusionary of others and oppressive towards its own members. This critique draws on a wider poststructuralist critique of modern theories of knowledge which assume that meaning is fully present in words and that creates meaning out of binary oppositions which value the core and devalue the excluded other. Thus community is a homogenizing meaning that denies difference. It also privileges face-to-face interaction at the expense of more distant and mediated relations. This again, according to Young, is part of a philosophy of consciousness that emphasizes the immediacy of meaning, whereas Derrida and the deconstructionists look for meaning from absences and meaning being endlessly deferred. Thus the meaning of community is through its mediated relations beyond its assumed boundaries.

The point about Young's critique is that she offers an ideal urban public relationship as the beginnings of a better politics beyond the oppression of community. By doing this she is also offering a notion of urbanity that is part of a poststructuralist critique of identity. She looks for the unoppressive city in which identity is not so firmly fixed in community and self-identity. The ideal urban relation is that of the openness to unassimilated otherness. This is a politics of the public that seeks not to define and delimit in the certainties of political constitution and prescribed public space. The ideal city is a being together of strangers who acknowledge and celebrate the ambiguities of identity and social life with which the city presents them.

While not privileging face-to-face contact in the constitution of the public, Young still does rely on the broader sociogeographic setting of the city to facilitate the types of relationships that might be more progressive. Poststructuralist theory has brought such a "ground" as the city into question. This is reflected in Virilio's work on technology and architecture. Virilio posits that the crisis in the conceptualization of dimension in architecture becomes the crisis of the whole, which we take to mean the crisis of representation that marked debates over postmodernism. The loss of perspective, of near and far, as a result of electronic, digital media opens out human experience and the conceptualization of architectural form. It makes constellations and collisions of information at the expense of meaning. The problem of visibility in public which Sennett alluded to is now accentuated into a form of hypervisibility, but at the same time a loss in the ability to visualize, an experience of overexposure. Here the city is in bits, set along planars of digital information. We lose all sense of a public that intersects with a city. Virilio seems to be suggesting a public beyond the city, or a public without a city, and perhaps not a public but a set a nodes in a constellation of communication. Whilst Virilio's argument might be overemphatic it remains to be seen whether the trends of time-space disruption he is pointing to will have progressive or destructive consequences for any notion of the public, and indeed the city.

REFERENCES

Arendt, H. 1958: *The Human Condition*. Chicago: Chicago University Press.

Davis, M. 1992: *City of Quartz*. London: Verso.

Fraser, N. 1990: Rethinking the public sphere: a contribution to the critique of actually existing democracy. *Social Text*, 25(6), 56–80.

Habermas, J. 1989: *The Structural Transformation of the Public Sphere*. Cambridge: Polity.

Lefebvre, H. 1991: *The Production of Space*. Oxford: Blackwell.

Mitchell, D. 1995: The end of public space? People's Park, definitions of the public, and democracy. *Annals of the Associations of American Geographers* 85: 108–33.

Sennett, R. 1970: *The Uses of Disorder*. Harmondsworth: Penguin.

Sennett, R. 1974: *The Fall of Public Man*. New York: Norton.

Sennett, R. 1990: *The Conscience of the Eye: The design and social life of cities*. London: Faber and Faber.

Sennett, R. 1994: *Flesh and Stone*. London: Faber and Faber.

Smith, N. 1996: *The New Urban Frontier*. London: Routledge.

Sorkin 1992: *Variations on a Theme Park: The New American city and the end of public space*. New York: Hill and Wang.

Zukin, S. 1991: *Landscapes of Power: From Detroit to Disneyland*. Berkeley: University of California Press.

Chapter 36

from *The Fall of Public Man*

Richard Sennett

Dead Public Space

Intimate vision is induced in proportion as the public domain is abandoned as empty. On the most physical level, the environment prompts people to think of the public domain as meaningless. This is in the organization of space in cities. Architects who design skyscrapers and other large-scale, high-density buildings are among the few professionals who are forced to work with present-day ideas of public life, such as they are, and indeed are among the few professionals who of necessity express and make these codes manifest to others.

One of the first pure International School skycrapers built after World War II was Gordon Bunshaft's Lever House on Park Avenue in New York. The ground floor of Lever House is an open-air square, a courtyard with a tower rising on the north side, and, one story above the ground, a low structure surrounding the other three sides. But one passes from the street underneath this low horseshoe to penetrate to the courtyard; the street level itself is dead space. No diversity of activity takes place on the ground floor; it is only a means of passage to the interior. The form of this International-type skyscraper is at odds with its function, for a miniature public square revivified is declared in form, but the function destroys the nature of a public square, which is to intermix persons and diverse activities.

This contradiction is part of a greater clash. The International School was dedicated to a new idea of visibility in the construction of large buildings. Walls almost entirely of glass, framed with thin steel supports, allow the inside and the outside of a building to be dissolved to the least point of differentiation; this technology permits the achievement of what S. Giedion calls the ideal of the permeable wall, the ultimate in visibility. But these walls are also hermetic barriers. Lever House was the forerunner of a design concept in which the wall, though permeable, also isolates the activities within the building from the life of the street. In this design concept, the aesthetics of visibility and social isolation merge.

The paradox of isolation in the midst of visibility is not unique to New York, nor are the special problems of crime in New York a sufficient explanation of the deadness of public space in such a design. In the Brunswick Centre built in the Bloomsbury section of London and in the Defense office complex being built on the edge of Paris, the same paradox is at work, and results in the same dead public area.

In the Brunswick Centre two enormous apartment complexes rise away from a central concrete concourse; the apartment buildings are stepped back story after story, so that each looks like a Babylonian terrace city sited on a hill. The terraces of the Brunswick Centre apartments are covered in glass for the most part; thus the apartment dweller has a greenhouse wall letting in a great deal of light and breaking down the barrier between inside and outside. This permeation of the house and the outside is curiously abstract; one has a nice sense of the sky, but the buildings are so angled that they have no relationship to, or view out on, the surrounding buildings of Bloomsbury. Indeed, the rear end of one of the apartment blocks, faced in solid concrete, gives on, or rather ignores, one of the most beautiful squares in all of London. The building is sited as though it could be anywhere, which is to say its siting shows its designers had no sense of being anywhere in particular, much less in an extraordinary urban milieu.

The real lesson of Brunswick Centre is contained in its central concourse. Here there are a few shops and vast areas of empty space. Here is an area to pass through, not to use; to sit on one of the few concrete benches in the concourse for any length of time is to become profoundly uncomfortable, as though one were on exhibit in a vast empty hall. The "public" concourse of the Centre is in fact shielded from the main contiguous Bloomsbury streets by two immense ramps with fences edging them; the concourse itself is raised several feet above street level. Everything has been done, again, to isolate the public area of Brunswick Centre from accidental street incursion, or from simple strolling, just as the siting of the two apartment blocks effectively isolates those who inhabit them, from street, concourse, and square. The visual statement made by the detailing of the greenhouse wall is that the inside and the outside of a dwelling have no differentiation; the social statement made by the concourse, the siting of the complex, and the ramps is that an immense barrier separates "within" the Brunswick Centre from "without."

The erasure of alive public space contains an even more perverse idea – that of making space contingent upon motion. In the Defense Center, as with Lever House and

Brunswick Centre, the public space is an area to move through, not be in. At Defense, the grounds around the mass of office towers which compose the complex contain a few stores, but the real purpose is to serve as a pass-through area from car or bus to office building. There is little evidence that the planners of Defense thought this space to have any intrinsic value, that people from the various office blocks might want to remain in it. The ground, in the words of one planner, is "the traffic-flow–support-nexus for the vertical whole." Translated, this means that the public space has become a derivative of movement.

The idea of space as derivative from motion parallels exactly the relations of space to motion produced by the private automobile. One does not use one's car to see the city; the automobile is not a vehicle for touring – or, rather, it is not used as such, except by joyriding adolescent drivers. The car instead gives freedom of movement; one can travel, uninhibited by formal stops, as in the subway, without changing one's mode of motion, from bus, subway, or elevated to pedestrian movement, in making a journey from place A to place B. The city street acquires, then, a peculiar function – to permit motion; if it regulates motion too much, by lights, one-ways, and the like, motorists become nervous or angry.

Today, we experience an ease of motion unknown to any prior urban civilization, and yet motion has become the most anxiety-laden of daily activities. The anxiety comes from the fact that we take unrestricted motion of the individual to be an absolute right. The private motorcar is the logical instrument for exercising that right, and the effect on public space, especially the space of the urban street, is that the space becomes meaningless or even maddening unless it can be subordinated to free movement. The technology of modern motion replaces being in the street with a desire to erase the constraints of geography.

Thus does the design concept of a Defense or a Lever House coalesce with the technology of transportation. In both, as public space becomes a function of motion, it loses any independent experiential meaning of its own.

"Isolation" has so far been used in two senses. First, it means that the inhabitants or workers in an urban high-density structure are inhibited from feeling any relationship to the milieu in which that structure is set. Second, it means that as one can isolate oneself, in a private automobile, for freedom of movement, one ceases to believe one's surroundings have any meaning save as a means toward the end of one's own motion. There is a third, rather more brutal sense of social isolation in public places, an isolation directly produced by one's visibility to others.

The design idea of the permeable wall is applied by many architects within their buildings as well as on the skin. Visual barriers are destroyed by doing away with office walls, so that whole floors will become one vast open space, or there will be a set of private offices on the perimeter with a large open area within. This destruction of walls, office planners are quick to say, increases office efficiency, because when people are all day long visually exposed to one another, they are less likely to gossip and chat, more likely to keep to themselves. When everyone has each other under surveillance, sociability decreases, silence being the only form of protection. The open-floor office plan brings the paradox of visibility and isolation to its height, a paradox which can also be stated in reverse. People are more sociable, the more they have some tangible barriers between them, just as they need specific places in public whose sole purpose is to bring them together. Let us put this another way again: Human beings need to have some distance from intimate observation by others in order to feel sociable. Increase intimate contact and you decrease sociability. Here is the logic of one form of bureaucratic efficiency.

Dead public space is one reason, the most concrete one, that people will seek out on intimate terrain what is denied them on more alien ground. Isolation in the midst of public visibility and overemphasis on psychological transactions complement each other. To the extent, for instance, that a person feels he must protect himself from the surveillance of others in the public realm by silent isolation, he compensates by baring himself to those with whom he wants to make contact. The complementary relation exists because here are two expressions of a single, general transformation of social relations. I have sometimes thought about this complementary situation in terms of the masks of self which manners and the rituals of politeness create. These masks have ceased to matter in impersonal situations or seem to be the property only of snobs; in closer relationships, they appear to get in the way of knowing someone else. And I wonder if this contempt for ritual masks of sociability has not really made us more primitive culturally than the simplest tribe of hunters and gatherers.

A relation between how people view their love-making and what they experience on the street may seem farfetched. And even if one grants there are such connections between modes of personal and public life, one might reasonably object that they have shallow roots historically. It is the generation born after World War II which has turned inward as it has liberated itself from sexual constraints; it is in this same generation that most of the physical destruction of the public domain has occurred. The thesis of this book, however, is that these blatant signs of an unbalanced personal life and empty public life have been a long time in the making. They are the results of a change that began with the fall of the *ancien régime* and the formation of a new capitalist, secular, urban culture.

The Changes in the Public Domain

The history of the words "public" and "private" is a key to understanding this basic shift in the terms of Western culture. The first recorded uses of the word "public" in

English identify the "public" with the common good in society; in 1470, for instance, Malory spoke of "the emperor Lucyos...dictatour or procurour of the publyke wele of Rome." Some seventy years later, there was added a sense of "public" as that which is manifest and open to general observation. Hall wrote in his *Chronicle* of 1542, "Their inwarde grudge could not refrayne but crye out in places publicke, and also private." "Private" was here used to mean privileged, at a high governmental level. By the end of the 17th Century, the opposition of "public" and "private" was shaded more like the way the terms are now used. "Public" meant open to the scrutiny of anyone, whereas "private" meant a sheltered region of life defined by one's family and friends; thus Steele, in an issue of the *Tatler* in 1709, "These effects...upon the publick and private actions of men," and Butler in the *Sermons* (1726), "Every man is to be considered in two capacities, the private and the publick." To go "out in publick" (Swift) is a phrase based on society conceived in terms of this geography. The older senses are not entirely lost today in English, but this 18th Century usage sets up the modern terms of reference.

The meanings accorded *le public* in French show something similar. Renaissance use of the word was largely in terms of the common good and the body politic; gradually *le public* became also a special region of sociability. Erich Auerbach once made a thorough study of this more modern definition of "the public," first appearing in France in the middle of the 17th Century, as it was related to the public that was the audience for plays. The theatrical public was referred to in the time of Louis XIV by the catch-phrase *la cour et la ville*, the court and the city. Auerbach discovered that this theatrical public in fact consisted of an elite group of people – an obvious finding in terms of court life, not so obvious in terms of urban life. *La ville* of 17th Century Paris was a very small group, whose origins were non-aristocratic and mercantile, but whose manners were

directed to obscuring this fact, not only out of shame but in order to facilitate interchanges with the court.

The sense of who "the public" were, and where one was when one was out "in public," became enlarged in the early 18th Century in both Paris and London. Bourgeois people became less concerned to cover up their social origins; there were many more of them; the cities they inhabited were becoming a world in which widely diverse groups in society were coming into contact. By the time the word "public" had taken on its modern meaning, therefore, it meant not only a region of social life located apart from the realm of family and close friends, but also that this public realm of acquaintances and strangers included a relatively wide diversity of people.

There is a word logically associated with a diverse urban public, the word "cosmopolitan." A cosmopolite, in the French usage recorded in 1738, is a man who moves comfortably in diversity; he is comfortable in situations which have no links or parallels to what is familiar to him. The same sense of the word appeared in English earlier than in French, but was not much employed until the 18th Century. Given the new terms of being out in public, the cosmopolitan was the perfect public man. An early English usage foreshadowed the commonplace sense of the word in 18th Century bourgeois society. In one of Howell's *Letters* (1645), he wrote, "I came tumbling out into the World, a pure Cadet, a true Cosmopolite, not born to Land, Lease, House, or Office." Without inherited wealth or inherited feudal obligation, the cosmopolitan, whatever his pleasure in worldly diversity, of necessity must make his way in it.

"Public" thus came to mean a life passed outside the life of family and close friends; in the public region diverse, complex social groups were to be brought into ineluctable contact. The focus of this public life was the capital city.

These changes in language were correlated with conditions of behavior and terms of belief in the 18th Century cosmopolis.

As the cities grew, and developed networks of sociability independent of direct royal control, places where strangers might regularly meet grew up. This was the era of the building of massive urban parks, of the first attempts at making streets fit for the special purpose of pedestrian strolling as a form of relaxation. It was the era in which coffeehouses, then cafes and coaching inns, became social centers; in which the theater and opera houses became open to a wide public through the open sale of tickets rather than the older practice whereby aristocratic patrons distributed places. Urban amenities were diffused out from a small elite circle to a broader spectrum of society, so that even the laboring classes began to adopt some of the habits of sociability, like promenades in parks, which were formerly the exclusive province of the elite, walking in their private gardens or "giving" an evening at the theater.

In the realm of necessity as in the realm of leisure, patterns of social interaction grew up which were suited to exchange between strangers and did not depend on fixed feudal privileges or monopolistic control established by royal grant. The 18th Century urban market was unlike its late medieval or Renaissance predecessors; it was internally competitive, those selling in it vying for the attention of a shifting and largely unknown group of buyers. As the cash economy expanded and modes of credit, accounting, and investment became more rationalized, business was carried on in offices and shops and on an increasingly impersonal basis. It would, of course, be wrong to see either the economy or the sociability of these expanding cities replacing at a stroke older modes of business and pleasure. Rather they juxtaposed still-surviving modes of personal obligation with new modes of interaction, suited to a life passed amidst strangers under conditions of poorly regulated entrepreneurial expansion.

Nor would it be correct to imagine that forging a social bond suited to an expanding city and expanded bourgeois class was either painless or just. People anxiously sought to create modes of speech, even of dress, which would give order to the new urban situation, and also demarcate this life from the private domain of family and friends. Often in their search for principles of public order they resorted to modes of speech, dress, or interaction logically suited to a vanishing era, and tried to force these modes to signify under new and antipathetic conditions. In the process many inequities of late medieval society, now transplanted to alien terrain, became all the more painful and oppressive. There is no need to romanticize the public life of the *ancien régime* cosmopolis to appreciate it; the attempt to create a social order in the midst of confusing and chaotic social conditions at one and the same time brought the contradictions of the *ancien régime* to a point of crisis and created positive opportunities for group life which have yet to be understood.

As in behavior, so in belief, the citizens of the 18th Century capitals attempted to define both what public life was and what it was not. The line drawn between public and private was essentially one on which the claims of civility – epitomized by cosmopolitan, public behavior – were balanced against the claims of nature – epitomized by the family. They saw these claims in conflict, and the complexity of their vision lay in that they refused to prefer the one over the other, but held the two in a state of equilibrium. Behaving with strangers in an emotionally satisfying way and yet remaining aloof from them was seen by the mid-18th Century as the means by which the human animal was transformed into a social being. The capacities for parenthood and deep friendship were seen in turn to be natural potentialities, rather than human creations; while man *made* himself in public, he *realized* his nature in the private realm, above all in his experiences within the family. The tensions between the claims of civility and the rights of nature, epitomized in the divide between public and private life in the cosmopolitan center, not only suffused the high culture of the era but extended into more mundane realms. These tensions appeared in manuals on child-rearing, tracts on moral obligation, and common-sense beliefs about the rights of man. Together, public and private created what would today be called a "universe" of social relations.

The struggle for public order in the 18th Century city, and the tension between the claims of public and private life, constituted the terms of a coherent culture, though there were, as there are in any period, exceptions, deviations, and alternative modes. But a balance of public and private geography in the Enlightenment did exist, and against it there stands out in relief the fundamental change in the ideas of public and private which followed upon the great revolutions at the end of the century and the rise of a national industrial capitalism in more modern times.

Three forces were at work in this change. They were, first, a double relationship which industrial capitalism in the 19th Century came to have with public life in the great city; second, a reformulation of secularism beginning in the 19th Century which affected how people interpret the strange and the unknown; third, a strength which became a weakness, built into the structure of public life itself in the *ancien régime*. This strength meant that public life did not die an instantaneous death under the weight of political and social upheaval at the end of the 18th Century. The public geography prolonged itself into the 19th Century, seemingly intact, in fact changing from within. This inheritance affected the new forces of secularism and capitalism as much as they were at work on it. The transformation of public life can be thought of as parallel to the collapse which comes to athletes who have been especially strong, so that they survive beyond youth with seemingly undiminished powers, and then all at once make manifest the decay which has been continuously eroding the body from within. Because of this peculiar form of survival, the signs of *ancien régime* publicness are not so far from modern life as might at first be imagined.

The double relation of industrial capitalism to urban public culture lay first in the pressures of privatization which capitalism aroused in 19th Century bourgeois society. It lay second in the "mystification" of material life in public, especially in the matter of clothes, caused by mass production and distribution.

The traumas of 19th Century capitalism led those who had the means to try to shield themselves in whatever way possible from the shocks of an economic order which neither victors nor victims understood. Gradually the will to control and shape the public order eroded, and people put more emphasis on protecting themselves from it. The family became one of these shields. During the 19th Century the family came to appear less and less the center of a particular, nonpublic region, more an idealized refuge, a world all its own, with a higher moral value than the public realm. The bourgeois family was idealized as life wherein order and authority were unchallenged, security of material existence could be a concomitant of real marital love, and the transactions between members of the family would brook no outside scrutiny. As the family became a refuge from the terrors of society, it gradually became also a moral yardstick with which to measure the public realm of the capital city. Using family relations as a standard, people perceived the public domain not as a limited set of social relations, as in the Enlightenment, but instead saw public life as morally inferior. Privacy and stability appeared to be united in the family; against this ideal order the legitimacy of the public order was thrown into question.

Industrial capitalism was equally and directly at work on the material life of the public realm itself. For instance, the mass production of clothes, and the use of mass-production patterns by individual tailors or seamstresses, meant that many diverse segments of the cosmopolitan public began in gross to take on a similar appearance, that public markings were losing distinctive forms. Yet virtually no one believed that society was becoming thereby homogenized; the machine meant that social differences – important differences, necessary to know if one were to survive in a rapidly expanding milieu of strangers – were becoming hidden, and the stranger more intractably a mystery. The machine production of a wide variety of goods, sold for the first time in a mass-merchandising setting, the department store, succeeded with the public not through appeals to utility or cheap price, but rather by capitalizing on this mystification. Even as they became more uniform, physical goods were endowed in advertising with human qualities, made to seem tantalizing mysteries which had to be possessed to be understood. "Commodity fetishism," Marx called it; he was only one among many who were struck by the confluence of mass production, homogeneity of appearance, and yet the investing in material things of attributes or associations of intimate personality.

The interaction of capitalism and public geography thus pulled in two directions; one was withdrawal from the public into the family, the other was a new confusion about the materials of public appearance, a confusion which, however, could be turned to a profit. It might therefore be tempting to conclude that industrial capitalism alone caused the public realm to lose legitimacy and coherence, but the conclusion would be inadmissible even on its own terms. What after all prompted people to believe these physical goods, so uniform, could have psychological associations? Why believe in a thing as though it were human? The fact that this belief was profitable for a few does not explain why it should be held by a multitude.

This question involves the second force which changed the public life inherited from the *ancien régime*, a change in the terms of belief about worldly life. This belief is secularity. As long as the secular is thought opposed in some way to the sacred, the word becomes one-dimensional and fixed. It is better used as the imagery and symbols which make things and people in the world understandable. I think

the following definition best: secularity is the conviction before we die of why things are as they are, a conviction which will cease to matter of itself once we are dead.

Secular terms changed drastically from the 18th to the 19th Century. "Things and people" were understandable in the 18th Century when they could be assigned a place in the order of Nature. This order of Nature was not a physical, tangible thing, nor was the order ever encapsuled by worldly things. A plant or a passion occupied a place in the order of Nature but did not define it in miniature and whole. The order of Nature was therefore an idea of the secular as the transcendental. Not only did this idea permeate the writing of scientists and other intellectuals, it reached into such daily affairs as attitudes toward the discipline of children or the morality of extramarital affairs.

The secularism which arose in the 19th Century was of a wholly antithetical sort. It was based on a code of the immanent, rather than the transcendent. Immediate sensation, immediate fact, immediate feeling, were no longer to be fitted into a pre-existent scheme in order to be understood. The immanent, the instant, the fact, was a reality in and of itself. Facts were more believable than system – or, rather, the logical array of facts became a system; the 18th Century order of Nature in which phenomena had a place but in which Nature transcended phenomena was thus overturned. This new measure of what could serve as materials for belief ruled psychology as much as it ruled the study of physical objects. By 1870 it appeared plausible to study "an emotion" as having a self-contained meaning, if one could find out all the tangible circumstances in which "the emotion" appeared and the tangible signs through which "the emotion" made itself manifest. No circumstance or sign could therefore be ruled out, a priori, as irrelevant. In a world where immanence is the principle of secular knowledge, everything counts because everything might count.

This restructuring of the code of secular knowledge had a radical effect on public life. It meant that appearances in public, no matter how mystifying, still had to be taken seriously, because they might be clues to the person hidden behind the mask. Any appearance a person made was in some way real, because it was tangible; indeed, if that appearance were a mystery, all the more reason for taking it seriously: on what grounds, a priori, would one put it out of mind, on what grounds discriminate? When a society dedicates itself to the principle of things having meanings in themselves, it thus introduces an element of profound self-doubt into its cognitive apparatus, for any exercise of discrimination may be a mistake. Thus arose one of the great and enriching contradictions of the 19th Century; even as people wanted to flee, to shut themselves up in a private, morally superior realm, they feared that arbitrarily classifying their experience into, say, public and private dimensions might be self-inflicted blindness.

To fantasize that physical objects had psychological dimensions became logical in this new secular order. When belief was governed by the principle of immanence, there broke down distinctions between perceiver and perceived, inside and outside, subject and object. If everything counts potentially, how am I to draw a line between what relates to my personal needs and what is impersonal, unrelated to the immediate realm of my experience? It may all matter, nothing may matter, but how am I to know? I must therefore draw no distinction between categories of objects and of sensations, because in distinguishing them I may be creating a false barrier. The celebration of objectivity and hardheaded commitment to fact so prominent a century ago, all in the name of Science, was in reality an unwitting preparation for the present era of radical subjectivity.

If the impact of industrial capitalism was to erode the sense of public life as a morally legitimate sphere, the impact of the new secularity was to erode this sphere by a contrary route, posing to mankind the dictum that nothing which arouses sensation, puzzlement, or simple notice may be excluded a priori from the realm of the private life of a person, or be bereft of some psychological quality important to discover. However, capitalism and secularism together still provide only an incomplete view of what agents of change were at work on the public domain, or rather a distorted picture. For the sum of these two forces would have added up to complete social and cognitive disaster. All the familiar catastrophic clichés – alienation, dissociation, etc. – would have to be trundled out. Indeed, if the story of how a public dimension was shattered stopped at this point, we should expect that there would have occurred among the bourgeoisie massive upheavals, political storms, and rages of a sort equal in passion, if different in substance, to those which socialists hoped would arise among the 19th Century urban proletariat.

The very extension of an established urban culture into the world of these new economic and ideological forces counterbalanced them, and maintained some semblance of order for a time in the midst of very painful and contradictory emotions. Historians promote blindness about this inheritance. When they speak of a revolution being a "water-shed," or the coming of industrial capitalism as being a "revolution," they often suggest to the imagination of their readers that beforehand there was one society, that during the revolution society stopped, and that afterward a new society began. This is a view of human history based on the life cycle of the moth. Nowhere, unfortunately, has the chrysalis theory of human history reigned to worse effect than in the study of the city. Phrases like "the urban-industrial revolution" and "the capitalist metropolis" (employed by writers of contrary political views) both suggest that before the 19th Century the city was one thing, after capitalism or modernism did its work, entirely another. The error is more than that of failing to see how one condition of life blurs into another; it is a failure to understand both the reality of cultural survival and the problems this legacy, like any inheritance, creates in a new generation.

The bourgeoisie continued to believe that "out in public" people experienced sensations and human relations which one could not experience in any other social setting or context. The legacy of the *ancien régime* city was united to the privatizing impulses of industrial capitalism in another way. Out in public was where moral violation occurred and was tolerated; in public one could break the laws of respectability. If the private was a refuge from the terrors of society as a whole, a refuge created by idealizing the family, one could escape the burdens of this ideal by a special kind of experience, one passed among strangers, or, more importantly, among people determined to remain strangers to each other.

The public as an immoral domain meant rather different things to women and men. For women, it was where one risked losing virtue, dirtying oneself, being swept into "a disorderly and heady swirl" (Thackeray). The public and the idea of disgrace were closely allied. The public for a bourgeois man had a different moral tone. By going out in public, or "losing yourself in public," as the phrase occurred in ordinary speech a century ago, a man was able to withdraw from those very repressive and authoritarian features of respectability which were supposed to be incarnate in his person, as father and husband, in the home. So that for men, the immorality of public life was allied to an undercurrent of sensing immorality to be a region of freedom, rather than of simple disgrace, as it was for women. For instance, in the restaurants of the 19th Century, a lone, respectable woman dining with a group of men, even if her husband were present, would cause an overt sensation, whereas the dining out of a bourgeois man with a woman of lower station was tacitly but studiously avoided as a topic of conversation among any of those near to him. For this same reason, the extramarital liaisons of Victorian men were sometimes conducted more publicly than one would in retrospect imagine, because they occurred in a social space which continued to be far away from the family; they were "outside," in a kind of moral limbo.

Moreover, by the middle of the last century, experience gained in the company of strangers came to seem a matter of urgent necessity in the formation of one's personality. One's personal strengths might not develop if one did not expose oneself to strangers – one might be too inexperienced, too naïve, to survive. In the child-rearing manuals and primers for juveniles of the 1870's or 1880's, we encounter again and again the contradictory themes of avoidance of worldly perils in the company of strangers and the command to learn so thoroughly the dangers of the world that one becomes strong enough to recognize these hidden temptations. In the *ancien régime*, public experience was connected to the formation of social order; in the last century, public experience came to be connected to the formation of personality. Worldly experience as an obligation for self-development appeared in the great monuments of the last century's culture, as well as in its more everyday codes of belief; the theme speaks in Balzac's *Illusions Perdues*, in Tocqueville's *Souvenirs*, in the works of the social Darwinists. This pervasive, painful, unreasonable theme was the conjunction of a surviving belief in the value of public experience with the new secular creed that all experiences may have an equal value because all have an equal, potential importance in forming the self. . . .

Chapter 37

from *The Death and Life of Great American Cities*

Jane Jacobs

The Uses of Sidewalks: Safety

Streets in cities serve many purposes besides carrying vehicles, and city sidewalks – the pedestrian parts of the streets – serve many purposes besides carrying pedestrians. These uses are bound up with circulation but are not identical with it and in their own right they are at least as basic as circulation to the proper workings of cities.

A city sidewalk by itself is nothing. It is an abstraction. It means something only in conjunction with the buildings and other uses that border it, or border other sidewalks very near it. The same might be said of streets, in the sense that they serve other purposes besides carrying wheeled traffic in their middles. Streets and their sidewalks, the main public places of a city, are its most vital organs. Think of a city and what comes to mind? Its streets. If a city's streets look interesting, the city looks interesting; if they look dull, the city looks dull.

More than that – and here we get down to the first problem – if a city's streets are safe from barbarism and fear, the city is thereby tolerably safe from barbarism and fear. When people say that a city, or a part of it, is dangerous or is a jungle, what they mean primarily is that they do not feel safe on the sidewalks.

But sidewalks and those who use them are not passive beneficiaries of safety or helpless victims of danger. Sidewalks, their bordering uses, and their users, are active participants in the drama of civilization versus barbarism in cities. To keep the city safe is a fundamental task of a city's streets and its sidewalks.

This task is totally unlike any service that sidewalks and streets in little towns or true suburbs are called upon to do. Great cities are not like towns only larger; they are not like suburbs only denser. They differ from towns and suburbs in basic ways, and one of these is that cities are, by definition, full of strangers. To any one person, strangers are far more common in big cities than acquaintances. More common not just in places of public assembly, but more common at a man's own doorstep. Even residents who live near each other are strangers, and must be, because of the sheer number of people in small geographical compass.

The bedrock attribute of a successful city district is that a person must feel personally safe and secure on the street among all these strangers. He must not feel automatically menaced by them. A city district that fails in this respect also does badly in other ways and lays up for itself, and for its city at large, mountain on mountain of trouble.

Today barbarism has taken over many city streets, or people fear it has, which comes to much the same thing in the end. 'I live in a lovely, quiet residential area,' says a friend of mine who is hunting another place to live. 'The only disturbing sound at night is the occasional scream of someone being mugged.' It does not take many incidents of violence on a city street, or in a city district, to make people fear the streets. And as they fear them, they use them less, which makes the streets still more unsafe.

To be sure, there are people with hobgoblins in their heads, and such people will never feel safe no matter what the objective circumstances are. But this is a different matter from the fear that besets normally prudent, tolerant, and cheerful people who show nothing more than common sense in refusing to venture after dark – or in a few places, by day – into streets where they may well be assaulted, unseen or unrescued until too late.

The barbarism and the real, not imagined, insecurity that gives rise to such fears cannot be tagged a problem of the slums. The problem is most serious, in fact, in genteel-looking 'quiet residential areas' like that my friend was leaving.

It cannot be tagged as a problem of older parts of cities. The problem reaches its most baffling dimensions in some examples of rebuilt parts of cities, including supposedly the best examples of rebuilding, such as middle-income projects. The police precinct captain of a nationally admired project of this kind (admired by planners and lenders) has recently admonished residents not only about hanging around outdoors after dark but has urged them never to answer their doors without knowing the caller. Life here has much in common with life for the three little pigs or the seven little kids of the nursery thrillers. The problem of sidewalk and doorstep insecurity is as serious in cities which have made conscientious efforts at rebuilding as it is in those cities that have lagged. Nor is it illuminating to tag minority groups, or the poor, or the outcast with responsibility for city danger. There are immense variations in the degree of civilization and safety found among such groups and among the city areas where they live. Some of the safest sidewalks in New York City, for example,

at any time of day or night, are those along which poor people or minority groups live. And some of the most dangerous are in streets occupied by the same kinds of people. All this can also be said of other cities.

Deep and complicated social ills must lie behind delinquency and crime, in suburbs and towns as well as in great cities. This book will not go into speculation on the deeper reasons. It is sufficient, at this point, to say that if we are to maintain a city society that can diagnose and keep abreast of deeper social problems, the starting point must be, in any case, to strengthen whatever workable forces for maintaining safety and civilization do exist – in the cities we do have. To build city districts that are custom made for easy crime is idiotic. Yet that is what we do.

The first thing to understand is that the public peace – the sidewalk and street peace – of cities is not kept primarily by the police, necessary as police are. It is kept primarily by an intricate, almost unconscious, network of voluntary controls and standards among the people themselves, and enforced by the people themselves. In some city areas – older public housing projects and streets with very high population turnover are often conspicuous examples – the keeping of public sidewalk law and order is left almost entirely to the police and special guards. Such places are jungles. No number of police can enforce civilization where the normal, casual enforcement of it has broken down.

The second thing to understand is that the problem of insecurity cannot be solved by spreading people out more thinly, trading the characteristics of cities for the characteristics of suburbs. If this could solve danger on the city streets, then Los Angeles should be a safe city, because superficially Los Angeles is almost all suburban. It has virtually no districts compact enough to qualify as dense city areas. Yet Los Angeles cannot, any more than any other great city, evade the truth that, being a city, it *is* composed of strangers not all of whom are nice. Los Angele's crime figures are flabbergasting. Among the seventeen standard metropolitan areas with populations over a million, Los Angeles stands so pre-eminent in crime that it is in a category by itself. And this is markedly true of crimes associated with personal attack, the crimes that make people fear the streets.

Los Angeles, for example, has a forcible-rape rate (1958 figures) of 31.9 per 100,000 population, more than twice as high as either of the next two cities, which happen to be St Louis and Philadelphia; three times as high as the rate of 10.1 for Chicago, and more than four times as high as the rate of 7.4 for New York.

In aggravated assault, Los Angeles has a rate of 185, compared with 149.5 for Baltimore and 139.2 for St Louis (the two next highest), and with 90.9 for New York and 79 for Chicago.

The overall Los Angeles rate for major crimes is 2,507.6 per 100,000 people, far ahead of St Louis and Houston, which come next with 1,634.5 and 1,541.1, and of New York and Chicago, which have rates of 1,145.3 and 943.5.

The reasons for Los Angeles's high crime rates are undoubtedly complex and, at least in part, obscure. But of this we can be sure: thinning out a city does not ensure safety from crime and fear of crime. This is one of the conclusions that can be drawn within individual cities too, where pseudo-suburbs or super-annuated suburbs are ideally suited to rape, muggings, beatings, hold-ups, and the like.

Here we come up against an all-important question about any city street: how much easy opportunity does it offer to crime? It may be that there is some absolute amount of crime in a given city, which will find an outlet somehow (I do not believe this). Whether this is so or not, different kinds of city streets garner radically different shares of barbarism and fear of barbarism.

Some city streets afford no opportunity to street barbarism. The streets of the North End of Boston are outstanding examples. They are probably as safe as any place on earth in this respect. Although most of the North End's residents are Italian or of Italian descent, the district's streets are also heavily and constantly used by people of every race and background. Some of the strangers from outside work in or close to the district; some come to shop and stroll; many, including members of minority groups who have inherited dangerous districts previously abandoned by others, make a point of cashing their pay-cheques in North End stores and immediately making their big weekly purchases in streets where they know they will not be parted from their money between the getting and the spending.

Frank Havey, director of the North End Union, the local settlement house, says, 'I have been here in the North End twenty-eight years, and in all that time I have never heard of a single case of rape, mugging, molestation of a child, or other street crime of that sort in the district. And if there had been any, I would have heard of it even if it did not reach the papers.' Half a dozen times or so in the past three decades, says Havey, would-be molesters have made an attempt at luring a child or, late at night, attacking a woman. In every such case the try was thwarted by passers-by, by kibitzers from windows, or shop-keepers.

Meantime, in the Elm Hill Avenue section of Roxbury, a part of inner Boston that is suburban in superficial character, street assaults and the ever-present possibility of more street assaults with no kibitzers to protect the victims, induce prudent people to stay off the sidewalks at night. Not surprisingly, for this and other reasons that are related (dispiritedness and dullness), most of Roxbury has run down. It has become a place to leave.

I do not wish to single out Roxbury or its once fine Elm Hill Avenue section especially as a vulnerable area; its disabilities, and especially its great blight of dullness, are all too common in other cities too. But differences like these in public safety within the same city are worth noting. The Elm Hill Avenue section's basic troubles are not owing to a criminal or a discriminated against or a poverty-stricken population.

Its troubles stem from the fact that it is physically quite unable to function safely and with related vitality as a city district.

Even within supposedly similar parts of supposedly similar places, drastic differences in public safety exist. An incident at Washington Houses, a public housing project in New York, illustrates this point. A tenants' group at this project, struggling to establish itself, held some outdoor ceremonies in mid December 1958, and put up three Christmas trees. The chief tree, so cumbersome it was a problem to transport, erect, and trim, went into the project's inner 'street', a landscaped central mall and promenade. The other two trees, each less than six feet tall and easy to carry, went on two small fringe plots at the outer corners of the project where it abuts a busy avenue and lively cross streets of the old city. The first night, the large tree and all its trimmings were stolen. The two smaller trees remained intact, lights, ornaments and all, until they were taken down at New Year's. 'The place where the tree was stolen, which is *theoretically* the most safe and sheltered place in the project, is the same place that is unsafe for people too, especially children,' says a social worker who had been helping the tenants' group. 'People are no safer in that mall than the Christmas tree. On the other hand, the place where the other trees were safe, where the project is just one corner out of four, happens to be safe for people.'

This is something everyone already knows: a well-used city street is apt to be a safe street. A deserted city street is apt to be unsafe. But how does this work, really? And what makes a city street well used or shunned? Why is the sidewalk mall in Washington Houses, which is supposed to be an attraction, shunned? Why are the sidewalks of the old city just to its west not shunned? What about streets that are busy part of the time and then empty abruptly?

A city street equipped to handle strangers, and to make a safety asset, in itself, out of the presence of strangers, as the streets of successful city neighbourhoods always do, must have three main qualities:

First, there must be a clear demarcation between what is public space and what is private space. Public and private spaces cannot ooze into each other as they do typically in suburban settings or in projects.

Second, there must be eyes upon the street, eyes belonging to those we might call the natural proprietors of the street. The buildings on a street equipped to handle strangers and to ensure the safety of both residents and strangers must be oriented to the street. They cannot turn their backs or blank sides on it and leave it blind.

And third, the sidewalk must have users on it fairly continuously, both to add to the number of effective eyes on the street and to induce the people in buildings along the street to watch the sidewalks in sufficient numbers. Nobody enjoys sitting on a stoop or looking out a window at an empty street. Almost nobody does such a thing. Large numbers of people entertain themselves, off and on, by watching street activity.

In settlements that are smaller and simpler than big cities, controls on acceptable public behaviour, if not on crime, seem to operate with greater or lesser success through a web of reputation, gossip, approval, disapproval, and sanctions, all of which are powerful if people know each other and word travels. But a city's streets, which must control not only the behaviour of the people of the city but also of visitors from suburbs and towns who want to have a big time away from the gossip and sanctions at home, have to operate by more direct, straightforward methods. It is a wonder cities have solved such an inherently difficult problem at all. And yet in many streets they do it magnificently.

It is futile to try to evade the issue of unsafe city streets by attempting to make some other features of a locality, say interior courtyards or sheltered play spaces, safe instead. By definition again, the streets of a city must do most of the job of handling strangers, for this is where strangers come and go. The streets must not only defend the city against predatory strangers, they must protect the many, many peaceable and well-meaning strangers who use them, ensuring their safety too as they pass through. Moreover, no normal person can spend his life in some artificial haven, and this includes children. Everyone must use the streets.

On the surface, we seem to have some simple aims: to try to secure streets where the public space is unequivocally public, physically unmixed with private or with nothing-at-all space, so that the area needing surveillance has clear and practicable limits; and to see that these public street spaces have eyes on them as continuously as possible.

But it is not so simple to achieve these objects, especially the latter. You can't make people use streets they have no reason to use. You can't make people watch streets they do not want to watch. Safety on the streets by surveillance and mutual policing of one another sounds grim, but in real life it is not grim. The safety of the street works best, most casually, and with least frequent taint of hostility or suspicion precisely where people are using and most enjoying the city streets voluntarily and are least conscious, normally, that they are policing.

The basic requisite for such surveillance is a substantial quantity of stores and other public places sprinkled along the sidewalks of a district; enterprises and public places that are used by evening and night must be among them especially. Stores, bars, and restaurants, as the chief examples, work in several different and complex ways to abet sidewalk safety.

First, they give people – both residents and strangers – concrete reasons for using the sidewalks on which these enterprises face.

Second, they draw people along the sidewalks past places which have no attractions to public use in themselves but which become travelled and peopled as routes to somewhere else; this influence does not carry very far geographically, so enterprises must be frequent in a city district if they are to populate with walkers those other stretches of street that lack public places along the sidewalk. Moreover, there should be many different kinds of enterprise, to give people reasons for criss-crossing paths.

Third, storekeepers and other small businessmen are typically strong proponents of peace and order themselves; they hate broken windows and holdups; they hate having customers made nervous about safety. They are great street watchers and sidewalk guardians if present in sufficient numbers.

Fourth, the activity generated by people on errands, or people aiming for food or drink, is itself an attraction to still other people.

This last point, that the sight of people attracts still other people, is something that city planners and city architectural designers seem to find incomprehensible. They operate on the premiss that city people seek the sight of emptiness, obvious order, and quiet. Nothing could be less true. People's love of watching activity and other people is constantly evident in cities everywhere. This trait reaches an almost ludicrous extreme on upper Broadway in New York, where the street is divided by a narrow central mall, right in the middle of traffic. At the cross-street intersections of this long north–south mall, benches have been placed behind big concrete buffers and on any day when the weather is even barely tolerable these benches are filled with people at block after block after block, watching the pedestrians who cross the mall in front of them, watching the traffic, watching the people on the busy sidewalks, watching each other. Eventually Broadway reaches Columbia University and Barnard College, one to the right, the other to the left. Here all is obvious order and quiet. No more stores, no more activity generated by the stores, almost no more pedestrians crossing – and no more watchers. The benches are there but they go empty in even the finest weather. I have tried them and can see why. No place could be more boring. Even the students of these institutions shun the solitude. They are doing their outdoor loitering, outdoor homework, and general street watching on the steps overlooking the busiest campus crossing.

It is just so on city streets elsewhere. A lively street always has both its users and pure watchers. Last year I was on such a street in the Lower East Side of Manhattan, waiting for a bus. I had not been there longer than a minute, barely long enough to begin taking in the street's activity of errand goers, children playing, and loiterers on the stoops, when my attention was attracted by a woman who opened a window on the third floor of a tenement across the street and vigorously yoo-hooed at me. When I caught on that she wanted my attention and responded, she shouted down, 'The bus doesn't run here on Saturdays!' Then by a combination of shouts and pantomime she directed me around the corner. This woman was one of thousands upon thousands of people in New York who casually take care of the streets. They notice strangers. They observe everything going on. If they need to take action, whether to direct a stranger waiting in the wrong place or to call the police, they do so. Action usually requires, to be sure, a certain self-assurance about the actor's proprietorship of the street and the support he will get if necessary, matters which will be gone into later in this book. But even more fundamental than the action and necessary to the action, is the watching itself. . . .

In some rich city neighbourhoods, where there is little do-it-yourself surveillance, such as residential Park Avenue or upper Fifth Avenue in New York, street watchers are hired. The monotonous sidewalks of residential Park Avenue, for example, are surprisingly little used; their putative users are populating, instead, the interesting store-, bar-, and restaurant-filled sidewalks of Lexington Avenue and Madison Avenue to east and west and the cross-streets leading to these. A network of doormen and superintendents, of delivery boys and nursemaids, a form of hired neighbourhood, keeps residential Park Avenue supplied with eyes. At night, with the security of the doormen as a bulwark, dog walkers safely venture forth and supplement the doormen. But this street is so blank of built-in eyes, so devoid of concrete reasons for using or watching it instead of turning the first corner off of it, that if its rents were to slip below the point where they could support a plentiful hired neighbourhood of doormen and elevator men, it would undoubtedly become a woefully dangerous street.

Once a street is well equipped to handle strangers, once it has both a good, effective demarcation between private and public spaces and has a basic supply of activity and eyes, the more strangers the merrier. . . .

Chapter 38

Spatializing Culture: The Social Construction of Public Space in Costa Rica

Setha M. Low

Setting

San José, Costa Rica, is the capital and largest city of this small Central American nation. Costa Rica – known for its beautiful scenery, protected natural environment, friendly people, and stable government – has become an ecotourism mecca and a desirable retirement site for middle-income North Americans who want to stretch their dollars while living in a warm climate. The rapid increase of tourism, the recent influx of refugees from Nicaragua and El Salvador, and the seemingly unending economic crises are blamed for what Josefinos (San José residents) perceive as an increase in crime and physical deterioration in the capital city of this erstwhile tropical paradise.

Two plazas in the center of the city were selected as field sites. Parque Central, the original Plaza Mayor, is one of the oldest plazas in San José and represents Costa Rica's Spanish colonial history in its spatial form and context. Its relatively long history spans the colonial, republican, and modern periods, and a number of historical photographs and portrayals of earlier periods of plaza design and social life were available in local archives. Parque Central remains a vibrant center of traditional Costa Rican culture and is inhabited by a variety of largely male workers, pen-

sioners, preachers and healers, tourists, shoppers, sex workers, and people who just want to sit and watch the action. When I returned in 1993 it was temporarily under reconstruction: the cement kiosk was being renovated and the surrounding benches, pathways, and gathering spaces had been redesigned since my previous visit.

The Plaza de la Cultura, a contemporary plaza only one block west and one block north of Parque Central, is a recently designed urban space heralded by Josefino boosters as an emblem of the "new Costa Rican culture." Because it was opened in 1982, I was able to interview individuals involved in its design and planning while at the same time I could study it as a well-established place. The Plaza de la Cultura proved to be an excellent comparison to Parque Central, providing contrasts in style of design, spatial configuration, surrounding buildings and institutions, activities, and the kinds of inhabitants and visitors. It is a site of modern consumption, an example of what Zukin (1991) calls a landscape of power. North American culture is "consumed" by Costa Rican teenagers carrying radios blaring rap music, and North American tourists "consume" Costa Rican culture by buying souvenirs, snacks, theater tickets, and artworks as well as the sexual favors and companionship of young Costa Ricans. These two urban spaces were socially produced – planned, built, designed, and maintained – in different historical and sociopolitical contexts, and both were constrained by limits imposed by the available resources as well as by the central government's political objectives. The environments thus produced are observably different: Parque Central is a furnished and enclosed space with trees, paths, and benches, while the Plaza de la Cultura is an open expanse that provides few places to sit but offers a magnificent open vista leading to a view of the National Theater.

These plazas were also socially constructed through contested patterns of use and attributed meanings. The social uses of the plazas, which at first glance appear similar, are fundamentally different according to the age, sex, ethnicity, and interests of the users. The degree and form of social contestation and conflict between the regular users and the agents of the municipal government – the police, the planning agency, and the directors of surrounding institutions – also vary, most visibly in terms of the kinds of spatial control maintained. Even the experience of being in the plaza (Richardson 1982) is distinct and voiced in different ways in the different spaces. The differences in the plazas' material production and symbolic and experiential construction have created very different urban spaces that are distinct in physical design as well as in the ways both users and nonusers control, experience, and think about them. These distinctions provide a vehicle to contrast the ways in which urban space is socially produced – both materially and symbolically – and socially constructed through experience and social interaction.

Parque Central

In 1751 Spanish colonists who had left the cacao-growing lowlands along the Caribbean coast established a new town, La Villa Nueva del Señor San José, in the central highland plateau of Costa Rica (González Víquez 1973, Vega Carballo 1981). In contrast to the Plaza de Armas, a plaza for military displays that was built a few blocks away, the Parque Central was designed as the ceremonial and civic center of the growing town. It began as a grassy, tree-covered rectangular public space that served as a weekend marketplace and was oriented as a square city block with north-south and east-west roads as its boundaries. Civic and religious institutions quickly surrounded it.... The remaining building sites were eventually filled with private residences and small businesses, including the Botica Francesa and a small hotel on the southern edge by the mid-nineteenth century. As early as the beginning of the nineteenth century, San José was a relatively urban center in comparison with other populated areas (Vega Carballo 1981).

The plan and urban design of Parque Central was part of the establishment of the Spanish American colonial empire, which repeatedly created a type of urban space that is still "produced despite the vicissitudes of imperialism, independence and industrialization" (Lefebvre 1991, 151)....

Lefebvre characterizes the building of Spanish American towns such as San José as the "production of a social space by political power – that is, by violence in the service of economic goals" (Lefebvre 1991, 151–2). While I agree with his theoretical analysis, the details of the origins of the plaza-centered grid-plan town deserve further examination.

I have argued elsewhere that the Spanish American plaza and gridplan town are syncretic spatial forms derived from a combination of European architectural traditions of medieval *bastides* (planned agricultural towns built by the French to protect their territory) and the Mesoamerican plaza-temple complexes and urban plans of the cities encountered during the conquest of the New World (Low 1993, Low 1995). Some of the earliest Spanish American plazas were in fact superposed on the ruins of their Aztec or Maya antecedents.

The European and Mesoamerican plaza designs had similar aims: both were produced to display military conquest and market domination by the conquering rulers, whether those rulers were Aztec, Mayan, or Spanish. Therefore, although the Spanish American plaza is a product of colonial control and consciously produced as a means of spatial domination, its form also derived from indigenous forms of political and economic control expressed in the Mesoamerican plaza-temple complex. Since the spatial relations of plaza to buildings, hierarchy of spaces, and functions of the plaza remained the same from the Mesoamerican models to their Spanish American successors, the symbolic meanings of the spatialized material culture reflect aspects of both cultural histories.

Parque Central retained its colonial form and meaning until the beginning of the republican era in 1823. In the mid-nineteenth century the plaza was redesigned and refurbished with all the trappings of European bourgeois elegance: a grand fountain was imported from England in 1859 to supply water to the city (and was completed in 1868); an elaborate iron fence was added in 1870; and a wooden "Victorian" kiosk in which the military band could play for the Sunday *retreta* was constructed in 1890. The plaza was also famous for its large fig, palm, and magnolia trees at this time, to the point that when one was cut down in 1902 a public protest ensued (Caja 1928).

It is in the late nineteenth century that we find textual and photographic evidence for class-based social constructions of the appropriate use (and appropriated use) of public space. The accumulated wealth of coffee growers and a republican government composed of members of the landed elite began to impose a class-biased conception of public space and spatial representation. Historical texts, retrospective interviews, and diaries from this period describe Parque Central as a place where the elite would gather and stroll in the evening and that was locked and patrolled

at night (Costa Rica en el Siglo XIX 1929). This elite image, however, is contested in other sources. For instance, photographs from 1870 show workers in open shirts and boys with bare feet resting in the plaza, and a well-known 1915 portrait of middle-class men with their children sitting on the ledge of the fountain captures a barefoot boy standing on the side of the scene. . . .

This conflict between the images of Parque Central as an elite strolling park and as a socially heterogeneous public gathering place has continued, manifesting itself most recently in the ongoing resistance to the replacement of the original 1890 kiosk. In 1944 a giant cement kiosk was donated by a Nicaraguan industrialist; this first housed a disco nightclub and later a children's library. By now, current daily users have incorporated the cement kiosk into their spatial pattern of activities. It makes a convenient stage and serves as a place to continue business on a rainy day. Children play on its ledges, and it is large enough to hold the orchestra and audience for the weekly Sunday concert.

As recently as the spring of 1992, however, a group of citizens formed a movement to tear down this cement structure and reconstruct the original Victorian one; the issue was so controversial that it provoked a series of well-attended town meetings. The cement kiosk and its current uses do not fit many Josefinos' idea of the appropriate architecture for the ceremonial and civic center of the city. The citizens who are attempting to reconstitute Parque Central in its elite turn-of-the-century image are not the daily users or the municipal designers but professional and middle-class residents who yearn for an idealized past. Thus the conflict over the architectural form of the kiosk reveals a struggle over the social construction of the meaning and appropriate use of public space. The symbolic contrasts of Victorian with modern, wooden with cement, and elite with working class provide architectural metaphors for class-based taste cultures, a forum for public conflict over appropriate modes of symbolic representation, and a convenient cover for broader class-based social meanings and conflicts.

Daily life in the Parque Central has changed over time. These changes appear in the architectural furnishings, the social class and gender composition of the users, the range of occupations and work sites, the nature of the policing and social control, and what people say about their experience of being in the plaza. Most of these changes are the end product of global economic and political forces, which have led to declining socioeconomic conditions and increasing cultural and social diversity. Dramatic economic changes in Costa Rica since the 1950s have led to increases in urban density as well as crowding, crime, and pollution. Most upper-class families have left the central city and moved to the western sector or to the suburbs, abandoning the central city – and thus Parque Central – to the poor and the working classes. The elite residences, symbols of the upper class's erstwhile presence in the central city, have been replaced by the symbols of a new kind of global economy, one based on debt and world-banking controls and dependent on foreign capital: national and international banks, movie theaters playing English-language movies, soda shops, and small businesses now surround Parque Central, replacing the civic and residential context of earlier plaza life. By 1985 the Latin American debt crisis had increased Costa Rica's dependence on United States AID funds (Shallat 1989), and the International Monetary Fund (IMF) had intervened to monitor Costa Rica's economy in order to ensure timely debt payments (Edelman and Kenen 1989).

The increase in unemployment that resulted from the decline in the value of agricultural exports has encouraged the growth of an informal economy. This informal economy is very visible in Parque Central. The plaza is used as an urban workplace of exchange and coexistence: shoeshine men control the northeast corner, ambulatory vendors use the sidewalks and pathways, salespeople use the benches as office space, construction workers wait for pickup jobs under the arbor, sex workers stand in the kiosk or sit on benches, and men move through the crowd selling stolen goods and gambling. The influx of refugees from Nicaragua, El Salvador, and Guatemala has increased both the number of vendors and the competition among them and has increased the presence of homeless adults and street children.

Middle-class businesspeople and nonusers, however, have used political pressure to increase the number of police in order to remove "undesirables." Concerned about the increase in crime and vagrancy that they associate with the ongoing economic crisis, the resulting numbers of people working in the plaza, homeless people, and their associated activities reflect their fears. The state is therefore attempting to constrain these uses in several ways. The police maintain open surveillance from the top of the cement kiosk, thus repeating and reiterating Parque Central's colonial history as a public space originally produced as a spatial representation of state domination and social control. In addition, plainclothes policemen look for drug transactions and the sale of stolen goods. . . . There are also municipal agents, representing a different kind of state control; they require vendors to pay for the right to sell on city streets and in the plazas. If vendors do not have the money to pay for a license – and they frequently do not – they forfeit their proceeds for that day.

Many of the older men are pensioners who come to spend the day on their regular benches with a group of cronies. One pensioner, Don Carlos, says that he is 86 years old. He comes to the plaza every day at about 10:00 A.M., after having his coffee, bread, and cheese – "something to nourish one" – at home. He sits with his friends on the southwest corner until the afternoon and then returns home to eat a late meal. When he was younger, he was employed by the civil police and at one time had worked as a guard in the plaza. He opened the gates at 6:00 A.M. and closed them at 10:00 P.M. When I asked how the plaza had changed, he replied, "The plaza was more strict before; they locked the gates at night. People of all kinds can come here now, but not before. It was a very polite place then, and not everyone was allowed in." Thus control over who is in the plaza is apparently maintained less openly and more subversively than it used to be.

We can see another example of coexistence and contestation in Parque Central in the number of evangelical healers and preachers who hold prayer meetings in the arbor and healing services on the northwest corner. These Protestant practitioners and their adherents can be seen as symbolically contesting the religious hegemony of the Catholic cathedral that flanks the eastern perimeter. Although the original Parque Central was designed as the "front garden" of the Catholic church (Richardson 1982), the diversity of religious beliefs and practices has now reconstituted the space as one of broadly defined religious heterodoxy. . . .

The actions of the plaza users also contest the hegemony of state Catholicism. Plaza users say that they enjoy the spectacle of the healing ceremonies, to which successful cures draw large crowds of believers. . . .

There is no unified experience of being in Parque Central, but fragments of its social production are reproduced in the everyday practices and feelings of its users. Many of the older men express considerable affection for and attachment to the plaza; often the sense of being comfortable is based on memories of being in the park at an earlier time or in different circumstances. One elderly man expressed his feelings when he began to cry upon seeing a giant palm cut down and reminisced about how it felt to sit in the shade of that tree. Women, however, often express a sense of unease and are rarely found sitting for very long, especially during the week. A woman who sat down next to me gave me her explanation when I asked her if she came there often. She replied, "No, but I am resting because my package is heavy." She said that she lived in an outlying suburb and was on her way home. "I normally only come to the plaza

on Sunday," she commented. I asked her why. "Because there are a lot of unemployed men here and women are usually working, or if they are not working, they are in the house. Sunday is when women come to Parque Central, with their children." Younger adult men are often found working in the plaza. One man was running his real estate business from a bench: "With the high price of rent, the electricity, water, and everything else, it is difficult to stay in business. Here my clients can find me, and I do not have all these other expenses." Other regular plaza workers include the food, candy, flower, lottery ticket, and newspaper vendors; shoeshine men; gamblers; sex workers; and day laborers waiting for casual work in the morning. These working users are territorial about their spaces and defend them both from new workers and from casual passersby. When asked about their work they express satisfaction with their working conditions, and in the case of the shoeshine men, say that they intend to hand down their work location to their children or friends.

Other plaza users come to participate in the illicit world of gambling and trade in stolen goods. . . .

According to some plaza users there is an increasing number of sex workers working in Parque Central. One afternoon I was working on a map sitting next to a man who asked me what I was doing. After I told him, I asked him who the women were in front of us. He replied, "Prostitutes, young prostitutes. They come every evening. There seem to be more [of them] than ever now for economic necessity." I also asked him about why there were so few women in the plaza. He replied that there was increasing unemployment and that the unemployed men in the plaza made women uneasy: "It is the government's fault. Have you heard that they want to build eighty thousand houses? You could not even do it physically! And the price supports for farmers and manufacturers just do not work." (Costa Rica had government subsidies for basic agricultural products such as beans, rice, and milk and high import taxes on foreign manufactured products to protect the development of local industry.)

Even the clowns who work in the Parque Central are concerned about the economic conditions of people who use it. In an interview with two clowns, I commented that they had cut their performance short the day before. The older clown responded by saying that they did not make much money in Parque Central and that they could earn more at the Plaza de la Cultura: "Because the people of the Plaza de la Cultura are of a higher social class and are richer...there are more tourists and foreigners. Here in the Parque Central they do not have the resources." An older man who had overheard us walked up and remarked: "I am a pensioner, and I enjoy the clowns and would like to give money, but I do not have enough to support even myself. That is how we are."

The experience of being in the plaza is sensory as well as social. When I returned to study the plaza during the dry season, I noticed that a group of pensioners had moved from the benches on the southwest corner (where I had always seen them) to the inner ring of benches near the kiosk. Until then the territories of different groups of people had been quite stable in terms of both location and time of day. When I asked them if I had been mistaken to assume that their preferred bench was on the southwest corner, they told me they had sat on that corner for the past five years but that the noise and fumes from increased bus traffic had become intolerable. The inner ring had benches where it was quieter and smelled better. I also noticed subtle sensory changes in the environment throughout the day: the bird songs early in the morning and at sunset, the bells of the cathedral at noon, and the smell of roasting candied peanuts and meats that announced the vendors who catered to the evening movie theater crowd. These sensory perceptions, although a valued part of the cultural landscape, are also undergoing change.

The ethnographic evidence for the transformation of the Parque Central into a workplace and a place mainly for pensioners and unemployed men on weekdays shows how the space is the object of conflicts over the nature of social and spatial representation in the urban center. The struggle over the design of the kiosk, the number of police and the kinds of state control, the increasing territoriality of the vendors and shoeshine men, the discomfort of women and children, and the heterodoxy of religious practitioners all illustrate how individuals and groups resist the consequences of larger sociopolitical, economic, and historical forces.

Plaza de la Cultura

The second case study, the more recently built Plaza de la Cultura, sheds further light on these processes by allowing us to observe how a new public urban space was created and defined and subsequently appropriated by a different group of users – who gave it quite distinct cultural meanings.

The Plaza de la Cultura is a modern paved plaza reminiscent of the futurist design of the Pompidou Center in Paris; it has bright chrome and yellow ventilation pipes, a shallow pool containing three water jets, metal pipe benches, and few trees. Beneath the plaza are a subterranean Gold Museum, exhibition spaces, and the Costa Rican tourist center, entered from the northern edge of the plaza by a series of grassy, sloping steps. The plaza is bordered on the south by the turn-of-the-century National Theater; on the west by the Gran Hotel, the major tourist hotel for North Americans; and on the north and east by busy shopping streets lined by McDonald's, Burger King, Pizza Hut, Sears, photographic supply stores, bookstores, and other local businesses. The few trees are in planters lining the western edge alongside the hotel shops, which include a newspaper stand carrying the *Miami Herald*, a clothing store, and a shop that sells the renowned Costa Rican ice cream, Pops.

The building of the Plaza de la Cultura was an inspiration of the minister of culture.

Costa Rica's world-famous collection of pre-Columbian gold artifacts was formerly stored in the Central Bank of Costa Rica. In 1975 the head of the Central Bank convinced the Legislative Assembly to allocate funds to build a Gold Museum in order to display the collection as a celebration of indigenous Costa Rican culture. The plan was supported by the "Liberationists," the political party in power at the time. The National Liberation Party (Liberación Nacional) represents a politically liberal coalition of professional, middle-class, and working-class Costa Ricans, whereas the Social Christians' Unity Party (Partido Unidad de Social Cristianos) – a more conservative party – had grown out of earlier political coalitions that included the landed gentry and coffee-growing elite. The minister of planning and the head of the Central Bank selected the land around the National Theater, already partly owned by the Central Bank, as an appropriate site for a cultural center that would accommodate tourists and visitors to the new Gold Museum. This desire for a new cultural center was also stimulated by the changes taking place in Parque Central, which was becoming inadequate as a cultural embodiment of the National Liberation Party ideals (Low 1996). Some structures already in place would remain: the new plaza would incorporate the already existing *parquecito* (little park) Juan Mora Fernandez in front of the Gran Hotel and the shopping structure known as the Arcades (Naranjo Coto 1982). Among the many structures to be demolished, however, were the homes of a few older residents (who were to be compensated by the state) and a number of small business establishments (Archivos 1993).

This initial design was radically changed and expanded. When the minister of culture went to the site to survey the progress of the demolition, he saw the National Theater isolated in the open space created by the destruction of the surrounding buildings. In an instant, he said, he realized that it would be a much more powerful plan to have an open public plaza with the Gold Museum underground, so that there would be an unobstructed view of the National Theater – the "architectural jewel" of San José. Thus the architectural plans for the original Gold Museum were scrapped and a new phase of planning and design began. The planning, design, and building of the Plaza de la Cultura began in 1976 and culminated in the plaza's inauguration in 1982. Although some of the buildings selected for demolition were deemed of historic significance, and despite local protest, the plan moved forward....

Both the location and design program were produced by a combination of local sociopolitical forces and global – particularly North American – capital. When the plaza was conceived, global capital was already fueling the Costa Rican economy and the IMF restrictions would soon be in place. Foreign as well as local interests thus influenced the siting of the plaza, placing it next to the major tourist hotel and the National Theater and in the center of North American businesses (including McDonald's, Burger King, and Sears) and tourist activity. The design, on the other hand, was influenced by the political ideology of the National Liberation Party under the leadership of a new professional class, which wanted Costa Rican culture to be represented as both modern in its reliance on modern European idioms of design and indigenous in its evocation of the pre-Columbian past.

The spatial form and design, however, were ultimately determined by a team of three architects who had won the design competition for the original plan, the above-ground Gold Museum. The architects themselves, although all Costa Rican, represented Costa Rican, European, and North American design training, blended to create what they defined as a new Costa Rican design idiom. From my interviews with them, it seems that each had a different vision of the plaza. Further, they produced design features best appreciated from a male point of view.

One of them imagined the plaza to be a place where men could watch women walk past; he designed a vast paved open space, providing the longest sight line available for watching women walk in the city. Another architect saw the plaza as a meeting place, symbolically linked to other plazas in the city by a second grid, with pedestrian walkways and trees. He imagined young men leaning on the outside rails of the perimeter piping and put a foot rail just where a man's foot might rest. The third architect thought that the new plaza should be a significant open space: "Costa Ricans have their gardens and their parks, and they have their special places, but they do not have a center for jugglers, music, political meetings and large gatherings as in New York." He wanted an open space for public performances: "But we did not want a huge dry space, so we put in trees along the edges." These different social imaginings and representations of space were integrated to create a rather eclectic space with a modernist style – a design idiom that many Costa Ricans neither liked nor understood. When the plaza first opened there were spontaneous demonstrations by people who came and tore out the plantings, started fires in the trash cans, and tried to destroy as many of the furnishings as possible. There is even conflict over the meaning of these demonstrations: It is not entirely clear either from the media reports or from firsthand accounts who the demonstrators were or what exactly they were protesting, but the media interpreted this demonstration as a protest against the plaza's stark modernity.

Nonetheless, the plaza appears to be successful in terms of the architects' objectives: the unusual modern and empty urban space produced by these sociopolitical and economic forces and professional imaginings has been rapidly appropriated by groups of users. The vast open space is used by street performers, religious singing groups, political speakers, and teenagers break dancing or playing soccer (to the delight of the third architect). These are all users who did not have a public place before this plaza was constructed, since the parklike atmosphere

of Parque Central does not accommodate these activities.

In addition, the small plazas created by the designers in front of the National Theater and Gran Hotel are used by officially licensed vendors who sell local crafts to tourists from their semipermanent stands. A seemingly endless stream of tourists from the Gran Hotel sit on the edges of the plaza watching people from the safety of the hotel's sidewalk café. Women and families bring their children, who run after pigeons and play in the fountain during the afternoon; in the late evening the plaza becomes a gay cruising area and social meeting place that is internationally known...

From interviews with key informants and conversations with users and friends one learns that this tranquillity is contested by a number of illicit activities that contribute to the perception that the Plaza de la Cultura is an unsafe and unpleasant place. This perception is reinforced in several ways. The newspapers regularly and frequently report mishaps and transgressions and criticize the municipal government's management of the plaza. The hotel bouncer remains posted at the edge of the plaza, ready to protect his customers from the sight of beggars or poor people looking for a place to rest. Official uniformed police stand outside the National Theater and refuse entrance to anyone who looks likely to cause a disturbance;... The intensity of social and spatial control appears even greater than in the Parque Central; here it is more visible and even more intensely contested.

These conflicting forces produce an ambivalent experience of being in the Plaza de la Cultura. Nonusers uniformly describe the plaza as dangerous, frightening, and uncomfortable. The media seem to have influenced many potential users in ways I found hard to understand, inasmuch as the bright, sunlit plaza never threatened me. Mothers and children do come to this plaza to play with the pigeons or splash in the low fountain. Many more young men and women, often students, stop there to meet one another or to have lunch or an ice cream cone in the afternoon sun than in the Parque Central. Tourists seem secure and comfortable.

Yet all my students at the Universidad de Costa Rica were uncomfortable there and unwilling to visit, even for a field visit. . . .

Frequent users also criticized the space, even though they admitted to spending a considerable amount of time there. For instance, an artist who said that he spent too much time in the plaza told me that he thought it was poorly designed: "It should have had a roof – a roof where artists could work and things could happen. This plaza is useless when the weather is forbidding and it is usually forbidding. We might as well have had a football stadium here." . . .

People who work in the Plaza de la Cultura express some of the same ambivalence about working there. While the clowns preferred the crowd there because they could collect more money that they could elsewhere, the vendors complained that they were charged a high fee for putting up a stall in the tourist area. These stalls are carefully regulated by the municipal government and have multiplied over time. During most of the time that I observed the vendors, they sat around, talked, and smoked cigarettes while waiting for the busy Saturday craft market held in front of the National Theater. During my last visit in December 1993, however, the plaza was crammed with stalls and vendors, most of whom were illegally selling clothes and souvenirs from other Central American countries. It seems that a Guatemalan vendor, who was fined for selling without a permit, sued the city and is bringing his case to court, arguing that the plaza should be a "free market" with no charge for selling in this "democratic" country. So even the vendors are contesting the city's control of the plaza to regulate their means of making a living. The Plaza de la Cultura also has a few child workers – young shoeshine boys in front of the Gran Hotel, and children who illegally sell gum and candy.

These young boys, who range in age from about seven to nine, are not found working in Parque Central.

There are nonetheless some who are happy with the plaza, often for very specific reasons. . . .

Probably the happiest group are the teenagers who hang out in the evenings along the pipe railing. One young man said that he found the spaciousness appealing. "Here," he said, "we feel at home." When I asked two young men what they were doing in the plaza, they replied, "Passing the time, shooting the breeze. What do young people do in the US?" Before the creation of this plaza, the teenagers were not a visible part of any park or plaza. You could see them walking down the streets or in couples, kissing or quietly talking in Parque España or Parque Morazon. But now they have their own space, designed to create a stage for their nightly performances. And they have successfully appropriated this public space for their activities in the evenings.

As in Parque Central, however, the visible presence of the Gran Hotel bouncer and the *guardia civil* (civil police), who question the youths (and in some cases stop or detain them), contests their symbolic dominance. For instance, one Friday night a young man with a bottle in a brown paper bag joined the line of teenagers along the railing. I was just wondering if they realized how many police were around when two came by, took the bag, frisked all of them, took their identity cards, and lined them up along the wall.

Compared with Parque Central, this urban space represents and accommodates more modern spatial practices, based on youth, foreign capital, tourism, and an ideology of liberal modernism but contested through the localized discourse about safety and comfort. The Plaza de la Cultura seems to be more about the consumption of culture than the working landscape of Parque Central is. Most important, the forces that produced this new plaza are reflected in its design and social use as well as in the ambivalence of being there. The teenagers and tourists are comfortable. while other Costa Ricans either fear the plaza and or wish that it were quieter, calmer, more shaded, and sedate.

Furthermore, the plaza is engendered in a distinct way: there are more women and children than in Parque Central, and fewer older men, except for the male North American tourists and pensioners who are looking at (or for) young Costa Rican women. The new public space thus appears to challenge the institutionalized weekday spatial segregation of domesticated women from plaza-frequenting men, a phenomenon that remains marked in more culturally traditional settings such as Parque Central. Since spatial arrangements reproduce gender differences in power and privilege, changing spatial relations such as the creation of public spaces that women can use may potentially change the status hierarchy and improve the position of women in Costa Rica (Spain 1992, 33).

Conclusion

In both places, however, there is a hiatus between what is experienced and socially constructed by the users on the one hand, and the circumstances that socially produced the space and its current physical form and design on the other. Furthermore, the designs and material conditions of these two worlds are subject to symbolic interpretation and manipulation by the users in such a way that they themselves become cultural representations to the users. Thus the contestation of the design, furnishings, use, and atmosphere of a plaza becomes a visible public forum for the expression of cultural conflict, social change, and attempts at class-based, gender-segregated, and age-specific social control.

These examples illustrate how an anthropological approach to the study of urban space would work ethnographically....

REFERENCES

Archivos, Censo Municipalidad. 1993. *Municipalidad de San José*. Departamento Financiero Sec. Censo. Distrito Catedral 4, Manzana 3, Propidad 2.

Caja. 1928. La capital de antaño. Nov. 30, 17–19.

Costa Rica en el Siglo XIX. 1929. *Costa Rica en el siglo XIX*. San José: Editorial Lehmann.

Edelman, Marc, and Joanne Kenen. 1989. *The Costa Rican reader*. New York: Grove Weidenfeld.

González Víquez, Cleto. 1973. San José y sus comienzos. In *Obras Históricas* I. San José: Universidad de Costa Rica.

Lefebvre, Henri. 1991. *The production of space*, trans. D. Nicholson-Smith. Oxford: Basil Blackwell.

Low, Setha M. 1993. Cultural meaning of the plaza: Origin and evolution of the Spanish American gridplan-plaza urban design. In *The cultural meaning of urban space*, eds. Gary McDonogh and Robert Rotenberg. Pp. 75–94. Westport, Conn.: Bergin and Garvey.

———. 1995. Indigenous architectural representations and the Spanish American plaza in Mesoamerica and the Caribbean. *American Anthropologist* 97: 748–62

———. 1996. Constructing difference: Spatial boundaries in the plaza. In *Setting boundaries*, ed. Deborah Pellow. Pp. 161–78. Westport, Conn.: Bergin and Garvey.

Naranjo Coto, Manuel. 1982. *Plaza de la Cultura*. Costa Rica: Litografia Trejos.

Richardson, Miles. 1982. Being-in-the-market versus being-in-the-plaza: Material culture and the construction of social reality in Spanish America. *American Ethnologist* 9: 421–36.

Shallat, Lezak. 1989. AID and the secret parallel state. In *The Costa Rican reader*, edited by Marc Edelman and Joanne Kenen. Pp. 221–8. New York: Grove Weidenfeld.

Spain, Daphne. 1992. *Gendered spaces*. Chapel Hill: University of North Carolina Press.

Vega Carballo, José Luis. 1981. *San José: Antecedentes coloniales y formación del estado nacional*. San José: Instituto de Investigaciones Sociales.

Zukin, Sharon. 1991. *Landscapes of power: From Detroit to Disney World*. Berkeley: University of California Press.

Chapter 39

The Right to the City

Henri Lefebvre

Theoretical thought sees itself compelled to redefine the forms, functions and structures of the city (economic, political, cultural, etc.) as well as the social needs inherent to urban society. Until now, only those individual needs, motivated by the so-called society of consumption (a bureaucratic society of managed consumption) have been prospected, and moreover manipulated rather than effectively known and recognized. Social needs have an anthropological foundation. Opposed and complimentary, they include the need for security and opening, the need for certainty and adventure, that of organization of work and of play, the needs for the predictable and the unpredictable, of similarity and difference, of isolation and encounter, exchange and investments, of independence (even solitude) and communication, of immediate and long-term prospects. The human being has the need to accumulate energies and to spend them, even waste them in play. He has a need to see, to hear, to touch, to taste and the need to gather these perceptions in a 'world'. To these anthropological needs which are socially elaborated (that is, sometimes separated, sometimes joined together, here compressed and there hypertrophied), can be added specific needs which are not satisfied by those commercial and cultural infrastructures which are somewhat parsimoniously taken into account by planners. This refers to the need for cre-

ative activity, for the *oeuvre* (not only of products and consumable material goods), of the need for information, symbolism, the imaginary and play. Through these specified needs lives and survives a fundamental desire of which play, sexuality, physical activities such as sport, creative activity, art and knowledge are particular expressions and *moments*, which can more or less overcome the fragmentary division of tasks. Finally, the need of the city and urban life can only be freely expressed within a perspective which here attempts to become clearer and to open up the horizon. Would not specific urban needs be those of qualified places, places of simultaneity and encounters, places where exchange would not go through exchange value, commerce and profit? Would there not also be the need for a time for these encounters, these exchanges?

At present, an analytical science of the city, which is necessary, is only at the outline stage. At the beginning of their elaboration, concepts and theories can only move forward with urban reality in the making, with the *praxis* (social practice) of urban society. Now, not without effort, the ideologies and practices which blocked the horizon and which were only bottlenecks of knowledge and action, are being overcome.

The *science of the city* has the city as object. This science borrows its methods, approaches and concepts from the fragmentary sciences, but synthesis escapes it in two ways. Firstly, because this synthesis which would wish itself as total, starting from the analytic, can only be strategic systematization and programming. Secondly, because the object, the city, as consummate reality is falling apart. Knowledge holds in front of itself the historic city already modified, to cut it up and put it together again from fragments. As social text, this historic city no longer has a coherent set of prescriptions, of use of time linked to symbols and to a style. This text is moving away. It takes the form of a document, or an exhibition, or a museum. The city historically constructed is no longer lived and is no longer understood practically. It is only an object of cultural consumption for tourists, for aestheticism, avid for spectacles and the picturesque. Even for those who seek to understand it with warmth, it is gone. Yet, the *urban* remains in a state of dispersed and alienated actuality, as kernel and virtuality. What the eyes and analysis perceive on the ground can at best pass for the shadow of a future object in the light of a rising sun. It is impossible to envisage the reconstitution of the old city, only the construction of a new one on new foundations, on another scale and in other conditions, in another society. The prescription is: there cannot be a going back (towards the traditional city), nor a headlong flight, towards a colossal and shapeless agglomeration. In other words, for what concerns the city the object of science is not given. The past, the present, the possible cannot be separated. What is being studied is a *virtual object*, which thought studies, which calls for new approaches.

The career of the old classical humanism ended long ago and badly. It is dead. Its mummified and embalmed corpse weighs heavily and does not smell good. It occupies many spaces, public or otherwise, thus transforms into cultural cemeteries under the guise of the human: museums, universities, various publications, not to mention new towns and planning procedures. Trivialities and platitudes are wrapped up in this 'human scale', as they say, whereas what we should take charge of are the excesses and create 'something' to the scale of the universe.

This old humanism died during the World Wars, during the demographic growth which accompanied great massacres, and before the brutal demands of economic growth and competition and the pressure of poorly controlled techniques. It is not even an ideology, barely a theme for official speeches.

Recently there have been great cries of 'God is dead, man too' as if the death of classical humanism was that of man. These formulae spread in best-sellers, and taken in by a publicity not really responsible, are nothing new. Nietzschean meditation, a dark presage for Europe's culture and civilization, began a hundred years ago during the 1870–1 Franco-Prussian war. When Nietzsche announced the death of God and man, he did not leave a gaping hole, or fill this void with makeshift material, language or linguistics. He was also announcing the Superhuman which he thought was to come. He was overcoming the nihilism he was identifying. Authors transacting these theoretical and poetic treasures, but with a delay of a century, plunge us back into nihilism. Since Nietzsche, the dangers of the Superhuman have been cruelly evident. Moreover, this 'new man' emerging from industrial production and planning rationality has been more than disappointing. There is still another way, that of urban society and the human as *oeuvre* in this society which would be an *oeuvre* and not a product. There is also the simultaneous overcoming of the old 'social animal' and man of the ancient city, the urban animal, towards a polyvalent, polysensorial, urban man capable of complex and transparent relations with the world (the environment and himself). Or there is nihilism. If man is dead, for whom will we build? How will we build? It does not matter that the city has or has not disappeared, that it must be thought anew, reconstructed on new foundations or overcome. It does not matter whether terror reigns, that the atomic bomb is dropped or that Planet Earth explodes. What is important? Who thinks? Who acts? Who still speaks and for whom? If meaning and finality disappear and we cannot even declare them in a praxis, nothing matters. And if the capacities of the 'human being', technology, science, imagination and art, or their absence, are erected as autonomous powers, and that reflective thought is satisfied with this assessment, the absence of a 'subject', what to reply? What to do?

Old humanism moves away and disappears. Nostalgia lessens and we turn back less and less often to see its shape lying across the road. It was the ideology of the liberal bourgeoisie, with its Greek and Latin quotes sprinkled with Judeo-Christianity, which bent over the people and human sufferings and which covered and supported the rhetoric of the clear consciences of noble feelings and of the sensitive souls. A dreadful cocktail, a mixture to make you sick. Only a few intellectuals (from the 'Left' – but are there still any intellectuals on the 'Right'?) who are neither revolutionary nor openly reactionary, nor Dionysiacs or Apollonians, still have a taste for this sad potion.

We thus must make the effort to reach out towards a new humanism, a new praxis, another man, that of urban society. We must avoid those myths which threaten this will, destroy those ideologies which hinder this project and those strategies which divert this trajectory. Urban life has yet to begin. What we are doing now is to complete an inventory of the remains of a millenarian society where the countryside dominated the city, and whose ideas, values, taboos and prescriptions were largely agrarian, with rural and 'natural' dominant features. A few sporadic cities hardly emerged from a rustic ocean. Rural society was (still is), a society of scarcity and penury, of want accepted or rejected, of prohibitions managing and regulating privations. It was also the society of the *Fête*, of festivities. But that aspect, the best, has been lost and instead of myths

and limitations, this is what must be revitalized! A decisive remark: for the crisis of the traditional city accompanies the world crisis of agrarian civilization, which is also traditional. It is up to us to resolve this double crisis, especially by creating with the new city, a new life in the city. Revolutionary societies (among which the USSR ten or fifteen years after the October Revolution), intimated the development of society based on industry. But they only intimated.

The use of 'we' in the sentences above has only the impact of a metaphor to mean those concerned. The architect, the planner, the sociologist, the economist, the philosopher or the politician cannot out of nothingness create new forms and relations. More precisely, the architect is no more a miracle-worker than the sociologist. Neither can create social relations, although under certain favourable conditions they help trends to be formulated (to take shape). Only social life (praxis) in its global capacity possesses such powers – or does not possess them. The people mentioned above can individually or in teams clear the way; they can also propose, try out and prepare forms. And also (and especially), through a maieutic nurtured by science, assess acquired experience, provide a lesson from failure and give birth to the possible.

At the point we have arrived there is an urgent need to change intellectual approaches and tools. It would be indispensable to take up ideas and approaches from elsewhere and which are still not very familiar.

Transduction. This is an intellectual operation which can be methodically carried out and which differs from classical induction, deduction, the construction of 'models', simulation as well as the simple statement of hypothesis. Transduction elaborates and constructs a theoretical object, a *possible* object from information related to reality and a problematic posed by this reality. Transduction assumes an incessant feed back between the conceptual framework used and empirical observations. Its theory (methodology), gives shape to certain spontaneous mental operations of the planner, the architect, the sociologist, the politician and the philosopher. It introduces rigour in invention and knowledge in utopia.

Experimental utopia. Who is not a *utopian* today? Only narrowly specialized practioners working to order without the slightest critical examination of stipulated norms and constraints, only these not very interesting people escape utopianism. All are utopians, including those futurists and planners who project Paris in the year 2000 and those engineers who have made Brasilia! But there are several utopianisms. Would not the worst be that utopianism which does not utter its name, covers itself with positivism and on this basis imposes the harshest constraints and the most derisory absence of technicity?

Utopia is to be considered experimentally by studying its implications and consequences on the ground. These can surprise. What are and what would be the most successful places? How can they be discovered? According to which criteria? What are the times and rhythms of daily life which are inscribed and prescribed in these 'successful' spaces favourable to happiness? That is interesting.

There are other indispensable intellectual approaches to identify without dissociating them from the three fundamental theoretical concepts of structure, function and form, and to know their import, the spheres of their validity, their limits and their reciprocal relations. To know that they make a whole but that the elements of this whole have a certain independence and relative autonomy. To not privilege one over the other, otherwise this gives an ideology, that is, a closed and dogmatic system of significations: structuralism, formalism, functionalism. To be used equally and in turn for the analysis of the real (an analysis which is never exhaustive or without residue), as well as for that operation known as 'transduction'. It is important to understand that a function can be accomplished by means of different structures, and that there is no unequivocal link between the

terms. That is, that functions and structures clothe themselves with forms which reveal and veil them – that the triplicity of these aspects make a whole which is more than these aspects, elements and parts.

We have among our intellectual tools one which deserves neither disdain nor privilege of the absolute: that of *system* (or rather *sub-system* of significations.

Policies have their systems of significations – ideologies – which enable them to subordinate to their strategies social acts and events influenced by them. At the ecological level, the humble inhabitant has his system (or rather, his sub-system) of significations. The fact of living here or there involves the reception, adoption and transmission of such a system, for example that of owner-occupied housing. The system of significations of the inhabitant tells of his passivities and activities: he is received but changed by practice. He is perceived.

Architects seem to have established and dogmatized an ensemble of significations, as such poorly developed and variously labelled as 'function', 'form', 'structure', or rather, functionalism, formalism, and structuralism. They elaborate them not from the significations perceived and lived by those who inhabit, but from their interpretation of inhabiting. It is graphic and visual, tending towards metalanguage. It is graphism and visualization. Given that these architects form a social body, they attach themselves to institutions, their system tends to close itself off, impose itself and elude all criticism. There is cause to formulate this system, often put forward without any other procedure or precaution, as *planning* by extrapolation.

This theory which one could legitimately call planning, close to the meanings of that old practice of *to inhabit* (that is, the human) which would add to these partial facts a general theory of urban *time-spaces*, which would reveal a new practice emerging from this elaboration can be envisaged only as the practical application of a comprehensive theory of the city and the urban which could go beyond current scissions and separations, particularly those existing between philosophy and the sciences of the city, the global and the partial. Current planning projects could figure in this development – but only within an unwavering critique of their ideological and strategic implications. Inasmuch as we can define it, our object – the urban – will never today be entirely present in our reflections. More than any another object, it possesses a very complex quality of totality in act and potential the object of research gradually uncovered, and which will be either slowly or never exhausted. To take this object as a given truth is [to] operate a mythifying ideology. Knowledge must envisage a considerable number of methods to grasp this object, and cannot fasten itself onto a particular approach. Analytical configurations will follow as closely as possible the internal articulations of this 'thing' which is not a thing; they will be accompanied by reconstructions which will never be realized. Descriptions, analyses and attempts at synthesis can never be passed off as being exhaustive or definitive. All these notions, all these batteries of concepts will come into play: form, structure, function, level, dimension, dependent and independent variables, correlations, totality, ensemble, system, etc. Here as elsewhere, but more than elsewhere, the residue reveals itself to be most precious. Each 'object' constructed will in turn be submitted to critical examination. Within the possible, this will be accomplished and submitted to experimental verification. The science of the city requires a historical period to make itself and to orient social practice.

This science is necessary but not sufficient. We can perceive its limits at the same time as its necessity. Planning thought proposes the establishment or reconstitution of highly localized, highly particularized and centralized social units whose linkages and tensions would re-establish an urban unity endowed with a complex interior order, with its hierarchy and a supple structure. More specifically, sociological thought seeks an understanding and reconstitution of the integrative capacities of the urban as well as the conditions of practical participation. Why not? But only under one condition: never to protect these fragmented and therefore partial attempts from criticism, practical assessment and global preoccupation.

Knowledge can therefore construct and propose models. In this sense each object is but a model of urban reality. Nevertheless, such a reality will never become manageable as a thing and will never become instrumental even for the most operational knowledge. Who would not hope that the city becomes again what it was – the act and *oeuvre* of a complex thought? But it cannot remain at the level of wishes and aspirations and an *urban strategy* is not defined. An urban strategy cannot take into account existing strategies and acquired knowledge: science of the city, with its disposition towards the planning of growth and the control of development. Whoever says 'strategies' says the hierarchy of 'variables' to be considered, some having a strategic capacity and others remaining at the tactical level – and says also the power to realize these strategies on the ground. Only groups, social classes and class fractions capable of revolutionary initiative can take over and realize to fruition solutions to urban problems. It is from these social and political forces that the renewed city will become the *oeuvre*. The first thing to do is to defeat currently dominant strategies and ideologies. In the present society that there exist many divergent groups and strategies (for example between the State and the private) does not alter the situation. From questions of landed property to problems of segregation, each project of *urban reform* questions the structures, the immediate (individual) and daily relations of existing society, but also those that one purports to impose by the coercive and institutional means of what remains of urban reality. In itself *reformist*, the strategy of urban renewal becomes 'inevitably' revolutionary, not by force of circumstance, but against the established order. Urban strategy resting on the science of the city needs a social support and political forces to be effective. It cannot act on its own. It cannot but depend on the presence and action of the working class, the only one able to put an end to a segregation directed essentially against it. Only this class, as a class, can decisively contribute to the reconstruction of centrality destroyed by a strategy of segregation and found again in the menacing form of *centres of decision-making*. This does not mean that the working class will make urban society all on its own, but that without it nothing is possible. Without it integration has no meaning and disintegration will continue under the guise of nostalgia and integration. There is there not only an option but an horizon which opens or closes. When the working class is silent, when it is quiescent and cannot accomplish what theory has defined as its 'historical mission', then both the 'subject' and 'object' are lacking. Reflection confirms this absence, which means that it is appropriate to consider two series of propositions:

1 *A political programme of urban reform* not defined by the framework and the possibilities of prevailing society or subjugated to a 'realism', although based on the study of realities. In other words, reform thus understood is not limited to reformism. This programme will therefore have a singular and even paradoxical character. It will be established to be proposed to political forces, parties. One could even add that preferentially it would be presented to 'left' parties, political formations representing or wishing to represent the working class. But it would not be established as a function of these forces and formations. It will have in relation to them a specific character which comes from knowledge, a scientific part. It will be *proposed* (free to be altered) by those who take control of it. Let political forces take their responsibilities. In this domain which engages the future of modern society and that of producers, ignorance and misunderstanding entail responsibilities before history.

2 Mature *planning projects* which consist of models and spatial forms and urban times without concern for their current feasibility or their utopian aspect. It does not seem possible that these models result either from a simple study of existing cities and urban typologies, or from a combination of elements. Other than contrary to experience, the forms of space and time will be invented and proposed to praxis. That imagination be deployed, not the imaginary of escape and evasion which conveys ideologies, but the imaginary which invests itself in *appropriation* (of time, space, physiolocal life and desire). Why not oppose ephemeral cities to the eternal city, and movable centrality to stable centres? All audacities can be premissed. Why limit these propositions only to the morphology of time and space? They could also include the way of living in the city and the development of the urban on this basis.

In these two series there will also be long, medium and short-term propositions constituting urban strategy understood as such.

The society in which we live appears to tend towards plenitude – or at least towards fullness (durable goods and objects, quantity, satisfaction and rationality). In fact it allows a colossal gulf to be dug into which ideologies agitate themselves and the fog of rhetoric spreads. Having left speculation and contemplation, incomplete knowledge and fragmentary divisions, one of the greatest projects active thought can propose for itself is to fill this lacuna – and not only with language.

In a period during which ideologists pronounce abundantly on structures, the destructuration of the city manifests the depth of phenomena, of social and cultural disintegration. Considered as a whole, this society finds itself *incomplete*. Between the sub-systems and the structures consolidated by various means (compulsion, terror, and ideological persuasion), there are holes and chasms. These voids are not there due to chance. They are the places of the possible. They contain the floating and dispersed elements of the possible, but not the power which could assemble them.

Moreover, structuring actions and the power of the social void tend to prohibit action and the very presence of such a power. The conditions of the possible can only be realized in the course of a radical metamorphosis.

In this conjuncture, ideology claims to provide an absolute quality to 'scientificity', science appertaining to the real, dissecting it, reconstituting it, and by this fact isolating it from the possible and closing the way. Now, in such a conjuncture science which is fragmentary science can only have a *programmatic* impact. It brings elements to a programme. If one concedes that these elements already constitute a totality, and one wishes to execute this programme literally, one treats the virtual object as a pre-existent technical object. A project is accomplished without criticism and this project fulfills an ideology by projecting it on the ground – that of the technocrats. Although necessary, policy is not enough. It changes during the course of its implementation. Only social force, capable of investing itself in the urban through a long political experience, can take charge of the realization of a programme concerning urban society. Conversely, the science of the city brings to this perspective a theoretical and critical foundation, a positive base. Utopia controlled by dialectical reason serves as a safeguard against supposedly scientific fictions and visions gone astray. Besides, this foundation and base prevent reflection from losing itself in pure policy. Here the dialectical movement presents itself as a relation between science and political power, as a dialogue which actualizes relations of 'theory–practice' and 'critical positive–negative'.

As necessary as science, but not sufficient, *art* brings to the realization of urban society its long meditation on life as drama and pleasure. In addition and especially, art restitutes the meaning of the *oeuvre*, giving it multiple facets of *appropriated* time and space; neither endured nor accepted by a passive resignation, metamorphosed as *oeuvre*. Music shows the appropriation of time, painting and sculpture that of space.

If the sciences discover partial determinisms, art and philosophy show how a totality grows out of partial determinisms. It is incumbent on the social force capable of creating urban society to make efficient and effective the unity of art, technique and knowledge. As much the science of the city, art and the history of art are part of a meditation on the urban which wants to make efficient the images which proclaim it. By overcoming this opposition, this meditation striving for action would thus be both utopian and realistic. One could even assert that the maximum of utopianism could unite with the optimum of realism.

Among the contradictions characteristic of our time there are those (particularly difficult ones) between the realities of society and the facts of civilization. On the one hand, genocide, and on the other, medical and other interventions which enable a child to be saved or an agony prolonged. One of the latest but not least contradictions has been shown in this essay: between the *socialization of society* and *generalized segregation*. There are many others, for example, the contradiction between the label of *revolutionary* and the attachment to an obsolete productivist rationalism. The individual, at the centre of social forces due to the pressure of the masses, asserts himself and does not die. *Rights* appear and become customs or prescriptions, usually followed by enactments. And we know how, through gigantic destructions, World Wars, and the terror of nuclear threats, that these concrete rights come to complete the abstract rights of man and the citizen inscribed on the front of buildings by democracy during its revolutionary beginnings: the rights of ages and sexes (the woman the child and the elderly), rights of conditions (the proletarian, the peasant), rights to training and education, to work, to culture, to rest, to health, to housing. The pressure of the working class has been and remains necessary (but not sufficient) for the recognition of these rights, for their entry into customs, for their inscription into codes which are still incomplete.

Over the last few years and rather strangely, the *right to nature* entered into social practice thanks to *leisure*, having made its way through protestations becoming commonplace against noise, fatigue, the concentrationary universe of cities (as cities are rotting or exploding). A strange journey indeed! Nature enters into exchange value and commodities, to be bought and sold. This 'naturality' which is counterfeited and traded in, is destroyed by commercialized, industrialized and institutionally organized leisure pursuits. 'Nature', or what passes for it, and survives of it, becomes the ghetto of leisure pursuits, the separate place of pleasure and the retreat of 'creativity'. Urban dwellers carry the urban with them, even if they do not bring planning with them! Colonized by them, the countryside has lost the qualities, features and charms of peasant life. The urban ravages the countryside: this urbanized countryside opposes itself to a dispossessed rurality, the extreme case of the deep misery of the inhabitant, the habitat, of to inhabit. Are the rights to nature and to the country-side not destroying themselves?

In the face of this pseudo-right, the *right to the city* is like a cry and a demand. This right slowly meanders through the surprising detours of nostalgia and tourism, the return to the heart of the traditional city, and the call of existent or recently developed centralities. The claim to nature, and the desire to enjoy it displace the right to the city. This latest claim expresses itself indirectly as a tendency to flee the deteriorated and unrenovated city, alienated urban life before at last, 'really' living. The need and the 'right' to nature contradict the right to the city without being able to evade it. (This does not mean that it is not necessary to preserve vast 'natural' spaces.)

The *right to the city* cannot be conceived of as a simple visiting right or as a return to traditional cities. It can only be formulated as a transformed and renewed *right to urban life*. It does not matter whether the urban fabric encloses the countryside and what survives of peasant life, as long as the

'urban', place of encounter, priority of use value, inscription in space of a time promoted to the rank of a supreme resource among all resources, finds its morphological base and its practico-material realization. Which presumes an integrated theory of the city and urban society, using the resources of science and art. Only the working class can become the agent, the social carrier or support of this realization. Here again, as a century ago, it denies and contests, by its very existence, the class strategy directed against it. As a hundred years ago, although under new conditions, it gathers the interests (overcoming the immediate and the superficial) of the whole society and firstly of all those who *inhabit*. Who can ignore that the Olympians of the new bourgeois aristocracy no longer inhabit. They go from grand hotel to grand hotel, or from castle to castle, commanding a fleet or a country from a yacht. They are everywhere and nowhere. That is how they fascinate people immersed into everyday life. They transcend everyday life, possess nature and leave it up to the cops to contrive culture. Is it essential to describe at length, besides the condition of youth, students and intellectuals, armies of workers with or without white collars, people from the provinces, the colonized and semi-colonized of all sorts, all those who endure a well-organized daily life, is it here necessary to exhibit the derisory and untragic misery of the inhabitant, of the suburban dweller and of the people who stay in residential ghettos, in the mouldering centres of old cities and in the proliferations lost beyond them? One only has to open one's eyes to understand the daily life of the one who runs from his dwelling to the station, near or far away, to the packed underground train, the office or the factory, to return the same way in the evening and come home to recuperate enough to start again the next day. The picture of this generalized misery would not go without a picture of 'satisfactions' which hides it and becomes the means to elude it and break free from it.

Chapter 40

from *Discipline and Punish: The Birth of the Prison*

Michel Foucault

3 Panopticism

The following, according to an order published at the end of the seventeenth century, were the measures to be taken when the plague appeared in a town.[1]

First, a strict spatial partitioning: the closing of the town and its outlying districts, a prohibition to leave the town on pain of death, the killing of all stray animals; the division of the town into distinct quarters, each governed by an intendant. Each street is placed under the authority of a syndic, who keeps it under surveillance; if he leaves the street, he will be condemned to death. On the appointed day, everyone is ordered to stay indoors: it is forbidden to leave on pain of death. The syndic himself comes to lock the door of each house from the outside; he takes the key with him and hands it over to the intendant of the quarter; the intendant keeps it until the end of the quarantine. Each family will have made its own provisions; but, for bread and wine, small wooden canals are set up between the street and the interior of the houses, thus allowing each person to receive his ration without communicating with the suppliers and other residents; meat, fish and herbs will be hoisted up into the houses with pulleys and baskets. If it is absolutely necessary to leave the house, it will be done in turn, avoiding any meeting. Only the intendants,

syndics and guards will move about the streets and also, between the infected houses, from one corpse to another, the 'crows', who can be left to die: these are 'people of little substance who carry the sick, bury the dead, clean and do many vile and abject offices'. It is a segmented, immobile, frozen space. Each individual is fixed in his place. And, if he moves, he does so at the risk of his life, contagion or punishment.

Inspection functions ceaselessly. The gaze is alert everywhere: 'A considerable body of militia, commanded by good officers and men of substance', guards at the gates, at the town hall and in every quarter to ensure the prompt obedience of the people and the most absolute authority of the magistrates, 'as also to observe all disorder, theft and extortion'. At each of the town gates there will be an observation post; at the end of each street sentinels. Every day, the intendant visits the quarter in his charge, inquires whether the syndics have carried out their tasks, whether the inhabitants have anything to complain of; they 'observe their actions'. Every day, too, the syndic goes into the street for which he is responsible; stops before each house: gets all the inhabitants to appear at the windows (those who live overlooking the courtyard will be allocated a window looking onto the street at which no one but they may show themselves); he calls each of them by name; informs himself as to the state of each and every one of them – 'in which respect the inhabitants will be compelled to speak the truth under pain of death'; if someone does not appear at the window, the syndic must ask why: 'In this way he will find out easily enough whether dead or sick are being concealed.' Everyone locked up in his cage, everyone at his window, answering to his name and showing himself when asked – it is the great review of the living and the dead.

This surveillance is based on a system of permanent registration: reports from the syndics to the intendants, from the intendants to the magistrates or mayor. At the beginning of the 'lock up', the role of each of the inhabitants present in the town is laid down, one by one; this document bears 'the name, age, sex of everyone, notwithstanding his condition': a copy is sent to the intendant of the quarter, another to the office of the town hall, another to enable the syndic to make his daily roll call. Everything that may be observed during the course of the visits – deaths, illnesses, complaints, irregularities – is noted down and transmitted to the intendants and magistrates. The magistrates have complete control over medical treatment; they have appointed a physician in charge; no other practitioner may treat, no apothecary prepare medicine, no confessor visit a sick person without having received from him a written note 'to prevent anyone from concealing and dealing with those sick of the contagion, unknown to the magistrates'. The registration of the pathological must be constantly centralized. The relation of each individual to his disease and to his death passes through the representatives of power, the registration they make of it, the decisions they take on it. . . .

This enclosed, segmented space, observed at every point, in which the individuals are inserted in a fixed place, in which the slightest movements are supervised, in which all events are recorded, in which an uninterrupted work of writing links the centre and periphery, in which power is exercised without division, according to a continuous hierarchical figure, in which each individual is constantly located, examined and distributed among the living beings, the sick and the dead – all this constitutes a compact model of the disciplinary mechanism. The plague is met by order; its function is to sort out every possible confusion: that of the disease, which is transmitted when bodies are mixed together; that of the evil, which is increased when fear and death overcome prohibitions. It lays down for each individual his place, his body, his disease and his death, his well-being, by means of an omnipresent and omniscient power that subdivides itself in a regular, uninterrupted way even to the ultimate determination of the individual, of what characterizes him, of what belongs to him, of what happens to him. Against the plague, which is a mixture, discipline brings into play its power, which is one of analysis. A whole literary fiction of the festival grew up around the plague: suspended laws, lifted prohibitions, the frenzy of passing time, bodies mingling together without respect, individuals unmasked, abandoning their statutory identity and the figure under which they had been recognized, allowing a quite different truth to appear. But there was also a political dream of the plague, which was exactly its reverse: not the collective festival, but strict divisions; not laws transgressed, but the penetration of regulation into even the smallest details of everyday life through the mediation of the complete hierarchy that assured the capillary functioning of power; not masks that were put on and taken off, but the assignment to each individual of his 'true' name, his 'true' place, his 'true' body, his 'true' disease. The plague as a form, at once real and imaginary, of disorder had as its medical and political correlative discipline. Behind the disciplinary mechanisms can be read the haunting memory of 'contagions', of the plague, of rebellions, crimes, vagabondage, desertions, people who appear and disappear, live and die in disorder. . . .

The constant division between the normal and the abnormal, to which every individual is subjected, brings us back to our own time, by applying the binary branding and exile of the leper to quite different objects; the existence of a whole set of techniques and institutions for measuring, supervising and correcting the abnormal brings into play the disciplinary mechanisms to which the fear of the plague gave rise. All the mechanisms of power which, even today, are disposed around the abnormal individual, to brand him and to alter him, are composed of those two forms from which they distantly derive.

Bentham's *Panopticon* is the architectural figure of this composition. We know the principle on which it was based: at the periphery, an annular building; at the centre, a tower; this tower is pierced with wide windows that open onto the inner side of the ring; the peripheric building is divided into cells, each of which extends the whole width of the building; they have two windows, one on the inside, corresponding to the windows of the tower; the other, on the outside, allows the light to cross the cell from one end to the other. All that is needed, then, is to place a supervisor in a central tower and to shut up in each cell a madman, a patient, a condemned man, a worker or a schoolboy. By the effect of backlighting, one can observe from the tower, standing out precisely against the light, the small captive shadows in the cells of the periphery. They are like so many cages, so many small theatres, in which each actor is alone, perfectly individualized and constantly visible. The panoptic mechanism arranges spatial unities that make it possible to see constantly and to recognize immediately. In short, it reverses the principle of the dungeon; or rather of its three functions – to enclose, to deprive of light and to hide – it preserves only the first and eliminates the other two. Full lighting and the eye of a supervisor capture better than darkness, which ultimately protected. Visibility is a trap.

To begin with, this made it possible – as a negative effect – to avoid those compact, swarming, howling masses that were to be found in places of confinement, those painted by Goya or described by Howard. Each individual, in his place, is securely confined to a cell from which he is seen from the front by the supervisor; but the side walls prevent him from coming into contact with his companions. He is seen, but he does not see; he is the object of information, never a subject in communication. The arrangement of his room, opposite the central tower, imposes on him an axial visibility; but the divisions of the ring, those separated cells, imply a lateral invisibility. And this invisibility is a guarantee of order. If the inmates are convicts, there is no danger of a plot, an attempt at collective escape, the planning of new crimes for the future, bad reciprocal influences; if they are patients, there is no danger of contagion; if they are madmen there is no risk of their committing violence upon one another; if they are schoolchildren, there is no copying, no noise, no chatter, no waste of time; if they are workers, there are no disorders, no theft, no coalitions, none of those distractions that slow down the rate of work, make it less perfect or cause accidents. The crowd, a compact mass, a locus of multiple exchanges, individualities merging together, a collective effect, is abolished and replaced by a collection of separated individualities. From the point of view of the guardian, it is replaced by a multiplicity that can be numbered and supervised; from the point of view of the inmates, by a sequestered and observed solitude (Bentham, 60–4).

Hence the major effect of the Panopticon: to induce in the inmate a state of conscious and permanent visibility that assures the automatic functioning of power. So to arrange things that the surveillance is permanent in its effects, even if it is discontinuous in its action; that the perfection of power should tend to render its actual exercise unnecessary; that this architectural apparatus should be a machine for creating and sustaining a power relation independent of the person who exercises it; in short, that the inmates should be caught up in a power situation of which they are them-selves the bearers. To achieve this, it is at once too much and too little that the pris-oner should be constantly observed by an inspector: too little, for what matters is that he knows himself to be observed; too much, because he has no need in fact of being so. In view of this, Bentham laid down the principle that power should be visible and unverifiable. Visible: the inmate will con-stantly have before his eyes the tall outline of the central tower from which he is spied upon. Unverifiable: the inmate must never know whether he is being looked at at any one moment; but he must be sure that he may always be so. In order to make the presence or absence of the inspector unveri-fiable, so that the prisoners, in their cells, cannot even see a shadow, Bentham envis-aged not only venetian blinds on the windows of the central observation hall, but, on the inside, partitions that inter-sected the hall at right angles and, in order to pass from one quarter to the other, not doors but zig-zag openings; for the slightest noise, a gleam of light, a brightness in a half-opened door would betray the pres-ence of the guardian.[2] The Panopticon is a machine for dissociating the see/being seen dyad: in the peripheric ring, one is totally seen, without ever seeing; in the central tower, one sees everything without ever being seen.[3]

It is an important mechanism, for it au-tomatizes and disindividualizes power. Power has its principle not so much in a person as in a certain concerted distribu-tion of bodies, surfaces, lights, gazes; in an arrangement whose internal mechanisms produce the relation in which individuals are caught up. The ceremonies, the rituals, the marks by which the sovereign's surplus power was manifested are useless. There is a machinery that assures dissymmetry, dis-equilibrium, difference. Consequently, it does not matter who exercises power. Any individual, taken almost at random, can operate the machine: in the absence of the director, his family, his friends, his visitors, even his servants (Bentham, 45). Similarly, it does not matter what motive animates

him: the curiosity of the indiscreet, the malice of a child, the thirst for knowledge of a philosopher who wishes to visit this museum of human nature, or the perversity of those who take pleasure in spying and punishing. The more numerous those an-onymous and temporary observers are, the greater the risk for the inmate of being surprised and the greater his anxious awareness of being observed. The Panopti-con is a marvellous machine which, what-ever use one may wish to put it to, produces homogeneous effects of power.

A real subjection is born mechanically from a fictitious relation. So it is not neces-sary to use force to constrain the convict to good behaviour, the madman to calm, the worker to work, the schoolboy to applica-tion, the patient to the observation of the regulations. Bentham was surprised that panoptic institutions could be so light: there were no more bars, no more chains, no more heavy locks; all that was needed was that the separations should be clear and the openings well arranged. The heavi-ness of the old 'houses of security', with their fortress-like architecture, could be replaced by the simple, economic geometry of a 'house of certainty'. The efficiency of power, its constraining force have, in a sense, passed over to the other side – to the side of its surface of application. He who is subjected to a field of visibility, and who knows it, assumes responsibility for the constraints of power; he makes them play spontaneously upon himself; he in-scribes in himself the power relation in which he simultaneously plays both roles; he becomes the principle of his own subjec-tion. By this very fact, the external power may throw off its physical weight; it tends to the non-corporal; and, the more it ap-proaches this limit, the more constant, pro-found and permanent are its effects: it is a perpetual victory that avoids any physical confrontation and which is always decided in advance....

So much for the question of observation. But the Panopticon was also a laboratory; it could be used as a machine to carry out experiments, to alter behaviour, to train or correct individuals. To experiment with medicines and monitor their effects. To try out different punishments on prisoners, according to their crimes and character, and to seek the most effective ones. To teach different techniques simultaneously to the workers, to decide which is the best. To try out pedagogical experiments – and in particular to take up once again the well-debated problem of secluded education, by using orphans. One would see what would happen when, in their sixteenth or eighteenth year, they were presented with other boys or girls; one could verify whether, as Helvetius thought, anyone could learn anything; one would follow 'the genealogy of every observable idea'; one could bring up different children according to different systems of thought, making certain children believe that two and two do not make four or that the moon is a cheese, then put them together when they are twenty or twenty-five years old; one would then have discussions that would be worth a great deal more than the sermons or lectures on which so much money is spent; one would have at least an opportunity of making discoveries in the domain of metaphysics. The Panopticon is a privileged place for experiments on men, and for analysing with complete certainty the transformations that may be obtained from them. The Panopticon may even provide an apparatus for supervising its own mechanisms. In this central tower, the director may spy on all the employees that he has under his orders: nurses, doctors, foremen, teachers, warders; he will be able to judge them continuously, alter their behaviour, impose upon them the methods he thinks best; and it will even be possible to observe the director himself. An inspector arriving unexpectedly at the centre of the Panopticon will be able to judge at a glance, without anything being concealed from him, how the entire establishment is functioning. And, in any case, enclosed as he is in the middle of this architectural mechanism, is not the director's own fate entirely bound up with it? The incompetent physician who has allowed contagion to spread, the in-

competent prison governor or workshop manager will be the first victims of an epidemic or a revolt. ' "By every tie I could devise", said the master of the Panopticon, "my own fate had been bound up by me with theirs" ' (Bentham, 177). The Panopticon functions as a kind of laboratory of power. Thanks to its mechanisms of observation, it gains in efficiency and in the ability to penetrate into men's behaviour; knowledge follows the advances of power, discovering new objects of knowledge over all the surfaces on which power is exercised.

The plague-stricken town, the panoptic establishment – the differences are important. They mark, at a distance of a century and a half, the transformations of the disciplinary programme. In the first case, there is an exceptional situation: against an extraordinary evil, power is mobilized; it makes itself everywhere present and visible; it invents new mechanisms; it separates, it immobilizes, it partitions; it constructs for a time what is both a counter-city and the perfect society; it imposes an ideal functioning, but one that is reduced, in the final analysis, like the evil that it combats, to a simple dualism of life and death: that which moves brings death, and one kills that which moves. The Panopticon, on the other hand, must be understood as a generalizable model of functioning; a way of defining power relations in terms of the everyday life of men. No doubt Bentham presents it as a particular instituion, closed in upon itself. Utopias, perfectly closed in upon themselves, are common enough. As opposed to the ruined prisons, littered with mechanisms of torture, to be seen in Piranese's engravings, the Panopticon presents a cruel, ingenious cage. The fact that it should have given rise, even in our own time, to so many variations, projected or realized, is evidence of the imaginary intensity that it has possessed for almost two hundred years. But the Panopticon must not be understood as a dream building: it is the diagram of a mechanism of power reduced to its ideal form; its functioning, abstracted from any obstacle, resistance or friction, must be represented as a pure architectural and optical system: it is in fact a figure of political technology that may and must be detached from any specific use.

It is polyvalent in its applications; it serves to reform prisoners, but also to treat patients, to instruct schoolchildren, to confine the insane, to supervise workers, to put beggars and idlers to work. It is a type of location of bodies in space, of distribution of individuals in relation to one another, of hierarchical organization, of disposition of centres and channels of power, of definition of the instruments and modes of intervention of power, which can be implemented in hospitals, workshops, schools, prisons. Whenever one is dealing with a multiplicity of individuals on whom a task or a particular form of behaviour must be imposed, the panoptic schema may be used. It is – necessary modifications apart – applicable 'to all establishments whatsoever, in which, within a space not too large to be covered or commanded by buildings, a number of persons are meant to be kept under inspection' (Bentham, 40; although Bentham takes the penitentiary house as his prime example, it is because it has many different functions to fulfil – safe custody, confinement, solitude, forced labour and instruction).

In each of its applications, it makes it possible to perfect the exercise of power. It does this in several ways: because it can reduce the number of those who exercise it, while increasing the number of those on whom it is exercised. Because it is possible to intervene at any moment and because the constant pressure acts even before the offences, mistakes or crimes have been committed. Because, in these conditions, its strength is that it never intervenes, it is exercised spontaneously and without noise, it constitutes a mechanism whose effects follow from one another. Because, without any physical instrument other than architecture and geometry, it acts directly on individuals; it gives 'power of mind over mind'. The panoptic schema makes any apparatus of power more intense: it assures

its economy (in material, in personnel, in time); it assures its efficacity by its preventative character, its continuous functioning and its automatic mechanisms. It is a way of obtaining from power 'in hitherto unexampled quantity', 'a great and new instrument of government . . . ; its great excellence consists in the great strength it is capable of giving to *any* institution it may be thought proper to apply it to' (Bentham, 66).

It's a case of 'it's easy once you've thought of it' in the political sphere. It can in fact be integrated into any function (education, medical treatment, production, punishment); it can increase the effect of this function, by being linked closely with it; it can constitute a mixed mechanism in which relations of power (and of knowledge) may be precisely adjusted, in the smallest detail, to the processes that are to be supervised; it can establish a direct proportion between 'surplus power' and 'surplus production'. In short, it arranges things in such a way that the exercise of power is not added on from the outside, like a rigid, heavy constraint, to the functions it invests, but is so subtly present in them as to increase their efficiency by itself increasing its own points of contact. The panoptic mechanism is not simply a hinge, a point of exchange between a mechanism of power and a function; it is a way of making power relations function in a function, and of making a function function through these power relations. Bentham's Preface to *Panopticon* opens with a list of the benefits to be obtained from his 'inspection-house': '*Morals reformed – health preserved – industry invigorated – instruction diffused – public burthens lightened –* Economy seated, as it were, upon a rock – the gordian knot of the Poor-Laws not cut, but united – all by a simple idea in architecture!' (Bentham, 39).

Furthermore, the arrangement of this machine is such that its enclosed nature does not preclude a permanent presence from the outside: we have seen that anyone may come and exercise in the central tower the functions of surveillance, and that, this being the case, he can gain a clear idea of the way in which the surveillance is practised. In fact, any panoptic institution, even if it is as rigorously closed as a penitentiary, may without difficulty be subjected to such irregular and constant inspections: and not only by the appointed inspectors, but also by the public; any member of society will have the right to come and see with his own eyes how the schools, hospitals, factories, prisons function. There is no risk, therefore, that the increase of power created by the panoptic machine may degenerate into tyranny; the disciplinary mechanism will be democratically controlled, since it will be constantly accessible 'to the great tribunal committee of the world'.[4] This Panopticon, subtly arranged so that an observer may observe, at a glance, so many different individuals, also enables everyone to come and observe any of the observers. The seeing machine was once a sort of dark room into which individuals spied; it has become a transparent building in which the exercise of power may be supervised by society as a whole.

The panoptic schema, without disappearing as such or losing any of its properties, was destined to spread throughout the social body; its vocation was to become a generalized function. The plague-stricken town provided an exceptional disciplinary model: perfect, but absolutely violent; to the disease that brought death, power opposed its perpetual threat of death; life inside it was reduced to its simplest expression; it was, against the power of death, the meticulous exercise of the right of the sword. The Panopticon, on the other hand, has a role of amplification; although it arranges power, although it is intended to make it more economic and more effective, it does so not for power itself, nor for the immediate salvation of a threatened society: its aim is to strengthen the social forces – to increase production, to develop the economy, spread education, raise the level of public morality; to increase and multiply.

How is power to be strengthened in such a way that, far from impeding progress, far from weighing upon it with its rules and regulations, it actually facilitates such progress? What intensificator of power will be able at the same time to be a multiplicator of production? How will power, by increasing its forces, be able to increase those of society instead of confiscating them or impeding them? The Panopticon's solution to this problem is that the productive increase of power can be assured only if, on the one hand, it can be exercised continuously in the very foundations of society, in the subtlest possible way, and if, on the other hand, it functions outside these sudden, violent, discontinuous forms that are bound up with the exercise of sovereignty. The body of the king, with its strange material and physical presence, with the force that he himself deploys or transmits to some few others, is at the opposite extreme of this new physics of power represented by panopticism; the domain of panopticism is, on the contrary, that whole lower region, that region of irregular bodies, with their details, their multiple movements, their heterogeneous forces, their spatial relations; what are required are mechanisms that analyse distributions, gaps, series, combinations, and which use instruments that render visible, record, differentiate and compare: a physics of a relational and multiple power, which has its maximum intensity not in the person of the king, but in the bodies that can be individualized by these relations. At the theoretical level, Bentham defines another way of analysing the social body and the power relations that traverse it; in terms of practice, he defines a procedure of subordination of bodies and forces that must increase the utility of power while practising the economy of the prince. Panopticism is the general principle of a new 'political anatomy' whose object and end are not the relations of sovereignty but the relations of discipline.

The celebrated, transparent, circular cage, with its high tower, powerful and knowing, may have been for Bentham a project of a perfect disciplinary institution; but he also set out to show how one may 'unlock' the disciplines and get them to function in a diffused, multiple, polyvalent way throughout the whole social body. These disciplines, which the classical age had elaborated in specific, relatively enclosed places – barracks, schools, workshops – and whose total implementation had been imagined only at the limited and temporary scale of a plague-stricken town, Bentham dreamt of transforming into a network of mechanisms that would be everywhere and always alert, running through society without interruption in space or in time. The panoptic arrangement provides the formula for this generalization. It programmes, at the level of an elementary and easily transferable mechanism, the basic functioning of a society penetrated through and through with disciplinary mechanisms....

NOTES

1   Archives militaires de Vincennes, A 1,516 91 sc. Pièce. This regulation is broadly similar to a whole series of others that date from the same period and earlier.
2   In the *Postscript to the Panopticon*, 1791, Bentham adds dark inspection galleries painted in black around the inspector's lodge, each making it possible to observe two storeys of cells.
3   In his first version of the *Panopticon*, Bentham had also imagined an acoustic surveillance, operated by means of pipes leading from the cells to the central tower. In the *Postscript* he abandoned the idea, perhaps because he could not introduce into it the principle of dis-symmetry and prevent the prisoners from hearing the inspector as well as the inspector hearing them. Julius tried to develop a system of dis-symmetrical listening (Julius, 18).

4   Imagining this continuous flow of visitors entering the central tower by an underground passage and then observing the circular landscape of the Panopticon, was Bentham aware of the Panoramas that Barker was constructing at exactly the same period (the first seems to have dated from 1787) and in which the visitors, occupying the central place, saw unfolding around them a landscape, a city or a battle. The visitors occupied exactly the place of the sovereign gaze.

REFERENCES

Bentham, J. 1843: *Works*, ed. J. Bowring. Edinburgh: William Tait.

Julius, N. H. 1831: *Leçons sur les prisons*, vol. I. Paris.

Chapter 41

from *The Practice of Everyday Life*

Michel de Certeau

Chapter VII: Walking in the City

Seeing Manhattan from the 110th floor of
the World Trade Center. Beneath the haze
stirred up by the winds, the urban island, a
sea in the middle of the sea, lifts up the
skyscrapers over Wall Street, sinks down
at Greenwich, then rises again to the crests
of Midtown, quietly passes over Central
Park and finally undulates off into the distance beyond Harlem. A wave of verticals.
Its agitation is momentarily arrested by
vision. The gigantic mass is immobilized
before the eyes. It is transformed into a
texturology in which extremes coincide –
extremes of ambition and degradation,
brutal oppositions of races and styles, contrasts between yesterday's buildings, already transformed into trash cans, and
today's urban irruptions that block out its
space. Unlike Rome, New York has never
learned the art of growing old by playing on
all its pasts. Its present invents itself, from
hour to hour, in the act of throwing away its
previous accomplishments and challenging
the future. A city composed of paroxysmal
places in monumental reliefs. The spectator
can read in it a universe that is constantly
exploding. In it are inscribed the architectural figures of the *coincidatio opposi-
torum* formerly drawn in miniatures and
mystical textures. On this stage of concrete,
steel and glass, cut out between two oceans
(the Atlantic and the American) by a frigid
body of water, the tallest letters in the
world compose a gigantic rhetoric of excess
in both expenditure and production.[1]

Voyeurs or walkers

To what erotics of knowledge does the ec-
stasy of reading such a cosmos belong?
Having taken a voluptuous pleasure in it, I
wonder what is the source of this pleasure
of "seeing the whole," of looking down on,
totalizing the most immoderate of human
texts.

To be lifted to the summit of the World
Trade Center is to be lifted out of the city's
grasp. One's body is no longer clasped by
the streets that turn and return it according
to an anonymous law; nor is it possessed,
whether as player or played, by the rumble
of so many differences and by the nervous-
ness of New York traffic. When one goes up
there, he leaves behind the mass that carries
off and mixes up in itself any identity of
authors or spectators. An Icarus flying
above these waters, he can ignore the
devices of Daedalus in mobile and endless
labyrinths far below. His elevation transfig-
ures him into a voyeur. It puts him at a
distance. It transforms the bewitching
world by which one was "possessed" into
a text that lies before one's eyes. It allows
one to read it, to be a solar Eye, looking
down like a god. The exaltation of a scopic

and gnostic drive: the fiction of knowledge is related to this lust to be a viewpoint and nothing more.

Must one finally fall back into the dark space where crowds move back and forth, crowds that, though visible from on high, are themselves unable to see down below? An Icarian fall. On the 110th floor, a poster, sphinx-like, addresses an enigmatic message to the pedestrian who is for an instant transformed into a visionary: *It's hard to be down when you're up*.

The desire to see the city preceded the means of satisfying it. Medieval or Renaissance painters represented the city as seen in a perspective that no eye had yet enjoyed.[2] This fiction already made the medieval spectator into a celestial eye. It created gods. Have things changed since technical procedures have organized an "all-seeing power"?[3] The totalizing eye imagined by the painters of earlier times lives on in our achievements. The same scopic drive haunts users of architectural productions by materializing today the utopia that yesterday was only painted. The 1370-foot-high tower that serves as a prow for Manhattan continues to construct the fiction that creates readers, makes the complexity of the city readable, and immobilizes its opaque mobility in a transparent text.

Is the immense texturology spread out before one's eyes anything more than a representation, an optical artifact? It is the analogue of the facsimile produced, through a projection that is a way of keeping aloof, by the space planner urbanist, city planner or cartographer. The panorama-city is a "theoretical" (that is, visual) simulacrum, in short a picture, whose condition of possibility is an oblivion and a misunderstanding of practices. The voyeur-god created by this fiction, who, like Schreber's God, knows only cadavers,[4] must disentangle himself from the murky intertwining daily behaviors and make himself alien to them.

The ordinary practitioners of the city live "down below," below the thresholds at which visibility begins. They walk – an elementary form of this experience of the city; they are walkers, *Wandersmänner*, whose bodies follow the thicks and thins of an urban "text" they write without being able to read it. These practitioners make use of spaces that cannot be seen; their knowledge of them is as blind as that of lovers in each other's arms. The paths that correspond in this intertwining, unrecognized poems in which each body is an element signed by many others, elude legibility. It is as though the practices organizing a bustling city were characterized by their blindness.[5] The networks of these moving, intersecting writings compose a manifold story that has neither author nor spectator, shaped out of fragments of trajectories and alterations of spaces: in relation to representations, it remains daily and indefinitely other.

Escaping the imaginary totalizations produced by the eye, the everyday has a certain strangeness that does not surface, or whose surface is only its upper limit, outlining itself against the visible. Within this ensemble, I shall try to locate the practices that are foreign to the "geometrical" or "geographical" space of visual, panoptic, or theoretical constructions. These practices of space refer to a specific form of *operations* ("ways of operating"), to "another spatiality"[6] (an "anthropological," poetic and mythic experience of space), and to an *opaque and blind* mobility characteristic of the bustling city. A *migrational*, or metaphorical, city thus slips into the clear text of the planned and readable city.

1 From the concept of the city to urban practices

The World Trade Center is only the most monumental figure of Western urban development. The atopia-utopia of optical knowledge has long had the ambition of surmounting and articulating the contradictions arising from urban agglomeration. It is a question of managing a growth of human agglomeration or accumulation. "The city is a huge monastery," said Erasmus. Perspective vision and prospective vision constitute the twofold projection of an opaque past and an uncertain future onto a surface that can be dealt with. They inaugurate (in the sixteenth century?) the transformation of the urban *fact* into the *concept* of a city. Long before the concept itself gives rise to a particular figure of history, it assumes that this fact can be dealt with as a unity determined by an urbanistic *ratio*. Linking the city to the concept never makes them identical, but it plays on their progressive symbiosis: to plan a city is both to *think the very plurality* of the real and to make that way of thinking the plural *effective*; it is to know how to articulate it and be able to do it.

An operational concept?

The "city" founded by utopian and urbanistic discourse[7] is defined by the possibility of a threefold operation:

1. The production of its *own* space (*un espace propre*): rational organization must thus repress all the physical, mental and political pollutions that would compromise it;

2. the substitution of a nowhen, or of a synchronic system, for the indeterminable and stubborn resistances offered by traditions; univocal scientific strategies, made possible by the flattening out of all the data in a plane projection, must replace the tactics of users who take advantage of "opportunities" and who, through these trap-events, these lapses in visibility, reproduce the opacities of history everywhere;

3. finally, the creation of a *universal* and anonymous *subject* which is the city itself: it gradually becomes possible to attribute to it, as to its political model, Hobbes' State, all the functions and predicates that were previously scattered and assigned to many different real subjects – groups, associations, or individuals. "The city," like a proper name, thus provides a way of conceiving and constructing space on the basis of a finite number of stable, isolatable, and interconnected properties.

Administration is combined with a process of elimination in this place organized by "speculative" and classificatory operations.[8] On the one hand, there is a differentiation and redistribution of the parts and functions of the city, as a result of inversions, displacements, accumulations, etc.; on the other there is a rejection of everything that is not capable of being dealt with in this way and so constitutes the "waste products" of a functionalist administration (abnormality, deviance, illness, death, etc.). To be sure, progress allows an increasing number of these waste products to be reintroduced into administrative circuits and transforms even deficiencies (in health, security, etc.) into ways of making the networks of order denser. But in reality, it repeatedly produces effects contrary to those at which it aims: the profit system generates a loss which, in the multiple forms of wretchedness and poverty outside the system and of waste inside it, constantly turns production into "expenditure." Moreover, the rationalization of the city leads to its mythification in strategic discourses, which are calculations based on the hypothesis or the necessity of its destruction in order to arrive at a final decision.[9] Finally, the functionalist organization, by privileging progress (i.e., time), causes the condition of its own possibility – space itself – to be forgotten; space thus becomes the blind spot in a scientific and political technology. This is the way in which the Concept-city functions; a place of transformations and appropriations, the object of various kinds of interference but also a subject that is constantly enriched by new attributes, it is simultaneously the machinery and the hero of modernity.

Today, whatever the avatars of this concept may have been, we have to acknowledge that if in discourse the city serves as a totalizing and almost mythical landmark for socioeconomic and political strategies, urban life increasingly permits the re-emergence of the element that the urbanistic project excluded. The language of power is in itself "urbanizing," but the city is left prey to contradictory movements that counter-balance and combine themselves outside the reach of panoptic power. The city becomes the dominant theme in political legends, but it is no longer a field of programmed and regulated operations. Beneath the discourses that ideologize the city, the ruses and combinations of powers that have no readable identity proliferate; without points where one can take hold of them, without rational transparency, they are impossible to administer.

The return of practices

The Concept-city is decaying. Does that mean that the illness afflicting both the rationality that founded it and its professionals afflicts the urban populations as well? Perhaps cities are deteriorating along with the procedures that organized them. But we must be careful here. The ministers of knowledge have always assumed that the whole universe was threatened by the very changes that affected their ideologies and their positions. They transmute the misfortune of their theories into theories of misfortune. When they transform their bewilderment into "catastrophes," when they seek to enclose the people in the "panic" of their discourses, are they once more necessarily right?

Rather than remaining within the field of a discourse that upholds its privilege by inverting its content (speaking of catastrophe and no longer of progress), one can try another path: one can try another path: one can analyze the microbe-like, singular and plural practices which an urbanistic system was supposed to administer or suppress, but which have outlived its decay; one can follow the swarming activity of these procedures that, far from being regulated or eliminated by panoptic administration, have reinforced themselves in a proliferating illegitimacy, developed and insinuated themselves into the networks of surveillance, and combined in accord with unreadable but stable tactics to the point of constituting everyday regulations and surreptitious creativities that are merely concealed by the frantic mechanisms and discourses of the observational organization.

This pathway could be inscribed as a consequence, but also as the reciprocal, of Foucault's analysis of the structures of power. He moved it in the direction of mechanisms and technical procedures, "minor instrumentalities" capable, merely by their organization of "details," of transforming a human multiplicity into a "disciplinary" society and of managing, differentiating, classifying, and hierarchizing all deviances concerning apprenticeship, health, justice, the army, or work.[10] "These often miniscule ruses of discipline," these "minor but flawless" mechanisms, draw their efficacy from a relationship between procedures and the space that they redistribute in order to make an "operator" out of it. But what *spatial practices* correspond, in the area where discipline is manipulated, to these apparatuses that produce a disciplinary space? In the present conjuncture, which is marked by a contradiction between the collective mode of administration and an individual mode of reappropriation, this question is no less important, if one admits that spatial practices in fact secretly structure the determining conditions of social life. I would like to follow out a few of these multiform, resistance, tricky and stubborn procedures that elude discipline without being outside the field in which it is exercised, and which should lead us to a theory of everyday practices, of lived space, of the disquieting familiarity of the city.

2 The chorus of idle footsteps

> "The goddess can be recognized by her step." Virgil, *Aeneid*, I, 405

Their story begins on ground level, with footsteps. They are myriad, but do not compose a series. They cannot be counted because each unit has a qualitative character: a style of tactile apprehension and kinesthetic appropriation. Their swarming mass is an innumerable collection of singularities. Their intertwined paths give their shape to spaces. They weave places together. In that respect, pedestrian movements form one of these "real systems whose existence in fact makes up the city."[11] They are not localized; it is rather they that spatialize. They are no more inserted within a container than those Chinese characters speakers sketch out on their hands with their fingertips.

It is true that the operations of walking on can be traced on city maps in such a way as to transcribe their paths (here well-trodden, there very faint) and their trajectories (going this way and not that). But these thick or thin curves only refer, like words, to the absence of what has passed by. Surveys of routes miss what was: the act itself of passing by. The operation of walking, wandering, or "window shopping," that is, the activity of passers-by, is transformed into points that draw a totalizing and reversible line on the map. They allow us to grasp only a relic set in the nowhen of a surface of projection. Itself visible, it has the effect of making invisible the operation that made it possible. These fixations constitute procedures for forgetting. The trace left behind is substituted for the practice. It exhibits the (voracious) property that the geographical system has of being able to transform action into legibility, but in doing so it causes a way of being in the world to be forgotten.

Pedestrian speech acts

A comparison with the speech act will allow us to go further[12] and not limit ourselves to the critique of graphic representations alone, looking from the shores of legibility toward an inaccessible beyond. The act of walking is to the urban system what the speech act is to language or to the statements uttered.[13] At the most elementary level, it has a triple "enunciative" function: it is a process of *appropriation* of the topographical system on the part of the pedestrian (just as the speaker appropriates and takes on the language); it is a spatial acting-out of the place (just as the speech act is an acoustic acting-out of language); and it implies *relations* among differentiated positions, that is, among pragmatic "contracts" in the form of movements (just as verbal enunciation is an "allocution," "posits another opposite" the speaker and puts contracts between interlocutors into action).[14] It thus seems possible to give a preliminary definition of walking as a space of enunciation.

We could moreover extend this problematic to the relations between the act of writing and the written text, and even transpose it to the relationships between the "hand" (the touch and the tale of the paintbrush) and the finished painting (forms, colors, etc.). At first isolated in the area of verbal communication, the speech act turns out to find only one of its applications there, and its linguistic modality is merely the first determination of a much more general distinction between the *forms used* in a system and the *ways of using* this system (i.e., *rules*), that is, between two "different worlds," since "the same things" are considered from two opposite formal viewpoints.

Considered from this angle, the pedestrian speech act has three characteristics which distinguish it at the outset from the spatial system: the present, the discrete, the "phatic."

First, if it is true that a spatial order organizes an ensemble of possibilities (e.g., by a place in which one can move) and interdictions (e.g., by a wall that prevents one from going further), then the walker actualizes some of these possibilities. In that way, he makes them exist as well as emerge. But he also moves them about and he invents others, since the crossing, drifting away, or improvisation of walking privilege, transform or abandon spatial elements. Thus Charlie Chaplin multiplies the possibilities of his cane: he does other things with the same thing and he goes beyond the limits that the determinants of the object set on its utilization. In the same way, the walker transforms each spatial signifier into something else. And if on the one hand he actualizes only a few of the possibilities fixed by the constructed order (he goes only here and not there), on the other he increases the number of possibilities (for example, by creating shortcuts and detours) and prohibitions (for example, he forbids himself to take paths generally considered accessible or even obligatory). He thus makes a selection. "The user of a city picks out certain fragments of the statement in order to actualize them in secret."[15]

He thus creates a discreteness, whether by making choices among the signifiers of the spatial "language" or by displacing them through the use he makes of them. He condemns certain places to inertia or disappearance and composes with others spatial "turns of phrase" that are "rare," "accidental" or illegitimate. But that already leads into a rhetoric of walking.

In the framework of enunciation, the walker constitutes, in relation to his position, both a near and a far, a *here* and a *there*. To the fact that the adverbs *here* and *there* are the indicators of the locutionary seat in verbal communication[16] – a coincidence that reinforces the parallelism between linguistic and pedestrian enunciation – we must add that this location (*here–there*) (necessarily implied by walking and indicative of a present appropriation of space by an "I") also has the function of introducing an other in relation to this "I" and of thus establishing a conjunctive and disjunctive articulation of places. I would stress particularly the "phatic" aspect, by which I mean the function, isolated by Malinowski and Jakobson, of terms that initiate, maintain, or interrupt contact, such as "hello," "well, well," etc.[17] Walking, which alternately follows a path and has followers, creates a mobile organicity in the environment, a sequence of phatic *topoi*. And if it is true that the phatic function, which is an effort to ensure communication, is already characteristic of the language of talking birds, just as it constitutes the "first verbal function acquired by children," it is not surprising that it also gambols, goes on all fours, dances, and walks about, with a light or heavy step, like a series of "hellos" in an echoing labyrinth, anterior or parallel to informative speech.

The modalities of pedestrian enunciation which a plane representation on a map brings out could be analyzed. They include the kinds of relationship this enunciation entertains with particular paths (or "statements") by according them a truth value ("alethic" modalities of the necessary, the impossible, the possible, or the contingent), an epistemological value ("epistemic" modalities of the certain, the excluded, the plausible, or the questionable) or finally an ethical or legal value ("deontic" modalities of the obligatory, the forbidden, the permitted, or the optional).[18] Walking affirms, suspects, tries out, transgresses, respects, etc., the trajectories it "speaks." All the modalities sing a part in this chorus, changing from step to step, stepping in through proportions, sequences, and intensities which vary according to the time, the path taken and the walker. These enunciatory operations are of an unlimited diversity. They therefore cannot be reduced to their graphic trail.

Walking rhetorics

The walking of passers-by offers a series of turns (*tours*) and detours that can be compared to "turns of phrase" or "stylistic figures." There is a rhetoric of walking. The art of "turning" phrases finds an equivalent in an art of composing a path (*tourner un parcours*). Like ordinary language,[19] this art implies and combines styles and uses. *Style* specifies "a linguistic structure that manifests on the symbolic level ... an individual's fundamental way of being in the world";[20] it connotes a singular. Use defines the social phenomenon through which a system of communication manifests itself in actual fact; it refers to a norm. Style and use both have to do with a "way of operating" (of speaking, walking, etc.), but style involves a peculiar processing of the symbolic, while use refers to elements of a code. They intersect to form a style of use, a way of being and a way of operating.[21]

In introducing the notion of a "residing rhetoric" ("*rhétorique habitante*"), the fertile pathway opened up by A. Médam[22] and systematized by S. Ostrowetsky[23] and J.-F. Augoyard,[24] we assume that the "tropes" catalogued by rhetoric furnish models and hypotheses for the analysis of ways of appropriating places. Two postulates seem to me to underlie the validity of this application: 1) it is assumed that practices of space also correspond to manipulations of the basic elements of a constructed order; 2) it is assumed that they are, like the tropes in rhetoric, deviations relative to a sort of "literal meaning" defined by the urbanistic system. There would thus be a homology between verbal figures and the figures of walking (a stylized selection among the latter is already found in the figures of dancing) insofar as both consist in "treatments" or operations bearing on isolatable units,[25] and in "ambiguous dispositions" that divert and displace meaning in the direction of equivocalness[26] in the way a tremulous image confuses and multiplies the photographed object. In these two modes, the analogy can be accepted. I would add that the geometrical space of urbanists and architects seems to have the status of the "proper meaning" constructed by grammarians and linguists in order to have a normal and normative level to which they can compare the drifting of "figurative" language. In reality, this faceless "proper" meaning (ce "propre" sans figure) cannot be found in current use, whether verbal or pedestrian; it is merely the fiction produced by a use that is also particular, the metalinguistic use of science that distinguishes itself by that very distinction.[27]

The long poem of walking manipulates spatial organizations, no matter how panoptic they may be: it is neither foreign to them (it can take place only within them) nor in conformity with them (it does not receive its identity from them). It creates shadows and ambiguities within them. It inserts its multitudinous references and citations into them (social models, cultural mores, personal factors). Within them it is itself the effect of successive encounters and occasions that constantly alter it and make it the other's blazon: in other words, it is

like a peddler, carrying something surprising, transverse or attractive compared with the usual choice. These diverse aspects provide the basis of a rhetoric. They can even be said to define it.

By analyzing this "modern art of everyday expression" as it appears in accounts of spatial practices,[28] J.-F. Augoyard discerns in it two especially fundamental stylistic figures: synecdoche and asyndeton. The predominance of these two figures seems to me to indicate, in relation to two complementary poles, a formal structure of these practices. *Synecdoche* consists in "using a word in a sense which is part of another meaning of the same word."[29] In essence, it names a part instead of the whole which includes it. Thus "sail" is taken for "ship" in the expression "a fleet of fifty sails"; in the same way, a brick shelter or a hill is taken for the park in the narration of a trajectory. *Asyndeton* is the suppression of linking words such as conjunctions and adverbs, either within a sentence or between sentences. In the same way, in walking it selects and fragments the space traversed; it skips over links and whole parts that it omits. From this point of view, every walk constantly leaps, or skips like a child, hopping on one foot. It practices the ellipsis of conjunctive *loci*.

In reality, these two pedestrian figures are related. Synecdoche expands a spatial element in order to make it play the role of a "more" (a totality) and take its place (the bicycle or the piece of furniture in a store window stands for a whole street or neighborhood). Asyndeton, by elision, creates a "less," opens gaps in the spatial continuum, and retains only selected parts of it that amount almost to relics. Synecdoche replaces totalities by fragments (a *less* in the place of a *more*); asyndeton disconnects them by eliminating the conjunctive or the consecutive (nothing in place of something). Synecdoche makes more dense: it amplifies the detail and miniaturizes the whole. Asyndeton cuts out: it undoes continuity and undercuts its plausibility. A space treated in this way and shaped by practices is transformed into enlarged singularities and separate islands.[30] Through these swellings, shrinkings, and fragmentations, that is, through these rhetorical operations a spatial phrasing of an analogical (composed of juxtaposed citations) and elliptical (made of gaps, lapses, and allusions) type is created. For the technological system of a coherent and totalizing space that is "linked" and simultaneous, the figures of pedestrian rhetoric substitute trajectories that have a mythical structure, at least if one understands by "myth" a discourse relative to the place/nowhere (or origin) of concrete existence, a story jerry-built out of elements taken from common sayings, an allusive and fragmentary story whose gaps mesh with the social practices it symbolizes.

Figures are the acts of this stylistic metamorphosis of space. Or rather, as Rilke puts it, they are moving "trees of gestures." They move even the rigid and contrived territories of the medico-pedagogical institute in which retarded children find a place to play and dance their "spatial stories."[31] These "trees of gestures" are in movement everywhere. Their forests walk through the streets. They transform the scene, but they cannot be fixed in a certain place by images. If in spite of that an illustration were required, we could mention the fleeting images, yellowish-green and metallic blue calligraphies that howl without raising their voices and emblazon themselves on the subterranean passages of the city, "embroideries" composed of letters and numbers, perfect gestures of violence painted with a pistol, Shivas made of written characters, dancing graphics whose fleeting apparitions are accompanied by the rumble of subway trains: New York graffiti.

If it is true that *forests of gestures* are manifest in the streets, their movement cannot be captured in a picture, nor can the meaning of their movements be circumscribed in a text. Their rhetorical transplantation carries away and displaces the analytical, coherent proper meanings of urbanism; it constitutes a "wandering of the semantic"[32] produced by masses that make some parts of the city disappear and exaggerate others, distorting it, fragmenting it, and diverting it from its immobile order.

3 Myths: what "makes things go"

The figures of these movements (synecdoches, ellipses, etc.) characterize both a "symbolic order of the unconscious" and "certain typical processes of subjectivity manifested in discourse."[33] The similarity between "discourse"[34] and dreams[35] has to do with their use of the same "stylistic procedures"; it therefore includes pedestrian practices as well. The "ancient catalog of tropes" that from Freud to Benveniste has furnished an appropriate inventory for the rhetoric of the first two registers of expression is equally valid for the third. If there is a parallelism, it is not only because enunciation is dominant in these three areas, but also because its discursive (verbalized, dreamed, or walked) development is organized as a relation between the *place* from which it proceeds (an origin) and the nowhere it produces (a way of "going by").

From this point of view, after having compared pedestrian processes to linguistic formations, we can bring them back down in the direction of oneiric figuration, or at least discover on that other side what, in a spatial practice, is inseparable from the dreamed place. To walk is to lack a place. It is the indefinite process of being absent and in search of a proper. The moving about that the city multiplies and concentrates makes the city itself an immense social experience of lacking a place – an experience that is, to be sure, broken up into countless tiny deportations (displacements and walks), compensated for by the relationships and intersections of these exoduses that intertwine and create an urban fabric, and placed under the sign of what ought to be, ultimately, the place but is only a name, the City. The identity furnished by this place is all the more symbolic (named) because, in spite of the inequality of its citizens' positions and profits, there is only a pullulation of passer-by, a network of residences temporarily appropriated by pedestrian traffic, a shuffling among pre-

tenses of the proper, a universe of rented spaces haunted by a nowhere or by dreamed-of places....

NOTES

1 See Alain Médam's admirable "New York City," *Les Temps modernes*, August–September 1976, 15–33; and the same author's *New York Terminal* (Paris: Galilée, 1977).

2 See H. Lavedan, *Les Représentations des villes dans l'art du Moyen Age* (Paris: Van Oest, 1942); R. Wittkower, *Architectural Principles in the Age of Humanism* (New York: Norton, 1962); L. Marin, *Utopiques: Jeux d'espaces* (Paris: Minuit, 1973); etc.

3 M. Foucault, "L'Oeil du pouvoir," in J. Bentham, *Le Panoptique* (Paris: Belfond, 1977), 16.

4 D. P. Schreber, *Mémoires d'un névropathe* (Paris: Seuil, 1975), 41, 60, etc.

5 Descartes, in his *Regulae*, had already made the blind man the guarantor of the knowledge of things and places against the illusions and deceptions of vision.

6 M. Merleau-Ponty, *Phénoménologie de la perception* (Paris: Gallimard Tel, 1976), 332–3.

7 See F. Choay, "Figures d'un discours inconnu," *Critique*, April 1973, 293–317.

8 Urbanistic techniques, which classify things spatially, can be related to the tradition of the "art of memory": see Frances A. Yates, *The Art of Memory* (London: Routledge and Kegan Paul, 1966).

9 See André Glucksmann, "Le Totalitarisme en effet," *Traverses*, no. 9, 1977, 34–40.

10 M. Foucault, *Surveiller et punir* (Paris: Gallimard, 1975); *Discipline and Punish*, trans. A. Sheridan (New York: Pantheon, 1977).

11 Ch. Alexander, "La Cité semi-treillis, mais non arbre," *Architecture, Mouvement, Continuité*, 1967.

12 See R. Barthes's remarks in *Architecture d'aujourd'hui*, no. 153, Dec. 1970–Jan. 1971, 11–13: "We speak our city... merely by inhabiting it, walking through it, looking at it." Cf. C. Soucy, *L'Image du centre dans quatre romans contemporains* (Paris: CSU, 1971), 6–15.

13 See the numerous studies devoted to the subject since J. Searle's "What is a Speech Act?" in *Philosophy in America*, ed. Max Black (London: Allen & Unwin; Ithaca, NY: Cornell University Press, 1965), 221–39.

14 E. Benveniste, *Problèmes de linguistique générale* (Paris: Gallimard, 1974), II, 79–88, etc.

15 R. Barthes, quoted in C. Soucy, *L'Image du centre*, 10.

16 "*Here* and *now* delimit the spatial and temporal instance coextensive and contemporary with the present instance of discourse containing I": E. Benveniste, *Problèmes de linguistique générale* (Paris: Gallimard, 1966), I, p. 253.

17 R. Jakobson, *Essais de linguistique générale* (Paris: Seuil Points, 1970), p. 217.

18 On modalities, see H. Parret, *La Pragmatique des modalités* (Urbino: Centro di Semiotica, 1975); A. R. White, *Modal Thinking* (Ithaca, NY: Cornell University Press, 1975).

19 See Paul Lemaire's analyses, *Les Signes sauvages. Une Philosophie du language ordinaire* (Ottawa: Université d'Ottawa et Université Saint-Paul, 1981), in particular the introduction.

20 A. J. Greimas, "Linguistique statistique et linguistique structurale," *Le Français moderne*, Oct. 1962, 245.

21 In a neighboring field, rhetoric and poetics in the gestural language of mute people, I am grateful to E. S. Klima of the University of California, San Diego and U. Bellugi, "Poetry and Song in a Language without Sound," an unpublished paper; see also Klima, "The Linguistic Symbol with and without Sound," in *The Role of Speech in Language*, eds. J. Kavanagh and J. E. Cuttings (Cambridge, Mass.: MIT, 1975).

22 *Conscience de la ville* (Paris: Anthropos, 1977).

23 See Ostrowetsky, "Logiques du lieu," in *Sémiotique de l'espace* (Paris: Denoël-Gonthier Médiations, 1979), 155–73.

24 *Pas à pas. Essai sur le cheminement quotidien en milieu urbain* (Paris: Seuil, 1979).

25 In his analysis of culinary practices, P. Bourdieu regards as decisive not the ingredients but the way in which they are prepared and used: "Le Sens pratique," *Actes de la recherche en sciences sociales*, Feb. 1976, 77.

26 J. Sumpf, *Introduction à la stylistique du français* (Paris: Larousse, 1971), 87.

27 On the "theory of the proper," see J. Derrida, *Marges de la philosophie* (Paris: Minuit, 1972), 247–324; *Margins of Philosophy*, trans. A. Bass (Chicago: University of Chicago Press, 1982).

28 Augoyard, *Pas à pas*.

29 T. Todorov, "Synecdoques," *Communications*, no. 16 (1970), 30. See also P. Fontanier, *Les Figures du discours* (Paris: Flammarion, 1968), 87–97; J. Dubois et al., *Rhétorique générale* (Paris: Larousse, 1970), 102–12.

30 On this space that practices organize into "islands," see P. Bourdieu, *Esquisse d'une théorie de la pratique* (Genève: Droz, 1972), 215, etc.; "Le Sens pratique," 51–2.

31 See Anne Baldassari and Michel Joubert, *Pratiques relationnelles des enfants à l'espace et institution* (Paris: CRECELE-CORDES, 1976); and by the same authors, "Ce qui se trame," *Parallèles*, no. 1, June 1976.

32 Derrida, *Marges*, 287, on metaphor.

33 Benveniste, *Problèmes*, I, 86–7.

34 For Benveniste, "discourse is language considered as assumed by the person who is speaking and in the condition of intersubjectivity" (ibid., 266).

35 See for example S. Freud, *The Interpretation of Dreams*, trans. J. Strachey (New York: Basic Books, 1955), ch. VI, § 1–4, on condensation and displacement, "processes of figuration" that are proper to "dreamwork."

from *The Arcades Project*

Walter Benjamin

Arcades[1]

On the Avenue Champs-Elysées, between modern hotels with Anglo-Saxon names, arcades were opened recently and the newest Parisian *passage* made its appearance. For its inaugural ceremony, a monster orchestra in uniform performed in front of flower beds and flowing fountains. The crowd broke, groaning, over sandstone thresholds and moved along before panes of plate glass, saw artificial rain fall on the copper entrails of late-model autos as a demonstration of the quality of the materials, saw wheels turning around in oil, read on small black plaques, in paste-jewel figures, the prices of leather goods and gramophone records and embroidered kimonos. In the diffuse light from above, one skimmed over flagstones. While here a new thoroughfare was being prepared for the most fashionable Paris, one of the oldest arcades in the city has disappeared – the Passage de l'Opéra, swallowed up by the opening of the Boulevard Haussmann. Just as that remarkable covered walkway had done for an earlier generation, so today a few arcades still preserve, in dazzling light and shadowy corners, a past become space. Antiquated trades survive within these inner spaces, and the merchandise on display is unintelligible, or else has several meanings. Already the inscriptions and signs on the entranceways (one could just

as well say "exits," since, with these peculiar hybrid forms of house and street, every gate is simultaneously entrance and exit), already the inscriptions which multiply along the walls within, where here and there between overloaded coatstands a spiral staircase rises into darkness – already they have about them something enigmatic. "Albert at No. 83" will in all likelihood be a hairdresser, and "Theatrical Tights" will be silk tights; but these insistent letterings want to say more. And who would have the courage to take the dilapidated stairs up one flight to the beauty salon of Professor Alfred Bitterlin? Mosaic thresholds, in the style of the old restaurants of the Palais-Royal, lead to a *dîner de Paris*; they make a broad ascent to a glass door – but can there really be a restaurant behind it? And the glass door next to it, which announces a casino and permits a glimpse of something like a ticket booth with prices of seats posted – would it not, if one opened it, lead one into darkness rather than a theater, into a cellar or down to the street? And on the ticket booth hang stockings once again, stockings as in the doll hospital across the way and, somewhat earlier, on the side table of the tavern. – In the crowded arcades of the boulevards, as in the semi-deserted arcades of the old Rue Saint-Denis, umbrellas and canes are displayed in serried ranks: a phalanx of colorful crooks. Many are the institutes of hygiene, where gladiators are wearing orthopedic belts and bandages wind round the white bellies of mannequins. In the windows of the hairdressers, one sees the last women with long hair; they sport richly undulating masses, petrified coiffures. How brittle appears the stonework of the walls beside them and above: crumbling papier-mâché! "Souvenirs" and bibelots take on a hideous aspect; the odalisque lies in wait next to the inkwell; priestesses in knitted jackets raise aloft ashtrays like vessels of holy water. A bookshop makes a place for manuals of lovemaking beside devotional prints in color; next to the memoirs of a chambermaid, it has Napoleon riding through Marengo and, between cookbook and dreambook, old-English burghers treading the broad and the narrow way of the Gospel. In the arcades, one comes upon types of collar studs for which we no longer know the corresponding collars and shirts. If a shoemaker's shop should be neighbor to a confectioner's, then his festoons of boot-laces will resemble rolls of licorice. Over stamps and letterboxes roll balls of string and of silk. Naked puppet bodies with bald heads wait for hairpieces and attire. Combs swim about, frog-green and coral-red, as in an aquarium; trumpets turn to conches, ocarinas to umbrella handles; and lying in the fixative pans from a photographer's darkroom is birdseed. The concierge of the gallery has, in his loge, three plush-covered chairs with crocheted antimacassars, but next door is a vacant shop from whose inventory only a printed bill remains: "Will purchase sets of teeth in gold, in wax, and broken." Here, in the quietest part of the side-alley, individuals of both sexes can interview for a staff position within the confines of a sitting room set up behind glass. On the pale-colored wallpaper full of figures and bronze busts falls the light of a gas lamp. An old woman sits beside it, reading. For years, it would seem, she has been alone. And now the passage is becoming more empty. A small red tin parasol coyly points the way up a stair to an umbrella ferrule factory; a dusty bridal veil promises a repository of cock-

ades for weddings and banquets. But no one believes it any longer. Fire escape, gutter: I am in the open. Opposite is something like an arcade again – an archway and, through it, a blind alley leading to a one-windowed Hôtel de Boulogne or Bourgogne. But I am no longer heading in that direction; I am going up the street to the triumphal gate that, gray and glorious, was built in honor of Louis the Great. Carved in relief on the pyramids that decorate its columns are lions at rest, weapons hanging, and dusky trophies.

The Arcades of Paris: Paris Arcades II[2]

"In speaking of the inner boulevards," says the *Illustrated Guide to Paris*, a complete picture of the city on the Seine and its environs from the year 1852, "we have made mention again and again of the arcades which open onto them. These arcades, a recent invention of industrial luxury, are glass-roofed, marble-paneled corridors extending through whole blocks of buildings, whose owners have joined together for such enterprises. Lining both sides of these corridors, which get their light from above, are the most elegant shops, so that the arcade is a city, a world in miniature, in which customers will find everything they need. During sudden rainshowers, the arcades are a place of refuge for the unprepared, to whom they offer a secure, if restricted, promenade – one from which the merchants also benefit." The customers are gone, along with those taken by surprise. Rain brings in only the poorer clientele without waterproof or mackintosh. These were spaces for a generation of people who knew little of the weather and who, on Sundays, when it snowed, would rather warm themselves in the winter gardens than go out skiing. Glass before its time, premature iron: it was one single line of descent – arcades, winter gardens with their lordly palms, and railroad stations, which cultivated the false orchid "adieu" with its fluttering petals. They have long since given way to the hangar. And today, it is the same with the human material on the inside of the arcades as with the materials of their construction. Pimps are the iron bearings of this street, and its glass breakables are the whores. Here was the last refuge of those infant prodigies that saw the light of day at the time of the world exhibitions: the briefcase with interior lighting, the meter-long pocket knife, or the patented umbrella handle with built-in watch and revolver. And near the degenerate giant creatures, aborted and broken-down matter. We followed the narrow dark corridor to where – between a discount bookstore, in which colorful tied-up bundles tell of all sorts of failure, and a shop selling only buttons (mother-of-pearl and the kind that in Paris are called *de fantaisie*) – there stood a sort of salon. On a pale-colored wallpaper full of figures and busts shone a gas lamp. But its light, an old woman sat reading. They say she has been there alone for years, and collects sets of teeth "in gold, in wax, and broken." Since that day, moreover, we know where Doctor Miracle got the wax out of which he fashioned Olympia. They are the true fairies of these arcades (more salable and more worn than the life-sized ones): the formerly world-famous Parisian dolls, which revolved on their musical socle and bore in their arms a doll-sized basket out of which, at the salutation of the minor chord, a lambkin poked its curious muzzle.

All this is the arcade in our eyes. And it was nothing of all this. They <the arcades> radiated through the Paris of the Empire like grottoes. For someone entering the Passage des Panoramas in 1817, the sirens of gaslight would be singing to him on one side, while oil-lamp odalisques offered enticements from the other. With the kindling of electric lights, the irreproachable glow was extinguished in these galleries, which suddenly became more difficult to find – which wrought a black magic at entrance-ways, and peered from blind windows into their own interior. It was not decline but transformation. All at once, they were the hollow mold from which the image of "modernity" was cast. Here, the century mirrored with satisfaction its most recent past. Here was the retirement home for infant prodigies . . .

When, as children, we were given those great encyclopedic works *World and Mankind*, *New Universe*, *The Earth*, wouldn't our gaze always fall, first of all, on the color illustration of a "Carboniferous Landscape" or on "Lakes and Glaciers of the First Ice Age"? Such an ideal panorama of a barely elapsed primeval age opens up when we look through the arcades that are found in all cities. Here resides the last dinosaur of Europe, the consumer. On the walls of these caverns, their immemorial flora, the commodity, luxuriates and enters, like cancerous tissue, into the most irregular combinations. A world of secret affinities: palm tree and feather duster, hair dryer and Venus de Milo, prosthesis and letter-writing manual come together here as after a long separation. The odalisque lies in wait next to the inkwell, priestesses raise aloft ashtrays like patens. These items on display are a rebus; and <how> one ought to read here the birdseed kept in the fixative-pan from a darkroom, the flower seeds beside the binoculars, the broken screws atop the musical score, and the revolver above the goldfish bowl – is right on the tip of one's tongue. After all, nothing of the lot appears to be new. The goldfish come perhaps from a pond that dried up long ago, the revolver will have been a corpus delicti, and these scores could hardly have preserved their previous owner from starvation when her last pupils stayed away. . . .

One knew of places in ancient Greece where the way led down into the underworld. Our waking existence likewise is a land which, at certain hidden points, leads down into the underworld – a land full of inconspicuous places from which dreams arise. All day long, suspecting nothing, we pass them by, but no sooner has sleep come than we are eagerly groping our way back to lose ourselves in the dark corridors. By day, the labyrinth of urban dwellings resembles consciousness; the arcades (which are galleries leading into the city's past) issue unremarked onto the streets. At night, however, under the tenebrous mass of the houses, their denser darkness bursts forth like a threat, and the nocturnal pedestrian hurries past – unless, that is, we have emboldened him to turn into the narrow lane.

Falser colors are possible in the arcades; that combs are red and green surprises no one. Snow White's stepmother had such things, and when the comb did not do its work, the beautiful apple was there to help out – half red, half poison-green, like cheap combs. Everywhere stockings play a starring role. Now they are lying under phonographs, across the way in a stamp shop; another time on the side table of a tavern, where they are watched over by a girl. And again in front of the stamp shop opposite, where, between the envelopes with various stamps in refined assortments, manuals of an antiquated art of life are lovelessly dispensed – *Secret Embraces* and *Maddening Illusions*, introductions to outmoded vices and discarded passions. The shop windows are covered with vividly colored Epinal-style posters, on which Harlequin betroths his daughter, Napoleon rides through Marengo, and, amid all types of standard artillery pieces, delicate English burghers travel the high road to hell and the forsaken path of the Gospel. No customer ought to enter this shop with preconceived ideas; on leaving, he will be the more content to take home a volume: Malebranche's *Recherche de la vérité*, or *Miss Daisy: The Journal of an English Equestrienne*.

To the inhabitants of these arcades we are pointed now and then by the signs and inscriptions which multiply along the walls within, where here and there, between the shops, a spiral staircase rises into darkness. The signs have little in common with the nameplates that hang beside respectable entryways but are reminiscent of plaques on the cages at zoos, put there to indicate not so much the dwelling place as the origin and species of the captive animals. Deposited in the letters of the metal or enameled signboards is a precipitate of all the forms of writing that have ever been in use in the West. "Albert at No. 83" will be a hairdresser, and "Theatrical Tights" will probably be silk tights, pink and light blue, for young chanteuses and ballerinas; but these insistent letterings want to say something more, something different. Collectors of curiosities in the field of cultural history have in their secret drawer broadsheets of a highly paid literature which seem, at first sight, to be commercial prospectuses or theatrical bills, and which squander dozens of different alphabets in disguising an open invitation. These dark enameled signs bring to mind the baroque lettering on the cover of obscene books. – Recall the origin of the modern poster. In 1861, the first lithographic poster suddenly appeared on walls here and there around London. It showed the back of a woman in white who was thickly wrapped in a shawl and who, in all haste, had just reached the top of a flight of stairs, where, her head half turned and a finger upon her lips, she is ever so slightly opening a heavy door to reveal the starry sky. In this way Wilkie Collins advertised his latest book, one of the greatest detective novels ever written, *The Woman in White*. Still color <less>, the first drops of a shower of letters ran down the walls of houses (today it pours unremittingly, day and night, on the big cities) and was greeted like the plagues of Egypt. – Hence the anxiety we feel when, crowded out by those who actually make purchases, wedged between overloaded coatstands, we read at the bottom of the spiral staircase: "Institut de Beauté du Professeur Alfred Bitterlin." And the "Fabrique de Cravates au Deuxième" – Are there really neckties there or not? ("The Speckled Band" from Sherlock Holmes?) Of course, the needlework will have been quite inoffensive, and all the imagined horrors will be classified objectively in the statistics on tuberculosis. As a consolation, these places are seldom lacking institutes of hygiene. There gladiators wear orthopedic belts, and bandages are wrapped round the white bellies of mannequins. Something induces the owner of the shop to circulate among them on a frequent basis. – Many are the aristocrats who know nothing of the Almanach de Gotha: "Mme. de Consolis, Ballet Mistress – Lessons, Classes, Numbers." "Mme. de Zahna, Fortuneteller." And if, sometime in the mid-Nineties, <we had> asked for a prediction, surely it would have been: the decline of a culture.

Often these inner spaces harbor antiquated trades, and even those that are thoroughly up to date will acquire in them something obsolete. They are the site of information bureaus and detective agencies, which there, in the gloomy light of the upper galleries, follow the trail of the past. In hairdressers' windows, you can see the last women with long hair. They have richly undulating masses of hair, which are "permanent waves," petrified coiffures. They ought to dedicate small votive plaques to those who made a special world of these buildings – to Baudelaire and Odilon Redon, whose very name sounds like an all too well-turned ringlet. Instead, they have been betrayed and sold, and the head of Salome itself made into an ornament – if that which sorrows there in the console is not the embalmed head of Anna Czyllak. And while these things are petrified, the masonry of the walls above has become brittle. Brittle, too, are the mosaic thresholds that lead you, in the style of the old restaurants of the Palais-Royal, to a "Parisian Dinner" for five francs; they mount boldly to a glass door, but you can hardly believe that behind this door is really a restaurant. The glass door adjacent promises a "Petit Casino" and allows a glimpse of a ticket booth and the prices of seats; but were you to open it – would it open into anything? Instead of entering the space of a theater, wouldn't you be stepping down to the street? Where doors and walls are made of mirrors, there is no telling outside from in, with all the equivocal illumination. Paris is a city of mirrors. The asphalt of its road-

ways smooth as glass, and at the entrance to all bistros glass partitions. A profusion of windowpanes and mirrors in cafés, so as to make the inside brighter and to give all the tiny nooks and crannies, into which Parisian taverns separate, a pleasing amplitude. Women here look at themselves more than elsewhere, and from this comes the distinctive beauty of the Parisienne. Before any man catches sight of her, she has already seen herself ten times reflected. But the man, too, sees his own physiognomy flash by. He gains his image more quickly here than elsewhere and also sees himself more quickly merged with this, his image. Even the eyes of passersby are veiled mirrors. And over that wide bed of the Seine, over Paris, the sky is spread out like the crystal mirror hanging over the drab beds in brothels. . . .

Ambiguity of the arcades as an ambiguity of *space*. Readiest access to this phenomenon would be afforded by the multiple deployment of figures in the wax museum. On the other hand, the resolute focus on the ambiguity of space, a focus obtained in the arcades, has to benefit the theory of Parisian streets. The outermost, merely quite peripheral aspect of the ambiguity of the arcades is provided by their abundance of mirrors, which fabulously amplifies the spaces and makes orientation more difficult. Perhaps that isn't saying much. Nevertheless: though it may have many aspects, indeed infinitely many, it remains – in the sense of mirror world – ambiguous, double-edged. It blinks, is always just this one – and never nothing – out of which another immediately arises. The space that transforms itself does so in the bosom of nothingness. In its tarnished, dirtied mirrors, things exchange a Kaspar-Hauser-look with the nothing: it is an utterly equivocal wink coming from nirvana. And here, again, we are brushed with icy breath by the dandyish name of Odilon Redon, who caught, like no one else, this look of things in the mirror of nothingness, and who understood, like no one else, how to join with things in their collusion with nonbeing. The whispering of gazes fills the arcades. There is no thing here that does not, where one least expects it, open a fugitive eye, blinking it shut again; and should you look more closely, it is gone. To the whispering of these gazes, the space lends its echo: "Now, what," it blinks, "can possibly have come over me?" We stop short in some surprise. "What, indeed, can possibly have come over you?" Thus we gently bounce the question back to it. Here, the coronation of Charlemagne could have taken place, as well as the assassination of Henri IV, the death of <Edward's> sons in the Tower, and the . . . That is why the wax museums are here. This optical gallery of princes is their acknowledged capital. For Louis XI, it is the throne room; for York, the Tower of London; for Abdel Krim, the desert; and for Nero, Rome. . . .

Streets are the dwelling place of the collective. The collective is an eternally wakeful, eternally agitated being that – in the space between the building fronts – lives, experiences, understands, and invents as much as individuals do within the privacy of their own four walls. For this collective, glossy enameled shop signs are a wall decoration as good as, if not better than, an oil painting in the drawing room of a bourgeois; walls with their "Post No Bills" are its writing desk, newspaper stands its libraries, mailboxes its bronze busts, benches its bedroom furniture, and the café terrace is the balcony from which it looks down on its household. The section of railing where road workers hang their jackets is the vestibule, and the gateway which leads from the row of courtyards out into the open is the long corridor that daunts the bourgeois, being for the courtyards the entry to the chambers of the city. Among these latter, the arcade was the drawing room. More than anywhere else, the street reveals itself in the arcade as the furnished and familiar interior of the masses. . . .

For the flâneur, a transformation takes place with respect to the street: it leads him through a vanished time. He strolls down the street; for him, every street is precipitous. It leads downward – if not to the mythical Mothers, then into a past that can be all the more profound because it is not his own, not private. Nevertheless, it always remains the past of a youth. But why that of the life he has lived? The ground over which he goes, the asphalt, is hollow. His steps awaken a surprising resonance; the gaslight that streams down on the paving stones throws an equivocal light on this double ground. The figure of the flâneur advances over the street of stone, with its double ground, as though driven by a clockwork mechanism. And within, where this mechanism is ensconced, a music box is palpitating <?> like some toy of long ago. It plays a tune: "From days of youth, / from days of youth, / a song is with me still." By this melody he recognizes what is around him; it is not a past coming from his own youth, from a recent youth, but a childhood lived before then that speaks to him, and it is all the same to him whether it is the childhood of an ancestor or his own. – An intoxication comes over the man who walks long and aimlessly through the streets. With each step, the walk takes on greater momentum; ever weaker grow the temptations of bistros, of shops, of smiling women, ever more irresistible the magnetism of the next streetcorner, of a distant square in the fog, of the back of a woman walking before him. Then comes hunger. He wants, however, nothing to do with the myriad possibilities offered to sate his appetite, but like an animal he prowls through unknown districts in search of food, in search of a woman, until, utterly exhausted, he stumbles into his room, which receives him coldly and wears a strange air. Paris created this type. What is remarkable is that it wasn't Rome. And the reason? Just this: does not dreaming itself take the high road in Rome? And isn't that city too full of themes, of monuments, enclosed squares, national shrines, to be able to enter *tout entière* – with every cobblestone, every shop sign, every step, and every gateway – into the passerby's dream? The national character of the Italians may also have much to do with this. For it is not the foreigners but they themselves, the Parisians, who have made Paris the holy city of the flâneur – the "landscape built of sheer life," as Hofmannsthal once put it. Landscape – that, in fact, is what Paris becomes for the flâneur. Or, more precisely, the city neatly splits for him into its dialectical poles: it opens up to him as a landscape, even as it closes around him as a room. – Another thing: that anamnestic intoxication in which the flâneur goes about the city not only feeds on the sensory data taking shape before his eyes but can very well possess itself of abstract knowledge – indeed, of dead facts – as something experienced and lived through. This felt knowledge, as is obvious, travels above all by word of mouth from one person to another. But in the course of the nineteenth century, it was also deposited in an immense literature. Even before Lefeuve (who quite aptly made the following formula the title of his five-volume work), "Paris street by street, house by house" was lovingly depicted as storied landscape forming a backdrop to the dreaming idler. The study of these books was, for the Parisian, like a second existence, one wholly predisposed toward dreaming; the knowledge these books gave him took form and figure during an afternoon walk before the apéritif. And wouldn't he necessarily have felt the gentle slope behind the church of Notre Dame de Lorette rise all the more insistently under his soles if he realized: here, at one time, after Paris had gotten its first omnibuses, the *cheval de renfort* was harnessed to the coach to reinforce the two other horses.

Boredom is a warm gray fabric lined on the inside with the most lustrous and colorful of silks. In this fabric we wrap ourselves when we dream. We are at home then in the arabesques of its lining. But the sleeper looks bored and gray within his sheath. And when he later wakes and wants to tell of what he dreamed, he communicates, by and large, only this boredom. For who would be able at one stroke to turn the

lining of time to the outside? Yet to narrate dreams signifies nothing else. And in no other way can one deal with the arcades – structures in which we relive, as in a dream, the life of our parents and grandparents, as the embryo in the womb relives the life of animals. Existence in these spaces flows then without accent, like the events in dreams. Flânerie is the rhythmics of this slumber. In 1839, a rage for tortoises overcame Paris. One can well imagine the elegant set mimicking the pace of this creature more easily in the arcades than on the boulevards. Boredom is always the external surface of unconscious events. For that reason, it has appeared to the great dandies as a mark of distinction....

Few things in the history of humanity are as well known to us as the history of Paris. Tens of thousands of volumes are dedicated solely to the investigation of this tiny spot on the earth's surface. For many streets, we know about the fate of every single house over a period of centuries. In a beautiful turn of phrase, Hugo von Hofmannsthal called this city "a landscape built of pure life." And at work in the attraction it exercises on people is the kind of beauty that is proper to great landscapes – more precisely, to volcanic landscapes. Paris is a counterpart in the social order to what Vesuvius is in the geographic order: a menacing, hazardous massif, an ever-active June of revolution. But just as the slopes of Vesuvius, thanks to the layers of lava that cover them, have been transformed into paradisal orchards, so the lava of revolution provides uniquely fertile ground for the blossoming of art, festivity, fashion.

Hasn't his eternal vagabondage everywhere accustomed him to reinterpreting the image of the city? And doesn't he transform the arcade into a casino, into a gambling den, where now and again he stakes the red, blue, yellow *jetons* of feeling on women, on a face that suddenly surfaces (will it return his look?), on a mute mouth (will it speak?)? What, on the baize cloth, looks out at the gambler from every number –

luck, that is – here, from the bodies of all the women, winks at him as the chimera of sexuality: as his type. This is nothing other than the number, the cipher, in which just at that moment luck will be called by name, in order to jump immediately to another number. His type – that's the number that blesses thirty-six-fold, the one on which, without even trying, the eye of the voluptuary falls, as the ivory ball falls into the red or black compartment. He leaves the Palais-Royal with bulging pockets, calls to a whore, and once more finds in her arms the communion with number, in which money and riches, otherwise the most burdensome, most massive of things, come to him from the fates like a joyous embrace returned to the full. For in gambling hall and bordello, it is the same supremely sinful, supremely punishable delight: to challenge fate in pleasure. That sensual pleasure, of whatever stripe, could determine the theological concept of sin is something that only an unsuspecting idealism can believe. Determining the concept of debauchery in the theological sense is nothing else but this wresting of pleasure from out of the course of life with God, whose covenant with such life resides in the name.

The name itself is the cry of naked lust. This holy thing, sober, fateless in itself – the name – knows no greater adversary than the fate that takes its place in whoring and that forges its arsenal in superstition. Thus in gambler and prostitute that superstition which arranges the figures of fate and fills all wanton behaviour with fateful forwardness, fateful concupiscence, bringing even pleasure to kneel before its throne. . . .

These notes devoted to the Paris arcades were begun under an open sky of cloudless blue that arched above the foliage and yet was dimmed by the millions of leaves from which the fresh breeze of diligence, the stertorous breath of research, the storm of youthful zeal, and the idle wind of curiosity have raised the dust of centuries. The painted sky of summer that looks down from the arcades in the reading room of the Bibliothèque Nationale in Paris has stretched its dreamy, unlit ceiling over the birth of their insight. And when that sky opened to the eyes of this young insight, there in the foreground were standing not the divinities of Olympus – not Zeus, Hephaestus, Hermes, or Hera, Artemis, and Athena – but the Dioscuri.

NOTES

1   This brief essay, dating from the summer or fall of 1927 (*Gesammelte Schriften*, vol. 5, [Frankfurt: Suhrkamp, 1982], pp. 1041–3), is the only completed text we have from the earliest period of work on *The Arcades Project*, when Benjamin was planning to write a newspaper article on the Paris arcades in collaboration with Franz Hessel. The article may have been written by Benjamin and Hessel together.

2   These originally untitled texts (*Gesammelte Schriften*, vol. 5, [Frankfurt: Suhrkamp, 1982], pp. 1044–59), written on loose sheets of expensive handmade paper folded in half, date from 1928 or, at the latest, 1929, when Benjamin was planning to write an essay entitled "Pariser Passagen: Eine dialektische Feerie" (Paris Arcades: A Dialectical Fairyland). In the manuscript

they are followed by citations which were largely transferred to the convolutes and which therefore are not reproduced in the German edition at this point. The ordering of the entries here is that of the German editor, who also gives their original order in the manuscript:

Ms. 1154 recto: a°,1; a°,3; b°,1; b°,2.
Ms. 1154 verso: c°,3; e°,1.
Ms. 1155 recto: c°,1; c°,4; d°,1; d°,2; c°,2.
Ms. 1155 verso: h°,5.
Ms. 1160 verso: h°,1; a°,2; f°,1; h°,2; h°,3; h°,4; a°,5.
Ms. 1161 verso: f°,2; e°,2; f°,3; a°,4; g°,1.

These texts were among those from which Benjamin read to Adorno and Horkheimer at Königstein and Frankfurt in 1929.

from *Evictions: Art and Spatial Politics*

Rosalyn Deutsche

Today, discourse about the problems of public spaces in American cities is dominated by the articulation of democracy in authoritarian directions. This movement is engineered in two interlocking steps. First, urban public spaces are endowed with substantive sources of unity. Particular uses of space are deemed self-evident and uniformly beneficial because they are said to be based on some absolute foundation – eternal human needs, the organic configuration and evolution of cities, inevitable technological progress, natural social arrangements, or objective moral values. Second, it is claimed that the foundation authorizes the exercise of state power in these spaces (or the power of such quasi-governmental entities as "business improvement districts").

But with this claim power becomes incompatible with democratic values, and public space is, to borrow a term from Lefort, "appropriated." When, that is, guardians of public space refer their power to a source of social unity outside the social, they attempt to occupy – in the senses of filling up, taking possession of, taking possession by filling up – the locus of power that in a democratic society is an empty place. Let us be clear. For Lefort, "appropriation" does not simply designate the exercise of power or the act of making a decision about the use of a space. Lefort does not deny the necessity of power or

political decision making. Appropriation is a strategy deployed by a distinctly undemocratic power that legitimates itself by giving social space a "proper," hence incontestable, meaning, thereby closing down public space.[1]

A single example should suffice to illustrate the appropriative strategy in contemporary urban discourse, since this strategy has become so familiar. Today it travels under the slogan "the quality of urban life," a phrase that in its predominant usage embodies a profound antipathy to rights and pluralism. Formulated in the singular, "the quality of life" assumes a universal city dweller who is equated with "the public" – identities that the phrase actually invents. The universality of this urban resident is called into question when we note that those who champion a better quality of life do not defend all public institutions equally. While conservative journalists routinely seek to protect municipal parks, they do not necessarily support public education, for example, or public housing. Yet how strongly do they even defend the publicness of parks?

In 1991 the *New York Times*, endorsing "The Public's Right to Put a Padlock On a Public Space,"[2] reported the triumph of a public space – Jackson Park, a tiny triangle in Greenwich Village that had previously fallen into disorder. Nearly a year later, a special "Quality of Urban Life" issue of

City Journal, the voice of neoconservative urban policy intellectuals, corroborated the *Times*'s positive judgment and further inflated the little plaza into a symbol of progress in the ongoing struggle to restore public space.[3] Located on a traffic island, Jackson Park is surrounded by upper-middle-class houses and apartments and by a substantial number of residents without apartments. Following a $1.2-million reconstruction of the park, a neighborhood group, Friends of Jackson Park – a group the *Times* consistently mistakes for both "the community" and "the public" – decided to lock the newly installed park gates at night. The City Parks Department, lacking sufficient personnel to close the park, welcomed "public" help in protecting public space, a defense they equated with evicting homeless people from city parks. "The people who hold the keys," announced the *Times*, "are determined to keep a park a park."[4]

A preordained public space, the *Times* tells us, is being defended by its natural owners – a statement that inverts the real sequence of events. For it is only by resorting to an argument outside argumentation – "a park is a park" – and so decreeing in advance which uses of public space are legitimate that such a space first becomes the property of an owner – "the people who hold the keys." Increasingly, conservative urbanists promote the transformation of public space into proprietary space – the occupation of public space – by conceding that public spaces are conflictual not harmonious terrains yet denying the legitimacy of spatial contests. *City Journal*, for instance, joining the *Times* in celebrating the "Jackson Park solution," notes that while urban analysts frequently ignore such problems, "what the homeless crisis has made unavoidable, is the clash of values created around contested spaces."[5] Whereupon, the *City Journal* avoids conflict by representing the decision to lock Jackson Park as the "reclamation" of "our" public space from "undesirables." The *Journal* portrays contests over city space as a war between two absolute, rather than political, forces: the Friends of Jackson Park, who are conflated with "the public" and who, backed by the local state, represent the proper uses that will restore the original harmony of public space and the park's enemies – homeless people who disrupt harmony.

In this scenario, recognition of conflict reassures observers that society might be free of division. The homeless person, represented as an intruder in public space, supports the housed resident's fantasy that the city, and social space in general, is essentially an organic whole. The person without a home is constructed as an ideological figure, a negative image created to restore positivity and order to social life. To appreciate this ideological operation, we might recall Theodor Adorno's postwar speculations about negative, that is anti-Semitic, images of Jews. Responding to the then prevalent idea that persisting German anti-Semitism could be defeated by acquainting Germans with "real" Jews – by, for instance, emphasizing the historical contribution of Jews or arranging meetings between Germans and Israelis – Adorno wrote: "This sort of activity depends too much upon the assumption that anti-Semitism essentially has something to do with Jews and could be combatted through an actual knowledge of Jews."[6] On the contrary, stated Adorno, anti-Semitism has nothing to do with Jews and everything to do with the psychic economy of the anti-Semite. Efforts to counteract anti-Semitism cannot, then, rely on the purportedly beneficial effects of education about "real" Jews. Such efforts must, rather, "*turn toward the subject*," scrutinizing the fantasies of the anti-Semite and the image of the Jew that he or she desires.[7]

Elaborating on Adorno's suggestion, Slavoj Žižek brilliantly analyzes the construction of the "Jew" as an ideological figure for fascism, a process that, though not identical to, has important parallels with current constructions of "the homeless person" as an ideological figure.[8] Disorder, unrest, and conflict in the social system are all attributed to this figure – properties that cannot be eliminated from the social system since, as Laclau and Mouffe argue, social space is structured around an impossibility and is therefore irrevocably split by antagonisms. But when public space is represented as an organic unity that the homeless person is seen to disrupt from the outside, the homeless person becomes a positive embodiment of the element that prevents society from achieving closure. The element thwarting society's ability to cohere is transformed from a negativity within the social itself into a presence whose elimination would restore social order. In this sense, negative images of the homeless person are images of a positivity. The homeless person becomes, as Žižek writes about the "Jew," "*a point at which social negativity as such assumes positive existence.*"[9] The vision of the homeless person as the source of conflict in public space denies that there is an obstacle to coherence at the very core of social life. The homeless person embodies the fantasy of a unified urban space that can – must – be retrieved.[10]

To challenge the image of the homeless person as a disruption of the normal urban order, it is crucial to recognize that this "intrusive" figure points to the city's true character. Conflict is not something that befalls an originally, or potentially, harmonious urban space. Urban space is the product of conflict. This is so in several, incommensurable senses. In the first place, the lack of absolute social foundations – "the disappearance of the markers of certainty" – makes conflict an ineradicable feature of all social space. Second, the unitary image of urban space constructed in conservative urban discourse is itself produced through division, constituted through the creation of an exterior. The perception of a coherent space cannot be separated from a sense of what threatens that space, of what it would like to exclude. Finally, urban space is produced by specific socioeconomic conflicts that should not simply be accepted, either wholeheartedly or regretfully, as evidence of the inevitability of conflict but, rather, politicized –

opened to contestation as social and therefore mutable relations of oppression. For, as I have argued elsewhere, the presence of homeless people in New York's public places today is the most acute symptom of the uneven social relations that determined the shape of the city throughout the 1980s, when it was redeveloped not, as promoters of redevelopment claimed, to fulfill the natural needs of a unitary society but to facilitate the restructuring of global capitalism.[11] As the specific form of advanced capitalist urbanism, redevelopment destroyed the conditions of survival for residents no longer needed in the city's new economy. The gentrification of parks played a key role in this process.[12] Homeless people and new public spaces, such as parks, are not, then, distinct entities, the first disrupting the peace of the second. The two are, rather, dual products of the spatioeconomic conflicts that constitute the contemporary production of urban space.

Yet, as I have also argued elsewhere, public art programs, serving as an arm of urban redevelopment, helped produce the opposite impression. Under several unifying banners – historical continuity, preservation of cultural tradition, civic beautification, utilitarianism – official public art collaborated with architecture and urban design to create an image of new urban sites that suppressed their conflictual character. In so doing, they also constructed the homeless person – a product of conflict – as an ideological figure – the bringer of conflict.[13]

In this pervasive atmosphere of conservative democracy, it might be seen as an encouraging sign that today's widespread enthusiasm for "public art" has been tempered from the beginning by uncertainty about the definition of the term. Artists and critics have repeatedly asked what it means to bring the word *public* into proximity with *art*. Writers alert to the problems that plague conventional concepts of publicness often begin their explorations of public art by questioning the identity, even the existence, of their object of study. In 1985 Jerry Allen, director of the Cultural Affairs Division of the City of Dallas, voiced this bewilderment: "Nearly 26 years after the passage of the first Percent for Art ordinance in Philadelphia, we still are unable to define exactly what public art is or ought to be."[14] Three years later, the critic Patricia Phillips concurred: "Though public art in the late 20th century has emerged as a full-blown discipline, it is a field without clear definitions."[15] Recent anxieties over the category "public art" could serve as a textbook example of the postmodern idea that objects of study are the effect, rather than the ground, of disciplinary knowledge.

Critics dedicated to public art's democratic potential but dissatisfied with its traditional classifications and uses have turned their uncertainty into a mandate to redefine the category. By 1988, writers like Kathy Halbreich of the National Endowment for the Arts had begun to insist that as an essential part of this redefinition "equal stress be placed on the words 'public' and 'art.'"[16] Soon the balance shifted even further, in favor of the first word. By now, attention to the term *public* is the touchstone of redefinitions of public art. Some writers have coined names, like Suzanne Lacy's "new genre public art," to designate the work of public artists who, as Lacy puts it, "adopt 'public' as their operative concept and quest."[17] Doubtless, these are steps in the direction of democratizing public art discourse. But critics often propose definitions of "public" that circumvent or eliminate what I, following Lefort, have called the question that gives rise to public space. Instead of describing public space so that it escapes appropriation altogether, those who challenge the conservative domination of public art discourse have largely reappropriated the term.

This tendency clearly dominates the principal forms of liberal public art discourse. For Allen, to give only one example, public art is a problem not because the meanings of art and public are uncertain or even subject to historical variation; on the contrary, problems arise because the meanings of the two terms are fixed in advance and inevitably clash:

> The very notion of a "public art" is something of a contradiction in terms. In it, we join two words whose meanings are, in some ways, antithetical. We recognize "art" [in the 20th century] as the individual inquiry of the sculptor or painter, the epitome of self-assertion. To that we join "public," a reference to the collective, the social order, selfnegation. Hence, we link the private and the public, in a single concept or object, from which we expect both coherence and integrity.[18]

This formulation ignores the forceful challenge that certain key branches of twentieth-century art and criticism have directed against individualistic notions of the artist as an autonomous self and of art as an expression grounded in this strictly private being. Individuals or artists may not be so securely private as Allen thinks. The dismissal of this possibility leads critics to support a rigid opposition between "art" and "public" that rephrases standard liberal dichotomies between individual and society, private and public. The public/private opposition has also been mobilized to unite, rather than polarize, "art" and "public." Critics often treat both art and the public as universal spheres that, harmonized by a common human essence, stand above the conflictual realm of atomized individuals, purely private differences, and special interests. In these cases, "public art" is not, as Allen assumes, a contradictory entity, but instead comes doubly burdened as a figure of universal accessibility.

Although the two formulations – art opposed to public, art united with public – place art on different sides of the public/private divide, they stay within the same polarizing framework. The failure to question this framework has led many critics to open and close the question of the public in a single gesture. While they note that public art is difficult to define and stress the incoherence of the contemporary public, they still equate public space with consensus, coherence, and universality and relegate pluralism, division, and difference to the realm of the private. They tacitly view the plurality and strife that characterize the public as problematic facts that supporters of public space must find procedures to reduce and finally eliminate. Allen, for instance, who offers a solution typically adopted by many public art advocates, initially acknowledges that art's "public context" is broad and heterogeneous. Public art cannot hope to express values held by everyone. Still, its goal should be to serve unified, if multiple, publics that, says Allen, can be found if artists suppress their individual egos and consult the people "immediately affected by the project" – preexisting groups or communities who use specific urban sites, distinct constituencies each defined by some common identification.[19]

Homogeneity and unanimity – frequently cast in the shape of "community" – become the object of quests for true publicness as some critics, while usefully documenting controversies fought over specific public artworks and even espousing controversy as a natural ingredient of the public art process, continue to associate public space and democracy with the goals of building consensus, consolidating communities, and soothing conflicts. At the same time they place the definition of democratic public space fundamentally outside controversy.

This dynamic is illustrated by a 1992 anthology titled *Critical Issues in Public Art: Content, Context, and Controversy.* In the book's opening sentence, the editors tie public art to democracy: "Public art with its built-in social focus would seem to be an ideal genre for a democracy."[20] They continue: "Yet, since its inception, issues surrounding its appropriate form and placement, as well as its funding, have made public art an object of controversy more often than consensus or celebration."[21] The conjunction *yet*, which links these two sentences, performs important ideological work. It joins democracy – introduced in the first sentence – and con-

troversy – introduced in the second – in an adverse relationship. Public art would be democratic *except* that it is controversial, or – in a more optimistic reading – public art retains its democratic potential *despite* the fact that it is controversial. "Yet" signals a reversal. Public art would seem to be democratic but instead turns out to be controversial. Controversy, moreover, serves as a foil for consensus, which consequently emerges as democracy's proper goal and is, further, associated with celebration. While the book's editors and many authors of the essays stress, or even valorize, disunity and antagonism, the word "yet" reveals an indecision at the heart of accounts of public art that interrogate the meaning of public space only to beg the question. "Yet" dissociates democracy from the fact of conflict and binds democracy to consensus-oriented, homogenizing notions of public space and public art. Conflict is simultaneously acknowledged and disavowed, a fetishistic process whose repressions generate certitudes about the meaning of public space. Later in *Critical Issues in Public Art*, for example, the editors simply repeat their universalizing assumptions: "The very concept of public art, defined in any meaningful way, presupposes a fairly homogeneous public and a language of art that speaks to all."[22]

Conservative and liberal aesthetic discourses are by no means alone in finding ways simultaneously to open and close the question of public space. Some of the most influential radical critiques of those discourses also try to dispel uncertainty. Many leftist cultural critics, for instance, search history to discover the origin and essence of democratic civic life. In the Athenian polis, the Roman republic, late-eighteenth-century France, and the commons of early American towns, critics locate the spatial forms that supposedly embody such a life. This quest has become especially common among left urban and architecture theorists who, driven by opposition to the newly homogenized, privatized, and state-regulated public spaces created by advanced capitalist urbanization, have formed influential alliances. Michael Sorkin, for example, introduces his interdisciplinary anthology of critical essays, *Variations on a Theme Park: The New American City and the End of Public Space*, with a plea for a return to "the familiar spaces of traditional cities, the streets and squares, courtyards and parks," that are "our great scenes of the civic."[23] Sorkin concludes that in the new "'public' spaces of the theme park or the shopping mall, speech itself is restricted: there are no demonstrations in Disneyland. The effort to reclaim the city is the struggle of democracy itself."[24]

When Sorkin treats public space as the site of political activity rather than as a universal domain that must be protected from politics, he significantly redirects mainstream discourse about public space. He is right to link public space to the exercise of free speech rights and to challenge the current proliferation of sanitized urban spaces that tolerate little resistance to the most circumscribed uses.[25] But when Sorkin idealizes traditional city space as a "more authentic urbanity,"[26] a space essential to democratic politics, he avoids the politics of *its* historical constitution as well as the possibility of its political transformation. Within this idealizing perspective, departures from established spatial arrangements inevitably signal the "end of public space." Edge cities, shopping malls, mass media, electronic space (even, for the right, "bizarrely shaped" voting districts) become tantamount to democracy's demise.

The cover of *Variations on a Theme Park* discloses certain problems with this approach. It depicts a group of Renaissance figures, the men and women normally seen in quattro- and cinquecento paintings disposed throughout the perspectival, orthogonally ordered, and visually unified outdoor squares of Italian cities. But on the book jacket these inhabitants of a stable public realm are spatially and temporally displaced. With patrician gestures and flowing drapery intact, they find themselves riding an escalator in a new "antiurban" structure – perhaps it is an "inward-looking atrium hotel" or multilevel shopping mall – a structure which, according to the book's thesis, signifies "the end of public space." Appropriated to visualize this thesis, providing the literal background of the book's subtitle, the illustration links Sorkin's trenchant critique of contemporary urbanism to a strong current of urban nostalgia that indeed pervades many of the essays in the book.

There are good reasons for radical urban critics to eschew this connection. Most obviously, the turn to the past brings them uncomfortably close to conservative urban discourse. Throughout the boom years of redevelopment, nostalgic images of the city were employed by real-estate developers, historic preservationists, and city officials to advertise individual redevelopment projects as advances in an ongoing struggle to restore an ideal city from the more or less remote past. In New York, these projects were promoted as piecemeal contributions to the city's own "renaissance," the rebirth of a lost urban tradition. Redevelopment projects, it was claimed, would help restore New York to its place in a lineage of earlier cities that, centered on expansive public spaces, were harmonious in their entirety.[27] The tradition continues. For Paul Goldberger, the newly renovated Bryant Park in midtown Manhattan is an "out-of-town experience." His appraisal, like so many contemporary accounts of the city, implies that homeless people control access to public space: Bryant Park, he says, is a place the poor have begun to "share." Now it "feels as if it has been ... dropped into some idyllic landscape far, far away."[28]

Public space, these comments suggest, is not only something we do not have. Rather, it is what we once had – a lost state of plenitude. Since it is lost, however, and not simply dead, we can recover it. "Whatever Became of the Public Square?" asked *Harper's Magazine*'s lead article in 1990 as a prelude to a search for new urban designs that will restore the public square – what *Harper's* calls "that great good place."[29]

What is pictured on the cover of *Variations on a Theme Park* if not a loss? We see, in absentia, a zone of safety, a great good place from which we have been banished – at least those of us who identify with Renaissance city dwellers as exiled inhabitants of a democratic public space.

This qualification should give us pause. Pursuing specificity, it raises two sets of questions that can help sharpen currently hazy images of public space. The first inquires into the concrete identity of the sketchy people who exemplify supposedly true publicness on the cover of Sorkin's book. Which social groups were actually included, and which excluded, in the purportedly fully inclusive, or at least more inclusive, urban public spaces of the near or distant past? Who counted as a citizen in the "great scenes of the civic" figured as missing? "*For whom*," as cultural critic Bruce Robbins asks, "was the city once more public than now? Was it ever open to the scrutiny and participation, let alone under the control, of the majority? ...

NOTES

1   Since I am applying Lefort's ideas to a discussion of contemporary urban discourse, it is important to note that Lefort uses the term *appropriation* in an opposite sense from Henri Lefebvre, whose concept of appropriation has been so compelling for critical urban thought. For Lefort, appropriation refers to an action of state power; for Lefebvre, it denotes an action against such power. This terminological difference does not mean that the ideas of the two writers are polarized. On the contrary, they have certain affinities. Although Lefort is not writing specifically about urban space, his appropriation – the occupation of public space by giving it an absolute meaning – resembles what Henri Lefebvre calls the domination of space – the technocratic designation of objective uses that bestow an ideological coherence on space. Moreover, Lefort's appropriation and Lefebvre's domination are similar to Michel de Certeau's notion of "strategy" as the relationship that becomes possible when a subject with power postulates a *place* that can be delimited as its *own*. See Henri Lefebvre, *The Production of Space*, trans. Donald Nicholson-Smith (Oxford: Basil Blackwell, 1991) and Michel de Certeau, *The Practice of Everyday Life* (Berkeley: University of California Press, 1984), 36. All three endow space with proper meanings and uses and, in this proprietary manner, set up a relation with an exterior that threatens those uses. In fact, de Certeau uses the adjective *appropriated* to delineate a space – "a place appropriated as one's own" – that serves from inception "as a base from which relations with an exteriority composed of targets of threats ... can be managed."

The actions described by Lefort, Lefebvre, and de Certeau call for countervailing democratic procedures: "depropriation" (a term that, as far as I am aware, Lefort does not explicitly use), Lefebvre's "appropriation," and what de Certeau calls "making do." In this context, depropriation and Lefebvre's appropriation have similar (though not identical) meanings. Like de Certeau's making do, they imply some kind of undoing by the outside of a space that has been made proper, a taking account of exclusions and differences, and consequent exposure of power where it has been naturalized and obscured.

2   Sam Roberts, "The Public's Right to Put a Padlock on a Public Space," *New York Times*, June 3, 1991, B1.

3   Fred Siegel, "Reclaiming Our Public Spaces," *The City Journal* 2, no. 2 (Spring 1992): 35–45.

4   Roberts, "The Public's Rights," B1.

5   Siegel, "Reclaiming Our Public Spaces," 41.

6   Theodor Adorno, "What Does Coming to Terms with the Past Mean?" in *Bitburg in Moral and Political Perspective*, ed. Geoffrey H. Hartman (Bloomington: Indiana University Press, 1986), 127–8; translated from *Gesammelte Schriften* 10, pt. 2 (Frankfurt am Main: Suhrkamp 1977), 555–72.

7   Ibid., 128.

8   Slavoj Žižek, *The Sublime Object of Ideology* (London: Verso, 1989), 128.

9   Ibid., 127.

10 The idea that the visibility of homeless people might reinforce the image of a unified urban space casts doubt on the more common assumption of critical urban discourse – that the mere presence of homeless people in public spaces challenges the appearance of harmony that official representations try to impose on dominated urban sites (I make this claim, for example, at the beginning of "Uneven Development: Public Art in New York City," in this volume). The visibility of homeless people neither guarantees the social recognition of homeless people nor legitimates conflicts over public space; it is just as likely to strengthen the image of an essentially harmonious public space, which legitimates the eviction of homeless people.

But raising questions about the conditions and consequences of visibility does not negate the importance of maintaining the visibility of homelessness, where visibility implies resistance to efforts to expel homeless people from public space and coercively assign them to shelters. The demand for visibility, understood as the declaration of the right of homeless people to live and work in public spaces, differs from a specular model of visibility, in which homeless people are constructed as objects for a viewing subject. The first demand challenges established legitimacy, questioning the legality of state power in evicting people from public spaces. The presence of homeless people can, then, reveal the presence of power in places, like parks, where it was formerly obscured. As power becomes visible and drops its veil of anonymity, the homeless person also emerges from her consignment to an ideological image into a new kind of visibility. It is, then, imperative to struggle against the possibility that, as the state exercises its monopoly on legitimate violence and evicts the homeless from public spaces, both state power and homeless people will fade into invisibility.

11 See "Krzysztof Wodiczko's *Homeless Projection* and the Site of Urban 'Revitalization,'" and "Uneven Development: Public Art in New York City," in [*Evictions*].

12 For a case study of the role played by parks in gentrification and redevelopment, see "Krzysztof Wodiczko's *Homeless Projec-tion* and the Site of Urban 'Revitalization,'" in [*Evictions*].

13 See "Uneven Development: Public Art in New York City," in [*Evictions*].

14 Jerry Allen, "How Art Becomes Public," 1985; reprinted in *Going Public: A Field Guide to Developments in Art in Public Places* (Arts Extension Service and the Visual Arts Program of the National Endowment for the Arts, 1988), 246.

15 Patricia Phillips, "The Public Art Machine: Out of Order," *Artforum* 27 (Dec. 1988): 93.

16 Kathy Halbreich, "Stretching the Terrain: Sketching Twenty Years of Public Art," in *Going Public: A Field Guide to Developments in Art in Public Places*, 9.

17 Suzanne Lacy, "Cultural Pilgrimages and Metaphoric Journeys," in Suzanne Lacy, ed., *Mapping the Terrain: New Genre Public Art* (Seattle: Bay Press, 1995), 20.

18 Allen, "How Art Becomes Public," 246.

19 Ibid., 250.

20 Harriet F. Senie and Sally Webster, ed., *Critical Issues in Public Art: Content, Context, and Controversy* (New York: Harper Collins, 1992), xi.

21 Ibid.

22 Ibid., 171.

23 Michael Sorkin, "Introduction: Variations on a Theme Park," in Michael Sorkin, ed., *Variations on a Theme Park: The New American City and the End of Public Space* (New York: The Noonday Press, 1992), xv.

24 Ibid.

25 The combination of profit-maximizing and desexualizing tendencies in contemporary urban planning is manifest both in the use of Disneyland as a model for contemporary urbanism and in the role played by the Disney Development Company in actual urban redevelopment. Since the publication of Sorkin's book, Disney has become financially and symbolically useful to the current partnership being forged in New York between real-estate interests and moral crusaders who want to repress urban sexual cultures. Disney's instrumentality emerged clearly in a recent *New York Times* article that announced the city's choice of the Disney Development Company and the Tishman Urban Development Corporation to rebuild the corner of 42nd Street and Eighth Avenue as part of the

redevelopment of Times Square: "The $303 million project is the centerpiece of state and city efforts to transform 42nd Street between Seventh and Eighth Avenues from a seedy strip with its ever-present hustlers and sex shops into a glitzy family-oriented entertainment center.... But perhaps of even more value is the Disney name. In its effort to turn around a neighborhood long synonymous with urban danger and degradation, the city now has a partner that is a symbol of wholesome entertainment worldwide." Shawn G. Kennedy, "Disney and Developer Are Chosen To Build 42nd Street Hotel Complex," *New York Times*, May 12, 1995, B1.

26   Sorkin, "Introduction: Variations on a Theme Park," xv.

27   For an analysis of the functions of the preservationist rhetoric that accompanied redevelopment, see my "Architecture of the Evicted," in *Krzysztof Wodiczko: New York City Tableaux and The Homeless Vehicle Project*, exhib. cat. (New York: Exit Art, 1989), 28–37, reprinted in *Strategies* 3 (1990): 159–83; and "Krzysztof Wodiczko's *Homeless Projection* and the Site of Urban 'Revitalization,'" in [*Evictions*].

28   Paul Goldberger, "Bryant Park, An Out-of-Town Experience," *New York Times*, May 3, 1992, H34.

29   "Whatever Became of the Public Square? New Designs for a Great Good Place," *Harper's* (July 1990): 49–60.

from *City of Dreadful Delight: Narratives of Sexual Danger in Late-Victorian London*

Judith R. Walkowitz

Urban Spectatorship

When Henry James arrived in London in 1876, he found the city "not a pleasant place" nor "agreeable, or cheerful, or easy, or exempt from reproach." He found it "only magnificent...the biggest aggregation of human life, the most complete compendium in the world." It was also the "largest chapter of human accidents," scarred by "thousands of acres covered by low black houses of the cheapest construction" as well as by "unlimited vagueness as to the line of division between centre and circumference." "London is so clumsy and brutal, and has gathered together so many of the darkest sides of life," that it would be "frivolous to ignore her deformities." The city itself had become a "strangely mingled monster," the principal character in its own drama: an "ogress who devours human flesh to keep herself alive to do her tremendous work."[1]

Despite its brutalities, London offered James an oasis of personal freedom, a place of floating possibilities as well as dangers. Alone in lodgings, James first experienced himself in London as "an impersonal black hole in the huge general blackness." But the streets of London offered him freedom and imaginative delights. "I had complete liberty, and the prospect of profitable work; I used to take long walks in the rain. I took possession of London; I felt it to be the right place." As an artist, bachelor and outsider, James aestheticized this "world city," the "center of the race," into a grand operatic panorama of movement, atmosphere, labyrinthine secrets and mysteries. London's "immeasurable circumference," argued James, gave him a "sense of social and intellectual elbow room"; its "friendly fogs," which made "everything brown, rich, dim, vague," protected and enriched "adventure." For the "sympathetic resident," such as James, the social ease of anonymity was matched by an ease of access to and imaginative command of the whole: one may live in one "quarter" or "plot" but in "imagination and by a constant mental act of reference...[inhabit] the whole."[2]

James celebrated the traditional prerogatives of the privileged urban spectator to act, in Baudelaire's phrase, as *flaneur*, to stroll across the divided spaces of the metropolis, whether it was London, Paris, or New York, to experience the city as a whole. The fact and fantasy of urban exploration had long been an informing feature of nineteenth-century bourgeois male subjectivity. Cosmopolitanism, "the experience of diversity in the city as opposed to a relatively confined localism," argues Richard Sennett, was a bourgeois male pleasure. It established a right to the city – a right not traditionally available to, often not even part of, the imaginative repertoire of the less advantaged. In literary and visual terms, observes Griselda Pollock, "being at home in the city" was represented as a privileged gaze, betokening possession and distance, that structured "a range of disparate texts and heterogeneous practices which emerge in the nineteenth-century city – tourism, exploration/discovery, social investigation, social policy."[3]

A powerful streak of voyeurism marked all these activities; the "zeal for reform" was often accompanied "by a prolonged, fascinated gaze" from the bourgeoisie. These practices presupposed a privileged male subject whose identity was stable, coherent, autonomous; who was, moreover, capable through reason and its "science" of establishing a reliable and universal knowledge of "man" and his world.[4] It was these powers of spectatorship that Henry James ascribed to his "sympathetic resident" who, while residing in one quarter of town, was capable "in imagination" of inhabiting "the whole" of it.

At odds with this rationalist sensibility was the flaneur's propensity for fantasy. As illusionist, the flaneur transformed the city into a landscape of strangers and secrets. At the center of his art, argues Susan Buck-Morss, was the capacity to present things in fortuitous juxtapositions, in "mysterious and mystical connection." Linear time became, to quote Walter Benjamin, "a dream-web where the most ancient occurrences are attached to those of today." Always scanning the gritty street scene for good copy and anecdote, his was quintessentially "consumerist" mode of being-in-the-world, one that transformed exploitation and suffering into vivid individual psychological experience.[5]

James's affectionate portrait of London, that "dreadfully delightful city," is dominated by the flaneur's attention to the viewer's subjectivity and by the capacity of the city to stimulate. In James's "strangely mingled monster," activities of manufacture, trade, and exchange were overshadowed by rituals of consumption and display. Extremes of wealth and poverty aroused the senses, for "the impression of suffering was part of the general vibration," while London's status as repository of continuous culture and national heritage – its "great towers, great names, great memories" – served as a further stimulant to his own consciousness and memory: "All history appeared to live again and the continuity of things to vibrate through my mind."[6]

The literary construct of the metropolis as a dark, powerful, and seductive labyrinth held a powerful sway over the social imagination of educated readers. It remained the dominant representation of London in the 1880s, conveyed to many reading publics through high and low literary forms, from Charles Booth's surveys of London poverty, to the fictional stories of Stevenson, Gissing, and James, to the sensational newspaper exposés by W. T. Stead and G. R. Sims. These late-Victorian writers built on an earlier tradition of Victorian urban exploration, adding some new perspectives of their own. Some rigidified the hierarchical divisions of London into a geographic separation, organized around the opposition of East and West. Others stressed the growing complexity and differentiation of the world of London, moving beyond the opposition of rich and poor, palace and hovels, to investigate the many class cultures in between. Still others among them repudiated a fixed, totalistic interpretive image altogether, and emphasized instead a fragmented, disunified, atomistic social universe that was not easily decipherable.

Historians and cultural critics have linked this contest over and "crisis" in representation to a range of psychological and social crises troubling literary men and their social peers in the 1880s: religious self-doubt, social unrest, radical challenges to liberalism and science, anxiety over imperial and national decline, as well as an imaginative confrontation with the defamiliarized world of consumer culture "where values and perception seem in constant flux."[7] Equally crucial may have been the psychic difficulties produced by the imperatives of a "hard" physical manliness, first developed in the mid-and late-nineteenth century public schools and then diffused among the propertied classes of the Anglo-Saxon world. The hallmarks of this "virile" ethos were self-control, self-discipline, and the absence of emotional expression.[8] Whatever the precipitating causes, the public landscape of the privileged urban flaneur of the period had become an unstable construct: threatened internally by contradictions and tensions and constantly challenged from without by social forces that pressed these dominant representations to be reworked, shorn up, reconstructed.

Middle-class men were not the sole explorers and interpreters of the city in the volatile decade of the 1880s. On the contrary, as the end of the century approached, this "dreadfully delightful city" became a contested terrain, where new commercial spaces, new journalistic practices, and a range of public spectacles and reform activities inspired a different set of social actors to assert their own claims to self-creation in the public domain. Thanks to the material changes and cultural contests of the late-Victorian city, protesting workers and "gents" of marginal class position, female philanthropists and "platform women," Salvation Army lasses and match girls, as well as glamorized "girls in business," made their public appearances and established places and viewpoints in relation to the urban panorama. These new entrants to the urban scene produced new stories of the city that competed, intersected with, appropriated, and revised the dominant imaginative mappings of London.

Before tracking the progress of these new urban travelers and their social visions, let us first examine the tradition of urban spectatorship embodied in Henry James's alter ego, the "sympathetic resident." As a cosmopolitan, the "sympathetic resident" could take up nightwalking, a male pursuit immortalized in urban accounts since Elizabethan times, but one that acquired a more active moral and emotional meaning for intrepid urban explorers in the Victorian period. Whereas Regency dandies of the

1820s like Pierce Egan's characters, Tom and Jerry, had experienced the streets of London as a playground for the upper classes, and interpreted streets sights and characters as passing shows, engaged urban investigators of the mid- and late-Victorian era roamed the city with more earnest (if still voyeuristic) intent to explain and resolve social problems. Frederick Engels, Charles Dickens, and Henry Mayhew were the most distinguished among a throng of missionaries and explorers, men who tried to read the "illegible" city, transforming what appeared to be a chaotic, haphazard environment into a social text that was "integrated, knowable, and ordered." To realize their subject, their travel narratives incorporated a mixture of fact and fancy: a melange of moralized and religious sentiment, imperialist rhetoric, dramatized characterization, graphic descriptions of poverty, and statistics culled from Parliamentary Blue Books.[9]

As early as the 1840s, these urban explorers adapted the language of imperialism to evoke features of their own cities. Imperialist rhetoric transformed the unexplored territory of the London poor into an alien place, both exciting and dangerous. As Peter Keating notes, urban explorers never seemed to walk or ride into the slums, but to "penetrate" inaccessible places where the poor lived, in dark and noisy courts, thieves' "dens," foul-smelling "swamps," and the black "abyss." To buttress their own "eye of power," these explorers were frequently accompanied by the state representative of order, a trusty policeman: in the 1860s, the journalist George Sims made excursions to East End taverns frequented by sailors and prostitutes, accompanied by a detective or professional "minder." As a master of disguise, the journalist James Greenwood felt comfortable enough to dispense with this latter precaution: "A private individual," he insisted, "suitably attired and of modest mien, may safely venture where a policeman dare not show his head."[10]

The literature of urban exploration also emulated the privileged gaze of anthropology in constituting the poor as a race apart, outside the national community.[11] Mayhew, for example, introduced his investigation in *London Labour and the London Poor* by linking the street folks of London to the ethnographic study of "wandering tribes in general," arguing that, like all nomads, costermongers had big muscles and small brains, and were prone to be promiscuous, irreligious, and lazy;[12] even Engels, who went to great lengths to expose the "culpability" of the bourgeoisie for the slums, still retained, according to Peter Stallybrass and Allon White, "an essentialist category of the sub-human nomad: the Irish."[13]

Mid-Victorian investigators represented the urban topography of the "gaslight era" as a series of social juxtapositions of "high" and "low" life. Observers in the 1860s and 1870s frequently reproduced a Dickensian cityscape of dirty, crowded, disorganized clusters of urban villages, each with its own peculiar flavor and eccentricity, where the Great Unwashed lived in chaotic alleys, courts, and hovels just off the grand thoroughfares. In the 1860s, for instance, James Greenwood began his tour of "Low Life Deeps" with a visit to the "notorious Tiger Bay" of the East End's Radcliffe Highway, but he soon moved westward to "Jack Ketch's Warren" in Frying Pan Alley, Clerkenwell, and then to a "West End Cholera Stronghold." Henry Mayhew also moved from place to place in his study of the urban poor, although he noticed a difference between the laboring classes in the East and the West: "In passing from the skilled operative of the West-end, to the unskilled workman of the Eastern quarter, the moral and intellectual change is so great, that it seems as if we were in a new land, and among another race."[14]

Mayhew's observations portended an important reconfiguration of London as a city divided into East and West. Mid-Victorian explorations into the *terra incognita* of the London poor increasingly relied on the East/West opposition to assess the connecting links between seemingly unrelated parts of society. One of the most powerful and enduring realizations of this opposition, Doré and Jerrold's *London: A Pilgrimage* (1872), envisioned London as two distinct cities, not of capital and labor, but of the *rentier* and the impoverished criminal. It juxtaposed a West End of glittering leisure and consumption and national spectacle to an East End of obscure density, indigence, sinister foreign aliens, and potential crime.[15]

This bifurcated cityscape reinforced an imaginative distance between investigators and their subjects, a distance that many urban explorers felt nonetheless compelled to transgress. Cultural critics Stallybrass and White offer a Bakhtinian explanation of the cultural dynamics at work in this "poetics" of transgression. In class society, they argue, the repudiation of the "low" by the dominant "top" of society was paradoxically accompanied by a heightened symbolic importance of the "low Other" in the imaginative repertoire of the dominant culture.

> A recurrent pattern emerges: the "top" attempts to reject and eliminate the "bottom" for reasons of prestige and status, only to discover not only that it is in some way frequently dependent on the low-Other..., but also that the top *includes* that low symbolically as a primary eroticized constituent of its own fantasy life. The result is a mobile, conflictual fusion of power, fear and desire in the construction of subjectivity.

For this reason, Stallybrass and White argue, "what is *socially* peripheral is so frequently *symbolically* central.... The low-Other is despised, denied at the level of political organization and social being whilst it is instrumentally constitutive of the shared imaginary repertoire of the dominant culture."[16]

Urban investigators not only distanced themselves from their objects of study; they also felt compelled to possess a comprehensive knowledge of the Other, even to the point of cultural immersion, social masquerade, and intrapsychic incorporation.[17] James Greenwood, for example, prided himself on his improvisational skills, on being able to mingle as "one of the crowd": as "The Amateur Casual," he achieved journalistic fame for gaining admission to a workhouse casual ward dressed as a "sly and ruffianly figure marked with every sign of squalor."[18] In his investigations of the London poor, Henry Mayhew also played a number of roles, including stage manager and director/voyeur. At a public meeting, he encouraged impoverished needlewomen who had been forced by economic distress to resort to the streets to "tell their own tale." Each recounted "her woes and struggles, and published her shame amid the convulsive sobs of the others," while Mayhew and one other gentlemen observed the scene, "scarcely" visible in the "dimly lighted" meeting place.[19]

No figure was more equivocal, yet more crucial to the structured public landscape of the male flaneur, than the woman in public. In public, women were presumed to be both endangered and a source of danger to those men who congregated in the streets. In the mental map of urban spectators, they lacked autonomy: they were bearers of meaning rather than makers of meaning. As symbols of conspicuous display or of lower-class and sexual disorder, they occupied a multivalent symbolic position in this imaginary landscape.[20]

The prostitute was the quintessential female figure of the urban scene, a prime example of the paradox, cited by Stallybrass and White, that "what is socially peripheral is so frequently symbolically central." For men as well as women, the prostitute was a central spectacle in a set of urban encounters and fantasies. Repudiated and desired, degraded and threatening, the prostitute attracted the attention of a range of urban male explorers from the 1840s to the 1880s. Leonore Davidoff assesses the "close affinity" among a long line of urban voyeurs and social investigators who eroticized working women. There is the "sexual scoring" noted by Walter in his notorious diary, *My Secret Life*, the streak of voyeurism that can be

sensed behind the work of a journalist such as Mayhew, the "detailed account of moral depravity in the pages of staid publications such as the *Journal of the Royal Statistical Society*," the "nocturnal wandering in search of conversation with 'women of the streets' which figure in the lives of men like Gladstone," and A. J. Munby's passion for collecting examples of muscular women at work. Uniting all these efforts was a similar "pattern of wandering from place to place in search of encounters, the emotional urgency and the sense of culmination with each 'find'."[21]

The public symbol of female vice, the prostitute established a stark contrast to domesticated feminine virtue as well as to male bourgeois identity[22] she was the embodiment of the corporeal smells and animal passions that the rational bourgeois male had repudiated and that the virtuous woman, the spiritualized "angel in the house," had suppressed. She was also a logo of the divided city itself. When commentators detailed the social geography of vice, extending from the courtesans of St. John's Wood, to the elegantly attired streetwalkers who perambulated around the fashionable shopping districts, to the impoverished women – the "kneetremblers" and "Round-the-corner-Sallies" – committing "acts of indecency" in the ill-lit back alleys and courts of the city's slums,[23] they brought into relief the class structure and general social distribution of London. In these accounts, prostitution appeared in two guises: as disorderly behavior on the part of "soiled doves," sauntering down the city thoroughfares, dangerous in their collectivity; or as the isolated activity of the lone streetwalker, a solitary figure in the urban landscape, outside home and hearth, emblematic of urban alienation and the dehumanization of the cash nexus.[24] In both cases, they stood in stark opposition to the classical elite bodies of female civil statuary that graced the city squares: they were female grotesques, evocative of the chaos and illicit secrets of the labyrinthine city.

By the 1840s, literary accounts invested considerable emotion and anxiety in the lonely figure of the streetwalker; she had become both an object of pity and a dangerous source of contagion. This new concern found powerful expression in Dickens' fiction and in the illustrations accompanying his texts: when in *David Copperfield* (1849–50), David and Mr. Peggotty seek out the streetwalker Martha to help them in their search for the seduced Emily, they spot a "solitary female figure" walking towards the Thames. Contemplating the scene at the river edge, an environmental nightmare of "ooze" and "slush," dominated by the "blighting influence" of the "polluting stream," David mentally associates "the girl" with "the refuse it had cast out and left to corruption and decay."[25]

Dickens' elision of prostitution and excrement was symptomatic of a middle-class concern with immorality, city waste, pollution, and infection emanating from the "Great Unwashed." In the wake of devastating cholera epidemics of 1831 and 1849, sanitary reformers and writers on "moral statistics" used this fear to promote interest in their cause: they identified the prostitute literally and figuratively as the conduit of infection to respectable society – a "plague spot," pestilence, a sore. Like the slums from which she emanated, she carried with her, argues Alain Corbin, the "heavy scents of the masses," with their "disturbing messages of intimate life." She evoked a sensory memory of all the "resigned female bodies" who serviced the physical needs of upper-class men in respectable quarters: in 1888 these resigned but disorderly bodies included the servant girls and nannies who brought the dangers of the streets into the bourgeois home by spreading the latest newspaper account of the Whitechapel "horrors" across the nursery tables.[26]

As the permeable and transgressed border between classes and sexes, as the carrier of physical and moral pollution, the prostitute was the object of considerable public inquiry as well as the object of individual preoccupation for respectable Victorians. Official concern over prostitution as a dangerous form of sexual activity, whose boundaries had to be controlled and defined by the state, led to the passage of the first Contagious Diseases Act in 1864 (followed by the Acts of 1868 and 1869), which provided for a medical and police inspection of prostitutes in garrison towns and ports.[27]

Regulationists praised the supervision and inspection of prostitutes as a defense of public health, public decency, and public order. In pressuring for the medical inspection of prostitutes while refusing to impose periodic genital examination on the enlisted men who were their clients, architects of the acts reinforced a double standard of sexual morality, which justified male sexual access to a class of "fallen" women. They were confident about the physiological imperative of sexual desire for men but often hedged their bets in relation to women. On the one hand, regulationists condemned prostitutes as so "unsexed" that they exhibited "male lust"; on the other hand, they insisted that sexual desire on the part of prostitutes did not enter into the picture at all. A report of the Royal Commission in 1871 insisted that there was "no comparison to be made between prostitutes and the men who consort with them. With the one sex the offense is a matter of gain; with the other it is an irregular indulgence of a natural impulse."[28]

Regulationists also exhibited considerable enthusiasm for state intervention into the lives of the poor. Although such Acts were ostensibly passed as sanitary measures to control the spread of venereal disease, their local administration extended well beyond the sanitary supervision of common prostitutes. The Acts were part of institutional and legal efforts to contain the occupational and geographic mobility of the casual laboring poor, to clarify the relationship between the unrespectable and respectable poor, and specifically to force prostitutes to accept their status as public women by destroying their private associations with the poor working-class community.

Regulation would also contribute to public decency, its defenders argued, by checking the public spectacle of vice. Middle-class commentators repeatedly complained of the physical and visual aggressiveness of the "painted creatures," with their "gaudy dress," aggressive gaze, and provoking deportment.[29] For this reason, London Metropolitan police eagerly awaited the extension of the Acts to London, where they hoped to institute a system of *police de moeurs* to supervise and contain the street disorder of West End prostitutes.[30]

The Metropolitan police's dreams were shattered, however, when a successful opposition of middle-class moral reformers, feminists, and radical workingmen forced the repeal of regulation in 1886. This political campaign impinged on the imaginary cityscape of the flaneur in two ways. The repeal campaign brought thousands of respectable women, the "shrieking sisterhood," into the political arena for the first time, thus disturbing the public/private division of space along gender lines so essential to the male spectator's mental mapping of the civic order. Moreover, the repeal campaign and the social purity movement which it inspired significantly impinged on the public face of London prostitution. With regulation and confinement out of the question, London police found themselves increasingly under pressure from social purity and antivice groups to suppress the indoor resorts of West End prostitutes – Cremorne Gardens, the Argyll Rooms, the Holborn dancing casino, the infamous nighthouses at Haymarket – as well as to clear public thoroughfares and theaters of street-walkers to make room for respectable women. For the next twenty years, the police would be forced to instigate periodic crackdowns which moved prostitutes temporarily to other quarters, or from sites of commercial sex into the streets, and subjected law enforcement authorities to outcries against the false arrests of respectable women. Crackdowns and ensuing scandals would keep prostitution before the "public" eye as a confusing and protean identity that invoked the larger question of women and civil society.[31] ...

NOTES

1 Henry James, "London," in *Essays in London and Elsewhere* (Freeport, NY: Books for Libraries, 1922 [first pub. 1893]) pp. 27, 32.
2 Henry James, *The Complete Notebooks of Henry James*, ed. Leon Edel (New York: Oxford University Press, 1987), pp. 215–18; James, "London," pp. 7, 14.
3 Richard Sennett, *The Fall of Public Man* (Cambridge: Cambridge University Press, 1973), pp. 135–37; Peter Stallybrass and Allon White, *The Politics and Poetics of Transgression* (Ithaca: Cornell University Press, 1986), p. 139; Griselda Pollock, "Vicarious Excitements: *London: A Pilgrimage* by Gustave Doré and Blanchard Jerrold, 1872," *New Formations 2* (Spring 1988): 28.
4 Jane Flax, "Postmodernism and Gender Relations in Feminist Theory," *Signs* 12, no. 4 (Summer 1987): 624.
5 Susan Buck-Morss, "The Flaneur, the Sandwichman, and the Whore: The Politics of Loitering," *New German Critique 13*, no. 39 (1986): 106; Walter Benjamin, quoted in ibid., 106, ibid., 105.
6 James, "London," p. 27.
7 Gareth Stedman Jones, *Outcast London: A Study in the Relationship Between Classes in Victorian Society* (Oxford: Clarendon Press, 1971); Frank Miller Turner, *Between Science and Religion: The Reaction to Scientific Naturalism in Late-Victorian England* (New Haven: Yale University Press, 1974); Colin Ford and Brian Harrison, *A Hundred Years Ago: Britain in the 1880s in Words and Photographs* (Cambridge: Harvard University Press, 1983); Norman MacKenzie and Jeanne MacKenzie, *The Fabians* (New York: Simon and Schuster, 1977); T. J. Jackson Lears, *No Place of Grace: Anti-modernism and the Transformation of American*

Culture, 1880–1920 (New York: Pantheon, 1981); Richard Wightman Fox and T. J. Jackson Lears, eds., *The Culture of Consumption: Critical Essays in American History, 1880–1980* (New York: Pantheon, 1983).

8   This norm involved the merger of aristocratic and middle-class norms; it was a secularized version of "muscular Christianity" with a decidedly greater emphasis on the muscular than the Christian. As historians note, it may have subjected men to a greater degree of emotional deprivation than the moral strictures of evangelical Christianity, which at least offered an outlet of intense emotion in religious expression. See J. A. Mangan and James Walvin, eds., *Manliness and Morality: Middle-Class Masculinity in Britain and America, 1800–1940* (New York: St. Martin's Press, 1987); Ronald Hyam, *Empire and Sexuality: The British Experience* (Manchester: Manchester University Press, 1990), pp. 71–3; Janet Oppenheim, *"Shattered Nerves": Doctors, Patients, and Depression in Victorian England* (New York: Oxford University Press, 1991), pp. 146–51.

9   On Tom and Jerry, see Deborah Epstein Nord, "The City as Theater: From Georgian to Early Victorian London," *Victorian Studies* 31, no. 2 (Winter 1988): 159–88. On reading the city, see William Sharpe and Leonard Wallock, "From 'Great Town' to 'Nonplace Urban Realm': Reading the Modern City," in *Visions of the Modern City: Essays in History, Art, and Literature*, ed. William Sharpe and Leonard Wallock (Baltimore: Johns Hopkins University Press, 1987), p. 9.

10 Peter Keating, ed., Introduction, *Into Unknown England, 1866–1913: Selections from the Social Explorers* (Glasgow: William Collins and Sons, 1976), p. 16; Pollock, "Vicarious Excitements," p. 28; George R. Sims, *My Life: Sixty Years' Recollections of Bohemian London* (London: Eveleigh Nash, 1917), p. 101; James Greenwood, *The Wilds of London* (1874; rpt., New York: Garland, 1985).

11 See Deborah Epstein Nord, "The Social Explorer as Anthropologist: Victorian Travellers among the Urban Poor," in *Visions of the Modern City*, ed. Sharpe and Wallock, pp. 122–34; George W. Stocking, *Victorian Anthropology* (New

York: The Free Press, 1987); Adam Kuper, *The Invention of Primitive Society* (London and New York: Routledge and Kegan Paul, 1988).

12 They did not always sustain this separation throughout the texts: as Mayhew detailed the lives of his street folk, observes Catherine Gallagher, "these charges evaporate." Mayhew's ethnography of wandering tribes conflicted with what Gareth Stedman Jones describes as Mayhew's understanding "in embryo" of the "specificity of the London economy," its prevalence of casual trades, low wages, underemployment, that explained the "improvident" habits of the London worker. Catherine Gallagher, "The Body versus the Social Body in the Works of Thomas Malthus and Henry Mayhew," in *The Making of the Modern Body: Sexuality and Society in the Nineteenth Century*, ed. Catherine Gallagher and Thomas Laqueur (Berkeley: University of California Press, 1987), pp. 83–106; Jones, *Outcast London*.

13 "By condensing the 'abnormal' practices of the slum in the figure of the savage Irishman," Engels attempted to protect the English proletariat from conflation with the filth and squalor of their environment (Stallybrass and White, *Politics and Poetics of Transgression*, p. 132). As Gertrude Himmelfarb observes, Mayhew imagined the costermongers more as "a species in the Darwinian sense than a class in the Marxian." As urban primitives, they were likened to the Bushmen and Hottentots of Africa, subjected to the same anthropological scrutiny and classification as subhuman. Commentators often fixed on their animalistic bodies; in Mayhew's case, on the unnaturally robust health of the street traders who parasitically lived off the labor of the productive poor; or, in the cases of Engels and Dickens, the starving, enfeebled bodies of the industrial classes. Gertrude Himmelfarb, "The Culture of Poverty," in *The Victorian City: Images and Realities*, 2 vols., eds. H. J. Dyos and Michael Wolff (London and Boston: Routledge and Kegan Paul, 1973), 2:712; Gertrude Himmelfarb, *The Idea of Poverty: England in the Early Industrial Age* (New York: Vintage, 1985).

14 James Greenwood, *Low Life Deeps: An Account of the Strange Fish to be Found There* (London: Chatto and Windus,

1876). Henry Mayhew, *London Labour and the London Poor*, 4 vols. (1861; rpt, New York: Dover, 1968), 3:233, quoted by Jones, *Outcast London*, p. 30.

15 Visual interpretations like *London: A Pilgrimage* helped to sustain nostalgic and anachronistic representations of London in the last decades of the century. See Pollock, "Vicarious Excitements."

16 Stallybrass and White, *Politics and Poetics of Transgression*, pp. 5–6.

17 Urban explorers' efforts to marginalize the "low-Other" reveals an "operative ambivalence," akin to the psychological conflict manifested by the imperialist towards the colonial Other. Stallybrass and White, *Politics and Poetics of Transgression*, p. 5. See also Edward Said, *Orientalism* (New York: Vintage Books, 1979), pp. 3, 7. "Orientalism," the myth of the Middle East constructed by Europe to justify its authority, explains Said, "depends for its strategy on a flexible *positional* superiority, which puts the Westerner in a whole series of possible relationships with the Orient without ever losing him the upper hand."

18 Greenwood, "A Night in the Workhouse" in Keating, *Into Unknown England*, p. 34.

19 This proved to be the sensational climax of his *Morning Chronicle* series in 1849 and 1850. Henry Mayhew, "Second Test – Meeting of needlewoman forced to take to the streets," in *The Unknown Mayhew*, ed. Eileen Yeo and E. P. Thompson (New York: Schocken Books, 1972), p. 168.

20 Mary P. Ryan, *Women in Public: Between Banner and Ballots, 1825–1880* (Baltimore: Johns Hopkins University Press, 1990); Laura Mulvey, "Visual Pleasure and Narrative Cinema," *Screen* 16, no. 3 (Autumn 1975): 6–18.

21 Leonore Davidoff, "Gender and Class in Victorian England: The Diaries of Arthur J. Munby and Hannah Cullwick," *Feminist Studies* 5 (Spring 1979): 87–141.

22 Feminist deconstructionists like Mary Poovey argue that men construct their own identities in opposition to what they have ascribed to women. See Mary Poovey, *Uneven Developments: The Ideological Work of Gender in Mid-Victorian England* (Chicago: University of Chicago Press, 1988), chap. 1.

23 See Judith R. Walkowitz, "Dangerous Sexualities," in *Storia delle Donne*, ed.

Michelle Perrot and Georges Duby (Rome: Laterza, 1991).

24 As Deborah Nord observes, early nineteenth-century observers interpreted the solitary prostitute as alter ego for the male spectator, himself an outsider and stranger. De Quincey, for example, has his "Opium Eater" observe: "Being myself at that time of necessity a peripatetic, or a walker of the streets, I naturally fell in more frequently with those female peripatetics who are technically called street walkers." Deborah Epstein Nord, "The City as Theater," p. 181.

25 Charles Dickens, *David Copperfield*, quoted in Lynda Nead, *Myths of Sexuality: Representations of Women in Victorian Britain* (Oxford: Blackwell, 1988), pp. 126–7.

26 Frank Mort, *Dangerous Sexualities: Medico-Moral Politics in England since 1830* (London: Routledge and Kegan Paul, 1987), p. 18; Deborah Epstein Nord, "The Urban Peripatetic: Spectator, Streetwalker, Woman Writer" (unpublished essay), p. 15; Alain Corbin, "Commercial Sexuality in Nineteenth-Century France: A System of Images and Regulations," trans. Katherine Streip, *Representations* 14 (Spring 1986): 212–13.

27 Judith R. Walkowitz, *Prostitution and Victorian Society: Women, Class, and the State* (New York: Cambridge University Press, 1980).

28 *Parliamentary Papers* (1871) 29, C.408, "Report of the Royal Commission on the Administration and Operation of the Contagious Diseases Acts 1868–69."

29 Cited in Henry Mayhew and Bracebridge Hemyng, "The Prostitute Class Generally," in Mayhew, *London Labour and the London Poor*, 4:205.

30 Robert D. Storch, "Police Control of Street Prostitution in Victorian London: A Study in the Context of Police Action," in *Police and Society*, ed. David H. Bayley (Beverly Hills and London: Sage, 1977), pp. 49–72.

31 Ibid.; Edward J. Bristow, *Vice and Vigilance: Purity Movements in Britain since 1700* (Dublin: Gill and Macmillan, 1977); Judith R. Walkowitz, "Male Vice and Feminist Virtue: Feminism and the Politics of Prostitution in Nineteenth-Century Britain," *History Workshop Journal* 13 (Spring 1982): 77–93.

from *The Sphinx in the City: Urban Life, the Control of Disorder, and Women*

Elizabeth Wilson

The City of the Floating World: Paris

I shall...only think of amusing myself; a business never performed anywhere with so much ease as at Paris...this gay, bright, noisy, restless city – this city of the living. Mrs Frances Trollope, *Paris and the Parisians* (1836)

Meanwhile the restaurants were closing and their lights began to go out. Under the trees of the boulevards there were still a few people strolling to and fro, barely distinguishable in the gathering darkness. From time to time the shadowy figure of a woman gliding up to Swann, murmuring a few words in his ear, asking him to take her home, would make him start. Anxiously he brushed past all these dim forms, as though among the phantoms of the dead, in the realms of darkness, he had been searching for a lost Eurydice. Marcel Proust, *Swann's Way* (1913)

Paris became 'the capital of the nineteenth century', the capital in terms of pleasure, excitement and consumption. Other European cities, Vienna, for example, cultivated an expansive public life, in promenades, cafés and theatres – unlike gloomy, reclusive London. Yet it was Paris that became the byword for everything that was enchanting and intoxicating about the urban scene.

The centralised nature of French life encouraged this especially rich and varied culture. Everything was drawn to Paris, which became the overheated source of all social, intellectual and artistic expression. The Goncourt brothers, Jules and Edmond, viewed this centralisation with alarm:

We talked about the absence of intellectual life in the French provinces, compared with all the active literary societies in the English counties and second or third-class German towns; about the way Paris absorbed everything, attracted everything, and did everything; and about the future of France which, in the circumstances, seemed destined to die of a cerebral haemorrhage. (Baldick, 1984, p. 83)

Above all, Paris was the city sexualised. Poets sometimes likened Paris to a prostitute, but more often sang her praises as a queen (Citron, 1961, ch. 17). Either way, the city was inescapably female.

Some of the nineteenth-century anti-urbanists saw cities as harbingers of death. On the other hand, the 1881 Census of Paris appeared to support the opposite view: that nineteenth-century urban civilisation was essentially 'erotic' because the age of the metropolitan population was skewed in the direction of the young and fit: there were fewer children and old people, and more adolescents and young adults. Therefore, the city's 'marriage and birth rates and its productive force should be greater...the population is of an age at which vigour, mental and physical activity and productive force, and consequently all the appetites and sexual needs are at their height' (Chevalier, 1973, pp. 20–1).

This cannot, though, explain the gaiety of Paris, since other cities experienced the same population patterns without gaining a similar reputation; 'erotic' was hardly the adjective that mid-nineteenth-century London called to mind, despite its prostitutes, nor was it a city of pleasure.

Paris the capital of pleasure was also Paris the city of revolutions and uprisings. For a century, France was periodically racked by revolution, interspersed with periods of political repression, and not until the Third Republic was thoroughly established in the 1880s were the competing spectres of monarchy and anarchy laid to rest.

These two aspects of Paris – pleasure and revolution – were closely linked. According to Victor Hugo's account, two of the first casualties of the 1848 uprising (which toppled Louis Philippe, the 'bourgeois' constitutional monarch, from his throne) were prostitutes, 'beautiful, dishevelled, terrible'. They mounted the barricades, raised their skirts to their waists and dared the National Guard to fire 'into the belly of a woman'. Both were shot down.

This account is probably inaccurate. A London journal of the period, reporting what is likely to have been the same incident, described the women as advancing respectably dressed and throwing stones at the soldiery. Hugo's embellishment of the incident is significant as an example of the way in which revolutionary activity was sexualised – to the nineteenth-century bourgeoisie the 'red whore' was one of the most frightening spectres of urban life (Hertz, 1983). Conservatives linked the political excesses of the 1789 French Revolution to sexual freedom and anarchy. And, if Paris was the crucible both of sexual freedom and of political revolution, the link that joined them was the female form. A woman was actually the symbol of the French Revolution.

During the Revolution, women had taken part in public pageants playing the part of the Goddess of Reason, and the spectacle that was Paris repeatedly assigned women a representational or symbolic role, which placed them firmly within a realm of pleasure for the most part devoid of real power. Statues of women, for example, adorned the often severe buildings of Paris in astonishing numbers, and from all periods. Sometimes they represented grandiose abstractions: Victory, Justice, France herself; but they might as easily appear to signify sheer lust and hedonism. The female form might even stand for such mundane enterprises as the telephone system, and by the turn of the century the art nouveau posters of Alphonse Mucha had introduced the commercialised seduction of womanhood into advertisements for cigarettes and railway travel.

Meanwhile, the lot of most working-class Parisiennes was, as in other cities, one of relentless toil. The main reason for prostitution, which was widespread, was poverty; many young women, and particularly those on their own without a family, were more or less starving.

As in London, men were usurping what had traditionally been women's work. In 1873 a detailed investigation of women's work in France revealed that women were crowded into the least skilled and most poorly paid sectors of employment, and that since a survey of 1847, women's employment opportunities had narrowed, and the number of woman workers had actually declined, proportionately. One consequence of this was that there were 68 per cent more female than male paupers. Although some women were still to be found in every kind of work, the author of the survey described woman roofers, for example, as 'deviations from the natural order of things, abnormal protestations against the physical weakness of the frail sex'.

Also as in London, the majority of women were employed in the needlework trades. Another important source of employment was in retail. Saleswomen formed an indeterminate class, and it was hard 'to decide whether they are workers, servants or clerks'. These young women put the finishing touches to goods for sale – decorating, wrapping and sometimes delivering. The author of the report noticed that some of these women were among the best dressed working women – in fact, their appearance in shops was part of the sales pitch – but were less well paid than many factory workers (Leroy-Beaulieu, 1873; Zola, 1970).

The social ambiguity of the salesgirl would have been impossible anywhere but in the huge and anonymous city. This ambiguity was a source of alarm to the moralist, and, as in London, the forces of order and reform sought ruthlessly to regulate the lives of women in the city. Prostitution was the subject, in France as in Britain, of persistent debate and moral outrage, and it was in fact from Paris that the first major investigation of prostitution emerged: Dr Parent-Duchâtelet's work *On Prostitution*, published in 1836, upon which many of the later English surveys were modelled.

Parent-Duchâtelet was a member of the Paris Board of Health, and voluntarily undertook a series of general reports on the consequences of urban growth. He investigated the sewers (Victor Hugo based his famous description of the Paris sewers in *Les Misérables* on Parent-Duchâtelet's (1836) reports), and drew a parallel between the study of drains and the study of prostitutes:

> If I have been able to creep into the sewers, handle putrid matter, spend some of my time on muck heaps and in some sort live in the midst of all that is most abject and disgusting...without scandalising anyone...why should I blush to approach a sewer of another kind (a sewer I admit, fouler than the rest) in the well founded hope of doing some good...If I engage in research on prostitutes, must I necessarily be sullied by my contact?

Officialdom saw prostitutes as simply a conduit of filth.

Parent-Duchâtelet returned again and again in his treatise to the 'disorder' that

prostitutes caused, a disorder which he linked directly to the political disorder of the French Revolution. It was to inaugurate a form of surveillance to control the 'disorder' that 'in 1796 the municipal authorities ordered a new census of all prostitutes. From 1816 all prostitutes were supposed to be officially registered, and after 1828 each had to produce a birth certificate, and had her own "dossier".' Parent-Duchâtelet argued that this individualisation of each woman was necessary because the better the authorities knew the women in question the more successful the surveillance would be.

Michel Foucault has discussed this insistence on the accumulation of facts and information in *Discipline and Punish* and other works, and has argued that it was (and is) a means of controlling the individual through knowledge. He sees it as a pervasive feature of nineteenth- and twentieth-century life. It appeared necessary because of the way in which urban life was breaking down the rigid distinctions between the classes, to create a disorientating confusion as to who was who. In such an ambiguous world, no wonder, wrote Parent-Duchâtelet, that working girls were drawn to prostitution out of vanity and because they wished to shine on this brightly lit stage:

> When simplicity of dress and even more strongly shabbiness of any kind are a source of absolute opprobrium, is it surprising that so many young girls slide into seduction for the sake of a costume they long for, and even more to the extent that this outfit enables them in a manner of speaking to escape from the station in life to which they were born and permits them to mingle with a class by which they might otherwise think themselves despised? (ibid. pp. 91–2)

This perception accurately linked the importance of dress with the uncertainty and anonymity of urban life. The city was a spectacle, and in the right costume a woman – or a man – could escape into a new identity. Such, at any rate, was a widely held belief about the great nineteenth-century city. To what extent individuals were really able to escape their origins is less certain (Clarke, 1984), but undoubtedly many reformers believed that anonymity not only made it possible, but also presented an insidious challenge to law and order.

Paris in the 1830s and 1840s was still a medieval city. Each neighbourhood was a maze of winding streets and hidden courtyards. Eugène Sue described the Ile de la Cité near Notre Dame Cathedral, a notorious haunt of criminals, as 'a labyrinth of obscure crooked and narrow streets... wretched houses with scarcely a window, and those of worm-eaten frames without any glass; dark, infectious looking alleys [leading] to still darker staircases' (Sue, n.d., p. 9). The lack of through roads meant that it was difficult to move freely from one's own *quartier* to another part of town.

The 1830s and 1840s in Old Paris were the great decades of the bohemians. Bohemian Paris was a Paris of students and artists, of poverty and desperate ambition. The students were wanderers (bohemians – gypsies) in their rejection of bourgeois stability, but they clung like limpets to the attics and cafés of the Latin Quarter.

Bohemian Paris sheltered many young women who lived outside the bounds of bourgeois respectability. Arsène Houssaye, who was a bohemian in his youth, but became director of the Comédie Française under Napoleon III, described the gaily dressed '*grisettes*' as 'janitors' daughters in rebellion, dressmakers' apprentices who had snapped their needles, chambermaids who had thrown their bonnets over the rooftops, governesses who had tasted too fully of the tree of knowledge, actresses without a theatre, romantics in search of Prince Charming' (Knepler, 1972, p. 38).

Jules Vallès, another bohemian, but a leftwing one – he played an active role in the 1870 Commune – painted a grimmer picture of the life of the *grisette*: 'If she flourished in the Latin Quarter it was certainly not in my time', he wrote. He described how one, Pavillon, who was said

to have been mistress to a whole circle of well-known bohemians (including Henri Murger himself, the author of the bestseller *La Bohème*), broke down completely, physically and mentally, and ended her life in an asylum (Richardson, 1969, p. 76).

Flora Tristan and George Sand, both of whom were feminists and also revolutionary socialists, represented a different model for emancipated womanhood in the romantic Bohemia of the 1830s and 1840s. George Sand openly took lovers, occasionally wore male dress and smoked in public. According to one (rather hostile) account, she inspired a generation of bohemian women, who showed 'disdain of what became their sex, and a pursuit of glaring eccentricity'. They were called Les Lionnes (the lionesses – as in 'literary lion'). They 'affected to disdain the feminine graces' and went in for sports, drinking and cigar-smoking (ibid., p. 41).

Whereas the dominant progressive trends in Britain were utilitarian reformism and evangelical Christianity, Frenchwomen were more likely to be influenced by utopian or revolutionary socialism. Both Flora Tristan and George Sand lived independent lives in the leftwing culture of Paris, although the existence of a strong socialist tradition did not mean that the equality of women was high on the agenda. The attitudes of socialist groups varied. The Saint-Simonians believed in the equality of women, but the followers of Charles Fourier were less egalitarian (Dijkstra, 1984, p. 21).

George Sand was one of the most successful of nineteenth-century French writers, yet is most remembered – and was famous at the time – for her love affairs and flouting of the conventions. She described how, disguised as a man, she could experience the pleasure of being a *flâneur* – a stroller, that quintessentially Parisian way of relating to the modern industrial city of the nineteenth century: 'no one knew me, no one looked at me...I was an atom lost in that immense crowd' (Moers, 1978, p. 9) – an experience denied most middle-class women.

As industrialisation proceeded and the bourgeoisie expanded and prospered, Paris became yet gayer. Café concerts, for example, which offered entertainment and refreshment in a sheltered yet open-air environment, became more and more popular. The French middle class lived in much more overcrowded circumstances than its London counterpart, in cramped apartments rather than large houses. Whole families were therefore more likely to go out together, to enjoy the vibrant street and café life offered by the capital. . . .

In the mid century, under the 'Second Empire' (1851–70) presided over by Louis Napoleon, Napoleon III, Paris was re-invented. The Second Empire was a hysterical spectacle of luxury borne aloft on a bubble of stockmarket and property speculation, yet it produced the very solid monument of a magnificently rebuilt city. Ironically, or perhaps appropriately, Georges Haussmann, the agent of this transformation, financed the whole enterprise by means of floating debts which led ultimately to his downfall.

Napoleon III had long cherished a dream of rebuilding Paris in a suitably imperial style, as his uncle, the great Napoleon, had planned. It seems possible that he was influenced by utopian socialist plans for ideal cities of the future, plans that were usually highly rationalistic and symbolic; the plan for the new Paris also incorporated a revival of Renaissance town planning.

In 1853 he appointed Georges Haussmann as Prefect of the Seine, and within the space of sixteen years Paris was transformed. Haussmann and Louis Napoleon drove wide new streets and boulevards through the densely crowded quarters of central Paris, connecting east to west and north to south. In place of the slums of the Ile de la Cité there rose uniform, imposing offices and apartment blocks. Les Halles, the old central markets (removed in the 1970s), and the rebuilt Opéra were among the most ambitious constructions. The Bois de Boulogne was designed on the 'romantic' English model of Hyde Park, and

became the parade ground of high society and the demimonde (Pinkney, 1958, passim).

Napoleon and Haussmann devised new building regulations prescribing the heights of buildings, the harmony and uniformity of the new frontages and rules regulating the maintenance of the exteriors. Behind the high façades of the new buildings, however, over-crowding was as bad as ever.

Many condemned the ruthless thrust of the boulevards as counter-revolutionary: in the old narrow streets it had been relatively easy to throw up barricades and for insurrectionaries to melt away and escape arrest. Permanent barracks were indeed built at strategic points, yet even more significant were the railway stations and railway lines that brought thousands of visitors and migrants to the city. New streets created a 'circulatory and respiratory system' for modern traffic and movement. In this way Haussmann, by means of the physical changes he wrought, enhanced the 'modern' quality of the nineteenth-century capital, with its constant flux and movement (Choay, 1969).

Haussmann was also accused of having built a second, industrial Paris in the plain of St Denis – what one writer described as a Siberia 'crisscrossed with winding unpaved paths, without lights, without shops, with no water laid on'. Whether or not there was a deliberate attempt to banish artisans and workers to the industrial suburbs, the classes in the city began to be more segregated. A further paradox of the 'modern' city was that even as its inhabitants experienced it as more fragmented and disorientating, the regulation of the new mass society tightened (Clarke, 1984, p. 29).

During the Second Empire political repression perhaps even, ironically, added to the gaiety of the capital. Jacques Offenbach's popular operettas, which incorporated veiled social satire, distilled the glittering hedonism of the 1850s and 1860s. Government censorship and repression created a depoliticised bohemia, in which opposition was stifled, or at least displaced, reappearing as frivolity and moral nihilism, and yet enriching the artistic atmosphere. (Kracauer, 1937, p. 202).

As the Parisian middle class grew rich, the classic bohemia went into decline. The growth of industry impoverished the artisan and petty bourgeois families from which many of the students and clerks of bohemian circles had come, and by the late 1840s the *flâneur* had replaced the bohemian of an earlier period.

The *flâneur* lived on the boulevards, and made the streets and cafés of Paris his drawing room. Like the bohemian, the *flâneur* often lived on his literary wits: the turbulence of the fast-expanding cities gave birth in Paris, as in London, to a whole new journalistic literature of vignettes, anecdotes and 'travellers' tales'.

The difference between the bohemian and the *flâneur* was that while the bohemian had been passionately emotional, the *flâneur* was a detached observer. He caught the fleeting, fragmentary quality of modern urban life, and, as a rootless outsider, he also identified with all the marginals that urban society produced. In particular he empathised not so much with the organised working class as with the down and outs: the ragpickers, the semi-criminal and the deviant.

The ragpickers were one of the most abject and notorious groups in Parisian society. They lived like nomads in shanty towns near the *barrières*, the areas close to the city limits and town gates; and of all the bizarre kinds of work that the growing urban scene produced at this period of early industrial capitalism, none was more symbolic than theirs.

In Paris, as in London, refuse, dirt and dust threatened to overwhelm the gaudy edifice of urban civilisation. Rubbish was the inevitable end product of the whirl of sensual fulfilment in the restaurants, concerts and brothels; and at the same time formed the foundations upon which the city of pleasure was built. The dust heap was the unspeakable aspect of the city of charm and light.

The ragpickers in their hovels represented the 'Other' of Paris, the underside of the city of gaiety and pleasure. Writers such as Charles Baudelaire and Gérard de Nerval were particularly drawn to these outcasts, because just as the scavengers searched the dust heaps for hidden silver cutlery, accidentally thrown away (Frégier, 1840, pp. 104–10), so did Baudelaire and de Nerval, as writers of the city, seek out the forgotten or unnoticed treasures of urban life to record and embellish.

For Baudelaire, both writers and ragpickers were outcasts to some extent. The writer understood the inner meaning of the city and revealed it in his poetry or prose; the ragpickers symbolised this inner meaning. Karl Marx, by contrast, detested the marginals, whether ragpickers or *flâneurs*, as counter-revolutionaries. He likened the anarchists – double agents and agents-provocateurs of the Parisian underworld – to prostitutes, whose painted faces concealed duplicity and evil (Marx, 1978, pp. 311–25). He saw them as the political rubbish thrown up by urban society. What is interesting about this much harsher and strictly political judgment is the way in which Marx nevertheless uses metaphors similar to those of Baudelaire: prostitution remains at the heart of the city's meaning.

Baudelaire, indeed, believed that poets resembled prostitutes. They had something to sell – their writing. Since this expressed their soul, their truest self, in selling it they were in a sense prostituting themselves.

They resembled prostitutes in another way, for if prostitutes were women of the streets, the poet in his guise as *flâneur* or dandy also walked the streets. Indeed, Baudelaire saw the essential condition of Parisian city life as a kind of universal prostitution created by consumerism, circulating 'securely in the city's clogged heart' (Benjamin, 1973, p. 57).

So, just as the *flâneur* was a prostitute, perhaps also the prostitute could be said to be the female *flâneur*. There were, of course, important differences, but both shared an intimate knowledge of the dark recesses of urban life. They understood, better than anyone, the pitiless way in which the city offered an intensity of joy that was never, somehow, fulfilled. The spectacle melted away just as you felt you had reached its centre; the bubble burst when you touched it. That was the source of the melancholy which lay at the heart of the city of pleasure. None felt this more keenly than Gervaise, the heroine of Emile Zola's novel of Parisian working-class life, as she touched rock bottom, crushed by what seemed like the insatiable appetite of the city itself:

> She walked slowly on. The gas lamps were being lit in the misty darkness, and the long avenues which had gradually disappeared into the shadow reappeared blazing with light, stretching out and slashing a way through the night as far as the vague darkness of the horizon. There was a great breath of life... This was the hour when from end to end of the boulevards pubs... [and] dancehalls flared up with the fun... of the first round of drinks... And the night was very dark, still and freezing... broken only by the fiery lines of the boulevards stretching to the four corners of heaven. (Zola, 1970, pp. 44–5)

In recent years feminists have argued that there could never be a female *flâneur*. They have gone further, to suggest that the urban scene was at all times represented from the point of view of the male gaze: in paintings and photographs men voyeuristically stare, women are passively subjected to the gaze. The public arena – cafés and places of public entertainment such as the Folies Bergères – offered a '*mise en scène*', or setting where men of the bourgeoisie could meet and seduce or purchase working-class women. Middle-class women were restricted to certain limited public spaces designated as respectable: parks and the opera, for example. This division is reflected in the subjects chosen by the Impressionists, painters who devised new techniques to capture the glittering visual fragmentation of the urban scene; Manet, Degas and others painted backstage scenes, bars and brothels, but Berthe Morisot's choice of locations and subject matter was necessar-

ily much more restricted; she often painted domestic scenes (Wolff, 1985; Pollock, 1985).

There has perhaps been a tendency for this argument to be overstated. Women did participate actively as well as passively in the spectacle, and the whole Parisian atmosphere of pleasure and excess, both sexual and political, did create an environment in which women were able to gain certain freedoms – even if the price of this was their over-sexualisation and their participation in what was often a voyeuristic spectacle. In this it was unlike London. There were, of course, important English woman writers – and of these, George Eliot lived with a man who was not her husband. There were also English demi-mondaines. Yet the whole atmosphere of mid-nineteenth-century London was worthier and more serious, and there was much less public life in the shape of concerts and spectacles. This difference was illustrated at the great 1867 Paris Exhibition, when the British pavilion, amid a riot of exotic and luxurious displays from other nations, consisted of 'a Bible Society kiosk, a Protestant church, agricultural machines, a model farm and a school' (Richardson, 1971, p. 149)....

The metaphor of the stock exchange symbolised the linked obsessions of frenzied speculation and sexual experience that gripped the Second Empire. On an unstable financial basis was built a society of consumerism and erotic illusion.

A whole class of demi-mondaines – financiers, entertainers and above all courtesans – occupied a central position in the society of the Second Empire. The courtesans played a directly economic role in two ways. They were the ultimate objects of conspicuous consumption; and they also intervened directly in the economics of speculation, often acting as agents for brokers and financiers, working on a commission basis among their clientele (Kracauer, 1937, pt. 2, ch. 6)....

Paris displayed as its charming everyday self the society of the spectacle in all its glory. Napoleon III inaugurated the Paris

Exhibitions, the first held in 1855. The 1867 International Exhibition in particular was 'the apotheosis of the Second Empire'. The display reached new heights with Chinese tea pavilions, Brazilian temples and Turkish tents: it was a dazzling dream world.

In Paris as in other great cities a more permanent form of the exhibition had also appeared: the department store. The department store was a public space pretending to be a private interior, just as the public street and the cafés became a kind of salon for the *flâneurs*. . . .

The department store created an 'aesthetic demi-monde' for the bourgeoisie in which beauty was for sale as a commodity. Consumption became a substitute for virtue. The department store offered the customer an imitation *vie de château*: shopwalkers and assistants were as if footmen and ladies' maids; the shop was as if an upper-class interior. Yet ultimately this masquerade was a dream, because the bourgeoisie, or at any rate its men, had to work for their wealth, yet longed to be like the leisured aristocracy who owned the ultimate luxury of consumption: time (Williams, 1982; Miller 1981; Bowlby, 1985). . . .

The presence of women created a special and ambiguous atmosphere in these zones, which were public, yet aimed at the intimacy of the private interior. The bourgeoisie, it is true, idealised the woman in the bosom of her family, and bourgeois culture made possible the immense elaboration of the private sphere – after all, what middle-class ladies purchased at The Ladies' Paradise was for the embellishment of themselves, their children and their homes. At the same time, bourgeois consumerism invaded the public sphere, and the very spaces that were permitted to respectable women were in many cases devoted to purchase and sale rather than to morally more elevated activities. There, women looked, as well as being looked at; in any case, it was above all the appearance of respectability that counted. In a sense, respectability itself was just another mask.

Despite the elaboration of the private sphere, women formed an essential element of the crowds in the streets, at the theatre and in the parks. Department stores in their seduction of women created zones such as restaurants, rest rooms and even reading rooms where they could, towards the end of the century, go unchaperoned or certainly free of men's protection. The carriages of fashionable women rolled along the promenades of the Bois de Boulogne, and, of course, women teemed through the *faubourgs*, or outlying working-class districts of Paris.

Not surprisingly, the Second Empire witnessed the development of fashion to an astonishing degree. Charles Frederick Worth (actually an Englishman) invented *haute couture* (high fashion) in the modern sense of the named designer, and created fabulous growns for the Empress Eugénie and her court. The mad extravagance found everywhere else appeared at its most dazzling and most ephemeral in the adornment both of the ladies at court and of the great courtesans.

Baudelaire and his contemporaries experienced the sensations of the new metropolis as 'modern', yet the changes already taking place in Paris generated the beginnings of a sensibility of nostalgia. As Paris was transformed architecturally, the surviving districts of 'Old Paris' became picturesque. This nostalgia became the 'charm' of Paris.

The charm of Paris combined overpowering melancholy at the loss of the past with the loneliness of the 'atom in the crowd'. It was the charm of the alleyways and courtyards lapped in shadow, the bridges and quays of Paris, which were beautiful especially *because* they seemed doomed to crumble before the developer's demolition squad. Shabby, forgotten corners of the city inhabited by the marginals became precious and magical (Citron, 1961, ch. 21).

After the end of the Second Empire, in 1870, Paris lost much of its gaiety, but by the 1890s, the capital was re-established as the city of pleasure. Pleasure now, however, was more fully commercialised, as Paris was becoming a tourist and consumerist mecca in the twentieth-century sense. As part of this, 'the charm of Paris' could itself be commercialised as a myth.

The cabarets and dance halls of Paris now offered the tourist a spectacle which consciously represented an image of 'gay Paree'. By the 1890s the famous Moulin Rouge cabaret was attracting nightly crowds and the Montmartre district, once a charming, semi-rustic backwater, had long since been brought within the city boundary. At the Moulin Rouge tourists crowded to the raucous, sweaty music-hall shows, whose dancers are still familiar today because the painter Henri de Toulouse-Lautrec drew them on his posters for the cabaret and in his paintings of Montmartre low life (Rudorff, 1972, ch. 2). What had once been spontaneous working-class entertainments were now reworked for the consumption of a class of spectators.

Quite apart from prostitution, urban life made possible the emergence of other forbidden sexualities, and in particular a 'gay subculture', first for men and later for women. Homosexuals had known places of rendezvous in the 1830s, and it was claimed that homosexuality was widespread among the dandies of the 1840s (Ibid, pp. 381–2). Baudelaire wrote some of his poems to lesbians; he addressed them as 'disordered souls', as sterile yet noble, devout satyrs, feverish and desiccated. He saw them as bachelors like him, and like him searching for the unattainable. Walter Benjamin, writing about Baudelaire, saw the 'mannishness' of the lesbian as a consequence of industrial work and urban life; this mannishness was part of the 'heroism of modern life'. It was also, nonetheless, another indication of the 'unnaturalness' of city life (Benjamin, 1973, pp. 90, 95).

By the time that Marcel Proust was describing Parisian lesbian and gay circles during the *belle époque* (the period 1890–1910), 'gay identities' were well established. Homosexuals were now a 'race

apart', one of the mysterious and, many felt, sinister groups that inhabited the endless labyrinth that was a great city.

A sexualisation of the spectacle of all aspects of life both degraded women and sometimes offered them the escape of wealth and the freedom of depravity. Toulouse-Lautrec often depicted his singers and prostitutes as lesbians. By 1900 *belle époque* 'pleasure guides' alerted readers to the existence of specialised brothels in which lesbian love played a special role.

At the same time, Paris provided a suitable environment for the growth of a genuine lesbian subculture. The American heiress Nathalie Clifford-Barney opened a lesbian salon. The poet Renée Vivien and the writer Colette lived in this world – which was both condoned and suppressed. Exploited as a titillating perversion, lesbianism was not acceptable as an open way of life. Colette described it as a 'marginal and timorous life, sustained by an out-of-date form of snobbishness'. Although Colette lived with her lesbian lover 'Missy', the Marquise de Belboeuf, for eight years, her recollections are rather mocking:

> How timid I was, at that period when I was trying to look like a boy, and how feminine I was beneath my disguise of cropped hair. 'Who would take us to be women? Why, women.' They alone were not fooled. With such distinguishing marks as pleated shirt front, hard collar, sometimes a waistcoat, and always a silk pocket handkerchief, I frequented a society perishing on the margin of all societies...The clique I am referring to...tried, trembling with fear, to live without hypocrisy, the breathable air of society. This...sect claimed the right of 'personal freedom' and equality with homo-sexuality, that imperturbable establishment. And they scoffed, if in whispers, at 'Papa' Lépine, the Prefect of Police, who never could take lightly the question of women in men's clothes. (Colette, 1971, p. 61)

According to Colette, her lesbian friends were afraid of appearing openly in public in male attire. They wore long trousers and dinner jackets at their private parties, but in the street they covered them with a long cloak, 'which gave them an excessively respectable look'. They did, however, have their own 'dives' – neighborhood cinemas, basement restaurants, a Montmartre cellar run by a woman who was a lesbian herself. . . .

Most of the women associated with St Germain des Prés were highly sexualised figures. Juliette Greco, the *chanteuse* of existentialism, shocked French (and international) society with her informal clothes, lack of make-up and unconventional life, but her role was a familiar one in bohemian terms. In early films by Claude Chabrol and other New Wave directors, Left Bank young women appeared faithless and frail – in Jean-Luc Godard's famous first film, *A bout de souffle* (*Breathless*), for example, Jean Seberg's heroine is responsible for the anti-hero's death. Like Greco, these film characters were sexually and (perhaps even more important) emotionally free, yet otherwise locked into traditional stereotypes (Greco, 1982; Webster and Powell, 1984).

Yet it was this Left Bank movement that provided the context for Simone de Beauvoir's pioneering feminist work *The Second Sex*. Simone de Beauvoir had from the beginning been passionately a Parisienne. Not only was she brought up in Paris, but the personal drama of her intellectual and sexual emancipation seemed inseparable from its setting in the hotels and cafés of Montparnasse and St Germain. In her autobiographies, her assignment to teaching posts in the provincial towns of Rouen

and Marseille appear as forms of exile. She enjoyed the conquest of nature when she climbed the Alpes-Maritimes near Marseille, or took skiing holidays, but real life was Paris. The city provided a world in which you could dispense altogether with the trappings of bourgeois privacy; for years her home was a hotel room; her base was a café; there she wrote her books, ate her meals, met her friends and lovers. The terraces of Les Deux Magots and Le Flore provided her with a role and a setting which de-emphasised her position as merely the partner of a well-known male writer. Unlike the wives and lovers of the American Beats and the English bohemians of 1950s Soho, a well-established public urban world offered her a stage on which she could appear in her own right. For Simone de Beauvoir (1984, pp. 11–12), Paris *was* freedom:

> The most intoxicating aspect of my return to Paris in September 1929, was the freedom I now possessed . . . From my fifth floor balcony I looked out over the Lion of Belfort and the plane trees on the rue Denfert-Rochereau . . . I was free to come and go as I pleased. I could get home with the milk, read in bed all night, sleep until midday, shut myself up for forty-eight hours at a stretch, or go out on the spur of the moment. My lunch was a bowl of borsch at Dominique's, and for supper I took a cup of hot chocolate at La Coupole.

So, in a perhaps unexpected way, Paris, the capital of sexual pleasure, gave birth to the most influential feminist text of all.

REFERENCES

Baldick, Robert (1984) *Pages from the Goncourt Journals*, Harmondsworth: Penguin

Beauvoir, Simone de (1984) *The Prime of Life*, Harmondsworth: Penguin (originally published 1960)

Benjamin, Walter (1973) *Charles Baudelaire: A Lyric Poet in the Era of High Capitalism*, London: New Left Books

Bowlby, Rachel (1985) *Just Looking: Consumer Culture in Dreiser, Gissing and Zola*, London: Methuen

Chevalier, Louis (1973) *Labouring Classes and Dangerous Classes in Paris during the First Half of the Nineteenth Century*, trans. Frank Jellinek, London: Routledge & Kegan Paul

Choay, Françoise (1969) *The Modern City: Planning in the Nineteenth Century*, London: Studio Vista

Citron, Pierre (1961) *La poésie de Paris dans la littérature française de Rousseau à Baudelaire*, Paris: Editions de Minuit

Clarke, T. J. (1984) *The Painting of Modern Life: Paris in the Art of Manet and his Followers*, London: Thames & Hudson

Colette (1971) *The Pure and the Impure*, trans. Herma Briffault, Harmondsworth: Penguin (originally published as *Ces Plaisirs*, 1932.)

Dijkstra, Sandra (1984) 'The City as Catalyst for Flora Tristan's Vision of Social Change', in Squier, ed. (1984)

Frégier, H. -A. (1840) *Des classes dangereuses de la population dans les grandes villes*, Paris: H. Baillière

Greco, Juliette (1982) *Jujube*, Paris: Editions Stock

Hertz, Neil (1983) 'Medusa's Head: Male Hysteria under Political Pressure', *Representations*, vol. 1, no. 4, Fall

Knepler, Henry, ed. (1972) *Man About Paris: The Confessions of Arsène Houssaye*, London: Victor Gollancz

Kracauer, Siegfried (1937) *Jacques Offenbach and the Paris of his Time*, London: Constable

Leroy-Beaulieu, Paul (1873) *Le travail des femmes au XIXe siècle*, Paris: Charpentier

Marx, Karl (1978) 'Review of *Les Conspirateurs* par A. Chenu, and *La Naissance de la république en Février 1848*, par Lucien de la Hodde', in Marx, Karl and Engels, Friedrich (1978) *Collected Works*, vol. 10 (originally published 1851)

Miller, Michael (1981) *The Bon Marché: Bourgeois Culture and the Department Store 1869–1920*, London: Allen & Unwin

Moers, Ellen (1978) *Literary Women*, London: The Women's Press

Parent-Duchâtelet, A. J. B. (1836) *De la prostitution dans la ville de Paris*, Paris: H. Baillière

Pinkney, David H. (1958) *Napoleon III and the Rebuilding of Paris*, Princeton, New Jersey: Princeton University Press

Pollock, Griselda (1985) *Vision and Difference: Femininity, Feminism and Histories of Art*, London: Routledge & Kegan Paul

Richardson, Joanna (1969) *The Bohemians: La Vie de Bohème in Paris 1830–1914*, London: Macmillan

Richardson, Joanna (1971) *La Vie Parisienne 1852–1870*, London: Hamish Hamilton.

Rudorff, Raymond (1972) *Belle Epoque: Paris in the Nineties*, London: Hamish Hamilton

Squier, Susan Merrill ed. (1984) *Women Writers and the City: Essays in Feminist Literary Criticism*, Knoxville: University of Tennessee Press

Sue, Eugène (n.d.) *The Mysteries of Paris*, New York: Daedalus/Hippocrene (originally published 1842–3)

Trollope, Mrs. Frances (1985) *Paris and the Parisiennes*, Gloucester: Alan Sutton.

Webster, Paul and Powell, Nicholas (1984) *Saint Germain-des-Prés*, London: Constable

Williams, Rosalind (1982) *Dream Worlds: Consumption in Late Nineteenth Century France*, Berkeley: University of California Press

Wolff, Janet (1985) 'The Invisible Flâneuse: Women and the Literature of Modernity', *Theory, Culture and Society*, special issue, vol. 2, no. 3, 'The Fate of Modernity'.

Zola, Emile (1970) *L'Assommoir*, trans. Leonard Tancock, Harmondsworth: Penguin (originally published 1876)

46

The Ideal of Community and the Politics of Difference

Iris Marion Young

The ideal of community privileges unity over difference, immediacy over mediation, sympathy over recognition of the limits of one's understanding of others from their point of view. Community is an understandable dream, expressing a desire for selves that are transparent to one another, relationships of mutual identification, social closeness and comfort. The dream is understandable, but politically problematic, I argue, because those motivated by it will tend to suppress differences among themselves or implicitly to exclude from their political groups persons with whom they do not identify. The vision of small, face-to-face, decentralized units that this ideal promotes, moreover, is an unrealistic vision for transformative politics in mass urban society. . . .

The Metaphysics of Presence

Western conceptualization, as expressed both in philosophical writing, other theoretical writing, and quite often everyday speech as well, exhibits what Derrida calls a logic of identity.[1] This metaphysics consists in a desire to think things together in a unity, to formulate a representation of a whole, a totality. It seeks the unity of the thinking subject with the object thought, that the object would be a grasping of the real. The urge to unity seeks to think everything that is a whole or to describe some ontological region, such as social life, as a whole, a system. Such totalization need not be restricted to synchronic conceptualization, moreover. The conceptualization of a process teleologically also exhibits the logic of identity, inasmuch as the end conceptually organizes the process into a unity.

The desire to bring things into unity generates a logic of hierarchical opposition. Any move to define an identity, a closed totality, always depends on excluding some elements, separating the pure from the impure. Bringing particular things under a universal essence, for example, depends on determining some attribute of particulars as accidental, lying outside the essence. Any definition or category creates an inside/outside distinction, and the logic of identity seeks to keep those borders firmly drawn. In the history of Western thought the metaphysics of presence has created a vast number of such mutually exclusive oppositions that structure whole philosophies: subject/object; mind/body, culture/nature, male/female. In the metaphysical tradition the first of these is elevated over the second because it designates the unified, the chaotic, unformed, transforming. Metaphysical thinking makes distinctions and formulates accounts by relying on such oppositions, where one side designates the pure, authentic, good, and the other the impure, inauthentic, bad.

The logic of identity also seeks to understand the subject, the person, as a self-identical unity. Beginning with Descartes, modern philosophy is particularly preoccupied with the unity of consciousness and its immediate presence to itself. The tradition of transcendental philosophy from Descartes through Kant to Husserl conceives the subject as a unity and an origin, the self-same starting point of thought and meaning, whose signification is never out of its grasp.

There are two sorts of criticisms Derrida, Adorno, Kristeva, and others make of the metaphysics of presence. First, its effort to bring things into unity is doomed to failure. The claim to totality asserted by this metaphysics is incoherent, because, as I have already discussed, the process of totalizing itself expels some aspects of the entities. Some of the experienced particulars are expelled to an unaccounted-for, "accidental" realm, what Derrida calls the supplement and Adorno calls the addendum. The move to create totality, as the logic of hierarchical opposition shows, creates not one, but two: inside and outside. The identity or essence sought receives its meaning and purity only by its relation to its outside. What Derrida calls the method of deconstruction consists in showing how with a concept or category what it claims to exclude is implicated in it. Dialectical logic, of course, makes a similar claim. The method of deconstruction, or what Adorno calls negative dialectic, however, rejects the Hegelian method of dialectic. For Hegelian dialectic is the ultimate totalizer, bringing the oppositions generated by metaphysical logic into ultimate unity within a totality.

Second, the metaphysics of presence represses or denies difference. This term has come to carry a great deal of meaning in these philosophical accounts. As I understand it, difference means the irreducible particularity of entities, which makes it impossible to reduce them to commonness or bring them into unity without remainder. Such particularity derives from the contextuality of existence, the being of a thing and what is said about it is a function of its contextual relation to other things. Adorno in particular contrasts the logic of identity with entities in their particularity, which for him also means their materiality. Idealism, which Adorno thinks exhibits the logic of identity, withdraws from such particularity and constructs unreal essences.[2]

Derrida defines difference primarily in terms of the functioning of language, expressing the irreducible spatiotemporality of language. The sign signifies, has meaning, by its place in the chain of signs, by differing from other signs. Any moment of signification also defers, holds in abeyance, any completion of its meaning. Any utterance has a multiplicity of meanings and directions of interpretation and development in which it can be taken. For Derrida, the metaphysics of presence seeks to detemporalize and despatialize this signifying process, inventing the illusion of pure present meaning which eliminates the referential relation. This is idealism: conceiving the being and truth of things as lying outside time and change.[3]

Kristeva more often uses the term *heterogeneity* than difference, but like Derrida and Adorno she suggests that a logic of identity represses heterogeneity, which she associates with the body as well as language. She too focuses on language and the process of signification, especially the speaking subject. The subject is never a unity, but always in process, for Kristeva, producing meaning through the play between the literal and figurative, representational and musical aspects that any speech simultaneously carries.[4]

Along with such writers as Anthony Giddens and Fred Dallmayr, I think the critique of the metaphysics of presence and the claim that we need to attend to the irreducibility of difference have important implications for social philosophy and social theory.[5] I will argue that the ideal of community exhibits the desire for unity these writers find in the metaphysics of presence. Community usually appears as one side of a dichotomy in which individualism is the opposite pole, but as with any such opposition, each side is determined by its relation to the other. I argue that the ideal of community exhibits a totalizing impulse and denies difference in two primary ways. First, it denies the difference within and between subjects. Second, in privileging face-to-face relations it seeks a model of social relations that are not mediated by space and time distancing. In radically opposing the inauthentic social relations of alienated society with the authentic social relations of community, moreover, it detemporalizes the process of social change into a static before and after structure....

Denying Difference Within and Between Subjects

...The communitarian ideal participates in the metaphysics of presence because it conceives that subjects no longer need be exterior to one another. They need no longer outrun one another in directions they do not mutually understand and affirm. The ideal, moreover, extends this mutuality to its conception of the good society as a telos, an end to the conflict and violence of human interaction. Community here is conceived as a totality in two ways. It has no ontological exterior, since it realizes the unity of general will and individual subjectivity. It also has no historical exterior, for there is no further stage to travel.

While she does not specifically speak of her ideal as community, Seyla Benhabib expresses a similar ideal of person relating to one another through reciprocal recognition of subjectivities as a particular standpoint of moral autonomy. Liberalism holds a conception of moral autonomy, what she calls the "standpoint of the generalized other," which abstracts from the difference, desires and feeling among persons, to regard all as sharing a common set of formal rights and duties. In contrast, what Benhabib calls the "standpoint of the concrete other" views each person in his or her concrete individuality.

In assuming this standpoint, we abstract from what continues our commonality and seek to understand the other as he/she understands himself/herself. We seek to comprehend the needs of the other, their motivations, what they search for and what they desire. Our relation to the other is governed by the norm of *complementary reciprocity*: each is entitled to expect and assume from the other forms of behavior through which the other feels recognized and confirmed as a concrete, individual being with specific needs, talents and capacities. Our differences in this case complement rather than exclude one another.[6]

...Many other writers express a similar ideal of relating to other persons internally, understanding them from their point of view. In the quotation previously cited, Sandel poses the elimination of the opacity of other persons as the ideal for community. Isaac Balbus represents the goal of radical politics and the establishment of community as the overcoming of the "otherness" of other in reciprocal recognition.[7] Roberto Unger articulates the ideal of community as the political alternative to personal love. In community persons relate to one another as concrete individuals who recognize themselves in each other because they have shared purposes. The conflict between the demands of individuality and the demands of sociability disappears in mutual sympathy.[8] Dorothy Allison proposes an ideal of community for feminists that is characterized by a "shared feeling of belonging and merging," with an "ecstatic sense of oneness."[9]

All these formulations seek to understand community as a unification of particular persons through the sharing of subjectivities: Persons will cease to be opaque, other, not understood, and instead become fused, mutually sympathetic, understanding one another as they understand themselves....

Such a concept of self-knowledge retains the Cartesian understanding of subjectivity basic to the modern metaphysics of presence. The idea of the self as a unified subject of desire and need and an origin of assertion and action has been powerfully called into question by contemporary philosophers.[10] I will rely on my reading of Julia Kristeva. . . .

. . . Kristeva relies on a psychoanalytic notion of the unconscious to assert that subjectivity is heterogeneous and de-centered. Consciousness, meaning, and intention are only possible because the subject-in-process slips and surpasses its intentions and meanings. Any utterance, for example, not only has a literal meaning, but is laden with ambiguities, embodied in gesture, tone of voice, and rhythm that all contribute to the heterogeneity of its meaning without being intended. So it is with actions and interactions with other persons. What I say and do always has a multiplicity of meanings, ambiguities, plays, and these are not always coher-ent.[11] . . .

If the subject is heterogeneous process, unable to be present to itself, then it follows that subjects cannot make themselves transparent, wholly present to one an-other. . . .

Not only does this ideal of shared sub-jectivity express an impossibility but it has undesirable political implications. Political theorists and activists should distrust this desire for reciprocal recognition and iden-tification with others, I suggest, because it denies difference in the concrete sense of making it difficult for people to respect those with whom they do not identify. I suggest that the desire for mutual under-standing and reciprocity underlying the ideal of community is similar to the desire for identification that underlies racial and ethnic chauvinism. . . .

Denial of Difference as Time and Space Distancing

Many political theorists who put forward an ideal of community specify small-group, face-to-face relations as essential to the realization of that ideal.

. . . I take there to be several problems with the privileging of face-to-face rela-tions by theorists of community. It pre-sumes an illusory ideal of unmediated social relations and wrongly identifies me-diation with alienation. It denies difference in the sense of time and space distancing. It implies a model of the good society as con-sisting of decentralized small units, which is both unrealistic and politically undesirable. Finally, it avoids the political question of the relation among the decentralized com-munities.

All the writers cited previously give pri-macy to face-to-face presence because they claim that only under those conditions can the social relations be *immediate*. I under-stand them to mean several things by social relations that are immediate. They are direct, personal relations, in which each understands the other in her or his individu-ality. This is an extension of the ideal of mutual understanding I have criticized in the previous section. Immediacy also here means relations of co-presence in which persons experience a simultaneity of speak-ing and hearing and are in the same space, that is, have the possibility to move close enough to touch.[12]

This ideal of the immediate presence of subjects to one another, however, is a meta-physical illusion. Even a face-to-face rela-tion between two people is mediated by voice and gesture, spacing and temporality. As soon as a third person enters the inter-action, the possibility arises of the relation between the first two being mediated through the third, and so on. The medi-ation of relations among persons by speech and actions of still other persons is a funda-mental condition of sociality. The richness, creativity, diversity, and potential of a soci-ety expand with growth in the scope and means of its media, linking persons across time and distance. The greater the time and distance, however, the greater the number of persons who stand between other per-sons.

The normative privileging of face-to-face relations in the ideal of community seeks to suppress difference in the sense of the time and space distancing of social processes, which material media facilitate and en-large. Such an ideal dematerializes its con-ception of interaction and institutions. For all social interaction takes place over time and across space. Social desire consists in the urge to carry meaning, agency, and the effects of agency beyond the moment and beyond the place. As laboring subjects we separate the moment of production from the moment of consumption. Even societies confined to a limited territory with few institutions and a small population devise means of their members communicating with one another over distances, means of maintaining their social relationships even though they are not face to face. Societies occupy wider and wider territorial fields and increasingly differentiate their activity in space, time, and function, a movement that, of course, accelerates and takes on qualitatively specific form in modern industrial societies.[13]

I suggest that there are no conceptual grounds for considering face-to-face relations more pure, authentic social relations than relations mediated across time and distance. For both face-to-face and non-face-to-face relations are mediated relations, and in both there is as much the possibility of separation and violence as there is communication and consensus. Theorists of community are inclined to privilege face-to-face relations, I suggest, because they wrongly identify mediation and alienation.

By alienation, I mean a situation in which persons do not have control either over their actions, the conditions of their action, or the consequences of their action, due to the intervention of other agents.[14] Social mediation is a condition for the possibility of alienation in this sense; media make possible the intervention of agents between the conditions of a subject's action and the action or between a subject's action and its consequences. Thus, media make domination and exploitation possible. In modern society the primary structures creating alienation and domination are bureaucracy and commodification of all aspects of human activity, including and especially labor. Both bureaucracy and commodification of social relations depend on complex structures of mediation among a large number of persons.

That mediation is a necessary condition of alienation, however, does not entail the reverse implication: That only by eliminating structures of mediation do we eliminate alienation. If temporal and spatial distancing are basic to social processes, and if persons always mediate between other persons to generate social networks, then a society of immediacy is impossible. While mediation may be a necessary condition for alienation, it is not sufficient. Alienation is that specific process of mediation in which the actions of some serve the ends of others without reciprocation and without being explicit, and this requires coercion and domination.

By positing a society of immediate face-to-face relations as ideal, community theorists generate a dichotomy between the "authentic" society of the future and the "inauthentic" society we live in, which is characterized only by alienation, bureaucratization, and degradation. Such a dichotomization between the inauthentic society we have and the authentic society of community, however, detemporalizes our understanding of social change. On this understanding, social change and revolution consist in the complete negation of this society and the establishment of the truly good society. In her scheme of social evolution, Gould conceives of "the society of the future" as the negated sublation of capitalist society. This understands history not as temporal process but as divided into two static structures: the before of alienated society and the after of community.

The projection of the ideal of community as the radical other of existing society denies difference in the sense of the contradictions and ambiguities of social life. Instead of dichotomizing the pure and the impure into two stages of history or two kinds of social relations, a liberating politics should conceive the social process in which we move as a multiplicity of actions and structures which cohere and contradict, some of them exploitative and some of them liberating. The polarization between the impure, inauthentic society we live in and the pure, authentic society we seek to institute detemporalizes the process of change because it fails to articulate how we move from one to the other. If institutional change is possible at all, it must begin from intervening in the contradictions and tensions of existing society. No telos of the final society exists, moreover; society understood as a moving and contradictory process implies that change for the better is always possible and always necessary.

The requirement that genuine community embody face-to-face relations, when taken as a model of the good society, carries a specific vision of social organization. Since the ideal of community demands that relations between members be direct and many-sided, the ideal society is composed of small locales, populated by a small enough number of persons so that each can be personally acquainted with all the others. For most writers, this implies that the ideal social organization is decentralized, with small-scale industry and local markets. Each community aims for economic self-sufficiency, and each democratically makes its own decisions about how to organize its working and playing life.

I do not doubt the desirability of small groups in which individuals have personal acquaintance with one another and interact in a plurality of contexts. Just as the intimacy of living with a few others in the same household has unique dimensions that are humanly valuable, so existing with others in communities of mutual friendship has specific characteristics of warmth and sharing that are humanly valuable. Furthermore, there is no question that capitalist patriarchal society discourages and destroys such communities of mutual friendship, just as it squeezes and fragments families. In our vision of the good society, we surely wish to include institutional arrangements that would nurture the specific experience of mutual friendship, which only relatively small groups interacting in a plurality of contexts can produce. Recognizing the specific value of such face-to-face

relations, however, is quite a different matter from proposing them as the organizing principle of a whole society.

Such a model of the good society as composed of decentralized, economically self-sufficient, face-to-face communities functioning as autonomous political entities is both wildly utopian and undesirable. To bring it into being would require dismantling the urban character of modern society, a gargantuan physical overhaul of living space, work places, places of trade and commerce. A model of a transformed better society must in some concrete sense begin from the concrete material structures that are given to us at this time in history, and in the United States these are large-scale industry and urban centers. The model of society composed of small communities is not desirable, at least in the eyes of many. If we take seriously the way many people live their lives today, it appears that people enjoy cities, that is, places where strangers are thrown together.

One final problem arises from the model of face-to-face community taken as a political goal. The model of the good society as usually articulated leaves completely unaddressed the question of how such small communities are to relate to one another. Frequently, the ideal projects a level of self-sufficiency and decentralization which suggests that proponents envision few relations among the decentralized communities except those of friendly visits. But surely it is unrealistic to assume that such decentralized communities need not engage in extensive relations of exchange of resources, goods, and culture. Even if one accepts the notion that a radical restructuring of society in the direction of a just and humane society entails people living in small democratically organized units of work and neighborhood, this has not addressed the important political question: How will the relations among these communities be organized so as to foster justice and prevent domination? When we raise this political question the philosophical and practical importance of mediation reemerges. Once again, politics must be conceived as a relationship of strangers who do not understand one another in a subjective and immediate sense, relating across time and distance.

City Life and the Politics of Difference

I have claimed that radical politics must begin from historical givens and conceive radical change not as the negation of the given but rather as making something good from many elements of the given. The city, as a vastly populated area with large-scale industry and places of mass assembly, is for us a historical given, and radical politics must begin from the existence of modern urban life. The material surroundings and structures available to us define and presuppose urban relationships. The very size of populations in our society and most other nations of the world, coupled with a continuing sense of national or ethnic identity with millions of other people, all support the conclusion that a vision of dismantling the city is hopelessly utopian.

Starting from the given of modern urban life is not simply necessary, moreover, it is desirable. Even for many of those who decry the alienation, massification, and bureaucratization of capitalist patriarchal society, city life exerts a powerful attraction. Modern literature, art, and film have celebrated city life, its energy, cultural diversity, technological complexity, and the multiplicity of its activities. Even many of the most staunch proponents of decentralized community love to show visiting friends around the Boston or San Francisco or New York in which they live, climbing up towers to see the glitter of lights and sampling the fare at the best ethnic restaurants. For many people deemed deviant in the closeness of the face-to-face community in which they lived, whether "independent" women or socialists or gay men and lesbians, the city has often offered a welcome anonymity and some measure of freedom.[15] To be sure, the liberatory possibilities of capitalist cities have been fraught with ambiguity.

Yet, I suggest that instead of the ideal of community, we begin from our positive experience of city life to form a vision of the good society. Our political ideal is the unoppressive city. In sketching this ideal, I assume some material premises. We will assume a productivity level in the society that can meet everyone's needs, and a physical urban environment that is cleaned up and renovated. We will assume, too, that everyone who can work has meaningful work and those who cannot are provided for with dignity. In sketching this ideal of city life, I am concerned to describe the city as a *kind of relationship* of people to one another, to their own history and one another's history. Thus, by "city" I am not referring only to those huge metropolises that we call cities in the United States. The kinds of relationship I describe obtain also ideally in those places we call towns, where perhaps 10,000 or 20,000 people live.

As a process of people's relating to one another, city life embodies difference in all the senses I have discussed in this chapter. The city obviously exhibits the temporal and spatial distancing and differentiation that I have argued, the ideal of community seeks to collapse. On the face of the city environment lies its history and the history of the individuals and groups that have dwelt within it. Such physical historicity, as well as the functions and groups that live in the city at any given time, create its spatial differentiation. The city as a network and sedimentation of discretely understood places, such as particular buildings, parks, neighborhoods, and as a physical environment offers changes and surprises in transition from one place to another.

The temporal and spatial differentiation that mark the physical environment of the city produce an experience of aesthetic *inexhaustibility*. Buildings, squares, the twists and turns of streets and alleys offer an inexhaustible store of individual spaces and things, each with unique aesthetic characteristics. The juxtaposition of incongruous styles and functions that usually emerge after a long time in city places contribute to this pleasure in detail and surprise. This is an experience of difference in the sense of always being inserted. The modern city is without walls; it is not planned and coherent. Dwelling in the city means always having a sense of beyond, that there is much human life beyond my experience going on in or near these spaces, and I can never grasp the city as a whole.

City life thus also embodies difference as the contrary of the face-to-face ideal expressed by most assertions of community. City life is the "being-together" of strangers. Strangers encounter one another, either face to face or through media, often remaining strangers and yet acknowledging their contiguity in living and the contributions each makes to the others. In such encountering people are not "internally" related, as the community theorists would have it, and do not understand one another from within their own perspective. They are externally related, they experience each other as other, different, from different groups, histories, professions, cultures, which they do not understand.

The public spaces of the city are both an image of the total relationships of city life and a primary way those relationships are enacted and experienced. A public space is a place accessible to anyone, where people engage in activity as individuals or in small groups. In public spaces people are aware of each other's presence and even at times attend to it. In a city there are a multitude of such public spaces: streets, restaurants, concert halls, parks. In such public spaces the diversity of the city's residents come together and dwell side by side, sometimes appreciating one another, entertaining one another, or just chatting, always to go off again as strangers. City parks as we now experience them often have this character.

City life implies a social exhaustibility quite different from the ideal of the face-to-face community in which there is mutual understanding and group identification and loyalty. The city consists in a great diversity of people and groups, with a multitude of subcultures and differentiated activities and functions, whose lives and movements mingle and overlap in public spaces. People belong to distinct groups or cultures and interact in neighborhoods and work places. They venture out from these locales, however, to public places of entertainment, consumption, and politics. They witness one another's cultures and functions in such public interaction, without adopting them as their own. The appreciation of ethnic foods or professional musicians, for example, consists in the recognition that these transcend the familiar everyday world of my life.

In the city strangers live side by side in public places, giving to and receiving from one another social and aesthetic products, often mediated by a huge chain of interactions. This instantiates social relations as difference in the sense of an understanding of groups and cultures that are different, with exchanging and overlapping interactions that do not issue in community, yet which prevent them from being outside of one another. The social differentiation of the city also provides a positive inexhaustibility of human relations. The possibility always exists of becoming acquainted with new and different people, with different cultural and social experiences; the possibility always exists for new groups to form or emerge around specific interests.

The unoppressive city is thus defined as openness to unassimilated otherness. Of course, we do not have such openness to difference in our current social relations. I am asserting an ideal, which consists in a politics of difference. Assuming that group differentiation is a given of social life for us, how can the relationships of group identities embody justice, respect, and the absence of oppression? The relationship among group identities and cultures in our society is blotted by racism, sexism, xenophobia, homophobia, suspicion, and mockery. A politics of difference lays down institutional and ideological means for recognizing and affirming differently identifying groups in two basic senses: giving political representation to group interests and celebrating the distinctive cultures and characteristics of different groups.

Many questions arise in proposing a politics of difference. What defines a group that deserves recognition and celebration? How does one provide representation to group interests that avoids the mere pluralism of liberal interest groups? What are institutional forms by which the mediations of the city and the representations of its groups in decision making can be made democratic? These questions, as well as many others, confront the ideal of the unoppressive city. They are not dissimilar from questions of the relationships that ought to exist among communities. They are questions, however, which appeal to community as the ideal of social life appears to repress or ignore. Some might claim that a politics of difference does express what the ideal of community ought to express, despite the meaning that many writers give the concept of community. Fred Dallmayr, for example, reserves the term *community* for just this openness toward unassimilated otherness, designating the more totalistic understanding of social relations I have criticized as either "communalism" or "movement."

As opposed to the homogeneity deliberately fostered in the movement, the communitarian mode cultivates diversity – but without encouraging willful segregation or the repressive preponderance of one of the social subsectors. . . . Community may be the only form of social aggregation which reflects upon, and makes room for, otherness or the reverse side of subjectivity (and inter-subjectivity) and thus for the play of difference – the difference between ego and Other and between man and nature.[16]

In the end it may be a matter of stipulation whether one chooses to call such politics as play of difference "community." Because most articulations of the ideal of community carry the urge to unity I have criticized, however, I think it is less confusing to use a term other than community rather than to redefine the term. Whatever the label, the concept of social relations that embody openness to unassimilated otherness with justice and appreciation needs to be developed. Radical politics, moreover, must develop discourse and institutions for bringing differently identified groups together without suppressing or subsuming the differences.

NOTES

1   The texts of these authors I am relying on primarily are Jacques Derrida, *Of Grammatology* (Baltimore, MD: Johns Hopkins University Press, 1976); Theodor Adorno, *Negative Dialectics* (New York: Continuum Publishing Company, 1973); Julia Kristeva, *Polylogue* (Paris: Editions du Seuil, 1977). These three writers have a similar critique of Western metaphysics. Several writers have noted similarities between Adorno and Derrida in this regard. See Fred Dallmayr, *Twilight of Subjectivity: Contributions to a Post-Structuralist Theory of Politics* (Amherst, MA: University of Massachusetts Press, 1981), pp. 107–14, 127–36; and Michael Ryan, *Marxism and Deconstruction* (Baltimore, MD: Johns Hopkins University Press, 1982), pp. 73–81. For an account that draws some parallel between Kristeva and Adorno in this respect, see Drucilla Cornell and Adam Thurschwell, "Feminism, Negativity and Intersubjectivity," *Praxis International*, vol. 5, no. 4, 1986, pp. 484–504. My account of metaphysics of presence is based on my reading of these three writers, but I do not claim to be "representing" what they say. Nor in this chapter am I claiming to appropriate all these writers say for social theory. While I do regard the critique of the ideal of community I engage in here loosely as a deconstructive critique along the lines of Derrida's method, I part ways with him and some of the other poststructuralists insofar as I think that it is both possible and necessary to pose alternative conceptualizations. Doing so is, of course, always a positing, and hence excludes and demarks,

thus always itself open to the possibility of deconstructive critique.

2 Adorno, *Negative Dialectics*, Part Two, pp. 134–210.

3 Derrida, *Of Grammatology*, pp. 12–87.

4 Kristeva, "Le sujet en procès," "L'expérience et la pratique," "Matière, sense, dialectique," *Polylogue* pp. 55–136, 263–86.

5 Anthony Giddens, *Central Problems in Social Theory* (Berkeley, CA: University of California Press, 1979), pp. 28–40; Dallmayr, *Twilight of Subjectivity*, pp. 107–115.

6 Seyla Benhabib, "Communicative Ethics and Moral Autonomy," presented at a meeting of the American Philosophical Association, Eastern Division, December 1982; See also "The Generalized and Concrete Other: Toward a Feminist Critique of Substitutionalist Universalism," *Praxis International*, vol. 5, no. 4, 1986, pp. 402–24.

7 Isaac Balbus, *Marxism and Domination* (Princeton: Princeton University Press, 1983).

8 Roberto Mangabeira Unger, *Knowledge and Politics* (New York: The Free Press, 1975), pp. 220–22.

9 Dorothy Alison, "Weaving the Web of Community," *Quest: A Feminist Quarterly*, vol. 4, 1978, p. 79.

10 Sandel, in *Liberalism and the Limits of Justice* (Cambridge: Cambridge University Press, 1982), levels a powerful critique against Rawls by arguing that his theory of justice presupposes a self as separated from and prior to the actions it undertakes as its unified origin. Sandel gives several arguments showing the incoherence of such a conception of the unified self prior to the context of action.

11 Kristeva, "Le sujet en procès," *Polylogue*, pp. 55–106.

12 Derrida discusses the illusory character of this ideal of immediate presence of subjects to one another in community in his discussion of Lévi-Strauss and Rousseau. See *Of Grammatology*, pp. 101–40.

13 Anthony Giddens, *Central Problems in Social Theory*, pp. 198–233.

14 For a useful account of alienation, see Richard Schmitt, *Alienation and Class* (Cambridge, MA: Schenkman Publishing Co., 1983), esp. ch. 5. In this book Schmitt, like many other of the writers I have cited, takes community to stand as the negation of the society of alienation. Unlike those writers discussed in this section, however, he does not take face-to-face relations as a condition of community. To the degree that he makes a pure/impure distinction and exhibits the desire for unity I have criticized, however, the critique articulated here applies to Schmitt's appeal to the ideal of community.

15 Marshall Berman presents a fascinating account of the attractions of city life in *All That Is Solid Melts Into Air* (New York: Simon & Schuster, 1982). George Shulman points to the open-endedness of city life as contrasted with the pastoral vision of community in "The Pastoral Idyll of Democracy," *Democracy*, vol. 3, 1983, pp. 43–54; for a similar critique, see David Plotke, "Democracy, Modernization, and Democracy," *Socialist Review*, vol. 14, March–April 1984, pp. 31–56.

16 Dallmayr, *Twilight of Subjectivity*, pp. 142–3.

47

The Overexposed City

Paul Virilio

At the beginning of the 1960s, with black ghettoes rioting, the mayor of Philadelphia announced: 'From here on in, the frontiers of the State pass to the interior of the cities.' While this sentence translated the political reality for all Americans who were being discriminated against, it also pointed to an even larger dimension, given the construction of the Berlin Wall, on 13 August 1961, in the heart of the ancient capital of the Reich.

Since then, this assertion has been confirmed time and again: Belfast, Londonderry where not so long ago certain streets bore a yellow band separating the Catholic side from the Protestant, so that neither would move too far, leaving a chain-link no man's land to divide their communities even more clearly. And then there's Beirut with its East and West sections, its tortured internal boundaries, its tunnels and its mined boulevards.

Basically, the American mayor's statement revealed a general phenomenon that was just beginning to hit the capital cities as well as the provincial towns and hamlets, the phenomenon of obligatory introversion in which the City sustained the first effects of a multinational economy modelled along the lines of industrial enterprises, a real urban redeployment which soon contributed to the gutting of certain worker cities such as Liverpool and Sheffield in England, Detroit and Saint Louis in the United States, Dortmund in West Germany, and all of this at the very moment in which other areas were being built up, around tremendous international airports, a METROPLEX, a metropolitan complex such as Dallas/Fort Worth. Since the 1970s and the beginnings of the world economic crisis, the construction of these airports was further subjected to the imperatives of the defence against air pirates.

Construction no longer derived simply from traditional technical constraint. The plan had become a function of the risks of 'terrorist contamination' and the disposition of sites conceived of as sterile zones for departures and non-sterile zones for arrivals. Suddenly, all forms of loading and unloading – regardless of passenger, baggage or freight status – and all manner of airport transit had to be submitted to a system of interior/exterior traffic control. The architecture that resulted from this had little to do with the architect's personality. It emerged instead from perceived public security requirements.

As the last gateway to the State, the airport came to resemble the fort, port or railway station of earlier days. As airports were turned into theatres of necessary regulation of exchange and communication, they also became breeding and testing grounds for high-pressured experiments in control and aerial surveillance performed for and by a new 'air and border patrol', whose anti-terrorist exploits began to make headlines with the intervention of the German GS.G9 border guards in the Mogadishu hijacking, several thousand miles away from Germany.

At that instant, the strategy of confining the sick or the suspect gave way to a tactic of mid-voyage interception. Practically, this meant examining clothing and baggage, which explains the sudden proliferation of cameras, radars and detectors in all restricted passageways. When the French built 'maximum security cell-blocks', they used the magnetized doorways that airports had had for years. Paradoxically, the equipment that ensured maximal freedom in travel formed part of the core of penitentiary incarceration. At the same time, in a number of residential areas in the United States, security was maintained exclusively through closed-circuit television hook-ups with a central police station. In banks, in supermarkets, and on major highways, where toll-booths resembled the ancient city gates, the rite of passage was no longer intermittent. It had become immanent.

In this new perspective devoid of horizon, the city was entered not through a gate nor through an *arc de triomphe*, but rather through an electronic audience system. Users of the road were no longer understood to be inhabitants or privileged residents. They were now interlocutors in permanent transit. From this moment on, continuity no longer breaks down in space, not in the physical space of urban lots nor in the juridical space of their property tax records. From here, continuity is ruptured in time, in a time that advanced technologies and industrial redeployment incessantly arrange through a series of interruptions, such as plant closings, unemployment, casual labour and successive or simultaneous disappearing acts. These serve to organize and then disorganize the urban environment to the point of provoking the irreversible decay and degradation of neighbourhoods, as in the housing development near Lyon where the occupants' 'rate of rotation' became so great – people staying for a year and then moving on – that it contributed to the ruin of a place that each inhabitant found adequate...

In fact, since the originary enclosures, the concept of boundary has undergone numerous changes as regards both the façade and the neighbourhood it fronts. From the palisade to the screen, by way of stone ramparts, the boundary-surface has recorded innumerable perceptible and imperceptible transformations, of which the latest is probably that of the interface. Once again, we have to approach the question of access to the City in a new manner. For example, does the metropolis possess its own façade? At which moment does the city show us its face?

The phrase 'to go into town', which replaced the nineteenth-century's 'to go to town', indicates the uncertainty of the encounter, as if we could no longer stand before the city but rather abide forever within. If the metropolis is still a place, a geographic site, it no longer has anything to do with the classical oppositions of city/country nor centre/periphery. The city is no longer organized into a localized and axial estate. While the suburbs contributed to this dissolution, in fact the intramural–extramural opposition collapsed with the transport revolutions and the development of communication and telecommunications technologies. These promoted the merger of disconnected metropolitan fringes into a single urban mass.

In effect, we are witnessing a paradoxical moment in which the opacity of building materials is reduced to zero. With the invention of the steel skeleton construction, curtain walls made of light and transparent materials, such as glass or plastics, replace stone façades, just as tracing paper, acetate and plexiglass replace the opacity of paper in the designing phase.

On the other hand, with the screen interface of computers, television and teleconferences, the surface of inscription, hitherto devoid of depth, becomes a kind of 'distance', a depth of field of a new kind of representation, a visibility without any face-to-face encounter in which the *vis-à-vis* of the ancient streets disappears and is erased. In this situation, a difference of position blurs into fusion and confusion. Deprived of objective boundaries, the architectonic element begins to drift and float in an electronic ether, devoid of spatial dimensions, but inscribed in the singular temporality of an instantaneous diffusion. From here on people can't be separated by physical obstacles or by temporal distances. With the interfacing of computer terminals and video monitors, distinctions of *here* and *there* no longer mean anything.

This sudden reversion of boundaries and oppositions introduces into everyday, common space an element which until now was reserved for the world of microscopes. There is no *plenum*; space is not filled with matter. Instead, an unbounded expanse appears in the false perspective of the machines' luminous emissions. From here on, constructed space occurs within an electronic topology where the framing of perspective and the gridwork weft of numerical images renovate the division of urban property. The ancient private/public occultation and the distinction between housing and traffic are replaced by an over-exposure in which the difference between 'near' and 'far' simply ceases to exist, just as the difference between 'micro' and 'macro' vanished in the scanning of the electron microscope.

The representation of the modern city can no longer depend on the ceremonial opening of gates, nor on the ritual processions and parades lining the streets and avenues with spectators. From here on, urban architecture has to work with the opening of a new 'technological space-time'. In terms of access, telematics replaces the doorway. The sound of gates gives way to the clatter of data banks and the rites of passage of a technical culture whose progress is disguised by the immateriality of its parts and networks. Instead of operating in the space of a constructed social fabric, the intersecting and connecting grid of highway and service systems now occurs in the sequences of an imperceptible organization of time in which the man/machine interface replaces the façades of buildings as the surfaces of property allotments.

Where once the opening of the city gates announced the alternating progression of days and nights, now we awaken to the opening of shutters and televisions. The day has been changed. A new day has been added to the astronomers' solar day, to the flickering day of candles, to the electric light. It is an electronic false-day, and it appears on a calendar of information 'commutations' that has absolutely no relationship whatsoever to real time. Chronological and historical time, time that passes, is replaced by a time that exposes itself instantaneously. On the computer screen, a time period becomes the 'support-surface' of inscription. Literally, or better cinematically, time surfaces. Thanks to the cathode-ray tube, spatial dimensions have become inseparable from their rate of transmission. As a unity of place without any unity of time, the City has disappeared into the heterogeneity of that regime comprised of the temporality of advanced technologies. The urban figure is no longer designated by a dividing line that separates here from there. Instead, it has become a computerized timetable.

Where once one necessarily entered the city by means of a physical gateway, now one passes through an audiovisual protocol in which the methods of audience and surveillance have transformed even the forms of public greeting and daily reception. Within this place of optical illusion, in which the people occupy transportation and transmission time instead of inhabiting space, inertia tends to renovate an old sedentariness, which results in the persistence of urban sites. With the new instantaneous communications media, arrival supplants departure: without necessarily leaving, everything 'arrives'.

Until recently, the city separated its 'intramural' population from those outside the walls. Today, people are divided according to aspects of time. Where once an entire 'downtown' area indicated a long historical period, now only a few monuments will do. Further, the new technological time has no relation to any calendar of events nor to any collective memory. It is pure computer time, and as such helps construct a permanent present, an unbounded, timeless intensity that is destroying the tempo of a progressively degraded society.

What is a monument within this regime? Instead of an intricately wrought portico or a monumental walk punctuated by sumptuous buildings, we now have idleness and monumental waiting for service from a machine. Everyone is busily waiting in front of some communications or telecommunications apparatus, lining up at tollbooths, poring over captains' checklists, sleeping with computer consoles on their nightstands. Finally, the gateway is turned into a conveyance of vehicles and vectors whose disruption creates less a space than a countdown, in which work occupies the centre of time while uncontrolled time of vacations and unemployment form a periphery, the suburbs of time, a clearing away of activities in which each person is exiled to a life of privacy and deprivation.

If, despite the wishes of postmodern architects, the city from here on is deprived of gateway entries, it is because the urban wall has long been breached by an infinitude of openings and ruptured enclosures. While less apparent than those of antiquity, these are equally effective, constraining and segregating. The illusion of the industrial revolution in transportation misled us as to the limitlessness of progress. Industrial time-management has imperceptibly compensated for the loss of rural territories. In the nineteenth century, the city/country attraction emptied agrarian space of its cultural and social substance. At the end of the twentieth century, urban space loses its geopolitical reality to the exclusive benefit of systems of instantaneous deportation whose technological intensity ceaselessly upsets all of our social structures. These systems include the deportation of people in the redeployment of modes of production, the deportation of attention, of the human face-to-face and the urban *vis-à-vis* encounters at the level of human/machine

interaction. In effect, all of this participates in a new 'posturban' and transnational kind of concentration, as indicated by a number of recent events.

Despite the rising cost of energy, the American middle classes are evacuating the cities of the East. Following the transformation of inner cities into ghettoes and slums, we now are watching the deterioration of the cities as regional centres. From Washington to Chicago, from Boston to Saint Louis, the major urban centres are shrinking. On the brink of bankruptcy, New York City lost 10 per cent of its population in the last ten years. Meanwhile, Detroit lost 20 per cent of its inhabitants, Cleveland 23 per cent, Saint Louis 27 per cent. Already, whole neighbourhoods have turned into ghost towns.

These harbingers of an imminent 'post-industrial' deurbanization promise an exodus that will affect all of the developed countries. Predicted for the last forty years, this deregulation of the management of space comes from an economic and political illusion about the persistence of sites constructed in the era of automotive management of time, and in the epoch of the development of audiovisual technologies of retinal persistence.

'Each surface is an interface between two environments that is ruled by a constant activity in the form of an exchange between the two substances placed in contact with one another.'

This new scientific definition of surface demonstrates the contamination at work: the 'boundary, or limiting surface' has turned into an osmotic membrane, like a blotting pad. Even if this last definition is more rigorous than earlier ones, it still signals a change in the notion of limitation. The limitation of space has become commutation: the radical separation, the necessary crossing, the transit of a constant activity, the activity of incessant exchanges, the transfer between two environments and two substances. What used to be the boundary of a material, its 'terminus', has become an entryway hidden in the most imperceptible entity. From here on, the appearance of surfaces and superficies conceals a secret transparency, a thickness without thickness, a volume without volume, an imperceptible quantity.

If this situation corresponds with the physical reality of the infinitesimally small, it also fits that of the infinitely large. When what was visibly nothing becomes 'something', the greatest distance no longer precludes perception. The greatest geophysical expanse contracts as it becomes more concentrated. In the interface of the screen, everything is always already there, offered to view in the immediacy of an instantaneous transmission. In 1980, for example, when Ted Turner decided to launch Cable News Network as a round-the-clock live news station, he transformed his subscribers' living space into a kind of global broadcast studio for world events.

Thanks to satellites, the cathode-ray window brings to each viewer the light of another day and the presence of the antipodal place. If space is that which keeps everything from occupying the same place, this abrupt confinement brings absolutely everything precisely to that 'place', that location that has no location. The exhaustion of physical, or natural, relief and of temporal distances telescopes all localization and all position. As with live televised events, the places become interchangeable at will.

The instantaneity of ubiquity results in the atopia of a singular interface. After the spatial and temporal distances, *speed distance* obliterates the notion of physical dimension. Speed suddenly becomes a primal dimension that defies all temporal and physical measurements. This radical erasure is equivalent to a momentary inertia in the environment. The old agglomeration disappears in the intense acceleration of telecommunications, in order to give rise to a new type of concentration: the concentration of a domiciliation without domiciles, in which property boundaries, walls and fences no longer signify the permanent physical obstacle. Instead, they now form an interruption of an emission or of an electronic shadow zone which repeats the play of daylight and the shadow of buildings.

A strange topology is hidden in the obviousness of televised images. Architectural plans are displaced by the sequence plans of an invisible montage. Where geographical space once was arranged according to the geometry of an apparatus of rural or urban boundary setting, time is now organized according to imperceptible fragmentations of the technical time span, in which the cutting, as of a momentary interruption, replaces the lasting disappearance, the 'program guide' replaces the chain link fence, just as the railroads' timetables once replaced the almanacs.

'The camera has become our best inspector,' declared John F. Kennedy, a little before being struck down in a Dallas street. Effectively, the camera allows us to participate in certain political and optical events. Consider, for example, the irruption phenomenon, in which the City allows itself to be seen thoroughly and completely, or the diffraction phenomenon, in which its image reverberates beyond the atmosphere to the farthest reaches of space, while the endoscope and the scanner allow us to see to the farthest reaches of life.

This overexposure attracts our attention to the extent that it offers a world without antipodes and without hidden aspects, a world in which opacity is but a momentary interlude. Note how the illusion of proximity barely lasts. Where once the *polis* inaugurated a political theatre, with its *agora* and its *forum*, now there is only a cathode-ray screen, where the shadows and spectres of a community dance amid their processes of disappearance, where cinematism broadcasts the last appearance of urbanism, the last image of an urbanism without urbanity. This is where tact and contact give way to televisual impact. While tele-conferencing allows long-distance conferences with the advantage derived from the absence of displacement, tele-negotiating inversely allows for the production of distance in discussions, even when the members of the conversation are right next to each other. This is a little like those telephone crazies for whom the receiver induces flights of verbal fancy amid the anonymity of a remote control aggressiveness.

Where does the city without gates begin? Probably inside that fugitive anxiety, that shudder that seizes the minds of those who, just returning from a long vacation, contemplate the imminent encounter with mounds of unwanted mail or with a house that's been broken into and emptied of its contents. It begins with the urge to flee and escape for a second from an oppressive technological environment, to regain one's senses and one's sense of self. While spatial escape may be possible, temporal escape is not. Unless we think of lay-offs as 'escape hatches,' the ultimate form of paid vacation, the forward flight responds to a post-industrial illusion whose ill effects we are just beginning to feel. Already, the theory of 'job sharing' introduced to a new segment of the community – offering each person an alternative in which sharing work-time could easily lead to a whole new sharing of space as well – mirrors the rule of an endless periphery in which the homeland and the colonial settlement would replace the industrial city and its suburbs. Consider, for example, the Community Development Project, which promotes the proliferation of local development projects based on community forces, and which is intended to reincorporate the English inner cities.

Where does the edge of the exo-city begin? Where can we find the gate without a city? Probably in the new American technologies of instantaneous destruction (with explosives) of tall buildings and in the politics of systematic destruction of housing projects suddenly deemed as 'unfit for the new French way of life', as in Venissieux, La Courneuve or Gagny. According to a recent French study, released by the Association for Community Development,

The destruction of 300,000 residential units over a five-year period would cost 10 billion francs per year, while creating 100,000 new jobs. In addition, at the end of the demolition/reconstruction, the fiscal receipts would be 6 to 10 billion francs above the sum of public moneys invested.

One final question arises here. In a period of economic crisis, will mass destruction of the large cities replace the traditional politics of large public works? If that happens, there will be no essential difference between economic-industrial recession and war.

Architecture or post-architecture? Ultimately, the intellectual debate surrounding modernity seems part of a de-realization phenomenon which simultaneously involves disciplines of expression, modes of representation and modes of communication. The current wave of explosive debates within the media concerning specific political acts and their social communication now also involves the architectural expression, which cannot be removed from the world of communication systems, to the precise extent that it suffers the direct or indirect fall-out of various 'means of communication', such as the automobile or audiovisual systems.

Basically, along with construction techniques, there's always the construction *of* techniques, that collection of spatial and temporal mutations that is constantly reorganizing both the world of everyday experience and the aesthetic representations of contemporary life. Constructed space, then, is more than simply the concrete and material substance of constructed structures, the permanence of elements and the architectonics of urbanistic details. It also exists as the sudden proliferation and the incessant multiplication of special effects which, along with the consciousness of time and of distances, affect the perception of the environment.

This technological deregulation of various milieux is also topological to the exact extent that – instead of constructing a perceptible and visible chaos, such as the processes of degradation or destruction implied in accident, aging and war – it inversely and paradoxically builds an imperceptible order, which is invisible but just as practical as masonry or the public high-ways system. In all likelihood, the essence of what we insist on calling urbanism is composed/decomposed by these transfer, transit and transmission systems, these transport and transmigration networks whose immaterial configuration reiterates the cadastral organization and the building of monuments.

If there are any monuments today, they are certainly not of the visible order, despite the twists and turns of architectural excess. No longer part of the order of perceptible appearances nor of the aesthetic of the apparition of volumes assembled under the sun, this monumental disproportion now resides within the obscure luminescence of terminals, consoles and other electronic nightstands. Architecture is more than an array of techniques designed to shelter us from the storm. It is an instrument of measure, a sum total of knowledge that, contending with the natural environment, becomes capable of organizing society's time and space. This geodesic capacity to define a unity of time and place for all actions now enters into direct conflict with the structural capacities of the means of mass communication.

Two procedures confront each other. The first is primarily material, constructed of physical elements, walls, thresholds and levels, all precisely located. The other is immaterial, and hence its representations, images and messages afford neither locale nor stability, since they are the vectors of a momentary, instantaneous expression, with all the manipulated meanings and mis-information that presupposes.

The first one is architectonic and urba-nistic in that it organizes and constructs durable geographic and political space. The second haphazardly arranges and de-ranges space-time, the continuum of soci-eties. The point here is not to propose a Manichaean judgment that opposes the physical to the metaphysical, but rather to attempt to catch the status of contempor-ary, and particularly urban, architecture within the disconcerting concert of ad-vanced technologies. If architectonics de-veloped with the rise of the City and the discovery and colonization of emerging lands, since the conclusion of that con-quest, architecture, like the large cities, has rapidly declined. While continuing to invest in internal technical equipment, architecture has become progressively in-troverted, becoming a kind of machinery gallery, a museum of sciences and technolo-gies, technologies derived from industrial *machinism*, from the transportation revo-lution and from so-called 'conquest of space'. So it makes perfect sense that when we discuss space technologies today, we are not referring to architecture but rather to the engineering that launches us into outer space.

All of this occurs as if architectonics had been merely a subsidiary technology, sur-passed by other technologies that produced accelerated displacement and sidereal pro-jection. In fact, this is a question of the nature of architectural performance, of the telluric function of the constructed realm and the relationships between a cer-tain cultural technology and the earth. The development of the City as the conserva-tory of classical technologies has already contributed to the proliferation of architec-ture through its projection into every spatial direction, with the demographic concentration and the extreme vertical den-sification of the urban milieu, in direct op-position to the agrarian model. The advanced technologies have since con-tinued to prolong this 'advance', through the thoughtless and all-encompassing ex-pansion of the architectonic, especially with the rise of the means of transporta-tion.

Right now, vanguard technologies, de-rived from the military conquest of space, are already launching homes, and perhaps tomorrow the City itself, into planetary orbit. With inhabited satellites, space shuttles and space stations as floating la-boratories of high-tech research and indus-try, architecture is flying high, with curious repercussions for the fate of post-industrial societies, in which the cultural markers tend to disappear progressively, what with the decline of the arts and the slow regression of the primary technologies.

Is urban architecture becoming an outmoded technology, as happened to extensive agriculture, from which came the debacles of megalopolis? Will architectonics become simply another decadent form of dominating the earth, with results like those of the uncontrolled exploitation of primary resources? Hasn't the decrease in the number of major cities already become the trope for industrial decline and forced unemployment, symbolizing the failure of scientific materialism?

The recourse to History proposed by experts of postmodernity is a cheap trick that allows them to avoid the question of Time, the regime of trans-historical temporality derived from technological ecosystems. If in fact there is a crisis today, it is a crisis of ethical and aesthetic references, the inability to come to terms with events in an environment where the appearances are against us. With the growing imbalance between direct and indirect information that comes of the development of various means of communication, and its tendency to privilege information mediated to the detriment of meaning, it seems that the *reality effect* replaces immediate reality. Lyotard's modern crisis of grand narratives betrays the effect of new technologies, with the accent, from here on, placed on means more than ends.

The grand narratives of theoretical causality were thus displaced by the petty narratives of practical opportunity, and, finally, by the micro-narratives of autonomy. At issue here is no longer the 'crisis of modernity', the progressive deterioration of commonly held ideals, the proto-foundation of the meaning of History, to the benefit of more-or-less restrained narratives connected to the autonomous development of individuals. The problem now is with the narrative itself, with an official discourse or mode of representation, connected until now with the universally recognized capacity to say, describe and inscribe reality. This is the heritage of the Renaissance. Thus, the crisis in the conceptualization of 'narrative' appears as the other side of the crisis of the conceptualization of 'dimension' as geometrical narrative, the discourse of measurement of a reality visibly offered to all.

The crisis of the grand narrative that gives rise to the micro-narrative finally becomes the crisis of the narrative of the grand and the petty.

This marks the advent of a disinformation in which excess and incommensurability are, for 'postmodernity', what the philosophical resolution of problems and the resolution of the pictorial and architectural image were to the birth of the Enlightenment.

The crisis in the conceptualization of dimension becomes the crisis of the whole.

In other words, the substantial, homogeneous space derived from classical Greek geometry gives way to an accidental, heterogeneous space in which sections and fractions become essential once more. Just as the land suffered the mechanization of agriculture, urban topography has continuously paid the price for the atomization and disintegration of surfaces and of all references that tend towards all kinds of transmigrations and transformations. This sudden exploding of whole forms, this destruction of the properties of the individual by industrialization, is felt less in the city's space – despite the dissolution of the suburbs – than in the time – understood as sequential perceptions – of urban appearances. In fact, transparency has long supplanted appearances. Since the beginning of the twentieth century, the classical depth of field has been revitalized by the depth of time of advanced technologies. Both the film and aeronautics industries took off soon after the ground was broken for the grand boulevards. The parades on Haussmann Boulevard gave way to the Lumière brothers' accelerated motion picture inventions; the esplanades of Les Invalides gave way to the invalidation of the city plan. The screen abruptly became the city square, the crossroads of all mass media.

From the aesthetics of the appearance of a *stable* image – present as an aspect of its static nature – to the aesthetics of the disappearance of an *unstable* image – present in its cinematic and cinematographic flight of escape – we have witnessed a transmutation of representations. The emergence of forms as volumes destined to persist as long as their materials would allow has given way to images whose duration is purely retinal. So, more than Venturi's Las Vegas, it is Hollywood that merits urbanist scholarship, for, after the theatre-cities of Antiquity and of the Italian Renaissance, it was Hollywood that was the first Cinecittà, the city of living cinema where stage-sets and reality, tax-plans and scripts, the living and the living dead, mix and merge deliriously.

Here more than anywhere else advanced technologies combined to form a synthetic space-time.

Babylon of filmic de-formation, industrial zone of pretence, Hollywood was built neighbourhood by neighbourhood, block by block, on the twilight of appearances, the success of magicians' tricks, the rise of epic productions like those of D. W. Griffith, all the while waiting for the megalomaniacal urbanizations of Disneyland, Disney World and Epcot Center. When Francis Ford Coppola, in *One From the Heart*, electronically inlaid his actors into a life-size Las Vegas built at the Zoetrope studios in Hollywood (simply because the director wanted the city to adapt to his shooting schedule instead of the other way around), he overpowered Venturi, not by demonstrating the ambiguities of contemporary architecture, but by showing the 'spectral' characters of the city and its denizens.

The utopian 'architecture on paper' of the 1960s took on the video-electronic special effects of people like Harryhausen and Tumbull, just at the precise instant that computer screens started popping up in architectural firms. 'Video doesn't mean I see; it means I fly,' according to Nam June Paik. With this technology, the 'aerial view' no longer involves the theoretical altitudes of scale models. It has become an opto-electronic interface operating in real time, with all that this implies for the redefinition of the image. If aviation – appearing the same year as cinematography – entailed a revision of point of view and a radical mutation of our perception of the world, infographic technologies will likewise force a readjustment of reality and its representations. We already see this in 'Tactical Mapping Systems', a video-disc produced by the United States Defense Department's Agency for Advanced Research Projects. This system offers a continuous view of Aspen, Colorado, by accelerating or decelerating the speed of 54,000 images, changing direction or season as easily as one switches television channels, turning the town into a kind of shooting gallery in which the functions of eyesight and weaponry melt into each other.

If architectonics once measured itself according to geology, according to the tectonics of natural reliefs, with pyramids, towers and other neo-gothic tricks, today it measures itself according to state-of-the-art technologies, whose vertiginous prowess exiles all of us from the terrestrial horizon.

Neo-geological, the 'Monument Valley' of some pseudo-lithic era, today's metropolis is a phantom landscape, the fossil of past societies whose technologies were intimately aligned with the visible transformation of matter, a project from which the sciences have increasingly turned away.

Part V   Reading Urban Interventions

Introduction: Reading Urban Interventions

Gary Bridge and Sophie Watson

Introduction

With unprecedented rates of urbanization, the twentieth century saw a multiplicity of interventions in the urban process that sought to influence city form and function. We use the term interventions to cover all forces impacting on the city, from the action of transnational corporations through to locally-based street protests, as well as the more traditional effects of urban planning and various forms of city governance. This section aims to capture some of the main trends behind direct interventions that shaped the city in the twentieth century. In particular, in light of the fact that it was the cities of the south that were the main engines of growth towards the end of the millennium, this section aims to consider these forces in a western and nonwestern context.

Cities in a World Economy

One of the main influences shaping the nature of urban interventions in the twentieth century was the opening out of the city to wider economic forces. As we have seen in the economy section, David Harvey has sought to identify the role of cities (or the urban process) in capitalist accumulation. This concentration on how the city connects to broader economic processes is in contrast to the earlier, neoclassical readings that concentrated on the city as a distinct market or positioned at the hub of a distinctive regional hinterland economy. The assets of land, capital, and labor were seen as resources for that region, coordinated through the city. The globalization of investment has meant that these city assets have become relational rather than endemic. Cities are increasingly competing with each other for flows of investment. Interurban competition for investments to spur economic growth can be seen as a move from the Keynesian to the neoliberal city. In the Keynesian city, assets were considered to be *in situ* resources to be supported by public investment in welfare and infrastructure. In the neoliberal city the assets of the city must compete for economic investments at a national and international scale (with welfare as a trickle-down effect). There has been a shift from the city being a site of managerial interventions by urban politicians and planners to the city as entrepreneur in the competition for capital investments operating at a global scale. This is a major trend that Harvey indentifies in the extract included here. Planners and politicians have been much more concerned with facilitating economic activity, rather than seeking to redress some of the social inequalities that came out of uneven economic development.

As urban space becomes part of the abstract marketplace for global capitalism, so the politics of place becomes more intense politically, involving a wide range of players. John Logan and Harvey Molotch's influential work on urban growth coalitions shows how a link between politicians and city business interests has been a long-standing feature of US cities. However, they suggest that urban boosterism has changed from a politics of personality in the early twentieth century to a more abstract alliance between business and city hall. There now exists a settled infrastructure of interests that does not question the pro-growth philosophy. Other players, such as cultural institutions, universities, and the unions, can take occasional roles. Logan and Molotch's other key argument is that urban growth coalitions treat urban space as exchange value in the wider marketplace for city assets. This is at the expense of the city as use value for the people that inhabit it, especially the working class and dispossessed who cannot influence the growth coalition and whose neighbourhoods are often most at risk from boosterist redevelopment.

Cities in the Planning Imagination

The previous pieces may make urban politics and planning seem like low-grade, Machiavellian activities. Yet behind urban planning there have been high-minded ideals of the good city. For Ebenezer Howard it meant combining elements of capitalism and communism in a compact city with plenty of green space (the Garden City). For Frank Lloyd Wright it involved the thinning out of the city into homestead-style lots joined by highways, with a spread of urban facilities in a form of integrated decentralization (his idea for the "democratic" Broadacre City – Wright 1945). Peter Hall makes the point that America got the form of Broadacre City, through developer-led postwar suburbanization, but without any of its idealistic content of decentralized independence and self-sufficiency for families. As Hall argues in the extract, both Howard and Wright's visions are anti-urban or at least against the big city. In this they stand in stark contrast to the large-scale, machine-like organization of the high rise, modernist architecture of the International School and in particular of Le Corbusier (see Chapter 2 above). Rather than the civilizing influence of rurality on the city inherent in the Howard and Wright plans, this was a vision of functionalist rationality and efficiency that could be achieved given the scale of architectural development that the large city afforded. These pro- and anti-urban sentiments represent the polarized imagining of cities that has been evident also in film and literature.

The extract from Hall serves to illustrate some of the anti-urban visions behind urban planning. It also shows how much of the actual urban development in the US in the second half of the twentieth century was in fact away from the city and not rigorously planned. Developer-led speculative suburbanization – as a result of more rapid transport, the baby-boom, and changing practices of mortage lending – was the prominent urban form of western cities at this time. Suburban sprawl offended pro- and anti-urbanists alike, but the "city on the highway", as Hall coins it, did influence a change in architectural sensibilities. The signscapes and low-rise architecture of the American strip began to be celebrated rather than condemned in a new postmodern architectural movement rising from the American west, against the ideas of European modernism (see Venturi et al. 1972).

The decline of modernism in planning is a pervasive theme in Patsy Healey's book *Collaborative Planning*, from which an extract is included here. Healey's argument picks out the wider philosophical critique of modernist systems of knowledge and in particular the dominance of instrumental rationality that separates fact from value and is premised on narrow notions of efficiency. This system of thought still dominates planning practice and is seen through the functional separation of land uses, a narrow range of factors to be taken into the development plan, and an idea of the city as some sort of functioning whole – either a machine, or more traditionally a human body. This rationalization of urban space through planning has been a dominant organizing force in urban interventions through planning, and more widely (see especially Boyer 1983), and has had a profound effect on many cities of the south (as many of the remaining extracts in this section attest). Another element of modernist thought is the separation of expert knowledge from lay knowledge. Planners are experts whose specialist knowledge enables them to conceive of the city as a whole and impose their visions upon it (allowing for the powerful influences of the market, of course). Healey's argument is that planning should more and more involve the contextual experience of urban dwellers and become more collaborative and participatory in character. Her vision of the good city is one that starts with the process of planning itself, rather than the visions of the experts. Healey argues that this collaborative change is necessary if planning is not to become wholly bankrupt in being unresponsive to the needs of citizens and completely overtaken by the pressures of the neoliberal agenda, which is to let the market decide.

A Postmodern Turn?

Bob Beauregard's piece is an important appraisal of modernist and postmodernist influences on planning. Part of his point is that planning has had to shake itself out of its modernist slumber because of what is happening to the economy and built form of cities. Economic restructuring and the growth of flexible specialization (see Cho's chapter 17 above) have had the effect of fragmenting the city, such that the comprehensive planning of modernism can no longer keep pace with the pressure of rapid economic change. Conceiving of the city as a whole is no longer possible in planning practice (see also Soja's chapter). Marxist influenced planning theory has been critiqued for its master narratives and the pragmatic planning approach that is suspicious of theory has been left high and dry. Planning theory seems to be caught between the (modernist) desire for a solid ground from which to operate and a postmodern sensitivity to other experiences of the city.

In his extract from *The Modernist City*, James Holston looks at the archetypical modernist city of Brasília, illustrating some of Beauregard's arguments on the ground. Brasília embodies, probably more than any other city, the urban form and organization espoused by Le Corbusier (and other members of the modernist movement) in his utopian blueprints (see Part I above). Central to these was the idea that modern architecture and planning could do away with urban disorder and heterogeneity, thereby creating new forms of collective association and transforming individual and social life. The separation of home and work through zoning was the key tenet. In the plan for Brasília, the national site of government bureaucracy, the residential units were to be exactly the same in every respect, avoiding any differentiation of social classes, and thus adopting an instrumental relation between architecture and society. The overwhelming experience for the residents thus became a sense of monotony and sameness. Yet a contradiction was inherent in the objective of egalitarianism. If residential relations are organized on the basis of work, which is based on the occupational stratification of the bureaucracy, hierarchical work relations are bound to contradict the egalitarian attempts to allocate the same housing conditions to different occupational strata. This reflects the problem with the modernist model's identification of the state as organizer of social life through work in every aspect of society.

Anthony King introduces a different kind of critique of modernist planning and its effects. His point is that planning is centrally embedded in the processes of colonialism, a point which is developed in the three extracts which follow. Colonial planning takes different forms in different colonial situations – for example, the length of colonial rule or number of indigenous people (Drakakis-Smith 1987). King distinguishes three phases of colonial planning: the period up to the early twentieth century where cities were laid out according to various military, technical, political, and cultural codes and principles; second, the early twentieth century, when the structure of colonial relationships conveyed town planning ideologies and practices to dependent territories; and a third post- or neocolonial period when cultural, political, and economic links within the wider global framework provided the means to convey planning models and ideologies in the "neocolonial modernization" of once-colonial cities. For King, colonialism provided the opportunity for urban planning to be exported to nonwestern societies. Central to its tenets was an obsessive concern with health and sanitation, which in the colonial context overrode local definitions and cultural practices. Thus the colonial population came to be monitored and analyzed in western terms, leading to the creation of new environments imposed externally which disregarded the local social, religious, symbolic, or political meaning of the indigenous built environments encountered. The central premise of this colonial planning was segregation, predominantly on racial grounds.

These processes of racialization which underpin imported planning ideas are central to Oren Yiftachel's arguments concerning the use of spatial policies to control ethnic minorities. Also critiquing modernist planning methods and ideologies, Yiftachel exposes the darker side of policies which ostensibly are cast in a discourse of reform. Instead in deeply divided societies occupied by non-assimilating ethnic groups, policies are devised to counter any serious challenge to the territorial integrity of the state. In this context planning shifts from being a progressive tool of reform to one of control and repression. This is enacted through spatial and land-use policies, through the control of access to decision-making processes, and socioeconomically through the long-term impact of planning on social and economic relations in society. As a result, planning in deeply divided societies, Yiftachel suggests, is at best ambiguous and at worst pernicious in its facilitation of domination of key societal resources: space, power, and wealth.

The encounter between western planning models and the presence of the Aboriginal sacred in the city provides a sharp illustration of local politics marked by the legacy of colonial dispossession of indigenous peoples. Jane M. Jacobs tells the story of the proposal to redevelop the site of the Swan Brewery in Perth, Western Australia, a city where the Aboriginal population through processes of colonization and segregation had been relegated to the margins of the city, or rendered invisible during the period of assimilation. The redevelopment of the old brewery is placed in the context of global urban transformations involving a property and development boom, and the diversification of capital into consumption industries which meant a revalorization of the heritage buildings and their incorporation into tourism and leisure sectors. For the urban Aborigines of Perth this revalued commercial space was set against their own claims about the sacredness of the site and their aspirations to see the land return to "nature." Two opposing and incommensurate notions of cultural heritage (but differently placed in the networks of power) thus collided.

The last piece by Badshah and Perlman in this final section of the *Reader* is both pragmatic and optimistic. The growth of megacities is one of the most pressing issues of the day, with more and more people in huge urban conglomerations experiencing rapidly deteriorating environments and greater and greater levels of economic stress and cultural and social alienation. This extract explores some significant initiatives to improve the urban social, physical, and economic environments. Many of these projects are initiated by the very people severely affected by poor urban conditions, representing important models of self-empowerment. Such an argument closes the *Reader* with a call for resistance in the face of domination, and possibilities for practical, often small-scale and local, change in the face of seemingly all-powerful global processes. This is a note we would like to support.

REFERENCES

Boyer, C. 1983: *Dreaming the Rational City.* Cambridge, MA: MIT Press.
Drakakis-Smith, D. 1987: *The Third World City.* New York: Methuen.
Howard, E. 1898: *Garden Cities of Tomorrow.* London: Swan Sonnenscein.
Venturi, R., Brown, D., and Izenour, S. 1972: *Learning From Las Vegas.* Cambridge, MA: MIT Press.
Wright, F. L. 1945: *When Democracy Builds.* Chicago: University of Chicago Press.

48

From Managerialism to Entrepreneurialism: The Transformation in Urban Governance in Late Capitalism

David Harvey

...

1 The Shift to Entrepreneurialism in Urban Governance

A colloquium held at Orleans in 1985 brought together academics, businessmen, and policy-makers from eight large cities in seven advanced capitalist countries (Bouinot, 1987). The charge was to explore the lines of action open to urban governments in the face of the widespread erosion of the economic and fiscal base of many large cities in the advanced capitalist world. The colloquium indicated a strong consensus: that urban governments had to be much more innovative and entrepreneurial, willing to explore all kinds of avenues through which to alleviate their distressed condition and thereby secure a better future for their populations. The only realm of disagreement concerned how this best could be done. Should urban governments play some kind of supportive or even direct role in the creation of new enterprises and if so of what sort? Should they struggle to preserve or even take over threatened employment sources and if so which ones? Or should they simply confine themselves to the provision of those infrastructures, sites, tax baits, and cultural and social at-

tractions that would shore up the old and lure in new forms of economic activity?

I quote this case because it is symptomatic of a reorientation in attitudes to urban governance that has taken place these last two decades in the advanced capitalist countries. Put simply, the "managerial" approach so typical of the 1960s has steadily given way to initiatory and "entrepreneurial" forms of action in the 1970s and 1980s. In recent years in particular, there seems to be a general consensus emerging throughout the advanced capitalist world that positive benefits are to be had by cities taking an entrepreneurial stance to economic development. What is remarkable, is that this consensus seems to hold across national boundaries and even across political parties and ideologies....

There is general agreement, of course, that the shift has something to do with the difficulties that have beset capitalist economies since the recession of 1973. Deindustrialisation, widespread and seemingly 'structural' unemployment, fiscal austerity at both the national and local levels, all coupled with a rising tide of neoconservatism and much stronger appeal (though often more in theory than in practice) to market rationality and privatisation, provide a backdrop to understanding why so many urban governments, often of quite different political persuasions and armed with very different legal and political powers, have all taken a broadly similar direction. The greater emphasis on local action to combat these ills also seems to have something to do with the declining powers of the nation state to control multinational money flows, so that investment increasingly takes the form of a negotiation between international finance capital and local powers doing the best they can to maximise the attractiveness of the local site as a lure for capitalist development. By the same token, the rise of urban entrepreneurialism may have had an important role to play in a general transition in the dynamics of capitalism from a Fordist–Keynesian regime of capital accumulation to a regime of "flexible accumulation" (see Gertler, 1988; Harvey, 1989; Sayer, 1989; Schoenberger, 1988; Scott, 1988; Swynge-douw, 1986, for some elaboration and critical reflection on this controversial concept). The transformation of urban governance these last two decades has had, I shall argue, substantial macro-economic roots and implications. And, if Jane Jacobs (1984) is only half right, that the city is the relevant unit for understanding how the wealth of nations is created, then the shift from urban managerialism to urban entrepreneurialism could have far reaching implications for future growth prospects.

If, for example, urban entrepreneurialism (in the broadest sense) is embedded in a framework of zero-sum inter-urban competition for resources, jobs, and capital, then even the most resolute and avantgarde municipal socialists will find themselves, in the end, playing the capitalist game and performing as agents of discipline for the very processes they are trying to resist. It is exactly this problem that has dogged the Labour councils in Britain (see the excellent account by Rees and Lambert, 1985). They had on the one hand to develop projects which could "produce outputs which are directly related to working people's needs, in ways which build on the skills of labour rather than de-skilling them" (Murray, 1983), while on the other hand recognizing

that much of that effort would go for nought if the urban region did not secure relative competitive advantages. Given the right circumstances, however, urban entrepreneurialism and even inter-urban competition may open the way to a non zero-sum pattern of development. This kind of activity has certainly played a key role in capitalist development in the past. And it is an open question as to whether or not it could lead towards progressive and socialist transitions in the future. . . .

First, the new entrepreneurialism has, as its centrepiece, the notion of a "public–private partnership" in which a traditional local boosterism is integrated with the use of local governmental powers to try and attract external sources of funding, new direct investments, or new employment sources. The Orleans colloquium (Bouinot, 1987) was full of references to the importance of this public–private partnership and it was, after all, precisely the aim of local government reforms in Britain in the 1970s to facilitate their formation (or in the end to by-pass local resistance by setting up the urban development corporations). In the United States the tradition of federally backed and locally implemented public–private partnership faded during the 1960s as urban governments struggled to regain social control of restive populations through redistributions of real income (better housing, education, health care, etc. all targeted towards the poor) in the wake of urban unrest. The role of the local state as facilitator for the strategic interests of capitalist development (as opposed to stabilizer of capitalist society) declined. The same dismissiveness towards capitalist development has been noted in Britain:

"The early 1970s was a period of resistance to change: motorway protest groups, community action against slum clearance, opponents of town centre redevelopment. Strategic and entrepreneurial interests were sacrificed to local community pressures. Conceivably, however, we are moving into a different period in which the entrepreneurial role becomes dominant." (Davies,

1980, p. 23; quoted in Ball, 1983, pp. 270–1).

In Baltimore the transition-point can be dated exactly. A referendum narrowly passed in 1978, after a vigorous and contentious political campaign, sanctioned the use of city land for the private development that became the highly spectacular and successful Harborplace. Thereafter, the policy of public–private partnership had a popular mandate as well as an effective subterranean presence in almost everything that urban governance was about (see Berkowitz, 1984; Levine, 1987; Lyall, 1982; Stoker, 1986).

Secondly, the activity of that public–private partnership is entrepreneurial precisely because it is speculative in execution and design and therefore dogged by all the difficulties and dangers which attach to speculative as opposed to rationally planned and coordinated development. In many instances this has meant that the public sector assumes the risk and the private sector takes the benefits, though there are enough examples where this is not the case (think, for example, of the private risk taken in Gateshead's Metrocenter development) to make any absolute generalization dangerous. But I suspect it is this feature of risk-absorption by the local (rather than the national or federal) public sector which distinguishes the present phase of urban entrepreneurialism from earlier phases of civic boosterism in which private capital seemed generally much less risk averse.

Thirdly, the entrepreneurialism focuses much more closely on the political economy of place rather than of territory. By the latter, I mean the kinds of economic projects (housing, education, etc.) that are designed primarily to improve conditions of living or working within a particular jurisdiction. The construction of place (a new civic centre, an industrial park) or the enhancement of conditions within a place (intervention, for example, in local labour markets by re-training schemes or downward pressure on local wages), on the other hand, can have impacts either smaller or greater than the specific territory within

which such projects happen to be located. The up-grading of the image of cities like Baltimore, Liverpool, Glasgow or Halifax, through the construction of cultural, retail, entertainment and office centres can cast a seemingly beneficial shadow over the whole metropolitan region. Such projects can acquire meaning at the metropolitan scale of public–private action and allow for the formation of coalitions which leap over the kinds of city-suburb rivalries that dogged metropolitan regions in the managerial phase. On the other hand, a rather similar development in New York City – Southstreet Seaport – constructs a new place that has only local impacts, falling far short of any metropolitan-wide influence, and generating a coalition of forces that is basically local property developers and financiers.

The construction of such places may, of course, be viewed as a means to procure benefits for populations within a particular jurisdiction, and indeed this is a primary claim made in the public discourse developed to support them. But for the most part, their form is such as to make all benefits indirect and potentially either wider or smaller in scope than the jurisdiction within which they lie. Place-specific projects of this sort also have the habit of becoming such a focus of public and political attention that they divert concern and even resources from the broader problems that may beset the region or territory as a whole.

The new urban entrepreneurialism typically rests, then, on a public–private partnership focussing on investment and economic development with the speculative construction of place rather than amelioration of conditions within a particular territory as its immediate (though by no means exclusive) political and economic goal.

3 Alternative Strategies for Urban Governance

There are . . . four basic options for urban entrepreneurialism. Each warrants some separate consideration, even though it is the combination of them that provides the clue to the recent rapid shifts in the uneven development of urban systems in the advanced capitalist world.

1. Competition within the international division of labour means the creation or exploitation of particular advantages for the production of goods and services. Some advantages derive from the resource base (the oil that allowed Texas to bloom in the 1970s) or location (e.g. favoured access to the vigour of Pacific Rim trading in the case of Californian cities). But others are created through public and private investments in the kinds of physical and social infrastructures that strengthen the economic base of the metropolitan region as an exporter of goods and services. Direct interventions to stimulate the application of new technologies, the creation of new products, or the provision of venture capital to new enterprises (which may even be cooperatively owned and managed) may also be significant, while local costs may be reduced by subsidies (tax breaks, cheap credit, procurement of sites). Hardly any large scale development now occurs without local government (or the broader coalition of forces constituting local governance) offering a substantial package of aids and assistance as inducements. International competitiveness also depends upon the qualities, quantities, and costs of local labour supply. Local costs can most easily be controlled when local replaces national collective bargaining and when local governments and other large institutions, like hospitals and universities, lead the way with reductions in real wages and benefits (a series of struggles over wage rates and benefits in the public and institutional sector in Baltimore in the 1970s was typical). Labour power of the right quality, even though expensive, can be a powerful magnet for new economic development so that investment in highly trained and skilled work forces suited to new labour processes and their managerial requirements can be well rewarded. There is, finally, the problem of agglomeration economies in metropolitan regions. The production of goods and services is often dependent not on single decisions of economic units (such as the large multinationals to bring a branch plant to town, often with very limited local spillover effects), but upon the way in which economies can be generated by bringing together diverse activities within a restricted space of interaction so as to facilitate highly efficient and interactive production systems (see Scott, 1988). From this standpoint, large metropolitan regions like New York, Los Angeles, London, and Chicago possess some distinctive advantages that congestion costs have by no means yet offset. But, as the case of Bologna (see Gundle, 1986) and the surge of new industrial development in Emilia Romagna illustrates, careful attention to the industrial and marketing mix backed by strong local state action (communist-led in this instance), can promote powerful growth of new industrial districts and configurations, based on agglomeration economies and efficient organisation.

2. The urban region can also seek to improve its competitive position with respect to the spatial division of consumption. There is more to this than trying to bring money into an urban region through tourism and retirement attractions. The consumerist style of urbanisation after 1950 promoted an ever-broader basis for participation in mass consumption. While recession, unemployment, and the high cost of credit have rolled back that possibility for important layers in the population, there is still a lot of consumer power around (much of it credit-fuelled). Competition for that becomes more frenetic while consumers who do have the money have the opportunity to be much more discriminating. Investments to attract the consumer dollar have paradoxically grown apace as a response to generalised recession. They increasingly focus on the quality of life. Gentrification, cultural innovation, and physical upgrading of the urban environment (including the turn to post-modernist styles of architecture and urban design), consumer attractions (sports stadia, convention and

shopping centres, marinas, exotic eating places) and entertainment (the organisation of urban spectacles on a temporary or permanent basis), have all become much more prominent facets of strategies for urban regeneration. Above all, the city has to appear as an innovative, exciting, creative, and safe place to live or to visit, to play and consume in. Baltimore, with its dismal reputation as "the armpit of the east coast" in the early 1970s has, for example, expanded its employment in the tourist trade from under one to over fifteen thousand in less than two decades of massive urban redevelopment. More recently thirteen ailing industrial cities in Britain (including Leeds, Bradford, Manchester, Liverpool, Newcastle and Stoke-on-Trent) put together a joint promotional effort to capture more of Britain's tourist trade. Here is how *The Guardian* (May 9th, 1987) reports this quite successful venture: "Apart from generating income and creating jobs in areas of seemingly terminal unemployment, tourism also has a significant spin-off effect in its broader enhancement of the environment. Facelifts and facilities designed to attract more tourists also improve the quality of life for those who live there, even enticing new industries. Although the specific assets of the individual cities are obviously varied, each is able to offer a host of structural reminders of just what made them great in the first place. They share, in other words, a marketable ingredient called industrial and/or maritime heritage." Festivals and cultural events likewise become the focus of investment activities. "The arts create a climate of optimism – the 'can do' culture essential to developing the enterprise culture," says the introduction to a recent Arts Council of Great Britain report, adding that cultural activities and the arts can help break the downward spiral of economic stagnation in inner cities and help people "believe in themselves and their community" (see Bianchini, forthcoming). Spectacle and display become symbols of the dynamic community, as much in communist controlled Rome and Bologna as in Baltimore, Glasgow and Liverpool. This way, an urban region can hope to cohere and survive as a locus of community solidarity while exploring the option of exploiting conspicuous consumption in a sea of spreading recession.

3. Urban entrepreneurialism has also been strongly coloured by a fierce struggle over the acquisition of key control and command functions in high finance, government, or information gathering and processing (including the media). Functions of this sort need particular and often expensive infrastructural provision. Efficiency and centrality within a worldwide communications net is vital in sectors where personal interactions of key decision makers is required. This means heavy investments in transport and communications (airports and teleports, for example) and the provision of adequate office space equipped with the necessary internal and external linkages to minimise transactions times and costs. Assembling the wide range of supportive services, particularly those that can gather and process information rapidly or allow quick consultation with 'experts', calls for other kinds of investments, while the specific skills required by such activities put a premium on metropolitan regions with certain kinds of educations provision (business and law-schools, hightech production sectors, media skills, and the like). Inter-urban competition in this realm is very expensive and peculiarly tough because this is an area where agglomeration economies remain supreme and the monopoly power of established centres, like New York, Chicago, London, and Los Angeles, is particularly hard to break. But since command functions have been a strong growth sector these last two decades (employment in finance and insurance has doubled in Britain in less than a decade), so pursuit of them has more and more appealed as the golden path to urban survival. The effect, of course, is to make it appear as if the city of the future is going to be a city of pure command and control functions, an informational city, a post-industrial city in which the export of ser-

vices (financial, informational, knowledge-producing) becomes the economic basis for urban survival.

4. Competitive edge with respect to redistributions of surpluses through central (or in the United States, state) governments is still of tremendous importance since it is somewhat of a myth that central governments do not redistribute to the degree they used to do. The channels have shifted so that in both Britain (take the case of Bristol) and in the United States (take the case of Long Beach–San Diego) it is military and defense contracts that provide the sustenance for urban prosperity, in part because of the sheer amount of money involved but also because of the type of employment and the spin-offs it may have into so-called "high-tech" industries (Markusen, 1986). And even though every effort may have been made to cut the flow of central government support to many urban regions, there are many sectors of the economy (health and education, for example) and even whole metropolitan economies (see Smith and Keller's 1983, study of New Orleans) where such a cut off was simply impossible. Urban ruling class alliances have had plenty of opportunity, therefore, to exploit redistributive mechanisms as a means to urban survival.

These four strategies are not mutually exclusive and the uneven fortunes of metropolitan regions have depended upon the nature of the coalitions that have formed, the mix and timing of entrepreneurial strategies, the particular resources (natural, human, locational) with which the metropolitan region can work, and the strength of the competition. But uneven growth has also resulted from the synergism that leads one kind of strategy to be facilitative for another. For example, the growth of the Los Angeles–San Diego–Long Beach–Orange County megalopolis appears to have been fuelled by interaction effects between strong governmental redistributions to the defence industries and rapid accrual of command and control functions that have further stimulated consumption-oriented activities to the point where there

has been a considerable revival of certain types of manufacturing. On the other hand, there is little evidence that the strong growth of consumption-oriented activity in Baltimore has done very much at all for the growth of other functions save, perhaps, the relatively mild proliferation of banking and financial services. But there is also evidence that the network of cities and urban regions in, say, the Sunbelt or Southern England has generated a stronger collective synergism than would be the case for their respective northern counterparts. Noyelle and Stanback (1984) also suggest that position and function within the urban hierarchy have had an important role to play in the patterning of urban fortunes and misfortunes. Transmission effects between cities and within the urban hierarchy must also be factored in to account for the pattern of urban fortunes and misfortunes during the transition from managerialism to entrepreneurialism in urban governance.

Urban entrepreneurialism implies, however, some level of inter-urban competition. We here approach a force that puts clear limitations upon the power of specific projects to transform the lot of particular cities. Indeed, to the degree that inter-urban competition becomes more potent, it will almost certainly operate as an "external coercive power" over individual cities to bring them closer into line with the discipline and logic of capitalist development. It may even force repetitive and serial reproduction of certain patterns of development (such as the serial reproduction of "world trade centers" or of new cultural and entertainment centres, of waterfront development, of post-modern shopping malls, and the like). The evidence for serial reproduction of similar forms of urban redevelopment is quite strong and the reasons behind it are worthy of note.

With the diminution in transport costs and the consequent reduction in spatial barriers to movement of goods, people, money and information, the significance of the qualities of place has been enhanced and the vigour of inter-urban competition for capitalist development (investment, jobs, tourism, etc.) has strengthened considerably. Consider the matter, first of all, from the standpoint of highly mobile multinational capital. With the reduction of spatial barriers, distance from the market or from raw materials has become less relevant to locational decisions. The monopolistic elements in spatial competition, so essential to the workings of Löschian theory, disappear. Heavy, low value items (like beer and mineral water), which used to be locally produced are now traded over such long distances that concepts such as the "range of a good" make little sense. On the other hand, the ability of capital to exercise greater choice over location, highlights the importance of the particular production conditions prevailing at a particular place. Small differences in labour supply (quantities and qualities), in infrastructures and resources, in government regulation and taxation, assume much greater significance than was the case when high transport costs created "natural" monopolies for local production in local markets. By the same token, multinational capital now has the power to organise its responses to highly localised variations in market taste through small batch and specialised production designed to satisfy local market niches. In a world of heightened competition – such as that which has prevailed since the post-war boom came crashing to a halt in 1973 – coercive pressures force multinational capital to be much more discriminating and sensitive to small variations between places with respect to both production and consumption possibilities.

Consider matters, in the second instance, from the standpoint of the places that stand to improve or lose their economic vitality if they do not offer enterprises the requisite conditions to come to or remain in town. The reduction of spatial barriers has, in fact, made competition between localities, states, and urban regions for development capital even more acute. Urban governance has thus become much more oriented to the provision of a "good business climate" and to the construction of all sorts of lures to bring capital into town. Increased entrepreneurialism has been a partial result of this process, of course. But we here see that increasing entrepreneurialism in a different light precisely because the search to procure investment capital confines innovation to a very narrow path built around a favourable package for capitalist development and all that entails. The task of urban governance is, in short, to lure highly mobile and flexible production, financial, and consumption flows into its space. The speculative qualities of urban investments simply derive from the inability to predict exactly which package will succeed and which will not, in a world of considerable economic instability and volatility.

It is easy to envisage, therefore, all manner of upward and downward spirals of urban growth and decline under conditions where urban entrepreneurialism and interurban competition are strong. The innovative and competitive responses of many urban ruling class alliances have engendered more rather than less uncertainty and in the end made the urban system more rather than less vulnerable to the uncertainties of rapid change....

REFERENCES

Ball. M. (1983): *Housing policy and economic power: the political economy of owner occupation*, London.

Berkowitz. B. (1984): 'Economic development really works: Baltimore, MD', in Bingham. R. and Blair. J. (eds): *Urban economic development*, Beverly Hills.

Bianchini. F. (forthcoming): 'The arts and the inner cities', in Pimlott, B. and Macgregor. S. (eds): *Tackling the inner cities*, Oxford.

Bouinot. J. (ed) (1987): *L'action economiques des grandes villes en France et a l'etranger*, Paris.

Davies. H. (1980): 'The relevance of development control', *Town Planning Review*, 51, pp. 7–24.

Gertler. M. (1988): 'The limits to flexibility: comments on the post-Fordist vision of production and its geography', *Transactions, Institute of British Geographers*, New Series, 13, pp. 419–32.

Gundle. S. (1986): 'Urban dreams and metropolitan nightmares: models and crises of communist local government in Italy', in Szajkowski, B. (ed.): *Marxist local governments in Western Europe and Japan*, London.

Harvey. D. (1989): *The condition of postmodernity*, Oxford.

Jacobs. J. (1984): *Cities and the wealth of nations*, New York.

Levine. M. (1987): 'Downtown redevelopment as an urban growth strategy: a critical appraisal of the Baltimore renaissance', *Journal of Urban Affairs*, 9 (2), pp. 103–23.

Lyall. K. (1982): 'A bicycle built for two: public-private partnership in Baltimore', in Fosler. S. and Berger. R. (eds): *Public-private partnerships in American cities*, Lexington, Mass.

Markusen. A. (1986): 'Defense spending: a successful industrial policy', *International Journal of Urban and Regional Research*, 10, pp. 105–22.

Murray. F. (1983): 'Pension funds and local authority investments', *Capital and Class*, 20, pp. 89–103.

Noyelle. T. and Stanback. T. (1984): *The economic transformation of American cities*, Totawa, NJ.

Rees. G. and Lambert. J. (1985): *Cities in crisis: the political economy of urban development in post-war Britain*, London.

Sayer. A. (1989): 'Post-Fordism in question', *International Journal of Urban and Regional Research*, forthcoming.

Schoenberger. E. (1988): 'From Fordism to flexible accumulation: technology, competitive strategies and international location', *Environment and Planning*, Series D. Society and Space, 6, pp. 245–62.

Scott. A. (1988): *New Industrial spaces: flexible production organisation and regional development in North America and Western Europe*, London.

Smith. M. and Keller. M. (1983): 'Managed growth and the politics of uneven development in New Orleans', in Fainstain. S. et al: *Restructuring the city: the poltical economy of urban redevelopment*, New York.

Stoker. R. (1986): 'Baltimore: the self-evaluating city?' in Stone. C. N. and Sanders. H. T. (eds): *The politics of urban development*, Lawrence, Kansas.

Swyngedouw. E. (1986): 'The socio-spatial implications of innovations in industrial organisation', *Working Paper*, No 20, *Johns Hopkins European Center for Regional Planning and Research*, Lille.

from *Urban Fortunes: The Political Economy of Place*

John R. Logan and Harvey L. Molotch

3 The City as a Growth Machine

Traditional urban research has had little relevance to the day-to-day activities of the place-based elites whose priorities affect patterns of land use, public budgets, and urban social life. It has not even been apparent from much of the scholarship of urban social science that place is a market commodity that can produce wealth and power for its owners, and that this might explain why certain people take a keen interest in the ordering of urban life.

Research on local elites has been preoccupied with the question "Who governs?" (or "Who rules?"). Are the politically active citizens of a city split into diverse and competing interest groups, or are they members of a coordinated oligarchy? Empirical evidence of visible cleavage, such as disputes on a public issue, has been accepted as evidence of pluralistic competition (Banfield, 1961; Dahl, 1961). Signs of cohesion, such as common membership in voluntary and policy groups, have been used to support the alternative view (see Domhoff, 1971).

We believe that the question of who governs or rules has to be asked in conjunction with the equally central question "For what?" With rare exceptions (see Smith and Keller, 1983), one issue consistently generates consensus among local elite groups and separates them from people who use the city principally as a place to live and work: the issue of growth. For those who count, the city is a growth machine, one that can increase aggregate rents and trap related wealth for those in the right position to benefit. The desire for growth creates consensus among a wide range of elite groups, no matter how split they might be on other issues. Thus the disagreement on some or even most public issues does not necessarily indicate any fundamental disunity, nor do changes in the number or variety of actors on the scene (what Clark [1968] calls "decentralization") affect the basic matter. It does not even matter that elites often fail to achieve their growth goal; with virtually all places in the same game, some elites will inevitably lose no matter how great their effort (Lyon et al., 1981; Krannich and Humphrey, 1983).

Although they may differ on which particular strategy will best succeed, elites use their growth consensus to eliminate any alternative vision of the purpose of local government or the meaning of community. The issues that reach public agendas (and are therefore available for pluralists' investigations) do so precisely because they are matters on which elites have, in effect, agreed to disagree (Molotch and Lester, 1974, 1975; see Schattschneider, 1960). Only under rather extraordinary circumstances is this consensus endangered.

For all the pluralism Banfield (1961) uncovered in Chicago, he found no disagreement with the idea that growth was good. Indeed, much of the dissension he did find, for example, on where to put the new convention center, was part of a dispute over how growth should be internally distributed. In his studies of cities on both sides of the southern US border, D'Antonio found that when community "knowledgeables" were "asked to name the most pressing problems facing their respective cities," they cited finding sufficient water for both farming and urban growth (Form and D'Antonio, 1970:439). Whitt (1982) found that in formulating positions on California transportation policies, elites carefully coordinated not only the positions they would take but also the amount of money each would give toward winning relevant initiative campaigns. Thus on growth infrastructure, the elites were united.

Similarly, it was on the primacy of such growth and development issues that Hunter found Atlanta's elites to be most unified, both at the time of his first classic study and during its replication twenty years later (Hunter, 1953, 1980). Hunter (1953:214) reports, "They could speak of nothing else" (cited in Domhoff, 1983:169). In his historical profiles of Dallas and Fort Worth, Melosi (1983:175) concludes that "political power in Dallas and Fort Worth has typically been concentrated in the hands of those people most willing and able to sustain growth and expansion." Finally, even the ecologically oriented scholars with a different perspective, Berry and Kasarda (1977:371), have remarked, "If in the past urbanization has been governed by any conscious public objectives at all, these have been, on the one hand, to encourage growth, apparently for its own sake, and on the other hand, to provide public works and public welfare programs to support piecemeal, spontaneous development impelled primarily by private initiative." And even Hawley (1950:429) briefly departs from his tight ecological schema to remark that "competition is observable . . . in the struggle for transportation and communication advantages and superior services of all kinds; it also appears in efforts to accelerate rates of population growth."

All of this competition, in addition to its critical influence on what goes on *within* cities, also influences the distribution of populations throughout cities and regions, determining which ones grow and which do not. The incessant lobbying, manipulating, and cajoling can deliver the critical resources from which great cities are made. Although virtually all places are subject to the pervasive rule of growth boosters, places with more active and creative elites may have an edge over other areas. In a comparative study of 48 communities, Lyon et al. (1981) indeed found that cities with reputedly more powerful elites tended to have stronger growth rates. This may mean that active elites stimulate growth, or it may mean that strong growth emboldens elites to actively maintain their advantage. Although we suspect that both perspectives are valid, we stress that the activism of entrepreneurs is, and always has been, a critical force in shaping the urban system, including the rise and fall of given places. . . .

The modern-day good business climate

The jockeying for canals, railroads, and arsenals of the previous century has given way in this one to more complex and subtle efforts to manipulate space and redistribute rents. The fusing of public duty and private gain has become much less acceptable (both in public opinion and in the criminal courts); the replacing of frontiers by complex cities has given important roles to mass media, urban professionals, and skilled political entrepreneurs. The growth machine is less personalized, with fewer local heroes, and has become instead a multifaceted matrix of important social institutions pressing along complementary lines.

With a transportation and communication grid already in place, modern cities typically seek growth in basic economic functions, particularly job intensive ones. Economic growth sets in motion the migration of labor and a demand for ancillary production services, housing, retailing, and wholesaling ("multiplier effects"). Contemporary places differ in the type of economic base they strive to build (for example, manufacturing, research and development, information processing, or tourism). But any one of the rainbows leads to the same pot of gold: more intense land use and thus higher rent collections, with associated professional fees and locally based profits.

Cities are in a position to affect the "factors of production" that are widely believed to channel the capital investments that drive local growth (Hawley, 1950; Summers et al., 1976). They can, for example, lower access costs of raw materials and markets through the creation of shipping ports and airfields (either by using local subsidies or by facilitating state and federal support). Localities can decrease corporate overhead costs through sympathetic policies on pollution abatement, employee health standards, and taxes. Labor costs can be indirectly lowered by pushing welfare recipients into low-paying jobs and through the use of police to constrain union organizing. Moral laws can be changed; for example, drinking alcohol can be legalized (as in Ann Arbor, Mich., and Evanston, Ill.) or gambling can be promoted (as in Atlantic City, NJ) to build tourism and convention business. Increased utility costs caused by new development can be borne, as they usually are (see, for an example, Ann Arbor, Michigan, Planning Department, 1972), by the public at large rather than by those responsible for the "excess" demand they generate. Federally financed programs can be harnessed to provide cheap water supplies; state agencies can be manipulated to subsidize insurance rates; local political units can forgive business property taxes. Government installations of various sorts (universities, military bases) can be used to leverage additional development by guaranteeing the presence of skilled labor, retailing customers, or proximate markets for subcontractors. For some analytical purposes, it doesn't even matter that a number of these factors have little bearing on corporate locational decisions (some certainly do; others are debated); just the *possibility* that they might matter invigorates local growth activism (Swanstrom, 1985) and dominates policy agendas.

Following the lead of St. Petersburg, Florida, the first city to hire a press agent (in 1918) to boost growth (Mormino, 1983:150), virtually all major urban areas now use experts to attract outside investment. One city, Dixon, Illinois, has gone so far as to systematically contact former residents who might be in a position to help (as many as twenty thousand people) and offer them a finder's fee up to $10,000 for directing corporate investment toward their old home town (*San Francisco Chronicle*, May 10, 1984). More pervasively, each city tries to create a "good business climate." The ingredients are well known in city-building circles and have even been codified and turned into "official" lists for each regional area. The much-used Fantus rankings of business climates are based on factors like taxation, labor legislation, unemployment compensation, scale of government, and public indebtedness (Fantus ranks Texas as number one and New York as number forty-eight). In 1975, the Industrial Development Research Council, made up of corporate executives responsible for site selection decisions, conducted a survey of its members. In that survey, states were rated more simply as "cooperative," "indifferent," or "antigrowth"; the results closely paralleled the Fantus rankings of the same year (Weinstein and Firestine, 1978: 134–44).

Any issue of a major business magazine is replete with advertisement from localities of all types (including whole countries) striving to portray themselves in a manner attractive to business....

While a good opera or ballet company may subtly enhance the growth potential of some cities, other cultural ingredients are crucial for a good business climate. There should be no violent class or ethnic conflict (Agger, Goldrich, and Swanson, 1964:649; Johnson, 1983:250–1). Rubin (1972:123) reports that racial confrontation over school busing was sometimes seen as a threat to urban economic development. Racial violence in South Africa is finally leading to the disinvestment that reformers could not bring about through moral suasion. In the good business climate, the work force should be sufficiently quiescent and healthy to be productive; this was the rationale originally behind many programs in work place relations and public health. Labor must, in other words, be "reproduced," but only under conditions that least interfere with local growth trajectories.

Perhaps most important of all, local publics should favor growth and support the ideology of value-free development. This public attitude reassures investors that the concrete enticements of a locality will be upheld by future politicians. The challenge is to connect civic pride to the growth goal, tying the presumed economic and social benefits of growth in general (Wolfe, 1981) to growth in the local area. Probably only partly aware of this, elites generate and sustain the place patriotism of the masses. According to Boorstin, the competition among cities "helped create the booster spirit" as much as the booster spirit helped create the cities (1965:123). In the nineteenth-century cities, the great rivalries over canal and railway installations were the political spectacles of the day, with attention devoted to their public, not private, benefits. With the drama of the new railway technology, ordinary people were swept into the competition among places, rooting for their own town to become the new "crossroads" or at least a way station. "The debates over transportation," writes Scheiber (1973:143), "heightened urban community consciousness and sharpened local pride in many western towns."

The celebration of local growth continues to be a theme in the culture of local-

ities. Schoolchildren are taught to view local history as a series of breakthroughs in the expansion of the economic base of their city and region, celebrating its numerical leadership in one sort of production or another; more generally, increases in population tend to be equated with local progress. Civic organizations sponsor essay contests on the topic of local greatness. They encourage public celebrations and spectacles in which the locality name can be proudly advanced for the benefit of both locals and outsiders. They subsidize soapbox derbies, parade floats, and beauty contests to "spread around" the locality's name in the media and at distant competitive sites....

The growth machine avidly supports whatever cultural institutions can play a role in building locality. Always ready to oppose cultural and political developments contrary to their interests (for example, black nationalism and communal cults), rentiers and their associates encourage activities that will connect feelings of community ("we feelings" [McKenzie, 1922]) to the goal of local growth. The overall ideological thrust is to deemphasize the connection between growth and exchange values and to reinforce the link between growth goals and better lives for the majority. We do not mean to suggest that the only source of civic pride is the desire to collect rents; certainly the cultural pride of tribal groups pre-dates growth machines. Nevertheless, the growth machine coalition mobilizes these cultural motivations, legitimizes them, and channels them into activities that are consistent with growth goals.

The organization of the growth coalition

The people who use their time and money to participate in local affairs are the ones who – in vast disproportion to their representation in the population – have the most to gain or lose in land-use decisions. Local business people are the major participants in urban politics (Walton, 1970), particularly business people in property investing, development, and real estate financing (Spaulding, 1951; Mumford, 1961). Peterson (1981:132), who applauds growth boosterism, acknowledges that "such policies are often promulgated through a highly centralized decision-making process involving prestigious businessmen and professionals. Conflict within the city tends to be minimal, decision-making processes tend to be closed." Elected officials, says Stone (1984:292), find themselves confronted by "a business community that is well-organized, amply supplied with a number of deployable resources, and inclined to act on behalf of tangible and ambitious plans that are mutually beneficial to its own members."

Business people's continuous interaction with public officials (including supporting them through substantial campaign contributions) gives them *systemic* power (Alford and Friedland, 1975; Stone, 1981, 1982). Once organized, they stay organized. They are "mobilized interests" (Fainstein, Fainstein, and Armistead, 1983:214). Rentiers need local government in their daily money-making routines, especially when structural speculations are involved. They are assisted by lawyers, syndicators, and property brokers (Bouma, 1962), who prosper as long as they can win decisions favoring their clients. Finally, there are monopolistic business enterprises (such as the local newspaper) whose futures are tied to the growth of the metropolis as a whole, although they are not directly involved in land use. When the local market is saturated with their product, they have few ways to increase profits, beyond expansion of their surrounding area. As in the proverbial Springdale, site of the classic Vidich and Bensman (1960:216) ethnography of a generation ago, there is a strong tendency in most cities for "the professionals (doctors, teachers, dentists, etc.), the industrial workers, the shack people and the lower middle-class groups [to be] for all intents and purposes disenfranchised except in terms of temporary issues."

Because so much of the growth mobilization effort involves government, local growth elites play a major role in electing local politicians, "watchdogging" their activities, and scrutinizing administrative detail. Whether in generating infrastructural resources, keeping peace on the home front, or using the city mayor as an "ambassador to industry" (Wyner, 1967), local government is primarily concerned with increasing growth. Again, it is not the only function of local government, but it is the key one. . . .

When elites come to see, for example, that inadequate public services are repelling capital investment, they can put the issue of raising taxes on the public agenda. Trillin (1976:154) reports on Rockford, Illinois, a city whose school system was bankrupted by an antitax ideology. Initially, local elites opposed taxes as part of their efforts to lure industry through a low tax rate. As a result, taxes, and therefore tax money for schools, declined. Eventually, the growth coalition saw the educational decline, not the tax rate, as the greatest danger to the "economic vitality of the community." But ironically, elites are not able to change overnight the ideologies they have put in place over decades, even when it is in their best interests to do so.[1] Unfortunately, neither can the potential *opponents* of growth. As the example of Rockford shows, even such issues as public school spending can become subject to the growth maximization needs of locality. The appropriate level of a social service often depends, not on an abstract model of efficiency or on "public demand" (cf. Tiebout, 1956), but on whether the cost of that service fits the local growth strategy (past and present).

By now it should be clear how political structures are mobilized to intensify land uses for private gain of many sorts. Let us look more closely, therefore, at the various local actors, besides those directly involved in generating rents, who participate in the growth machine.

Politicians

The growth machine will sustain only certain persons as politicians. The campaign contributions and public celebrations that build political careers do not ordinarily come about because of a person's desire to save or destroy the environment, to repress or liberate the blacks or other disadvantaged groups, to eliminate civil liberties or enhance them. Given their legislative power, politicians may end up doing any of these things. But the underlying politics that gives rise to such opportunities is a person's participation in the growth consensus. That is why we so often see politicians springing into action to attract new capital and to sustain old investments. Even the pluralist scholar Robert Dahl observed in his New Haven study that if an employer seriously threatened to leave the community, "political leaders are likely to make frantic attempts to make the local situation more attractive" (quoted in Swanstrom, 1981:50)....

Local media

One local business takes a broad responsibility for general growth machine goals – the metropolitan newspaper. Most newspapers (small, suburban papers are occasionally an exception) profit primarily from increasing their circulation and therefore have a direct interest in growth.[2] As the metropolis expands, the newspaper can sell a larger number of ad lines (at higher per line cost), on the basis of a rising circulation base; TV and radio stations are in a similar situation. In explaining why his newspaper had supported the urbanization of orchards that used to cover what is now the city of San Jose, the publisher of the *San Jose Mercury News* said, "Trees do not read newspapers" (Downie, 1974:112, as cited in Domhoff, 1983:168). Just as newspaper boosterism was important in building the frontier towns (Dagenais, 1967), so today "the hallmark of media content has been peerless boosterism: congratulate growth rather than calculate consequences; compliment development rather than criticize its impact" (Burd, 1977:129; see also Devereux, 1976; Freidel, 1963). The media "must present a favorable image to outsiders" (Cox and Morgan, 1973:136),[3]

and only "sparingly use their issue-raising capacities" (Peterson, 1981:124)....

Utilities

Leaders of "independent" public or quasi-public agencies, such as utilities, may play a role similar to that of the newspaper publisher: tied to a single locale, they become growth "statesmen" rather than advocates for a certain type of growth or intralocal distribution of growth.

For example, a water-supplying agency (whether public or private) can expand only by acquiring more users. This causes utilities to penetrate deep into the hinterlands, inefficiently extending lines to areas that are extremely costly to service (Gaffney, 1961; Walker and Williams, 1982). The same growth goals exist within central cities. Brooklyn Gas was an avid supporter of the movement of young professionals into abandoned areas of Brooklyn, New York, in the 1970s, and even went so far as to help finance housing rehabilitation and sponsor a traveling slide show and open houses displaying the pleasant life styles in the area. All utilities seem bent on acquiring more customers to pay off past investments, and on proving they have the good growth prospects that lenders use as a criterion for financing additional investments. Overall efficiencies are often sacrificed as a result....

Auxiliary players

Although they may have less of a stake in the growth process than the actors described above, certain institutions play an auxiliary role in promoting and maintaining growth. Key among these auxiliary players are the cultural institutions in an area: museums, theaters, universities, symphonies, and professional sports teams. An increase in the local population may help sustain these institutions by increasing the number of clients and support groups. More important, perhaps, is that such institutions often need the favor of those who are at the heart of local growth machines – the rentiers, media owners, and politicians, who can make or break their institutional goals. And indeed, cultural institutions do have something to offer in return.

Organized labor

Although they are sometimes in conflict with capitalists on other issues, labor union leaders are enthusiastic partners in growth machines, with little careful consideration of the long-term consequences for the rank and file. Union leadership subscribes to value-free development because it will "bring jobs," particularly to the building trades, whose spokespersons are especially vocal in their support of development. Less likely to be openly discussed is the concern that growth may bring more union members and enhance the power and authority of local union officials.[4] ...

Self-employed professionals and small retailers

Retailers and professionals ordinarily have no clear interest in the generation of aggregate rents. The stake of these groups in growth depends on their particular situation, including the possibility that growth may displace a clientele upon which they are dependent. Any potential opposition from these groups is, however, blunted by a number of factors, two of which are especially important. Retailers need customers and this often leads them to equate aggregate growth in a locality with an increase in sales and profits for themselves. They also have social ties with local rentier groups, whose avid growth orientation may have a strong influence.

By contrast, larger but locally based retailing chains with substantial local market shares have a direct interest in local growth. They can grow more cheaply by expanding in their own market area (where media and other overhead costs can be spread among existing stores) than by penetrating distant regions. But a larger population base also draws new competitors, since retailing is more competitive than most other business. ...

Well-paid professionals such as doctors and lawyers sometimes invest their own high salaries in property syndicates (often unprofitable ones) that are put together for them by brokers and financial advisers. This gives the professionals the direct stake in growth outcomes that we ordinarily associate with place entrepreneurs. As social peers of the rentiers, and as vague supporters of value-free production generally, these professionals are often sympathetic to growth. ...

The effects of growth

By claiming that more intensive development benefits virtually all groups in a locality, growth machine activists need pay no attention to the distinction between use and exchange values that pervades our analysis. They assert that growth strengthens the local tax base, creates jobs, provides resources to solve existing social problems, meets the housing needs caused by natural population growth, and allows the market to serve public tastes in housing, neighborhoods, and commercial development. Similarly, Paul Peterson speaks of development goals as inherently uncontroversial and "consensual" because they are aligned with the "collective good" (1981:147), "with the interests of the community as a whole" (1981:143). Speaking in characteristically sanguine terms even about urban renewal (widely known by then for its detrimental effects on cities), Peterson says in his celebrated book: "Downtown business benefits, but so do laborers desiring higher wages, homeowners hoping house values will rise, the unemployed seeking new jobs, and politicians aiming for reelection" (1981:147).

Some of these claims, for some times and places, are true. The costs and benefits of growth depend on local circumstance. Declining cities experience problems that might be eased by replacement investments. Even in growing cities, the costs of growth can conceivably be limited by appropriate planning and control techniques. Nevertheless, for many places and times, growth is at best a mixed blessing and the growth machine's claims are merely legitimating ideology, not accurate descriptions of reality. Residents of declining cities, as well as people living in more dynamic areas, are often deceived by the extravagant claims that growth solves problems. These claims demand a realistic evaluation.

Fiscal health

Systematic comparative analyses of government costs as a function of city size and growth have found that cost is positively related to both size of place and rate of growth, at least for middle-size cities (see Appelbaum et al., 1976; Follett, 1976). Of course, the *conditions* of growth are important. The overall fiscal state of a city depends on the kind of growth involved (industrial versus residential, and the subtypes of each) and the existing capacities of the local infrastructure. In general, most studies (see Stuart and Teska, 1971) conclude that housing development represents a net fiscal loss because of the service costs that residents require, although housing for the rich is more lucrative than housing for the poor. Industrial and commercial growth, on the other hand, tends to produce net benefits for the tax base, but only if the costs of servicing additions to the local labor force are omitted from the calculations. If local government provides special tax incentives or other sorts of subsidies to attract new industries, the fiscal costs of development will obviously be higher.

Growth can also at times save a local government money. A primary factor in this possibility is the existence of "unused capacities." If a town has a declining birth rate and thus a school district with empty classrooms, officials may try to attract additional families to increase the efficient use of the physical plant and thereby reduce the per capita costs. If a city is paying off a bonded debt on a sewer plant that could

serve double its present demand, officials may seek additional users in order to spread the costs to a larger number and thus decrease the burden for current residents.

Under other conditions, however, even small increases in demand can have enormous fiscal costs if the increases entail major new public expenditures. In many cases infrastructures must be built "all at once"; these are "lumpy" costs. . . .

Costs to existing residents can be particularly high if the anticipated growth does not materialize. In what Worster (1982:514) calls the "infrastructural trap," localities that place bets on future growth by investing in large-scale capacities then must move heaven and earth to make sure they get that growth. Whether through deceitful plot or inadvertent blunder, the results can be a vicious cycle of crisis-oriented growth addiction as various infrastructures collapse from overuse and are replaced by still larger facilities, which then can only be paid for with additional growth that again creates another crisis of overuse. . . .

Employment

A key ideological prop for the growth machine, especially in appealing to the working class, is the assertion that local growth "makes jobs." This claim is aggressively promulgated by developers, bankers, and Chamber of Commerce officials – people whose politics otherwise reveal little concern for problems of the working class. The emphasis on jobs becomes a part of the statesmanlike talk of media editorialists. Needless to say, the benefits in profits and rents are seldom brought up in public.

The reality is that local growth does not make jobs: it only distributes them. In any given year the United States will see the construction of a certain number of new factories, office units, and highways – regardless of where they are put. Similarly, a given number of automobiles, missiles, and lamp shades will be made in this country, regardless of where they are manufactured.

The number of jobs in this society, whether in the building trades or in any other economic sector, will therefore be determined by rates of return on investments, national trade policy, federal decisions affecting the money supply, and other factors unrelated to local decision making. Except for introducing draconian measures that would replicate Third World labor conditions in US cities, a locality can only compete with other localities for its share of newly created US jobs. Aggregate employment is unaffected by the outcome of this competition among localities to "make" jobs. . . .

Job and income mobility

. . .Whatever the specific reasons for the differences among places, Greenberg's findings indicate that "growth *per se* is no panacea for urban poverty" (Greenberg, n.d.:26). Instead, the issue is the *kind* of growth that is involved, and the degree (ordinarily, limited) to which local residents are given an advantage over migrants in the competition for jobs. Otherwise, local growth may be only a matter of making the local rich even richer, or, alternatively, of moving those already privileged in their jobs from one part of the country to another part of the country. To stay with our metaphor of musical chairs, the number of *comfortable* chairs and the basis for allocating them does not change; only their *location* is altered. As Summers and Branch conclude on the basis of their own growth studies, "Industrial location has a small or even negative effect on the local public sector and on economically disadvantaged citizens" (1984:153; see also Garrison, 1971). This is hardly consistent with the myth of opportunity promoted by supporters of the growth machine.

Eliminating social problems

The idea that an increase in numbers and density leads to severe social pathology has been, at long last, thoroughly discredited (see, for example, Fischer, Baldasarre, and Ofshe, 1975). We do believe, however, that size and rate of growth have a role in creating and exacerbating urban problems such as segregation and inequality.

The great population explosions that marked America's industrial cities earlier in this century cannot be said to have increased levels of either equality or class and racial integration. Instead, greater numbers seem to have increased spatial and social segregation between rich and poor, black and white (Lieberson, 1980; Zunz, 1982). In a more contemporary context, Sternlieb and Hughes (1983) have studied the social effects of the growth of gambling in Atlantic City, New Jersey – the revitalization of a service sector industry. Sternlieb and Hughes report that the consequences have been extremely negative for existing residents. The growth boom has set up "walled off universes" of casino-generated wealth, with the old people and poor finding their former "dismal comforts being swept away," without the compensation of better jobs. (*Los Angeles Times*, 1983). The original residents are not participating in the new economy, except at the bottom (as is consistent with Greenberg's findings, discussed above), and the overall effect of the gambling boom on the community is to exacerbate visible cleavages between the rich and the poor (see also Markusen, 1978).

More generally, growth may not be the cause of problems, but increases in scale make it more difficult to deal with those that do exist. Racial integration is more difficult when members of a minority are concentrated in large ghettos within a vast, and often politically divided, region. . . .

Environment

Growth has obvious negative consequences for the physical environment; growth affects the quality of air and water, and the ease of getting around in a town or city. Growth obliterates open spaces and damages the aesthetic features of a natural terrain. It decreases ecological variety with a consequent threat to the larger eco-system.

Though sometimes viewed as trivial concerns of an idle middle class ("rich housewives," according to the stereotype), these blows to the physical environment most heavily affect the less well to do. A high-quality physical environment constitutes a free public good for those who have access to it (Harvey, 1973). Those who are unable to buy amenities in the market lose most from the unavailability of such resources. More concretely, since the poor are most likely to live and work in close proximity to pollution sources, the poor are more affected by growth-induced environmental decay than are the rich.

Perhaps nowhere are the effects of environmental decline more dramatically displayed than in those places with the most rapid growth experiences....

Accommodating natural increase

Growth activists incessantly raise the problem of providing "homes and jobs for our children." To avoid the forced exile of their youth, towns and cities might reasonably have as a goal the maintenance of economic expansion sufficient to provide jobs and housing for new generations. These expansions would be modest in scale, given the low rates of birth that are characteristic of US urban populations. The difficulty is "reserving" the right openings for the right youths, a goal that is unrealistic given the nature of the hiring queue and the constitutional limitations on restraint of trade. Virtually no local growth policy could effectively guarantee local jobs for local people. Many of the young prefer, of course, to leave their home town anyway, and this in itself probably eliminates the problem of having to create large numbers of jobs to accommodate local youth.

Growth trade-offs

Although there is clear evidence on some of the effects of growth, urban size is fundamentally a political or value issue in which one person's criteria are lined up against another's (see Duncan, 1957). It may, for example, be necessary to sacrifice clean air to build a population base large enough to support a major opera company. If one loves music enough, the price may be worth paying. But in reality, differential material interests influence the trade-offs. If one happens to be on the winning side of the rent intensification process (or in the opera business), the pleasures of cleaner air or lower taxes will be easier to forgo.

Besides the variations between individuals and groups, the actual price to be paid for growth and the willingness to pay it will vary somewhat. Having an opera house is probably more important to the Viennese than to the residents of Carmel, California, and in the same way the preferred trade-offs in population size will vary. On more prosaic grounds, certain places may need additional population to absorb the costs of existing road and sewer systems, however misguided the initial commitment to build them. People in some small towns may want a population increase in order to make rudimentary specialization possible in their public school system. In other instances, a past history of outmigration may have left behind a surplus of unused capacities, which would easily accommodate additional growth and provide public benefits of various sorts.

These variations notwithstanding, the evidence on fiscal health and economic or social problems indicates clearly that the assumptions of value-free development are false. In many cases, probably in most, additional local growth under current arrangements is a transfer of wealth and life chances from the general public to the rentier groups and their associates. Use values of a majority are sacrificed for the exchange gains of the few. To question the wisdom of growth for any specific locality is to threaten a benefit transfer and the interests of those who gain from it.

NOTES

1   Trillin remarks that rejection of high taxes by the citizens of Rockford is "consistent with what the business and industrial leadership of Rockford has traditionally preached. For years, the industrialists were considered to be in complete control of the sort of local government industrialists traditionally favor – a conservative, relatively clean administration committed to the proposition that the highest principle of government is the lowest property tax rate" (Trillin, 1976:150).

2   Although many suburban newspapers encourage growth, especially of tax-generating business, the papers of exclusive suburban towns may instead try to guard the existing land-use patterns and social base of their circulation area. Rudel (1983:104) describes just this sort of situation in Westport, Connecticut. There are a number of reasons for this occasional deviation from the rule we are proposing. When trying to attract advertising dollars, newspapers prefer a small, rich readership to a larger but poorer one. Maintaining exclusivity is itself occasionally a growth strategy for smaller communities. Opposition to growth in these cases is consistent with the desires of local elites.

3   Cox and Morgan's study of British local newspapers indicates that the booster role of the press is not unique to the United States.

4   Unions oppose growth projects that bring nonunion shops; the UAW did not welcome Japanese-owned auto plants that would exclude the union.

REFERENCES

Agger, Robert, Daniel Goldrich, and Bert E. Swanson. 1964. *The Rulers and the Ruled: Political Power and Impotence in American Communities*. New York: Wiley.

Alford, Robert, and Roger Friedland. 1975. "Political Participation and Public Policy." *Annual Review of Sociology* 1: 429–79.

Ann Arbor, Michigan, Planning Department. 1972. *The Ann Arbor Growth Study*. Ann Arbor, Mich.: City Planning Department.

Appelbaum, Richard P., Jennifer Bigelow, Henry Kramer, Harvey Molotch, and Paul Relis. 1976. *The Effects of Urban Growth*. New York: Praeger.

Banfield, Edward C. 1961. *Political Influence*. New York: Macmillan.

Berry, Brian J. L., and John Kasarda. 1977. *Contemporary Urban Ecology*. New York: Macmillan.

Boorstin, Daniel. 1965. *The Americans: The National Experience*. New York: Random House.

Bouma, Donald. 1962. "Analysis of the Social Power Position of a Real Estate Board." *Social Problems* 10(Fall): 121–32.

Brower, John. 1972. *The Black Side of Football*. Ph.D. dissertation, Department of Sociology, University of California, Santa Barbara.

Burd, Gene. 1977. "The Selling of the Sunbelt: Civic Boosterism in the Media." Pp. 129–50 in David Perry and Alfred Watkins (eds.), *The Rise of the Sunbell Cities*. Beverly Hills, Calif.: Sage.

Clark, Terry. 1968. "Community Structure, Decision-Making, Budget Expenditures, and Urban Renewal in Fifty-one American Cities." *American Sociological Review* 33(August): 576–93.

Cox, Harvey, and David Morgan. 1973. *City Politics and the Press: Journalists and the Governing of Merseyside*. Cambridge: Cambridge University Press.

Dagenais, Julie. 1967. "Newspaper Language as an Active Agent in the Building of a Frontier Town." *American Speech* 42(2): 114–21.

Dahl, Robert Alan. 1961. *Who Governs?* New Haven: Yale University Press.

Devereux, Sean. 1976. "Boosters in the Newsroom: The Jacksonville Case." *Columbia Journalism Review* 14: 38–47.

Domhoff, G. William. 1971. *The Higher Circles: The Governing Class in America*. New York: Random House.

Domhoff, G. William. 1983. *Who Rules America Now? A View for the 80's*. Englewood Cliffs, NJ: Prentice-Hall.

Downie, Leonard, Jr. 1974. *Mortgage on America*. New York: Praeger.

Duncan, Otis Dudley. 1957. "Optimum Size of Cities." Pp. 759–73 in Paul K. Hatt and Albert J. Reiss, Jr. (eds.), *Readings in Urban Sociology*, 2d ed. Glencoe, Ill.: Free Press.

Fainstein, Susan, Norman Fainstein, and P. Jefferson Armistead. 1983. "San Francisco: Urban Transformation and the Local State." Pp. 202–44 in Susan Fainstein (ed.), *Restructuring the City*. New York: Longman.

Fischer, Claude S., Mark Baldasarre, and R. J. Ofshe. 1975. "Crowding Studies and Urban Life – A Critical Review." *Journal of the American Institute of Planners* 41(6): 406–18.

Follett, Ross. 1976. "Social Consequences of Urban Size and Growth: An Analysis of US Urban Areas." Ph.D. dissertation, Dept. of Sociology, University of California, Santa Barbara.

Form, William H., and William V. D'Antonio. 1970. "Integration and Cleavage among Comunity Influentials in Two Border Cities." Pp. 431–42 in Michael Aiken and Paul E. Mott (eds.), *The Structure of Community Power*. New York: Random House.

Freidel, Frank. 1963. "Boosters, Intellectuals and the American City." Pp. 115–20 in Oscar Handlin and John Burchard (eds.), *The Historian and the City*. Cambridge, Mass.: MIT Press.

Gaffney, M. Mason. 1961. "Land and Rent in Welfare Economics." Pp. 141–67 in *Land Economics Research* (papers presented at a symposium on land economics research, Lincoln, Neb. June 16–23). Washington, DC: Resources for the Future. Distributed by Johns Hopkins University Press, Baltimore.

Garrison, Charles B. 1971. "New Industry in Small Towns: The Impact on Local Government." *National Tax Journal* 21(4): 493–500.

Greenberg, Stephanie. n.d. "Rapid Growth in a Southern Area: Consequences for Social Inequality." Unpublished manuscript, Denver Research Institute, University of Denver, Denver, Colorado.

Harvey, David. 1973. *Social Justice and the City*. Baltimore: Johns Hopkins University Press.

Hawley, Amos. 1950. *Human Ecology: A Theory of Community Structure*. New York: Ronald Press.

Hunter, Floyd. 1953. *Community Power Structure: A Study of Decision Makers*. Chapel Hill: University of North Carolina Press.

Hunter, Floyd. 1980. *Community Power Succession*. Chapel Hill: University of North Carolina Press.

Johnson, David R. 1983. "San Antonio: The Vicissitudes of Boosterism." Pp. 235–54 in Richard M. Bernard and Bradley R. Rice (eds.), *Sunbelt Cities: Politics and Growth since World War II*. Austin: University of Texas Press.

Krannich, Richard S., and Craig R. Humphrey. 1983. "Local Mobilization and Community Growth: Toward an Assessment of the 'Growth Machine' Hypothesis." *Rural Sociology* 48(1): 60–81.

Lieberson, Stanley. 1980. *A Piece of the Pie: Blacks and White Immigrants since 1800*. Berkeley and Los Angeles: University of California Press.

Los Angeles Times 1983 "Atlantic City Hurt By Gambling, Study Finds." Nov. 2, Sec. 1, p. 11.

Lyon, Larry, Lawrence G. Felice, M. Ray Perryman, and E. Stephen Parker. 1981. "Community Power and Population Increase: An Empirical Test of the Growth Machine Model." *American Journal of Sociology* 86 (6): 1387–1400.

McKenzie, R. D. 1922. "The Neighborhood: A Study of Local Life in the City of Columbus Ohio – Conclusion." *American Journal of Sociology* 27: 780–99.

Markusen, Ann. 1978. "Class, Rent and Sectoral Conflict: Uneven Development in Western US Boomtowns." *Review of Radical Political Economics* 10(3): 117–29.

Melosi, Martin. 1983. "Dallas-Fort Worth: Marketing the Metroplex." Pp. 162–95 in Richard M. Bernard and Bradley R. Rice (eds.), *Sunbelt Cities: Politics and Growth since World War II*. Austin: University of Texas Press.

Molotch, Harvey, and Marilyn Lester. 1974. "News as Purposive Behavior: On the Strategic Use of Routine Events, Accidents, and Scandals." *American Sociological Review* 39(1): 101–13.

Molotch, Harvey, and Marilyn Lester. 1975. "Accidental News: The Great Oil Spill as Local Occurrence and National Event." *American Journal of Sociology* 81(2): 235–60.

Mormino, Gary R. 1983. "Tampa: From Hell Hole to the Good Life." Pp. 138–61 in Richard M. Bernard and Bradley R. Rice (eds.), *Sunbelt Cities: Politics and Growth since World War II*. Austin: University of Texas Press.

Mumford, Lewis. 1961. *The City in History*. New York: Harcourt.

Peterson, Paul E. 1981. *City Limits*. Chicago: University of Chicago Press.

Rubin, Lillian B. 1972. *Busing and Backlash: White against White in an Urban School District*. Berkeley and Los Angeles: University of California Press.

Rudel, Thomas K. 1983. "Managing Growth: Local Governments and the Social Control of Land Use." Unpublished ms., Dept. of Human Ecology, Rutgers University.

San Francisco Chronicle. 1984. "Reagan's Hometown Offers Bounty to Lure More Business to the Area." *San Francisco Chronicle*, May 10, p. 4.

Schattschneider, Elmer Eric. 1960. *The Semisovereign People*. New York: Holt, Rinehart and Winston.

Scheiber, Harry N. 1973. "Urban Rivalry and Internal Improvements in the Old Northwest, 1820–1860." Pp. 135–46 in Alexander Callow, Jr. (ed.), *American Urban History: An Interpretive Reader with Commentaries*, 2d ed. New York: Oxford University Press.

Smith, Michael Peter, and Marlene Keller. 1983. "Managed Growth and the Politics of Uneven Development in New Orleans." Pp. 126–66 in Susan Fainstein (ed.), *Restructuring the City*. New York: Longman.

Spaulding, Charles. 1951. "Occupational Affiliations of Councilmen in Small Cities." *Sociology and Social Research* 35(3): 194–200.

Sternlieb, George, and James W. Hughes. 1983. *The Atlantic City Gamble*. Piscataway, NJ: Center for Urban Policy Research.

Stone, Clarence N. 1981. "Community Power Structure – A Further Look." *Urban Affairs Quarterly* 16(4):505–15.

Stone, Clarence N. 1982. "Social Stratification, Non-Decision-Making and the Study of Community Power." *American Politics Quarterly* 10(3):275–302.

Stone, Clarence N. 1984. "City Politics and Economic Development: Political Economy Perspectives." *Journal of Politics* 46(1): 286–99.

Stuart, Darwin, and Robert Teska. 1971. *Who Pays for What: Cost Revenue Analysis of Suburban Land Use Alternatives*. Washington, DC: Urban Land Institute.

Summers, Gene F., and Kristi Branch. 1984. "Economic Development and Community Social Change." *Annual Review of Sociology* 10: 141–66.

Summers, Gene F., et al. 1976. *Industrial Invasion of Nonmetropolitan America: A Quarter Century of Experience*. New York: Praeger.

Swanstrom, Todd. 1981. "The Crisis of Growth Politics: Cleveland, Kucinich, and the Challenge of Urban Populism." Ph.D. dissertation, Princeton University.

Swanstrom, Todd. 1985. *The Crisis of Growth Politics: Cleveland, Kucinich, and the Challenge of Urban Populism*. Philadelphia: Temple University Press.

Tiebout, Charles M. 1956. "A Pure Theory of Local Expenditures." *Journal of Political Economy* 64(October):416–24.

Trillin, Calvin. 1976. "US Journal: Rockford, Illinois – Schools without Money." *New Yorker* 52(38):146–54.

Vidich, Arthur J., and Joseph Bensman. 1960. *Small Town in Mass Society: Class, Power and Religion in a Rural Community*. Garden City, NY: Doubleday.

Walker, Richard A., and Matthew J. Williams, 1982. "Water from Power: Water Supply and Regional Growth in the Santa Clara Valley." *Economic Geography* 58(2):95–119.

Walton, John. 1970. "A Systematic Survey of Community Power Research." Pp. 443–64 in Michael Aiken and Paul Mott (eds.), *The Structure of Community Power*. New York: Random House.

Weinstein, Bernard L., and Robert E. Firestine. 1978. *Regional Growth and Decline in the United States*. New York: Praeger.

Whitt, J. Allen. 1982. *Urban Elites and Mass Transportation: The Dialectics of Power*. Princeton, NJ: Princeton University Press.

Wolfe, Alan. 1981. *America's Impasse: The Rise and Fall of the Politics of Growth*. New York: Pantheon.

Worster, Donald. 1982. "Hydraulic Society in California: An Ecological Interpretation." *Agricultural History* 56(July):503–15.

Wyner, Allen. 1967. "Governor-Salesman." *National Civic Review* 16(Feb.): 81–6.

Zunz, Olivier. 1982. *The Changing Face of Inequality: Urbanization, Industrial Development, and Immigrants in Detroit, 1880–1920*. Chicago: University of Chicago Press.

from *Cities of Tomorrow: An Intellectual History of Urban Planning and Design in the Twentieth Century*

Peter Hall

9 The City on the Highway

The automobile suburb: Long Island, Wisconsin, Los Angeles, Paris, 1920–1987

... [M]ass motorization had already begun to impinge on American cities by the mid-1920s, in a way the rest of the world would not know until the 1950s and 1960s. By 1923, traffic congestion in some cities was already so bad that there was talk of barring cars from downtown streets; by 1926, Thomas E. Pitts had closed his cigar store and soft-drink bar at a major intersection in the centre of Atlanta because congestion made it impossible to operate.[1] In the same decade, Sears Roebuck and then Montgomery Ward planned their first automobile-oriented suburban stores[2] When the Lynds came to make their classic sociological study of 'Middletown' (actually, Muncie in Indiana), at the end of the 1920s, they found that already car ownership was allowing the ordinary worker to live farther from his work.[3] And, by that time, already in some cities – Washington, Kansas City, St Louis – downtown commuters by automobile outnumbered those coming by transit. Unsurprisingly, then, the 1920s were the first decade when the Census-takers noticed that the suburbs were growing much faster than the central

cities: by 39 per cent, more than 4 million people, as against 19 per cent or 5 million in the cities. In some cities the suburbanization trend was even more marked: the relative rates of growth in New York City were 67 against 23 per cent, in Cleveland 126 against 12 per cent, in St Louis 107 against 5 per cent.[4]

The remarkable fact was that some American planners, at any rate, greeted this trend with equanimity, even with enthusiasm. At the National Conference of City Planners in 1924, Gordon Whitnall, a Los Angeles planner, proudly declared that western planners had learned from eastern mistakes, and would now lead the way to the horizontal city of the future. During the 1920s, as transit systems for the first time reported falling ridership and loss of profits, Detroit and Los Angeles considered large-scale support for transit investment in order to support their downtown areas, but found that voters would not support it.[5]

This ever-growing volume of car traffic for the most part travelled on ordinary city streets, widened and upgraded to cope with the flood. By the end of the 1920s there were few examples even of simple underpasses or overpasses on American highways.[6] The outstanding exception was New York, which during the 1920s followed a distinctive path, deriving directly from an older tradition: the parkway. First used by Olmsted in his design for New York's Central Park in 1858, the parkway had been widely employed by landscape architects in the planning of parks and new residential areas in cities as diverse as Boston, Kansas City and Chicago.[7] But, beginning with William K. Vanderbilt's Long Island Motor Parkway (1906–11), which can claim to be the world's first limited-access motor highway, and the 16-mile Bronx River Parkway (1906–23), followed by the Hutchinson River Parkway of 1928 and the Saw Mill Parkway of 1929, this distinctively American innovation was rapidly adapted to a new function: extended continuously for 10 or 20 miles into open countryside – and sometimes, as in the Bronx Parkway, used to clear up urban blight – it now gave rapid access from the congested central city both to new suburbs and to rural and coastal recreation areas.[8]

The moving spirit was New York's Master Builder, Robert Moses. Using a State Act of 1924, which he had personally drafted to give him unprecedented (and, to the hapless legislators, unappreciated) powers to appropriate land, he proceeded to drive his parkways across the cherished estates of the Long Island millionaires – the Phippses, the Whitneys, the Morgans, the Winthrops – to give New Yorkers access to the ocean beaches. It was done, like most other things Moses did, for the highest public-spirited motives; and it established the base of his unprecedented public support, which he then skilfully extended through his management of the Triborough Ridge and Tunnel Authority, tying his parkway system together and linking it to the teeming tenements of Manhattan and the Bronx.[9]

But there were limits to public spirit: deliberately, Moses built the parkway bridges too low not only for trucks, but also for buses. The magnificent bathing beaches that he created at the ends of the parkways would thus be strictly reserved for middle-class car owners; the remaining two-thirds of the population could con-

tinue to ride the subway to Coney Island. And, when in the 1930s Moses extended his system down the west side of Manhattan island to create the Henry Hudson Parkway, the world's first true urban motorway, the same applied: Moses was now consciously planning a system for car commuters.[10]

The point about Moses's gigantic public works of these years was indeed precisely this: whatever their ostensible original purpose, once linked by the Triborough Bridge they constituted a vast network of urban expressways, making it possible to commute to Manhattan offices from distances up to 20, even 30 miles: three or four times the effective radius of the subway system. There was an immediate effect: the population of Westchester and Nassau counties, served by the new roads, increased by 350,000 during the 1920s.[11] But the full implications would emerge only in the suburban building boom after World War Two. It was no accident that the most celebrated of all the resulting developments, the one that came almost to symbolize the whole process, was located where it was: the original Levittown stands just off an interchange on Moses's Wantagh State Parkway, built nearly twenty years earlier as one of the approaches to Jones Beach State Park.

Some planners, even then, embraced the idea of new roads as the basis of a new urban form. One of the founding fathers of the Regional Planning Association of America, Benton MacKaye, had developed the idea of a townless highway, or 'motorway'. Seizing upon the plan of Radburn – developed by two other RPAA stalwarts, Clarence Stein and Henry Wright – he argued for its extension to the regional scale.

> The townless highway is a motorway, in which the adjoining towns would be in the same relationship to the road as the residential cul-de-sacs in Radburn are to the main traffic avenues. What Radburn does in the local community, the townless highway would do for the community at large.... Instead of a single roadtown

slum, congealing between our big cities, the townless highway would encourage the building of real communities at definite and favorable points *off* the main road.[12]

The concept was clear and consistent:

the abolition of approaches to the main highway except at certain points; public ownership, or effective public control through rigorous zoning, of the foreground along the right-of-way... proper landscape development of the foreground, including the culture of shade trees and the strict regulation of telephone and electric-light lines; and finally, strict control of highway service station development.[13]

All that, of course, came to pass – but first in other places, and only long afterwards in the United States. And the other part of the prescription, the ultimate RPAA dream – 'to stimulate the growth of the distinct community, compactly planned and limited in size, like the old New England village or the modern Radburn'[14] – was to remain unrealized in the land of its origin. ...

... Apart from a longer-distance extension of the New York Parkway system into the neighbouring state of Connecticut – the Merritt and Wilbur Cross Parkways, which were toll roads, restricted to private motor traffic – America's first true intercity motorway, the Pennsylvania Turnpike through the Appalachians from Carlisle near Harrisburg to Irwin near Pittsburgh, opened only in 1940[15] December of that same year marked another milestone in the automobile age: Los Angeles completed its Arroyo Seco Parkway, now part of the Pasadena Freeway. Like the early *Autobahnen*, it was under-designed; in an extraordinary re-run of the opening of the first Autobahn, the opening ceremony was marked by a multiple shunt collision involving three car-loads of dignitaries.[16] Thereafter, war intervened: at its end, Los Angeles had precisely 11 miles of freeway.[17] Its 1939 freeway plan, which had been produced by the City Engineer Lloyd

Aldrich with the aid of downtown business after the City had denied the money, was implemented only over the subsequent two decades.[18] Only then did the city of freeways deserve its appellation.

But perhaps what gave Los Angeles its mythical reputation was not the extent of its network – the New York metropolitan area, with the head start Moses gave it, could always win on that score – but the total dependence of its citizens on it, revealed by the rarity of public transportation and by that telling phrase of Angelenos who talk of 'going surface' as if it were an eccentric undertaking. It was also the distinctive lifestyle that ensued: a style exemplified by the heroine of Joan Didion's novel *Play It As It Lays*, who, deserted by her husband, 'turns to the freeways for sustenance', and is finally initiated:

Again and again she returned to an intricate stretch just south of the interchange where a successful passage from the Hollywood onto the Harbor required a diagonal move across four lanes of traffic. On the afternoon when she finally did it without once braking or once losing the beat on the radio she was exhilarated, and that night slept dreamlessly.[19]

It was also the resulting pattern of urban growth. The opening of the Arroyo Seco was followed almost immediately by higher land values in Pasadena. Thence, wherever the freeways went, the developers followed. And, unlike Moses's network in New York, this system was not radial – or at most, only partially so; it rather formed a loose trapezoidal grid, giving roughly equal accessibility from anywhere to anywhere. True, this had also been a feature of the old Big Red Cars of the Pacific Electric Railway; Los Angeles's celebrated polycentric, dispersed quality antedated the freeway era by many decades, and, as the urban area tripled in population in the 1930s and 1940s, downtown traffic stayed constant. And, ironically, as the rail system decayed under the pressure of rising car ownership from the mid-1920s, its abandoned rights of way provided ideal routes for the new freeways.[20] But the automobile revolution, coming much earlier here than in most American cities – there were already close on 800,000 cars, two to every five people, in Los Angeles County by 1930 – brought early thrombosis to the downtown area and the early spread of business activities outside it, thus contributing to the city's conscious decision in the mid-1920s not to support transit, and to the business pressures in the next decade to build a freeway system.[21] . . .

Frank Lloyd Wright and the Soviet deurbanists

In America . . . automobile-oriented suburbs were being consciously planned. . . . Thus in Kansas City, George E. Kessler's great city-parks plan of 1893–1910, which included recreational parkways, provided a basis for the developer Jesse Clyde Nichols's Country Club District begun in 1907–8; influenced both by the City Beautiful movement and by a bicycle tour of European Garden Cities, designed by Kessler to integrate with his parks, it was the first garden suburb specifically based on the automobile. Nichols deliberately bought cheap land outside the range of the city's streetcar system, allowing him to build at low density – first at six houses per acre, then even less; at the centre, the brilliant Country Club Plaza (originated by the architect Edward Buhler Delle in 1923–5) was the world's first car-based shopping centre.[22] In Los Angeles both Beverly Hills (1914) and Palos Verdes Estates (1923) followed similar planning principles; though the first was originally based on a Pacific Electric Railway station, both soon became classic early automobile suburbs.[23]

All these were private speculative developments pure and simple. They were designed to make money and they did. They owed their outstanding success to the quality of their design and to the use of private covenants to guarantee that this quality would be maintained. But there was also a highly idealized version of the automobile city, and a rationale for it. Appropriately enough, the most complete formulation of it came from America's outstanding native architect, Frank Lloyd Wright. But another, uncannily similar version came from a source as unlikely as could be imagined: the Soviet Union.

The Soviet deurbanists of the 1920s, led by Moisei Ginsburg and Moisei Okhitovich, argued – like Wright, and perhaps influenced by him – that electricity and new transportation technologies, above all the car, would allow cities to empty out.[24] They too were essentially individualistic and anti-bureaucratic; they similarly argued for new kinds of built form based on factory-produced materials, with individual lightweight transportable homes located in natural countryside, thus creating a 'townless, fully decentralized, and even populated country',[25] they even envisaged the eventual razing of the cities to form huge parks and urban museums.[26] But these were Soviet planners, and their version of individualism was curiously collective: all activities, save sleeping and repose, would be communal.[27] The technological imperative was identical to that of Frank Lloyd Wright, the moral order was – at least superficially – quite different.

In the event, given material conditions in the Soviet Union at the time, it was all quite fantastic. There were hardly any cars, and not much electricity. Well might Corbusier, who was of course allied to the opposite urbanist camp, parody the deurbanist vision:

> The cities will be part of the country; I shall live 30 miles from my office in one direction, under a pine tree; my secretary will live 30 miles away from it too, in the other direction, under another pine tree. We shall both have our own car. We shall use up tires, wear out road surfaces and gears, consume oil and gasoline. All of which will necessitate a great deal of work . . . enough for all.[28]

Perhaps such a vision was all conceivable in America; even in the depression-ridden America of the early 1930s. But in the Soviet Union, even given the appalling condition of Moscow's housing and infrastructure at the time, it was not. The historic 1931 Party Congress determined that anyone who denied the socialist character of existing cities was a saboteur; from 1933, a decree laid it down that city centres should be rebuilt to express 'socialist greatness'.[29] Stalin had spoken; the great Soviet urban debate was stilled for a generation.

Frank Lloyd Wright's vision, in contrast, was perfectly attuned not only to its author's personal philosophy, but also to the conditions of its time. It was, indeed, the distillation of almost everything that he felt and had expressed about the theory of built form. In the process, it managed in a rather extraordinary way to weave together almost every significant strain of American urban – more precisely, anti-urban – thinking.

Wright began to conceive of Broadacre City as early as 1924, and soon afterwards coined the title in a lecture at Princeton University[30] The conception shares many philosophical affinities with the ideas of the Regional Planning Association of America, and some of these with Ebenezer Howard. There is the same rejection of the big city – specifically, New York – as a cancer, a 'fibrous tumour'; the same populist antipathy to finance capital and landlordism; the same anarchist rejection of big government; the same reliance on the liberating effects of new technologies; the same belief in the homesteading principle and the return to the land; there is even that distinctively American transcendentalism that derives from writers like Emerson, Thoreau and Whitman.[31]

But there are also differences, particularly in comparison with Howard (as indeed with the Soviet deurbanists): Wright claimed to liberate men and women not in order to join in co-operation, but to live as free individuals; he desired not to marry town and country, but to merge them.[32] Above all, there is the notion that the new technological forces could recreate in America a nation of free independent farmers and proprietors: 'Edison and Ford

would resurrect Jefferson.'[33] In this regard, the similarity is rather with the Greenbelt communities of Rexford Tugwell; but Tugwell shared with Mumford, Stein and Chase a belief in community planning, hard to trace in Wright. Rather, Wright shares with the RPAA a common background of experience: the slow decay of rural America, ground down between the soul-destroying drudgery of the pre-electric farm and the welcoming bright lights of the city, as poignantly recorded by Hamlin Garland in his autobiographical *A Son of the Middle Border*:

> In those few days, I perceived life without its glamor. I no longer looked upon these toiling women with the thoughtless eyes of youth. I saw no humor in the bent forms and graying hair of the men. I began to understand that my own mother had trod a similar slavish round with never a full day of leisure, with scarcely an hour of escape from the tugging hands of children, and the need of mending and washing clothes.[34]

Liberated at last by World War One and the automobile, they left the farms 'in rattle-trap automobiles, their fenders tied with springs, and curtains flapping in the breeze ... with no funds and no prospects'.[35] And then, the migration turned into sheer necessity, as depression brought farm foreclosures and the forced conversion of proprietors into sharecroppers.[36] Yet, as Charles Abrams put it at the time, 'Not only is the frontier closed, but the city is closed'; the farmer had nowhere to go.[37] Hence the Resettlement Administration's greenbelt towns, hence Broadacre City.

But Broadacre would be different. The new technologies, as Kropotkin had argued more than three decades earlier, were transforming, even abolishing, the tyranny of geography. 'Given electrification, distances are all but eliminated as far as communication goes.... Given the steamship, airship, and the automobile, our human sphere of movement immeasurably widens by many mechanical modes, by wheel or air.'[38] Now, 'not only thought but speech and movement are volatile: the telegraph, telephone, mobilization, radio. Soon, television and safe flight.'[39] Modern mobility was available even for the poor man, 'by means of a bus or a model A Ford'.[40]

Coupled with this, new building materials – high-pressure concrete, glass and 'innumerable broad, thin, cheap sheets of wood, metal or plastics' – made a new kind of building possible: 'buildings may be made by machinery going to the building instead of the building going to machinery.'[41] And at the same time, 'machine-shop fabrication' made water and gas and electricity cheaply 'available in quantity for all instead of still more questionable luxuries for the few.'[42] So 'the congested verticality of any city is now utterly inartistic and *unscientific*!'[43]

Out of these technological ingredients, Wright constructed what he called his 'Usonian Vision':

> Imagine, now, spacious, well-landscaped highways, grade crossings eliminated by a new kind of integrated by-passing or over-or under-passing all traffic in cultivated or living areas....Giant roads, themselves great architecture, pass public service stations no longer eyesores but expanded as good architecture to include all kinds of roadside service for the traveller, charm and comfort throughout. These great roads unite and separate, separate and unite, in endless series of diversified units passing by farm units, roadside markets, garden schools, dwelling places, each on its acres of individually adorned and cultivated ground, developed homes all places for pleasure in work or leisure. And imagine man-units so arranged that every citizen as he chooses may have all forms of production, distribution, self-improvement, enjoyment within the radius of, say, ten to twenty miles of his own home. And speedily available by means of his private car or public conveyance. This integrated distribution of living related to ground composes the great city that I see embracing this country. This would be the Broadacre City of tomorrow that is the nation. Democracy realized.[44]

Broadacre, of course, would be a city of individuals. Its houses would be designed

> not only in harmony with greenery and ground but intimate with the pattern of the personal life of the individual on the ground. No two homes, no two gardens, none of the farm units on one – to two, three – to ten acres or more; no two farmsteads or factory buildings need be alike.... Strong but light and appropriate houses, spacious convenient workplaces to which all would be tributary, each item would be solidly and sympathetically built out of materials native to Time, Place, and Man.[45]

All this was the physical shell. But for Wright, just as for Mumford or for Howard, the built forms were merely the appropriate expression of a new kind of society. The skyscraper city, for him, represented 'the end of an epoch! The end of the plutocratic republic of America'.[46] Through another mass migration, as huge and as momentous as the original homesteading of America, the new pioneer would replace the plutocracy of the landlords and the giant corporations by 'a more simple, natural-basis right to live by and enough to live upon according to his better self'.[47] The vision is almost identical to Howard's:

> Emancipated from rent, were good ground made available to him, he – the machine worker rented by wages – paying toll to the exaggerated city in order that the city give him work to do – why should not he, the poor wage-slave, go forward, not backward, to his native birthright? Go to the good ground and grow his family in a free city?[48]

There, he would rediscover the quintessential American democracy 'the ideal of re-integrated decentralization...many free units developing strength as they learn by function and grow together in spacious mutual freedom.'[49] It was the vision of his Wisconsin boyhood, recaptured through the new technology.

No one liked it. For his pains, he was attacked by almost everyone: for naïvety, for architectural determinism, for encouraging suburbanization, for wasteful use of resources, for lack of urbanity, above all for being insufficiently collective in his philosophy.[50] He developed no movement to realize his ideas, received no commissions from Tugwell's Resettlement Administration, and got no moral support at all from the other powerful figures – above all the leaders of the RPAA – who were working in favour of planned decentralization.[51]

And, as Herbert Muschamp has eloquently argued, there was finally a contradiction in the whole vision: the free commonwealth of individuals would live in houses designed by the master architect:

> ... when all the Whitmanesque windbag rhetoric extolling the pioneer spirit is swept away, what remains is a society constructed upon the strict hierarchical principle of Wright's own Taliesin Fellowship: a government of architecture, a society in which the architect is granted ultimate executive power... It is easy, therefore, to view Broadacre as proof that within every self-styled individualist is a dictator longing to break free.[52]

The heart of the contradiction, for Muschamp, lay in the belief that the architect could control the whole process. In fact, by the early 1950s, the American actuality 'threatened to liquidate his own Romantic dream in a vista of carports, split-levels, lawn sprinklers washing away the Usonian dream to make way for the weekend barbecue.'[53] The final irony came at the end of the 1950s: Wright unsuccessfully sued the local county to remove the pylons that disfigured the view from Taliesin III, erected to carry power to new Phoenix suburbanites. Yet, in the same decade, driving Alvar Aalto around the Boston suburbs, he could claim that he had made all this possible. Muschamp comments:

> Didn't the Adventurer in Wright want to roar with laughter at the thought that the greatest architect of all time had made

possible the conversion of America's natural paradise to an asphalt continent of Holiday Inns, Tastee-Freeze stands, automobile graveyards, billboards, smog, tract housing, mortgaged and franchised coast to coast.[54]

Perhaps. There was a contradiction, to be sure: Wright wanted it all architect-designed, sanitized, in uniform good taste; it came out anything but. Perhaps he did have more in common with the Soviet deurbanists than either would have admitted; they were all architects, after all. Yet Broadacre City is significant for the nature of its vision. It probably could not have occurred in just that way, when it did, in any other country. It seized the American future, embodied it in a vision. The remarkable fact is just how visionary it proved to be.

'The suburbs are coming!'

This then was the ironic outcome: after World War Two a suburban building boom created a kind of Broadacre City all over America, but entirely divorced from the economic basis or the social order Wright had so steadfastly affirmed. In the late 1940s and the 1950s, thousands of square miles of American farmland disappeared under it; one *New Yorker* cartoon showed a traditional farm family sitting on their porch with a bulldozer rearing over the brow of the near-by hill, as the wife shouts 'Pa, get your gun! The suburbs are coming.' But the people who moved into the new tract homes typically owed their living to those very mammoth corporations which Wright assailed; their homes were mortgaged to giant financial institutions; and in no sense did they constitute a society of sturdy self-sufficient proprietors. Americans had got the shell without the substance.

There were four main foundations for the suburban boom. They were new roads, to open up land outside the reach of the old trolley and commuter rail routes; zoning of land uses, to produce uniform residential tracts with stable property values; government-guaranteed mortgages, to make possible long-repayment low-interest mortgages that were affordable by families of modest incomes; and a baby boom, to produce a sudden surge in demand for family homes where young children could be raised....

...The industry spectacularly responded: as against a mere 515,000 starts in 1939, there were 1,466,000 by 1949, 1,554,000 by 1959.[55] And in the 1949 Housing Act – as well as initiating the urban renewal process, chronicled in chapter 7 – Congress massively increased FHA's lending powers.[56] As before, this money went into the suburbs. By 1950, the suburbs were found to be growing at ten times the rate of the central cities; by 1954, it was estimated that in the previous decade 9 million people had moved into the suburbs.[57]

The 1950s, as the 1960 Census showed, was the decade of the greatest suburban growth in American history: while the central cities grew by 6 million or 11.6 per cent, the suburbs grew by a dizzy 19 million, or by 45.9 per cent. And ominously, for the first time, some of the nation's greatest cities recorded actual population decline: Boston and St Louis each lost 13 per cent of their population.[58]

This huge migration was made possible by a new breed of builder: large scale, economy-and efficiency-conscious, capable of building houses like refrigerators or cars. The archetypal firm, which became a legend in its own time, had been founded by Abraham Levitt and his sons William and Alfred, as a small family firm on Long Island outside New York City in 1929. During World War Two they learned how to build workers' housing fast, and rapidly waxed larger. In the town of Hempstead on Long Island, 23 miles from midtown Manhattan, they began in 1948 a suburb based on the techniques they had learned: flow production, division of labour, standardized designs and parts, new materials and tools, maximum use of prefabricated components, easy credit, good marketing. The people came and queued in long lines for hours to buy their houses; when the Levitts had finished, they had completed more than 17,000 homes

housing some 82,000 people: the largest single housing development in history[59] They went on to develop similar Levittowns in Pennsylvania and New Jersey....

It was, and is, also rigidly segregated by age, income and race. Those who came here were overwhelmingly young married couples in the lower-middle income range, and without exception they were white: as late as 1960, Levittown had not a single black, and in the mid-1980s it does not have conspicuously many. As the elder Levitt put it, 'We can solve a housing problem, or we can try to solve a racial problem. But we cannot combine the two.'[60] So Levittown, and all its countless imitators, were homogeneous places: like lived with like. And, as places like St Louis eloquently showed, a large part of the suburban flight from the city was white flight: here as elsewhere, the blacks were coming from the countryside to the city, the whites were simultaneously leaving the city for the suburbs.[61]

The question will be asked and should be asked: what has all this to do with planning? Does a place like Levittown belong in a history of city planning at all? Insofar as Long Island had both planners and plans, then – at least in a formal sense – it does. But Gottdiener's exhaustive analysis suggests that in practice Long Island's planners had little power: 'The decisions made by the politicians, speculators and housing developers lead to the same land-use pattern', he concludes, 'as would result from no planning or zoning.'[62] This leads him to ask: 'if planners do not implement land-use decisions nor guide directly social growth in our society, we are left with the intriguing question – what, then, do planners do?'[63] His answer is that they produce plans: 'The planning process, as it is usually practised in the society, makes planners advisory bystanders to decisions that are being carried out elsewhere – by political leaders and private businessmen';[64] their ideas – whether on physical matters, or on social – find little favour among the majority of white middle-class suburban residents, who would like yet more low-density suburban sprawl. Which, after all, is hardly surprising.

Suburbia: the great debate

But – here, or elsewhere – the planners had some vocal people on their side; while those who built the suburbs, and those who lived in them, were either too preoccupied or not sufficiently voluble to defend them. So, as it burgeoned, American suburbia came to be almost universally vilified in the public prints. What condemned it was the fact that it failed to conform to traditional – that is to say, European – notions of urbanity. Here are three representative critiques:

> In every department, form disintegrated: except in its heritage from the past, the city vanished as an embodiment of collective art and technics. And where, as in North America, the loss was not alleviated by the continued presence of great monuments from the past and persistent habits of social living, the result was a raw, dissolute environment and a narrow, constricted, and baffled social life.[65]

> Sprawl is bad aesthetics; it is bad economics. Five acres are being made to do the work of one, and do it very poorly. This is bad for the farmers, it is bad for communities, it is bad for industry, it is bad for utilities, it is bad for the railroads, it is bad for the recreation groups, it is bad even for the developers.[66]

> The question is, shall we have 'slurbs', or shall we plan to have attractive communities which can grow in an orderly way while showing the utmost respect for the beauty and fertility of our landscape? If present trends continue, we shall have slurbs.[67]

Many points of attack recur here: waste of land, increased commute times, higher service costs, lack of parkland. But the central criticism is that the suburbs lack *form*. As usual, Mumford puts it best, in his appreciation of the garden-city alternative: 'A modern city, no less than a medieval town...must have a definite size, form, boundary. It was no longer to be a mere

sprawl of houses along an indeterminate avenue that moved towards infinity and ended suddenly in a swamp.'[68] Ian Nairn, similarly, criticized the suburban landscape for the fact that 'each building is treated in isolation, nothing binds it to the next one', for 'togetherness in the landscape or townscape, like the coexistence of opposites, is essential.'[69]

The interesting fact is that the intellectual counter-attack, when it finally came, originated from the American west. James E. Vance, a Berkeley geographer, argued for the San Francisco Bay Area that

> It is fashionable, if extremely trite, to refer to the urban area as a shapeless sprawl, as a cancer, as an unrelieved evil.... The erroneous notion that no such structure exists must result from a failure to study the dynamics of urban growth, or possibly from the desire to put forward a doctrine of what is 'right' or 'good' in urban growth.[70]

And Robert Riley similarly defended the 'new' cities of the American southwest, like Houston and Dallas and Phoenix:

> The new city has been damned simply because it is different.... The planning proposals made for these cities – and, largely, too, for Eastern megalopolises – are based on nothing more or less than channelling growth back into a form that we recognize as the only true city – the traditional city.[71]

Taking up the case for the defence, Melvin Webber of Berkeley argued,

> I contend that we have been searching for the wrong grail, that the values associated with the desired urban structure do not reside in the spatial structure per se. One pattern and its internal land use form is superior to another only as it better serves to accommodate ongoing spatial processes and to further the nonspatial ends of the political community. I am flatly rejecting the contention that there is an overriding universal spatial or physical aesthetic of urban form.[72]

New communications technologies, he argued, had broken down the age-old connection between community and propinquity: the urban place was being replaced by the nonplace urban realm.[73] Early the next decade, Reyner Banham wrote his appreciative essay on Los Angeles;[74] the year after that, Robert Venturi and Denise Scott Brown published their celebrated exercise in architectural iconoclasm, boldly proclaiming across its dust jacket: 'A Significance for A&P Parking Lots, or *Learning from Las Vegas*...Billboards are Almost All Right'.[75] The battle lines could not be more clearly drawn: the West Coast had at last reasserted itself against the traditions of Europe.

The defection of Venturi, one of America's most distinguished architects, was especially significant. For he and his colleagues were passionately arguing that the roadside civilization of American suburbia, most exuberantly exemplified by the great neon-lit Strip at Las Vegas, should no longer be judged by the functionalist criteria that had ruled ever since the triumph of the international style in the 1930s.

'Learning from the existing landscape', they began, 'is a way of being revolutionary for an architect. Not the obvious way, which is to tear down Paris and begin again, as Corbusier suggested in the 1920s, but another, more tolerant way; that is, to question how we look at things.'[76] They studied Las Vegas 'as a phenomenon of architectural communication';[77] because people now moved in cars at high speeds and often in complex patterns, a whole new architecture of signs had arisen to guide and to persuade: 'the graphic sign in space has become the architecture of this landscape',[78] while the building itself is set back, half hidden – like most of the environment – by parked cars:

> The A & P parking lot is a current phase in the evolution of vast space since Versailles. The space that divides high-speed highway and low, sparse buildings produces no enclosure and little direction. To move through a piazza is to move

through high enclosing forms. To move through this landscape is to move over vast expansive texture: the megastructure of the commercial landscape...Because the spatial relationships are made by symbols more than by forms, architecture in this landscape becomes symbol in space rather than form in space. Architecture defines very little. The big sign and the little building is the rule of Route 66.[79]

This analysis, notice, represents the perfect analogue at the micro-, or urban-design, scale of the Berkeley geographer-planners' argument at the wider urban-structural scale: the new landscape is not worse, it is different; it cannot be appreciated and should not be judged by the traditional rules, but by its own.

The result, for international architecture, was cataclysmic: *Learning from Las Vegas* is one of the distinct breakpoints that mark the end of the modern architectural movement and its displacement by postmodernism, with its new stress on architecture as symbolic communication.[80] For the student of urbanism, it likewise marked a revolution: henceforth, the artefacts of roadside civilization were worthy of study for their own sake. So, by the mid-1980s, a scholarly treatise could trace the evolution of the 1920s motor court into the 1930s motel and finally into the 1950s motor hotel; this last mutation represented by the historic first Holiday Inn, developed by Kemmons Wilson and the prefabricated home-builder Wallace E. Johnson in Memphis, Tennessee, in 1952.[81] Or it could analyse the evolution of the fast-food outlet from the White Castle chain started by Edgard Ingram and Walter Anderson at Kansas City in 1921, via Howard Johnson's pioneering efforts in Massachusetts in 1929–30 and the historic McDonalds drive-in at San Bernardino, California, in 1948, to their standard design of 1952, first marketed nationally by Ray Kroc at Des Plaines, Illinois, in 1955.[82] Such work revealed just how long and rich this tradition of roadside architecture had been, making it the more remarkable that previously no one had possessed the sens-

ibility or the energy to see or to analyse the landscape in front of them....

NOTES

1 Flink, 1975, 163, 178.
2 Dolce, 1976, 28.
3 Ibid. 157.
4 Tobin, 1976, 103–4.
5 Foster, 1981, 80–5, 88–9.
6 Hubbard and Hubbard, 1929, 208.
7 Scott, 1969, 13–15, 22, 38–9; Dal Co, 1979, 177.
8 Rae, 1971, 71–2; Dolce, 1976, 19; Jackson, K., 1985, 166; Gregg, 1986, 38–42.
9 Caro, 1974, 143–57, 174–7, 184–5, 208–10, 386–8.
10 Ibid. 318, 546–7.
11 Dolce, 1976, 25.
12 MacKaye, 1930, 94.
13 Ibid. 95.
14 Ibid.
15 Rae, 1971, 79–81.
16 Jackson, K., 1985, 167.
17 Brodsly, 1981, 112.
18 Rae, 1971, 82–3; Brodsly, 1981, 101–2.
19 cit. Brodsly, 1981, 56; cf. Banham, 1971, 214–15.
20 Fogelson, 1967, 92, 175–85; Rae, 1971, 243; Warner, 1972, 138–41; Brodsly, 1981, 4; Foster, 1981, 17; Wachs, 1984, 303; Jackson, K., 1985, 122.
21 Fogelson, 1967, 92, 177–8.
22 Stern and Massingdale, 1981, 76; Jackson, K., 1985, 177–8, 258.
23 Stern and Massingdale, 1981, 78; Jackson, K., 1985, 179–80.
24 Parkins, 1953, 24; Frampton, 1968, 238; Bliznakov, 1976, 250–1; Starr, 1977; 90–1; Thomas, 1978, 275.
25 Bliznakov, 1976, 250.
26 Thomas, 1978, 275.
27 Bliznakov, 1976, 251.
28 Le Corbusier, 1967, 74.
29 Bliznakov, 1976, 252–4.
30 Wright, 1945, 138.
31 White and White, 1962, 193; Grabow, 1977, 116–17; Fishman, 1977, 124–7; Ciucci, 1979, 296–300, Muschamp, 1983, 75.
32 Fishman, 1977, 92–4.
33 Ibid. 123.
34 Garland, 1917, 366.
35 Fogelson, 1967, 74.
36 Abrams, 1939, 68.
37 Ibid.
38 Wright, 1945, 34.
39 Ibid. 36.
40 Ibid. 86.
41 Ibid. 37.
42 Ibid.
43 Ibid. 34.
44 Ibid. 65–6.
45 Ibid. 66.
46 Ibid. 120.
47 Ibid. 121.
48 Ibid. 86.
49 Ibid. 45–6.
50 Grabow, 1977, 119–22.
51 Fishman, 1977, 146–8.
52 Muschamp, 1983, 79–80.
53 Ibid. 93.
54 Ibid. 185.
55 Checkoway, 1984, 154.
56 Ibid. 161.
57 Jackson, K., 1985, 238.
58 Tobin, 1976, 106.
59 Checkoway, 1984, 158; Jackson, K., 1985, 234–5.
60 Jackson, K., 1985, 241.
61 Montgomery, 1985, 236.
62 Gottdiener, 1977, 111.
63 Ibid. 116.
64 Ibid. 143.
65 Mumford, 1938, 8.
66 Whyte, 1958, 117.
67 Wood and Heller, 1962, 13.
68 Mumford, 1938, 397.
69 Nairn, 1965, 13.
70 Vance, 1964, 68–9.
71 Riley, 1967, 21.
72 Webber, 1963, 52.
73 Webber, 1964b, *passim*.
74 Banham, 1971.
75 Venturi, Brown and Izenour, 1972.
76 Venturi *et al.*, 1972, o [*sic*].
77 Ibid.
78 Ibid.
79 Ibid.
80 Jencks, 1981, 45
81 Liebs, 1985, 182–5
82 Ibid. 185, 202, 206–8, 212–13; Langdon, 1986, 29–55, 81–109.

REFERENCES

Abrams, C. 1939: *Revolution in Land*. New York and London: Harper and Brothers.

Banham, R. 1971: *Los Angeles: The Architecture of Four Ecologies*. London: Allen Lane.

Bliznakov, M. 1976: Urban Planning in the USSR: Integration Theories. In: Hamm, M. F. (ed.), 1976: *The City in Russian History*. Lexington: University of Kentucky Press, 243–56.

Brodsly, D. 1981: *L. A. Freeway: An Appreciative Essay*. Berkeley: University of California Press.

Caro, R. A. 1974: *The Power Broker: Robert Moses and the Fall of New York*. New York: Alfred A. Knopf.

Checkoway, B. 1984: Large Builders, Federal Housing Programs, and Postwar Suburbanization. In: Tabb, W., Sawers, L. (eds), 1978, *Marxism and the Metropolis: New Perspectives on Urban Political Theory*, 2nd edn. New York: OUP, 152–73.

Checkoway, B., Patton, C. V. (eds) 1985: *The Metropolitan Midwest: Policy Problems and Prospects for Change*. Urbana: University of Illinois Press.

Ciucci, G. 1979: The City in Agrarian Ideology and Frank Lloyd Wright: Origins and development of Broadacres. In: Ciucci, G. et al., 1979, 293–387.

Ciucci, G., Dal Co, F., Manieri-Elia, M., Tafuri, M., 1979: *The American City: From the Civil War to the New Deal*. Cambridge, Mass.: MIT Press.

Dal Co, F. 1979: From Parks to the Region: Progressive Ideology and the Reform of the American City. In: Ciucci, G. et al., 1979, 143–291.

Dolce, P. C. (ed.) 1976: *Suburbia: The American Dream and Dilemma*. Garden City, NY: Anchor.

Fishman, R. 1977: *Urban Utopias in the Twentieth Century: Ebenezer Howard, Frank Lloyd Wright and Le Corbusier*. New York: Basic Books.

Flink, J. J. 1975: *The Car Culture*. Cambridge, Mass.: MIT Press.

Fogelson, R. M. 1967: *The Fragmented Metropolis: Los Angeles, 1850–1930*. Cambridge, Mass.: Harvard UP.

Foster, M. S. 1981: *From Streetcar to Superhighway: American City Planners and Urban Transportation, 1900–1940*. Philadelphia: Temple UP.

Frampton, K. 1968: Notes on Soviet Urbanism, 1917–32. *Architects' Yearbook*, 12, 238–52.

Garland, H. 1917: *A Son of the Middle Border*. London: John Lane, The Bodley Head.

Gottdiener, M. 1977: *Planned Sprawl: Private and Public Interests in Suburbia*. Beverly Hills: Sage.

Grabow, S. 1977: Frank Lloyd Wright and the American City: the Broadacres Debate. *Journal of the American Institute of Planners*, 43, 115–24.

Gregg, D. J. 1986: The Origins and Philosophy of Parkways with particular Reference to the Contribution of Barry Parker. *Planning History Bulletin*, 8.1, 38–50.

Hubbard, T. K., Hubbard, H. V. 1929: *Our Cities, Today and Tomorrow: A Study of Planning and Zoning Progress in the United States*. Cambridge, Mass.: Harvard UP.

Jackson, K. T. 1985: *Crabgrass Frontier: The Suburbanization of the United States*. New York: Oxford UP.

Jencks, C. 1981: *The Language of Post-Modern Architecture*. New York: Rizzoli.

Langdon, P. 1986: *Orange Roofs, Golden Arches: The Architecture of American Chain Restaurants*. New York: Knopf.

Le Corbusier 1967 (1933): *The Radiant City*. London: Faber and Faber.

Liebs, C. H. 1985: *Main Street to Miracle Mile: American Roadside Architecture*. Boston: Little, Brown.

MacKaye, B. 1930: The Townless Highway. *New Republic*, 62, 93–5.

Montgomery, R. 1985: Pruitt–Igoe: Policy Failure or Societal Symptom. In: Checkoway, B., Patton, C. V. (eds), 1985, 229–43.

Mumford, L. 1938: *The Culture of Cities*. London: Secker and Warburg.

Muschamp, H. 1983: *Man About Town: Frank Lloyd Wright in New York City*. Cambridge, Mass.: MIT Press.

Nairn, I. 1965: *The American Landscape: A Critical View*. New York: Random House.

Parkins, M. F. 1953: *City Planning in Soviet Russia: with an interpretative bibliography*. Chicago: University of Chicago Press.

Rae, J. B. 1971: *The Road and the Car in American Life*. Cambridge, Mass.: MIT Press.

Riley, R. B. 1967: Urban Myths and the New Cities of the South-West. *Landscape*, 17, 21–3.

Schwartz, B. (ed.) 1976: *The Changing Face of the Suburbs*. Chicago: University of Chicago Press.

Scott, M. 1969: *American City Planning since 1890: A History commemorating the Fiftieth Anniversary of the American Institute of Planners*. Berkeley: University of California Press.

Starr, S. F. 1977: L'Urbanisme utopique pendant la révolution culturelle soviétique. *Annales: Économies, Sociétés, Civilizations*, 32, 87–105.

Stern, R. A. M., Massingale, J. M. (eds) 1981: The Anglo American Suburb. *Architectural Design*, 50.10–11, entire double issue.

Thomas, M. J. 1978: City Planning in Soviet Russia (1917–1932) *Geoforum*, 9, 269–77.

Tobin, G. A. 1976: Suburbanization and the Development of Motor Transportation: Transportation Technology and the Suburbanization Process. In: Schwartz, B. (ed.), 1976, 95–111.

Vance, J. E., Jun. 1964: *Geography and Urban Evolution in the San Francisco Bay Area*. Berkeley: Institute of Governmental Studies.

Venturi, R., Brown, D. S., Izenour, S. 1972: *Learning from Las Vegas*. Cambridge, Mass.: MIT Press.

Wachs, M. 1984: Autos, Transit, and the Spread of Los Angeles: The 1920s. *Journal of the American Planning Association*, 5, 297–310.

Warner, S. B. Jun. 1972: *The Urban Wilderness: A History of the American City*. New York: Harper and Row.

Webber, M. M. 1963: Order in Diversity: Community without Propinquity. In: Wingo, L., Jun. (ed.), 1963, 23–54.

Webber, M. M. (ed.) 1964a: *Explorations into Urban Structure*. Philadelphia: University of Pennsylvania Press.

Webber, M. M. 1964b: The Urban Place and the Nonplace Urban Realm. In: Webber 1964a, 79–153.

White, M. G., White, L. 1962: *The Intellectual versus the City: From Thomas Jefferson to Frank Lloyd Wright*. Cambridge, Mass.: Harvard UP and the MIT Press.

Whyte, W. H. 1958: Urban Sprawl. In: Editors of *Fortune* (eds), 1958, *The Exploring Metropolis*. Garden City, NY: Doubleday Anchor. 115–39.

Wingo, L., Jun. (ed.) 1963: *Cities and Space: The Future Use of Urban Land*. Baltimore: Johns Hopkins UP.

Wood, S. E., Heller, A. E. 1962: *California Going, Going . . .* Sacramento: California Tomorrow.

Wright, F. L. 1945: *When Democracy Builds*. Chicago: University of Chicago Press.

from *Collaborative Planning: Shaping Places in Fragmented Societies*

Patsy Healey

Three Planning Traditions

The culture of spatial planning as it has arrived in our times has been woven together out of three strands of thought which have grown up in the context of this inheritance. The first is that of *economic planning*, which aims to manage the productive forces of nations and regions. It is this form of planning which Mannheim had primarily in mind, linked to social policies which together would form the framework of a 'welfare state'. The second strand is that of the management of the *physical development* of towns which promotes health, economy, convenience and beauty in urban settings (Abercrombie, 1944; Keeble, 1952; Adams, 1994). The third is the management of *public administration* and *policy analysis*, which aims to achieve both effectiveness and efficiency in meeting explicit goals set for public agencies.

Economic planning

The tradition of economic planning is a vivid expression of the materialist and rationalist conception of a planned social order. The processes of production and distribution had to be planned to ensure efficient production and continuing growth, and, for some protagonists of economic planning, a fair distribution of the benefits of growth. It was preoccupied with both the economic failures of capitalistic market processes and their social costs.

The interest in *economic planning* arose in part from a general critique of the processes of industrial capitalism. Karl Marx mounted a devastating attack on the social costs of industrial development driven by the striving of capitalist entrepreneurs to maximise profits in competitive markets by exploiting people's labour and destroying resources (Giddens, 1987; Kitching, 1988). His analysis of capitalist processes of production, distribution and exchange was immensely powerful because it combined empirical perception with intellectual coherence, and was informed by a deeply humanitarian concern with the recovery of human dignity, which he saw attacked and degraded by the production processes he observed in nineteenth-century England (Kitching, 1988). His answer, articulated as a political programme in the *Communist Manifesto*, was to replace the marketplace and the processes of production driven by capitalistic competition with a governance system which was run by the people. Initially, and in order to break the power of capitalists on governance, Marx argued that the forces representing labour should engage in 'class struggle' with the objective of taking control of the state. Ultimately, the state too should wither away, leaving economic activity and governance to be managed by local communities.

Marx's political strategy underpinned the communist political movement, which gained enormous leverage in the early part of the twentieth century as labour movements across the world struggled to improve working conditions. But where communist regimes or socialist regimes, inspired by similar ideas of class struggle, came to power, they tended to reinforce the state, and the original Marxist idea of withering away was forgotten. In the economic arena, capitalist production processes were replaced with centralised planning and programming by the state, with individual enterprises driven by centrally-established production targets rather than the drive for profitability. Economic activity was typically seen to consist of a number of production sectors, usually based on a conventional division between primary, secondary and tertiary, or service industries. Co-ordination in space was subordinated to relatively independent development programmes of the different national ministries, representing economic *sectors*. In theory, production targets were to be informed by scientific research and technical understanding. In practice, building up an adequate knowledge base at the centre proved enduringly difficult and the logic of effective and efficient production quickly got replaced by a 'politics of meeting targets'. Further, such a concentration of economic and political power at the apex of a national system not only encouraged forms of governance unresponsive to people's needs. It also provided many opportunities for corrupt practice (Bicanic, 1967). As a result, centralised 'command and control' planning was increasingly discredited, from the point of view of economic efficiency, democratic practice and social welfare. Those who criticise planning still often have this model of planning in mind.

The communist model was not the only one which proposed replacing capitalistic economic organisation. Many writers who saw problems in large scale organisation outlined proposals for 'alternative' lifestyles, characterised by forms of self-governance. These have at various times been taken up by those working within the town planning tradition (Hall, 1988). For instance, Ebenezer Howard, famous for his development of the idea of the *Garden City*, was strongly influenced by such ideas (Beevers, 1988). These ideas challenged the notion of state management and bureaucratic organisation as likely to compromise the freedom of individuals and communities to determine the conditions of their own existence. What they were searching for were ways of interacting among small groups with respect to those matters in which individuals had shared concerns. ... This kind of 'bottom up' economic planning represented a challenge both to capitalist societies and communist ones, and remains an important strand of thought in planning today. It has many links to the 'new' radical environmental movements which are searching for different and more environmentally sustainable ways of organising economic life (Beatley, 1994; Goodin, 1992).

Meanwhile, the problems of economic organisation also came to pre-occupy the advocates of capitalist production processes and market societies. The problems here arose from the repeated experience of periodic *market failures*. The ideal of the marketplace is that it provides a mechanism for the continual readjustment of production in relation to consumers' preferences and ability to pay. It is efficient in that it encourages innovative production methods, to reduce costs and introduce new and better products, and it in theory maximises welfare, being driven by consumer demand. And all this happens without the need for complex bureaucracy and the politics which go with state management. However, this marketplace balancing act can get upset for all sorts of reasons (Harrison, 1977; Harvey, 1987). Sometimes markets can be dominated by the producers, in a situation of monopoly or oligopoly. Or there may be too few transactions and too little knowledge available about them. People may come to the marketplace with very different capacities to pay. Market processes will tend to exacerbate these inequalities. Consumers may decide not to purchase and producers not to invest in new equipment or expand production because there is too much uncertainty to predict future expenditure patterns. Or there may be problems in the supply and maintenance of goods and services that everyone benefits from but which are very costly for any one person to supply. Some of these problems are short term, and are 'cleared' over time. But others are more deep-seated and can lead to a general slump in economic activity. By the middle of the twentieth century, there had been several such 'depressions'. The experience of these fostered ideas which suggested that economies could be 'managed' to avoid market failure.

The most influential ideas at this time were those of John Maynard Keynes, who argued that economies slumped because of a crisis in consumer demand. If people did not have the resources to buy goods, and/or they did not have the confidence in their longer term future to be prepared to invest in purchases, then production would sag. His solution, widely adopted in western economic management in the 1950s and 1960s, was to stimulate demand (Gamble, 1988; Thornley, 1991). A key element in his solution was the maintenance of 'full employment', a term meaning unemployment levels of 2 to 4%, regarded by economists as representing necessary labor turnover, flexibility and availability. Such policies were buttressed by social welfare policies to assist people to acquire education, to maintain health, and to get housing. The welfare states established in the post-Second World War period in many European countries served to keep the costs of labour low for companies, while enabling reasonable wages. (They also provided benefits to workers, and could be viewed as a strategy to fend off the more radical demands which some workers' groups were advocating at the time.) These wages could

then be ploughed back into the marketplace to stimulate production of consumer goods, and hence economic activity generally. In many countries, and notably Britain, the US and Australia, subsidies were provided to encourage people to purchase housing, generating the expansion of a residential development industry (see Ball, 1983).

Although rarely called planning, these demand promotion strategies created what came to be known as a 'mixed economy', with economic policy – planning by another name – being driven by a mixture of economic analysis of market conditions and political sensitivity to electoral consequences. As with the centrally planned economies, the 'economy' was conceptualised in terms of sectors of production. This approach provided a governance regime which seemed to have advantages for the kinds of companies and capital accumulation strategies which operated on 'Fordist' production lines (Harvey, 1989; Boyer, 1991; Amin (ed.), 1994).

However, by the 1970s, these demand-stimulation strategies seemed to have run out of steam. An increasingly interrelated global economy enabled those countries with cheaper labour costs to undercut the high wage economies. Consumer demand, and its accompanying demand for state spending, was growing energetically, creating conditions of rising inflation. At the same time, new technology was reducing the demand for, and therefore the power of, labour. Meanwhile, as companies sought to cut costs to be more competitive, questions were raised about the scale of tax demands needed to support the various demand-stimulation strategies, and about the various regulations on working conditions which had built up over the years to protect labour. The Keynesian strategy seemed to have ground to a halt in 'stagflation' – a situation of economic slow-down combined with rising inflation. This reaction provided fertile ground for the reappearance of liberal ideas about economic organisation. By this time, state intervention itself was seen as the problem. Articulated by the neo-liberal political movements, especially in the US and Britain, new economic strategies focused on the supply side of the economy, and the reduction of constraints on adaptation and innovation (Gamble, 1988). A major objective was to reduce the role of bureaucracy and politics in the management of the economy, and to 'unfetter' business from the burdens imposed upon it by the regulatory environment built up through the welfare state. Economic planning, and spatial and environmental planning, were considered one such burden, and a particular target during the period of the neo-liberal Thatcher administration in Britain in the 1980s.

Britain under the Conservative Prime Minister, Margaret Thatcher, became the arena for the wholesale introduction of these ideas. Through strategies of privatisation and deregulation, companies and market processes generally were to be freed up, to cut costs and to innovate in the globalising marketplace (Gamble, 1988; Thornley, 1991). The role of government was restricted to the management of the money supply to squeeze inflation out of national economies and to hold exchange rates at competitive positions in the international market place. Any government programmes which created 'blockages' to supply-side activity were to be reduced or removed. This included 'bureaucratic' regulations, such as land use controls, and the concentration of the ownership of development land in public hands in cities. The adverse social and environmental consequences of such a strategy were presented as necessary costs of transition to a more soundly-based economy, which would generate the wealth to put them right in due course. Planning, or co-ordinated economic management of the economy, in this context, was seen not just as unnecessary, but as counterproductive to the project of the recovery of a growth dynamic through market processes.

This neo-liberal strategy has had enormous influence across the world at the end of this century. It offers a way to transform governance to make it more relevant to the dynamics of contemporary economies. It pro-active elements promote entrepreneurial rather than regulatory styles in governance (Harvey, 1989; Healey, Khakee, Motte and Needham, 1996). It suggested an end of planning, and the return of the market as the key organising principle of economic life. Yet this strategy is also running into problems. Flexible labour markets create impoverished and insecure workers, unable or afraid to spend on consumption. Individualistic competitive firm behaviour undermines the delicate relations between firms which encourage knowledge flow and creative innovation. Attention is now turning to the institutional preconditions for economic growth. The deregulation impetus itself has changed into a project of regulatory reform, changing the target and process of regulation (Vickers, 1991; Thompson et al., 1991). This rediscovery of the institutional preconditions for market 'health' and 'vitality' has awakened interest once again in strategies which might foster economic *development*. Further, the increasing concern with environmental quality has created a climate within which there is more rather than less demand for the regulation of economic activity. So planning and the strategic management of urban region change are once again being discussed with regard to the management of economies. . . .

Underpinning the approaches are different social theories – of class struggle for the Marxists; of communitarian self-management for the anarchists; and of individualism for the Keynesians and neo-liberals. Despite their different emphases, however, the debates and practices of economic management have shared some common characteristics. Their focus has been on the material well-being of consumers and the generation of profits for producers. Their practices have drawn on the vocabulary of neo-classical economies, even in Eastern European economies, with its metaphors of utility-maximising, rational individuals making trade-off between their preferences. Through the science of economics, policy programmes can be developed objectively, without the need to test ideas out with the different interested parties. Governance becomes a technocratic exercise in economic management. All these assumptions are challenged by contemporary institutionalist analysis and the communicative approach now emerging in planning theory.

The debates on economic management provide a context for the discussion of the physical development of towns and cities, and the management of spatial change in urban regions, and hence for any exercise in spatial and environmental planning. But the connection between these two arenas has been persistently neglected. Economic analysis has focused on economic sectors, and has tended to neglect how economic activities occur in space and time. As a result, it has paid little attention to the co-existence of different economic activities in shared space, except at the level of the micro-analysis of labour market dynamics, or the agglomeration economies and diseconomies of particular clusters of economic activities. It was left to the field of regional economic analysis and regional location geography to articulate these connections through the elaboration of location models for urban regions.…

Physical development planning

Whereas the economic planning tradition has been dominated by economists and political philosophers, the arena of physical development planning was shaped for many years by engineers and architects, and by utopian images of what cities could be like. Utopian dreams of urban form, and architects to build them, have been around since long before the Enlightenment. What modernity and industrial urbanisation brought with them was a more material and functional concern with the qualities of city development. These influences led to practical interest in building regulation and in the strategic regulation of the location of development. Land use zoning was introduced, aimed to prevent the pollution of residential neighbourhoods by dirty industry, and to limit development location to enable adequate services to be provided. Ways of providing infrastructure and measures for land assembly, to allow land pooling among owners, or the purchase by the state of sites needed for public projects, were also introduced in early planning systems. Urban master plans, layout plans for 'greenfield' subdivision and projects for the reorganisation of the urban fabric became part of the management of the physical development process in many places from the late nineteenth century (Ward, 1994; Sutcliffe, 1981).

This of course implied affecting the structure of land and property rights and the interests of land and property owners. However, until the 1970s, and even later, there was little discussion of the nature of the development process and land and property markets in debates on physical development planning (see Adams, 1994). These were relegated to an arena of 'planning practice', concerned primarily with tools (Lichfield and Darin-Drabkin, 1980). The tools available were usually presented by the physical development planners as inadequate for the task in hand. The tradition of physical development planning instead tended to focus on broad policy objectives, and on the 'ideal city'. In their Utopian dreams, the most influential thinkers in the tradition harked back to the pre-Enlightenment days. They were largely disinterested in an analysis of the *processes* of physical development unfolding before them (see Hall, 1995 on Abercrombie). Instead, the idea of modernity entered into their discourse through ways of thinking about the shape and form of cities and the qualities of neighbourhood organisation. Cities were seen as an amalgam of economic, cultural and household activities. The challenge was to find a way of organising activities which was functionally efficient, convenient to all those involved, and aesthetically pleasing as well. The objective was to promote and accommodate modern life, as both a project in economic progress and an opportunity to provide good living conditions for urban populations (Healey and Shaw, 1994). The aim was to build a functionally rational city for economic and social life (Boyer, 1983). There were vigorous debates on how this could be done, which reflected different attitudes to the nature of urbanity, the proper relation between people and nature, and how far to welcome new building technologies and motorised transport. In these debates, the 'British' tradition was often contrasted with the continental, the former celebrating a nostalgia for an urban form in a rural setting, and a life in balance with the natural order, as expressed in Howard's ideas for a social garden city; the latter emphasising the tradition of high density apartment life, as encapsulated in Le Corbusier's Ville Radieuse (Hall, 1988; Ward, 1994).

As a result of these influences, planning theory became in the mid-twentieth century a discussion about urban form. This generated some of the most powerful urban spatial organising ideas of the century (Keeble, 1952; Hall, 1988). The dominant idea in the British tradition has been the conception of the urban region as centripetal, focused on a city core, with a hierarchy of district and subcentres developed in an urban form which spreads out with radial routes, interlinked by concentric ringroads, and contained by a green belt to give a clearly defined urban edge. This image is particularly associated with the work of the great English planner of the first part of the twentieth century, Patrick Abercrombie. These spatial organising ideas not only provided a vocabulary of urban spatial forms. The spatial plans for particular cities have in many instances provided enduring and popular principles in local debates on the development of particular cities, for example Burnham's plan for Chicago, Abercrombie's for London and Stephenson's for Perth. Such plans have had effects by *framing* how key players in urban regions have thought about place and location (Rein and Schon, 1993; Faludi, 1996; Healey, Khakee, Motte and Needham, 1996). This is currently recognised by politicans and planners in many places

in Europe, in efforts to recast spatial planning policies and practices...But by the late 1960s, the physical development tradition came to be heavily criticised, in part for the arrogant confidence of the planners who promoted it (Boyer, 1983; Davies, 1972; Ravetz, 1980), but also for the lack of any social scientific understanding of the dynamics of urban region change which the planning ideas set out to manage (Hall, 1995; McLoughlin, 1992).

In some countries, the tradition of planning as urban form dominates planning thought and practice to this day, for example in Italy. Elsewhere, the tradition has been relegated to questions of the design of neighbourhoods, or major projects, or urban design. Through this tradition, ideas about architectural style, and particularly the debate about modern and post-modern style, have infiltrated into planning discourse – the latter challenging the functionalism of the modernist preoccupation with the spatial order of the city. Postmodern thinking has also challenged rationalist conceptions of the social science of city management (Boyer, 1983; Moore Milroy, 1991). The urban form tradition has nevertheless kept active an aesthetic consciousness within urban planning, repeatedly sidelined in more utilitarian planning traditions, such as the British. Even in Britain, however, physical development planning incorporated concepts of stewardship of the environment, which have salience in the light of contemporary concerns about environmental sustainability. Thus, despite its rationalising and modernist origins, the physical development planning tradition embodies a critique of materialist rationalism. . . .

Policy analysis and planning

The science of policy analysis is of American origin, and grew out of a search for ways of making public administration more efficient and effective. In Britain, central and increasingly local government were transformed from the late nineteenth century by the development of an administrative class at national level, with substantial capability, good pay and a commitment to a service ethic. Local government was increasingly professionalised, challenging local politics with formalised expertise (Laffin, 1986; Rhodes, 1988). On the European continent, administration was formally governed by legal rules, developed from the Napoleonic code, which gave authority to administrative action. Both systems helped to constrain the play of political power games and to limit the subversion of administrative systems to private and political party objectives, except in places such as Southern Italy, where the administrative rules were typically bypassed or surrounded with powerful alternative practices.

In the US, however, local administrations were much more open to the whims of local politics. Many US studies of local politics describe alliances within which local politicians collude with local development interests to promote speculative land profits. Logan and Molotch (1987) argued that US local governance was dominated by property development and investment interest – a *rentier* politics. Stone (1989) develops the analysis of such alliances further to examine more enduring relations between local government and business. In their discussion of local politics, Lauria and Whelan (1995) refer to such alliances as *urban regimes*. Or local government could be driven by simple political objectives of maximising electoral advantage. This was described in a famous case study of Chicago, where decisions on the location of low cost housing were made entirely with electoral advantage in mind (Meyerson and Banfield, 1955). This led to pressure to make public administration more efficient and less corrupt (Friedmann, 1973). The ideal local government balanced the demands of a pluralistic polity through technical analysis and management. Policy analysis offered rational techniques for this purpose. The core of the approach developed in the 1960s focused on identifying objectives, and developing

and implementing appropriate means to achieve them. Its principles drew on Herbert Simon's ideas of management by objectives, rather than by setting legal rules for administrators to follow. This approach offered flexibility to address the particularity of decision circumstances while constraining corruption by clear accountability of actions to policy criteria. The decision model was the foundation for what became known as the *rational planning process*.

The resultant debates on planning as a policy process have been enormously influential, structuring the American planning tradition, and providing a point of reference for any planning culture open to American influence. They built on the pioneering experience in regional economic development of the Tennessee Valley Authority in the 1930s, and drew on ideas about efficient business management. Models for public planning and management were developed, based on the rational relation of means to ends (Friedmann, 1973). By 'rational' in this context was meant both a form of deductive logic, and the use of instrumental reason as a form of argument, drawing upon scientific analysis. As Davidoff and Reiner (1962) stress in their articulation of the approach as a 'choice theory of planning', a strict separation of fact from value was to be maintained. Values were seen as originating within the political process, and were provided by the 'clients' of the technicians of the policy process. Policy analysis work was seen to take place in a defined 'action space', cut out from the political and institutional context in which goals were articulated (Faludi, 1973). The planner as policy analyst was a specialist in helping clients articulate their goals, and translating these into alternative strategies to maximise, or at least 'satisfice', the achievement of these goals, through careful analysis and systematic evaluation.

. . . In the US in particular, it stimulated an explosion of work on the 'science' of decision-making, with much discussion on the forms the rational planning process could take and on the kinds of urban systems models which were needed to underpin analyses of the consequences of alternative actions. The model itself was challenged by those who argued that it was idealistic, with unrealistic expectations of the political willingness to stick to rational planning processes, and of the conceptual and empirical knowledge capacity to understand situations sufficiently to be able to identify and evaluate all possible alternatives. The most famous challenge was that by Charles Lindblom, who argued for an alternative approach of 'disjointed incrementalism' – approaching problems in small steps rather than big steps towards grand goals (Braybrook and Lindblom, 1963). Later he argued for a more negotiative approach, a form of 'partisan mutual adjustment' (Lindblom, 1965). Lindblom's ideas in this respect are an innovative precursor of the current discussion of interactive approaches to developing planning strategies.

Lindblom's arguments still propose a planning process dominated by the techniques of instrumental rationality (Sager, 1994). His approach looked rather like a sort of 'market adjustment' within the public sector, produced by a form of technical analysis which drew on microeconomics rather than management theory. Other American contributions to the debate on policy processes in the later 1960s raised more fundamental questions. These focused on questions of value. In the early post-war period, there was a powerful 'mood' in political debate that issues of value were no longer controversial. The West had chosen the capitalist path to peace and prosperity. Citizens were assumed to share broadly common interests, while arguing over the details of pluralistic interest conflicts. The planner or policy analyst was thus merely a technician of means committed to the values of scientifically-based and rationally-deduced policy choices, but neutral as regards ends. Davidoff and Reiner, writing in 1962, implied that this was indeed the case. But by the end of the 1960s, and linked to the reanalysis

of poverty in American cities at this time, Paul Davidoff himself had come to a different view. In a famous paper, 'Advocacy and pluralism in planning' (Davidoff, 1965), he argued that it was impossible for the planner to be entirely value-free as regards ends, since planners as people had values. Implicitly, he acknowledged that these values divided people. In particular, the interests of poorer people in inner-city neighbourhoods were not the same as those of local business interests. He sought a way of planning which opened up the value diversity among the plurality of interests within a political community. In this context, he argued that planners should not stay value-neutral, given that they too had substantive values, values about ends. They should instead become value-conscious, declare their values and make themselves available to clients who wished to pursue such values. This approach had a powerful influence on American planning practice and thought in the early 1970s....

Around the same time, the sociologist-planner Herbert Gans was arguing that planners had a moral responsibility to argue in favour of improving conditions for the disadvantaged. He argued, as Davidoff and Reiner had done, that planners needed to be aware of a double client, an employer, or 'customer' for the planner's services, and, more broadly, the citizens affected by the 'direct' client's proposals (Gans, 1969). Both Gans and Davidoff and Reiner were responding to the increasing political and popular interest in local environmental questions, and to the resultant pressure for more active citizen involvement in planning strategies and their implementation. In both the US and Britain, this led to ideas about the procedures for citizen participation in the planning process. This in turn generated critiques which challenged the pluralistic conception of local politics, presenting it instead as a power game, in which elites held on to power which citizens struggled to gain access to. This is encapsulated in Sherry Arnstein's *Ladder of Citizen Participation*

(1969), with its metaphoric reference to the 1968 student protests in France.

Both Davidoff and Gans assumed a pluralistic polity as idealised in dominant US political thinking at the time. They also continued to advocate the techniques of rational scientific analysis. Their objective was to shift the approach to fit the pluralistic context better. In seeking to fit the planning model to the 'action space' of the institutional context, they thus shifted away from earlier conceptions of the transformative power of planning. For the urban designer planners, and for the early advocates of the rational planning process, planning approaches were in the vanguard of the transformation of cities, and the transformation of the management of local governance. Davidoff and Gans, in contrast, saw planning as a tool which citizens could use in extracting a more democratic pluralist polity from the clutches of dominant elites.

During the 1970s in the US and in Western Europe, the discussion of appropriate planning process models moved on from this position to question both the model of a pluralistic polity itself and the value of techniques based on scientific knowledge and means-oriented or 'instrumental' rationality. The first was most strongly developed in Europe, and drew on Marxist-inspired theories to analyse the structural bases for the unequal distribution of power (Castells, 1977). The second challenge reached planning from several directions and reflected a much broader questioning of the role of science and instrumental reason in Western thought generally. An early paper by Rittel and Webber (1973) argued for a more interactive and enabling approach to planning since facts and values were intertwined in people's consciousness. Others, interested in how policies influenced subsequent events, in how they were 'implemented', showed that policies were continually being reinterpreted by those involved in carrying them forward (Pressman and Wildavsky, 1984)....

The Interpretive, Communicative Turn in Planning Theory

All these traditions, as they have evolved, provide pointers to the development of institutionalist analysis and communicative approaches. The economic planning tradition, as it has evolved in both national economic management and local economic development, incorporates an increasing appreciation of the institutional preconditions for economic health. The physical development planning tradition has moved both to recognise the social processes underpinning spatial organisation and urban form, and the range and complexity of the demands for local environmental management generated by interconnecting social, economic and biospheric processes. The policy analysis tradition is seeking both to escape from its predominant emphasis on instrumental reason and scientific knowledge to incorporate greater understanding of how people come to have the ways of thinking and ways of valuing that they do, and how policy development and policy implementation processes can be made more interactive. But these directions were not unchallenged. A new reassertion of market liberal notions of governance was also emerging in parallel with these. The current period is above all one of tension between these two rapidly developing approaches in public policy.

Neo-liberal theorisation involves a reassertion of instrumental rationality, but in a narrow form grounded in microeconomics. The neo-liberal turn in public policy in Britain was promoted by the growing influence of economists in the public policy arena. This in effect abandoned the idea of policy formulation as a technical task, and concentrated instead on policy evaluation, both before policies were put into place, and in assessing their performance over time. This has generated a body of technique and evaluation criteria now used extensively by government agencies, particularly where neoliberal policy interests predominate. It deliberately eschews a co-ordinative role with respect to public policy, leaving any necessary co-ordination to voluntaristic action, through the dynamics of market processes and community self-help. These ideas provide a foil against which the communicative approach developed in this book is developed.

The second direction shifts the conceptual ground firmly into a phenomenological interpretation of the relationship of knowledge to action. It builds on the realisation that knowledge and value do not merely have objective existence in the external world, to be 'discovered' by scientific inquiry. They are, rather, actively constituted through social, interactive processes (Berger and Luckman, 1967; Latour, 1987; Shotter, 1993). Public policy, and hence planning, are thus social processes through which ways of thinking, ways of valuing and ways of acting are actively constructed by participants.

This recognition is part of a broad wave of reflection on identity (ways of being – ontology) and the bases of knowledge (ways of knowing – epistemology) which is influencing western thought in general these days. This intellectual wave has been building up in the planning theory field since the 1970s. It is now labelled argumentative, communicative or interpretive planning theory. It has many different strands, but the key emphases are as follows:

- a recognition that all forms of knowledge are socially constructed; and that the knowledge of science and the techniques of experts are not as different from 'practical reasoning' as the instrumental rationalists had claimed;
- a recognition that the development and communication of knowledge and reasoning take many forms, from rational systematic analysis, to storytelling, and expressive statements, in words, pictures or sound;

- a recognition, as a result, of the social context within which individuals form interests; individuals thus do not arrive at their 'preferences' independently, but learn about their views in social contexts and through interaction;
- a recognition that, in contemporary life, people have diverse interests and expectations, and that relations of power have the potential to oppress and dominate not merely through the distribution of material resources, but through the finegrain of taken-forgranted assumptions and practices;
- a realisation that public policies which are concerned with managing coexistence in shared spaces which seek to be efficient, effective and accountable to all those with a 'stake' in a place need to draw upon, and spread ownership of, the above range of knowledge and reasoning;
- a realisation that this leads away from competitive interest bargaining towards collaborative consensus-building and that, through such consensus-building practices, organising ideas can be developed and shared which have the capacity to endure, to coordinate actions by different agents, and to transform ways of organising and ways of knowing in significant ways, in other words, to build cultures;
- a realisation that, in this way, planning work is both embedded in its context of social relations through its day to day practices, and has a capacity to challenge and change these relations through the approach to these practices; context and practice are not therefore separated but socially constituted together.

This summary draws upon ideas developed by a number of contemporary planning theorists, notably Bengt Flyvberg, John Forester, John Friedmann, Charlie Hoch, Judy Innes, and Tore Sager. However, the planning theorists developing a communicative approach have given little attention in their work to the changing understanding of urban region dynamics evolving in regional economic analysis, urban geography and urban sociology (Lauria and Whelan, 1995). This too emphasises the active social processes through which everyday life and economic activity are accomplished. Intellectually, there are close links between the two emerging bodies of thought, grounded in the recognition of the social construction of meaning and the social embeddedness of ways of thinking and acting. A major objective of this book [i.e. Healey's *Collaborative Planning*] is to bring these two strands together and thus overcome the persistent tendency in planning thought and practice to separate the understanding of urban and regional change from the processes of governance through which political communities can collectively address their common dilemmas about what is happening to their neighbourhoods....

REFERENCES

Abercrombie, P. (1944) *Town and Country Planning* (Oxford: Oxford University Press (orig. publ. 1933)).

Adams, D. (1994) *Urban Planning and the Development Process* (London: UCL Press).

Amin, A. (ed.) (1994) *Post-Fordism: A Reader* (Oxford: Blackwell).

Arnstein, S. (1969) 'The ladder of citizen participation', *Journal of the Institute of American Planners*, vol. 35(4), pp. 216–24.

Ball, M. (1983) *Housing Policy and Economic Power* (London: Methuen).

Beatley, T. (1994) *Ethical Land Use* (Baltimore: Johns Hopkins University Press).

Beevers. R. (1988) *The Garden City Utopia: a critical biography of Ebenezer Howard* (London: Macmillan).

Berger, P. and Luckman, T. (1967) *The Social Construction of Reality* (Harmondsworth: Penguin).

Bicanic, R. (1967) *Problems of Planning: East and West* (The Hague: Mouton Press).

Boyer, C. (1983) *Dreaming the Rational City* (Boston, Mass.: MIT Press).

Boyer, R. (1991) 'The eighties: the search for alternatives to Fordism', in *The Politics of Flexibility*, eds. Jessop, B., Kastendiek, H., Nielsen, K., and Petersen, I.K. (Aldershot, Hants: Edward Elgar).

Braybrook, D. and Lindblom, C. E. (1963) *A Strategy for Decision* (New York: Free Press).

Castells, M. (1977) *The Urban Question* (London: Edward Arnold).

Davidoff, P. (1965) 'Advocacy and pluralism in planning', *Journal of the American Institute of Planning*, vol. 31 (Nov), pp. 331–8.

Davidoff, P. and Reiner, T. (1962) 'A choice theory of planning', *Journal of the American Institute of Planners*, vol. 28 (May), pp. 103–15.

Davies, J. G. (1972) *The Evangelistic Bureaucrat* (London: Tavistock Press).

Faludi, A. (1996) 'Framing with images', *Environment and Planning B: Planning and Design*, vol. 23, pp. 93–108.

Friedmann, J. (1973) *Retracking America* (New York: Anchor Press).

Friedmann, J. (1987) *Planning in the Public Domain* (New Jersey: Princeton University Press).

Gamble, A. (1988) *The Free Economy and the Strong State* (London: Macmillan).

Gans, H. (1969) 'Planning for people, not buildings', *Environment and Planning A*, vol. 1, pp. 33–46.

Giddens, A. (1987) *Social Theory and Modern Sociology* (Cambridge: Polity Press).

Goodin, R. (1992) *Green Political Theory* (Cambridge: Polity Press).

Hall, P. (1988) *Cities of Tomorrow* (Oxford: Blackwell).

Hall, P. (1995) 'Bringing Abercrombie back from the shades', *Town Planning Review*, 663, pp. 227–42.

Harrison, A. (1977) *The Economics of Land Use Planning* (London: Croom Helm).

Harvey, J. (1987) *Urban Land Economics* (London: Macmillan).

Harvey, D. (1989) 'From managerialism to entrepreneurialism: the formation of urban governance in late capitalism', *Geografisker Annaler*, 71B, pp. 3–17.

Healey, P. and Barrett, S. (1990) 'Structure and agency in land and property development processes', *Urban Studies*, vol. 27(1), pp. 89–104.

Healey, P., Khakee, A., Motte, A. and Needham, B. (1996) *Making Strategic Spatial Plans: Innovation in Europe* (London: UCL Press).

Healey, P. and Shaw, T. (1994) 'Changing meanings of "environment" in the British planning system', *Transactions of the Institute of British Geographers*, vol. 19(4), pp. 425–38.

Keeble, L. (1952) *Principles and Practice of Town and Country Planning* (London: Estates Gazette).

Kitching G. (1988) *Karl Marx and the Philosophy of Praxis* (London: Routledge).

Laffin, M. (1986) *Professionalization and Policy: the role of the professions in central–local relationships* (Aldershot, Hants: Gower).

Latour, B. (1987) *Science in Action* (Cambridge: Mass.: Harvard University Press).

Lauria, M. and Whelan, R. (1995) 'Planning theory and political economy: the need for reintegration', *Planning Theory*, vol. 14.

Lefebvre, H. (1991) *The Production of Space* (London: Blackwell).

Lichfield, N. and Darin-Drabkin, H. (1980) *Land Policy and Urban Growth* (London: George Allen & Unwin).

Lindblom, C. E. (1965) *The Intelligence of Democracy* (New York: Free Press).

Logan, J. R. and Molotch, H. (1987) *Urban Fortunes: the political economy of place* (Berkeley, Calif.: University of California Press).

McLoughlin, B. (1992) *Shaping Melbourne's Future? Town planning, the state and civic society* (Cambridge: Cambridge University Press).

Meyerson, M. and Banfield, E. (1955) *Politics, Planning and the Public Interest* (New York: Free Press).

Moore Milroy, B. (1991) 'Into postmodern weightlessness', *Journal of Planning Education and Research*, 10(3), pp. 181–7.

Pressman, J. and Wildavsky, A. (1984) *Implementation*, 3rd ed. (Berkeley, Calif.: University of California Press).

Ravetz, A. (1980) *Remaking Cities* (London: Croom Helm).

Reade, E. (1987) *British Town and Country Planning* (Milton Keynes, Bucks: Open University Press).

Rein, M. and Schon, D. (1993) 'Reframing policy discourse', in F. Fischer and J. Forester (eds.), *The Argumentative Turn in Policy Analysis and Planning* (London: UCL Press).

Rhodes, R. (1988) *Beyond Westminster and Whitehall: the sub-central governments of Britain* (London: Unwin Hyman).

Rittel, H. and Webber, M. (1973) 'Dilemmas in a general theory of planning', *Policy Sciences*, vol. 4, pp. 155–69.

Sager, T. (1994) *Communicative Planning Theory* (Aldershot, Hants: Avebury).

Shotter, J. (1993) *Conversational Realities: constructing life through language* (London: Sage).

Stone, C. (1989) *Regime Politics: Governing Atlanta 1946–1988* (Kansas: University of Kansas Press).

Sutcliffe, A. (1981) *Towards the Planned City* (Oxford: Blackwell).

Thompson, G., Frances, J., Levacic, R. and Mitchell, J. (1991) *Markets, Hierarchies and Networks* (Milton Keynes: Open University Press).

Thornley, A. (1991) *Urban Planning under Thatcherism* (London: Routledge).

Vickers, J. (1991) 'New directions for industrial policy in the area of regulatory reform', in G. Thompson, J. Francis, R. Levacic and J. Mitchell (eds.), *Markets, Hierarchies and Networks* (London: Sage), pp. 163–70.

Wannop, U. (1995) *The Regional Imperative* (Cambridge: Cambridge University Press).

Ward, S. (1994) *Planning and Urban Change* (London: Paul Chapman Publishing).

52

Between Modernity and Postmodernity: The Ambiguous Position of US Planning

Robert Beauregard

Introduction

From the early decades of the twentieth century through the 1960s, state planning in the United States of America was able to maintain the integrity of its modernist project.[1] In that project, planners strove to (*a*) bring reason and democracy to bear on capitalist urbanization, (*b*) guide state decisionmaking with technical rather than political rationality, (*c*) produce a coordinated and functional urban form organized around collective goals, and (*d*) use economic growth to create a middle-class society. Planners took on the challenge of an industrial capitalism forged in the 19th century, and shaped a response to the turmoil of modernization. They did so shrouded in modernism, the "*cultural* precipitates of this socio-historical period" (Schulte-Sasse, 1987, p. 6).

By the 1980s, the modernist planning project was under attack. Some even talked about a crisis of state planning (Friedmann, 1987) emanating from a series of profound changes involving urban restructuring, state politics, and cultural practices; each related to new activities and sensibilities often subsumed under a postmodern rubric. The landscape of postmodernity with its hypermobile capital, concentrations of advanced services, juxtaposition of vast wealth and extreme poverty, downscaled and customized production complexes, and deconcentrated central cities (Cooke, 1988) poses novel and difficult problems for modernist planners. Moreover, the cultural practices of postmodernists undermine earlier commitments to a middle-class society, a disciplined urban form, the efficacy of rationalism, and political neutrality. US planning thus finds itself suspended between modernity and postmodernity, with its practitioners and theorists astride an everwidening chasm....

The Modernist Project of Planning

The initial thrusts of the modernist project of planning were to diminish the excesses of industrial capitalism while mediating the intramural frictions among capitalists that had resulted in a city inefficiently organized for production and reproduction. Planners were to do this from within local and, less so, state governments. Their planning project was modernist because it engaged the city of industrial capitalism and became institutionalized as a form of state intervention. Underlying these concrete manifestations are procedural assumptions and substantive commitments that sealed the fate of planning as a modernist project.

Procedural assumptions

In the modernist planning project, reality that can be controlled and perfected is assumed. The world is viewed as malleable, and it is malleable because its internal logic can be uncovered and subsequently manipulated. Thus modernist planners rejected the alienation that is often viewed as part of modernization (Schulte-Sasse, 1987) yet adopted a viewpoint, also modernist, that overcomes alienation through a belief in the efficacy of human action and the importance of commitment (Kraushaar, 1988; Orwell, 1953). Modernist planners believe in a future in which social problems are tamed and humanity liberated from the constraints of scarcity and greed (Hutcheon, 1987; Jencks, 1985). Social control is wielded in order to drive society forward along a path of progress; planning is part of the modern "struggle to make ourselves at home in a constantly changing world" (Berman, 1988, p. 6).

Planners' involvement in this modernist struggle was not as people of action. Rather their contribution was utilitarian understanding. Knowledge in planning would precede and shape the actions taken by investors, households, and governments. In effect, planning would liberate through enlightenment (Albertsen, 1988; Friedmann, 1987). Knowledge and reason would free people from fatalism and ideologies, allowing the logic intrinsic to an industrial society to be uncovered and exploited. Modernist planners thus situated themselves clearly within both a European rationalism and an American pragmatism (Hofstadter, 1958; Scott and Shore, 1979). To this extent, knowledge in planning had to be evaluated on a performative criterion, based as it was within a scientific mode of legitimation (Lyotard, 1984). As such, planners were somewhat anti-intellectual; impatient with abstract theorizing and thus with social theory. Nevertheless, the aim of modernist planners was to act as experts who could utilize the laws of development to provide societal guidance.

Fostering the faith of modernist planners in the liberating and progressive potential of knowledge was their corresponding belief in their ability to maintain a critical distance (Bernstein, 1987; Jameson, 1984b). Planners laid claim to a scientific and objective logic that transcended the interests of capital, labor, and the state. This logic allowed modernist planners to disengage themselves from the interests of any particular group, avoid accusations of self-interest, and identify actions in the public interest, that is, actions that benefit society as an organic whole. Such an ideology served modernist planners in two ways: first, they could position themselves within the state without having to be labeled 'political', and, second, they could assert a mediative role between capital and labor.

Last, both the practice and theory of modernist planning revolves around the use of master narratives (Jameson, 1984b). For practice, the narrative synthesizes developmental processes and the built environment into a coherent urban form that fulfills the functional necessities of the city. The text is the master plan. For theory, it involves the formulation of a dominant paradigm – comprehensive rationalism – that focuses the normal science of theorists. The 'planning process' is its plot (Beauregard, 1984). In essence, modernist planners believe in totalizing what planners call 'comprehensive' solutions that have a unitary logic.

Substantive commitments

Such bowing to modernization is reflected in the substantive orientation of planning to the city and the state. As already mentioned, the modernist project is based upon a belief in the 'synthetic' city; that is, the city of singular form invariant over time. This holistic and ahistoric perspective is derived from a revealed internal logic of how a city (under capitalism) functions. The task for planners is to take the fragments produced by the contradictions and struggles of capitalism and integrate them into a unique and orderly whole. As with modern art, "the unity of [planners'] work was assembled from fragments and juxtapositions" (Gitlin, 1988, p. 35). This in turn enabled modernist planners to claim a privileged position in the realm of specialists; planners were to transcend specializations and provide the contextual integration for numerous experts involved in the reform of the industrial city.

The holism that modernist planners propounded was dependent both on the economic dynamics of the industrial city and on the parallel rise of a middle class. The 'spatial paradigm' of modernist planning (Cooke, 1988) was focused on the production of standard commodities for large markets, the importance of transportation infrastructure for the circulation of commodities, and the location of investment in proximity to labor. As well as disciplining the city for capital accumulation (Boyer, 1983) and assuring an adequate supply of labor for the factories, however, planners had to meet the demands of a new administrative work force and an emerging professional stratum desirous of urban amenities (such as parks) and residential areas isolated from manufacturing districts. The contradiction between demands made on the work force by industrialists and the consumption demands of an emerging professional – managerial elite were reconciled in the minds of planners by a belief in the *embourgeoisement* of the working class. As capitalism was tamed, the city organized, and prosperity diffused socially and spatially; the lower classes would rise to affluence and take on the values and behaviors of the middle class (Gans, 1968).

The expansion of the middle class also validated the belief that society was not riven by contradictions, and thus the city could be organized physically for 'public' purposes. Invidious class distinctions were being erased by economic growth, thus the city could be viewed as the physical container for the workings of a conflict-free society (Hayden, 1984). Modernization, and thus progress, meant that the good

life diffused across all groups, natives and immigrants alike.

Moreover, modernization was possible because the state had progressive tendencies to be reformist and serve the long-run needs of all groups. From the 'progressive' perspective, the state could be an instrumentality representative of the interests of all its citizens as disclosed by the expertise of planners. In this way, modernist planners skirt the ideological issue of the compatibility of planning and democracy (Aptheker, 1967; Hayek, 1944). Instead, they rest easy on the democratic pretensions of the state and their privileged insights into the public interest.

Intrinsic to this perspective is a need for functional equilibrium. The singular, organic, and totalizing view taken of the city leaves little leeway for chaos and indeterminacy.[2] For the great majority of planners involved with the 'city functional', the efficient organization of the city was the preferred social interest (Hall, 1989). Reason replaced greed, and a nonpartisan logic displaced self-regarding behavior. The public interest would be revealed through a scientific understanding of the organic logic of society.

In terms of its interests in growth and quest for efficiency, the logic of planning overlapped with that of capital, but it denied capital's way of achieving them. The ideology of planning was more attuned to political reform embedded within the state, thus reinforcing the substantive commitment to a state that is external to the economy, a further manifestation of the adherence to the idea of keeping a critical distance. Without this understanding, planners could not view themselves as interceding without bias in the workings of capitalism, nor could they be reformers and governmental employees. Modernist planners thus adopted the separation of the political from the economic – the capitalist trenches (Katznelson, 1981) – that channels oppositional movements and enables the capitalist state to be viewed as an arena for reform.

In sum, the modernist project is derived from beliefs about knowledge and society and is inextricably linked to the rise of capitalism, the formation of the middle class, the emergence of a scientific mode of legitimation, the concept of an orderly and spatially integrated city that meets the needs of society, and the fostering of the interventionist state. Technical rationality is viewed as a valid and superior means of making public decisions, and information gathered scientifically is regarded as enlightening, captivating, and convincing. The democratic state contains an inherent tendency to foster and support reform, whereas its planners maintain a critical distance from specialized interests. Such beliefs repeat and mimic beliefs about enlightenment which are associated with the rise of capitalist democracies and with the modernist quest for control and liberation.

Modernist Planning Besieged

Modernist planning began to come apart in the 1970s and 1980s (Dear, 1986). Novel political forms, economic relations, and restructured cities posed new difficulties for the premises that underlie practice. The critical distance that modernist planners attempted to maintain was radically altered, and the emancipatory potential of planning was virtually abandoned. Numerous commentators began to ask "who controls planning?" In turn, the theoretical quest for a master narrative which could be applied both to the city and to planning thought was brought to an end by eclecticism and a reluctance to embrace social theory. Such changes reflect the realities of a post-Fordist political economy and postmodern cultural sensibilities.[3]

Practice

There are numerous versions of the most recent round of capital restructuring (Beauregard, 1989; Bluestone and Harrison, 1982; Bradbury, 1985; Castells, 1985; Chase-Dunn, 1984; Fainstein and Fainstein, 1989; Harrison and Bluestone, 1988; Peet, 1987; Soja et al., 1983). One

dominant interpretation is that Fordist means, techniques, and social relations of production have been superseded by post-Fordist and postmodern forms: high-technology products and processes, an expanded emphasis on the financial circuit of capital, more flexible procedures in the workplace, and a defensive and weakened labor force (Albersten, 1988; Cooke, 1988). The state has become more ideologically conservative and more subservient to the needs and demands of capital, turning away from the simultaneous pursuit of both economic growth and welfare. Although the needs and demands of capital are (still) achieved through state assistance, the state has turned away from simultaneous pursuit of welfare and economic growth (Kantor, 1988; Smith, 1988). Local politics, moreover, increasingly pivots around economic development and jobs (Stone and Sanders, 1987). New spatial forms also have appeared (Conzen, 1988; Cooke, 1988): a postmodern city to join the postmodern political economy of flexible accumulation and the globalization of capital (Harvey, 1987; Soja, 1986).

Whether one accepts this or another version of 'late capitalism', contemporary restructuring of capital has made the practice of modernist planning more precarious. On the one hand, planners are increasingly vulnerable to property and industrial capital through the state's deepening involvement in capital accumulation. Thus planners are less able to maintain a desired critical distance. Economic development is so highly valued by elected officials that planners, even if they were not to share this ideology of growth, would find it difficult, if not impossible, to oppose the state's complicity. The result has been a peculiar form of nonplanning in which planners participate in individual projects, often attempting to temper the most egregious negative externalities, while failing to place these projects into any broader framework of urban development, a basic tenet of modernist planning (Fainstein and Fainstein, 1987; Goldberger, 1989).

The totalizing vision and the reformist tendencies of modernist planning have been undermined. Comprehensive planning that articulates the organic integrity of the city has become politically untenable. Such planning requires a balancing of interests and a taming of the excesses of capital, thereby hindering economic expansion. Planners, however, are less and less able to maintain even the facade of being concerned with those outside the 'loop' of economic prosperity. No longer is the idea to improve society. The new strategy is to flee the problems of society by creating wider and wider circles of growth (Logan and Molotch, 1987). Economic development, not reform, is the political aim of the 1980s, and it sacrifices regulation and the welfare state to the lure of new investment and jobs.

Under modernist planning, reform and growth were viewed as compatible even if they were not pursued equally. This distinguished planners from property developers. Now, the two groups have formed public–private partnerships. Even the schools train students in real-estate development, the cutting edge of planning education. Planning has become entrepreneurial and planners have become dealmakers rather than regulators (Fainstein, 1988). The critical distance cherished by modernist planners is eroding.

In turn, the proponents of policies to promote local growth attempt, often unsuccessfully, to conduct their business outside the realm of public scrutiny and debate. Private–public partnerships and public authorities isolate development politics from democratic politics (Friedland et al., 1978). Decisions about subsidies to private property, industrial investment, and public infrastructure are cast as technical decisions, and thereby depoliticized and confined to the deliberations of experts. Yet, because planners still talk about the public interest and the negative consequences of development, if not reform, they are also kept to the fringes of the discussion. Development politics are for development-oriented individuals trained in business schools and housed in quasi-public economic development agencies.

More than the politics of the modernist project have been undermined by the recent capital restructuring. The form and dynamics of the city have changed to such an extent that the principles of modernist planning are less credible (Cooke, 1988; Simonsen, 1988; Soja, 1986; Zukin, 1988). First, whereas modernist planners had assumed that local actions were determinative of local conditions, thus partially justifying local planning, that fiction has been severely compromised. The heightened spatial mobility of capital has made large-scale property development and industrial investment into affairs of regional, national, and even international proportions. Locational determinants of investment are increasingly ephemeral. State subsidies are ubiquitous, and the quality-of-life factors that attract 'advanced service' industries and educated labor are hardly confined to a few global cities.

In addition, and in order to attract capital investment, civic boosters and economic development officials attempt to commodify the 'particularities of place' through public spectacles and festival marketplaces (Harvey, 1987). To the extent that communities rely on cultural conditions and social amenities to generate growth, they are even more vulnerable to the influence of capital over consumption and 'life-styles'. Accumulation and consumption have become more flexible and less place-bound (Harvey, 1987), and planners lack the legal capacity and political weight to reshape the investment and employment prerogatives of capital.

Second, planners' grasp of a functional and unitary notion of urban development is even less justifiable. The expanding urban economies of 'progressive era' cities and of metropolitan economies of the postwar period seemed to offer opportunities to maximize the interests of all classes, but the increasing fragmentation of capital and labor in the postmodern era and the failure of growth to eliminate or even ameliorate tenacious inequalities of class, race, and gender make ludicrous any assumption of unitary planning. The emergence of the modern city neither brought forth a society whose many groups participated equally in affluence nor erased the manifestation of past injustices. Rather, the postmodern city is layered with historical forms and struggled over by fractions of capital and labor, each of which is dependent upon economic activities that are industrial and postindustrial, formal and informal, primary and secondary (Davis, 1987; Soja, 1986). Under such conditions, it is difficult to maintain a modernist commitment to a conflict-free public interest.

National attempts to obliterate class distinctions through prosperity and collective consumption and the local attempts to provide events (for example, multiethnic fairs) that celebrate yet minimize differences have not led to the *embourgeoisement* of the working class. Neighborhoods of 'displaced' blue-collar workers in marginalized households, recent immigrants from Asia and Latin America, and the extremely wealthy coexist in numerous cities. Even more compelling is the continued existence and expansion of the black 'underclass' and the poverty and unemployment experienced by white and nonwhite working-class households alike (Wilson, 1987). The fringes of black, Hispanic, and other immigrant areas, moreover, are increasingly the sites of racial confrontations.

Last, the lessening of state controls and the deepening obeisance to capital investment have exacerbated the negative consequences of rapid economic growth and have even intensified the 'seesaw' effect of uneven development (Smith, 1984). Fueled by the hypermobility of capital, cities like Houston have experienced prosperity but not without wide-ranging social and environmental costs (Feagin, 1988). Such conditions thwart movement to an ideal city. Instead, the city functions as a locus of unending struggle around the distribution of the costs and benefits of growth and decline. The implications for modernist planning are profound. Without a conflict-free society and the possibility of a single textual response, the modernist planning project is cut adrift.

In essence, the master narrative of modernist planning is incompatible with a spatially problematic and flexible urban form whose articulations are intrinsically confrontational and whose purposes are more and more the ephemeral ones of consumption. Subsequently, a modernist striving for orderlines, functional integration, and social homogeneity is unlikely to succeed, as is the desire on the part of planners to maintain a critical distance and apply technical rationalism. Broadly cast, modernist planners are in the grip of a postmodern helplessness (Gitlin, 1988).

Theory

Theoretically, planning remains in a modernist mode. The literature on planning theory is devoid of attempts to view planning theory through the lens of the postmodern cultural critique. Rather, this theoretical investigation has been initiated by urban geographers, mainly Michael Dear, Phillip Cooke, David Harvey, Edward W. Soja, and Edward Relph. This does not mean that planning theory has remained unaffected. The turmoil attendant to modernist planning practice reverberates into academe as planning theorists reflect upon the nature of planning practice and consider how to educate students. Moreover, the work of the above mentioned urban geographers has begun to diffuse into the literature on planning theory, posing a postmodern challenge to planning theorists as they look towards the social sciences for theoretical guidance.

The postmodernist cultural critique is a complex one. It includes a turn to historical allusion and spatial understandings, the abandonment of critical distance for ironic commentary, the embracing of multiple discourses and the rejection of totalizing ones, a skepticism towards master narratives and general social theories, a disinterest in the performativity of knowledge, the rejection of notions of progress and enlightenment, and a tendency towards political acquiescence (Bernstein, 1987; Cooke, 1988; Dear, 1986; Gregory, 1987; Jameson, 1984a; Jencks, 1985; Lyotard, 1984; Relph, 1987; Soja, 1989). Each aspect challenges modernist planning theory.

To begin, the postmodern interest in space and time would seem, at first glance, to be supportive of modernist planning. Planners have made location central to their work, and always have had a strong need to relate past trends to future possibilities. The postmodern debate is filled with commentary on the new hyperspaces of capitalism (Jameson, 1984a), with the more empirical literature extolling the uniqueness of localities. At the same time, postmodernism involves a turn to the past, particularly in terms of urban design and architectural styles.

Excluding neo-Marxist political economy, modernist planning has been dominated by procedural theories; that is, generic, paradigmatic theories meant to be applicable regardless of context, thus leaving space and time unattended. Moreover, the space and time of postmodernism are not the space and time of modernist planning. Planning theorists and practitioners cling to relativist and physically inert notions of space and a linear sense of time. The postmodern challenge is to conceive of space and time dialectically, socially, and historically; and to integrate such conceptions into a critical social theory. In turn, even though planning in the United States of America has been a local project, focusing mainly on communities, planning theorists have rejected materialist perspectives for idealistic ones and thus have difficulty relating to postmodern locality studies. Rather, too little attention is given to spatial scales and the interaction of the structural and the particular.

This theoretical stance indicates the way in which modernist planning theorists have interpreted the notion of maintaining a critical distance. With few exceptions (Davidoff, 1965; Goodman, 1971), they rejected the role of social critic. Despite the need for a radical critique of US society, and the

potential to do so when subsidized and protected by an academic position, theorists did not challenge the prevailing orthodoxy concerning the domestic benefits of economic growth. Rather, most retreated from political involvement, content to accept the 'end of ideology' and thus to abandon a modernist commitment to reform. Prior to the 1960s, then, criticism centered on planning theories, specifically the comprehensive rational model. Modernist planning theorists turned away from the realities of planning practice and engaged in internal academic debates. Any commitment to being 'public' was cast aside (Jacoby, 1987). The critics within planning that emerged in the 1960s to debunk the conservative politics and middle-class bias of planning, made explicit connections between the racism and inequality of US society and planning, but did not venture outside the profession to share their criticism with a wider public.

For theorists, the modernist commitment to a master narrative became easier and more difficult as academic forces increasingly distanced them from practitioners, and isolated theorists from public debates. Practice no longer constrained their thoughts with pragmatic, political economic realities. As a body, planning theorists became highly eclectic, pursuing theoretical projects for their own sake. Collectively, they lost the object, the city, that had given planning its legitimacy. Their new objects – the planning process, policymaking, decisionmaking, and so on – were only tangentially the objects of practitioners; they were procedurally relevant but not substantively so.

This postmodern fragmentation of planning theory would have been acceptable if it had paralleled a corresponding adoption of an integrative framework that critiqued society and advanced planning practice. Theorists did look towards economics, management science, and mathematics for a synthesis. However, the modernist disciplinary blinders that come with these bodies of knowledge only narrowed the theoretical perspectives of planners. The great nineteenth-century theories of Charles Darwin, Emile Durkheim, Sigmund Freud, and Max Weber, for example, have not been plumbed for their views on society and relevance for planning. References to twentieth-century grand theorists such as Michel Foucault, Claude Lévi-Strauss, Ferdinand Braudel, and even Lewis Mumford are just as rare.

Planning theorists operating with a Left or neo-Marxist perspective have been more sensitive to integrative social theories and to broad and significant transformations underway in society. Friedmann (1987) is certainly attuned to deep intellectual currents, Forester (1989) has made major advances in planning theory by building on the ideas of Habermas, and Boyer's history of US planning (1983) owes much to the structuralism of Foucault. The neo-Marxists (for example, Fainstein and Fainstein, 1979; Harvey, 1978) have prepared a powerful critique of the function of planning under capitalism, but offer little guidance in practical affairs. Hayden's feminist analysis (1984) and Clavel's (1986) investigation of progressive planning have been successful at linking social theory to planning practice. Neither, however, has crystallized planning thought or attracted many adherents.

Planning theorists, with the above exceptions, have thus avoided the task of making sense of the post-Fordist economy and the postmodern city. They are silent about spatiality and treat planning ahistorically, despite a recent surge of interest in planning history. While other disciplines look outward (Dear, 1988; Soja, 1989), most planning theorists turn inward to planning pedagogy rather than to the social context of practice.

The postmodern cultural and literary theories that speak of the demise of the master narrative, the bankruptcy of positivism, and the political deficiencies of technical expertise are of little moment amongst planning theorists. A tinge of anti-intellectualism characterizes planning theory as a whole, at least if one interprets this as an unfamiliarity with and avoidance of current intellectual debates and the foundations of modern social thought. Planning theorists tend to carry on a dialogue among themselves, reflecting in their insularity the ambiguous and the peripheral social position of planning in the United States of America. The little enlightenment that is generated is thus confined to theorists rather than extended to practitioners and citizens. This further distances theorists from society, and makes a clear political statement.

The postmodern debate, nonetheless, is not simply an issue of theoretical possibilities and cultural practices, but also a political agenda, muddled though it is, that has implications for planning theory (Smith, 1987). On the one hand, political and economic reform are not high on that agenda, and political acquiescence seems to extend from the celebration of multiple discourses. Such political inclinations coincide well with the directions taken by most modernist planning theorists who have abandoned any critical role and turned to academic debates. To the extent that planning education, however, trains its students to think in terms of dampening the excesses of capitalism, improving society, and understanding the political role of the expert, a tension exists between modernist and postmodernist political sensibilities. On the other hand, the postmodern debate does offer a useful antidote to planners' belief in the *embourgeoisement* of the working class and the conflict-free homogeneity of social interests.

Overall, then, the modernist planning project has disintegrated but not disappeared. Practice has lost its 'neutral' mediative position, forsaken its clear object of the city, abandoned its critical distance, and further suppressed reformist and democratic tendencies. Yet, practitioners still cling to a modernist sensibility and search for ways to impose expertise on democracy and to integrate their many specialties around a grand vision such as the master plan. Theory, on the other hand, has undergone centrifugal disintegration without a corresponding refocusing of knowledge around social theories and a broadening of the planning debate. Neither does one find a theoretical commitment to more than a pragmatic political agenda. From this perspective, planning seems suspended between modernity and postmodernity, with practitioners and theorists having few clues as to how to (re)establish themselves on solid ground.[4]

NOTES

1 Throughout the text, state planning is synonymous with planning undertaken by the various levels of government in the United States of America. When state planning refers to planning by the state-level government in contrast to the federal or local levels, the context will make the distinction clear. I use state in a similar fashion.

2 Pluralist political theorists in the postwar period, of course, interpreted this ostensible cacophony of voices as simply the workings of democracy.

3 For a similar argument concerning human geography, see Dear (1988) and Soja (1989).

4 This is also to say that postmodernism is not "modernism at its end" (Lyotard, 1984); there is as much continuity as discontinuity. On this point, see Soja (1989) and the essays in the fourth 1987 issue of *Environment and Planning D: Society and Space* (*EPD*, 1987).

REFERENCES

Albertsen N., 1988, "Postmodernism, post-Fordism, and critical social theory", *Environment and Planning D: Society and Space* 6, 339–65.

Aptheker H., 1967 *The Nature of Democracy, Freedom and Revolution* (International Publishers, New York).

Beauregard R. A., 1984, "Making planning theory: a retrospective" *Urban Geography* 5, 255–261.

Beauregard R. A., 1989, "Space, time, and economic restructuring", in *Economic Restructuring and Political Response*, ed. R. A. Beauregard (Sage, Beverly Hills, CA), pp. 209–240.

Berman M., 1988 *All that is Solid Melts into Air* (Penguin Books, New York).

Bernstein C., 1987, "Centering the postmodern", *Socialist Review* 17, 45–56.

Bluestone B., Harrison B., 1982 *The Deindustrialization of America* (Basic Books, New York).

Boyer M. C., 1983 *Dreaming the Rational City* (MIT Press, Cambridge, MA).

Bradbury J. H., 1985, "Regional and industrial restructuring processes in the new international division of labor", *Progress in Human Geography* 9, 38–63.

Castells M., 1985 *High Technology, Space, and Society* (Sage, Beverly Hills, CA).

Chase-Dunn C. K., 1984, "The world-system since 1950: what has really changed?", in *Labor in the Capitalist World-Economy*, ed. C. Bergquist (Sage, Beverly Hills, CA), pp. 75–104.

Clavel P., 1986 *The Progressive City* (Rutgers University Press, New Brunswick, NJ)

Conzen M. P., 1988, "American cities in profound transition", in *The Making of Urban America*, ed. R. A. Mohl (Scholarly Resources, Wilmington, DE), pp. 277–89.

Cooke P., 1988, "Modernity, postmodernity and the city", *Theory, Culture and Society* 5, 475–92.

Davidoff P., 1965, "Advocacy and pluralism in planning", *Journal of the American Institute of Planners* 31, 596–615.

Davis M., 1987, "Chinatown, part two?: the 'internationalization' of downtown Los Angeles", *New Left Review* 164, 65–86.

Dear M., 1986, "Postmodernism and planning", *Environment and Planning D: Society and Space* 4, 367–84.

Dear M., 1988, "The postmodern challenge: reconstructing human geography", *Transactions of the Institute of British Geographers* 13, 262–74.

EPD, 1987, "Reconsidering social theory: a debate", *Environment and Planning D: Society and Space* 5, 367–434.

Fainstein N. I., Fainstein S. S., 1979, "New debates in urban planning: the impact of Marxist theory", *International Journal of Urban and Regional Research* 3, 381–401.

Fainstein N. I., Fainstein S. S., 1987, "Economic restructuring and the politics of land use planning in New York City", *Journal of the American Planning Association* 53, 237–48.

Fainstein S. S., 1988, "Urban transformation and economic development policy", paper presented at the annual meeting of the Association of Collegiate Schools of Planning, Buffalo, NY; copy available from author.

Fainstein S. S., Fainstein N. I., 1989, "Technology, the new international division of labor, and location", in *Economic Restructuring and Political Response*, ed. R. A. Beauregard (Sage, Beverly Hills, CA), pp. 17–39.

Feagin J. R., 1988 *Free Enterprise City* (Rutgers University Press, New Brunswick, NJ).

Forester J., 1989 *Planning in the Face of Power* (University of California Press, Berkeley, CA).

Friedland R., Piven F. F., Alford R., 1978, "Political conflict, urban structure, and the fiscal crisis", in *Comparing Urban Policies*, ed. D. Ashford (Sage, Beverly Hills, CA), pp. 175–225.

Friedmann J., 1987 *Planning in the Public Domain* (Princeton University Press, Princeton, NJ).

Gans H. (ed.), 1968, "City planning in America: a sociological analysis", in *Essays on Urban Problems and Solutions: People and Plans* (Basic Books, New York), pp. 50–70.

Gitlin T., 1988, "Hip-deep in post-modernism", *The New York Times*, 6 Dec. pp. 1, 35, and 36.

Goldberger P., 1989, "When developers change the rules during the game", *The New York Times*, 19 March, pp. 36 and 38.

Goodman R., 1971 *After the Planners* (Touchstone Books, New York).

Gregory D., 1987, "Postmodernism and the politics of social theory", *Environment and Planning D: Society and Space* 5, 245–8.

Hall P., 1989, "The turbulent eighth decade: challenges to American city planning", *Journal of the American Planning Association* 55, 275–82.

Harrison B., Bluestone B., 1988 *The Great U-turn* (Basic Books, New York).

Harvey D., 1978, "On planning the ideology of planning", in *Planning Theory in the 1980s*, eds. R. W. Burchell, G. Sternlieb (Center for Urban Policy Research, Rutgers University, New Brunswick, NJ), pp. 213–34.

Harvey D., 1987, "Flexible accumulation through urbanization: reflections on 'postmodernism' in the American city", *Antipode* 19, 260–86.

Hayden D., 1984 *Redesigning the American Dream* (W. W. Norton, New York).

Hayek F., 1944 *The Road to Serfdom* (University of Chicago Press, Chicago, IL).

Hofstadter R., 1958 *Social Darwinism in American Thought* (Beacon Press, Boston, MA).

Hutcheon L., 1987, "The politics of postmodernism: parody and history", *Cultural Critique* 5, 179–207.

Jacoby, R., 1987 *The Last Intellectuals* (Farrar, Straus and Giroux, New York).

Jameson F., 1984a, "Postmodernism, or the cultural logic of late capitalism", *New Left Review* 146, 53–92.

Jameson F., 1984b, "Foreword", in *The Postmodern Condition*, J. -F. Lyotard (University of Minnesota Press, Minneapolis, MN), pp. vii–xxi.

Jencks C., 1985 *Modern Movements in Architecture* (Viking Press, New York).

Kantor P., 1988 *The Dependent City* (Scott Foresman, Glenview, IL).

Katznelson I., 1981 *City Trenches* (University of Chicago Press, Chicago, IL).

Kraushaar R., 1988, "Outside the whale: progressive planning and the dilemmas of radical reform", *Journal of the American Planning Association* 54, 91–100.

Logan J. R., Molotch H. L., 1987 *Urban Fortunes* (University of California Press, Berkeley, CA).

Lyotard J.-F., 1984 *The Postmodern Condition* (University of Minnesota Press, Minneapolis, MN).

Orwell G., 1953, "Inside the whale", in *A Collection of Essays by George Orwell* (Harcourt Brace Jovanovich, New York), pp. 210–52.

Peet R., 1987 *International Capitalism and Industrial Restructuring* (Allen and Unwin, Winchester, MA).

Relph E., 1987 *The Modern Urban Landscape* (The Johns Hopkins University Press, Baltimore, MD).

Schulte-Sasse J., 1987, "Modernity and modernism, postmodernity and postmodernism: framing the issue", *Cultural Critique* 5, 5–22.

Scott R. A., Shore A. R., 1979 *Why Sociology Does Not Apply* (Elsevier, New York).

Simonsen K., 1988, "Planning on 'postmodern' conditions", paper presented at the International Sociological Association Research Committee on the Sociology of Urban and Regional Development Conference, "Trends and Challenges of Urban Restructuring", Rio de Janeiro; copy available from author.

Smith M. P., 1988 *City, State, and Market* (Blackwell, New York).

Smith N., 1984 *Uneven Development* (Blackwell, Oxford).

Smith N., 1987, "Rascal concepts, minimalizing discourse and the politics of geography", *Environment and Planning D: Society and Space* 5, 377–83.

Soja E. W., 1986, "Taking Los Angeles apart: some fragments of a critical human geography", *Environment and Planning D: Society and Space* 4, 255–72.

Soja E. W., 1989 *Postmodern Geographies* (Verso, London).

Soja E. W., Morales R., Wolff G., 1983, "Urban restructuring: an analysis of social and spatial change in Los Angeles", *Economic Geography* 59, 195–230.

Stone C. N., Sanders H. T., 1987 *The Politics of Urban Development* (University Press of Kansas, Lawrence, KN).

Wilson W. J., 1987 *The Truly Disadvantaged* (University of Chicago Press, Chicago, IL).

Zukin S., 1988, "The postmodern debate over urban form", *Theory, Culture and Society* 5, 431–46.

from *The Modernist City: An Anthropological Critique of Brasília*

James Holston

The Idea of Brasília

To understand the intentions of building Brasília, it is first necessary to see the city as the acropolis of an enormous expanse of emptiness. The Federal District in which the capital lies is an area of 5,771 square kilometers plotted at the approximate center of the Central Plateau. Around it is nearly 2 million square kilometers of stunted scrub vegetation called *cerrado*, lying without significant modulation between 1000 and 1300 meters above sea level. This vast tableland includes areas within three of Brazil's five great regions – the Central West, the Northeast, and the Southeast – and comprises almost all of the states of Mato Grosso, Mato Grosso do Sul, and Goiás in the West and parts of Bahia and Minas Gerais in the East. Although it represents 23% of Brazil's surface area, in 1980 it contained only 6% of its population, mostly found in the isolated boom towns and agricultural stations of pioneer zones. The rest survive as pastoralists and subsistence cultivators sparsely distributed across the land. At the time of Brasília's construction, its average population density was less than one person per square kilometer. Today, it is only four. As one journeys across this desolate flatness, any interruption in the landscape – a twisted palm or a chain of voluminous clouds – becomes a welcome figure of life.

It is in this tradition of desert sculpture that the steel and glass oasis of Brasília arises, almost 1000 kilometers from the coastline to which, in the metaphor of Frei Vicente do Salvador (1931: 19), Brazilian civilization has for over four centuries "clung like crabs."

Since the middle of the eighteenth century, the idea of transferring Brazil's capital from the coast to the center of this uninhabited interior has been the dream of numerous visionaries. Their combined legacy to Brasília is that of a New World mythology in which the construction of a capital city at the heart of the Central Plateau is the means of launching a great civilization to flourish in a paradise of plenty. One of these visionaries, the Italian João Bosco, became the patron saint of Brasília for such a prophecy. According to interpretors of his revelation, he envisaged the site of the city 75 years before its construction as that of the Promised Land. On 30 August 1883, the saint dreamed that he was traveling by train across the Andes to Rio de Janeiro in the company of a celestial guide. As they crossed the Central Plateau, they surveyed not only the land's surface but also its subterranean features:

I saw the bowels of the mountains and the depths of the plains. I had before my eyes the incomparable riches ... which would one day be discovered. I saw numerous mines of precious metals and fossil coals, and deposits of oil of such abundance as had never before been seen in other places. But that was not all. Between the fifteenth and the twentieth degrees of latitude, there was a long and wide stretch of land which arose at a point where a lake was forming. Then a voice said repeatedly: when people come to excavate the mines hidden in the middle of these mountains, there will appear in this place the Promised Land, flowing with milk and honey. It will be of inconceivable richness. (Cited in Silva 1971: 34)

Official interpretation holds that the topography of this vision corresponds pre-

cisely to the site of Brasília, constructed between the fifteenth and the sixteenth latitudes, and that its "lake in the process of forming" refers to the city's man-made Lake Paranoá. Moreover, as one of Brasília's founding fathers and local historians writes: "To confirm once again that Saint João Bosco was referring to our capital, to the Great Civilization that is now arising on the Central Plateau of Brazil, the Saint affirmed that these dreams... would be lived in the third generation" after his own (Silva 1971: 35). Brasilienses – as the people of Brasília are called – consider this prognostication to indicate a period of 75 years. This establishes the late 1950s as the

Figure 53.1 Distances between Brasília and state capitals. This map frequently illustrates discussion of "Brasília and national development." For example, in a social studies textbook for elementary school children, it accompanies the following passage: "The transfer of the capital brought progeress to the central west region and contributed to the settlement and development of a great part of Brazil's territory. The new capital is linked by great highways to all the regions of Brazil" (Perugine et al. 1980: 15).

date of the prophecy's realization, exactly the years of Brasília's construction. João Bosco's prophecy is one of several foundation myths officially recognized in the city's history books and monuments. These myths are various versions of the same theme: they present Brasília as the civilizing agent of the Central Plateau, as the harbinger of an inverted development in which the capital creates the civilization over which it exercises a radiant sovereignty....

The Instruments of Change

> The apartment blocks of a *superquadra* [the city's basic residential unit] are all equal: same façade, same height, same facilities, all constructed on *pilotis* [columns], all provided with garages and constructed of the same material – which prevents the hateful differentiation of social classes; that is, all the families share the same life together, the upper-echelon public functionary, the middle, and the lower.
>
> As for the apartments themselves, some are larger and some are smaller in number of rooms. [They] are distributed, respectively, to families on the basis of the number of dependents they have. And because of this distribution and the inexistence of social class discrimination, the residents of a *superquadra* are forced to live as if in the sphere of one big family, in perfect social coexistence, which results in benefits for the children who live, grow up, play, and study in the same environment of sincere camaraderie, friendship, and wholesome upbringing.... And thus is raised, on the plateau, the children who will construct the Brazil of tomorrow, since Brasília is the glorious cradle of a new civilization. (*Brasília* 1963 [65–81]: 15)

This description of "perfect social coexistence" comes neither from the pages of a utopian novel, nor from the New World annals of Fourierite socialism. Rather, it is taken from the periodical of the state corporation that planned, built, and administered Brasília – from a "report" on living conditions in the new capital. Nevertheless, it presents a fundamentally utopian prem-

ise: that the design and organization of Brasília were meant to transform Brazilian society. Moreover, it does so according to the conventions of utopian discourse: by an implicit comparison with and negation of existing social conditions. In this case, the subtext is the rest of Brazil, where society is stratified into pernicious social classes, where access to city services and facilities is differentially distributed by class, and where residential organization and architecture are primary markers of social standing. Brasília is put forth not merely as the antithesis of this stratification, but also as its antidote, as the "cradle" of a new society. Thus, when the city's planners presuppose that lower-level government employees live "the same life together" with higher officials, it is not because they assume that such egalitarianism already exists as a basic value in Brazilian society. They know that it does not. Rather, they are presupposing the value they *want* to create among the residents, especially the children, of Brasília. To complete the deliberate *petitio principii* – the assumption of what one wishes to prove – which seems fundamental to this sort of discourse, they state their intention as fact, as a transformation in the present tense: they claim that the unequal distribution of advantage due to differences in class, race, employment, wealth, and family that structures urban life elsewhere in Brazil is in Brasília already negated.

The mechanism of this negation is its embodiment in the residential organization of the city. It lies not only in the distribution of apartments according to need but moreover in their design. Thus, the planners claim that the "equality" or standardization of architectural elements "prevents" social discrimination. In this embodiment of intention, they propose an instrumental relation between architecture and society: the people who inhabit their buildings will be "forced" to adopt the new forms of social experience, collective association, and personal habit their architecture represents. This forced conduction to radical changes in social values and relations is the essential means by which Brasília's planners hoped to institute their egalitarian prescriptions for a new Brazilian society. It is in this sense that they considered architecture an instrument of social change. Moreover, in designing an entire city, a total environment, they viewed this conduction as an inescapable inversion of social evolution in which architects and city planners would design fundamental features of society. . . .

Brasília serves in this book as a case study of the modernist city proposed in the manifestos of the Congrès Internationaux d'Architecture Moderne (CIAM). It embodies in form and organization CIAM's premise of social transformation: that modern architecture and planning are the means to create new forms of collective association, personal habit, and daily life. . . .

Brasília's Pedigree

Brasília is a CIAM city. In fact, it is the most complete example ever constructed of the architectural and planning tenets put forward in CIAM manifestos. From 1928 until the mid-1960s, CIAM remained the most important forum for the international exchange of ideas on modern architecture. CIAM's meetings and publications established a worldwide consensus among architects on the essential problems confronting architecture, giving special attention to those of the modern city. Brazil was represented in the congress as early as 1930, and Brasília's architects Lúcio Costa and Oscar Niemeyer have practiced its principles with renowned clarity.[1]

The Brasília's design derives from CIAM proposals is easily demonstrated. Its most significant manifesto, *The Athens Charter*, defines the objectives of city planning in terms of four functions: "The keys to city planning are to be found in the four functions: housing, work, recreation (during leisure) and traffic" (Le Corbusier 1957 [1941]: art. 77). The last function, traffic,

"bring[s] the other three usefully into communication" (ibid., art. 81). A later CIAM meeting augmented these to include a "public core" of administrative and civic activities. Planners refer to the organization of these functions into typologies of social activity and building form as zoning. What distinguishes modernist zoning from its precursors is the conception that urban life may be understood for planning purposes in terms of these four or five functions and, more important, that they should be organized as mutually exclusive sectors within the city. Together with circulation, this organization determines both the internal order and the overall shape of the CIAM city.

Now consider the Plan of Brasília (figures 53.2 and 53.3): it is a perfect illustration of how the zoning of these functions can generate a city. A circulation cross of speedways determines the organization and shape of the city exactly as Le Corbusier (1971 [1924]: 164), the guiding hand of CIAM, proposes in an earlier publication: "Running north and south, and east and west, and forming the two great axes of the city, there would be great *arterial roads for fast one-way traffic*" (figure 53.4). Residential super-blocks are placed along one axis; work areas along the other. The public core is located to one side of the axial crossing. Recreation in the form of a lake and green belt surrounds the city. *Et voilà* – total city planning.

Next, compare views of Brasília with those of two ideal cities by Le Corbusier, A Contemporary City for Three Million Inhabitants of 1922 and The Radiant City of 1930. These two projects became prototypes both for and of the CIAM model defined in *The Athens Charter*. Note the explicit similarities between the two and Brasília: the circulation cross of speedways; the dwelling units of uniform height and appearance grouped into residential superblocks with gardens and collective facilities; the administration, business, and financial towers around the central crossing; the recreation zone surrounding the city. Brasília's pedigree is evident. . . .

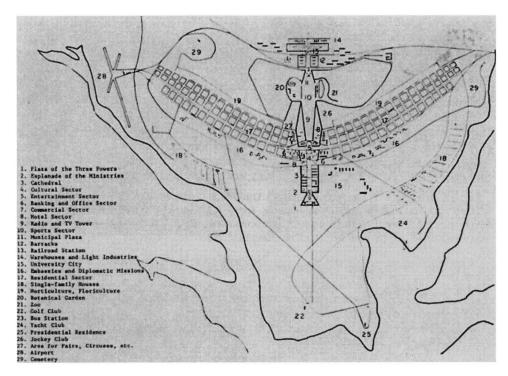

1. Plaza of the Three Powers
2. Esplanade of the Ministries
3. Cathedral
4. Cultural Sector
5. Entertainment Sector
6. Banking and Office Sector
7. Commercial Sector
8. Hotel Sector
9. Radio and TV Tower
10. Sports Sector
11. Municipal Plaza
12. Barracks
13. Railroad Station
14. Warehouses and Light Industries
15. University City
16. Embassies and Diplomatic Missions
17. Residential Sector
18. Single-family Houses
19. Horticulture, Floriculture
20. Botanical Garden
21. Zoo
22. Golf Club
23. Bus Station
24. Yacht Club
25. Presidential Residence
26. Jockey Club
27. Area for Fairs, Circuses, etc.
28. Airport
29. Cemetery

Figure 53.2   Lúcio Costa, master plan of Brasília, 1957

Figure 53.3   Lúcio Costa, perspective sketch of Brasília, 1957. AU–Arquitetura e Urbanismo

Figure 53.4   Le Corbusier, A Contemporary City for Three Million Inhabitants, perspective sketch, 1922

To those familiar with the apparent disorder of other cities, in Brazil or elsewhere, Brasília presents the radically unfamiliar view of total urban order. The Master Plan creates order by organizing city life in terms of several basic proposals. I analyzed one of these proposals ... that of replacing the street and its system of public spaces with a new system of traffic circulation. The all-figural city that results features a new and total order of parts, one comprehensively structured by the bureaucratic state. How does the Master Plan, on behalf of the state, organize this city of objects? [Here] I shall evaluate its proposals to structure Brasília in terms of the modernist functions of work and residence. These proposals are three: (1) to organize the city into exclusive and homogeneous zones of activity based on a predetermined typology of urban functions and building forms; (2) to concentrate the function of work in relation to dispersed dormitory settlements; and (3) to institute a new type of residential architecture and organization based on the concept of the *superquadra*. ...

Zoning the City: A Typology of Form and Function

The preindustrial Brazilian city is typically organized into three or four domains of institutional influence, that is, areas of the city in which the affairs of one institution or another dominate daily activities. These domains are distinguished by a customary spatial distribution of urban institutions, one established at the outset of colonization and based on Iberian models. Thus, the principal institutions of church and state occupy a pivotal square (*a praça*), those of commerce, finance, and light manufacturing are in a central area around it (*o centro*), and those of residence surround these (*os bairros residenciais*). Sometimes, an additional domain of recreation is important in the spatial conception of the city, such as the municipal park or the beach in Rio de Janeiro (but here the beach is less important as a preserve of nature within the

city than as a domain of sociality similar to that of the public square). Thus, the municipal square, the downtown, and the residential neighborhood are both spatial categories and domains of predictable social activities, distinguished in both instances by virtue of their landmark institutions.

Although these categories are conceptually distinct in terms of the characteristic institutions to which they refer, they are not mutually exclusive in terms of either activities or institutions. Fundamental to preindustrial urban organization is the heterogeneity of functions, activities, and institutions in all areas of the city. Thus, municipal squares and downtowns are also places of residence for certain classes of people. Similarly, residential neighborhoods are usually organized around small squares which reiterate on a local scale the institutional organization of the municipal square: they feature parish churches, headquarters of neighborhood social and political associations, and houses of prominent members of the community. Moreover, residential neighborhoods always support a variety of commercial establishments – typically on the ground floor of houses – for the everyday needs of the community. Although small cities often do not have a commercial center distinct from a municipal square, the terms *o centro* and *a praça* are, nevertheless, used in different situations to refer to different aspects and expectations about the same place.

Similarly, in those cities where spatial distinctions based on industrial class relations have arisen, the actual experience of the city is still one of a mixing of classes in most areas. Thus, although such oppositions as "center and periphery" (São Paulo), "city and suburb" (Rio de Janeiro, Recife), and "South Zone and North Zone" (Rio de Janeiro) differentiate areas of relative wealth and poverty, all classes have neighborhoods *within* these cities. Moreover, wealthy neighborhoods are often immediately contiguous with poor ones, and in the most dramatic examples of the spatial proximity of socially distant strata, the poorest (illegal but often permanent) squatter communities are found inside middle-class districts. While Brazilian cities are historically differentiated into several domains of institutional influence, the experience of each, and the quality of its daily life, are a heterogeneous mix of functions, activities, institutions, and classes.

Unlike its precursors in the nineteenth century, modernist planning homogenizes this preindustrial heterogeneity into exclusive "sectors" of "urban functions." It achieves uniformity in the structure and configuration of its sectors by reconceiving city organization in a number of ways. To rethink the city, to destroy the past and begin anew, it turns preindustrial urban order inside out by eliminating the street system of circulation. Producing a new type of cityscape with this inversion, it attempts to preclude class-based spatial differentiations through the agencies of total planning and architectural standardization. Having eliminated discriminations between public space and private building as a basis of urban order, it organizes its city of objects on the basis of a concept of zoned functions.

We may define zoning as the correlation, or typologizing, of social activities, building forms, and planning conventions. Modernist architecture redefines each of these elements and develops their classification as an instrument both of social transformation and of the rational organization of daily life transformed. It classifies urban social activities into the four functions of housing, work, recreation, and traffic, at times adding a fifth function termed the "public core of administrative and civic affairs." However, the fifth is never well defined, and its problematic status will become significant in our evaluation of modernist planning. Correlated with this typology of urban social life is a classification of building types and spatial conventions – the apartment block raised on columns, the office building, the transparent façade, the free plan, and the like – a correlation motivated by the idea that a new physical environment will create new

types of association and habit. Thus, the typologies of modernist master planning are not only total in the sense that they impose a totally planned city. They are also totalizing in the sense that the new architecture always refers to some aspect of the new society; that is, the classification of form always refers to the classification of function.

The purpose of a master plan is therefore to achieve a rationally structured homology between social-functional and architectural-formal organizations. The zone is the basic unit of such a structure and is conceived of as a single correlation of function and form, for example, of housing and the *superquadra*. As the zone is its conceptual unit, the sector is its unit of spatial organization. Ideally, each zone is comprised of a single sector, or area, of the city. Thus, the place of work is separated from the place of residence. Where zones must mesh, as with traffic circulation, every effort is made to keep the activities of each as independent as possible. Therefore, pedestrians are given one system of circulation and cars another. As each of the basic urban functions comprehends numerous types of activities, each zone is subdivided. Each subdivision of activity, with its assigned architectural form, is given a separate, self-contained sector within the encompassing zone. Thus, within the housing zone, there is one sector for actual residence (the *superquadra*) and one for local commerce. Ideally, each sector within the city has a unitary definition, based on a single correlation of form and function. It is this uncompromising rationality in the planning of its parts that gives the modernist city the quality of total and totalizing order.

When we turn to the case of Brasília, there is an additional factor that increases its totalizing aspect: all of its sectors are organized into a single architectural and schematic image, that of a great cross of speedways. The cross is the most encompassing correlation of form and function. It serves both as the organizational spine for the distribution of social functions and building forms and as the symbol of the city's total organization. Thus, Brasília's planning achieves total order through two types of totalizations: by typologizing social functions, building types, and spatial conventions, and by subsuming the distribution of social and architectural typologies into a single urban form.

Advocates of this kind of total urban order commonly argue that its rationality increases the legibility of the city's plan and thus inhabitants' knowledge of the city. We may therefore note at this point the way in which Brasília's typologies of order affect both abstract and practical orientation. As we might expect, its total order inverts the problems of orientation associated with other cities. It increases the legibility of the whole but decreases that of its parts, producing a peculiar set of navigational dilemmas. Most cities are not identified with a total shape. They present a nonfigural conglomeration of sprawling districts within which, however, individual neighborhoods are identified by distinctive landmarks of one kind or another (including place names which are temporal markers of personages and events in the collective memory). The idiosyncrasies of place are memorable in these cities and therefore crucial in one's knowledge of them. In contrast, Brasilienses understand Brasília as a single, legible image – commonly read as a cross, an airplane, or a bird – composed of neighborhood units that with very few exceptions they find uniform, undistinguishable, and land-markless.[2]

When one asks them for directions, for example, they will inevitably reckon by the whole first, describing the cross in some fashion and then locating the desired point within it. Or, they will simply give the address, which again depends on a knowledge of the whole. Both modes of reckoning are entirely abstract. Indeed, it is almost impossible to give practical directions because there are very few memorable reference points. Moreover, people can't say "go to the corner and turn at the light." In such a situation, even long-time residents regularly have difficulty finding the location of a place even though they grasp it in their mental map of the whole city and have been to it many times. Thus, while the typologies of total order produce an unusual, abstract awareness of the plan, practical knowledge of the city actually decreases with the imposition of systemic rationality.

This disjunction between abstract knowledge and practical experience is exacerbated by the impeccably rational address system, which confronts people with an entirely new vocabulary to describe urban location. What was once a street address in Rio de Janeiro like Rua Montenegro 87 becomes in Brasília an apartment address of such complex denotation as SQS 106–F–504. Even after one knows what it means, which in the abstract depends on seven different discriminations of information, it helps very little in correlating a sense of real place with its position on the mental map of the whole, or even in actually finding the apartment. The address system is especially disastrous in the commercial sectors. Not only do Brasilienses have difficulty remembering the exact location of shops in look-alike blocks (what is the memorable difference between CLS 403–A–33 and CLS 405–A–33?) but the merchants, too, exhibit their ambivalence toward the system by idiosyncratically using different versions of the code in their advertisements.[3]

Further investigation into this new vocabulary of orientation reveals that Brasilienses also encounter a bewildering array of sector abbreviations: the telephone directory lists 70 unpronounceable acronyms such as SQS, CLN, QL, HCGN, and MSPW. These are universally used in place names and address codes, for there are no other available designations short of writing out the entire phrase. In sum, Brasilienses confront not only a correlation of form and function based on an unfamiliar logic, but an equally strange language to describe it. As a result, the total order of Brasília may increase their abstract knowledge of the plan, but it also alienates them from their own experiences of it.

This total order has a functional organization in relation to the axial plan:

the function of work concentrated in sectors along the Monumental Axis, that of housing along the Residential Axis, and that of recreation surrounding both axes.[4] Corresponding to this typology of functions, the Master Plan proposes to give each axis, and each major sector within them, distinguishing architectural and spatial characteristics. According to Costa (1962: 343–5), these are determined by a typology of shapes and by a set of scales – the residential, the monumental, the gregarious, and the bucolic. The planner's intention is to differentiate the functions of the city's figural buildings by assigning different shapes and patterns of shapes to each sector. . . . I demonstrated that in terms of the basic logic of the plan (i.e., the solid–void/figure–ground relations) such differentiation is semantically inefficacious: regardless of their sector, the buildings are all freestanding objects, and as such they are all monumental. At most, we may say that the sectors of the Monumental Axis are designed to make some of their monumental objects appear even more monumental (in the sense of being the most conspicuous, dramatic, and exceptional gestures in a field of exceptional gestures), while the sectors of the Residential Axis are only less so. This paradox of anonymous monumentality suggests that Costa's intended correlation of form and function is spurious if its purpose is to differentiate function in terms of form.

What it suggests instead is that the correlation modernism makes between form and function is most fundamentally based on equivalence rather than difference. It applies the same formal conception of object as figure to buildings destined for different use and applies the same strategies of defamiliarization to different functions (such as the use of the transparent façade in both the office building and the apartment block). This uniform application reduces the perception and the experience of difference in form and, significantly, in function: the formal equivalence of all the buildings in the various sectors implies an equivalence among their functions as well. It is

the merging, the homogenization, and not the differentiation, of function that residents experience in the city's architecture. Brasilienses especially note, and dislike, the merging of the functions of work and residence – a complaint directed primarily at the *superquadras* that Congressman Ulysses Guimarães, president of the opposition party during the years of military rule, epitomizes when he observes that "no one likes to sleep in the office" (*Veja*, 18 April 1984, p. 37).

This reduction of difference derives from two sources. On the one hand, as we have seen, modernist ideology sets out to reduce architectural discriminations as a means of reducing social discriminations. This correlation is based on the vision of an egalitarian society in which status differences traditionally associated with the private domain of family and residence do not determine an individual's rights to the city and in which these rights are instead determined by new collective identities based on work – which is to say, ultimately on affiliation in the institutions of the bureaucratic state. This transformation entails a collectivization of residence that we shall discuss later. As this collectivization is in turn based on work, it is not surprising that Brasilienses experience a deep penetration of the roles and identities of work into residential life (hence Guimarães's observation). . . . the federal government's initial organization of residence in Brasília actually accomplished what modernist theory proposed: it distributed the apartments on the basis of work affiliations. Thus, there appeared in Brasiliense society an *equivalence* of the principles on which the functions of work and residence were organized – that the architecture both helped create and also reflected and reinforced. While the functions remained spatially separate, their organizational principles appeared similar.

This formal and functional equivalence reveals a number of basic contradictions both in the planners' intentions and in the means by which they sought to realize them. On the one hand, if the intention of the modernist concept of zoned functions is to differentiate function by form, then we must conclude that in a city of figural objects the concept fails. It remains an illusion created on paper, on a blueprint in which different sectors are drawn in different colors and labeled "residence," "work," "recreation," and so on. In terms of the most basic object-space relations, there is in fact nothing different in the treatment of these sectors. Hence, the overwhelming sense of monotony and sameness that Brasilienses experience in the city.[5]

On the other hand, if the intention of the concept of zoned functions is to reduce differences between the principles on which various functions are organized – which amounts to equating the functions of urban life uniformly for all residents in terms of the principles of a collectivized, egalitarian social structure – then we must conclude that the generalization of work relations to the other functions may not accomplish this end if work is based on a stratified hierarchy of command and status relations. This is precisely the contradiction faced in Brasília between the actual organization of work and the intended organization of residence ... If residential relations are established on the basis of work relations and the latter are based on the occupational stratification of the bureaucracy, then hierarchic work relations are bound to contradict egalitarian attempts to allocate the same residential conditions to different occupational strata. This problem is not unique to Brasília because the kind of collectivization that the ideology of the modernist city entails depends on the centralization of authority at the level of the state. Rather, it reflects the merging of state and society that the modernist model presupposes: the identification of the state as the organizer of social life, through work, in every sector of society....

NOTES

1 For a history of modern architecture and urban planning in Brazil, see Bruand 1981.

2 Without doubt, the Monumental Axis, especially the eastern, federal half, is for Brasilienses the most memorable part of the city. In their reading of the city's form as an airplane, the plane's body is taken as a metaphor for the body politic of the city: its cockpit, the center of command, corresponds to the Plaza of the Three Powers; its fuselage, to the ministerial and service sectors; its tail section to the municipal administration ("at the back of the plane" politically); and, in the wings, with no voice along the axis of command, the residents in their *superquadras*.

3 In the Commercial Sector South, the rational address system has been altogether abandoned and replaced by a landmark-type system: buildings are named after companies and capitalists, states and statesmen, and the like. Thus, one finds the Antonio Venâncio Building, the Gilberto Salamão Building, (named after local entrepreneurs), the President Dutra Building, the JK Building (for President Juscelino Kubitschek), the City Bank Building, the São Paulo Building, and so on. In other words, there has been a return to the use of buildings as monuments of individual privilege and of collective memory. Nevertheless, the result is a kind of oversubscribed "valley of the kings" in which so many monuments shoulder each other that it becomes very difficult to remember, identify, or even find one of them.

4 These functions are divided into approximately 80 sectors according to the most comprehensive survey of the city (Geipot 1975: 57). A full listing may be found in Holston 1986: table 5.2.

5 An example of this illusion of the plan is the way in which maps of the Plano Piloto (e.g., the one in Brasília's telephone directory) label the two strips of grass on either side of the Bus Terminal Platform as *praças*, 'squares'. These strips border the upper-level parking lots ... To my knowledge they are not used by human beings for any sort of activity. Nor are they identified in peoples'

minds as particular places, certainly not as squares. The same deception occurs with the Square (*read* parking lot) of the Superior Tribunals. If such areas can be called squares, then one wonders about the impoverishment of architectural concepts – not to mention the quality of city life – in modernist planning.

REFERENCES

Brasília (Journal of Companhia Urbanizadora da Nova Capital do Brasil – Novacap)

Bruand, Yves. 1981. *Arquitetura Contemporânea no Brasil*. São Paulo: Editora Perspectiva.

Costa, Lúcio. 1957. O relatório do Plano Piloto de Brasília [multilingual edition]. *Módulo 8.*

——. 1962. *Sôbre Arquitura*. Porto Alegre: Centro dos Estudantes de Arquitetura.

Geipot (Ministério dos Transportes). 1975. *Plano Director de Transportes Urbanos do Distrito Federal: Levantamentos, Pesquisas e Estudos Básicos*. Brasília: Geipot.

Holston, James. 1986. The Modernist City: Architecture, Politics, and Society in Brasília. Ph.D. diss., Department of Anthropology, Yale University.

Le Corbusier (Charles Edouard Jeanneret). 1957. *La Charte d'Athenes*. [1941.] Paris: Editions de Minuit.

——. 1971. *The City of Tomorrow*. [1924.] Cambridge: MIT Press.

Perugine, Erdna, and Maria Luísa C. Aroeira, Maria José Caldeira. 1980. *Gente, Terra Verde, Céu Azul: Estudos Sociais*. São Paulo: Editora Ática.

Salvador, Frei Vicente do. 1931. *História do Brasil, 1500–1627*. São Paulo: Cia. Melhoramentos.

Silva, Ernesto. 1971. *História de Brasília: Um Sonho, Uma Esperança, Uma Realidade*. Brasília: Coordenada-Editora de Brasília.

from *Urbanism, Colonialism, and the World-economy*

Anthony D. King

Incorporating the Periphery (2):
Urban Planning in the Colonies

...

Planning and imperialism

The last fifteen or twenty years have seen the growth of a new academic specialization, the history of urban and regional planning. Until the early 1980s, the focus of these studies had principally been on the development of urban planning in the core countries of Europe and North America but in recent years, there has been increasing interest in planning history in the Third World (see *Third World Planning Review*, 1979–present)

These are not two spheres of operation, however, but one.... urban-industrial development in the core depended on the materials and markets in the periphery just as peripheral cities depended on the injection of capital and 'professional' expertise from the core. Colonial economies played a role in the industrial urbanization of Europe, especially Britain, and hence, indirectly as well as directly, in the development of 'modern' urban planning. With regard to, for example, two early influential examples of planning, where did Bournville's cocoa come from, or, in relation to Port Sunlight, the coconut oil for Lever's soaps? This chapter, therefore, examines urban plan-

ning in the colonies and some of the issues that research in this area needs to raise.

Conceivably, the scope of such a theme would cover the activities of those metropolitan societies – France, Britain, Belgium, Portugal, Spain, the Netherlands, Italy, Germany, the United States, and also South Africa, with colonial possessions in South and South-East Asia, middle America, and Africa over the last hundred or more years. (In Africa in 1919 this included Algeria, Tunisia, Morocco, French West Africa, French Equatorial Africa, Somaliland, Togoland, Cameroon, Madagascar, Congo, Guinea, Angola, Mozambique, Cabinda, Rio de Oro, Rio Muni, Spanish Guinea, Eritrea, Italian Somaliland, Gambia, Sierra Leone, the Gold Coast, Nigeria, South-West Africa, Bechuanaland, Swaziland, Basutoland, Southern Rhodesia, Northern Rhodesia, Nyasaland, Tanganyika, Zanzibar, Uganda, Kenya, the Sudan, and Egypt.) To be technically correct, it would be necessary to include other continents – such as Australasia – politically defined as 'colonies' during part of the period. It should purportedly deal, not only with the 'grand designs' for Delhi, Lusaka, Canberra, Salisbury, Nairobi, Kaduna, or Kuala Lumpur, but with a myriad cases from Fez to Djibouti, Casablanca to Luanda, where some forms of conscious planning took place, if not in the particular British manner of town-planning ordinances, improvement trusts, or master plans (Alcock and Richards; 1953; Atkinson, 1953). It would deal with the activities of Lutyens, Baker, Geddes, and Lanchester in India (Delhi, Calcutta, Madras), with Baker or White in South and East Africa (Pretoria, Nairobi), with Reade in Malaya, Adshead in Northern Rhodesia (now Zambia), Ashbee in Palestine, Gardner-Medwin in the West Indies, or their American, Italian, French, Portuguese, Dutch, German, Belgian, or other counterparts in the Philippines, Morocco, Algeria, other parts of colonial Africa, in Saigon, Cholon, or the Treaty Ports of China or other parts of the colonial urban world (see Abu-Lughod, 1975; 1976; 1978; 1980; Boralévi, 1980; Christopher, 1988; Davies, 1969; Dethier, 1973; *Garden City*, 1904–10; *Garden Cities and Town Planning*, 1911–32; *Town and Country Planning*, 1932–80; Gardner-Medwin, et al., 1948; Fetter, 1976; Ginsburg, 1965; Hines, 1972; Home, 1983; Langlands, 1969; Lewcock, 1963; Rabinow, 1989a, b; Reitani, 1980; Sandercock, 1975; Shapiro, 1973; Simon, 1986; Soja and Weaver, 1976; Wright, 1987; Wright and Rabinow, 1981; Western, 1985). If this is the possible scope for the field, this chapter is limited to the British colonial experience as it relates to those areas where subject populations were incorporated on a large scale into the political, economic, social, and cultural systems of the metropolitan society.

Two conceptual clarifications are needed. . . . colonialism is understood as 'the establishment and maintenance, for an extended time, of rule over an alien people that is is separate from and subordinate to the ruling power' (Emerson, 1968). In this case, we are referring to 'modern' industrial colonialism, mainly of the nineteenth and twentieth centuries. For a proper understanding of the processes of 'colonial planning', some basic conceptual distinctions would need to be made between different colonial situations, for example, colonies of settlement, and those of exploitation of the indigenous inhabitants, as also the

number of indigenous people in a colonized territory, their state of economic development, and the length of colonial rule (see Chapter 1 [of King's *Urbanism*]; also Christopher, 1988; Drakakis-Smith, 1987).

Second, what is to be understood by 'urban and regional planning'? The history of urban planning in any society demonstrates a continuity, in terms of the distribution of political and economic power, and in social and cultural values, between an age when there was no 'town planning' as such, and a period (after 1909 in Britain) when there was. This continuity in practice is especially evident in colonial territories (King, 1976) where the urban assumptions of industrial capitalism combine with cultural practice to produce particular spatial forms well before a 'professional' expertise of 'town planning' is constructed. In this context, therefore, the modern history of colonial planning can be usefully divided into three phases:

1　A period up to the early twentieth century when settlements, camps, towns, and cities were consciously laid out according to various military, technical, political, and cultural codes and principles, the most important of the latter being military and political dominance. These practices are the outcome of the state of development in the core society (economic, social, and political), the mode of production on which this was based and the (often military) context in which they had developed.

2　A second period, beginning in the early twentieth century that coincides with the development of formally stated 'town-planning' theory, ideology, legislation, and professional knowledges in Britain, when the structure of colonial relationships was used to convey such phenomena, on a selective and uneven basis, to the dependent territories.

3　A third period of post-, or neocolonial developments, after 1947 in Asia and 1951 in Africa, when cultural, political, and economic links have, within a larger network of global communications and a situation of economic dependence, provided the means to continue the transplantation of ideologies, values, and planning models, generally in the 'neocolonial modernisation' of once-colonial cities (Steinberg, 1984).

This periodization can be matched with classical, monopoly (or imperialist), and multinational phases in the development of capitalism and classical, 'modern', and most recently, 'post-modern' phases in the development of culture, particularly as it relates to architecture and planning (see comments on Jameson, 1985: 11–12).

Moreover, in discussing urban planning in relation to colonial territories, it is impossible to disassociate a more limited notion of 'planning' from, at one level, a range of related topics such as architectural style, health, house form, legislation, building science, and technology and these, at another level, from the total cultural, economic, political, and social system of which they are a part. The introduction of 'modern' 'planned' environments based on 'Western' (and capitalist) notions of civilization, when compared to the 'traditional' (non-capitalist) indigenous city of Kano (northern Nigeria) or the Malayan village, has obviously modified far more than just the physical environment.

The aim of this chapter, therefore, is to suggest five interrelated themes that are central to any discussion regarding urban planning in a colonial and neocolonial situation.

The political-economic framework

Colonialism, as a political, economic, and cultural process, was the vehicle by which urban planning was exported to many non-Western societies. How were the aims and activities of planning affected by this? How did urban and regional planning contribute to or modify the larger colonial situation? What is the present-day structure of political and economic relationships that enables the assumptions and aims of plan-ning to be transferred to ex-colonial societies?

A consideration of these questions presupposes an intellectual and moral stance. Stated as a simplistic dichotomy, this may be an analysis that treats imperialism as 'the highest state of capitalism' (Lenin) where subject populations (and environments) were incorporated into the metropolitan capitalist economy with the attendant consequences for good or ill inherent in that system; at the other end of the spectrum, colonialism can be seen as the primary channel by which the benefits of Western civilization, 'the ideas and techniques, the spiritual and material forces of the West' have been brought to a large portion of humankind (Emerson, 1968), a viewpoint shared by some African scholars whether Black or White (Adu Boahen, 1987; Christopher, 1988). There are also, of course, positions in between.

In the simplest analysis, colonialism was a means by which the metropolitan power extended its markets for manufactured goods and by which the colonies, in turn, supplied raw materials to the metropolis. Though this oversimplifies the historical situation, economic dependency characterizes both colonial and post-colonial situations, with the concomitant phenomenon of what Castells (1977) has termed 'dependent urbanization', i.e. industrialization that historically was related to urbanization in the development of core Western societies, which, in the colonial case, took place in the metropolitan society, whilst urbanization (without industrialization) took place in the dependent colonial society. Urban planning in the colonies, along with its associated activities such as housing and transport developments, in any of the three periods indicated, may be viewed as part of 'dependent urbanization'. The evolution of urban systems (regional planning) and the organization of urban space (urban planning) in the colonial society can be accounted for by 'the internal and (especially) the external distribution of power' (Friedmann and Wulff, 1976: 13–14). Despite criticisms of the dependency paradigm (see Corbridge, 1986) Friedmann and Wulff's comments on it still have salience for the understanding of historic colonial environments:

> Basically, it involves the notion that powerful corporate and national interests, representing capitalist society at its most advanced, established outposts in the principal cities of Third World countries, for three interrelated purposes: to extract a sizable surplus from the dependent economy, in the form of primary products, through principally a process of 'unequal exchange'; to expand the market for goods and services produced in the home countries of advanced monopoly capitalism; and to ensure stability of an indigenous political system that will resist encroachment by ideologies and social movements that threaten to undermine the basic institutions of the capitalistic system. All three forms of penetration are ultimately intended to serve the single purpose of helping to maintain expanding levels of production and consumption in the home countries of advanced capitalism.
>
> (Later versions of this theory see the domination of peripheral economies primarily of help in the expansion of multinational corporations that exhibit a growing independence of action from national commitments and control.)
>
> In the course of this process, local élites are co-opted. Their life-style becomes imitatively cosmopolitan . . . As part of this process massive transfers of rural people are made to the urban enclave economy. (Friedmann and Wulff, 1976)

According to Friedmann and Wulff, this theory of dependency, or more accurately, dependent capitalism, seems to account for certain forms of spatial development in newly-industrializing societies (ibid.).

These theoretical generalizations can be translated more specifically into colonial built forms and urban spaces. Colonial forms of urbanism and urbanization are evident not only in Latin America, Asia, and Africa (Basu, 1985; Castells, 1972; Harvey, 1973; King, 1976; Mabogunje, 1980; Ross and Telkamp, 1985) but also in the early-eighteenth-century American colonies (Foglesong, 1986; Gordon, 1984; Lampard, 1986) as well as in Australia.

In India, the most widespread example of conscious urban planning prior to the twentieth century is the location and lay-out of military cantonments, the primary purpose of which was to provide for the ultimate sanction of force over the colonized population. The informally planned 'civil station', located alongside, accommodated the political-administrative 'managers' of the colonized society. The major cities resulting from the colonial connection (Madras, Bombay, and Calcutta), were not industrial centres but commercial, entrepôt ports oriented to the metropolitan economy (Brush, 1970; Kosambi, 1985) subject to nineteenth-century planning exercises to optimize their function in the colonial economy (Dossal, 1989). The major city-building exercise during two hundred years of informal and formal colonial rule – the planning and construction of New Delhi (1911–40) – involved the creation of a capital city almost entirely devoted to administrative, political, and social functions with virtually no attempt made to plan for industrial development. The so-called 'hill stations' – a major example of specifically colonial urban development – had primarily political and sociocultural, consumption-oriented functions, the most famous of them, Simla, described by Learmouth and Spate (1965) as 'parasitic' in relation to India's economy (King, 1976: 156–79).

In Africa, for much of the colonial period, the functions of newly established centres were political, administrative, and commercial. The built environment of the 'ideal-type', political, administrative capital was characterized by those buildings housing the key institutions of colonialism: the government or state house, the council or assembly buildings (if any), the army barracks or cantonment, the police lines, the hospital, the jail, the government offices, and the road system, housing, and recreational space for the ex-patriate European bureaucracy, and occasionally, housing for local-government employees. At its most extreme, as at Lagos, the place of the central business district was occupied by the race course.

The economic institutions of colonialism were expressed in physical and spatial form: the penetration of finance capital in the construction of banks, insurance buildings, and the headquarters of multinational corporations; the incorporation of labour power in the 'native townships', mining compounds and the 'housing for labour'. The whole relationship between the economic system, the supply of 'native labour' by induced migration from rural areas, and the provision or, more accurately, lack of provision for their accommodation is too large an issue to be discussed here, 'having', to quote Collins (1980), 'a literature of its own' (see also Amin, 1974; Gugler, 1970; Rex, 1973). The underlying assumption of the system of circulatory labour migration in the Copperbelt was that:

> the towns were for Europeans and the rural areas were for Africans. It followed that no African should be in town except to provide labour as and when required by a European employer. Only men were required. . . . Urban housing was therefore rudimentary. (Collins, 1980: 232)

In the pre-independence phase in Africa, considerable effort was placed in planning and construction of low-cost and 'planned' 'African housing'. Such efforts can be viewed on the one hand as evidence of changing values and priorities, concern for what were seen as the unsatisfactory conditions of indigenous rural migrants living in shanty towns on the edge of the city: 'planned' housing, with sanitation, electricity, and a water supply constructed as part of a new social welfare programme of the Colonial Office. It can also, however, be seen as a means of incorporating labour into the colonial economy. Thus, 'social housing' built in the Gold Coast in the 1950s is 'to house labour required at the harbour'; housing in Jinja, Uganda, are 'units for Labourers, Waluka Labour Estate'. Housing in Nairobi in the late 1920s, and elsewhere, was constructed on the 'bed space' principle to accommodate single male labourers (*Colonial Building Notes. passim*). Built and let by the metropolitan government, housing in this sense represented a subsidy to wages – either to government employees or metropolitan enterprises – as well as a potential instrument of social control. The planning, design, and building of such housing estates – as also of 'Asian' and 'European' housing (of a somewhat different order) – in separate parts of the town is patently 'town planning' and the nature of the activities are part of the larger colonial enterprise. . . .

The metropolitan government, in developing these low-cost housing programmes, generates and exchanges information on standards, costs, and design with other European powers with interests in Africa: the Belgian Office des Cités Africaines in the Congo (later Zaïre); the French Bureau Central d'Etudes pour les Equipments d'Outre-Mer (on 'tropical housing') of the Secrétariat des Missions d'Urbanisme et d'Habitat; and the South African National Housing and Planning Commission (on minimum standards for housing non-Europeans). Information is also exchanged with major metropolitan multinational companies with their own housing programmes for African workers: Imperial Tobacco, Fyffes, or the Union Minère (later, Gecamines) in the Congo (*Colonial Building Notes, passim*). In brief, 'official' housing and planning policy is primarily directed to ensuring basic minimum standards for the local labour force and government employees as well as government buildings, administrative buildings, and, for collective consumption, welfare buildings (schools, hospitals, and colleges). Industrial development, such as it is, is the responsibility of local, or more usually, metropolitan based multinationals.

The cultural, social, and ideological context of colonial planning

The history of 'town and country planning' in Britain in the industrial-capitalist and post-industrial era is, in one sense, a unique and culture-specific historical experience. True, common factors resulting from the influence of industrialization or modern automative transport may induce a structural similarity in urban environments of different industrial and capitalist societies: in some respects, Birmingham is like Berlin in the same way as pre-industrial Fez is like pre-industrial Baghdad or Katmandu. Yet given such economic or technological influences, the extent to which urban forms and planned environments differ clearly depends on political and economic factors, cultural values, historical experience, geography, and the values and ideological beliefs of those power-holding groups and professional elites responsible for structuring and implementing decisions about urban planning and the overall shape of towns.

The particular ideological and cultural context of British planning in the first half of the twentieth century, as dominated by the 'Garden City movement', is well known. The primacy of 'health, light and air', combined with a set of social and aesthetic beliefs, as a reaction to the nineteenth-century industrial city was expressive of an implicit environmental determinism that pursued physicalist solutions to social, economic, and political ills ('the peaceful path to reform'). It was a strategy of power exercised by municipal authorities to alleviate what were defined as social pathologies.

From this nineteenth- and early-twentieth-century experience grew the theory of physical planning, as well as planning legislation and the mechanisms to implement it, a form of social technology in which environments, and people, were modelled or controlled in accordance with an assumed 'public good'. It was this 'expertise' that, with its assumptions, values, and practices and partly modified by local conditions, was exported to colonial societies. There are many aspects of this process only some of which can be touched on here.

... physical-planning notions and legislation were introduced as part of the overall situation of colonial power. The basic divisions of the society, political, social, and racial, inherent in the colonial process, between ruler and ruled, Black (Brown) and White, rich and poor, 'European' and 'native', were taken as givens. In this situation, the 'techniques' and goals of planning – 'orderly' development, easing traffic flows, physically 'healthy' environments, planned residential areas, reduced densities, and zoning of industrial and residential zones were introduced, each according to the standards deemed appropriate to the various segregated populations in the city – and all without disturbing the overall structure of power.

Second, the overriding, even obsessive concern with 'health' (referred to by Swanson (1970) as the 'sanitation syndrome') was, after the implicit political and economic function of planning, taken as the driving force behind planning in all colonial territories. The creation of physically 'healthy' environments, defined according to the cultural criteria of the metropolitan power, became a major objective. It is 'health' rather than health because the basically relative nature of health states and their overall cultural and behavioural context, if appreciated at some times, were ignored at others. Indigenous definitions of health states, the means for achieving them, and the environments in which they existed were replaced by those of the incoming power in a total ecological transformation.

Thus, vital statistics from the metropolitan society are used as the reference point to 'measure' health states in the colonial population; historically and socially derived concepts of 'overcrowding' developed in the metropolitan society are applied to the indigenous environment and people. In the interests of 'health' and the new economic and social order, new environments are created – rows of minimal 'detached' housing units, surrounded by 'light and air', 'open space', gardens, and recreational areas in total disregard of the religious, social, symbolic, or political meaning of built environments as expressed in the indigenous villages and towns. ...

Health care defined according to metropolitan cultural norms, with its systems of inspections, regulated environments, and controls over behaviour becomes, like the police, housing, or employment, another means of discipline and social control. Because of the racially segregated nature of the society, as Swanson (1970) points out, 'problems of public health and sanitation, overcrowding, slums, public order and security are perceived in terms of racial differences'. Though many of the objectives of municipal government (abatement of health dangers, slum clearance and housing) were legitimate, in a colonial society the pursuit of class interest and the exercise of prejudice regarding race, culture, and colour mixed up these objectives with racial and social issues (ibid.). The culture and class-specific *perception* of health hazards more than the actual health hazards themselves was instrumental in determining much colonial, urban-planning policy.

From a purely physical and spatial viewpoint, environmental standards, norms of building and design (as well as the urban institutions themselves) derived from the historical experience of the capitalist industrial State and overlaid with its particular cultural preferences, were transferred to societies with totally different economic and cultural experience (United Nations, 1971; Mabogunje et al., 1978).

Where substantial numbers of 'expatriates' or 'settlers' were involved as in Lusaka, Nairobi, or Delhi, very low-density residential developments were built to suit their convenience. In the Master Plan for Nairobi of 1948, revisions to the original lay-out of the town, founded in 1896, suggested that densities in the European area be raised from 1 to 15 per acre (White et al., 1948). Low densities, extensive intra-urban distances, large housing plots, and lavish recreational space were all based on the assumption of the availability of motorized transport and the telephone, as well as cheap 'native labour'; i.e. on a technology for which the colonized country was dependent on the metropolitan. The assumption in such plans was presumably that the 'industrial', fully motorized society was inevitable, an assumption which, in the postcolonial era of independent development has meant not only vast journeys to work, but excessive expenditure on basic services (water, sewers, roads, electricity), inefficient land use and a need for fundamental redensification.

As metropolitan environments were introduced, or rather, colonial versions of such environments, so metropolitan legislation was necessary to maintain them; hence, the widespread introduction of the 1932 Act and other legislative codes. Here, two points can be mentioned. The first concerns the transfer of particular social and environmental categories from the metropolitan to the colonial society, of which the basic dichotomy between 'town' and 'country' was one of the more important.

Another is the transfer of particular culture-specific practices, and especially, those values of historicism and sentiment expressed in the 'preservation' syndrome. In the colonial context, this has a double irony. Not only does planning effort go into inculcating the colonized culture with similar values but the criteria of the colonial power are used to define and 'preserve' 'buildings of architectural and historic importance', while remnants of the indigenous culture are allowed to disappear. Thus, the Ministry of Overseas Development-sponsored Survey and Plan for Kaduna, Northern Nigeria, 1967 (Max Lock and Partners, 1967) suggests the retention of a small iron bridge erected by Lord Lugard, the previous colonial Governor; the Secretary of the Georgian Group visits the West Indies to advise on the preservation of military officers' quarters from the eighteenth century. In Delhi, various 'sacred' sites, associated with the 'Mutiny' are preserved throughout colonial rule, indirectly affecting the location of the new capital (King, 1976: 234).

Colonial planning: social space

The central social fact of colonial planning was segregation, principally, though not only, on racial lines. The segregated city not only resulted from but in many cases, created the segregated society. In southern Africa, the indigenous population was kept out of cities; here and elsewhere it was confined to 'native locations' or 'townships' (Soweto, of course, stands for the South West Township), or it 'squatted' on the perimeter. In India, an implicit apartheid based on economic and cultural criteria governing occupation of residential areas was practised. In other south-east Asian cities zoning of Asian and European areas was the norm (McGee, 1967).

In South Africa, as labour migration increased, 'native housing' was provided in locations on the edge of the city. As urbanization proceeded, Africans were 'brought into' the urban systems in the form of segregated cities, thus, as Swanson (1970) describes, learning to see themselves in the new social categories imposed by the ruling White minority. 'The urban nexus explains why the policies of segregation and separate development emerged as the dominant concerns of local and national government', the *Native (Urban) Areas Act* of 1923 embodying, for the first time, national recognition of the impact of urbanization. The segregated city has been fundamental in the development of 'categorical' relationships, the stereotyping of one race and its behaviour by another (Mitchell, 1966).

Even within the larger racial divisions, transformations have also occurred as a result, in later times, of particular planning and housing policies that have allocated different social groups to housing types and residential areas built and allocated according to economic (i.e. income-bracket) criteria. Because of the lack of finance or capacity in the private sector, in many colonial and ex-colonial societies, a large proportion of housing has been undertaken by government, particularly in newly created urban centres. The design and allocation of housing and area according to occupation and income group have been significant in structuring perceptions of social stratification (King, 1976; Little, 1974; Nilsson, 1973). Similar

practices – a continuation of the colonial Public Works Department tradition – can be found in Chandigarh or Islamabad.

Nothing could be more different than the traditional Ashanti village and the low-cost, gridiron, planned, suburban housing-unit estate of Accra. The symbolic meaning of space in the traditional village, whether expressed in terms of house or compound size, dwelling form, or distance between dwellings, in all cultures relates to social, cultural, or religious meanings. New urban environments based on income and occupational differentials clearly affect both the construction and self-perception of social classes and categories. Yet in Ghana, it was assumed that such planned housing could be used as a means to break down traditional tribal and kinship bonds and help to establish a 'law-abiding' and, with the introduction of privately owned, single-family dwellings, an implicitly consumer society:

> As urbanization takes effect in Ghana, tribal ties and discipline must be superseded by other loyalties if a coordinated law-abiding society is to emerge. It is therefore important to give the urban Ghanaian a sense of community membership. The policy in Tema has been to discourage racial, tribal, religious or class segregation, in the hope that the citizens' loyalty will be to neighbourhood, community and town. This policy requires non-traditional types of housing accommodation. The tribal compound has no place in Tema and is replaced by the private family dwelling. Differentiation of dwelling standards is purely by income and all income groups are represented in each community. (*Tema, 1951–61, A Report on the Development of the Town of Tema*, prepared for the Ghana Government by D. C. Robinson and R. J. Anderson)

...

The interaction of environment and behaviour

Urban planning relates, on the one hand to the actual creation of planned space and, on the other, to the regulation and modification of existing areas by means of statutory legislation and municipal controls. In democratic societies, it is assumed that statutory control – the law – represents the 'collective will' of society, the contested outcome of economic and political interests, but which also has the power to change it. In theory, therefore, members of the society are, by and large, in agreement with the law and, in a stable polity, accept it as legitimate.

A more important factor controlling the use and modification of the environment – determining how houses are built, how public space is used, how people behave in specific areas – is the whole realm of 'unwritten law', the taken-for-granted rules and codes, based on shared values that are part of everyday cultural practices and behaviour.

In the case of planned environments as well as planning legislation exported to culturally different, pre-capitalist societies, neither of these two assumptions applies. By definition, such societies are not democratically governed. Legislation is imposed after being conceived for the interests of the ruling elite. In ensuring that such legislation is enforced, resort must be had to the instruments of such control – the police, the army, and the judiciary, or the informal, but effective, para-judicial policing by members of the ex-patriate community.

In a totally different culture, the taken-for-granted codes and cultural rules governing people's relation to their environment simply do not apply to culturally different 'imposed' environments; indigenous codes conflict with those of the newcomers, most obviously, in pre-capitalist, pre-industrial situations, with the entire building process and the way that space is organized and used. Hence, over time, two interrelated processes take place. New laws and regulations are enforced by municipal or State authorities by a mixture of penalty and example; second, the life style and cultural behaviour of local populations may be modified as they emulate the ruling colonial elite. These regulatory mechanisms are buttressed by the power of the State: in cases, keeping indigenous populations out of cities and/or distributing resources in favour of colonial populations.

REFERENCES

Abu-Lughod, J. (1975) 'Moroccan cities: apartheid and the serendipity of conservation', in I. Abu-Lughod (ed.) *African Themes*, Northwestern University Studies in honour of G. M. Carter, Evanston, pp. 77–111.

Abu-Lughod, J. (1976) 'Developments in North African urbanism. The process of decolonization', in B.J.L. Berry (ed.) *Urbanization and Counterurbanization*, Beverly Hills, CA and London: Sage, pp. 191–211.

Abu-Lughod, J. (1978) 'Dependent urbanism and decolonization: the Moroccan case', *Arab Studies Quarterly* 1: 49–66.

Abu-Lughod, J. (1980) *Rabat. Urban Apartheid in Morocco*, Princeton, NJ: Princeton University Press.

Adu Boahen, A. (1987) *African Perspectives on Colonialism*, Baltimore, MD: Johns Hopkins Press.

Alcock, A. E. S. and Richards, H. (1953) *How to Plan Your Village. A Handbook for Villages in Tropical Countries*, London: Longmans, Green.

Amin, S. (1974) *Accumulation on a World Scale. A Critique of the Theory of Underdevelopment*, New York: Monthly Review Press.

Atkinson, G. A. (1953) 'British architects in the tropics', *Architectural Association Journal* 69 (773): 7–21.

Basu, D. K. (ed.) (1985) *The Rise and Growth of Colonial Port Cities in Asia*, Santa Cruz: Center for South Pacific Studies, University of California (1st edn, 1979).

Boralévi, A. (1980) 'Le "Citta' dell' impero": Urbanistica fascista in Etiopia, 1936–41', in A. Moini (ed.) *Urbanistica Fascista*, Milan: Cinta.

Brush, J. E. (1970) 'The growth of the Presidency Towns', in R. G. Fox (ed.) *Urban India: Society, Space and Image*, Durham, NC: Duke University Press, pp. 91–114.

Castells, M. (1972) *Imperialismo y Urbanizacion en America Latina*, Barcelona: Editorial Gustava Gili.

Castells, M. (1977) *The Urban Question*, London: Edward Arnold (first published as *La Question Urbaine*, Paris: Francis Maspero (1972)).

Christopher, A. J. (1988) *The British Empire at its Zenith*, London: Croom Helm.

Collins, J. (1980) 'Lusaka: urban planning in a British colony' in G. E. Cherry (ed.) *Shaping an Urban World*, London: Mansell.

Colonial Building Notes, 1950–7 (later, *Overseas Building Notes*, 1959–present), Building Research Station, Garston, Watford.

Corbridge, S. (1986) *Capitalist World Development*, London: Macmillan.

Davies, D. H. (1969) 'Lusaka, Zambia: some town-planning problems in an African capital city at Independence', *Zambian Urban Studies*, Lusaka: Zambian Institute of Social Research.

Dethier, J. (1973) 'Evolution of concepts of housing, urbanism and country planning in a developing country: Morocco', in L. C. Brown (ed.) *From Madina to Metropolis*, Princeton: Darwin Press, pp. 197–243.

Dossal, M. (1989) 'Colonial urban planning in Bombay, 1860–1880', *International Journal of Urban and Regional Research* 13, 1 (in press).

Drakakis-Smith, D. (1987) *The Third World City*, New York: Methuen.

Emerson, R. (1968) 'Colonialism', in *International Encyclopaedia of Social Sciences*, New York: Macmillan.

Fetter, B. (1976) *The Creation of Elizabethville, 1910–40*, Stanford: Hoover Institute Press.

Foglesong, R. E. (1986) *Planning the Capitalist City: the Colonial Era to the 1920s*, Princeton, NJ: Princeton University Press.

Friedmann, J. and Wulff, G. (1982) 'World city formation: an agenda for research and action', *International Journal of Urban and Regional Research* 6: 309–44.

Friedmann, J. and Wulff, G. (1976) The Urban Transition: *Comparative Studies of Newly Industrializing Societies*, London: Arnold.

Gardner-Medwin, R. et al. (1948) 'Recent planning developments in the colonies', *RIBA Journal 55*, Feb.

Ginsburg, N. (1965) 'Urban geography in non-Western areas', in P. M. Hauser and L. F. Schnore (eds) *The Study of Urbanization*, New York: Wiley, pp. 311–46.

Gordon, D. (1984) 'Capitalist development and the history of American cities', in W. K. Tabb and L. Sawers (eds) *Marxism and the Metropolis: New Perspectives in Urban Political Economy*, Oxford: Oxford University Press.

Gugler, J. (ed.) (1970) *Urban Growth in Sub-Saharan Africa*, Kampala: Makere Institute of Social Research.

Harvey, D. (1973) *Social Justice and the City*, London: Edward Arnold.

Hines, T. (1972) 'The imperial facade: D. H. Burnham and American architectural planning in the Philippines', *Pacific Historical Review* 61: 35–53.

Home, R. K. (1983) 'Town planning, segregation and indirect rule in colonial Nigeria', *Third World Planning Review* 5 (2): 165–75.

Jameson, F. (1985) 'Postmodernism and consumer society', in H. Foster (ed.) *Postmodern Culture*, London: Pluto Press, pp. 111–25.

King A. D. (1976) *Colonial Urban Development: Culture, Social Power and Environment*, London: Routledge & Kegan Paul.

Kosambi, M. (1985) 'Commerce, conquest and the colonial city: the role of locational factors in the rise of Bombay', *Economic and Political Weekly* 5: 31–7, Jan.

Lampard, E. E. (1986) 'The New York metropolis in transformation: history and prospect', in H. J. Ewers, J. B. Goddard, and H. Matzerath (eds) *The Future of the Metropolis*, Berlin and New York: de Gruyter.

Langlands, B. (1969) 'Perspective on urban planning for Uganda', in M. Safier and B. W. Langlands (eds) *Perspectives on Urban Planning for Uganda*, Uganda: Department of Geography, Makerere University College.

Learmouth, A. T. L. and Spate, O. U. K. (1965) *India: A Regional Geography*, London: Methuen.

Lewcock, R. (1963) *Early Nineteenth Century Architecture in South Africa*, Cape Town: Hobbema.

Lewcock, R. (1979) Review of King, *Colonial Urban Development (1976)*, in *Modern Asian Studies* 13: 164–7.

Little, A. (1974) *Urbanisation as a Social Process*, London: Routledge & Kegan Paul.

Lock, Max, and Partners (1967) *Survey and plan for Kaduna, Northern Nigeria*, London: Faber & Faber.

Mabogunje, A. L. (1980) *The Development Process: a Spatial Perspective*, London: Hutchinson.

Mabogunje, A. L., Hardoy, J. E., and Misra, R. P. (1978) *Shelter Provision in Developing Countries: The Influence of Standards and Criteria*, Chichester: Wiley.

McGee, T. G. (1967) *The South East Asian City*, London: Bell.

Mitchell, J. C. (1966) 'Theoretical orientations in African urban studies', in M. Banton (ed.) *The Social Anthropology of Complex Societies*, London: Tavistock.

Nilsson, S. (1973) *The New Capitals of India, Pakistan and Bangladesh*, Lund: Scandinavian Institute of South Asian Studies.

Rabinow, P. (1989a) 'Modernity and difference: French colonial planning in Morocco', *International Journal of Urban and Regional Research* 13 (1).

Rabinow, P. (1989b) *French Modern. Norms and Forms of Missionary and Didactic Pathos*, Cambridge, MA: MIT Press (forthcoming).

Reitani, G. (1980) 'Politica territoriale e urbanistica in Tripolitania, 1920–40', in A. Moini (ed.) *Urbanistica Fascista*, Milan: Cinta.

Rex, J. (1973) *Race, Colonialism and the City*, London: Routledge.

Ross, R. and Telkamp, G. (eds) (1985) *Colonial Cities*, Boston, Lancaster, Dordrecht: Martinus Nijhoff.

Sandercock, L. (1975) *Cities for Sale*, Melbourne: Melbourne University Press.

Shapiro, S. G. (1973) 'Planning Jerusalem: the first generation, 1917–1968', in D. H. K. Amiran et al. (eds) *Urban Geography of Jerusalem*, Jerusalem: Massada Press, pp. 139–53.

Simon, D. (1986) 'Desegregation in Namibia: the demise of urban apartheid?', *Geoforum* 17 (2) 289–307.

Soja, E. W. and Weaver, C. E. (1976) 'Urbanization and underdevelopment in East Africa', in B. J. L. Berry (ed.) *Urbanization and Counter-Urbanization*, Beverly Hills, CA and London: Sage, pp. 233–66.

Steinberg, F. (1984) 'Town planning and the neocolonial modernization of Colombo', *International Journal of Urban and Regional Research* 8 (4) 530–48.

Swanson, M. W. (1970) 'Reflections on the urban history of South Africa', in H. L. Watts (ed.) *Focus on Cities*, Durban: Institute of Social Research, University of Natal.

United Nations (1971) *Climate and House Design*, New York: United Nations.

Western, J. (1985) 'Undoing the colonial city', *Geographical Review* 73 (3): 335–57.

White, L. W. T. et al. (1948) *Nairobi: Master Plan for a Colonial Capital*, London: HMSO.

Wright, G. (1987) 'Tradition in the service of modernity: architecture and urbanism in French colonial policy, 1900–1930', *Journal of Modern History* 59: 291–316.

Wright, G. and Rabinow, P. (1981) 'Savoir et pouvoir dans l'urbanisme moderne colonial d'Ernest Hebrard', *Cahiers de la Recherche Architecture*.

55

The Dark Side of Modernism: Planning as Control of an Ethnic Minority

Oren Yiftachel

Introduction

Urban and regional planning as an organized field of human endeavour came into being as an integral part of what is often termed 'the modernist project' (Dear 1986; Hall 1988). Consequently, it has been conceived, by planners and public alike, as a rational, professional activity, aimed at producing a 'public good' of one kind or another. Research into the theory and practice of urban and regional planning has therefore tended to concentrate on its capacity to contribute to the attainment of well-established societal (modernist) goals, such as residential amenity, economic efficiency, social equity, or environmental sustainability. Far less attention has been devoted to the ability of planning to promote goals of an opposite nature, such as social repression, economic retardation or environmental degradation. In particular, the links between planning policy, the problems of ethnic minorities and the political impact of modernist concepts in developing societies are yet to be explored fully. . . .

'Planning' is defined here as the formulation, content and implementation of spatial policies. 'Reform' implies 'making things better', affecting amendment or improvement in the affairs of subject groups. 'Control' means the regulations of development enforced from above, with the aim of maintaining existing patterns of social, political and economic domination. 'Ethnicity' is defined as a set of group characteristics, based on belief in a common history and place, and usually including language, culture, race and/or religion. . . .

Planning and the Control of Minorities: Some Theoretical Observations

Planning: reform or control?

Urban and regional planning emerged out of the unacceptable and inhumane living conditions prevalent in the rapidly expanding industrial cities of the eighteenth and nineteenth centuries. The emergence of planning was intimately linked to a broader reform movement, which sought to redress the ills of unconstrained capitalism, through changes to the politics, economy and geography of cities (Cherry 1988; Hall 1988; Schaffer 1988). While early planning thinkers (like later ones) were clearly divided along ideological lines, a discernable consensus underlaid the development of planning thought and the emergence of the planning profession: planning should, first and foremost, act to improve people's (mainly physical) living conditions. This basic assumption formed the foundation for theories and tools which were later developed to guide public intervention in the development process and the land market. Most of the theoreis and concepts developed in planning during subsequent decades focused on two key questions: what is a good city? What is good planning? (see Cherry 1988; Hall 1988; Schaffer 1988; Yiftachel 1989).

Recent studies on the performance of planning systems clearly attest to the pervasive understanding of 'planning as reform'. Pearce (1992) and Healey (1992), for example, examine the historical performance of the British planning system by using as yardsticks the progressive concepts of amenity, order, efficiency, distributive justice and environmental protection. The recent evaluative works of Burgess (1993), Cherry (1988), Carmon (1990) and Schaffer (1988) also predominantly assess planning according to its ability to deliver improvement in the lives of subject populations. Even the thoroughly reflective work of Friedmann (1987) delineates four main perspectives which have dominated the development of planning theories and concepts: social reform, policy analysis, social learning and social mobilization. These are characterized, to varying degrees, by a view that planning has the capacity to reform and improve cities, regions and society. I argue here that this view of planning is narrow, too idealistic and often *unrealistic*. Furthermore, because planning has been widely interpreted as reform, relatively little research has focused on the instances when it acts as a regressive agent of change, particularly in the context of ethnic relations.

To be sure, the reformist-benevolent interpretation of planning is not universal. Contrasting accounts exist, particularly from Marxist, feminist and racial perspectives (see, for example: Dear and Scott 1981; Harvey 1992; Huxley 1993; Jackson 1986, 1987; Sandercock 1990; S. Smith 1989). However, even those explaining planning as assisting the domination of powerful interests observe that planners and politicians have shared a belief in its contribution to a 'better society', through development which would – if properly planned – maximize benefits for the largest number of people (for this popular utilitarian view, see Huxley 1994). The main argument of such critics has focused on planning's *unintentional* (or implicit) regressive consequences. Thus, planning has been widely perceived as part and parcel of the *modernization* of society, a process requiring the preparation of urban and regional plans (Cherry 1988; Hall 1988).

Planning in deeply divided societies

Urban and regional planning in the form known today in the West first emerged in the Anglo-Saxon world, particularly in Great Britain. Subsequently, the debate over the goals, achievements and effectiveness of planning has been mainly confined to the institutional and political settings usually defined as 'liberal democracy'. This setting is characterized by a capitalist economy, a subsequent dominance of the market in politics (Lindblom 1977), a promotion of individualism, and a two-party political system with little minority representation (Lijphart 1984).

A fundamental difference exists between these liberal democracies and other, more collectively segmented societies. This difference can be highlighted by differentiating between two main types of multiethnic society: *pluralistic* and *deeply divided* (or plural). Pluralistic societies are typically composed of immigrant groups which tend to assimilate over time, and are usually governed by a liberal-democratic regime. In such societies, one's ethnic affiliation is a private matter, and ethnic movements mainly focus on the attainment of civil and economic equality. Ethnic affairs are often interwoven with *class issues*, which are the most dominant social cleavage in such societies.

On the other hand, deeply divided societies are composed of non-assimilating ethnic groups which occupy their historical (real or mythical) homeland. Hence, ethnic movements in such societies tend to promote goals of cultural and regional autonomy, recognition of national minority status for sizeable ethnic groups, and at times ethnic separatism. In deeply divided societies, ethnic conflicts are potentially more explosive, often threatening the very structure or unity of the state (Connor 1987). For that reason, government policies in such societies often attempt to *control* ethnic minorities, hoping to prevent serious challenge to the character or the territorial integrity of the state. Control policies typically attempt to retard the minority's economic development, contain its territorial expression, and exclude it from the state's centres of power and influence.

Notably, the Western countries where planning has flourished, as either an organized profession or a field of active research (Britain, Australia or New Zealand, the USA and Canada), are all pluralistic societies governed by liberal-democratic regimes. However, following British colonialism and the global spread of Western influence and capitalism, the ideas, concepts, methods and institutions of urban and regional planning have spread to many developing countries. Western planning ideas thus found their way to many deeply divided societies, where ethnic groups have often had a long history of struggles over land control, and where local political systems were far from the Western version of liberal democracy. The introduction of Anglo-Saxon planning ideas to these fundamentally different societies has created a set of problems and contradictions.

One of the most obvious problems has been the conversion of planning from a progressive tool of reform to an instrument of control and repression. This became possible because, in most post-colonial societies, one ethnic group came to dominate the state, using its apparatus (including planning) to maintain and strengthen this domination (Demaine 1984; Smooha 1990). While such ethnic domination may occur in Western pluralistic societies, it is usually more subtle, and is often constrained in such societies by the dominance of markets in politics (Lindblom 1977), and by legal mechanisms which protect

civil rights. In many deeply divided societies – even those with formal democratic systems – these constraints to majority dominance are either weak or lacking all together (Esman 1985). In addition, the substance matter of planning – the use of land – is a vital issue in deeply divided societies, due to the historical attachment of ethnic groups to their homeland, which assumes extreme political importance, particularly in the current 'ethnic revival' age (A. Smith 1981).

As mentioned; the use of planning to control segments of the population has not been confined to deeply divided societies. It has undoubtedly occurred in Western (pluralistic) democratic societies, although this has usually transpired in relatively subtle ways, mainly through market mechanisms (see, for example: Harvey 1973; Huxley 1994; McLoughlin 1992) or male domination (Fincher 1990; Sandercock and Forsythe 1992; Little 1993). In such societies, the consequences of 'control through planning' have been usually manifested through class and gender relations, which are less tangible or visible than the primordial ethnicity characteristic of deeply divided societies. Even ethnic and racial discrimination has largely been expressed in Western-liberal societies through (usually distorted) market outcomes, rather than explicit ethnically based legislation and policies (S. Smith 1989; Thomas 1988). In contrast, the structural importance of ethnicity in deeply divided societies has meant that the use of planning as control has in many cases become quite explicit and blatant.

The very same planning tools usually introduced to assist social reform and improvement in people's quality of life can be used as a means of controlling and repressing minority groups. This explicitly regressive face of planning has yet to be widely studied or theorized. Studies of the impact of public policy on ethnic and racial relations abound, although they mostly address ethnic issues in pluralistic (not deeply divided) societies, and few specifically address the influence of land use (or spatial) planning policies (see Eyles 1990; Jackson 1986; S. Smith 1989; Thomas 1988; Williams 1985). The approach of many planners to the problem is typically summarized by Thomas and Krishnarayan (1993: 17), who claim that 'a positive approach to racial and ethnic equality in planning follows from taking principles and good professional practice seriously.'

The issue goes beyond the ethical and professional aspects of planning and planners, especially in deeply divided societies. It is directly linked to a *structural* understanding of the relations between the state, society and space. Constant use of planning as a tool for control is likely to exacerbate social tensions. This, in turn, can lead to increasing levels of intergroup conflict and violence, thereby undermining the entire 'modernist project'. This is particularly the case in deeply divided democracies, where ethnic (and not class) cleavages dominate, and where changes to the balance of ethnic relations may have an explosive potential. The sections below attempt to begin the task of defining and theorizing the control aspect of planning, by positing that function against the original ideas of reform and progress. . . .

The three dimensions of planning control

The use of urban and regional planning as a means of control can be usefully studied by examining three key dimensions of planning policy: *territorial, procedural* and *socioeconomic*. These dimensions embody the most critical aspects of planning as an organized field of policy and professional practice: its spatial content (the territorial dimension); its power relations and decision-making processes (the procedural dimension); and its long-term consequences (the socioeconomic dimension).

The territorial dimension is defined as the spatial and land use content of plans and policies. This may include the location of settlements, neighbourhoods, industries, communal and social facilities, infrastructure services, and employment centres. It also includes the demarcation of administrative boundaries, according to which land use, development, and the provision of facilities and services are usually determined. Territorial policies can be used as a most powerful tool of control over minorities, particularly in deeply divided societies, where ethnic groups often reside in 'their own' regions. Planning policies can be used in such regional contexts to *contain* the territorial expression of such minorities, typically by imposing restrictions on minority land ownership, restricting the expansion of minority settlements, and settling members of the majority group within the minority region for control and *surveillance* (see Marcuse 1995). This is believed to impede the emergence of a powerful, regionally based, counter-culture, which may challenge the social and political order espoused by the central (majority controlled) state (Mikessel and Murphy 1991; Williams 1985; Yiftachel 1992). On an urban scale, too, majority-controlled authorities can exercise (more subtle) forms of planning control, through land-use and housing policies, with the effect of creating *segregation* between social groups, usually according to class, race and/or ethnicity (Eyles 1990; S. Smith 1989). This process is elsewhere described as the recreation of walled cities, in which patterns of domination are expressed by physical division and spatial fragmentation (Marcuse 1995). This, in turn, may further increase intergroup inequalities, as powerful groups would generally occupy the most desirable locations nearly exclusively, denying other groups the full share of the city's benefits and opportunities (Badcock 1984). The imposition of complex, inconsistent and unstable administrative boundaries can also function as a powerful tool of control, as ordinary citizens may encounter difficulties in dealing with such systems, which are usually more familiar to the wealthy and the powerful.

The procedural dimension covers the formulation and implementation processes of plans and policies. Here planning can directly affect power relations in society by controlling access to decision-making processes (Forester 1989). The procedural dimension includes statutory aspects which formally determine the relationship between various authorities and the public, and less formal aspects such as the rate of public participation, consultation and negotiation in policy making, and the ongoing relations between authorities and communities. Planning processes can be used for the *exclusion* of various segments and groups from meaningful participation in decision making, thereby contributing to their *marginalization* and repression. This form of control can be explicit, as in the case of decisions imposed 'from above', or implicit, through sophisticated methods of information distortion and meaningless forms of public consultations (Forester and Krumbholtz 1990; Friedmann 1992; Hillier 1993).

The socioeconomic dimension is expressed as the long-term impact of planning on social and economic relations in society (as distinct from the immediate spatial impact). Bound up with the concept of 'planning externalities', land-use changes result in (usually indirect) positive or negative impact on neighbouring people or communities. That impact, which may include consequences such as improved accessibility, or proximity to environmental nuisance, forms an integral part of people's real income, whether it can or cannot be directly expressed in monetary terms. In that way, resources may shift between societal groups in what Harvey (1973: 100) termed 'the quiet distributive mechanism of land use planning'. Therefore, planning can be used as a tool of socioeconomic control and domination by helping to maintain and even widen socioeconomic gaps through the location of development costs and benefits in accordance with the interests of dominant groups (McLoughlin 1992). The systematic *deprivation* of subordinate groups by spatial policies often results in a growing level of *dependence* by weaker groups on dominant interests. This dependence, in turn, forms another powerful tool of socioeconomic control (Friedmann 1992; Harvey 1992).

The fact that ethnicity is the most pronounced cleavage in deeply divided societies does not reduce the importance of the socioeconomic consequences of planning. In such societies, the 'spin-offs' of negative externalities often add a class dimension to what was previously defined as a cultural-ethnic conflict (Mabin 1995; Yiftachel 1992). In general, and contrary to conventional wisdom, urban and regional planning is not just an arm of government which may or may not contribute to societal (modernist) reform, but also a public policy area with a potential for controlling subordinate groups, particularly in deeply divided societies (see also Mabin 1995). This control can be exercised through the three dimensions of planning: territorial (affecting containment, surveillance and segregation), procedural (exclusion and marginalization), and socioeconomic (deprivation and dependence). Planning can therefore facilitate domination and control of three key societal resources: space, power and wealth...

REFERENCES

Badcock, B. 1984: *Unfairly Structured Cities*, London: Blackwell.

Burgess, P. 1993: 'City Planning and the Planning of Cities: The Recent Historiography', *Journal of Planning Literature*, 7, 4: 314–27.

Carmon, N. (ed.) 1990: *Neighbourhood Policy and Programmes: Past and Present*, London: Macmillan.

Cherry, G. 1988: *Cities and Plans*, Oxford: Blackwell.

Connor, W. 1987: 'Ethnonationalism', in E. Weiner and S. Huntington (eds), *Understanding Political Development*, Boston: Little, Brown.

Dear, M. 1986: 'Planning and Postmodernism', *Environment and Planning D: Society and Space*, 4: 367–84.

Dear, M. and Scott, A. 1981: 'Introduction', in M. Dear and A. Scott (eds), *Urbanisation and Urban Planning under Capitalism,* New York: John Wiley.

Demaine, H. 1984: 'Furnivall Reconsidered: Plural Societies in South-East Asia in the Post-Colonial Era', in C. Clarke, D. Ley and C. Peach (eds), *Geography and Ethnic Pluralism,* Boston: George Allen & Unwin.

Esman, M. 1985: 'Two Dimensions of Ethnic Politics: Defence of Homeland and Immigrant Rights', *Ethnic and Racial Studies,* 8: 438–41.

Eyles, J. 1990: 'Group Identity and Urban Space: The North American Experience', in M. Chisholm and D. Smith (eds), *Shared Space, Divided Space,* London: Unwin Hyman.

Fincher, R. 1990: 'Women in the City', *Australian Geographical Studies,* 28: 29–37.

Forester, J. 1989: *Planning in the Face of Power,* Berkeley: University of California Press.

Forester, J. and Krumbholtz, N. 1990: *Making Equity Planning Work,* Philadelphia: Temple University Press.

Friedmann, J. 1987: *Planning in the Public Domain: From Knowledge to Action,* Princeton, NJ: Princeton University Press.

Friedmann, J. 1992: *Empowerment: The Politics of Alternative Development,* Oxford: Blackwell.

Hall, P. 1988: *Cities of Tomorrow,* New York: Blackwell.

Harvey, D. 1973: *Social Justice and the City,* London: Edward Arnold.

Harvey, D. 1992: 'Social Justice, Postmodernism and the City', *International Journal of Urban and Regional Research,* 16: 588–601.

Healey, P. 1992: 'The Reorganisations of State and Markets in Planning', *Urban Studies,* 29: 411–34.

Hillier, J. 1993: 'To Boldly Go Where No Planner...', *Environment and Planning D: Society and Space,* 10: 377–92.

Huxley, M. 1993: 'Panoptica: Utilitarianism and Land Use Control', *Proceedings of the Conference on Postmodern Cities,* University of Sydney.

Huxley, M. 1994: 'Panoptica: Utilitarianism and Land Use Control', in K. Gibson and S. Watson (eds), *Metropolis Now,* Sydney: Pluto Press.

Jackson, P. 1986: 'Social Geography: Race and Racism', *Progress in Human Geography,* 10: 99–110.

Jackson, P. (ed.) 1987: *Race and Racism,* London: Allen and Unwin.

Lijphart, A. 1984: *Democracies,* New Haven: Yale University Press.

Lindblom, C. 1977: *Politics and Markets,* New York: Basic Books.

Little, J. 1993: *Gender, Planning and the Policy and the Policy Process,* Oxford: Pergamon.

Mabin, A. 1995: 'On the Problems and Prospects of Overcoming Segregation and Fragmentation in Southern Africa's Cities in the Postmodern Era', in S. Watson and K. Gibson (eds.), *Postmodern Cities and Spaces,* Oxford: Blackwell.

Marcuse, P. 1995: 'Not Chaos, but Walls: Postmodernism and the Partitioned City', in S. Watson and K. Gibson (eds.), *Postmodern Cities and Spaces,* Oxford: Blackwell.

McLoughlin, B. 1992: *Shaping Melbourne's Future?,* Sydney: Cambridge University Press.

Mikessel, M. and Murphy, A. 1991: 'A Framework for Comparative Study of Minority-group Aspirations', *Annals of the Association of American Geographers,* 81: 581–604.

Pearce, B. 1992: 'The Effectiveness of the British Land Use Planning System', *Town Planning Review,* 63: 13–28.

Sandercock, L. 1990: *Property, Politics and Urban Planning: A History of Australian Planning 1890–1990,* New Brunswick: Transactions.

Sandercock, L. and Forsythe, A. 1992: 'Gender: A New Agenda for Planning Theory', *Journal of the American Planning Association,* 58: 49–60.

Schaffer, D. (ed.) 1988: *Two Centuries of American Planning,* London: Mansell.

Smith, A. 1981: *The Ethnic Revival,* Cambridge: Cambridge University Press.

Smith, S. 1989. 'The Politics of Race and a New Segregationism', in J. Mohan (ed.), *The Political Geography of Contemporary Britain,* London: Macmillan.

Smooha, S. 1990: 'Minority Status in an Ethnic Democracy: The Arab Minority in Israel', *Ethnic and Racial Studies,* 13: 389–412.

Thomas, J. 1988: 'Racial Crisis and the Fall of the Detroit City Plan Commission', *Journal of the American Planning Association,* 48: 150–61.

Thomas, H. and Krishnarayan, V. 1993: 'Race Equality and Planning', *The Planner,* 79: 17–21.

Williams, C. H. 1985: 'Minority Groups in the Modern State', in M. Pacione (ed.), *Progress in Political Geography*, London: Croom Helm.

Yiftachel, O. 1989: 'Towards a New Typology of Urban Planning Theories', *Environment and Planning B: Planning and Design*, 16: 23–39.

Yiftachel, O. 1992: 'The State, Ethnic Relations and Democratic Stability: Lebanon, Cyprus and Israel', *Geojournal*, 21: 212–25.

from *Edge of Empire: Postcolonialism and the City*

Jane M. Jacobs

Urban Dreamings: The Aboriginal Sacred in the City

> Peter Weir's film *The Last Wave* (1977) opens with an Aboriginal elder painting sacred symbols on a rock face in outback Australia. For non-Aboriginal Australians this is a familiar image of Aboriginality: a male embodiment, a remote setting, a 'tribal' practice. The horror of *The Last Wave* comes from the uncanny movement of this spiritualised and remote Aboriginality into the modern city. A young Aboriginal man has taken some objects from a sacred site hidden under the architecture of Sydney. He is punished by his tribe, the victim of a 'tribal' killing, and the city is beset by the strange weather of an unleashed Aboriginal spirituality: an apocalyptic deluge of rain, hail, black rain and, finally, the 'last wave'. In *The Last Wave*, past time and distant people inhabit a modern Australian city. The film unsettles the familiar Manichaean geography of colonialism.... (McLean, 1993: 18)

On a bend on the Swan River, within view of the central business district of Perth, capital city of Western Australia, lies the Old Swan Brewery. Standing alone, flanked by the bushland of an urban park, it is a 'focal point' visible from the nearby city centre, a landmark for Perth residents as they speed past in their cars on their way from suburb to city. The distinctive group of nineteenth-

and early twentieth-century industrial buildings is considered to be part of the European heritage of Perth. By the mid-1980s brewing had ceased on the site and the State government of Western Australia, through its newly formed Western Australia Development Corporation, planned to adapt the buildings for use as a tourist/leisure centre featuring restaurants, retail outlets and galleries. This vision was confounded by Aboriginal claims that the site was the home of the Waugal serpent. From January to October 1989 Aborigines from the Perth region occupied this site in protest against the proposed redevelopment. They appealed to State and federal agencies concerned with the protection of Aboriginal sites of significance and launched several legal appeals to the courts. The 'Aboriginal Fringe Dwellers of the Swan Valley', as they called themselves, not only opposed redevelopment of the Brewery buildings, they wanted the buildings pulled down and the area (re)turned to parkland. In 1980s Perth, the fantastic narrative of Weir's *The Last Wave* became strangely real. Residents and urban authorities in Perth were confronted with the unlikely presence of the Aboriginal sacred in the city.

The conflict that developed around the proposed redevelopment of the Old Swan Brewery takes my general argument about the (post)colonial politics of urban space to a site on the geographical edge of the former British empire. The contest over this place elaborates my case for understanding cities in terms of the ongoing structures and cultures of colonialism and the oppositional negotiations of its persistent force. The urban transformations that gave rise to the Old Swan Brewery conflict are most certainly a product of a property and development boom and a diversification of capital accumulation into industries of consumption. In this sense, the contemporary trajectory of this site is connected to global economic transformations which, in part, transcend the spatial, political and economic logic of nineteenth-century colonialism. Yet this most 'global' development negotiated a very specific local politics deeply marked by the historical legacy of the colonial dispossession of indigenous peoples.[3]

Ordering the urban

The colonisation of Australia was based on establishing a white settler colony in a land previously occupied by an indigenous peoples, the Aborigines. The desire to establish settler colonies depended upon the will of erasure or, when this failed, systematic containment of indigenous peoples. In the case of Australia, this 'erasure' was inaugurated by the notion of *terra nullius*, land unoccupied, which became the foundational fantasy of the Australian colonies. The justice of *terra nullius* was debated in the British Parliament and its truth was daily challenged by the undeniable presence of Aborigines in the colonies. From the outset it has been a most unstable foundation for the nation. Its tenuous and debated reality was necessarily shored up by a whole range of spatial technologies of power such as the laws of private property, the practices of surveying, naming and mapping and the procedures of urban and regional planning. In the areas where cities grew, those areas of first settlement, quick and comprehensive colonisation was necessary to create the material preconditions for the realisation of a 'settler' colony. Towns provided the

home for settler 'authority'; they were administrative hubs of colonial governmentality and orchestrated the acquisition and redistribution of material resources. From these secure administrative centres settler expansion could move outward into those lands where the fantasy of *terra nullius* was less surely inscribed.

The 'city' of Perth was ritualistically marked on 12 August 1829, the birthday of King George IV, when the Lieutenant-Governor of the colony, James Stirling, led a small group to the elevated ground chosen for the city. A Mrs Dance was given the honour of striking the first blow to a tree which was felled to mark the commencement of the comprehensive land clearances which made room for the city to be called 'Perth' after the Scottish city of the same name (Green 1984: 51). In this event of colonial commencement, a woman took the symbolic edge of/off the masculinist conquest of territory. Like other cities in the emergent colonies of Australia, Perth was based on British colonial planning wisdom. An ordered grid was emphatically placed over the land and provided the spatial skeleton for an embodied settlement. Colonisation brought the city to 'a country without cities' and constructed 'little copies' that mimicked the imperial heart (Muecke 1992: 5). Paul Carter's spatial history of Australia has shown how the logic of the grid, most clearly and immediately articulated in relation to the townships of colonisation, worked like the map to connect and give unity to space 'in advance' (Carter 1987: 204). Gridded urban plans were undoubtedly imported spatial orderings intended to realise colonial authority. Yet, as Carter argues, their symbolic functioning was far from stable. The grid did connect Australian cities to a wider order of power which led back to the imperial heart but the local purchase of this authority was a more ambiguous matter. Colonists 'succumbed' to the gridded city, but not because they were responding to the orders of imperial authority. They settled comfortably into these cities because the grid was recognisable, it was a familiar spatiality in an unfamiliar land. It was for them 'the traditional matrix of new urban beginnings' (ibid.: 210). For Aborigines, the corners and lines which began to be carved into their land did not herald a familiar order that need only be awaited. This new geometry quite literally marked an unknowable future of imperfect encounters with those who sought, ceaselessly, to realise the perfection of the grid.

Aborigines were both necessary and problematic in the colonial occupation of Australia. 'Exploration' of the Australian continent was most often under the guidance of Aborigines and settlement often traced the spatiality of Aboriginal knowledge of available water and pasture. But 'possession' of the Australian continent required the Aboriginal presence, at the very least, to be contained and, at its most thorough, to be eradicated. From the moment of 'settlement', the Australian nation has realised itself through regularly intractable and frequently violent interactions between Aborigines and colonial settlers. The case of south-west Australia was no exception.... The early colonial ordering of urban space, the making of Perth the city, sought to eliminate indigenous people and indigenous meanings, those 'local authorities' which might compromise the mimetic transfer of imperial urban models to the colonies (de Certeau 1984: 106). Aborigines were positioned outside the 'civilisation' of the emergent city: a pure negativity against which settlers constituted their sense of Self. If not eradicated, then they were to be kept 'distant' by a process of spatial containment. Urban planning became the vehicle for what Bauman (1992: xv) describes as the 'perfect world that would know no misfits...no disorder...no vagabonds, vagrants or nomads', where there were 'no unattended sites left to chance'.

The land upon which the Old Swan Brewery was later built played an important role in the initial measures used in Perth to contain Aborigines. It was at this site, in 1833, that the colonial government established the Mount Eliza Depot for Aborigines (Vin-

nicombe 1989: 22). 'Public' access to this space was prohibited and it was hoped that Aborigines would settle permanently at the depot. But the colonial will to contain Aborigines and keep them separate contradicted the material needs of settlement and underestimated the reluctance of Aborigines to 'enjoy' colonial protection. Segregation was never fully realised and quickly gave way to more disorderly and permeable spatial arrangements....

By the early twentieth century, Aboriginal prior occupation was only vaguely traced on the official maps of Perth.... Aborigines were not eliminated from the Perth scene, but lived on designated reserves, in state-allocated houses or as 'fringedwellers' in informal camps in 'unseen' parts of the city. By the mid-1950s the early segregation and protection policies towards Aborigines gave way to an official policy of assimilation. Assimilation was intent on orchestrating the 'disappearance' of Aborigines through their absorption or integration into 'mainstream' Australia. In Perth, as elsewhere, Aborigines who were considered 'white' enough (a judgement based largely on skin colour) or 'civilised' enough (a judgement based on their adoption of European ways) were encouraged to leave reserves and move into suburban housing modelled on the British notion of the Garden Suburb. State-owned houses, strategically scattered through the lower income areas of cities, were offered to Aboriginal families in the belief that spatial integration would lead to social integration. The conditions under which Aborigines could 'dwell' in the city of Perth forced them, by exclusion or assimilation, to become an 'invisible', but menacingly present, citizenry.

Visioning development

...The redevelopment of the Old Swan Brewery was a small but controversial component in a larger process of restructuring. From the moment the site came onto the market in 1978, private development aspirations and notions of public amenity were blurred. the site was originally purchased by a private developer for A$4 million. But after public concerns were voiced about 'insensitive' foreshore development, the government purchased the land for 'public use' and declared it a Reserve for the purpose of government requirements. Under this designation the land was removed from the jurisdiction of normal town planning regulations. Within the entrepreneurial logic of the moment, 'public amenity' was readily translated into a government-led tourism and service industry development. In 1986 the Western Australian Development Corporation announced the site would be developed by the brewery and hotel chain, Brewtech. Initial plans included office space, a 450-vehicle car park, a 500-seat theatre, a museum display, a boutique brewery, various 'multicultural' food outlets and a 'genuine Aussie pub'.

Urban nomadism

The Aboriginal protest against the Old Swan Brewery redevelopment was led by Robert Bropho. He describes himself as a 'fringedweller' and has spent most of his life living on the 'margins' of the city (Bropho 1980). His precarious dwelling in the city was shaped by the historical fact of dispossession and his own negotiation of the permissible places for Aborigines to be, namely on institutionalised reserves, in allocated housing or homeless. For most of his life he lived in places inbetween; vacant land on the urban fringe, lands which were the marginal spaces, the 'dirty' spaces, of the city.... As a youngster with his family, fringedwelling was not by choice: Aborigines were the 'banned' people of the city. Under assimilationist policies which encouraged Aborigines to live by Anglo-Australian protocols of urban dwelling, Bropho's fringedwelling became a strategic refusal of state regulation. It provided a way for him and his family to 'return to where we knew we belonged ... back into the past where we came from' (ibid.: 56). Through fringedwelling Bropho removed his family from the expectations of assimilationist

suburban living and the everyday prejudices of life in predominantly Anglo-Australian suburbs. Bropho's fringedwelling was a way of avoiding the suburban version of what hooks (1992: 344) has described as the 'terrorism of whiteness'. For Bropho the closure of Aboriginal reserves and the promotion of assimilation was just another phase of colonialism which took from Aborigines the little land they had left, the final gesture in a process which had rendered him and his people 'a race ... without a country' (Bropho 1980: 15).

In Australia, efforts to acknowledge Aboriginal land interests and to provide some form of rights over land began in the 1970s. These provisions are notoriously inadequate in terms of Aborigines with interests in urban lands. The majority of lands returned to Aboriginal ownership have been in central and northern Australia, far from the urbanised coastal regions. This specific geography is a product of the limitations within various land rights provisions. On the one hand, the lands designated as available for claim are largely those not currently leased for productive use such as existing Aboriginal reserve lands, vacant Crown lands or national parks. Urban land, which is incorporated into multiple and productive uses and is largely under private ownership, is rarely available for land claim. On the other hand, the more comprehensive and potentially generous of the land rights provisions have been biased in favour of those Aboriginal groups who can prove or have an undisputed traditional way of life and association with the land. Land rights success in Australia was, and still is, linked to specific constructions of Aboriginality in which 'traditional' Aborigines are privileged over those Aborigines who have had their way of life most seriously disrupted by contact (Jacobs 1988).

For urban Aborigines rights over land have been piecemeal and incomplete. Their interests in land have been recognised, in part, through state-sponsored land purchase programmes working within the limits and opportunities of the private land market. Alternatively, urban Aborigines have had land interests recognised through programmes that record and give legal protection, but no proprietorial rights, to sites of cultural significance. Even within the provisions of site recording programmes, it has been those Aboriginal communities who conform to traditionalist notions of Aboriginal associations with the land who have been best served. The emphasis of much site recording and protection policy was initially on archaeological sites or sites that were significant in terms of clearly traditional practices and beliefs. Only recently have site registration and protection mechanisms expanded to include a more flexible notion of what a site of cultural significance might be for Aboriginal communities.

The limits of existing land rights provisions were unbound in 1992 when the High Court of Australia handed down a decision that found in favour of Eddie Mabo's claim that his people's entitlement to the Murray Islands in the Torres Strait had not been extinguished by the settlement of Australia by the British. In reaching this decision the Court held that the common law in Australia recognises a form of native title which is also applicable to mainland Australia. This decision displaced the fallacy of *terra nullius*, land unoccupied. It opened the way for the implementation of the Native Title Act 1993 (Lavarch 1994: iv). The Mabo decision implied that all lands, including urban lands, were once legitimately native lands and potentially open to claim. It heralded the possibility of a more equitable and uniformly applied land rights provision, including the possibility of meaningful urban land rights.

The requirements of the Native Title Act suggest that in practice those Aboriginal communities which can prove a traditional and uninterrupted interest in land will still be best served by the legislation and that lands not under long-term non-Aboriginal use will remain difficult to claim. That is, it is unlikely that Native Title will open the way for claims over urban lands. Despite these limitations the Mabo decision gener-

ated an intense anxiety among many non-Aboriginal Australians, especially around the possibility that – in principle if not in practice – claims might be made over city and suburban lands. As one press editorial noted:

> There is a significant gulf between recognising Aborigines' rights to something like Ayers Rock [*sic* – Uluru] and to allowing them open slather... encouraging militant Aboriginal groups to lay claim to sites such as the heart of Collins Street in Melbourne or Bennelong Point in Sydney. (*The Australian*, 23 July 1989: 3)

The Mabo decision and Native Title Act dismantled the established spatial architecture of existing land rights provisions in Australia which comfortably placed a spiritualised, 'tribalised', land-rights deserving, Aboriginality well away from the urban centres.

The disturbance of this moment comes not simply from the possible reterritorialisation of urban space by Aborigines, but also from the unpredictable and often unknowable sacredness such claims bring with them. Richard Sennett (1990: 16) has argued that the development of the modern western city saw the marking-off of sanctioned and ordered sites of the sacred from the threateningly disorganised spatiality of the secular. Kong (1993), using the example of multi-religious Singapore, shows how the religious geography of the contemporary city is controlled by the secular state in much the same way as any other land use. In the contemporary city sacredness is planned for, not to protect it from the threat of the secular but because the secular, the accumulative drive of the urban, needs to be protected from the irreverence (unproductivity) of the sacred. Yet such divides are always fragile....

The Aboriginal sacred is deeply antagonistic to urban modernity's need to keep the sacred apart from the secular and to regulate it as if it were just another land use. This is in part because of its 'hidden' quality. Aboriginal sites are often subject to strict protocols of disclosure and many are 'secret' sites known only to properly authorised individuals. The 'hidden' status of the sacred is also, and in a paradoxical sense, elaborated by a history of non-Aboriginal repression – the failure of colonial Australia to recognise and give legal status to such sites. In recent years various provisions have been made to recognise and protect, to recover, Aboriginal sites. . . .

Both site-recording procedures and Aboriginal strategies of non-disclosure create conditions in which something once repressed or secreted suddenly manifests itself. Modern Australia is now haunted by the possibility that 'new' sites will be discovered or made known. In this sense, the Aboriginal sacred is omnipresent in its absence (Taussig 1987: 78). The Aboriginal sacred has a 'nomadic' geography which is not derived from a pre-modern character but is produced by the conditions of articulation established under modernity. The possibility of sacred space simply appearing, coming from 'below ground' as the 'hidden' Aboriginal sacred appears to do, is radically unsettling to contemporary practices of allocating space. . . .

Brewery Dreamings

The plans to redevelop the Old Swan Brewery buildings were consistent with global processes of revalorising heritage buildings and incorporating them into the new service industries of tourism and leisure. Indeed, the classification of these buildings as part of the non-aboriginal 'heritage' of Perth was inextricably entwined with development aspirations for the site. When development was initially proposed there had been no official recognition of the heritage status of the buildings on the site. In 1986, soon after the unveiling of development plans, the National Trust of Western Australia conducted an assessment of the site and declared the Brewery and surrounding area as a Historic Site and classified the old stable, which was to be demolished in the redevelopment plans, as

a historic building in its own right (National Trust of Western Australia 1987). The Trust warned against over-development but encouraged the government to proceed with 'the presentation of the site and its surrounds as an historic site as well as a major landmark for the City and the river' (National Trust of Western Australia to Minister for Education and Planning 6 February 1986). . . .

In official assessments of the social relevance of the Brewery, the buildings came to mark an 'Australian ethos' of 'beer, work, tourism and sport' (Heritage Council of Western Australia 1991: sec. 4.8.2). Western Australians, the official assessment noted, were once ranked among the biggest consumers of alcohol in the world and could proudly claim to have drunk twice as much as their nearest rivals in Queensland. Swan brand beer is, in the words of the report, 'synonymous with Western Australia'. Once this may have been a local assemblage of a beer brand and State identity, but now it is registered on a global scale. Under the guidance of Alan Bond, Perth's favoured man of 'beer, work, tourism and sport', Swan beer has long departed from its historic site of production on the banks of the Swan River and entered a global circuit of production and consumption. It is not simply the globalisation of the Swan brand that unsettles official claims about the 'Australianness' of this site. Beer itself is less a signifier of a unified 'Australian ethos' than it is of a masculinist and racist 'ethos' of being Australian. For Aborigines in particular beer has marked not the forging of identity, but the ravaging of identity. Alcohol dependency among sections of the Aboriginal community has provided the basis for the elaboration of negative stereotyping of Aborigines and is now considered by Aborigines to have contributed to the breakdown of their traditional culture. Alcohol also marks the contingent nature of Aboriginal citizenry in the Australian nation: Aborigines were not legally entitled to buy alcohol until 1967 when they were finally given full rights of citizenship.

The site was quickly incorporated into what Urry (1990) refers to as the 'tourist gaze'. Jolly Jumbuck and Captain Cook cruises passed the site, but their commentaries were just as likely to speak about a present sensationalised by Aboriginal protest as a past tranquillised by the tourist gaze.

Under the conditions of development the Old Swan Brewery buildings were produced as non-Aboriginal 'heritage', a place where cultural and economic value excited each other. This revalued space was set against Aboriginal claims about the sacredness of the site and their aspirations to see the land returned to 'nature'. Foucault (1986: 23) suggests that the in-

violable spatial oppositions of contemporary society are those that are underpinned by the 'hidden presence of the sacred', that which is valued. This spatial controversy emerged not only because an incommensurate sacred and secular met, but because of a sudden proliferation of sacredness: the production of sanctioned heritage which was closely tied to development aspirations, alongside the sudden 'appearance' of an Aboriginal sacred which was irreverent to development. This was, as the then Premier of Western Australia suggested, an 'unfortunate clash between European heritage and Aboriginal heritage' (Western Australia House of Assembly 1990: 1659).

REFERENCES

Bauman, Z. (1992) *Imitations of Postmodernity*, London and New York: Routledge.

Bropho, R. (1980) *Fringedweller*, Sydney: Alternative Publishing Co-operative Ltd.

——(1992) No Title, in Nyungah People of the Swan River (eds) *The Brewery Picket*, People of the Swan River. [Political broadsheet.]

Carter, P. (1987) *The Road to Botany Bay*, London: Faber and Faber.

de Certeau, M. (1984) *The Practice of Everyday Life*, Berkeley: University of California Press.

Foucault, M. (1986) 'Of other spaces', trans. J. Miskowiec, *diacritics* 16: 22–7.

Green, N. (1984) *Broken Spears: Aboriginals and Europeans in Southwest of Australia*, Perth: Focus Education Services.

Heritage Council of Western Australia (1991) *Swan Brewery. Perth: Conservation Analysis*. Draft report by Clive Lucas, Stapleto and Partners, Pty Ltd, Sydney. Perth: Heritage Council of Western Australia.

hooks, b. (1992) 'Representing whiteness in the black imagination', in L. Grossberg, C. Nelson and P. Treichler (eds), *Cultural Studies*, London and New York: Routledge, 338–46.

Jacobs, J. M. (1988) 'The construction of identity', in J. R. Beckett (ed.), *Past and Present: the Construction of Aboriginality*, Canberra: Aboriginal Studies Press.

Kong, L. (1993) 'Ideological hegemony and the political symbolism of religious buildings in

Singapore', *Environment and Planning D: Society and Space* 11, 1: 23–46.

Lavarch, M. (1994) 'Foreword', in Attorney-General's Department *Native Title, Native Title Act* 1993, Canberra: Australian Government Press.

Muecke, S. (1992) *Textual Spaces: Aboriginality and Cultural Studies*, Sydney: University of New South Wales Press.

National Trust of Western Australia (1987) 'Swan Brewery site'. Press release, 11 Feb.

Sennet, R. (1990) *The Conscience of the Eye: The Design and Social Lives of Cities*, New York: Knopf.

Taussig, M. (1987) *Shamanism, Colonialism and the Wild Man*, Chicago and London: University of Chicago Press.

Urry, J. (1990) *The Tourist Gaze: Leisure and Travel in Contemporary Societies*, London: Sage.

Vinnicombe, P. (1989) *Goonininup: An Historical Perspective of Land Use and Associations in the Old Swan Brewery Area*, Perth: Department of Aboriginal Sites, Western Australian Museum.

Weir, P. (1977) *The Last Wave*. Screenplay: Peter Weir, Tony Morphett and Petru Popesou. Director: Peter Weir.

Western Australia House of Assembly (1990) *Hansard*, 31 May: 1659.

57

Mega-cities and the Urban Future: A Model for Replicating Best Practices

Akhtar A. Badshah and Janice E. Perlman[1]

Citizens of Berlin, Bombay, Boston, and Bogota all face problems of severely stressed urban infrastructure, poverty, political disillusionment, and social and cultural alienation. The world's largest metropolises – the mega-cities – are experiencing even more economic stress and cultural alienation. As the global economy produces benefits for the elite in mega-cities, most citizens face rapidly deteriorating urban environments.

Despite these trends, there are promising developments and visible changes in a multitude of new developments originating in the voluntary or non-profit sector. The majority of these programs have been initiated by the people who live in the most severe conditions, as they take the lead in making significant improvements in their physical, economic and social environment. In these times of severe resource constraints, citizens need to discover new ways to learn from each other's successes and to multiply the impact of approaches that work. It is through replication and adaptation that innovative solutions can have a significant and sustainable impact on our cities.

Peer-to-peer transfer promotes the kind of technical *cooperation* – as opposed to technical assistance – that leads to appropriate adaptation, new problem-solving, and longer term relationships between innovators. Teaching and mentoring is done by those who have first hand experience of the problem, and who have invented and implemented the solution.

Even if they are small in scale, tested solutions multiply their effects through replication which brings about broader practice. Micro-level change matters in three ways: First, transfers and adaptation can cause a ripple effect. Second, the impact of micro-level change can be enhanced through system-challenging transfers. And third, micro-level changes can reach the institutional level by affecting public policy.

...In other areas, such as the computer industry, copying is the norm, and companies go to great lengths to glean intelligence about innovations their counterparts have devised. Similarly, in popular culture, 'innovations' such as the Teenage Mutant Ninja Turtles and fashion trends are copied by people in the most remote corners of the world. Urban innovations, on the other hand, appear to be some of the best-kept secrets in the world, and urban leaders worldwide seem to constantly reinvent the wheel.

One reason for this phenomenon lies in the fact that successful solutions addressing pressing social problems, have until now largely remained undocumented and inaccessible to others who could benefit from the experience. With UNCHS (Habitat) institutionalizing the process of docu-

United Nations estimates indicate that at mid-1990, 43 percent (2.3 billion) of the world's population lived in urban areas. With the urban population growing two and a half times faster than its rural counterpart, the level of urbanization is projected to cross the 50 percent mark in 2005. UN projections further show that by 2025, more than three-fifths of the world's population will live in urban areas. The urban population in that year will be approximately 5.2 billion, of whom 77 percent will live in developing countries.[2]

Just over 20 years ago, more than half the world's urban population lived in developed countries. This balance has shifted by 1975 largely due to rapid population growth in developing countries, along with the movement of migrants from farms to cities. By 1990, far more of the world's population – 61 per cent – lived in developing countries. In 2025, it is projected that developing countries will have nearly four times as many urban dwellers as developed countries.[3]

It is also important to note that the pattern of migration identified in many developed countries: growth in large metropolitan areas has now become the norm in developing countries. Worldwide, the number of cities comprising 5 to 10 million inhabitants grew from 18 cities in 1970 to 22 cities in 1990. It is expected that by 2010, there will be 33 megacities – cities with more than 5 million inhabitants – and 21 of them will be in developing countries. Of the 26 expected urban agglomerations to have 10 million or more inhabitants by 2010, 21 will be in developing countries: Asia will be home to 14 of the very large cities; 5 will be in Latin America and 2 in Africa.[4]

We must, therefore, intensify and improve the global effort to address population, consumption and distribution trends in our cities if we are to preserve a livable future for all humanity.

Global Population Trends[5] (in millions)
Total increase of 2,713 Billion People – more than 10 times the current population of the US

Region	1995	2025	Country	1995	2025
Asia	3,282	4,773	USA	263	322
			Percent of World	4.57%	3.80%
Africa	744	1,583			
			Europe	516	541
Latin America	475	690			
			Japan	125	127
Oceania / Other	66	92			
			Ex-USSR	288	344
World	5,759	8,472			
			Sub Total	1,192	1,334
			Percent of World	20.60%	15.75%

menting and recording 'Best Practices, innovative solutions are more likely to become available to others.

However, without a mechanism for exchanging successes and failures, innovations often die out when funding agencies move on to other projects: the chance for reaching scale and having a major impact is lost. This is unacceptable in today's climate of exacerbated social needs and extreme budgetary constraints.

Another critical obstacle to this type of exchange is that innovative problem-solvers in the social sector are usually too beleaguered in fighting for survival and handling crises to be concerned with the replication of urban innovative projects.

It is now conspicuously clear that the innovation diffusion process is not self-propelling. It is time to take a strategic look at how the process can be supported and stimulated, so that urban leaders can develop more effective cross-sectoral partnerships and participate more efficiently in technical cooperation.

The Intermediary – A Catalyst for Change

In order for transfer and adaptation to be achieved, a network of different sectors within and among societies needs to be established; creating a sort of 'network of networks.' An intermediary agency would facilitate the coordination between individuals within sectors or cities (see Figure 57.1). The Mega-Cities Project is one such intermediary. Headquartered in New York City, it has a network of 18 'city coordinators' world-wide. On a local scale, the coordinator identifies, distills,

and disseminates positive approaches among sectors; and strengthens the capacity of urban leaders and groups by finding sources of support for them. On the inter-city or international scale, the coordinator can act as a transfer agent among cities by coordinating with his or her 'city coordinator' counterparts in the other cities.

The achievement of active linkages within and between sectors or cities is facilitated through a four-part strategy. As illustrated in Figure 57.2, the process begins with matching the innovation to the need by documenting and exchanging successful solutions through the Mega-Cities network. For example, current international transfers are written up, and presented as case studies at annual coordinators' meetings.

The second stage involves building a transfer task force, which adapts the innovation to the local context, and implements the transfer. In the third stage, the innovation is adapted to local conditions, and finally, the transfer is implemented in the

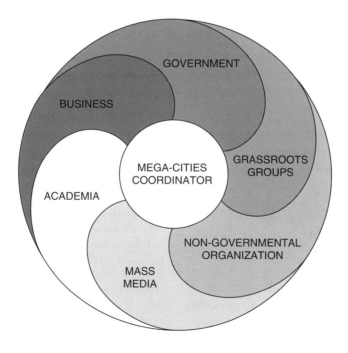

Figure 57.1

Stages	Match innovation to need	Build transfer task force	Adaptation	Implement transfer
	• Document solutions • Disseminate through innovation transfer marketplace (annual coordinator's meeting) • Identify problem • Match solution to problem	• Introduce concept to stake holders • Negotiate preliminary transfer commitment (between city coordinators) • Secure commitment from stake holders and decision makers	• Conduct site visits • Survey local conditions • Develop transfer implementation plan • Mobilize resources • Publicize transfer plan	• Pilot demonstration project • Implement full-scale transfer • Trace and evaluate results
Intermediary's role	"Catalyst"	"Broker"	"Facilitator"	"Supporter"

Figure 57.2 A 4-Stage Methodology for Innovation Transfer and Adaptation. The transfer procedure not only depends on the 'network of networks,' it also becomes a mechanism for strengthening the flexible, long-term partnerships which comprise that network.

fourth stage and traced through ongoing evaluations.

Once established, a single partnership may be re-utilized in the transfer of additional innovations and in the ongoing impacting of public policy. The 'network of networks' can function as an independent transnational voice for urban civil society. Paralleling that of the private and public sectors, it develops links between local innovation and global impact. While network members certainly act as catalysts in the transfer of projects to other communities, they also have an impact as leaders on the policy arena; they can access decision-makers, change official mind-sets, and de-centralize the problem-solving process.

The Transfer and Adaptation of Successful Innovations (Cross-cultural Learning)

The Mega-Cities Project has initiated the transfer of 37 innovations: 10 between cities internationally, 9 between New York and Los Angeles, 8 within Los Angeles, and 10 within New York. For this paper we are describing the transfer of the Zabbaleen Environmental Development Program from Cairo to Bombay and Manila with

the aim of laying out the major issues faced and the results of each approach.

The Zabbaleen Environmental Development Program from Cairo to Manila and Bombay: Background [6]

Cairo's population of 15 million is currently growing at a rate of almost one million every 8 months, and greater Cairo generates around 6,000 tons of solid waste per day. Waste collection has been traditionally conducted by the 'Wahi' and the 'Zabbaleen' people, who have worked together to collect and remove the city's trash. The Wahis control the routes and contract with homeowners, while the Zabbaleen collect the waste and transport it to their settlements, where the waste is sorted and recycled or used for animal fodder.

Cairo's high population growth rate and resultant increase in municipal waste began to supersede the capacity of the Zabbaleen waste pickers. Moreover, little of recyclable value was expected from the garbage which provided few incentives for the Zabbaleen to pick the waste. A marginalized community with little organization, the Zabbaleen were living in settlements with few basic services, and facing environmental devastation, little economic opportunity, lack of education, and a host of other problems endemic to urban slums. When the government threatened to look to more modern and efficient systems of municipal waste disposal, the Zabbaleen faced the possible loss of their traditional livelihood.

The Zabbaleen Environment and Development Program was started to improve the living conditions and build the capacity of the Zabbaleen in one of their settlements, the Moqattam settlement, while creating a more efficient solid waste management system for Cairo. The Moqattam settlement houses half of Cairo's Zabaleen garbage collectors, and is the largest of the seven settlements of its kind. Prior to 1981, there was no local government, school, health clinic, pharmacy, sewage system, telephone system, or means of transporting emergency patients to hospitals. The absence of a water supply resulted in frequent fires which destroyed large sections of the community on several occasions.

The program consisted of a number of projects initiated over a span of ten years, and was based on an exploratory, experimental approach. Activities were targeted at improving environmental and living conditions, promoting enterprise development, increasing the service capacity of the Zabbaleen, and instituting low cost technological innovations.

The program was first conceptualized by the Governor of Cairo and the World Bank in 1976. It was initiated and managed by Environmental Quality International (EQI), a Cairo based consulting firm specializing in solid waste management and urban renewal, with the assistance of the Moqattam Garbage Collectors' Association, the Gameya. Numerous government and non-government organization also participated in one or more aspects of the program.

The Area Upgrading and Infrastructure Extension Project was initiated in 1982, financed by the Government of Egypt in cooperation with the International Development Association of the World Bank.

EQI mapped out the settlement, and with the assistance of a consultant, the government constructed basic infrastructure and facilities, including piped water, electricity, sewerage networks, paved roads, a primary school and a health center. In an attempt to recover costs for the infrastructure and facilities construction and to provide residents with land security, community members were offered a 30 year installment plan for the purchase of land on which their families resided. Work then began towards meeting the goal of an improved solid waste collection system for Cairo.

In 1982, a Route Extension Project funded by Oxfam was conducted, which extended the Zabbaleen collection routes to 8,000 new homes in the neighboring low-income area. In order to provide incentives for collecting trash in areas which produced little valuable garbage, a fee-collection system was also put in place.

In an effort to diversify income generating possibilities, two new projects were introduced. The Small Industries Project, funded by Oxfam, offered credit and technical expertise to small community-based recycling industries in order to maximize the resource value of waste. The Income Generating Project for Female-Headed Households, funded by the Ford Foundation extended credit to widows, divorcees, and women with unemployed or disabled husbands.

In an effort to clean up the community while generating income, a Composting Plant was constructed in 1986, funded by the European Community, the Ford Foundation and the Soeur Emmanuelle Fund. Using simple rudimentary technology, organic waste in the settlement was removed, composted to make fertilizer, and sold to fund other development projects. The Association for the Protection of Environment (APE) was established to run the plant, and was eventually able to help initiate programs for women such as rug weaving and literacy classes, a paper recycling project, and a health awareness program for pregnant women.

Based on the success of the Zabbaleen experience, Mega-Cities obtained funding from UNDP-LIFE to facilitate the transfer and adoption of the project to Manila, in the Philippines, and Bombay, India.

Transfer from Cairo to Manila[7]

The Payatas Environmental Development Program (PEDP) was established, using a similar approach to the Zabbaleen Project. The Payatas project aimed at creating a sustainable community for the Payatas waste pickers in Manila, while providing more effective waste collection services to the public.

There are about 3,000 Payatas waste pickers who work in a 13-hectare open pit dumpsite in Quezon City which receives approximately 35% of the city's collected garbage. Metropolitan Manila has an estimated population of 13 million people that generate 5,000 tons of waste daily. Of the entire waste generated, only 85% is effectively collected. The remaining 15% are scattered throughout the capital and pollute waterways.

The first phase in the transfer process was to initiate the project and develop local transfer partnerships. A local coordinator for the transfer, Ms. Me-An Ignacio, the director of the Partnership for Philippine Support Service Agencies (PHILSSA), was selected. In the second phase of the project, funding was secured by PHILSSA from the local United Nations Volunteers office. After Ms. Ignacio's one-week visit to the Moqattam settlement in Cairo, a task force was created, consisting of the Vincentian Missionaries Social Development Foundation, the Kapatirsan ng mga Mangangalahig or KHALIG (the association of waste pickers in Payatas), PHILSSA, and Green Forum Philippines. A 9 member transfer team, including KHALIG representatives, also visited Cairo for 2 weeks. After the site-visit the Zabbaleen approach was readjusted and adapted to Manila's local context. A feasibility study was conducted, and local partnerships developed as well.

Among the local partnerships formed is the Payatas Environmental Development Program (PEDP) team. This team, composed of PO's and NGOs, is focused on installing people and environment friendly Solid Waste Management techniques in Payatas. PEDP is composed of PHILSSA, The Vincentian Missionaries Social Development Foundation, the Payatas Scavengers Association Incorporated, UNICONSULT, and Green Forum Philippines. Aside from, and in conjunction with the PDEP team, the OPLAN BASURA Network has been strengthened. OPLAN BASURA is also a network of environmental groups and NGOs unified in the advocacy for sustainable solid waste management. They are composed of the following groups: Concerned Citizens Against Pollution, Assorted Waste Administration and Recovery, Recycling Movement of the Philippines, and Artists for the Environment.

Phase Three, the longest of the three phases, was comprised of identifying a vision and objectives and crafting a strategy for implementation. The vision for Manila was a sustained human settlement in Payatas with the objectives of upgrading the status of Payatas community members and improving solid waste management. The strategy employed was a market, or enterprise, approach. This meant setting up a materials recovery center in Payatas that would include community-based enterprises. The task force decided that the transfer project was to consist of four main components: organizational development, technical input, capital formation, and marketing.

Recent innovations, in line with the Zabbaleen-Payatas innovation transfer and the PEDP plan to develop micro-enterprises related to recycling, have led to the creation of the following community based guilds:

1) Guild of Paper Makers
- 6 Payatas youths underwent intensive training on paper recycling for a month.

- Trainees set up a small paper recycling facility in Payatas.
- This facility is now fully operational.

2) Guild of Water Drillers
- A team of 4 Payatas waste pickers have just completed an intensive 6 month training on water drilling with the help of a Japan based NGO School of the Wind.
- A water facility has been set up in one area in Payatas, which is now providing potable water for the Payatas community plus water supply for recycling activities.

3) Guild of Compost Managers
- A team of 10 Payatas waste pickers are to be selected for an intensive training on composting in preparation for the establishment of a compost facility in Payatas.

The 'bottom up' initiative conceived by the task force met with immediate success, and, as a result, PEDP is in the process of scaling up, with plans for a Metro Wide Material Recovery Center. The center will eventually handle collection, transport, sorting, recycling, composting and marketing of recycled products. The PEDP team hired local experts earlier this year to conduct a feasibility study to determine the most effective way for setting up the Center. Preliminary plans for the Center have been approved by the ministry of the local government.

PEDP has targeted 68 markets as the next step in their recycling initiatives. The waste pickers plan to segregate and compost the markets' wet waste in machines which they are currently raising the funds to buy. The PEDP has also completed a study for marketing the compost as fertilizer. It is expected that part of the financing for the project will come from a debt swap that has been arranged with the Swiss Government.

Transfer from Cairo to Bombay

Each of Bombay's 14.5 million citizens produce one pound of waste a day. The Muni-

cipal Corporation of Greater Bombay spends 20–30% of its total budget on waste management, and only serves 60–70% of the urban population. Approximately 56,000 waste pickers in Bombay compete for valuable trash, which they sell to middlemen, who in turn employ scavengers to separate and reprocess waste materials, finally selling them to manufacturers of consumer goods. The trash in Bombay is contained in roadside dumpsters, and scavengers separate the trash by strewing valueless trash onto the streets. Most of the uncollected refuse lies in slum areas, worsening living conditions in already impoverished communities and creating public health hazards.

The Bombay–Cairo transfer was coordinated by Sneha Palnitkar, the Bombay coordinator, and the Additional Commissioner of the Municipal Corporation of Greater Bombay (MCGB). They both visited Cairo in September 1994 to study the Zabbaleen project, and concluded that some components of the Zabbaleen Project could be implemented with modifications in the solid waste management area of Greater Bombay.

The approach devised by the MCGB sought to improve living and social conditions for large numbers of urban poor and disadvantaged groups working in the waste collection and recycling industries; to reduce the cost of garbage disposal; and to benefit the municipal crew involved in the process of waste management and waste recycling.

An initial 24-month plan was completed and presented at the Mega-Cities Coordinators meeting in December 1994. The approach taken for the transfer to Bombay was different from Cairo in that its initial stages relied more on support from government officials than from community based organizations.

The Bombay coordinator prepared a situational analysis of solid waste management and networks in the waste recycling trade in Greater Bombay. She also discussed the transfer with concerned voluntary agencies and community based organizations as well as with activists in selected localities. Discussions were held with the Chief Engineer and Officials of Solid Waste Management of MCGB, the Mayor of Bombay, local NGOs (Stree Mukti Sanghatana, DEW and CORO), members of the State Women's Commission, and the Secretary of Women and Child Development of the Government of Maharashtra as well as field level activists in the area.

Suggestions emerged from the discussions that changes should be made in the existing pattern of waste management and that waste pickers – men and women – should be involved in primary collection. The pilot areas selected included the Churchgate area, the central business district; Dharavi, where there is a concentration of waste recycling trade; Shivaji Nagar, a residential area of rag-pickers; the Deonar Dumping Site; and Andheri.

The resulting strategy for the Bombay transfer contained two parts. The first component involved working with the Municipal Corporation of Greater Bombay (MCGB) – which runs solid waste collection in the city – to introduce separation of waste within households. It was proposed that in the two residential target areas in downtown Bombay, waste pickers would go to households to collect recyclable waste instead of rummaging through roadside dumpsters and leaving waste on the roadways. Surveys conducted among residents and waste pickers in the Churchgate area showed that this approach was feasible.

The second part of the strategy was to work with Jyoti Mhapsekar, President of Stree Mukti Sanghatana, to provide an integrated social services program for the waste pickers living at the Deonar dumping ground. After the plan of action was in place, however, state and local elections in Bombay essentially froze the transfer process. This demonstrated the impact political conditions can have on large scale transfers. The transfer task force, composed mainly of government of-ficials, had been busy preparing for upcoming elections, and thus had little time to contribute to the transfer process. Immediately after the elections, there was little incentive to continue projects as government offices preferred to wait for the new government to start new projects. As a result, the transfer plan was delayed and proved to be a major obstacle to the initial plan.

In July 1995, the Bombay multi-sectoral task force met and agreed to continue the plan of action for the Cairo–Bombay transfer that was interrupted by the elections. The British Council has initially approved funding for a two year project at the Deonar site. The Bombay coordinator, is currently completing further feasibility studies and detailed work plans.

Lessons learned

1 *'Product Champions' play a critical role in the transfer process.*
It is possible to identify one or more individuals in each transfer who push the transfer forward with a disproportionate level of determination and dedication. These charismatic individuals also tend to be gifted at drawing others into the process. Many times the success of the transfers depends on the dedication of the product champion. The persistence of Me-An Ignacio and her network to keep the Cairo–Manila transfer momentum, for example, was crucial to the transfer's success.

2 *Successful implementation of transfers requires partnerships, a participatory methodology, and an integrated and flexible approach.*
Successful transfer initiatives involve some degree of community involvement and participation. For instance, although the Zabbaleen transfer from Cairo to Bombay met with extremely positive official response, there was no community involvement in the initial planning phases. Had the community been involved in the process, it is likely the outcome would have been different.

3 *Importing ideas is preferable to exporting them.*

It is more effective to import an innovation and fit to the context of the community than for the originator of the innovation to convince others to replicate it. This is not to say that a leader cannot promote or disseminate their successes, but that the choice of who adapts an idea and where it is adapted must come from the adaptor. In addition, it is necessary that those undertaking the transfer grasp not only their own urban context, but that of the disseminating city as well.

4 *Transfer provides a non-crisis incentive for cross-cultural collaboration.*

In the Philippines, NGOs and community organizations have been antagonistic to local government efforts, however, during the transfer of the Zabbaleen project some of these differences were set aside and traditionally hostile groups came together to arrive at mutually acceptable solutions.

5 *Failures teach as much as success.*

Even when transfer attempts did not succeed, the organizations and their leaders attested to the important lessons they learned and the impact the experience had on their development as leaders and on their organization. For example, the derailed first attempt of the Zabbaleen transfer from Cairo to Bombay led to many important lessons regarding the importance of developing partnerships between different sectors in society. It became clear that independent bodies are crucial if transfers rely on government officials.

Challenges and Opportunities: Scaling Up into Public Policy

For almost a decade, the approach of urban innovation has been focused on peer-to-peer transfers with the dual objective of scaling out horizontally through replication and scaling up vertically into public policy. Transferring an idea from one community to another does more than simply expand the reach of a particular solution, it also broadens the focus of urban leaders from their immediate geographical vicinity to their entire city or society. Next on the agenda is a clearer understanding of the relationship between innovation transfer and the impact on public policy, in the quest for positive social change and the transformation of urban practices from the neighborhood level all the way to the city, national and international level.

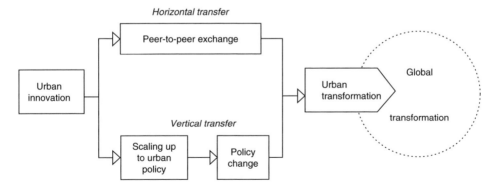

Figure 57.3 An approach to urban transformation

REFERENCES

1 This paper builds upon ongoing intellectual work on the transfer process by Jane Sweeney, Marianne Cocchini, Elwood Hopkins, Reena Lazar, and Robert Riggs. We would also like to acknowledge the contribution of the New York City and Los Angeles Leaders, Maria-Anna de Rosas Ignacio, the Metro-Manila Mega-Cities Coordinator, Mounir Neamatalla the Cairo Mega-Cities Coordinator and Sneha Palnitkar the Bombay Mega-Cities Coordinator.

2 United Nations, *World Urbanization Prospects* (New York, 1993).

3 Ibid.

4 Ibid.

5 UNCHS, Foundation Executives Briefing, Feb. 24, 1995.

6 See the Mega-Cities Project's *Monograph on the Inter-Regional Exchange and Transfer of Effective Practices for Urban Management*, funded by the UNDP Special Unit for TCDC and the UNDP Urban Development Unit, August 1995. In this monograph the Zabbaleen Environment and Development Program is one of 30 case studies documented.

7 A detailed evaluation of the transfer processes from Cairo to Manila and Cairo to Bombay was conducted in 1995 by a team of graduate students from Columbia University for the Mega-Cities Project. Their evaluation provides an assessment of the transfer project and offers recommendations for future transfers based on the case studies presented.

Index

NOTE: Page numbers in **bold** indicate a chapter (which may be an extract) by an author; page numbers followed by *n* indicate information is in a note; page numbers followed by *ill* indicate information is in an illustration or its caption.

A bout de souffle (film), 428
"abandoned city," 238
Abbott, Carl, 251
Abercrombie, Patrick, 495
Aboriginal people, 454–5, 542–3, 544; alcohol dependency, 547; land rights, 545–7; sacred sites, 546–7, 548
Abrams, Charles, 481
abstract art, 46
abstraction: and agoraphobia, 46–8; economic abstracts, 111–12; in planning, 39, 40
access: for disabled people, 304–5; to cities, 441–3
accumulation theory: regulation and post-Fordism, 147–9, 195; transition to entrepreneurialism, 457, 506; and the urban process, 109, 116–24
activism: community resistance in New York, 282–3, 285; disability activism, 307–9
Addams, Jane, 122
address codes in Brasília, 520
Adorno, Theodor, 400*n*, 402, 431
"advanced services city," 238
advertising: development of, 220; posters in Paris arcades, 396, 420
aerodrome: Le Corbusier's city, 21–2, 24
aesthetic *see* esthetic

Africa: colonial planning, 527–8, 530–1
African Americans: disadvantaged by globalization, 162, 170, 239
African Renaissance, 215
agglomeration of centralizing activities, 163
agglomeration economies, 459
agoraphobia, 6, 46–8
agricultural merchants, 172–3
agriculture: fields system, 171–2; grain trade, 111, 172–182; impact on cities, 171
ahistorical planning, 39, 40, 42
AIDS: opposition to siting of treatment centers, 285, 286; rhetoric of, 242, 321
airports: designed for security, 440–1
al-Shaykh, Hanan, 9–10, **93–103**
Albert, Prince Consort, 223*n*
Alcock, P., 305
Aldrich, Lloyd, 479
alienation: in community relations, 433, 434; in literature, 63–4; overcome by modernist planning, 503
Allen, Jerry, 404, 405
Allison, Dorothy, 432
ambiguity of space, 397–8
American Disabled for Accessible Public Transportation (ADAPT), 307
American Federation of Labor (AFL), 255–6
amusement parks *see* theme parks

ancien régime: public life in, 346–7, 348, 350
Anderson, Walter, 486
anonymity of urban life, 421–2, 436
anthropology: critique of Brasília, 513–23; Victorian views on poor, 412–13
anti-Semitism, 402–3
antiurbanism, 39–40, 241, 281, 406–7, 452–3; deurbanization movement, 480–3
anxiety, 47
apartheid *see* racial/ethnic divisions in cities
appropriation of time and space, 337–8, 372, 373, 387, 401
arcades, 219, 220, 338, 393–400
architectonics, 442, 446–7, 448
architecture, 5–6; crisis of conceptualization in, 340; for cyberspace cities, 55; of "defensible space," 324; effect of market economy, 43–4; influence of suburbanization, 452–3; split with planning, 41–2; systems of signification, 370; visibility in, 340, 342–3, 344, 377–8; *see also* urban planning and design
Arendt, Hannah, 335
argumentative planning theory, 499–500
Arnstein, Sherry, 497–8
art: abstract, 46; and appropriation of time and space, 373, 401; public art, 403–5; views of cities, 384
arterial roads, 22, 23
asyndeton, 389–90
Athens, 3, 16; Le Corbusier at Acropolis, 49, 50
Athens Charter, The (CIAM manifesto), 516
Atlantic City: gambling boom, 472
Auerbach, Erich, 345
Augoyard, J.-F., 389
Australia: Aboriginal land rights, 545–7; colonial history, 543–4; Old Swan Brewery development, 454–5, 542–3, 544–5, 547–8; symbolism of beer, 547
automobile suburbs, 477–80
Aymonino, Carlos, 42, 43–4

Bacon, Edmund, 40
Badshah, Akhtar A., 455, **549–58**
Bagehot, W., 8
Balbus, Isaac, 432
Ball, Benjamin, 47
Balzac, Honoré de, 7, 350
Banfield, Edward C., 465

Bangladesh: *bastees*, 240, 270–7
Banham, Rayner, 486
Baraka, Amiri, 280
Barbari, Jacopo dei, 316*ill*
barbarism vs. civilization, 351–4
Barker, Robert, 382*n*
Barnes, C., 311
Barnes, Djuna: "The Hem of Manhattan," 9, **71–5**
Barnes, T., 145
Barnum, Phineas, 223*n*
bastees in Bangladesh, 240, 270–7; forcible eviction from, 270, 271–3, 274, 275, 276; solutions to problem, 274–7
Baudelaire, Charles, 8, 397, 410, 424, 426, 427; *see also flâneur*
Baudrillard, Jean, 194–5
Bauman, Z., 544
bear traders, 181
Beard, George, 47
Beauregard, Robert A., 210, 280, 453, **502–12**
Beauvoir, Simone de, 428
Beirut: "Beirut Blues" (al-Shaykh), 10, **93–103**
Belboeuf, Marquise de ("Missy"), 427
belle époque Paris, 426–7
Bellow, Saul, 3
benevolent societies in early US, 256–7
Benhabib, Seyla, 432
Benjamin, Walter, 4, 8, 61, 63, 113–14, 411, 427; arcades project, 219–24, 338, **393–400**
Bennett, Arnold, 64
Bensman, Joseph, 468
Bentham, Jeremy, 242, 377, 378, 380, 381–2; *see also* panopticon
Benveniste, E., 391*n*, 392*n*
Berkeley Community Memory, 57, 59
Berman, Marshall, 439*n*
Berry, Brian J. L., 465
bid–rent land model, 108–9
Big Sky Telegraph, Montana, 57
Birmingham, UK: gun and jewelry manufacture, 136–9
Blake, William, 4
Bleak House (Dickens), 8, 76–9
body in urban theory, 225–8, 241–2, 293–4, 297–303; body defined, 298; fear of touching in Renaissance Venice, 317–18
body-politic, 300
bohemian life in Paris, 422–3, 423–4
"boiler rooms," 195

Bolan, Richard, 41
Bombay: waste management projects, 555–6
Bond, Alan, 547
Boorstin, Daniel, 467
boosterism, 211–12, 452, 457, 464–74
Booth, Charles, 411
boredom, 399
Bosco, Joao, 513–15
Boston: city image, 31, 32, 33, 35, 36; safety
    on streets of, 353–4
boundaries of city, 441–2, 443–4
Bourdieu, Pierre, 207n, 392n
Bourne, Larry, 279
Boyer, M. Christine, 6, **39–45**, 509
Branch, Kristi, 472
Brasília, 370, 513–23; Joao Bosco's
    prophecy, 513–15; zoning, 453–4, 516,
    518–22
Braudel, Ferdinand, 509
Bremner, Lindsay, 113, **208–18**
Bridge, G., 241
Bright Lights, Big City (McInerney), 200
Broadacre City plan, 452, 481–3
Broadway, New York, 355
Bropho, Robert, 545
Brown, Denise Scott, 486
Brueghel, Pieter, the Elder, 317
Brunswick Centre, London, 342–3
Bryant Park, New York, 406
Buck-Morss, Susan, 113–14, **219–24**, 411
Budgen, Frank, 60
bull traders, 181
Bunshaft, Gordon, 342
Burgess, Ernest, 237, **244–50**
Burgess, P., 536
Burgin, Victor, 3
Burnham, Daniel, 59, 495
Burrows, John, 172
bus stops: Le Corbusier's city, 21–2
business climate, 465–7
Butler, Joseph, 345

Cable News Network (CNN), 444
cafeteria culture, 197–8
Cairo: Zabbaleen Project, 552–3
Campbell, Beatrix, 238
Campbell, J., 308
canal investment, 118
capitalism: accumulation theory, 116–24,
    147–9, 195, 457; capital rights in global
    economy, 165–7; circulation of capital,
    109, 122–3, 462; class struggle under, 116,
    120–3; on display, 220–1; global economy,

111, 126–7; Identity of, 114, 225, 226,
    227; and modernist planning, 504–5; and
    public domain, 347–8; restructuring of,
    126, 128, 133; transformation in urban
    governance, 456–62; women in discourse
    of, 225–8; *see also* market economy;
    Marxist political economic theory
"carceral archipelagos," 190, 194; in Los
    Angeles, 323–4
Cardoso, Diego, 331n
Carmon, N., 536
cars and urban planning, 477–80
Carter, Paul, 543
Castells, Manuel, 114, 189, 191, 238–9, 290,
    526; on Africa, 215; network society, 110,
    125–34
Cavell, Edith, 65
centrality, geography of, 161, 164–5, 166
centralized control: during plague outbreaks,
    375–7, 379, 381; for global corporate
    management, 162–4, 239; and layout of
    imperial Paris, 222
Chabrol, Claude, 428
Chalmers, Revd. Thomas, 122
Chamberlin, Joseph, 122
champions, 556
Chandigarh, India, 5
Chandler, Raymond, 203
Chaplin, Charlie, 387
Charcot, Jean Martin, 47
charity in US, 256–7
Charles, Prince of Wales, 193
Charter of Athens, 42
Cherry, G., 536
Chevalier, Michel, 222
Chicago: city image, 33; downtown
    liminality, 200, 201; grain trade
    development, 111–12, 171–85; urban
    development and divisions, 135–6,
    244–50
Chicago Board of Trade, 176–7, 179, 180,
    181
Chicago School of urban studies, 194, 200,
    237–8
children: secluded education experiment,
    379
Cho, Myung-Rae, 111, **147–60**
Christaller, W., 108
church and working classes, 122
CIAM, 516
cinema *see* film
citizen participation in planning process,
    497–8

city: defined, 298–9; as operational concept, 384–6
City of Quartz (Davis), 112, 190, 193, 242, 280, 323–31; romanticization of, 194
city trenches, 251–9, 504
civic pride, 467
civilization vs. barbarism, 351–4
Clark, T., 464
class *see* social class
claustrophobia, 47
Clavel, P., 509
Cleveland Free-Net, 57
Clifford-Barney, Nathalie, 427
clothing production in New York, 140–5
clubs in downtown Manhattan, 198–9
clustering, 110, 111; of industrial processes, 136–45, 423; *see also* zoning
CNN, 444
coalitions for urban growth, 452, 461, 464–74, 505–6
Colette, 427
Collins, J., 528
Collins, Wilkie: *Woman in White* poster, 396
colonialism: colonial planning, 454, 524–32; in Costa Rica, 358–9
command and control functions, 460–1, 491; in global economy, 163–4
commodification of public space, 338
communications systems *see* information and communications technologies; telecommunications systems
communicative planning theory, 499–500
communism: economic planning, 490–1
communitarianism, 310, 432, 438
community: deconstructed meaning of, 339–40; ideal of, 339–40, 432–6, 438; improvement and class struggle, 122; networks in cyberspace, 53, 56–8, 59; and politics in US, 251–2, 254–5, 256, 257; site of resistance, 282–3, 285
Community Development Project, 445
commuting: effect on urban planning, 477–80; *see also* transport
competitiveness between urban areas, 459–62
computers, 52–9; *see also* cyberspace; hyperreality; information and communications technologies; internet
concentric–zone model, 237, 245–6
conflict in public space, 338–9, 401–3
Congrès Internationaux d'Architecture Moderne (CIAM), 516

conservatism: and homeless problem in US, 286–7; and public space, 405–6; view of ghetto underclass in US, 262, 265–7
consumerism/consumption: competition for consumers, 459–60; critical infrastructure for, 201–2; and downtown space, 200, 201–2, 206; market economy, 107–8, 113–14; in Marxist political economic theory, 117; and public domain, 347–8; of public space in Costa Rica, 357–8; in Second Empire Paris, 425–6; in Seoul, 153–4, 156–7; shopping malls, 338; visual consumption of landscape, 203–4, 205; women as embodiment of, 225, 226
control *see* centralized control; power relations
"controlling city," 238
Cooke, Phillip, 507
Coppola, Francis Ford, 448
Corbin, Alain, 415
Corbusier *see* Le Corbusier
Corker, M., 310
"corridor-streets," 22, 28*ill*
"cosmopolis," 112, 190, 192
cosmopolitanism, 17, 345, 410
Costa, Lúcio, 516, 517*ill*, 521
Costa Rica: control of public space, 336–7, 357–66
Cox, Harvey, 474*n*
Crane, Stephen, 3
Crenson, M., 254
crime: against homeless people, 328; crime rates in LA, 352–3; fear of in LA, 324; in global cities, 169–70; and mobility, 249; police force in early US, 254, 256; "scamscapes," 195–6; on streets, 352–3; violence against women, 227; and zoning, 336
Critical Issues in Public Art (anthology), 405
critical urban studies, 189–90, 196
Cronon, William, 111–12, **171–87**
cross-roads: Le Corbusier's plans to reduce, 21–2; as nodes in city image, 35
Crystal Palace, 219
cultural social movements, 126, 134
culture: and business climate, 466–7, 469–70; critical infrastructure for consumption of, 201–2; cultural codes, 134; in downtown Manhattan, 198–9; and economy, 112–14; individual vs. objective, 18–19; of information age, 129; multiculturalism in global cities,

168; and nature, 300; planning and indigenous heritage, 454–5, 542–8
culture of poverty argument, 265
Cyberion City (MUD), 54
cyberspace, 6, 52–9; access to, 55–6; customs and controls, 58–9; global interaction in, 168–9; MUDs, 53–5; public/private spaces, 55–9
Czyllak, Anna, 397

Dahl, Robert, 255, 469
Dallmayr, Fred, 431, 438
D'Antonio, William V., 465
Darwin, Charles, 509
David Copperfield (Dickens), 415
Davidoff, Leonore, 414
Davidoff, Paul, 496, 497, 498
Davies, H., 457–8
Davis, Mike: *City of Quartz*, 112, 190, 193, 194, 242, 280, **323–31**, 336; on LA uprisings, 280
de Certeau, Michel, 189, 337–8, **383–92**, 407*n*
De Quincey, Thomas, 418*n*
de Selincourt, Basil, 70*n*
dead public space, 336, 342–4
Dear, Michael, 306, 507
decentralization: ideal communities, 435, 452, 482; in New York clothing industry, 141–5
deconstruction, 339–40, 431
deeply divided societies, 536–7, 538–9
Defense Center complex, Paris, 342, 343
"defensible space," 324
Degas, Edgar, 425
degentrification, 241, 279–80, 287–8
deinstitutionalization of disabled people, 306–7
delinquency in global cities, 169–70
Delle, Edward Buhler, 480
democracy: and modernist planning, 504–5; and public art, 405; and public space, 405–7
department store in Paris, 426
"dependent urbanization," 526–7
deregulation, 166, 493
Derrida, Jacques, 339–40, 430–1
Descartes, René, 391*n*, 431
design *see* urban planning and design
desire, 113–14
deurbanization movement, 443, 480–3
Deutsche, Rosalyn, 48, 338–9, **401–9**
devaluation of built environment, 119

Dhaka: *bastee* eviction in, 270–7
dialecticism, 431
Dickens, Charles: *Bleak House*, 8, 76–9; prostitution depicted in *David Copperfield*, 415; representations of London, 7–8, 76–9, 412, 413
Didion, Joan, 479
difference in urban theory, 241–2, 290–331; community denial of, 433–6; highlighted in global cities, 169–70; ideal city embodies, 436–8; *see also* gender; racial/ ethnic divisions in cities
differences as mental stimuli, 11–12
Dinkins, Mayor David, 282, 286, 287; Dinkinsville, 283
"direct production city," 238
disability oppression, 242, 304–12; deinstitutionalization failure, 306–7; physical inaccessibility, 304–5; resistance to, 307–9; sociospatial exclusion, 304, 305–7
disaffected in global cities, 169–70
disciplinary control: of space, 337, 375–82, 386; through knowledge, 421
Disney, Walt, 203, 204–5
Disneyfication of public space, 338, 408–9*n*, 448
Disneyland, USA, 113, 204–6, 448
disorder: control of, 376–7; prostitutes as source of, 421
districts in city image, 30, 33–4, 43
divided societies: planning as control, 535–9
division of labor, 17–18, 117, 135–45; competition in, 459; and division of cities, 238–9, 247–8
divisions in cities, 237–41, 244–89; downtown liminality, 113, 197–201; as frontiers, 440; moral divisions in Victorian London, 410–18; *see also* racial/ethnic divisions in cities
Dolfin, Zacaria, 320
Domhoff, G., 469
Donald, James, 3, 4–5, 8
Doré, Gustave, 413
Dorn, M., 306, 307, 312*n*
downtown: as central space, 246; as liminal space, 113, 197–201; redevelopment in LA, 325–8, 329–30
dreaming, 4; cities as dreamscapes, 203; and discourse, 390
dress and identity, 421–2
drug treatment centers: lack of in LA, 331*n*

Dublin: Joyce's representation, 8–9, 60, 61–4, 69, 80–5
Dubliners (Joyce), 8–9, 61–2, 62–3, 80–5
Dunbar, William, 64
Duras, Marguerite, 9; The Sea Wall, 9, 90–2
Durkheim, Emile, 509
dust heaps of Paris, 424
dystopia: city as, 3, 323–4

ecological model of urban growth, 237–8
"economic city," 238
economy: economic cycles, 118, 119, 120, 123; economic planning, 490–4, 498; global economy, 111, 126–7, 162–70; growth imperative, 464–74, 505–6; and mental life, 12–13, 14, 17; and poverty in US underclass, 267; urban economies, 107–233; women's economic bodies, 225–8; see also capitalism; globalization; market economy
"edge cities," 112, 190, 192
edges in city image, 30, 31, 32, 33, 43
education: panopticon as site for experimentation, 379; politics of in US, 257
Egan, Pierce, 412
Eiffel Tower, Paris, 223n
electronic newsgroups, 52–3
elevator warehouse system, 175–7, 178, 181
Eliot, George, 68n, 425
Eliot, T. S., 43
elites and growth imperative, 464–5, 467–70
Elizabeth I, queen of England, 315
Emerson, Ralph Waldo, 481
Emery, Henry Crosby, 178, 181
emotional reactions to city, 12
employment: and division of cities, 238–9, 247–8, 252; effect of economic planning on, 492, 493; effect of growth on, 471–2, 473; in network society, 127–8; see also labor
enabling justice, 309–12
Engels, Friedrich, 224n, 238, 284, 412, 413
entrepreneurialism in urban governance, 451–2, 456–62, 506
environment: effect of growth on, 472–3; waste management projects, 552–6
Environmental Quality International (EQI), 553
Erasmus, Desiderius, 384
esthetic abstraction, 39
esthetic economy, 113–14
esthetics of Le Corbusier's city, 25–9

ethnic minorities see immigration; racial/ethnic divisions in cities
eviction: of basteebashees in Bangladesh, 270, 271–3, 274, 275, 276; of homeless from public parks, 281–5, 286, 402, 403
exchange relationship, 108
exhibitions: Great Exhibition (1851), 219; Paris Exhibition (1867), 425–6
"exopolis," 112, 190, 192–3
expansion of cities, 244–50
experience and personality, 350
experimental utopia, 370
expositions: world expositions, 219–21, 222
"eyes on the street" surveillance, 336, 353, 354, 355–6

face-to-face relations ideal, 339, 433–4, 435
Fainstein, S., 238, 239
Fales, R. L., 135
familiarity, 71–2
family and private domain, 347
fantasy: in cities, 113–14, 203; fantasy economies, 112–13; as landscape of power, 204–6; phantasmagoria of display, 219–21
farming see agriculture
fashion in Second Empire Paris, 426
feminist theory: censored in cyberspace, 59; Parisian origins, 428; on political economy, 225–8; on space, 48, 290–1; urban theory, 241, 291–5
"feminization" of culture, 47
Ferguson, Sarah, 282–3
Ferrabosco, Alfonso, 316
fields system, 171–2
film: carceral inner cities, 323; Parisian women in, 428; representations of city, 3, 4, 7; as symbol of overexposed city, 447–8
Fincher, R., 241
Finger, A., 311
Finkelstein, V., 310
FIRE sector, 192
fixed capital, 119
flâneur, 4, 63, 64, 189, 339; on streets of London, 410–14; on streets of Paris, 398–9, 422, 424–6
"flexcity," 112, 190
flexibilization in post-Fordist regulatory practices, 148, 151–8
flexible accumulation, 457, 506
flexiworkers, 128
Fliess, Wilhelm, 47

Florio, John, 316
Flyvberg, Brent, 499
fog: Dickens on London fog, 76–7
Fondaco dei Tedeschi, 318–19
Fordism, 110, 135, 147; late modern metropolis, 189, 191
Forester, John, 499, 509
formalism, 39, 41–2, 370
Forster, J., 8
fortress cities, 112, 194, 241; Los Angeles as, 323–4, 325–30
Foucault, Michel, 44, 298, 509, 548; disciplinary power, 337, **375–82**, 386; knowledge and power, 421; panopticon, 112, 242, 293, 337, 377–82
Fountainhead, The (Rand), 48–9, 50
Fourier, Charles, 422
fourth world exclusion, 127
Fraser, Nancy, 307–8, 309, 339
free indirect discourse, 69*n*
free-nets, 53, 56–9
freedom in city life, 16
freeway system in US, 479–80
French Revolution, 420, 421
French School of regulation theory, 147, 195
Freud, Sigmund, 4, 6, 47, 50, 509
Friedmann, John, 499, 509, 527, 536
fringe settlements: *bastees* in Bangladesh, 240, 270–7; fringedwelling Aborigines, 544, 545; ragpickers of Second Empire Paris, 424; townships in Africa, 209, 285, 528, 531
functionalism, 41, 370, 452; zoning in Brasília, 518–22
futures trading, 111; grain trade, 111, 178–182
"fuzes," 195

Gallagher, Catherine, 417*n*
Galsworthy, John, 64
gamblers, 399–400
Gans, Herbert, 266, 497, 498
garbage *see* waste
garden city movement, 5, 452, 495, 529; in Le Corbusier's plans, 21, 24, 25
Garland, Hamlin, 481
gated communities, 112, 194
Gateway to Africa initiative, 210–12, 214–15
gay subculture in Paris, 427
gaze: male gaze on streets of London, 411
Gehry, Frank, 323

gender: feminist urban theory, 241, 291–5; gendered spaces, 290–1, 425; *see also* feminist theory; male domination; women
gentrification, 113, 197–202, 240–1; degentrification, 241, 279–80, 287–8; displacing homeless people, 199–200, 241, 281–4, 286, 402, 403; of downtown Los Angeles, 325–8, 329–30; reflexive consumption, 201–2; women reclaim central space, 226
"gentrified city," 238
geography of centrality, 161, 164–5, 166
geometry in Le Corbusier's plans, 25, 26*ill*, 27*ill*, 29
George, Henry, 258
German community in Renaissance Venice, 318–19
Ghana: planned housing, 531
ghettos: community improvement principle, 122; as division of city, 247; Jewish Ghetto in Renaissance Venice, 242, 315–22; as racial division, 239–40, 261–9
Gibson, Kathie, 294
Gibson-Graham, J. K., 114, **225–8**, 295
Giddens, Anthony, 431
Giedion, Sigfried, 48, 220, 342
Gilderbloom, J. I., 305–6
"gilding the ghetto," 122
Gilmore, Ruth, 280, 288
Ginsburg, Moisei, 480
Gissing, George, 411
Giuliani, Mayor Rudolph, 287
Gladstone, W. E., 414
Glass, Ruth, 240
glass cities, 48
Gleeson, Brendan, 242, **304–14**
global cities, 164–5, 166, 167, 168, 169–70; costs to cities, 169; Johannesburg's reinvention initiative, 210–12, 214–15; narrow focus of study, 192; New York as, 286–7
globalization: class processes, 109; "cosmopolis" concept, 112, 190, 192; effect on New York, 286–7; and entrepreneurialism, 451–2; geography of centrality, 161, 164–5, 166, 239; global economy, 111, 126–7, 162–70; and place, 161–70
glocalization, 112, 190; in Seoul, 153–4
God, death of, 368
Godard, Jean-Luc, 428

Golab, Caroline, 256
Gold Museum, Costa Rica, 362, 363
Goldberger, Paul, 406
Golden Heartbeat initiative, 212–14
Goncourt, Edmond, 419
Goncourt, Jules, 419
Gordon, I., 238, 239
Gotbaum, Betsy, 282
Gottdiener, M., 484
governance *see* urban governance
Graham, Stephen, 133
grain trade, 172–85; Board of Trade central
    market and regulation, 176–8, 179, 180,
    181; elevator warehouse system, 175–7,
    178, 181; futures market, 111–12,
    178–82; grading scales, 177–8, 180, 181;
    impact of telegraph system, 178–80; "to
    arrive" contracts, 180–1; transportation
    changes, 172–6
Gramsci, Antonio, 147
Grand Central Station, New York: homeless
    problem, 199–200, 284
grand narratives, 447, 503
Great Exhibition (1851), 219
Great Society program, 266
Greco, Juliette, 428
Greenbelt communities, 481
Greenberg, Stephanie, 472
Greenstein, Robert, 267
Greenwood, James, 412, 413–14
grid structure, 6, 23, 29, 358–9, 543–4
Griffith, D. W., 448
grisettes, 422
Gropius, Walter, 42
Grosz, Elizabeth, 241–2, 294, **297–303**
growth of cities: costs of, 471–4, 507;
    economic growth, 452, 461, 464–74,
    505–6; expansion process, 244–50;
    political growth, 254–5
growth coalitions, 452, 461, 464–74, 505–6
Guimaraes, Ulysses, 521
gun industry in Birmingham, 136, 137,
    138*ill*, 139

Haagen, Alexander der, 323
Habermas, Jürgen, 339, 509
Habitat (MUD), 54–5
Hahn, H., 304–5
Haig, R. M., 140
Halbreich, Kathy, 404
Hall, Edward, 345
Hall, G. B., 306
Hall, Peter, 452–3, **477–89**

Hamnett, C., 240–1
Harloe, M., 238, 239
Harvey, David, 48, 131, 189, 238, 311, 507;
    entrepreneurialism, 451–2, **456–63**;
    hyperspeculation, 111; spectacle and
    oppression, 113–14, 158; urban process
    under capitalism, 108–9, **116–24**
Haussmann, Baron Georges Eugène, 59,
    221–2, 423
haute couture, 426
Havey, Frank, 353
Hawley, Amos, 465
Hayden, Dolores, 292, 509
Hayes, Ted, 330
Healey, Patsy, 453, **490–501**, 536
healing ceremonies, 361
health: planning for, 529–30; *see also* garden
    city movement; physical development
    planning
heaven: city as, 3; *see also* utopias
Hegelian dialectic, 431
hegemonic practices, 148
Helfgott, R. B., 140
Helvetius, 379
Hemingway, Ernest, 9
Herbert, Frank, 54
heritage planning, 454–5, 542–8
Hesse, B., 240
heterogeneity, 431, 433
Hill, Octavia, 122
Hillis Miller, J., 60, 61, 63
Himmelfarb, Gertrude, 417*n*
Hippodamos, 59
Hirsch, Susan, 259*n*
Hirsh, J., 148
history: and planning, 39, 40, 42–3, 477–87;
    of public life, 342–50; in Virginia Woolf's
    writing, 64–5
Hitchcock, Alfred, 7
Hitchcock, Henry-Russell, 41–2
Hoch, Charlie, 499
Hofmannsthal, Hugo von, 399
Hollywood, 448
Holston, James, 453–4, **513–23**
home, 71–2, 75; as gendered space, 290–1,
    291–2, 293; home/work divisions,
    252–9
homelessness: control of public space, 336–7,
    402; as disruptive influence in public
    space, 402, 403; in division of city, 247,
    281–4; eviction of homeless from public
    parks, 241, 281–5, 286, 402, 403; in

Grand Central Station, 199–200, 284; on Skid Row, 328–30; visibility of, 408*n*

homeownership, 121–2

homosexuality: gay subculture in Paris, 427; Jews as other in Renaissance Venice, 242, 321; mental collapse, 47–8

Honour, Hugh, 318–19

Horkheimer, Max, 40–1, 400*n*

household dependencies: changing situation in Tanzania, 229–32

housing: *bastees* in Bangladesh, 240, 270–7; Brasília social ideal, 453–4, 515–16, 521–2; in colonial Africa, 528, 530; destruction and rebuilding, 445; discrimination against disabled people, 305; effects of growth on, 473; housing for labor question, 121–2; labor migration problems, 209, 270–7, 528, 531; marginalized urban dwellers, 240; regeneration in Johannesburg, 213–14; women discriminated against, 291; *see also* fringe settlements; gated communities; gentrification; home; homelessness; slums; suburbs/suburbanization

Houssaye, Arsène, 422

Howard, Ebenezer, 5, 452, 481, 482, 491, 495

Howell, James, 345

Hughes, James W., 472

Hugo, Victor, 50, 222, 420, 421

human rights: disability rights, 305; right to shelter, 273

humanism: body in relation to city, 299; death of, 368–9; humanist planning, 6, 45

Hunter, Floyd, 465

Huriot, J. M., 145

Husserl, Edmund Gustav Albrecht, 431

Huxley, Margo, 293

hyperreality, 4–5, 190, 194–6; overexposed city, 302–3, 440–8

hyperspeculation, 111

hysteria, 47

idealism, 431; ideal city, 436–8, 452, 494–5; ideal of community, 432–6, 438

identity: anonymity of urban life, 421–2, 436; and community, 339–40; in cyberspace, 54; and globalization, 162, 167–8, 169; Identity of Capitalism, 114, 225, 226, 227; logic of, 339, 430–1; in network society, 134

image/imagining of the city: elements of, 6, 30–8, 43; gentrification and restructuring of, 113, 197–202, 240–1, 402, 403; negative image of homelessness, 402, 403; polarization of, 452

imagination and the city, 3–103

immanence, 348–9

immigration: immigrant workers in global economy, 162, 164, 170, 239, 286; into Great West of US, 172; into Johannesburg, 209; in "postmetropolis," 192; and social organization of cities, 247–8, 249, 256; *see also* migration

imperialism: Victorian discourse on poor, 412; *see also* colonialism

Imrie, R. F., 305, 307

independent living (IL) movement, 308

India: colonial planning, 527

individual culture, 18–19

individualism, 11, 16, 18, 19; in Broadacre City, 482; and community, 431–2

individualization of labor, 128

industrial zones, 42, 135–6; clustering, 110, 111, 136–45; "flexcity," 112; in Le Corbusier's contemporary city, 21, 24, 25, 29*n*; in Second Empire Paris, 423

industrialization: impact on urban development, 135–6; restructuring in "postmetropolis," 189, 190, 191–2, 196; restructuring in Seoul, 149–58

informal economy: in public spaces of Costa Rica, 360–1, 365; Seoul labor market, 155; women's role in Tanzania, 114–15, 229–32

information *see* knowledge

information age, 110, 125–34

information and communications technologies, 4–5; Castells' network society, 110, 125–34; centralized infrastructures, 162–3; interface with bodies and cities, 302–3; as mobility indicator, 250; overexposed city, 302, 440–8; in post-Fordist Seoul, 150–1; virtual communities, 6, 53, 56–8, 59; *see also* cyberspace; hyperreality; telecommunications systems

information technology revolution, 126

informational economy, 126

Ingram, Edgard, 486

"inner cities," 4

Innes, Judy, 499

Innis, Harold, 132

innovation, 110; in Seoul, 150; transfer
    initiatives, 549–58
Inouye, Senator, 56
insanity, 73–4
instrumental rationality, 497, 498; critique
    of, 453–4; *see also* modernism
interfirm linkages in Seoul, 151–3
International School, 5, 41, 342, 452
International Workingman's Association,
    220–1
internet, 52–9; controls, 58–9; global
    interaction, 168–9
interpretative planning theory, 499–500
interurban competition, 459–62
interventions in urban life, 451–558
investment: in built environment, 117–120;
    cities compete for, 451–2, 457; urban
    growth coalitions, 464–74; *see also*
    public–private partnerships
isolation and public space, 342–4

Jackson Park, New York, 401–3
Jacobs, Jane M., 241, 336, 457; sidewalks
    and safety, 351–6; Swan Brewery
    conversion, 454–5, **542–8**
Jakobson, R., 388
James, Henry, 8, 203, 412; on London, 410,
    411
Jaye, M.C., 7
Jerrold, Blanchard, 413
Jersey City, 31–2, 33
Jessop, B., 147
jewelry manufacture in Birmingham, 136,
    137–8, 139
Jews: ghetto in Renaissance Venice, 242,
    315–22; ideology of anti-Semitism,
    402–3
Joao Bosco, Saint, 513–15
Johannesburg, 208–15; black population and
    apartheid, 209; economic development,
    208, 209–10; historical development,
    208–9; reimaging the city, 113, 210–15
Johnson, Howard, 486
Johnson, Jeri, 8–9, **60–70**
Johnson, Philip, 41–2
Johnson, Wallace E., 486
Jones, Gareth Stedman, 417*n*
Jones, Inigo, 316
Joseph, A. E., 306
Journal of the Royal Statistical Society,
    414
Joyce, James, 68; accuracy of Dublin
    depiction, 60, 61–3; *Dubliners*, 8–9, 61–2,

62–3, **80–5**; *Ulysses*, 8, 43, 61, 62,
    63–4
Joyce, Stanislaus, 61–2
Juglar cycles, 118
junctions in city image, 30–1, 34–5, 36
Jünger, Ernst, 49
justice *see* social justice

Kant, Immanuel, 431
Kaplan, Sam Hall, 326
Kasarda, John, 465
Katznelson, Ira, 239, **251–60**
Keating, Peter, 412
Kelly, John, 257
Kendall, Revd Michael S., 285
Kennedy, John F., 444
Kessler, George E., 480
Keynes, John Maynard, 492
King, Anthony, 454, **524–34**
King, Rodney, 280
Klima, E. S., 391*n*
Knights of Labor, 255–6
knowledge: in cyberspace, 52–3; as
    disciplinary control, 421; and image of
    city, 31; informational economy, 126;
    interpretative communicative planning
    theory, 499–500; production and
    accumulation, 110; science of the city,
    367–8, 371, 373; secular knowledge,
    348–9; separation in planning, 453; as tool
    of modernist planning, 503
Kondratieff long waves, 118, 119, 120, 123
Kong, L., 546
Kracauer, Siegfried, 39
Krier, Leon, 42, 44
Krishnarayan, V., 538
Kristeva, Julia, 431, 433
Kroc, Ray, 486
Kuhn, Father, 283, 286
Kuznets cycles, 118

labor: and class struggle under capitalism,
    116, 120–3; discrimination against
    disabled people, 305, 311;
    flexibilization in Seoul, 148, 154–8;
    flexiworkers in network society, 128; in
    information age, 127–8; migration
    creates housing problems, 209, 270–7,
    528, 531; "others" as, 164, 168, 170;
    and social structure of cities, 238–9,
    247–8; specialized labor markets,
    136–45; trade union development in US,
    253–4, 255–6; transnationalization of,

167–8; women disadvantaged as, 162,
170, 227, 230–1; women in Tanzanian
informal economy, 114–15, 229–32; *see
also* division of labor
Laclau, Ernesto, 403
Lacy, Suzanne, 404
land rights in Australia, 545–7
landmarks: in city image, 31, 33, 35–7, 43; of
downtown as liminal space, 197–8
landscapes of power, 204–6, 357
land-use models, 108–9, 139, 484
Las Vegas, 448, 486
Lash, Scott, 131
Last Wave, The (film), 542
late modern metropolis, 189, 191
Lateran Council (1179), 317–18
Latinization of US cities, 240
Lauria, M., 496
Le Corbusier, 5–6, 42, 452, 486; at Athenian
Acropolis, 49, 50; on deurbanists, 480;
ineffable space, 49–50; plans for
contemporary city, **20–9**, 453, 495, 516,
517*ill*
Learmouth, A. T. L., 527
Lebanon *see* Beirut
Leborgne, D., 147, 152
Lefebvre, Henri, 337, 358, **367–74**, 407*n*
Lefort, Claude, 401, 404
Leibniz, Gottfried Wilhelm, 131, 132; on
space, 134*n*
lesbian subculture in Paris, 427–8
Lessing, Julius, 219
Lever House, New York, 342
Lévi-Strauss, Claude, 509
Levitt family firm, 484
Levittowns, 478, 484
Lewis, C. S., 54
Lewis, Oscar, 265
Liachowitz, C. H., 305
liberalism: anti-homeless policies in US, 282,
283–6, 287, 328–9; moral autonomy,
432; view of ghetto underclass, 261–5,
266–7
liminality: downtown as liminal space, 113,
197–201
Lindblom, Charles, 497
linguistics: walking compared with, 387–90
Lionnes, Les, 422
Lipietz, A., 147, 152
list servers, 52
literature: representations of city, 3–4, 7–10,
60–70; extracts, 71–103; *see also*
Dublin; London

local government: in early US, 254–5, 256–7;
entrepreneurialism in, 456–62, 506;
growth imperative, 464–74, 505–6;
influence on planning, 496
loft living, 113
Logan, John, 452, **464–77**, 496
logic of identity, 339, 430–1
London: in comparison with Paris, 425;
Dickens' representation, 7–8, 76–9;
Henry James on, 410, 411; sexual
danger in late-Victorian literature,
414–16; Victorian study of poverty in,
412–14; Virginia Woolf's representation,
8, 60, 61, 64–8, 86–9
lone mothers: discrimination against, 291
Long, Larry, 279
Long Island: suburban growth, 484–5
Long Island Motor Parkway, 478
long waves, 118, 119, 120, 123
Lopez, Dr (physician to Elizabeth I), 315
Los Angeles: "carceral archipelagos," 194,
323–4; city image, 32, 33, 34, 35, 36,
113; crime on streets of, 352–3;
downtown redevelopment, 325–8,
329–30; as fortress city, 323–4, 325–30;
nature's influence on landscape of, 202,
203–4; Orange County, 112, 195–6;
parkways and freeways in, 479–80; riots
(1992), 280; Skid Row homeless issues,
328–30; urban/suburban transposition,
193; *see also City of Quartz*
Los Angeles Times, The, 325–6
Louis Napoleon *see* Napoleon III
Low, Setha M., 336–7, **357–66**
Lukács, Georg, 40
Lynch, Kevin, 54; city image, 6, **30–8**, 43
Lyon, Larry, 465
Lyotard, Jean-François, 447

Mabo, Eddie, 546
McInerney, Jay: *Bright Lights, Big City*,
200
MacKaye, Benton, 478–9
macro-urban studies, 189–90
Maitland, Barry, 330*n*
male domination: in design of Plaza de la
Cultura, Costa Rica, 363–4; *flâneur* as
personification of, 339, 411, 422, 425;
Phallic landscape of cities, 114, 225; of
urban space, 48–50, 290–1, 291–2
Malinowski, B., 388
malls, 338
Malory, Sir Thomas, 345

managerialism in government, 456
Manet, Edouard, 425
Manhattan: clothing industry, 140–5;
  gentrification, 113, 197–201, 241; literary
  representation, 9, 71–5; view from World
  Trade Center, 383–4
Manila: Payatas Environmental
  Development Program (PEDP), 554–5
manual trades: women in, 292
maps: sketch maps and city image, 37
Marcuse, Peter, 238
market economy: basis of neoclassical
  economics, 107; city as site of, 107–8;
  critiques of see Marxist political economic
  theory; effect on architecture, 43–4; grain
  futures market, 111–12, 178–82;
  inequalities of globalization, 163–4, 165,
  166; management of, 491–3; and mental
  life, 12–13
Martinotti, Guido, 168–9
Marvin, Simon, 133
Marx, Karl, 194, 238, 424; accumulation
  theory, 116, 118, 119; economic planning,
  490–1
Marxist political economic theory, 107,
  108–10, 116–34; critiques of, 110,
  114–15; divisions in cities, 238–40
masks of self, 344
Matrix collective, 292
Mayhew, Henry, 238, 412, 413, 414
Médam, A., 388–9
media: attitude to growth, 469, 470; on
  homeless problem in US, 285–6; in
  information age, 129–30; panic over
  crime, 324; xenophobic reaction to terror
  attacks, 280–1
mega-cities, 455, 549–58
Mega-Cities Project, 551–8
Melosi, Martin, 465
memory of the city, 4, 43, 44
mental life and the city, 4, 11–19, 46, 47; in
  literature, 61, 63, 66–8
mercantile cities, 251–2
Merchant of Venice, The (Shakespeare),
  315–17, 318
merchants, agricultural, 172–3
metabolism metaphor, 246–50
metaphysics of presence, 430–3
Metro-North Commuter Railroad, 200
"metropolarities," 112, 190, 193–4
metropolitan area measure, 244
metropolitan dualism, 132
metropolitan networks in Seoul, 151–3

Miami: nature's influence on landscape of,
  202–3, 204; restructuring of image, 113
micro-urban studies, 189–90
Mies Van der Rohe, Ludwig, 49
migration and housing, 209, 270–7, 528, 531
Miller, J. Hillis, 60, 61, 63
Milligan, C., 306–7
mind see mental life and the city;
  psychoanalysis
mirrors, 338, 397
Mitchell, W. J., 6, 52–9, 133, 336
mixed economy, 492
mobility in cities, 249–50
modernism: in architecture, 5–6, 452–3;
  Brasília as archetypical city, 453–4,
  513–23; crisis of, 39–45, 453, 502–10;
  critiques of modernist planning, 453–4,
  495, 505–10; decline of, 453; in literature,
  8–9; modernist planning in US, 502–10;
  and physical development planning,
  494–5, 498, 529; planning as control, 454,
  535–9
Modjeska, D., 4
Mollenkopf, J., 238–9
Molotch, Harvey, 452, 464–77, 496
money and mental life, 12–13, 14
morality: double standard for Victorian men,
  412–13, 415; moral autonomy, 432; and
  public domain, 350
Moretti, Franco, 7, 60, 61
Morgan, David, 474n
Morisot, Berthe, 425
Moses, L. N., 135
Moses, Robert, 478, 479
motion and space, 343–4
Mouffe, Chantal, 403
Moulin Rouge, Paris, 427
movement in cities, 249, 250; plague control
  measures, 375–7, 379; public space as
  function of, 343–4; as resistance, 337–8;
  see also transport; walking
Mrs Dalloway (Woolf), 9, 86–9
Mucha, Alphonse, 420
MUDs (Multi-User Dungeons), 53–5
multiculturalism, 168
multiethnic society formation, 536–7
Mumford, Lewis, 54, 481, 482, 485, 509
Munby, A. J., 414
municipal services: development in US, 254,
  256
Murger, Henri, 422
Murray, Charles, 266–7
Murray, Josephine (Joyce's aunt), 62

Muschamp, Herbert, 483
muscular Christianity, 417n
music, 373
Musto, Michael, 198–9, 201

Nairn, Ian, 485
Napoleon III, 219, 221, 423
narrative theory, 447, 503
nation state: effect of globalization on
    economies, 161, 165–7; identification
    with, 162; world expositions promote,
    221
National Council on Disability (US), 306
nature: and cities, 112; and culture, 300;
    influence on urban landscape, 202–4;
    order of, 348; right to, 374
negative dialectic, 431
neoclassical economics, 107–8, 166, 493–4
neocolonial planning, 454, 525–6
neoliberal economics, 451, 492–3, 498–9
neo-Marxist theory: and planning, 509; see
    also Marxist political economic theory
Nerval, Gérard de, 424
nervous disorders, 47
network enterprises, 127, 128
network society, 110, 125–34; space of flows
    theory, 130, 131–3
networks: in cyberspace, 53, 56–9; and
    flexible production in Seoul, 151–3,
    154–6
neurasthenia, 47
New Delhi, 527
new urbanism, 188, 193
New York: city image, 34; clothing
    production, 140–5; compactness,
    251–2; as global city, 286–7; homeless in
    landscape of, 199–200, 241, 281–5,
    286, 402, 403; literary representations,
    9, 71–5; nostalgic redevelopment, 406;
    parkways in, 478–9; political party system
    in, 257; social structure, 238–9;
    see also Manhattan
Newman, Oscar, 331n
niche markets in Tanzania, 231–2
Nichols, Jesse Clyde, 480
Niemeyer, Oscar, 516
Nietzsche, Friedrich Wilhelm, 11, 14, 19, 47,
    49, 50, 368
nightclubs in downtown Manhattan, 198–9
nightwalking in Victorian London, 412–13
nihilism, 368–9
Nixon, Richard, 323–4
nodes in city image, 30–1, 33, 34–5, 36, 43

Nolli, Giambattista, 59
Nord, Deborah, 418n
Nordau, Max, 47
Noyelle, T., 461

Oates, Joyce Carol, 3, 8
objective culture, 18–19
objectivity of modernist planning, 503
O'Connor, Cardinal, 286
oeuvre, 367, 368, 371, 373
Offenbach, Jacques, 423
office design: open-plan visibility, 344
Okhitovich, Moisei, 480
Old Swan Brewery, Perth, 454–5, 542–3,
    544–5, 547–8
Oliver, M., 305, 307–8, 311
Olmsted, Frederick Law, 5, 325, 478
open spaces: in Le Corbusier's city, 21–2, 23,
    24, 29; to restore mental health, 48, 325;
    see also parks
operational concept of city, 384–6
Orange County, Los Angeles, 112, 195–6
Orientalism, 418n
Orwell, George, 238
Ostrogorski, M., 257
Ostrowetsky, S., 389
other: in global cities/workforce, 164, 168,
    170; Jews as in Renaissance Venice, 242,
    317–18, 319–21; low-life as in Victorian
    London and Paris, 413–14, 424
Otis, General, 325–6, 327
"outer cities," 190, 192
overexposed city, 302, 440–8
Oxfam, 553

Pagan, Antonio, 286–7
Paik, Nam June, 448
Palnitkar, Sneha, 555
panopticon, 112, 242, 293, 337, 377–82
panoramas, 382n
Parent-Duchâtelet, Dr., 421
Paris: of belle époque, 426–7; Benjamin's
    arcades project, 219, 220, 338,
    393–400; bohemian life, 422–3, 423–4;
    consumption in, 425–7; economic cycles
    and working-class struggle, 121, 123;
    gay subculture, 427; phantasmagoric
    display, 219, 220–1, 338; prostitutes on
    streets of, 420, 421, 424–5; ragpickers,
    424; regeneration scheme under
    Haussmann, 221–2, 423–4; revolution,
    420, 421; of Second Empire, 221–2,
    423–6; women in, 419–28

Paris Exhibition (1867), 425–6
Park, Robert, 5, 237
Parkman, Francis, 8
parks: control of public space in Costa Rica,
    336–7, 357–66; eviction of homeless
    people, 281–5, 286, 402, 403; in Le
    Corbusier's city, 21–2, 23, 24, 29; and
    spatial politics, 401–3
parkways, 478–9
Parque Central, Costa Rica, 357, 358–62,
    365, 366
party system: growth in US, 254–6, 257–8
paths in city image, 30, 31–3, 43; see also
    sidewalks
patriarchy, 291–2; see also male domination
Paul IV, pope, 321
pavements see sidewalks
Pavillon (grisette), 422
Payatas Environmental Development
    Program (PEDP), 554–5
Pearce, B., 536
Peck, J. A., 148
pedestrian speech acts, 387–8
PEN (Public Electronic Network), Santa
    Monica, 53, 57
people of color: disadvantaged by
    globalization, 162, 239
people-watching, 355–6
Perlman, Janice E., 455, **549–58**
permeable walls, 342–3, 344
personality: effect of city on, 11–19;
    experience of world, 350
Perth, Australia, 454–5, 542–8
Peterson, Paul E., 468, 470
Phallocentrism, 300
Phallus, Identity of, 114, 225, 226, 227
phantasmagoria of display, 219–21, 338
Philadelphia: as a community, 251, 252;
    Polish community in, 256
Phillips, Patricia, 404
philosophy: logic of identity, 430–1
phobias of city life, 46–8
physical development planning, 494–5, 498,
    529
physical inaccessibility, 304–5
Piazza San Marco, Venice, 35
Pitts, Thomas E., 477
place: and globalization, 161–70; political
    economy of, 464–73
plague control measures, 375–7, 379, 381
Plaza de la Cultura, Costa Rica, 357–8,
    362–6
plazas: control of public space, 357–66

Plekhanov, George, 221
pluralistic societies, 536, 537–8
poetry: representations of city, 3–4
police force: and control of prostitutes in
    Victorian London, 416; control of
    public space in Costa Rica, 360;
    development of in US, 254, 256; eviction
    of homeless in New York, 281–5;
    protection of Los Angeles elites, 323,
    324, 329, 330
policy analysis and planning, 495–8
Polish community in Philadelphia, 256
political correctness in underclass debate,
    261, 262
political parties: development in US, 254–6,
    257–8
politicians: attitudes to growth, 468–9
politics: body–politic, 300; of difference,
    436–8; local politics and planning, 496;
    and media in information age, 129–30;
    political economy of place, 464–73; of
    social organization of cities, 251–9;
    spatial politics, 401–9; of transnational
    economic geography, 161–2, 169; of
    urbanism, 221–2; views of ghetto
    underclass, 261–9; see also
    antiurbanism
Pollock, Griselda, 411
poor relief in US, 256–7
Poovey, Mary, 418n
population: density in Dublin of Ulysses, 64;
    density in Le Corbusier's city, 21, 23, 24;
    deurbanization, 443; effect on social
    organization of cities, 246–7, 249; Le
    Corbusier's classification of, 21; of
    mega–cities, 550; mobility of, 250; see also
    immigration
Populopolis (MUD), 54
postcolonialism: global cities as site of, 168;
    postcolonial planning, 454, 525–6
poster advertisements, 396, 420
post-Fordism, 110–11; "flexcity" concept,
    112, 190; and planning, 505–7; and
    regulation theory, 147–9, 195; in Seoul,
    111, 149–58
"postmetropolis," 112, 188–96
postmodernism: planning practice and
    theory, 495, 502–10; postmodern city,
    42–3, 294–5
poststructuralism, 339–40; see also
    deconstruction; Foucault
poverty: negative impact of social policy on,
    266–7; study of poor in Victorian

London, 412–14; in US ghetto underclass, 263–4; *see also* homelessness; slums

power relations: control of public space in Costa Rica, 336–8, 357–66; in control of Victorian prostitution, 415–16, 421; fantasy as landscape of power, 204–6; in network society, 132–3; panopticism, 112, 293, 337, 377–82

Pred, A., 252

presence, metaphysics of, 430–3

"private": meaning of term, 345

private investment *see* public–private partnerships

private space: in cyberspace, 55–6, 59

process planning, 39, 41–2

product champions, 556

professional sector and economic growth, 470

profit accumulation, 109, 116–23

progress on display, 219–21, 222

property market *see* real estate

prostitutes in public space, 294, 339, 361; in Paris, 420, 421, 424–5; on streets of Victorian London, 414–16; unsanitary imagery, 415, 421

protected zone: Le Corbusier's city, 21, 24

Proust, Marcel, 47–8, 419, 427

Pruitt-Igoe housing project, 6

psychoanalysis: agoraphobia, 47; desire, 113–14; heterogeneity of subjectivity, 433; uncanny, 4, 6

"public': composition of, 338–9; development of term, 344–50

public buildings: Le Corbusier's city, 22, 23, 24

Public Electronic Network (PEN), Santa Monica, 53, 57

public–private partnerships: in entrepreneurialist governance, 457–8, 506; Johannesburg regeneration schemes, 211, 212

public space, 335–448; appropriation of, 337–8, 372, 373, 387, 401; art in, 403–5; commodification of, 338; conflicts in, 338–9, 401–3; control of in Costa Rica, 336–7, 357–66; in cyberspace, 56–9; dead public space, 336, 342–4; destruction of, 324–5, 338; development of public life, 344–50; difference and diversity in, 437; Disneyfication of, 338, 408–9n; exclusion from, 338–9, 402, 403,

406–7; as function of movement, 343–4; history of, 342–50; homeless people in, 199–200, 241, 242, 281–5, 286, 328–30, 336–7, 402, 403; loss of, 335–6, 340, 342–50, 405–7; meaning of "public," 344–50; and memory, 44; and private life in Virginia Woolf's literature, 66–8; prostitutes in, 294, 339, 361, 414–16, 420, 421, 424–5; *see also* open spaces; parks

Pullan, Brian, 320

"quality of urban life," 401–2

quatorzièmes, 17

racial/ethnic divisions in cities: apartheid in Johannesburg, 209; in colonial Africa, 530–1; German community in Renaissance Venice, 318–19; ghetto underclass in US, 239–40, 261–9; planning for control of ethnic minorities, 454, 535–9; Polish community in Philadelphia, 256; segregation in Los Angeles, 324, 325, 327; Victorian racial classification of poor, 412–13; white flight to suburbs in US, 484; xenophobia in US, 280–1; *see also* ghettos; immigration

radical social geography, 309–10

Rae, Douglas, 258

ragpickers in Paris, 424

Rahman, Mohammed Mahbubur, 240, 270–8

railroads: competition from, 467; impact on agriculture, 174–5; impact on cities, 171, 175; as instrument of progress, 222; investment in, 119

railway stations: homeless in Grand Central, 199–200, 284; in Le Corbusier's city, 21–2, 24; as node in city image, 35

Rand, Ayn: *The Fountainhead*, 48–9, 50

rape: crime rates, 353; rape space/script, 225–6, 227

rational reactions to city, 12

rationality and planning, 39–45, 453; rational planning process, 496–8

real estate: C19th investment in, 118–19; as indicator of mobility, 250; in market economy, 108

real virtuality, 129

redistribution mechanisms, 461

Redon, Odilon, 397–8

reflexive consumption, 201–2

Reformulation School, 147
refuse *see* waste
regeneration schemes: in Johannesburg, 210–15; in Second Empire Paris, 221–2; to increase competitiveness, 459–60
regional economic development, 459–60, 496, 500
Regional Planning Association of America (RPAA), 479, 481, 483
regulation: of difference in urban space, 293, 294; in global economy, 166, 167; of prostitution, 415–16, 421
regulation theory, 147–9, 195
Reiner, T., 496, 497
religion: Aboriginal sacred sites, 546–7, 548; church and working classes, 122; contesting public space in Costa Rica, 361; muscular Christianity, 417*n*
Relph, Edward, 507
Renaissance: Jewish Ghetto in Venice, 242, 315–22
reserve of city–dwellers, 15
"residential city," 238
"residual city," 238
resistance: community resistance, 282–3, 285; in megacities, 455, 549–58; to disability oppression, 307–9; to surveillance, 293; walking as, 337–8, 383–91
restructuring: economic restructuring in Seoul, 111, 149–58; in postmetropolis, 189, 190, 191–2, 196
retail sector and economic growth, 470
"revanchist city" (Smith), 279–88
revolution: Paris as revolutionary city, 420, 421
rhetoric of walking, 388–90
Riazanov, David, 220–1
Richards, Grant, 62
rights: and the city, 373–4; *see also* human rights
Riley, Robert, 485
Rilke, Rainer Maria, 390
Rittel, H., 498
rivers: for transportation, 172, 173–4
roads: freeway system in US, 479–80; in Le Corbusier's city, 22, 23, 29; parkways in US, 478–9
roadside architecture, 486–7
Roark, Howard (fictional architect), 48–9, 50
Robbins, Bruce, 407
Robbins, Kevin, 5

Roberts, George, 62
Rockford: antitax ideology in, 468
Romantic poetry, 4
Rome: Jewish ghetto, 317–18, 321
Ronan Point, Britain, 6
Rosentraub, M. S., 305–6
Rossi, Aldo, 42, 44
Royal Statistical Society: *Journal*, 414
Rubin, Lillian B., 467
Rudel, Thomas K., 474*n*
rural communities, 5, 481
Ruskin, John, 14, 43

Sabot, R. H., 230
sack system for grain, 172–4, 175
sacred sites of Aborigines, 546–7, 548
safety/security: and airport design, 440–1; lack of for women, 290; and sidewalks, 351–6; *see also* fortress cities
Sager, Tore, 499
Said, Edward, 10, 418*n*
Saigon: literary representation, 9, 90–2
St Brigid's Church, New York, 282–3, 285, 286
St Louis: grain trade, 172, 173, 174–5, 176
Saint-Simonians, 222, 422
Salvador, Frei Vicente do, 513
San José, Costa Rica, 336–7, 357–66
Sand, George, 422
Sandel, M., 310, 432, 439*n*
sanitation: imagery associated with prostitutes, 415, 421; obsession with in colonial planning, 529–30
Sassen, Saskia, 111, **161–70**, 239
Saulle, Legrand du, 47
Saunders, Pete, 192
Savage, Mike, 191
Savings and Loans scandal, 112, 195
"scamscapes," 195–6
Schaffer, D., 536
Scheiber, Harry N., 467
Schmitt, Richard, 439*n*
Schuré, Edouard, 50
science of the city, 367–8, 371, 373
Scott, Allen J., 110, **135–46**
Sea Wall, The (Duras), 9, 90–2
Seberg, Jean, 428
secluded education experiment, 379
Second Empire Paris, 221–2, 423–6
secularism and public domain, 347, 348–9
security *see* safety/security
self-employed sector and economic growth, 470

Sennett, Richard, 410, 546; Jewish ghetto in Renaissance Venice, 242, **315–22**; loss of public space, 335–6, 340, **342–50**

Seoul: economic restructuring, 111, 149–58

service industries: growth in Seoul, 153, 154, 155

sexuality: and agoraphobia, 47–8; body in urban theory, 241–2, 293–4, 297–303; sexual danger in Victorian London, 414–16; women and Paris, 419–28; *see also* homosexuality; prostitutes

Shakespeare, William: *The Merchant of Venice*, 315–17, 318

shanty towns, 240, 283–4, 424

Shapiro, J. P., 308

al-Shaykh, Hanan, 9–10, **93–103**

Shefter, M., 254

Sheppard, E., 145

shopping malls, 338

Shulman, George, 439*n*

sidewalks: and safety, 351–6; *see also* paths; streets

Siegel, Philip, 197–8

signification: and metaphysics of presence, 431; systems of, 370

Simcities, 112, 190, 194–6

Simmel, Georg, 5, 40; blasé attitude, 14–15, 63, 64; mental life and the city, 4, **11–19**, 46, 47, 61, 63, 66

Simon, Herbert, 496

Simone, A. M., 215

Sims, George R., 411, 412

simulacra, 194–6

Sinclair, Upton, 3

Singer, Isaac Bashevis, 198

single mothers: discrimination against, 291

site: Aboriginal sacred sites impede development, 546–7, 548; selection for Le Corbusier's city, 21, 25, 28*ill*

Sitte, Camillo, 46–7

sketch maps and city image, 37

Skid Row, Los Angeles: homeless issues, 328–30

skyscrapers: architecture and public space in, 342; in Le Corbusier's city, 22, 23, 24, 25, 29, 452

slums: *bastees* in Bangladesh, 240, 270–7; as division of city, 240, 247; Haussmann's clearance scheme in Paris, 222; of late-Victorian London, 412–13; in Second Empire Paris, 424

Smith, Neil, 240, 241, **279–89**, 336

social class: cleavages in Seoul labor market, 156; critiques of capitalist economy, 109, 116, 120–3; and divisions in cities, 238–41, 246–9, 251–9; escape from origins, 421–2; and Haussmann's Parisian project, 221–2; modernist egalitarian planning, 453–4; planning for postmodern city, 506–7; in postmetropolis, 112; and public space, 325, 328–30; social organization of cities, 246–9, 251–9, 345–50; social transformation in Brasília, 515–16, 521; Victorian view of poor, 412–13; in Virginia Woolf's London, 65–6; *see also* gentrification; homelessness; underclass discourse; working classes

social Darwinism, 350

social exclusion: effect of growth on, 472; global scale, 127; in information age, 128–9; socio–spatial exclusion of disability, 304, 305–7

social justice: geographical perspective, 309–10

social movements: cultural social movements, 126, 134; disability social movements, 307–9

social organization of cities, 246–9, 251–9, 345–50; Brasília ideal, 515–16, 521; effect of growth on, 472; evolution of, 15–16, 434; ideal city, 436–8; ideal of community, 432–6, 438

social polarization, 238, 472; in information age, 128–9; "metropolarities," 112, 190, 193–4

social policy: discriminates against women, 291, 292; negative impact on poverty in US, 266–7

social production of space in Costa Rica, 357–66

socialism: economic planning, 490–1; resisted in US, 258; Soviet urbanism, 481

socialization: evolution of, 15–16, 434; face–to–face relations ideal, 339, 433–4, 435; in post-Fordist Seoul, 156–8

Societalization School, 147

sociologism, 191–2, 194

sociospatial dialectic, 188

sociospatial exclusion, 304, 305–7

Soja, Edward W., 48, 112, **188–96**, 507

Sombart, Werner, 258

Sorkin, Michael, 202–3, 338, 406–7

sottoportegho, 319–20

South Africa: segregated cities, 531; *see also* Johannesburg
Soviet Union: deurbanization movement, 480–3
space: agoraphobia, 6, 46–8; ambiguity of, 397–8; appropriation of, 337–8, 372, 373, 387, 400; disciplinary control, 337, 375–82, 386; divisions in cities, 237–41, 244–89; gendered space, 290–5; ineffable space, 49–50; liminal space, 113, 197–201; male domination, 48–50; and motion, 343–4; in postmodern planning theory, 508; social production of, 357–66; socio–spatial exclusion of disability, 304, 305–7; spatial plans for cities, 495; spatial politics, 401–9; spatialization of post-Fordism, 148–9, 191–2; women defined in, 225–6, 227, 290–5; *see also* cyberspace; open spaces; public space
space of flows theory, 130, 131–3, 133–4
Spain: colonial architecture and urban planning, 358–9
spamming, 58
Spate, O. U. K., 527
specialization: and global economy, 164; and labor markets, 136–45
spectacle and cities, 113–14, 158, 425–6, 426–7; phantasmagoria of display, 219–21, 338; on streets of Victorian London, 410–18
speculative markets, 111, 181–2
speech acts and walking, 387
speed distance, 444
Speed Racer (TV series), 54
Spencer, Herbert, 50
Spender, Stephen, 3–4
Spinoza, Baruch, 3
sponsorship and economic growth, 470
squatters: in African townships, 531; anti-squatter policy in New York, 283, 286; *basteebashees* in Bangladesh, 240, 270–7
"stagflation," 492
Stallybrass, Peter, 413, 414
Stanback, T., 461
Star Trek (TV series), 54
Stead, W. T., 411
Steele, Sir Richard, 345
Stein, Clarence, 478, 481
Sternlieb, George, 472
Stevenson, Robert Louis, 411
Stirling, James, 543

Stone, Clarence N., 468, 496
strangers: compose ideal city, 437; contribution to experience, 350; and safety on streets, 336, 353, 354–5, 356
"strategic beautification," 222
streets: concentration of use gives image to, 32; *flâneur* on streets of Paris, 398–9, 422, 424–6; in Le Corbusier's city, 21–2, 28*ill*, 29; safety of, 351–6; sexual danger on streets of Victorian London, 414–16; *see also* paths; roads; sidewalks
streetwalkers, 294, 339; and agoraphobia in women, 47; *see also* prostitutes
structuralism, 370
Stuart, O., 310
subaltern counter publics, 339
subjectivity, 432–3
"suburban city," 238
suburbs/suburbanization: automobile suburb, 477–80; Broadacre City plan, 452, 481–3; critiques of, 485–6; growth of, 477, 483–5; influence on architecture, 452–3; moral influence of, 121–2; urban/suburban transposition, 192–3; women in relation to, 225, 226, 290–1, 292, 293
subway system: nodes in city image, 35
Sue, Eugène, 422
Summers, Gene F., 472
Sunbelt cities, 202–3
Superhuman, 368
superquadra concept, 518, 519, 521
supply-side economics, 493
surveillance: "eyes on the street' surveillance, 336, 353, 354, 355–6; of Other in Renaissance Venice, 319, 320; panopticon, 337, 377–82; Parisian census of prostitutes, 421; plague control measures, 375–7, 379, 381; in "postmetropolis," 112, 194; of public space in Costa Rica, 360; removal of difference, 242; resistance to, 293; in security-obsessed Los Angeles, 323, 324; to protect women, 227
Swan Brewery, Perth, 454–5, 542–3, 544–5, 547–8
Swanson, M. W., 529, 530, 531
Swift, Jonathan, 345
synchrony, 385
synecdoche, 389

Tactical Mapping Systems, 448
Tafuri, Manfredo, 39–40, 42, 325

"Take back the night" rallies, 227
Tanzania: women in informal economy, 229–32
Taut, Bruno, 49
technological time, 442–3, 444
telecommunications systems: and overexposed city, 444–5; telegraph system and grain trade, 178–80; telephone use in Chicago, 250; *see also* information and communications technologies
"tenement city," 238
terra nullius fallacy in Australia, 543, 546
terrorism: airport antiterrorist measures, 440–1; World Trade Center bomb attack (1993), 280–1
textile industry in New York, 140–5
Thackeray, William Makepeace, 350
Thatcher, Margaret, 493
theme parks: as landscapes of power, 113, 204–6; *see also* Disneyfication of public space
Thomas, H., 538
Thompson, Susan, 293
Thoreau, Henry, 481
Thunen, J. H. von, 108
Tickell, A., 148
time: appropriation of, 373; and functionality of cities, 13; impact of hyperreality, 302, 303; juxtaposition of, 411; in postmodern planning theory, 508; technological time, 442–3, 444
timeless time theory, 130–1
Tocqueville, Alexis de, 350
toilets in public space, 329
Tomlinson, R., 215
Tompkins Square Park, New York: eviction of homeless people, 281–5, 286; restoration of, 287
Torchiana, Donald T., 63
totally planned cities: Brasília as, 515–22
Toulouse-Lautrec, Henri de, 427
tourism: competition to attract, 459–60
townless highway, 478–9
townships, 209, 285, 528, 531
trades union movement in US, 253–4, 255–6, 470
traffic: Le Corbusier's decongestion plans, 22–3, 24, 29
tramway: anathema to Le Corbusier, 23
transcendental philosophy, 431, 481
transduction, 369–70
transfer initiatives, 549–58

transnational political economy, 161–70
transparency, 48
transport: cars and urban planning, 477–80; discrimination against disabled people, 304, 305–6, 307; impact on agriculture, 172–6; industrialization and urban development, 135–6, 423; investment in, 119–20; junctions and city image, 30–1, 34–5; in Le Corbusier's city, 21, 22–3; male-oriented services, 290; as mobility indicator, 250; scene of violence against women, 227; *see also* railroads; roads
trenches: city trenches, 251–9, 504
Trillin, Calvin, 468
Tripp, Aili Mari, 114–15, **229–33**
Tristan, Flora, 422
Trollope, Anthony, 175
Trollope, Frances, 419
Tugwell, Rexford, 481
Turkle, Sherry, 133
Turner, Ted, 444
turnpike investment, 119
Tyack, David, 257

Ulysses (Joyce), 8–9, 43, 61, 62, 63–4
uncanny, 4, 6
UNCHS, 549–50
underclass discourse, 193, 194; architecture designates as Other, 324; ghetto underclass, 239–40, 261–9; race in, 240
underground building: in Le Corbusier's city, 22, 24
unemployment: in information age, 127–8; and poverty rate in US, 267
Unger, Roberto, 432
United States: literary representations of city, 3
unity: metaphysical desire for, 430–3; in modernist planning, 503–4, 506–7
unoppressive city, 436–8
"unskilled work city," 238
urban economics, 107–233
urban exploration in Victorian London, 410–18
urban governance: growth coalitions, 452, 461, 464–74, 505–6; transformation in, 456–62
urban planning and design, 5–6, 452–3; anti-intellectualism in, 509; antiurbanism in, 452–3; Brasília as archetypical modernist city, 453–4, 513–23; by extrapolation, 370–1; citizen

urban planning and design (*contd*)
  participation in, 497–8; colonial
  planning, 454, 524–32; as control, 535–9;
  crisis of modernism, 39–45, 453–4, 495,
  502–10; for cyberspace
  cities, 55; for difference, 294–5;
  discriminates against disabled people,
  304–5; economic planning, 490–4, 498;
  and history, 39, 40, 42–3, 477–87;
  interpretative communicative planning
  theory, 499–500; Le Corbusier's
  contemporary city, 20–9, 453, 516,
  517*ill*; physical development planning,
  494–5, 498, 529; physical inaccessibility
  for disabled people, 304–5; and policy
  analysis, 495–8; and postmodern theory,
  507–10; rationality in, 39–45, 453–4,
  496–8; split with architecture, 41–2;
  suburban development, 477–87; theory
  of, 507–10; *see also* architecture
urban reform, 371–2
urban strategy, 371–2
urban studies: Chicago School, 194, 200,
  237–8; feminist urban theory, 241, 291–5;
  Lefebvre's view of, 367–8; micro-and
  macro-viewpoints, 189–90; need for
  change, 188–9, 196
Urry, John, 131, 548
utilities, 244, 246, 469
utopias: city as, 3, 5; experimental utopia,
  370; ideal city, 436–8, 452, 494–5; ideal of
  community, 432–6, 438

Vallès, Jules, 422
Vallier, Dora, 46
Vance, James E., 485
Vanderbilt, William K., 478
Veltz, P., 151, 154
Venice: city image, 35; Jewish Ghetto in, 242,
  315–22
Venturi, Robert, 486
vertical building: Le Corbusier's plans, 22,
  23, 24, 25, 29, 452; *see also* skyscrapers
vertically disintegrated production: clothing
  industry, 140–5
Vidich, Arthur J., 468
Vidler, Antony, 4, 6, **46–51**
Vienna: Ringstrasse induces agoraphobia,
  46–7
"view from below" approach, 189–90
violence: against women, 227; on streets, 352
Virilio, Paul, 302–3, 340, **440–8**
virtual communities, 6, 53, 56–8, 59

visibility: in architecture, 340, 342–3, 344,
  377–8; of homeless people, 408*n*;
  overexposed city, 440–8
visions of the city, 5–6
visual consumption of landscape, 203–4, 205
Vivien, Renée, 427
Von Thunen, J. H., 108, 139
voyeurism: on streets of London, 411,
  412–14; in view of city, 383–4

walking: as resistance, 337–8, 383–91
WalKowitz, Judith, 339, **410–18**
Wallerstein, Immanuel, 189
Walpole, Hugh, 223*n*
Walzer, M., 310
war zones: Beirut, 10, 93–103
Warde, Alan, 191
Warner, S. B., 252
Washington Houses project, 354
waste disposal, 73
waste management projects, 552–6
watercourses: for transportation, 172, 173–4
Watson, Sophie, 241, **290–6**
Watts, A. Chalmers, 7
Webber, Melvin, 485, 498
Weber, Max, 509
Weiner, Annette B., 229–30
Weininger, Otto, 47
Weir, Peter, 542
Welfare Geography, 309
welfare services: dependency in US ghetto
  underclass, 263–4; in early US, 256–7;
  Great Society program, 266; inadequate
  support for disabled people, 306
Wells, H. G., 64
Wells, P. E., 307
Westphal, Carl Otto, 47
Wharton, Edith, 202
wheat trade *see* grain trade
Whelan, R., 496
White, Allon, 413, 414
Whitman, Walt, 481
Whitnall, Gordon, 477
Whitt, J. Allen, 465
Whyte, William, 324, 328
Williams, Raymond, 8, 60–1, 251, 258
Wilson, Elizabeth, 293–4, 339, **419–29**
Wilson, Kemmons, 486
Wilson, William Julius, 194, 237, 240, 241,
  261–9
Wirth, Louis, 237
Wise, M. J., 138
Wodiczko, Krzysztof, 57

Wolch, Jennifer, 306
Wolff, Janet, 48
Woman in White poster, 396
women: agoraphobia in, 6, 47–8; in capitalist discourse, 225–8; disadvantaged by globalization, 162, 170, 239; fourth world exclusion, 127; "inner cities," 4; in Paris, 419–28; peripheralization of, 114; and space, 225–6, 227, 290–1; in Tanzanian informal economy, 114–15, 229–32; uncomfortable in public space, 361; violence against, 227; *see also* prostitutes
Woolf, Leonard, 66
Woolf, Virginia, 10, 64, 291; *Mrs Dalloway*, 9, 64, **86–9**; *The Years*, 8, 61, 64–5, 66–8
work/home divisions, 252–9
working classes: "city trenches," 252–4; effect of world expositions on, 220–1, 222; marginalization of, 238, 240; struggle under capitalism, 120–3; *see also* capitalism; labor
world expositions, 219–21, 222
World Trade Center, New York: 1993 bomb attack, 280–1; view of Manhattan from, 383–4

World Wide Web (www), 53
Worringer, Wilhelm, 46
Worster, Donald, 471
Worth, Charles Frederick, 426
Wright, Frank Lloyd, 5, 6, 50; Broadacre City plan, 452, 481–3
Wright, Henry, 478
Wulff, G., 527

xenophobia in US, 280–1

Years, The (Woolf), 8, 61, 64–5, 66–8
Yiftachel, Oren, 454, **535–41**
Young, Iris Marion, 309, 339–40, **430–9**

Zabbaleen Environmental Project, 552–7
Zizek, Slavoj, 402–3
Zola, Emile, 330, 425
zoning: in Brasília, 453–4, 516, 518–22; concentric-zone model, 237, 245–6; destructive effect, 42, 336; Le Corbusier's application, 21, 24, 25, 29n, 42; resistance to, 293
Zukin, Sharon, 112–13, **197–207**, 357